Insight in Psychotherapy

Insight in Psychotherapy

Edited by **Louis G. Castonguay**
and **Clara E. Hill**

American Psychological Association • Washington, DC

KH

Published by
American Psychological Association
750 First Street, NE
Washington, DC 20002
www.apa.org

To order
APA Order Department
P.O. Box 92984
Washington, DC 20090-2984
Tel: (800) 374-2721; Direct: (202) 336-5510
Fax: (202) 336-5502; TDD/TTY: (202) 336-6123
Online: www.apa.org/books/
E-mail: order@apa.org

In the U.K., Europe, Africa, and the Middle East, copies may be ordered from
American Psychological Association
3 Henrietta Street
Covent Garden, London
WC2E 8LU England

Typeset in Goudy by Stephen McDougal, Mechanicsville, MD

Printer: Bookmart Press, North Bergen, NJ
Cover Designer: Naylor Design, Washington, DC
Technical/Production Editor: Devon Bourexis

The opinions and statements published are the responsibility of the authors, and such opinions and statements do not necessarily represent the policies of the American Psychological Association.

Library of Congress Cataloging-in-Publication Data

Insight in psychotherapy / edited by Louis G. Castonguay and Clara E. Hill. — 1st ed.
     p. cm.
   Includes bibliographical references and index.
   ISBN-13: 978-1-59147-477-7
   ISBN-10: 1-59147-477-9
   1. Insight in psychotherapy. 2. Psychotherapy. I. Castonguay, Louis Georges. II. Hill, Clara E., 1948- .
   [DNLM: 1. Psychotherapy—methods WM 420 I5936 2007]

   RC480.I57 2006
   616.89'14—dc22   2006013194

British Library Cataloguing-in-Publication Data
A CIP record is available from the British Library.

Printed in the United States of America
First Edition

7/29/08

CONTENTS

CONTRIBUTORS

Lynne Angus, York University, Toronto, Ontario, Canada

Diane B. Arnkoff, Catholic University of America, Washington, DC

Jacques P. Barber, University of Pennsylvania, Philadelphia

Thomas Berger, Université de Genève, Geneva, Switzerland

Kuldhir S. Bhati, University of Wisconsin—Madison

Arthur C. Bohart, Saybrook Graduate School and Research Center, San Francisco, CA

Thomas D. Borkovec, The Pennsylvania State University, State College

James F. Boswell, The Pennsylvania State University, State College

Elizabeth A. Bowman, The New School for Social Research, New York, NY

Meredith Glick Brinegar, Miami University, Oxford, OH

Franz Caspar, Université de Genève, Geneva, Switzerland

Louis G. Castonguay, The Pennsylvania State University, State College

Mary Beth Connolly Gibbons, University of Pennsylvania, Philadelphia

Paul Crits-Christoph, University of Pennsylvania, Philadelphia

Rachel E. Crook-Lyon, Brigham Young University, Provo, UT

Joslyn M. Cruz, The Pennsylvania State University, State College

Robert Elliott, University of Toledo, OH; Katholieke Universiteit Leuven, Leuven, Belgium

Greg C. Feldman, Massachusetts General Hospital, Harvard Medical School, Boston

Myrna L. Friedlander, University at Albany, State University of New York, Albany

Charles J. Gelso, University of Maryland, College Park

Carol R. Glass, Catholic University of America, Washington, DC

Melissa K. Goates-Jones, University of Maryland, College Park

Marvin R. Goldfried, State University of New York at Stony Brook

Leslie S. Greenberg, York University, Toronto, Ontario, Canada

Martin Grosse Holtforth, University of Bern, Bern, Switzerland

James Harbin, University of Maryland, College Park

Karen Hardtke, York University, Toronto, Ontario, Canada

Beth E. Haverkamp, University of British Columbia, Vancouver, Canada

Adele M. Hayes, University of Delaware, Newark

Jeffrey A. Hayes, The Pennsylvania State University, State College

Laurie Heatherington, Williams College, Williamstown, MA

Shirley A. Hess, Shippensburg University, Shippensburg, PA

Clara E. Hill, University of Maryland, College Park

Zac E. Imel, University of Wisconsin—Madison

Michelle D. Johnson-Jennings, University of Wisconsin—Madison

Aphrodite A. Kakouros, The Pennsylvania State University, State College

Sarah Knox, Marquette University, Milwaukee, WI

Nicholas Ladany, Lehigh University, Bethlehem, PA

Nancy McWilliams, Rutgers University, Piscataway, NJ

Stanley B. Messer, Rutgers University, Piscataway, NJ

Antonio Pascual-Leone, University of Windsor, Windsor, Ontario, Canada

Jeremy D. Safran, The New School for Social Research, New York, NY

Megan Schamberger, University of Pennsylvania, Philadelphia

Michele A. Schottenbauer, Catholic University of America, Washington, DC

Wonjin Sim, University of Maryland, College Park

William B. Stiles, Miami University, Oxford, OH

Ty D. Tashiro, University of Maryland, College Park

R. Fox Vernon, Capella University, Minneapolis, MN

Bruce E. Wampold, University of Wisconsin—Madison

Leslie A. Wilson, The Pennsylvania State University, State College

PREFACE

It is frequently argued that although we know that psychotherapy works, a great deal of uncertainty about *how* it works remains. We have devoted a large part of our respective careers trying to understand what seems to facilitate and what appears to interfere with client improvement. In doing so, we have read each other's conceptual and empirical work on the process of change. Over the years, we have also attended many of the same scientific and professional meetings where we discussed the role of variables (e.g., participant characteristics, client and therapist in-session experience, relationship factors, technical interventions) potentially involved in therapeutic change. It was during one of these discussions that the seeds for this book were planted.

We had just attended a symposium during the Mid-Atlantic Society for Psychotherapy Research Meeting at Lehigh University in October 2000. At the end of the symposium, we approached the presenters and a small number of other attendees to further discuss the findings that had just been presented. After 10 or 15 minutes of engaging and stimulating discussion, however, the other people involved gradually excused themselves and left to attend the next scheduled presentation. As we continued our discussion, one of us commented that good conferences always seem to involve two different types of meetings. One type is the formal presentation, in which ideas or projects are described in almost prescriptive ways and a limited amount of time is allowed for questions and open-ended interaction between the presenters and the audience. However, within these conferences a more interesting type of meeting generally takes place. This is the type of meeting we just had: a spontaneous, lively discussion among a small group of individuals who gathered close to the podium, just after the end of a formal presentation. We agreed that this type of informal meeting is often more exciting and informative than activities included in the conference program because presenters tend to be less nervous, less apprehensive of difficult questions, and thus more at ease to expand on their ideas, their clinical observations, or the implications of their studies. We also agreed that this type of meeting rarely attracts audience members who have a strong inclination for hostile questions or comments designed to display their conceptual brilliance, clinical acuteness, or statistical prowess (small, engaging, and informative discussions may well defeat the purpose of such comments). In our experience, these meetings are usually characterized by genuine interest, open-mindedness, and friendly interactions and can lead to fresh, new, and exciting ideas about what is going on in therapy and what facilitates a positive outcome. However, these meetings tend to be of short duration as many people eventually need to rush to the next conference activity: "Hey, this was a great discussion. I would like to talk more about these issues, but I've got to run to another panel."

We contemplated how exciting it would be to organize and attend a conference specifically built around the second type of meeting. Wouldn't it be great to convene in one room, for a day or two, a relatively small group of smart, knowledgeable, friendly people to simply talk about the process of change in therapy? We finally agreed (just before rushing to another presentation!), that one of us (Castonguay) would try to get financial support from his university to invite colleagues from not too distant academic institutions who are known for their expertise in process research and who, as a group, would represent an array of theoretical perspectives in psychotherapy, to a meeting based on informal, open discussions.

The impromptu conversation between the two of us led to three meetings, held at Pennsylvania State University (March 2001, May 2003, and May 2005), that brought together some of the most well-known psychotherapy researchers in the eastern United States and Canada. Before inviting these researchers, however, we decided that we should choose a specific aspect of the process of change to address in order to provide focus for our group meeting. For reasons described in the introduction to this book, we chose insight. On the basis of our conversation at the Mid-Atlantic conference, we also agreed that our meetings would not feature a series of formal presentations that recapitulate positions, arguments, or ideas already firmly held; instead, these meetings were organized primarily around open discussions. We assumed that open interactions among leading thinkers would provide the best conditions to delineate different aspects of the nature and role of insight, to creatively and nondefensively explore the processes facilitating and following insight, and to generate new ideas about this challenging construct. We were also convinced that the breadth and depth of the participants' expertise would allow us to examine insight with the pluralistic approach it deserves; that is, not only from different theoretical orientations but also from different perspectives of knowledge acquisition (conceptual, empirical, and clinical).

These meetings did lead to exciting exchanges and creative ideas related to the conceptualization, investigation, and clinical implications of insight in psychotherapy. After the first two conferences, the group decided that the next step should be to have each person engage in an in-depth exploration of a particular perspective or specific issues related to insight in psychotherapy. These explorations, which go well beyond what was covered at our conferences, form the first 20 chapters of this book. The last chapter, based on the third and final conference at Pennsylvania State University, attempts to integrate the discussions of these meetings and the ideas in the previous chapters of this book by articulating points of agreement on central issues about insight, while pointing the way to future research on this important event in psychotherapy.

ACKNOWLEDGMENTS

This book, as well as the three Pennsylvania State University conferences on which it is based, would not have been possible without the contribution and support of many people. We first need to acknowledge the generous help (in time and financial assistance) and strong encouragement that we received from three colleagues at The Pennsylvania State University: Gowen Roper (director of the Psychology Clinic), Keith Crnic (former head of the Department of Psychology), and Raymond Lombra (associate dean at the College of Liberal Arts). We deeply appreciate the fact that they understood from the beginning of this project how unique the conferences would turn out to be as well as how much creative impact they may end up having on our understanding of insight. We are also grateful to the conferences' participants and authors. It is difficult to express how pleased we have been with the level of involvement and depth of contribution they have shown during (and after) our meetings as well as by the amount of work they have dedicated to writing (and revising numerous times!) what we truly believe to be exquisite and innovative chapters. We also want to thank Susan Reynolds in the Books Department at the American Psychological Association for her full dedication to this project, constant attention to details, and outstanding expertise. She has been crucial in making this project a delightful and successful experience. Several graduate students have attended the Pennsylvania State University conferences, and some (Gloria Gia Maramba and Jay Reid) have devoted a substantial amount of time transcribing hours of recorded discussions. We are grateful for their help, as well as for the enthusiasm with which they interacted with participants. Their active engagement helped to make the conferences such special events. We are also deeply indebted to our respective spouses, Michelle Newman and Jim Gormally, for adding so much insight, as well as love and friendship, into our lives.

Finally, we want to recognize how much we both owe to the Society of Psychotherapy Research (SPR). As is true for most participants at the Pennsylvania State University conferences and authors in this book, SPR has had an indelible influence on our professional development. Over many years we have felt stimulated, supported, and encouraged in our scholarly and research endeavors by a large number of SPR members. In many ways, the degree of involvement and openness that prevailed at the Pennsylvania State University conferences and that allowed this book to happen is a reflection and a tribute to the spirit at SPR. As such, it seems only fit to dedicate this book to SPR and its members.

Insight in Psychotherapy

INTRODUCTION: EXAMINING INSIGHT IN PSYCHOTHERAPY

LOUIS G. CASTONGUAY AND CLARA E. HILL

Throughout history, the willingness and capacity to achieve personal insight has been valued as one of the most noble and meaningful features, or gifts, of human life. "The unexamined life," Socrates claimed, "is not worth living." Many of us prize, if not cherish, our ability to self-examine. How else to explain that one of the most memorable and intriguing words of the English literature might well be Shakespeare's inescapable inquiry, "To be, or not to be: that is the question," if not for our deeply held belief that we can, should, and will benefit from gaining a new understanding of who we are and why we are the way we are? Is there a better way to explain why readers (especially adult readers) resonate so deeply to the secret that the Little Prince has learned from Saint-Exupéry's fox ("what is the essential is invisible to the eye"), than to recognize the profoundly meaningful and fulfilling experiences we get from discovering new things about ourselves and others?

Self-understanding has also been viewed as a remedy for mental illness as far back as the age of antiquity. As noted by Mora (1975), the therapeutic power ascribed to words in the Greek culture is reflected by the motto "Know yourself" on the door of the Delphic temple, as well as by Heraclitus's statement, "I have explored myself." In our modern society, Frank and Frank (1991)

3

have argued that psychotherapy is the sanctioned method for healing through self-understanding. They noted that insight increases a client's sense of security, mastery, and self-efficacy by providing labels for experiences that seem confusing, haphazard, or inexplicable.

This book attempts to identify what is currently known about insight in psychotherapy and tries to generate theoretical and research directions to better understand this complex phenomenon. We chose to examine insight for two main reasons. First, as a process associated with the client's involvement in therapy (as opposed to an aspect of specific techniques favored by some therapists), insight seems to cut across different forms of therapy. Thus, we felt that what would be learned about insight would likely be perceived as relevant by most clinicians. We also decided to focus on insight because it is a rich and complex process that is not fully understood. Insight can vary considerably in terms of content (e.g., links between past and present, links between conscious thoughts and underlying assumptions). Insight also seems to involve several dimensions (e.g., emotional vs. intellectual, explicit vs. implicit, sudden vs. gradual). It is not surprising that, as illustrated in several chapters of this book, many definitions have been proposed for the construct of insight (e.g., *meta-awareness, learning of new connections, new understanding*). Furthermore, different factors appear to facilitate insight and numerous types of changes seem to result from it. Hence, given its centrality and complexity, we felt that a delineation and integration of what is known about insight could increase the understanding of the process of change in psychotherapy.

The book is composed of five sections. Part I focuses on theoretical perspectives. It includes chapters that describe how insight is defined and valued within four major contemporary traditions in psychotherapy: psychodynamic, humanistic–experiential, cognitive–behavioral, and systemic (i.e., couple and family therapy). This part also includes a chapter on the assimilation model, a theory of the process of change in which insight is featured as an important phase of therapy. The final chapter offers an integrative theoretical perspective by approaching insight as a common factor across orientations. Charting the rich tradition of several theories, these chapters illustrate how insight is relied on in numerous therapeutic approaches, even though these approaches might emphasize different dimensions in defining insight or encourage the use of diverse methods to foster it.

Part II is devoted to research. The first chapter of this section provides a review of the empirical literature that summarizes what has been learned from research about insight in psychotherapy. The second chapter focuses on a linguistic analysis of terms involving insight, followed by an examination of events in therapy during which clients indicated they gained insight. The remaining three chapters present different empirical methods that have been used to investigate insight within therapy sessions. They illustrate how both quantitative and qualitative methods of analyses can reveal the multifaceted nature of insight, as well as the complexity of the various processes involved in this mechanism of change.

Part III addresses clinical issues related to insight as they are manifested in the practice and learning of psychotherapy. The first chapter provides an overview of how clients are active agents in the insight process. In contrast, the next chapter discusses the therapist's role in promoting insight. The third chapter examines the fundamental interplay between insight and action (or the synergetic relationship between understanding and behavioral change). The fourth chapter provides a reminder that insight is not just the province of psychotherapy as insight is often developed, consolidated, and destroyed between sessions. Finally, the last chapter presents a model for understanding how supervisors help to facilitate insight within their supervisees, which can then be applied to the therapy setting. These chapters demonstrate how the adequate understanding and successful fostering of insight involve different facets of psychotherapy, thereby reflecting the intrinsic complexity and importance of this clinical phenomenon.

In an effort to avoid becoming insular in our thinking and to gain a fuller perspective on insight, Part IV of the book addresses this phenomenon from perspectives outside of psychotherapy. The four chapters in this section demonstrate how social psychology, cognitive psychology, developmental psychology, and philosophy of science have indeed generated a considerable amount of theory and research that can shed light on the understanding of insight in psychotherapy. As a whole, these chapters clearly convey how several constructs and findings that have emerged from basic areas of psychology, as well as some of the epistemological challenges raised by philosophical analyses, offer exciting ideas and methods to open ways of conceptualizing and investigating insight.

Needless to say, all of these chapters provide a wealth of information about insight. In an effort to integrate such rich and complex information, we invited authors of these chapters to reflect on their experiences, read the other chapters, and begin to integrate what is known about the definition of insight, the process of gaining insight, and the consequences of insight. Part V, the final chapter of this book, is the result of these efforts. We believe it provides a window on the current state of knowledge about insight in psychotherapy, as well as a substantial number of exciting directions for future theoretical, empirical, and clinical efforts related to this process of change.

REFERENCES

Frank, J. D., & Frank, J. B. (1991). *Persuasion and healing: A comparative study of psychotherapy* (3rd ed.). Baltimore: Johns Hopkins University Press.

Mora, G. (1975). Historical and theoretical trends in psychiatry. In A. M. Freedman, H. I. Kaplan, & B. J. Sadock (Eds.), *Comprehensive textbook of psychiatry: Vol. I* (2nd ed., pp. 1–75). Baltimore: Williams & Wilkins.

I
THEORETICAL PERSPECTIVES

1

INSIGHT IN PSYCHODYNAMIC THERAPY: THEORY AND ASSESSMENT

STANLEY B. MESSER AND NANCY McWILLIAMS

The pursuit of insight is generally regarded as a defining feature of psychoanalytic psychotherapy, which is often referred to as *insight-oriented* therapy (Frank, 1993). By the 1950s, most psychoanalytic authors writing about the therapy process assumed that insight is critical in effecting therapeutic change (e.g., Eissler, 1953). In addition, they viewed the attainment of insight as a superordinate goal of psychoanalytic therapy, an ideal that goes beyond symptom relief (e.g., Kris, 1956). More recent works in this field have noted that increased insight is an effect of psychodynamic treatment, an indication that some kind of change has taken place. A tendency to frame therapeutic issues in terms of the concept of insight is so closely associated with dynamic approaches that alternative therapies such as experiential, family systems, and behavioral arose at least in part from their founders' skepticism about whether insight into sources of one's mental, emotional, and behavioral problems is necessarily therapeutic in itself or indicative of a successful therapeutic process.

In this context, it is interesting to note that Freud (1900/1953) used the German term for insight only once, in an informal way. In a preface to an edition of his book on dreams, he wrote, "Insight such as this falls to one's lot but once in a lifetime" (p. xxxvi). In his psychoanalytic writings, even references to *interpretation*—the analyst's effort to promote the patient's insight into feelings, thoughts, and behaviors—are surprisingly scant, limited mostly to one essay on technique (Freud, 1913/1958). It remains a mystery how the psychoanalytic love affair with the concept of insight began. The best guess (e.g., Sandler, Holder, & Dare, 1973) is that the term was borrowed from psychiatry, whose conventional mental status assessment included *insight into illness* (i.e., awareness that one has a problem). Despite the absence of the term in Freud's writings, however, the reverence for the process of learning and the attainment of knowledge that infuses Freudian theory probably laid the groundwork for the assumption that achieving insight into one's psychic processes correlates with mental health. Later in this chapter we present our attempt to assess this construct in a way that will capture its central features.

The chapter begins with an overview of the roots of insight in Freud's early writings. It then chronicles the meanings of insight in ego psychology as both a process of looking inward and the content of what one discovers there. The acknowledgment that one has a problem and its prognostic value for successful psychoanalytic therapy is another use of the term *insight* within ego psychology. We next describe the relational paradigm, in which *insight* is regarded as an effect of a safe therapeutic relationship and a consequence of the effort to make sense of the playing out of the patient's difficulties in that relationship. The chapter then includes a brief review of early attempts to define insight operationally. This is presented as a backdrop to our effort and that of our students to devise a measure of insight as part of a scale that assesses patient progress in psychotherapy. We describe how degree of insight is rated on this scale and give examples from therapy sessions of each rating score. We conclude the chapter by recommending directions for future research on insight in psychodynamic therapy.

INSIGHT IN EARLY FREUDIAN THEORY

Freud's bedrock identity was that of a scientist. Like many intellectuals influenced by the ideals of the Enlightenment, he consistently framed his ideas in terms of the victory of rationality over irrationality, mind over body, and objective, "civilized" faculties over experiential, "primitive" human processes. Freud liked to see himself as a kind of conquistador overthrowing the superstitions of the dark past and leading the way to a bright future in which scientific explanation would replace seductive illusions. Attaining insight into the workings of the mind and conveying his discoveries to others was his life's work. With his patients he often spoke didactically, trying to get them to see what sense he had made of their problems. Over time, Freud increasingly valued their coming up with their own discoveries about their motivations. Thus, conveying his own insights and encouraging those of his patients were central to his effort, even if he did not say so explicitly.

Another precursor to the later psychotherapeutic emphasis on insight was Freud's tendency to equate therapy with the search for truth. Freud described the therapeutic relationship as "based on a love of truth" (1937/1964a, p. 248) and embraced the Delphic, Platonic, and biblical equation of truth with freedom (or *agency* in current psychoanalytic parlance). He frequently stated that to be free of neurosis, one has to confront unpleasant truths. Freud (1917/1955) viewed himself as the messenger of a highly unpalatable but scientifically unassailable truth, namely that most human motivation is unconscious. He boasted that psychoanalysis had delivered a third devastating insult to human vanity: "the universal narcissism of men, their self-love, has up to the present suffered three severe blows from the researches of science" (p. 139), the first being Copernicus's discovery that the earth is not the center of the universe and the second being Darwin's revelation that human beings are simply animals among animals and not a superior, qualitatively different kind of being. In these postmodern times, people are reluctant to talk blithely about "the truth," and the horrors perpetrated by the Nazis have laid to rest any confidence that science is always working for the good of humanity. However, the intellectual currency of Freud's era glittered with optimism that accumulating scientific knowledge would liberate humanity from the shackles of unreason.

Like most seminal theorists of personality and psychotherapy, Freud was highly influenced by his initial experiences with mentally troubled people. Thus, another source of the psychoanalytic focus on insight was the fact that Freud's earliest psychiatric patients were "hysterics" (an interesting contrast, e.g., to Jung's early experiences with psychotic patients or Carl Rogers's early work with children and adolescents, the impact of which can be seen in their respective theories). Individuals diagnosed as hysterical in the late 19th century experienced severe, complex dissociative and somatic syndromes that would today be seen as posttraumatic. Such problems are caused by events that are too overwhelming when experienced to assimilate emotionally or process verbally. Freud could not have found a better group to support his preexisting conviction that knowledge liberates. Not only is insight into the traumatic origins of their suffering therapeutic to patients with hysterical disorders (e.g., Horowitz, 1991; van der Kolk, McFarlane, & Weisaeth, 1996) but their recovery from specific symptoms (albeit not from their overall tendency to dissociate or develop new symptoms) also can be stunning. Freud's mentor Charcot was known for demonstrations in which hysterical symptoms were "cured" with hypnosis. Paralyzed women walked again, the blind were able to see, and the mute spoke. Such dramatic changes, later echoed when psychoanalytic therapists treated traumatized soldiers in both world wars, had a lot to do with the luster of psychoanalysis in the early to mid-20th century.

The nature of hysterical problems contributed in another way to the good press insight has enjoyed. From a structural psychoanalytic perspective, hysterical symptoms (e.g., numbness in an arm) are created by a compromise between the sexual or aggressive drive (e.g., a desire to strike someone) and the defense mechanisms of repression and dissociation. These defenses, which keep knowledge out of awareness, differ from defenses such as projection, which is implicated in paranoia, or idealization and devaluation, which are associated with narcissistic problems. Clinical experience suggests that repression and dissociation can be slowly reduced by integrating cognition and strong affect in the context of a safe relationship. The association of symptom reduction with the facing of painful truths (whether it be the "truth" of Freud's early conclusion that hysterical symptoms result from childhood molestation or of his later belief that they express traumatically disturbing fantasies) paved the way for analysts to cast insight in a starring role in their formulations.

It is intriguing that in his last years Freud (1937/1964b) did not consider the veridical recollection of traumatizing events or fantasies necessary for psychological healing. Increasingly, he wrote about *construction* or *reconstruction* of the childhood scenarios he assumed gave rise to neurotic symptoms. Like many contemporary analytic therapists treating individuals with probable trauma histories (e.g., Davies & Frawley, 1994), Freud (1937/1964b) felt that the analyst and patient can reconstruct enough to make sense of the patient's suffering and to reduce it significantly:

> The path that starts from the analyst's construction ought to end in the patient's recollection; but it does not always lead so far. Quite often we do not succeed in bringing the patient to recollect what has been repressed. Instead of that, if the analysis is carried out correctly, we produce in him an assured conviction of the truth of the construction which achieves the same therapeutic results as a recaptured memory. (p. 265)

Such construction is not the same kind of insight as a memory that emerges in treatment, but surely it constitutes a kind of insight or insightful therapeutic activity (see Bouchard & Guerette, 1991, on Freud's use of both empiricist–realist and hermeneutic approaches). Because Freud did not discuss *insight* per se in his theoretical writings, he never defined the word. If he had, we believe he would have construed it in terms of the replacement of unconscious, conflictual wishes, motives, and fantasies by conscious, rational understanding.

INSIGHT ACCORDING TO EGO PSYCHOLOGY

Freud's (1923/1961) theoretical change from a topographical (conscious, preconscious, unconscious) to a structural (id, ego, superego) model ushered in the era of ego psychology, dominated by such luminaries as Heinz Hartmann, Ernst Kris, and Rudolph Loewenstein. The metaphor of the id, ego, and superego captured the psychoanalytic imagination, mainly because of its clinical applicability: Freud and his followers had learned that it was more helpful for patients to work with their defenses against anxiety than to work directly with the material about which they were presumably anxious. In the language of the new paradigm, they addressed the ego rather than the id.

Along with Freud's shift from excavating the contents of the id to exploring the defensive operations of the ego, he had become increasingly appreciative of the phenomenon of transference by the 1920s. In addition to noting more frequent instances in which his patients transferred to him feelings and expectations that belonged to their early experiences with caregivers, he was slowly seeing the therapeutic implications of their investing him with this transferred authority. Although he initially found transferential reactions a distraction from the content he wanted to expose and tried unsuccessfully to argue his patients out of experiencing him as father, mother, or other primary love object, Freud began to realize that their imbuing him with the emotional power of childhood authorities was an asset to the therapeutic work. If he simply let the transference feelings strengthen (as they tend to do when a person reveals more and more intimate material to a sympathetic stranger), insights that arose in the process tended to be suffused with the strong affects characteristic of childhood.

It is one thing to talk dispassionately about one's vulnerability to feelings of shame but quite another to find oneself terrified that the analyst will respond to one's disclosures by shaming, despite evidence to the contrary. Experiences of insight intensified by transference feelings make strong impressions on patients. Such discoveries feel more organic and less cerebral than ordinary conjectures, and they cannot be easily brushed aside. Gradually, there arose in the analytic community a conviction that some of the most valuable insights occur within the affectively rich transference relationship. As the patient's long-standing maladaptive patterns repeat themselves within treatment (the *transference neurosis*), analyst and patient can make the patient's old story turn out differently. The belief that psychological problems will be most effectively examined and healed as they appear within the treatment relationship remains a defining feature of some prominent psychodynamic approaches.

Although he did not showcase the term *insight*, James Strachey (1934) is usually credited with articulating the first ego psychological theory of healing in which insight is implicitly central. In a seminal article on the therapeutic action of psychoanalysis, he coined the term *mutative interpretation*, noting the superiority of interventions that integrate affect and cognition (as interpretations of transference attempt to do) over those that engage cognitive faculties alone. Since his article appeared, most psychodynamic therapists have distinguished between intellectual and emotional (or experiential) insight. After 1934, many psychoanalytic conferences included a panel on the role of insight. In 1952, Reid and Feinsinger, perhaps evidencing some wishful thinking, announced that "with advances in data gathering, logical thinking, and hypothesis testing, we may reasonably look forward to a time, in the not too distant future, when we can really answer the question, what is the role of insight in psychotherapy?" (p. 734).

During the many years when ego psychology was the preeminent psychoanalytic paradigm, the word *insight* appeared with diverse connotations (e.g., Kris, 1956; Poland, 1988; Richfield, 1954). Sometimes the term was used nontechnically, to mean "awareness of one's feelings" or "self-understanding." It was used to convey both the process of looking at oneself and the content of what is seen. It could denote the means of therapeutic progress as well as the overall goal of therapy. This last use had unmistakable moral overtones, certainly related to the value Freud placed on self-knowledge and perhaps related to the psychoanalytic consensus that therapists should undergo analysis themselves before treating others. Self-understanding is presumably more important to one's ability to function as an analyst than is the reduction of one's depression or anxiety. Whether or not a concern with training analyses was a factor, self-understanding generally received more emphasis in the ego psychology literature than relief of symptoms. There is an echo of Freud's veneration of the examined life in the latter use of *insight* as referring to the aim of treatment.

One likely reason that the theories of ego psychologists highlighted insight involves an influential book by Alexander and French (1946), who argued that psychoanalytic treatment is effective because it offers a "corrective emotional experience" (p. 22). In other words, lived experience with a therapist who differs from one's childhood caregivers has more curative impact than the interpretations of the analyst or the growing self-knowledge of the patient. Although Alexander and French did not advocate outright manipulation, many ego psychologists, who had taken to heart Freud's image of the dispassionate scientist, reacted with dismay to the idea that the analyst might behave with an attitude other than one of utmost neutrality. In the context of the controversy, they attested to the primacy of insight with the fervor of true believers (e.g., Eissler, 1953).

By the middle of the 20th century, there was another use of *insight* that was more consistent with its psychiatric origins. As therapists compared notes on which patients seemed to profit from psychoanalysis and how quickly they responded (the question of "analyzability"), they agreed that insight into the fact that one has a problem is a good prognostic sign. In other words, in an initial interview such insight marks a patient as a good candidate for psychoanalytic treatment. As exploratory and supportive psychodynamic therapies joined classical psychoanalysis as available modalities in long- and short-term versions and with couples, families, and groups, analytic therapists observed that people with some insightful perspective on their problems tended to get better faster in any kind of therapy. Such patients may be contrasted with those who cannot grasp the nature or psychic cost of their problems and therefore require a long period of making symptoms ego-alien.

Thus, insight had several critical niches in what was written about the ego psychological take on therapy. By the late 20th century, there were scores of psychoanalytic papers with *insight* in the title. When insight was discussed as the goal rather than the means of treatment, that goal was usually described as the comfortable incorporation of previously unconscious drives, wishes, fantasies, conflicts, and other irrational strivings into the reality-oriented part of the self (the ego). "Where id was, there shall ego be," a comment Freud (1933/1964c, p. 80) made late in his career, was an organizing shibboleth of the ego psychology phase of the psychoanalytic movement whenever the process of therapeutic change was discussed. As recently as the late 1970s, however, Neubauer (1979) stated that "no satisfactory analytic definition of insight exists" (p. 29).

INSIGHT ACCORDING TO RELATIONAL THEORISTS

From the early days of psychoanalysis there has been a tension between analytic theorists, who attribute changes in the patient to systematic interpretation of drive and conflict, and relational theorists, who attribute these changes to the experience of a particular kind of relationship. This dispute can be seen in the protracted disagreement between Freud and his friend Ferenczi about what accounts for therapeutic progress. Freud's professional development reflects this conflict: He began his career emphasizing the former view, but by the end, he emphasized the latter. Members of the analytic community who viewed relationship variables to be more consequential than insight, especially when accounting for change, include the American interpersonal group (e.g., Sullivan, Horney, Fromm, Fromm-Reichmann, Thompson, Searles, Levenson), the British object relations theorists (e.g., Fairbairn, Winnicott, Bion, Guntrip), therapists identified with Heinz Kohut's self psychology and the related intersubjective orientation (e.g., the Ornsteins, the Shanes, Fosshage, Stolorow, Atwood, Orange), psychoanalytic researchers in infant development and attachment (e.g., Greenspan, Stern, Beebe, Tronick, Emde, Fonagy, Target), and therapists who identify with the relational movement (e.g., Mitchell, Greenberg, Aron, Benjamin, Hoffman, Bromberg, Ehrenberg, Slavin, Renik).

As relational ideas have become accepted as mainstream, there has been an increase in attention to insight as an outcome of psychotherapy. Relational analysts have challenged the assumption that it is the therapist's role to interpret the patient's unconscious material. These analysts question whether the analyst's understanding is necessarily superior to the patient's and have thus de-emphasized the therapist's responsibility to convey insight through interpretation. Rather, they view insight as a product of the therapeutic collaboration that emerges organically in both patient and therapist after an authentic and reliable relationship is established between them. In other words, instead of being seen as the cause of intrapsychic change, insight is viewed as one of its consequences, as evidence that change has occurred.

In this respect, the arguments of some relational analysts parallel early behaviorist critiques of the assumption by the ego psychological school of thought that insight is required to change behavior. (Chap. 3 in this volume, by Grosse Holtforth et al., contains a valuable review of this movement.) "Change the behavior, and insight may follow" was a common challenge of the early behavioral therapists. Relational therapists agree in principle but view the site of behavior change as within the therapeutic dyad: When the patient feels safe relating to the therapist in ways that differ from his or her past behavior with important people, insight follows.

Relational articles often note that insight emerges as therapy partners struggle to make sense of their mutual enactments (Hirsch, 1998)—that is, the inevitable ways in which both parties find themselves playing out a theme from the patient's life. This kind of insight differs, of course, from the traditional notion that the patient needs to become conscious of his or her impulses, affects, fantasies, or memories. Relationally oriented therapists assume that both parties are always contributing to what occurs in the therapy dyad; therefore, insights that arise are generally framed relationally (e.g., "Looks like you and I are repeating some emotional patterns from your relationship with your father"), rather than viewed as proceeding only from therapist to patient ("You're experiencing me as being like your father").

The extraction of meaning from experience, the central hermeneutic task, is the focus of relational writing more than is relief from symptoms of psychopathology (e.g., Hoffman, 1998; Mitchell, 1997; Ogden, 1997). This emphasis is not specific to the relational movement, although it is more clearly articulated by relational authors than by most ego psychologists. It continues the ongoing psychoanalytic disposition to understand specific psychopathologies in the larger context of an individual's personality and situation and to assume that the effort to derive meaning is a fundamental human need.

Unlike ego psychologists, who stressed the analyst's systematic interpretation of defenses against insight, relational therapists see insight as an outcome that does not have to be explicitly pursued and for which the groundwork does not have to be self-consciously laid. Therapeutic changes in the patient allow the emergence of an insightful orientation and the specific insights that arise once it exists. Many relational theorists, especially those inclined toward self psychology, credit the advent of insight to the reduction of shame; others connect it with natural human curiosity and creativity that are unleashed in a context of sufficient emotional authenticity (e.g., Kohut,

1977; Orange, 1995). By associating the emergence of insight with emotional honesty of both therapist and patient, the relational movement has reaffirmed, in a postmodern context, the emphasis on truthfulness that characterized Freud's original psychoanalytic project.

INSIGHT IN PSYCHOANALYTIC RESEARCH: EMPIRICAL CONSIDERATIONS

In a 1988 review, Luborsky lamented that there was little empirical investigation into the roles of insight or accuracy of interpretation in therapy. This is still the case, at least regarding the study of insight. Empirical investigations of the therapy process, however, give robust support to the relational perspective or *corrective emotional experience* position. Regardless of the theoretical orientation of the therapist and whether insight is specifically pursued (as it would be by cognitive therapists and psychodynamic practitioners in the ego psychology tradition, although not by others), what appears to make a difference to clients are (a) the practitioner's qualities as a human being (warmth, empathy, respect, flexibility, and so forth) and (b) the extent of attention given to establishing and maintaining a therapeutic alliance (e.g., Castonguay, Goldfried, Wiser, Raue, & Hayes, 1996; Lambert & Okiishi, 1997; Martin, Garske, & Davis, 2000; Norcross, 2002).

There is also empirical evidence that stable characteristics of patients account for a significant portion of the degree of change possible in therapy (Blatt, Shahar, & Zuroff, 2002; Bohart, chap.12, this volume), a finding that may vindicate the long-standing psychoanalytic effort to understand individual differences and their implications for treatment. One area in which patients differ widely is the extent to which they can see, at the beginning of therapy, that they have a problem. To our knowledge and according to Connolly Gibbons, Crits-Christoph, Barber, and Schamberger (see chap. 7, this volume), little research has been conducted on the specific question of whether insight into illness correlates with a positive response to psychoanalysis and psychoanalytic therapies, as the clinical experience of most psychoanalytic practitioners has suggested. There are few studies of insight per se as a factor in change, though we suspect that if researchers were to investigate therapies with individuals similar to those originally treated by Freud (i.e., those with hysterical and dissociative problems), they might find that for this patient group, insight is as important as the quality of the therapeutic relationship.

In recent years, empirical data suggested that increased insight is, as relational analysts and others have posited, an outcome of successful psychoanalytic therapy. Members of the San Francisco Psychotherapy Research Group, who have conducted research on psychoanalytic therapies (Weiss, Sampson, & the Mt. Zion Psychotherapy Research Group, 1986), have concluded that patients come to treatment with an unconscious idea or plan about the kind of experience they need to unlearn maladaptive childhood beliefs. Such beliefs exist outside their conscious awareness and are seen as responsible for their psychological suffering. Patients unconsciously devise tests that the therapist must pass to reduce their anxiety that their history (the experiences that created the pathogenic beliefs and associated painful emotions) will be repeated. If the therapist is successful in understanding the plan and passes the tests, which differ from person to person, the patient experiences a *condition of safety* in which psychopathology diminishes. Along with such changes, previously warded-off contents of the mind emerge. Thus, insight arises as an outcome of therapy as the patient learns that the world is not necessarily dangerous in the ways the patient previously assumed.

In a critique of this literature, Eagle (1984) suggested that "test-passing and the establishment of conditions of safety can lead to amelioration of symptoms (and other changes) without the intervening step of the emergence of warded-off contents into awareness and without articulated insight" (p. 103). However, most clinical experience suggests that insight usually does arise after an experience of progress in analytic therapy—perhaps because talk is the medium in which therapy is conducted, and the two parties are likely to reflect verbally on any improvements in the patient.

DEFINING AND MEASURING INSIGHT

Whether one agrees with the conclusions that Weiss, Sampson, and the Mt. Zion Psychotherapy Research Group (1986) have drawn about the process by which insight arises as therapy progresses, it would be valuable to have more empirical data about the role of insight in a positive therapy experience. Some years ago at Rutgers University, we set out to devise a measure of insight that would be part of a general measure of patient progress in psychotherapy. Before describing that measure, we give an overview and critique of the major efforts to operationalize and measure insight from a psychoanalytic perspective that existed (see Spillman, 1991, for more details regarding the supporting data for these measures). In constructing our scale, we tried to consider what we regarded as shortcomings of previous scales. This covers the period from 1959 to 1988; more recent efforts are described in chapter 7 of this volume.

Speisman (1959) started with a general attempt to measure insight, which he defined as

> the degree to which the patient is examining himself. He may be reacting to his own statements or those of the therapist, but in each case he is investigating reasons for, or expressing reactions to, his own feelings or statements. (p. 94)

A measure more indicative of insight as it was generally understood at the time was developed by Garduk and Haggard (1972):

> Patient shows understanding or insight in regard to what has apparently been communicated to him. This category includes both "simple" understanding ("Yes, I can understand that.") and insight ("I would not have thought that but I recognize it now."). (p. 45)

Garduk and Haggard's measure of insight, however, is very general, includes intellectual understanding only, and leaves too much room for clinical inference.

In their study of the immediate effects of interpretations, Luborsky, Bachrach, Graff, Pulver, and Christoph (1979) extended Garduk and Haggard's (1972) definition to include an affective component. A measure of insight that took multiple forms of insight into account was subsequently developed by the Penn Psychotherapy Project in connection with its work on the helping alliance (Morgan, Luborsky, Crits-Christoph, Curtis, & Solomon, 1982). The scale consisted of seven categories of behavior that measured the degree to which the patient recognized affects, patterns of behavior, defenses, and connections between present and past, on the basis of Reid and Feinsinger's (1952) definition. Broitman (1986) subsequently used the scale to study the immediate effects of accurate interventions on levels of insight in three short-term psychotherapy cases. The high intercorrelations among individual items led him to question the usefulness of the individual items and to reconsider the value of a single global score.

Joyce, Piper, McCallum, and Azim (1988) developed a measure of psychoanalytic work—a concept roughly equivalent to insight—defined as the degree to which the patient made productive use of the analyst's interpretations. It was developed as a means of measuring patients' responses to interpretations. For a response to qualify as work, it had to (a) maintain a focus on the self, (b) be related to the content of the interpretation, and (c) add something new to the interpretation. If the response failed to meet any one of these criteria, it was categorized as nonwork. They further categorized types of work on the basis of the content of the patient's response. *Descriptive work* simply added material to the interpretation and appeared roughly equivalent to patient exploration. *Relational work* applied to the recognition of interpersonal patterns. *Dynamic work* referred to a response that identified a facet of the patient's conflict other than that identified by the therapist's intervention. The researchers gave greater importance in the scoring to dynamic and relational work compared with descriptive work. They found that the distinction between a response that added something new to an interpretation (descriptive work) and one that did not (nonwork) was often difficult to make. Furthermore, a distinction not picked up by this scale was that descriptive, relational, and dynamic material all may be used in the service of resistance, that is, nonwork.

In addition to the latter measures, general patient progress measures such as the Vanderbilt Psychotherapy Process Scale (O'Malley, Suh, & Strupp, 1983) contain items that are roughly equivalent to insight, such as the effort to understand the reasons behind problematic feelings and behaviors. Some components of the Allen, Newsom, Gabbard, and Coyne (1984) Patient Collaboration Scale also tap into the construct of insight. For example, one of the dimensions of collaboration is defined as follows:

> He or she works actively and reflectively with the material of the sessions; for example, he or she spontaneously makes useful observations about his or her behavior and feelings, analyzes his or her own functioning. At this level, the patient actively identifies, discusses and explores resistances. (p. 386)

One key problem with previous measures of insight is that they typically rely on general terms that may carry different meanings for different research raters. The Rutgers Psychotherapy Research Group believed that a better approach to measuring insight would involve clearer, more concrete, descriptive terms referring to insightful verbal behavior. Perhaps one reason the empirical measures are rather general in their treatment of insight is that the theoretical literature tends to be diverse and somewhat abstract, offering little in the way of concrete markers. In addition, previous measures did not take into account the context of patient verbal material, which we regarded as essential. Our goal was to capture the main elements of insight as it is presented in the psychoanalytic literature in a way that could be measured reliably and meaningfully as part of a general psychotherapy process instrument.

THE RUTGERS PSYCHOTHERAPY PROGRESS SCALE AND THE DEVELOPMENT OF INSIGHT

The Rutgers Psychotherapy Progress Scale (RPPS) was developed to measure patient progress during the conduct of psychodynamic psychotherapy. The scale consists of eight items that are rated on a Likert-type scale. Each item is meant to measure some aspect of patient progress as it is conceptualized in the psychoanalytic literature. The eight items are as follows: (a) Significant Material, (b) Development of Insight, (c) Focus on Emotion, (d) Direct Reference to the Therapist and/or Therapy, (e) New Behavior in the Session, (f) Collaboration, (g) Clarity and Vividness of Communication, and (h) Focus on the Self. Definitions of each item, along with scale points and guidelines for assigning numeric scores, are contained in the scoring manual, which can be obtained from Stanley B. Messer. (For studies on the reliability and validity of the RPPS and its earlier version, the Rutgers Psychotherapy Progress and Stagnation Scale, see Holland, Roberts, & Messer, 1998; Messer, Tishby, & Spillman, 1992; Tishby, Assa, & Shefler, 2006; Tishby & Messer, 1995).

A unique aspect of the RPPS is that it was designed to measure patient progress using everything that has been said, either by the patient only or by both therapist and patient, up to the point of the patient material being rated. It was our belief that the best way to judge accurately whether a patient was making progress at a specific point in therapy was to know what had previously been said. Considering context allows raters to have a fuller understanding of the meaning of a patient's utterances and to make an informed judgment concerning movement toward therapeutic goals. We now focus on the item Development of Insight to briefly discuss the use of the scale. Our purpose in presenting this item and the way it is scored is to show how one may translate the psychoanalytic notion of insight into a useful empirical construct. It should be kept in mind that the Development of Insight item was developed and has been used only in the context of the other seven items.

Definition

Insight refers to the development of new understanding on the part of the patient, which is related to the issues he or she is presenting in therapy.

Criteria

All of the following are considered indications of insight:

1. *Recognition of patterns or connections*—The patient comes to see a link between current and past relationships, between two or more current relationships, between the transference relationship and a significant other, or between how others have treated the patient and how he or she treats him- or herself (i.e., internalizations). For example, a patient came to recognize that her passive behavior with the male therapist paralleled her behavior with her boyfriend. This passive behavior, in turn, stemmed from her response to her highly critical father, whom she feared.

2. *Ability to observe one's own internal processes, personality, or psychopathology*—The presence of insight is suggested when patients are able to distance themselves enough from their problems to observe them. For example, a patient may realize that she is being defensive in the midst of a session, or that he is repeating a pathological identification by being excessively compliant.

3. *Revision of pathological beliefs*—Insight is also working when the patient begins to question and revise pathological beliefs. For example, the patient may say, "Maybe it's not really my

fault that my mother is so depressed," or "Perhaps it is possible to experience feelings without anything catastrophic happening."

4. *Recognition of motivations of the self*—The patient may come to a new understanding about his or her motives. This may involve a recognition of wishes being expressed, fears that are involved, or the defensive function of behavior. For example, a patient came to understand that he avoided writing because he was afraid to find out that he had no talent.

5. *Recognition of motivations of others*—Insight is indicated when the patient shows fresh understanding about the motives and feelings of significant others or a change in his or her perception of others. For example, a patient who continually blamed her mother for her misfortunes gradually became aware of her mother's good intentions. Beliefs about the motives of others must be accompanied by evidence or examples that support the veracity of the attributions.

In deciding on the degree of insight, the following criteria are used:

1. *Historical significance*—Other things being equal, insight into patterns involving important figures from childhood is rated higher than insight involving only current relationships.

2. *Motivation of the self*—Other things being equal, insight into motivations of the self are rated higher than insight into motivations of others.

3. *Centrality*—Insight that relates to issues that are central to the patient's presenting complaints is rated higher than insight related to tangential issues.

4. *Depth*—Insight may vary on how close it gets to the core of a presenting problem. Consider, for example, the case of a female patient who has trouble being sexual with men. The recognition that the problem occurs only when she begins to feel emotionally involved in the relationship, though important, would not be rated as highly as the realization of an unconscious fear that if she allows herself to be truly in love with a man her father would disown her.

5. *Conviction*—Sometimes an insight will be stated tentatively before it is fully accepted. This would be rated lower than an insight that is fully accepted.

Additional guidelines for measuring insight include the following: Insight is not rated if a patient merely repeats or agrees with an interpretation offered by the therapist. For insight to be considered present, patients have to provide some degree of elaboration or exploration of their own. Conversely, patients may receive a high score for an insight that they accept and elaborate on even if it is first suggested by the therapist.

If it seems clear that patients are discussing an understanding that they had before they came into therapy (as often happens in early sessions), the score for insight would be zero. Insight is rated only when the understanding is new to the patient. However, insights that occur between sessions and are reported during a subsequent session are given full credit as insight.

Sometimes a patient will have an "insight" that seems inaccurate. In this case, the rating for insight is zero. Other times, a patient may offer an insight that seems accurate but is being used, in part, defensively. For example, insight that is somewhat intellectualized and uttered by a patient with an obsessive style may serve the purpose of defending against feeling and is generally less indicative of progress than if it were uttered by a patient who relied on histrionic defenses. To the extent that insight serves a defensive function, it receives a lower rating.

It is expected that patients will have insights about material they have already been exploring. Thus, it may appear that insights are gradually built up, rather than occurring suddenly. As long as a patient is making new connections or strengthening his or her understanding, the block of material is rated for insight, even if there has been exploration of the material in previous blocks. How highly Development of Insight should be rated depends on what portion of the insight appears to be new in the block being rated. For example, if a patient has been exploring material related to two different areas of his or her life and makes a connection based on a similar pattern in both areas, this insight would receive a high rating.

EXAMPLES OF MEASURING DEGREE OF INSIGHT

The following examples of insight are taken from transcripts of brief psychodynamic therapy conducted by experienced psychologists at a university counseling center. In a single-case design research project investigating factors contributing to progress in this mode of therapy, a 5-point scale was used to rate the peak expression of insight in each 5 minute block of patient talk: 0 = *not insightful*; 1 = *slightly insightful*; 2 = *moderately insightful*; 3 = *very insightful*; and 4 = *extremely insightful*. The following examples are presented verbatim, with all the usually unnoticed, disjointed aspects of speech.

The client in the first example is in the process of working on problems in her relationship with her father.

Score = 1

    Client: . . . and I sit there and realize that my dad just wants me to say, oh this is such a good meal, ya know, this is wonderful. And I wonder, like, is this really his hobby or is this just his way of like, ya know, like why. . .why does he do this, what is his reason for it?

Therapist: What is your fantasy about why he's doing it?

Client: Now I'm starting to think that he does it just because he wants us to be grateful to him.

The patient then provided examples that corroborated her statement. The patient is beginning "recognition of the motivation of others" and thus gets a score indicating that her insight is *slightly insightful.*

The next client is the daughter of a Chinese mother and a Caucasian father. She has been struggling against her mother's culturally derived concerns about "saving face" and expectations she felt were placed on her as a pastor's daughter.

Score = 2

Client: . . . I'm doing that mother, daughter, grandmother paper? [*sigh*]. I have all these direct quotes from my mom and she knows so much and she's writing about, um, it's this Chinese idea of saving face, and just always looking good to people [*sigh*] and because you fear their disapproval and . . . the . . . fear of disapproval and embarrassment to the family . . . [*sigh*] and that my mother praises this [*sigh*] and I'm reading this. I'm like, this is what I do too, ya know, like I've been taught this, ya know, that I have to . . . I have to make everything look good for the family and ya know, we have, we have to go to church, everything has to look like we're the perfect family because our father is the pastor, ya know, it's just I'm realizing more and more that it's just not that way, ya know, my things are covered up and that I believed them because my parents like foster this, ya know . . .

In this case the client is coming to understand how she has covered up her feelings about the way she has been affected by the family's emphasis on outward appearances and fear of others' disapproval. The criteria for insight that apply here include "recognition of motivations of the self" and "recognition of motivations of others." This moderate degree of insight touches on the client's central pattern of falling in with her parents' wishes because she fears their disapproval, although she also wishes to rebel against them.

The following example is taken from the therapy of a young woman who presented with bulimia. She experiences feelings of powerlessness and lack of control and is usually submissive in her relationship with men.

Score = 3

Client: I see now that I don't do much to assert myself when I'm on a date, that I just go along with him and just, like, hope that he likes me. But then I get mad that he doesn't treat me better and it's confusing because I also see how I get mad at me when this happens—it's like then I feel bad and like that maybe I deserve how I'm treated. Ya know, I don't think I try to be more—ya know, assert myself more because I don't want to be disliked and maybe dumped . . . but I also somehow feel that I deserve not to be liked and so when I get treated bad it feels like it was supposed to happen.

The client recognizes a pattern in which she treats herself as badly as others treat her. In saying that she feels she deserves not to be liked she is recognizing both a "motivation of the self" and "an ability to observe her own psychopathology," which merits a rating of *very insightful*.

The following example is of a man whose chief presenting complaint is impotence and difficulty committing to relationships. His mother has been diagnosed with schizophrenia.

Score = 4

Therapist: You said you sometimes feel like your mother's watching you while you're having sex?

Client: It's not really that I feel like she's watching. It's . . . it's more like . . . well, I just feel she'd be disgusted or something. No . . . I guess . . . it's . . . you know what it is . . . I never really thought about this but . . . it's . . . it's like I'm being unfaithful somehow . . . like she has so little in her life . . . she's driven everyone away . . . I'm really all she has . . . so it feels like every little thing I take away from her is that much bigger . . . and so if I . . . you know . . . then she would have nothing . . . and then maybe she would go crazy and lose it all.

In this example the client is observing his internal processes and recognizes a major motive for his presenting complaints in connection with a major figure in his life, a person whose impact on him is both in the past and in the present. Having sex with a woman, he believes, is tantamount to being unfaithful to his mother, abandoning her and causing her mental anguish This passage reflects a high score on centrality and depth as it goes to the core of the client's problem. Therefore, it is scored as *extremely insightful*.

FUTURE DIRECTIONS FOR RESEARCH ON INSIGHT IN PSYCHODYNAMIC THERAPY

The Development of Insight scale contains only one item because it was constructed as part of a general psychotherapy progress scale. Given the complexity of the concept of insight, the scale might be fruitfully expanded to include about 8 to 10 items to enhance its reliability and validity. As

Connolly Gibbons et al. (see chap. 7, this volume) conclude in their review of the empirical research on insight, there have been few studies measuring insight and these are seriously flawed methodologically. This makes it difficult to draw firm conclusions about insight or its sister concepts, self-understanding and self-awareness. Yet, as Gelso and Harbin (see chap. 14, this volume) cogently point out, insight, especially when integrated with affect, constitutes a central feature of several prominent forms of therapy. Insight appears to be a concept begging for proper measurement and study.

There are many hypotheses that can be pursued empirically with the aid of a methodologically sound scale. Such hypotheses can be derived from the theoretical review of psychoanalytic notions of insight with which we began this chapter, as well as from Gelso and Harbin's (see chap. 14, this volume) theoretical propositions about the relation of insight to action. For example, does insight lead to symptom alleviation and other kinds of progress in psychoanalytic therapy as suggested by Freud and the ego psychologists? Does affect play an important role in potentiating intellectual insight and, if so, in what kinds of personality disorders? Are the relational theorists correct in claiming that insight is a natural product of the therapeutic collaboration that emerges from an authentic and trusting patient–therapist relationship? Should insight, then, be regarded more as an outcome than as a process measure? Is insight mainly a matter of becoming conscious of that which was previously unconscious, or is it a way of describing and making sense of mutual enactments that occur in therapy? Does insight, if viewed as a process, develop over the course of therapy, and is that development correlated with outcome? Do accurate interpretations lead to insight?

CONCLUDING COMMENTS

The concept of insight appears in many different contexts in the history of the psychodynamic psychotherapies. Although it began with Freud's hope that insight into the source of a disabling symptom would remove that symptom, the emphasis on insight became generalized to fit many features of the therapy process. The analytic literature has treated insight both as a means to an end (symptom relief) and as an end in itself, as the cause of change and as the result of change. Although a high value on insight has characterized the psychoanalytic movement from its inception through its most recent theoretical developments, there have been few empirical attempts to operationalize the concept. Because we were specifically interested in the increase in insight that psychoanalytic clinical theorists consider a product or by-product of successful therapy, we devised an instrument that has shown promise in examining this phenomenon in the context of overall progress. We hope that some readers will find themselves interested enough to measure the concept of insight more fully and examine it empirically in the ways described.

REFERENCES

Alexander, F., & French, T. M. (1946). *Psychoanalytic therapy: Principles and application*. New York: Ronald Press.

Allen, J. G., Newsom, G. E., Gabbard, G. O., & Coyne, L. (1984). Scales to assess the therapeutic alliance from a psychoanalytic perspective. *Bulletin of the Menninger Clinic, 48*, 383–399.

Blatt, S., Shahar, G., & Zuroff, D. C. (2002). Anaclitic/sociotropic and introjective/autonomous dimensions. In J. C. Norcross (Ed.), *Psychotherapy relationships that work: Therapist contributions and responsiveness to patients* (pp. 315–333). New York: Oxford University Press.

Bouchard, M. A., & Guerette, L. (1991). Psychotherapy as an hermeneutic experience. *Psychotherapy: Theory, Research, Practice, Training, 28*, 385–394.

Broitman, J. (1986). *Insight, the mind's eye: An exploration of three patients' process of becoming insightful*. Unpublished doctoral dissertation, The Wright Institute, Berkeley, CA.

Castonguay, L. G., Goldfried, M. R., Wiser, S., Raue, P. J., & Hayes, A. M. (1996). Predicting the effect of cognitive therapy for depression: A study of unique and common factors. *Journal of Consulting and Clinical Psychology, 65*, 497–504.

Davies, J. M., & Frawley, M. G. (1994). *Treating the adult survivor of childhood sexual abuse: A psychoanalytic perspective*. New York: Basic Books.

Eagle, M. N. (1984). *Recent developments in psychoanalysis: A critical evaluation*. Cambridge, MA: Harvard University Press.

Eissler, K. (1953). The effect of the structure of the ego on psychoanalytic technique. *Journal of the American Psychoanalytic Association, 1*, 104–143.

Frank, K. A. (1993). Action, insight, and working through: Outlines of an integrative approach. *Psychoanalytic Dialogues, 3*, 535–577.

Freud, S. (1953). The interpretation of dreams. In J. Strachey (Ed. & Trans.), *The standard edition of the complete psychological works of Sigmund Freud* (Vols. 4–5, pp. i–627) London: Hogarth Press. (Original work published in 1900)

Freud, S. (1955). A difficulty in the path of psycho-analysis. In J. Strachey (Ed. & Trans.), *The standard edition of the complete psychological works of Sigmund Freud* (Vol. 17, pp. 137–144). London: Hogarth Press. (Original work published in 1917)

Freud, S. (1958). On beginning the treatment (Further recommendations on the technique of psycho-analysis I). In J. Strachey (Ed. & Trans.), *The standard edition of the complete psychological works of Sigmund Freud* (Vol. 12, pp. 123–144). London: Hogarth Press. (Original work published 1913)

Freud, S. (1961). The ego and the id. In J. Strachey (Ed. & Trans.), *The standard edition of the complete psychological works of Sigmund Freud* (Vol. 19, pp. 3–66). London: Hogarth Press. (Original work published 1923)

Freud, S. (1964a). Analysis terminable and interminable. In J. Strachey (Ed. & Trans.), *The standard edition of the complete psychological works of Sigmund Freud* (Vol. 23, pp. 211–253). London: Hogarth Press. (Original work published 1937)

Freud, S. (1964b). Construction in analysis. In J. Strachey (Ed. & Trans.), *The standard edition of the complete psychological works of Sigmund Freud* (Vol. 23, pp. 256–269). London: Hogarth Press. (Original work published 1937)

Freud, S. (1964c). New introductory lectures in psycho-analysis. In J. Strachey (Ed. & Trans.), *The standard edition of the complete psychological works of Sigmund Freud* (Vol. 22, pp. 3–182). London: Hogarth Press. (Original work published 1933)

Garduk, E. L., & Haggard, E. A. (1972). Immediate effects on patients of psychoanalytic interpretations. *Psychological Issues, 7*, 1–85.

Hirsch, I. (1998). The concept of enactment and theoretical convergence. *Psychoanalytic Dialogues, 4*, 171–192.

Hoffman, I. Z. (1998). *Ritual and spontaneity in the psychoanalytic process: A dialectical constructivist view.* Hillsdale, NJ: Analytic Press.

Holland, S. J., Roberts, N. E., & Messer, S. B. (1998). Reliability and validity of the Rutgers Psychotherapy Progress Scale. *Psychotherapy Research, 8*, 104–110.

Horowitz, M. J. (Ed.). (1991). *Hysterical personality style and the histrionic personality disorder.* Northvale, NJ: Jason Aronson.

Joyce, A. S., Piper, W. E., McCallum, M., & Azim, H. F. A. (1988). *A measure of patient response to interpretation.* Unpublished manuscript, University of Alberta Hospitals, Edmonton, Canada.

Kohut, H. (1977). *The restoration of the self.* New York: International Universities Press.

Kris, E. (1956). On some vicissitudes of insight in psycho-analysis. *International Journal of Psycho-Analysis, 37*, 445–455.

Lambert, M. J., & Okiishi, J. C. (1997). The effects of the individual psychotherapist and implications for future research. *Clinical Psychology: Science and Practice, 4*, 66–75.

Luborsky, L. (1988). [Review of the book *Psychotherapy research: Where we are and where should we go?*]. *Journal of the American Psychoanalytic Association, 36*, 219–224.

Luborsky, L., Bachrach, H., Graff, H., Pulver, S., & Christoph, P. (1979). Preconditions and consequences of transference interpretations: A clinical–quantitative investigation. *Journal of Nervous and Mental Disease, 167*, 391–401.

Martin, D. J., Garske, J. P., & Davis, M. K. (2000). Relation of the therapeutic alliance with outcome and other variables: A meta-analytic review. *Journal of Consulting and Clinical Psychology, 68*, 438–450.

Messer, S. B., Tishby, O., & Spillman, A. (1992). Taking context seriously in psychotherapy research: Relating therapist interventions to patient progress in brief psychodynamic therapy. *Journal of Consulting and Clinical Psychology, 60*, 678–688.

Mitchell, S. A. (1997). *Influence and autonomy in psychoanalysis.* Hillsdale, NJ: Analytic Press.

Morgan, R. W., Luborsky, L., Crits-Christoph, P., Curtis, H., & Solomon, J. (1982). Predicting the outcomes of psychotherapy using the Penn Helping Alliance rating method. *Archives of General Psychiatry, 39*, 397–402.

Neubauer, P. B. (1979). The role of insight in psychoanalysis. *Journal of the American Psychoanalytic Association, 27*(Suppl.), 29–40.

Norcross, J. C. (Ed.). (2002). *Psychotherapy relationships that work: Therapist contributions and responsiveness to patients.* New York: Oxford University Press.

Ogden, T. H. (1997). *Reverie and interpretation: Sensing something human.* Northvale, NJ: Jason Aronson.

O'Malley, S. S., Suh, C. S., & Strupp, H. H. (1983). The Vanderbilt Psychotherapy Process Scale: A report of the scale development and a process-outcome study. *Journal of Consulting and Clinical Psychology, 51,* 581–586.

Orange, D. M. (1995). *Emotional understanding: Studies in psychoanalytic epistemology.* New York: Guilford Press.

Poland, W. S. (1988). Insight and the analytic dyad. *Psychoanalytic Quarterly, 57,* 341–369.

Reid, J. R., & Feinsinger, J. E. (1952). The role of insight in psychotherapy. *American Journal of Psychiatry, 108,* 726–734.

Richfield, J. (1954). An analysis of the concept of insight. *Psychoanalytic Quarterly, 23,* 390–408.

Sandler, J., Holder, A., & Dare, C. (1973). *The patient and the analyst.* New York: International Universities Press.

Speisman, J. C. (1959). Depth of interpretation and verbal resistance in psychotherapy. *Journal of Consulting Psychology, 23,* 93–99.

Spillman, A. (1991). *The development of a scale for measuring patient progress and patient stagnation in psychodynamic psychotherapy.* Unpublished doctoral dissertation, Graduate School of Applied and Professional Psychology, Rutgers University, New Brunswick, NJ.

Strachey, J. (1934). The nature of the therapeutic action of psycho-analysis. *International Journal of Psycho-Analysis, 15,* 127–159.

Tishby, O., Assa, T., & Shefler, G. (2006). Patient progress during two time-limited psychotherapies as measured by the Rutgers psychotherapy progress scale. *Psychotherapy Research, 16,* 80–90.

Tishby, O., & Messer, S. B. (1995). The relationship between plan compatibility of therapist interventions and patient progress: A comparison of two plan formulations. *Psychotherapy Research, 5,* 76–88.

van der Kolk, B. A., McFarlane, A. C., & Weisaeth, L. (Eds.). (1996). *Traumatic stress: The overwhelming experience on mind, body, and society.* New York: Guilford Press.

Weiss, J., Sampson, H., & the Mt. Zion Psychotherapy Research Group (1986). *The psychoanalytic process: Theory, clinical observation, and empirical research.* New York: Guilford Press.

2

INSIGHT AND AWARENESS IN EXPERIENTIAL THERAPY

ANTONIO PASCUAL-LEONE AND LESLIE S. GREENBERG

Traditionally, *insight* has been used as a global term referring to a new change in consciousness. However, qualitatively different processes of insights can be understood as falling on a continuum from *experience-near* to *experience-distant*. Experience-near insight, emphasized by experiential therapies, involves symbolizing the emergence of a new experience as it occurs. Through lived experiences, the client "discovers" new ways of being by a variety of different processes. This felt discovery of new aspects of self is central to experiential therapies (L. S. Greenberg & van Balen, 1998). In contrast, experience-distant insight involves conceptually considering one's experience from a bird's-eye view and often formulating an abstracted understanding of why one has a given experience.

This chapter delineates a number of different processes subsumed under the label *insight* and explores how they function in therapeutic change. In doing so, we review the perspectives on insight offered within the humanistic tradition. We begin by summarizing briefly how past experiential therapists described insight and its role in change processes. Next, we elaborate different insight processes more fully. Awareness and experiential meta-awareness are the two types of experience-near insight discussed in detail in this chapter. They are contrasted with two kinds of more experience-distant insight: rational meta-awareness and conceptual linking. In short, the chapter contrasts the experiential forms of insight, which emphasize a lived experience, with the traditional psychodynamic conceptualization of insight, which emphasizes linking pieces of knowledge into conceptual formulations (Malan, 1979). In the final part of this chapter, we describe causal processes and clinical implications for facilitating experience-near insights as well as emerging research directions.

One of the most identifying features of humanistic treatments such as client-centered, gestalt, process–experiential, and certain existential schools of therapy is that they focus on client experience. For this reason, we address these therapeutic orientations in this chapter under the rubric *experiential therapies*. Among experiential therapies, insight is usually referred to as *awareness*, *re-owning*, or *meta-awareness*. *Awareness* denotes explicitly attending to certain aspects of one's ongoing experience that may otherwise go unidentified, whereas the term *re-owning* implies that aspects of how one experiences oneself that have remained unaddressed or warded off are now accepted into awareness. We will call *meta-awareness* the special awareness of how one perceives things, processes information, or constructs one's own experience. Thus, some types of experience-near insight involve awareness of discovering something new (e.g., "I experience feeling sad about a loss"). Other types of insight involve meta-awareness, the gaining of a new perspective in vivo (e.g., "I realize I put up a wall to avoid closeness") or the awareness of one's awarenesses (e.g., "I notice that I'm always attentive to any hint of abandonment").

INSIGHT IN EXPERIENTIAL THERAPIES

The concept of insight in experiential therapies has been used with ambivalence. The term itself most often appears as a theoretical vestige inherited from psychoanalysis. Many important authors from humanistic–existential traditions, including Rogers, Perls, May, and Yalom, were trained to some extent in psychoanalytic and neo-Freudian approaches. Their initial attempts at describing therapeutic shifts were strongly influenced by this, and their early efforts at describing change used the concept of insight. For most of these authors, the manner in which the term *insight* was used metamorphosed substantially into the concepts of awareness and meta-awareness. To complicate matters further, these new conceptual variations of insight have found their way into modern psychodynamic schools of thought and are now used alongside the earlier sense of psychoanalytic insight as conceptual linking.

Client-Centered Therapy

The initial work of Rogers (1942) describes insight as "an experience which the client achieves" (p. 177). This early publication attempts to articulate the initial ideas of client-centered therapy and gives detailed examples of how insight develops within and across sessions. During this period, Rogers refers to insight as a form of connecting and acceptance but always with the insistence that insight is a felt, rather than an intellectual, experience. Thus, for Rogers insight is a process of discovering something new through experiential awareness and gaining a new perspective in vivo (i.e., meta-awareness). "While . . . insight appears simple enough, it is the fact that it comes to have *emotional and operational meaning* [italics added], which gives it its newness and vividness" (Rogers, 1951, p. 119). All leading experiential theorists have emphasized this distinction between the felt and the known.

Although Rogers used the term *insight* in his early work (albeit in a unique sense), his later works refer to insight sparingly and in a manner that is interchangeable with terms such as *awareness* and *felt experience*. In Rogers's final works (i.e., Raskin & Rogers, 1989), the term *insight* is dropped from the conceptual vocabulary of client-centered therapy altogether. The authors instead use the notion that clients symbolize their unfolding experience and that client experiencing deepens (Rogers, 1959). In therapy, *symbolization* "is the process by which the individual [usually] becomes aware or conscious of an experience" (Raskin & Rogers, 1989, p. 169). Experiencing, in turn, is the process of attending to that unverbalized yet ongoing visceral flow and using it as a referent against which one can check tentative symbolizations, thereby recursively discovering the meanings and significance of what one is feeling (Gendlin, 1981; Raskin & Rogers, 1989).

According to Rogers (1959), a forward shift in client-centered therapy has four qualities. These qualities essentially describe the role of awareness as a kind of insight: (a) It is not thinking about something, it is an experience of something at this instant in the relationship; (b) it is consciously feeling as much as one feels, without holding back and without exaggeration; (c) this is the first time it has been experienced completely; and (d) the experience is welcomed and acceptable to the client (pp. 52–53). Thus, the four qualities of a therapeutic shift capture the newness of perception and the lived understanding of an experience-near insight. In short, these features set awareness processes apart from the verbal and intellectual shift that is described as an experience-distant insight.

Focusing

Experiential schools following the work of Gendlin emphasized the experiencing process and *focusing* on the *bodily felt sense* to carry forward experience. Making the implicit explicit was the central idea in this school. *Insight* came to be seen as the product of explicating and creating new meaning in an ongoing process of awareness, rather than the product of an act of linking of elements (Gendlin, 1981). In a seminal chapter, Gendlin (1964) explained the role of attending to and symbolizing experience through awareness, as contrasted with a conceptual understanding of insight:

> Hence we often discuss self-exploration as if it were purely a logical inquiry in search of conceptual answers. However, in psychotherapy (and in one's private self-exploration as well) the logical contents and insights are secondary. Process has primacy. We must attend and symbolize in order to carry forward the process and thereby reconstitute it in certain new aspects. *Only then*, as new contents come to function implicitly in feeling, can we symbolize them. (p. 158)

The 7-point Experiencing Scale subsequently became the gold standard of the change process in experiential therapies. It defines Level 4 as a pivotal step of focusing on a bodily felt sense and symbolizing it in awareness. Level 6 represents a deeper level of experiencing in which clients use currently accessible feelings to solve problems or create new meanings (Klein, Mathieu-Coughlan, & Kiesler, 1986). This line of work was a dramatic help in elaborating the experiential conceptualization of insight.

Existential Psychotherapy

According to existentially oriented therapists and philosophers, awareness is achieved more often than not through confrontation with ultimate concerns (i.e., death, isolation, meaninglessness, and freedom). However, existentialists opposed the belief that reality can be understood in an abstract, detached way. By definition, confrontations are experiential and in the moment. Thus, existential confrontations of these ultimate concerns occur as visceral, emotional experiences. The *I-am* is an experience of reality "as such" (i.e., an ontological experience) and is the central concern of an existential therapy (May & Yalom, 1989). The awareness and subsequent existential awareness of one's own freedom, connectedness, or disconnectedness is an emotionally rooted perspective of life and living (i.e., the I-am experience). This existential insight is a particular type of awareness that engenders a new perspective (i.e., experiential meta-awareness).

This particular form of experience-near insight is one of awareness and lived appreciation for the nature of one's existence. This does not preclude the fact that insights regarding mortality or interpersonal connection could also be understood through forms of conceptual linking. However, the truly existential insight is experience-near and is an in-the-moment meta-awareness of oneself as both the reader and the author of one's life story. Yalom (1981) describes four insights (experiential types of meta-awareness) that are of special importance to the existential approach. When they are experience-near, these are highly complex affective-meaning states that serve to organize the individual in the moment. These prototypical existential insights are (a) "only I can change the world I have created," (b) "there is no danger in change," (c) "to get what I want I must change," and (d) "I have the power to change" (Yalom, 1981, pp. 340–432). Reflexive states such as these are simple yet profound. Although they can be entertained from an experience-distant position as theoretical possibilities (as with the acknowledgment of one's mortality), their full and real impact is appreciated only when they are lived moments of awareness rather than items of conceptual or behavioral learning. This is highlighted by the fact that from an existential perspective the content of an insight is considered to be largely unimportant. What is important is the effect such an insight has on a client in providing the experience of empowerment, agency, and a sense of the possibility of change (Yalom, 1981).

In short, intentionality is what gives existential insights (i.e., meta-awareness) their substance. May (1983) argued that decision actually precedes knowledge and insight, if decision is taken to mean a decisive attitude toward existence, an attitude of commitment. Similarly, when Rogers (1942) discussed insight in his early work he referred to the embodiment of choice and action as the true indicator of insight. An example of existential insight given by Schneider and May (1995) shows it to be an immediate, lived, and experience-near form of self-understanding: "I never realized how deeply these feelings affected me and how strongly I want to experience them again in my life" (p. 171). This example captures a client's sudden meta-awareness of his immediate experience in the context of both his worldview and his usual manner of processing such feelings. In this statement the client not only indicates self-understanding but also embodies intentionality toward new goals in a lived experience.

Gestalt Therapy

Gestalt therapy is both an experiential and an existential therapy (May & Yalom, 1989; Perls, 1969). As such, it typifies awareness as the experiential discovery of a previously unacknowledged feeling (i.e., "I feel angry"). It also typifies meta-awareness, in the form of existential insights (i.e., the *I-am* experience and awareness of oneself as a participant in the *I–Thou* encounter). Perls, Hefferline, and Goodman (1951) also acknowledged the subtle distinction between these and the traditional form of insight as conceptual linking. They make a case that a verbal and theoretical type of insight, though perfectly correct, does not contain the felt significance, which is a prerequisite to genuine change. The distinction between knowing something versus owning it is apparent (L. S. Greenberg & van Balen, 1998).

The emphasis in gestalt and other experientially oriented therapies is on experience and process (what the client feels and how it is experienced and done), over content and cause (what is being talked about and why the client experiences and does things). Moments of insight in these therapies are essentially unconcerned with the question *why*. Discovering *what* one feels and does, as well as *how* one does what one does, is necessarily part of awareness and meta-awareness, rather than causal knowledge (L. S. Greenberg & van Balen, 1998; Yontef & Simkin, 1989).

Gestaltist interventions of focused awareness and playful experimentation are intended to produce insight—awareness of what one is experiencing and how one interrupts that experience as well as awareness of the awareness process itself (i.e., meta-awareness). This phenomenological perspective of Gestalt therapy means that insight is achieved through an experience-near process; the traditional understanding of insight as linking has only an incidental place (Perls et al., 1951; Stevens, 1971).

INSIGHT: AWARENESS, META-AWARENESS, AND LINKING

To consider how insight is manifested in general and in experiential therapy specifically, one must accept that insight is not a singular phenomenon. This section will delineate a number of different processes subsumed under the label *insight* and explore how they function in relation to each other. This exploration is imperative for a deeper understanding of what insight is and what experiential therapies do to promote this process (L. S. Greenberg & van Balen, 1998). *Awareness* and *meta-awareness* can be contrasted with *linking and connecting*, the process that a traditional conceptualization of insight tends to emphasize. Notwithstanding the recognition of emotional insight as an important phenomenon in psychoanalytic literature, the emphasis on conceptual linking rests on providing explanations of why.[1]

Despite piecemeal attempts at identifying this loose assembly of phenomena, the three processes of awareness, meta-awareness and conceptual linking commonly are lumped together as *insights*. It is likely that a general integrated framework for encompassing this family of concepts has not been put forward because it emerged from different therapeutic orientations. Figure 2.1 offers a schematic representation of the distinct types of insight. In this diagram we see that the global term *insight* is used to refer to phenomena that vary on two process dimensions: level of abstraction (low, concrete experiential content vs. high, abstract linking across elements) and type of processing (near, perceptual–emotional vs. distant, conceptual–rational).

Abstraction is the process of internalizing concrete invariances across situations, over space and time, so that the higher the level of abstraction,

---

[1]It is important to realize that the term *emotional insight* does not necessarily capture central experiential aspects of the phenomena we discuss in this chapter. Moreover, that term has not been used consistently across the literature. In psychodynamic and body-based therapies, emotional insight is used to refer to cathartic processes that accompany understanding (Singer, 1970; Gelso, Kivlighan, Wine, Jones, & Friedman, 1997). In rational–emotive therapies, it refers to the sense of conviction that accompanies rationally derived insights (Ellis, 2001).

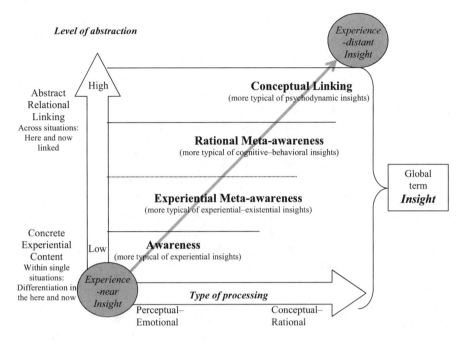

Figure 2.1. Types and dimensions of insight.

the broader the scope of the induction set, and the larger the set of elements abstracted from (J. Pascual-Leone, 2002; J. Pascual-Leone & Irwin, 1998). Low levels of abstraction have a direct bearing on concrete experiential content. In contrast, high levels of abstraction no longer have an impact only on direct concrete experience but rather on the relationship between elements— a relationship that is only apparent *across* different types of situations (J. Pascual-Leone, 2002; J. Pascual-Leone & Irwin, 1998). *Type of processing* refers to the relative weight of affective versus cognitive processes. Thus, processing an experience can occur either by living an experience through the immediacy of perception and emotion or by thinking about it from a conceptual and rational position (L. S. Greenberg, 2002). The two dimensions (which are not entirely orthogonal) are related to overall therapeutic styles and manifest themselves in what we have identified as four kinds of insight (middle section of Figure 2.1).

The types of insight identified here are tacitly constructed using different information-processing strategies: *top-down* versus *bottom-up.* These are different implicit approaches to making sense of one's experience and are reflected in each of the two dimensions we described. In a top-down strategy one begins with an overall conceptual formulation, such as the identification of a general theme occurring across situations, after which one follows with the gradual elaboration of details. Bottom-up processing begins by exploring individual and idiosyncratic details, such as one's moment-by-moment feelings, that are eventually combined to create a larger unit of general meaning.

The way different types of insight emerge and function in relation to one another is described by the model in Figure 2.1. Conceptual linking—such as between a current relationship, a past relationship, and the relationship with the therapist—is typified by the psychodynamic insight (at top of Figure 2.1) and is formulated at a high level of abstraction. That is, it includes integrating information through a top-down development of relational links made across different situations, from *here and now* to *there and then* (see left side of Figure 2.1). Psychodynamic forms of conceptual linking often are more experience-distant—although links can be constructed close to experience. The counterpoint to this is the insight of new awareness, such as experiencing that one feels angry at one's father, which is a mainstay of experiential schools. Awareness is constructed through a bottom-up process and is rooted in the concrete perceptual and emotional content of experience (i.e., in differentiating the here and now) rather than in abstract conceptual formulations. In the middle area of this continuum we find meta-awareness bridging top-down and bottom-up constructions. Depending on the perceptual–emotional versus conceptual–rational nature of this kind of insight, meta-awareness may be more rational, as in identifying a core belief or considering the rationality of an automatic thought as a cold cognition, which are more representative of the cognitive–behavioral schools. Alternatively, a meta-awareness can be more experiential, such as noticing in a felt manner that "I am seeing the world as a rejecting place," and is more representative of the experiential–existential schools.

Finally, the two dimensions, abstraction and type of processing, act together to define the nature of experience-near versus experience-distant insights. Experience-near and experience-distant are two contrasting poles on a structural (i.e., qualitative) continuum of processes that have been sweepingly regarded as insights. Experience-near insights are relatively more perceptual and emotional and reflect experiential content (i.e., they are synthesized at a low level of abstraction), whereas experience-distant insights are more conceptual and rational and reflect relational connections (i.e., synthesized at a high level of abstraction).

EXPERIENCE-NEAR VERSUS EXPERIENCE-DISTANT

In the integrative model of insight presented in Figure 2.1, insights that occur in-session can vary on a qualitative continuum that ranges from experience-near to experience-distant. This section elaborates on different types of insight using case illustrations to show that although they are qualitatively distinct, they hold positions relative to one another on an ordered series of epistemological levels, as defined by the levels of abstraction and the types of processing. One of the most important differences among the types of insight presented lies in the degree to which a client's insight is abstracted from his or her moment-by-moment experience, which often is related to the type of processing. The overall effect is that insights tend to be either more experience-near or more experience-distant, which is a way of understanding the type of self-knowledge clients are creating.

Awareness as a Low-Level Abstraction

In experiential therapies *awareness* refers to the process of symbolizing some internally felt experience, the content of which is perceived concretely and in the given moment. Focusing, for example, is a task that seeks to accomplish this result (Cornell, 1996; Gendlin, 1981). Thus, when a client comes to a realization (e.g., "I'm scared"), it is actually a form of experience-near, bottom-up insight (see Awareness in Figure 2.1). Clients are synthesizing various aspects of their immediate psychophysical experience with their linguistic-based understanding and find they are suddenly able to adequately capture an aspect of their subjective world (Gendlin, 1964; Leijssen, 1998). Gestalt therapy also provides a wealth of awareness exercises that similarly facilitate low-level insights (Perls et al., 1951; Stevens, 1971). Sometimes this involves re-owning unclaimed or sequestered aspects of one's conscious experience. Other times, it is simply managing to symbolize something that has not previously been symbolized (L. S. Greenberg & van Balen, 1998). The notion of awareness was elaborated by Gestalt psychotherapy as the forming of a new figure against the background of one's ongoing experience (Perls et al., 1951; Stevens, 1971). Thus, the concept of bringing into awareness or re-owning unclaimed aspects of oneself requires an experience in vivo but does not necessarily require connecting or linking to already established self-understandings (L. S. Greenberg & van Balen, 1998). In emotion-focused therapy, for example, naming or labeling a feeling is possibly the simplest form of new awareness (L. S. Greenberg 2002). Of course, not all forms of perceptual–emotional awareness should be regarded as insights: Only those that are truly novel and emerging for the first time can be viewed as insights (as suggested by Rogers's description of the forward shift, discussed previously in this chapter). When emotional awareness introduces a new trajectory of self-organization in the client (i.e., a new way of perceiving and engaging the self, world, or other), it is regarded as an experience-near insight.

An example of awareness taken verbatim from clinical archives of the York forgiveness studies is given here (L. S. Greenberg, Warwar, & Malcolm, 2003). In midsession, the client shows his usual angry stance as he speaks to an imagined sibling in an empty chair. As he does this he becomes aware of incipient sadness for the first time:

> *Client:* Well, I'm really angry. I'm angry enough that I don't want to see you. And I would, ah, be very happy not to see you ever again. [*He frowns.*]

Therapist:	What happens inside you when you say that?
Client:	Um . . . Oh, tremendous sadness. [*He shakes his head, sighs deeply.*]
Therapist:	Sadness.
Client:	Yeah, because we have been, since 1986. . . .
Therapist:	Speak from there. Tell her about the sadness.
Client:	Well, it just is, uh. . . . [*long pause*]. . . . It means we won't ever get together again, to have a swim, to have a barbeque, to . . . talk. . . .
Therapist:	So it's like, "I'm sad about losing you."
Client:	Yes. I'm very sad about losing you. [*Nodding slowly, he is deeply moved. He closes his eyes.*] I, I, ah. . . . .Oh! [*He sighs deeply, opens his eyes, and turns to address the therapist.*] She more than anybody.

This type of new awareness results from the exploration of a single situation rather than across situations and is formulated at a relatively low level of abstraction. Even so, clients often experience the newness felt in such an emerging experience as a tangible moment of insight. This excerpt would be rated as Level 4 on the Experiencing Scale, involving an awareness of an inner state from a focus on a bodily felt sense. In another example, a client elaborates on what it is like to have a moment of awareness after she had become aware of a previously unexplored aspect of her experience.

Client:	I'm not sure how I get to that sad feeling. [*She wipes tears from her face, and her voice continues to be emotional but she is no longer crying.*]
Therapist:	Did you feel like you touched a little bit of that today?
Client:	It's there. But I think that's the first time I've ever *felt* it. I mean, I knew it was there. I just never felt it there. Such a big empty space . . . [*She points to the center of her chest.*] . . . but not knowing what it is or what will fill it. The only way I've been able to explain it to people is as a lack of direction—but that's not really it. It's an emotional void.
Therapist:	. . . longing for something more tangible, more solid, more meaningful.
Client:	Yeah.

In this segment of transcript from the York depression project (L. S. Greenberg & Watson, 1998), the client describes feeling something she always knew was true but had never fully experienced. The feeling has been symbolized, yet the client describes not having a meta-perspective or any links regarding those feelings. She states a problem or proposition about the self and explores it, making it a Level 5 on the Experiencing Scale.

Meta-awareness as a Mid-level Abstraction

When clients develop meta-awareness—an emerging new view of themselves or the world—they are creating a more encompassing meaning, one that involves a new view or new way of perceiving self, world, or other. Evocatively elaborating clients' problematic reactions is a task designed to facilitate mid-level insight of new meaning about how one construes a specific situation (L. S. Greenberg, Rice, & Elliott, 1993; Rice, 1974; Watson & Rennie, 1994). Thus meta-awareness, which in many ways is synonymous with an existential insight, is an in vivo experience of, "Oh, so this is my perspective!" Nevertheless, when clients arrive at a new, fresh, and lived perspective such as, "I can see that I view the world as persecutory," they do not necessarily know why or how that came to be. The existential–phenomenological schools also stress the meta-awareness of an authentic interpersonal encounter as an important form of experience-near insight (Buber, 1957; May & Yalom, 1989; Sartre, 1956). Examples of such an experience are captured by I–Thou encounters (Buber, 1957) between client and therapist, such as "I feel we are able to be real with each other."

When clients experience a meta-awareness they suddenly see their personal constructs as generating their ongoing experience, and they see how they are functioning as agents in the creation of their experience. In this manner clients experience themselves as responsible for their own framework of awareness. With depressed clients, for example, this may appear as an awareness of how their self-critical processes play a role in producing their ongoing sense of hopelessness. Alternatively, clients may momentarily become aware of self-interruptive processes and the automatic ways in which they avoid painful or threatening content. These are often characterological processes that clients are able to consider in vivo.

The experience-near insights of awareness and experiential meta-awareness are generally *lived* or *experiential insights*: They are anchored in a specific situation. Following the elaboration of a puzzling personal reaction in a specific, context-bound situation, the client creates a meaning bridge, one that may later be extended to a broader context (L. S. Greenberg et al., 1993; Rice, 1974). Having an experiential insight does not require connecting or conceptual linking at an abstract level as much as it requires an actual shift in the client's perception and affective-meaning state (Gendlin, 1964). Here, insight refers to a client's moment-by-moment creation of new meanings, something that has been described as levels of client perceptual processing (Toukmanian, 1986).

It is interesting to note that meta-awareness can be facilitated from either a top-down, rational approach or a bottom-up, emotional approach (see middle of Figure 2.1). The rational meta-perspective is the anchor of cognitive–behavioral interventions. It is achieved through rational procedures and highlights, for example, that a belief that one is unworthy is irrational or inconsistent with evidence. The bottom-up, emotional approach, a more experience-near insight, is a common part of experiential therapy and involves a lived experience that one is worthwhile.

As the brief survey of experiential approaches shows, therapeutic interventions target self-understanding in a manner that is experience-near, emotionally evocative, and does not necessarily involve any logical, rational, or conceptual connecting. In short, they are a bottom-up approach to the construction of new meaning (L. S. Greenberg & Pascual-Leone, 1995); this is illustrated on the left side of Figure 2.1. From an experiential perspective, meaning is best constructed by exploring specific situations in depth to discover what one is, in fact, experiencing (L. S. Greenberg et al., 1993). Clients are better able to "taste" their immediate experience by exploring a single experience in depth; subsequently, clients make use of an inherent, spontaneous, and adaptive self-organizing process to promote survival and growth (L. S. Greenberg, 2002). The drawback of such an approach is that clients might find it difficult to discern a pattern or theme across situations in their lives without the benefit of an external, bird's-eye view. Recent efforts in experiential therapy highlight the benefit of promoting reflection and narrative reconstruction to remedy this potential pitfall (L. S. Greenberg & Angus, 2003; L. S. Greenberg & Watson, 2005; Watson & Rennie, 1994).

Linking as a High-Level Abstraction

Linking is a way of construing self-knowledge from a high level of abstraction and refers to the recognition of a personal, usually relational, theme (Binder & Strupp, 1991; Luborsky, Popp, Luborsky, & Mark, 1994). The top-down insight in that case occurs by connecting either different psychological components to one another (i.e., defenses—impulses—anxiety) or through connecting temporal relationship events to one another (i.e., distant past—recent past—here and now; past other—current other—therapist; J. R. Greenberg & Mitchell, 1983; Malan, 1979). This traditional type of conceptual linking insight, which is privileged by psychodynamic approaches, could be described as taking a supraperspective—going beyond the immediate experience of a new perspective (see L. S. Greenberg & Elliott, 1997). Thus, when clients arrive at conclusions such as "I feel persecuted because of the following autobiographical reasons . . . " they have a better self-understanding, although it is often from a conceptual vantage point—an experience-distant position. This distinction holds true, notwithstanding the acknowledgment of emotional insights as valuable to psychodynamic approaches. In fact, the client may subsequently appreciate a new understanding in an experience-near manner as an emotional insight. In such a case, what is often actually felt is a sense of the deep significance that the conceptual insight has to offer. By contrast, what is felt in awareness is the very referent of the connecting insight.

Linking insights are most often experience-distant because the thematization of experience requires a broader level of analysis and a connection between elements that takes precedence over the client's actual moment-by-moment experience of any particular element (J. Pascual-Leone & Irwin, 1998). The facilitation of high-level insight (often through an outside interpretation) is by its nature somewhat removed from the immediate experience. The risk is that conceptual linking could become excessively intellectualized or rationalized, thereby becoming unfastened from the experiential–empirical grounding where therapy matters most. There is also the risk of distorting a client's experience or being less attuned to a client's idiosyncratic experience (L. S. Greenberg & Elliot, 1997).

Thus, linking insights are often conceptual, but clients can have linking insights that are experiential in nature. This depends on the skill and the timing of an interpretation—of delivering it at the right depth when the client is ready to experience its significance. When linking occurs in experiential therapies it comes without explicit interpretation. It is constructed bottom-up by the client rather than being offered by the therapist, which would necessarily involve more top-down processing by the client. Thus, *experiential linking*, which unfolds spontaneously from some clients, is a form of insight that is high in abstraction while still in the purview of perceptual–emotional processing. Following is another verbatim example taken from clinical archives of the York depression project (L. S. Greenberg & Watson, 1998). The client began by discussing her marital difficulties, a topic that led her to discuss her relationship with her children. She notes a theme and goes on to elaborate an experiential linking insight: This would be rated as a Level 6 on the Experiencing Scale, as there is a new understanding and synthesis based on readily accessible feelings.

> Therapist: Oh, so you can't accept love just for being who you are.
>
> Client: [talking rapidly] No. I owe them. Somebody . . . I owe my children when they do something nice for me. I owe them so big I could never buy them enough gifts. I am so touched that somebody bothers to love me. It's so big for me. I think . . . I'm starting to formulate something here in my mind. [Her speech slows and becomes focused.] Give me a second . . . I think I turn people off so I don't have to owe. I'm just realizing that at this moment in time . . . I turn a lot of people off. And it seems to me—why would I do that? I mean that's like shooting yourself in the foot . . . But I think I do that simply for the purpose of not having to owe them. I just discovered that.

This example of a linking insight involves a more top-down, but still somewhat experience-near insight, in which the client makes connections and identifies a pattern that applies across situations. Taking a bird's-eye view can have powerful advantages: Clients have a more contextualized self-understanding and self-interpretative framework. A link that is self-discovered, or better yet self-created, will always fit one's own experience best. Moreover, knowledge that is attained through one's own efforts is more likely to be retained than if it has been conveyed by others.

Insights on Qualitative Continuum

From the viewpoint of the client's cognitive processes, the chief difference between high- and low-level insights is in the scope of mental attention they require (J. Pascual-Leone, 1990). On the one hand, processes at a low level of abstraction, such as awareness, require clients to focus their attention on a narrow level of analysis, the immediate moment-by-moment unfolding of experience. On the other hand, high-level processes such as linking require clients to open their focus of attention to a broad level of analysis. Thus, for high-level insights a client must bear in mind many remotely similar situations and consider past and current relationships, recurrent concerns, overarching experiences, and so forth. In contrast, insights at a low level of abstraction demand that the client remain fully present and focus exclusively on the holistic sense of what it is like to *be* in a particular moment or situation.

The fact that these processes occur at different levels of analysis indicates that one can have distinct types of insight (i.e., awareness, meta-awareness, or linking) with respect to the same content area; moreover, this indicates that insights can differ according to their place on a spectrum, from experience-near to experience-distant. A comparative example illustrates this as follows: Consider a client with a quiet, pleasant demeanor who can be relied on to assist those around her. She suffers from depression and usually talks about her sense of hopelessness. However, at some point in the session she begins to feel angry for the first time at the demands that providing care for a friend places on her. This newly emerging experience of anger is a low-level abstraction, an awareness insight. A meta-awareness at a mid level of abstraction may also emerge through more complex processes over longer periods of time. In its most succinct form her meta-awareness insight might be captured in the realization that "I realize I ignore my own needs and always give to others rather than paying attention to my own limits." At various times she may explore her life story and in doing so gradually formulates an understanding of why and how this came to be. That high-level formulation is a linking insight:

> I always put myself second because I always played 'helper' in my family. I was afraid that the whole family would fall apart if I didn't take care of my parents. Mom and Dad seemed so incompetent that I always ended up holding the bag.

Although these comparative illustrations have been presented in order of increasing abstraction (from low to high) and to some degree in increasing distance from experience (i.e., from experience-near to experience-distant), each insight could occur in isolation or in any sequential order. On a similar note, a client may experience some or all of these insights and each would contribute differently and uniquely toward personal development and change. The fact that each type of insight addresses a client's concern at a different (epistemological) level of discourse has ramifications for how one might best facilitate different types of insight.

MECHANISMS OF EXPERIENCE-NEAR INSIGHT

In this section we take a psychogenetic perspective to examine how one becomes aware of facets of experience that previously went unnoticed. This discussion describes causal processes and has clinical implications for how experience-near insights are facilitated.

Creating Newness Through Being Present

In the awareness and focusing exercises of experiential therapy, symbolizing one's complex and freshly emerging experience with new images or words is a truly novel performance or representation (Cornell, 1996; Gendlin, 1981; L. S. Greenberg et al., 1993; Perls et al., 1951; Stevens, 1971). When therapists who use focusing ask their clients to "check inside" or Gestalt therapists ask their clients to "experiment and try it on, see if those words fit," they are encouraging their clients to verify and test the viability of a truly novel performance–representation.

For a client who is striving to engage the self, world, or other in increasingly productive ways, the newly symbolized experience or new way of perceiving one's internal world eventually proves either useful or useless. In that effort, new ways of perceiving one's internal world will improve the representational repertoire that a client has available to articulate his or her experience. Thus, a truly novel performance–representation will only be retained as part of the client's development if it is an enhancement to the client's repertoire for engaging and experiencing the object of awareness. This is the process of self-development through symbolization.

To the extent that they capture the actual resistances of an internal reality through an evolving psychological construction, experience-near insights are functional and adaptive events that actually assist clients in positive development (L. S. Greenberg & Pascual-Leone, 1995, 2001). Accordingly, experiential schools produce insight through what is better referred to as the specific processes of awareness and the experiential meta-awareness of one's self-organization. Exploring and deepening clients' experiences facilitates these experience-near forms of insight.

Accommodation of Emerging Emotion: The Mini *Aha!* Experience

Emerging emotion is a form of information about the self that must be both differentiated and then integrated into one's representational–functional repertoire. In an experiential view, a client's problems arise because affective information goes unrecognized or is restricted so it is not available to inform and organize the individual adaptively (L. S. Greenberg, 2002; L. S. Greenberg & Safran, 1989, 1990). The creation by awareness of newly emerging emotion schemes in one's repertoire is achieved in experiential therapy through a unique process of accommodation.

In a study of how sensory perception is refined Gibson introduced an understanding of accommodation distinct from that of Piaget (Gibson, 1950; J. Pascual-Leone, 2002); this new type of accommodation best describes the effect of experiential interventions. In an experiential tradition the aim is to explore, elaborate, and expand the client's experience until it spontaneously splits into multiple schemes, that is, differentiates into new, unique schematic units of meaning and relevance (J. Pascual-Leone, 1990, 1991). Thus, the essence of an experiential understanding (i.e., awareness or meta-awareness insights) is to explore the individual instances of experiences right to their edges; that is, incorporating sensory images, episodic memory, symbolic significances, and so on (L. S. Greenberg, 2002; L. S. Greenberg et al., 1993). This is in lieu of linking elements or finding patterns that may exist across situations. An exploratory non-content-directive approach helps to elaborate aspects of a client's emotional experience in the moment, that is, her or his sadness, hurt, or frustration (L. S. Greenberg & van Balen, 1998).

Gibson (1950) first introduced his understanding of how awareness develops in a discussion of sensory and perceptual experiences (for an overview see Nakayama, 1994). In short, he believed individuals become aware of experiential objects by perceiving invariant relationships (i.e., reliable relational patterns) among figural objects and their perceptual–emotional background, which provides a rich experiential structure. Consequentially, the focal aspects of one's ongoing experiential activity are progressively differentiated relative to one another. In conveying this concept it is useful to draw an analogy between the experiential process in therapy and in a strictly sensory venture, such as wine tasting. To the uninitiated, all red wines taste more or less the same and perhaps are only slightly distinguishable from white wines. As one tastes supposedly different wines in blind faith, gradually distinct features of flavor come to one's attention. With greater and repeated exposure the original monolithic gustatory experience of red wine develops into a variety of subtly and increasingly differentiated experiences of flavor that, for the individual, simply did not exist before.

In this analogy, the original flavors of wine are now slightly changed by virtue of their being more refined for the individual; the same process holds true for the experiential "flavors" of affect and meaning (J. Pascual-Leone, 1991). A change in one's experiential landscape happens by virtue of it having been explored (Gendlin, 1981; Rennie, 1998; Stevens, 1971). Thus, in a session,

> If the listener's responsiveness makes it possible, the individual finds himself moving from one referent movement and unfolding to another and another. Each time the inward scene changes, new felt meanings are there for him. The cycles of [focusing] set into motion an overall feeling process. This feeling process has a very striking, concretely felt, self-propelled quality. (Gendlin, 1964, p. 151)

Thus, one must continually return to explore a client's feelings to make use of his or her expanding panoply of meanings.

The progressive unfolding of experience described here is well-known to client-centered and experiential therapists (L. S. Greenberg & van Balen, 1998; Rennie, 1998; Rogers, 1951). In this approach, client feelings are addressed and re-addressed; in doing so the feelings actually metamorphose, becoming more personally significant and tangible. The metamorphosis of that meaning structure occurs through the splintering of general schemes into specific subschemes. The result is the creation of a nested hierarchy of affective-meaning schemes—that is, more meaning and deeper feeling (J. Pascual-Leone, 1990).

Experiential awareness is neither associative linking nor the uncovering of meaning; rather, it is the progressive cocreation of meaning in a single moment as a therapist facilitates the elaboration of a client's ongoing experience. For example, consider a client who feels generally anxious about an impending interpersonal encounter. When the anxiety is first aroused, the therapist encourages this client to describe in the moment how he or she notices that nervousness inside his or her body and any thoughts or images the anxiety may be related to. In this task of elaboration the client begins to describe and experience the nervousness in slightly different ways. Describing the feeling changes it, and it becomes somewhat shame-based for this client. As the bad feeling unfolds, the client continually symbolizes it in words: "I'm tense. I guess. . .it's a bit of fear but a bit of shame too. I feel that I screwed up and wish I hadn't. I'm embarrassed and afraid that I'll never be able to wash that stain clean." In this example, symbolizing new and more differentiated meaning is, in and of itself, an insight from emerging emotional experience. This type of learning is Gibsonian accommodation in action.

Tentativeness

The experiential therapist is continually confronted by the elusiveness and complexity of a client's emotion that results from its spontaneous, changing, and very subjective nature. Therefore, facilitating insight in an experiential framework requires a great deal of tentativeness on the part of the therapist. This means that the therapist must handle the client's emerging awareness in a manner that is non-content-directive and exploratory, rather than prescriptive. As we note, the source of experience-near insights does not come from collating observations across situations or from associating a chain of cognitive–behavioral acts. Therapists must rely on clients themselves as the main source of material from which insights stem. In experiential therapies, the client (rather than the therapist) is the original author of any insight. Thus, the therapist has the precarious job of helping the client discover something that the therapist is not privy to. Therapists are always working from the concrete features of experience presented by clients in any given moment. This means collaboratively searching with clients to symbolize in words what the clients have previously been unable to say. Therefore, the nature and style of experiential interventions, which are tentative and person-centered, are particularly suited to facilitating experience-near insights.

INSIGHT AND CHANGE

In addition to referring to the four client processes of (a) awareness, (b) experiential meta-awareness, (c) rational meta-awareness, and (d) linking (either conceptual or experiential), the term *insight* has also been used to loosely refer to (e) therapeutic change itself. This may be because in the classical (i.e., psychoanalytic) tradition, insight (referring to linking) has been seen as the sine qua non of change. In experiential therapy, however, this is not the case.[2] The global term *insight* is often erroneously used to refer to changes in states of mind or experiential changes in self-organization, such as a client changing from an unentitled, passive position to an assertive, active position—even though linking is not directly involved.

We believe that insight, the forms of awareness, meta-awareness, and linking need to be distinguished from experiential or behavioral change proper. These various forms of insight should be thought of as initial process steps that often lead toward other, more transformational processes of change through choice or restructuring. After insight has taken place and an individual understands something differently (e.g., that one is feeling angry, or that childhood experiences have led one to keep one's guard up for fear of disappointment), the subsequent change may require that the individual is able to respond differently. An individual requires more than insight to be able to move beyond responding angrily and to open up and express needs.

---

[2]Gendlin (1964) has already pointed out that the conflation of a client's process with the contents of change is highly problematic. He refers to this as the *content paradigm* problem.

Modern experiential approaches create change by evoking affect to promote emotional processing and access to additional material (L. S. Greenberg, 2002). After accessing previously unacknowledged experience (i.e., insight), the focus shifts to transforming this experience by using those alternative emotion-based schemes to expand the person's response repertoire. Attending to a current (maladaptive) self-organization that is in need of transformation, such as feeling worthless, makes it accessible to new inputs that might change it. Identification and attention to unfulfilled needs that are embedded in a maladaptive state stimulates alternative self-organizations. These alternative self-organizations are tacit, emotionally based, and begin to organize the individual toward meeting the identified need. It is the synthesis of this new possibility with the old that leads to structural change (L. S. Greenberg, 2002; L. S. Greenberg & Pascual-Leone, 1995; L. S. Greenberg & Watson, 2005). Thus, emotion-focused approaches make use of affect's power to catalyze change, producing a restructuring of core emotion-based schemes. This access to alternative responses and the synthesis of old with new schemes is viewed as central to change, in addition to awareness or insight.

RESEARCH DIRECTIONS

Research on experience-near insights has largely been conducted within the framework of experiential therapies. A number of meta-analyses have been done on the outcome research of experiential treatments that facilitate awareness and meta-awareness; they reliably show large pre- to posteffect sizes (Elliott, 1996, 2001; L. S. Greenberg, Elliott, & Lietaer, 1994). When we discussed focusing and described case illustrations earlier in this chapter we introduced the 7-point Experiencing Scale (Klein, Mathieu-Coughlan & Kiesler, 1986; Klein, Mathieu, Kiesler, & Gendlin, 1969). Research on experience-near insights has measured awareness, meta-awareness, and even experiential moments of linking by way of the Experiencing Scale and has been useful in providing a closer view of the relationship between these processes and therapeutic outcome.

Key Findings

Early research on the Experiencing Scale (i.e., Gendlin, Jenney, & Shlien, 1960; Kiesler, 1971; Rogers, Gendlin, Kiesler, & Truax, 1967) was designed to test the hypothesis that deep levels of experiencing (i.e., complex experience-near insights) occurring across therapy was related to therapeutic change. Reviews of past process and outcome studies testing this claim have shown a strong relationship between experience-near processes occurring in-session, as measured by the Experiencing Scale, and therapeutic gain in experiential, psychodynamic, and cognitive therapies (Castonguay, Goldfried, Wiser, Raue, & Hayes, 1996; Orlinsky & Howard, 1986; Silberschatz, Fretter, & Curtis, 1986). This suggests that the experiencing variable may represent a common factor that helps explain change across approaches.

Kiesler (1971) found that more successful cases had deeper levels of experiencing than less successful cases at all measured points in therapy, but he was unable to show that a relative increase in experiencing over therapy related to positive outcome. He recommended that a more accurate picture of the trend in experiencing might be found by measuring it in relation to isolated therapeutic themes rather than in relation to randomly selected segments. Following this recommendation, researchers studying emotion focused therapy for depression (also known as process experiential therapy) found that a relative increase in theme-related experiencing from early to late in therapy predicted treatment outcome (Goldman, Greenberg, & Pos, 2005; Pos, Greenberg, Goldman, & Korman, 2003).

Pos et al. (2003) showed that increases in experiencing during emotional episodes in-session (whether they were theme-related or not) was a better predictor of outcome. This suggests that insight during the ongoing expression and articulation of emotion may be more central to therapeutic change than the theme-related content. Expanding this line of inquiry, Warwar and Greenberg (2003) found that emotional arousal at midtreatment predicted outcome and depth of experiencing later in treatment further enhanced that effect, a finding that indicates that making sense of aroused experience by reflecting on it (i.e., experience-near processing) predicts outcome.

Moreover, in the studies by Goldman et al. (2005) and Pos et al. (2003), clients' levels of experiencing on core themes also accounted for outcome variance above that accounted for by the alliance. This suggests that the type of experience-near awareness and meta-awareness a client has, as measured by the Experiencing Scale, is a unique predictor of outcome. The relationship between experience-near processing and alliance was further articulated in a study by Adams and Greenberg (1996). By examining moment-by-moment turn-taking, they found that when therapists focused on deeper levels of experience, clients were about eight times more likely to follow suit and deepen their own experience.

Current and Future Directions

There are several avenues of future research that would be particularly fruitful. A good alliance has been shown to be a precondition of experience-near insights; there is also reason to believe that an early emphasis on this type of experiencing may be important to alliance development (Pos & Greenberg, 2005). For these reasons, it would be useful to study closely exactly how interrelated the alliance and experiences of this type might be.

The work of Adams and Greenberg (1996) should be elaborated to study the impact that different types of therapist interventions have on a client's quality and degree of insight when the client is emotionally aroused. To that end, current work by Ellison et al. (2005) is examining how therapists' focus in emotion-focused therapy, cognitive–behavioral therapy, or interpersonal therapy might differentially predict clients' depth of experiencing. Finally, the manner in which a series of experience-near insights can cumulatively lead to transformational change has not been fully elucidated and is a central enigma in process research. Moreover, these shifts in awareness are likely to occur in nonlinear, sequential patterns (A. Pascual-Leone, 2005). Therefore, empirically examining the role of awareness and meta-awareness as ordered processes in moment-by-moment therapeutic transformations would be an important contribution to understanding how clinicians might better facilitate therapeutic change.

CONCLUDING COMMENTS

Traditionally, insight has been used liberally as a global term referring to a new change in consciousness. To adequately present an experiential therapy view of insight one must delineate a number of different processes subsumed under the label *insight*. In experientially oriented therapies, insight is generally referred to as awareness. Awareness includes immediate awareness of a current bodily felt sense or what one is feeling, as well as a slightly more abstract awareness of how one perceives things (i.e., awareness of one's awarenesses), which we call meta-awareness. The former involves discovering and experiencing something new in one's bodily felt experience; the latter involves gaining a lived new perspective.

Discovering *what* one feels as well as *how* one does what one does are the objectives of experiential therapies. By concentrating on increasing a client's awareness and meta-awareness over making conceptual links, experiential therapies are essentially unconcerned with the question of why a client has the experience. This is in contrast to the traditional psychoanalytic emphasis on insight as conceptual linking or the emphasis in cognitive therapy on gaining rational insights into one's beliefs, both of which rest on providing explanations of *why* experiences occur.

Moreover, the psychogenetic mechanisms that lead to different types of insight are brought about by different implicit information processing strategies. Experience-distant insights (i.e., linking) formulate self-knowledge top-down, whereas experience-near insights (i.e., awareness) approach self-knowledge bottom-up by starting with the idiosyncratic details of a client's subjective experience. It follows then that experience-near insights of awareness and meta-awareness are best facilitated by therapists in a tentative, moment-by-moment, and exploratory manner, a style most typified by humanistic–experiential treatments.

We suggest an integrative model of insight based on two dimensions: the degree of abstraction (abstracting from within a single situation vs. across different types of situations) and the type of processing (perceptual–emotional vs. rational–conceptual). This theoretical conceptualization helps delineate characteristics of the three processes of awareness, meta-awareness, and conceptual linking. Thus, qualitatively different processes of insight are understood as falling on a continuum from experience-near (i.e., emotional awareness and a more existential meta-awareness) to experience-far (i.e., linking pieces of knowledge into conceptual formulations). The model has ramifications for psychotherapy integration by shedding light on the types of process steps (insights) that different therapeutic orientations target in an effort to help clients create lasting, positive change.

REFERENCES

Adams, K. E., & Greenberg, L. S. (1996, June). *Therapists' influence on depressed clients' therapeutic experiencing and outcome.* Paper presented at the 43rd annual convention of the Society for Psychotherapeutic Research, St. Amelia, FL.

Binder, J. L., & Strupp, H. H. (1991). The Vanderbilt approach to time-limited dynamic psychotherapy. In P. Crits-Christoph & J. P. Barber (Eds.), *Handbook of short-term dynamic psychotherapy* (pp. 137–165). New York: Basic Books.

Buber, M. (1957). *I and thou.* New York: Scribner.

Castonguay, L. G., Goldfried, M. R., Wiser, S., Raue, P. J., & Hayes, A. M. (1996). Predicting the effect of cognitive therapy for depression: A study of unique and common factors. *Journal of Consulting and Clinical Psychology, 64,* 497–504.

Cornell, A. W. (1996). *The power of focusing: A practical guide to emotional self-healing.* Oakland, CA: New Harbinger.

Elliott, R. (1996). Are client-centered–experiential therapists effective? A meta-analysis of outcome research. In U. Esser, H. Pabst, & G. W. Speierer (Eds.), *The power of the person-centered approach: New challenges, perspectives, answers* (pp. 125–138). Koln, Germany: GwG Verlag.

Elliott, R. (2001). Research on the effectiveness of humanistic therapies: A meta-analysis. In D. J. Cain & J. Seeman (Eds.), *Humanistic psychotherapies: Handbook of research and practice* (pp. 57–81). Washington, DC: American Psychological Association.

Ellis, A. (2001). "Intellectual" and "emotional" insight revisited. *NYS Psychologist, 13,* 2–6.

Ellison, J., Greenberg, L. S., & Toukmanian, S. (2005). *Client–therapist interactions during emotion episode in EFT, CBT, and IPT.* Panel discussion at the Conference of the Society for Psychotherapy Research (SPR), Montreal, Canada.

Gelso, C. J., Kivlighan, D. M., Wine, B., Jones, A., & Friedman, S. C. (1997). Transference, insight, and the course of time-limited therapy. *Journal of Counseling Psychology, 44,* 209–217.

Gendlin, E. T. (1964). A theory of personality change. In P. Worchel & D. Byrne (Eds.), *Personality change* (pp. 129–173). New York: Wiley.

Gendlin, E. T. (1981). *Focusing* (2nd ed.). New York: Bantam Books.

Gendlin, E. T., Jenney, R. H., & Shlien, J. M. (1960). Counselor ratings of process and outcome in client-centered therapy. *Journal of Clinical Psychology, 16,* 210–213.

Gibson, J. J. (1950). *The perception of the visual world.* Boston: Houghton Mifflin.

Goldman, R. N., Greenberg, L. S., & Pos, A. E. (2005). Depth of emotional experience and outcome. *Psychotherapy Research, 15,* 248–260.

Greenberg, J. R., & Mitchell, S. A. (1983). *Object relations in psychoanalytic theory.* Cambridge, MA: Harvard University Press.

Greenberg, L. S. (2002). *Emotion-focused therapy: Coaching clients to work through their feelings.* Washington, DC: American Psychological Association.

Greenberg, L. S., & Angus, L. (2003). The contributions of emotion processes to narrative change in psychotherapy: A dialectical constructivist approach. In L. Angus and J. McLeod (Eds.), *The handbook of narrative and psychotherapy: Practice, theory and research* (pp. 331–349). Toronto, Ontario, Canada: Sage.

Greenberg, L. S., & Elliott, R. (1997). Varieties of empathic responding. In A. C. Bohart & L. S. Greenberg (Eds.), *Empathy reconsidered: New directions in psychotherapy* (pp. 167–186). Washington, DC: American Psychological Association.

Greenberg, L. S., Elliott, R., & Lietaer, G. (1994). Research on humanistic and experiential psychotherapies. In A. E. Bergin & S. L. Garfield (Eds.), *Handbook of psychotherapy and behavior change* (4th ed., pp. 509–539). New York: Wiley.

Greenberg, L. S., & Pascual-Leone, J. (1995). A dialectical constructivist approach to experiential change. In R. A. Neimeyer & M. J. Mahoney (Eds.), *Constructivism in psychotherapy* (pp. 169–191). Washington, DC: American Psychological Association.

Greenberg, L. S., & Pascual-Leone, J. (2001). A dialectical constructivist view of the creation of personal meaning. *Journal of Constructivist Psychology, 14,* 165–186.

Greenberg, L. S., Rice, L. N., & Elliott, R. (1993). *Facilitating emotional change: The moment-by-moment process.* New York: Guilford Press.

Greenberg, L. S., & Safran, J. D. (1989). Emotion in psychotherapy. *American Psychologist, 44,* 19–29.

Greenberg, L. S., & Safran, J. D. (1990). Emotional-change processes in psychotherapy. In R. Plutchik & H. Kellerman (Eds.), *Emotion: Theory, research, and experience* (Vol. 5., pp. 59–85). San Diego, CA: Academic Press.

Greenberg, L. S., Safran, J. D., & Rice, L. (1989). Experiential therapy: Its relation to cognitive therapy. In A. Freeman, K. M. Simon, L. E. Beutler, & H. Arkowitz (Eds.), *Comprehensive handbook of cognitive therapy* (pp. 169–187). New York: Plenum Press.

Greenberg, L. S., & van Balen, R. (1998). The theory of experience-centered therapies. In L. S. Greenberg, J. C. Watson, & G. Lietaer (Eds.), *Handbook of experiential psychotherapy* (pp. 28–57). New York: Guilford Press.

Greenberg, L. S., Warwar, S. H., & Malcolm, W. (2003). *The differential effects of emotion-focused therapy and psychoeducation for the treatment of emotional injury: Letting go and forgiving.* Panel Discussion at the Conference of the Society for Psychotherapy Research (SPR), Weimar, Germany.

Greenberg, L. S., & Watson, J. C. (1998). Experiential therapy in the treatment of depression: Differential effects of the client-centered relationship conditions and active experiential interventions. *Psychotherapy Research, 2,* 210–224.

Greenberg, L. S., & Watson, J. C. (2005). *Emotion-focused therapy of depression.* Washington, DC: American Psychological Association.

Kiesler, D. J. (1971). Patient experiencing level and successful outcome in individual psychotherapy of schizophrenics and psychoneurotics. *Journal of Consulting and Clinical Psychology, 37,* 370–385.

Klein, M. H., Mathieu, P. L., Kiesler, D. J., & Gendlin, E. T. (1969). *The Experiencing Scale: A research and training manual.* Madison: University of Wisconsin, Bureau of Audiovisual Research.

Klein, M. H., Mathieu-Coughlan, P., & Kiesler, D. J. (1986). The Experiencing Scales. In L. S. Greenberg & W. M. Pinsof (Eds.), *The psychotherapeutic process: A research handbook* (pp. 21–71). New York: Guilford Press.

Leijssen, M. (1998). Focusing microprocesses. In L. S. Greenberg, J. C. Watson, & G. Lietaer (Eds.), *Handbook of experiential psychotherapy* (pp. 121–154). New York: Guilford Press.

Luborsky, L., Popp, C., Luborsky, E., & Mark, D. (1994). The core conflictual relationship theme. *Psychotherapy Research, 4,* 172–183.

Malan, D. H. (1979). *Individual psychotherapy and the science of psychodynamics.* London: Butterworth-Heineman.

May, R. (1983). *The discovery of being: Writings in existential psychology.* New York: Norton.

May, R., & Yalom, I. D. (1989). Existential psychotherapy. In R. J. Corsini & D. Wedding (Eds.), *Current psychotherapies* (4th ed., pp. 363–402). Itasca, IL: F. E. Peacock Publishers.

Nakayama, K. (1994). James J. Gibson: An appreciation. *Psychological Review, 10,* 140–152.

Orlinsky, D. E., & Howard, K. I. (1986). The relation of process to outcome in psychotherapy. In S. L. Garfield & A. E. Bergin (Eds.), *Handbook of psychotherapy and behavior change: An empirical analysis* (3rd ed., pp. 311–381). New York: Wiley.

Pascual-Leone, A. (2005). *Emotional processing in the therapeutic hour: Why "the only way out is through."* Unpublished doctoral dissertation, York University, Toronto, Ontario, Canada.

Pascual-Leone, J. (1990). An essay on wisdom: Toward organismic processes that make it possible. In R. J. Sternberg (Ed.), *Wisdom: Its nature, origins, and development* (pp. 244–278). New York: Cambridge University Press.

Pascual-Leone, J. (1991). Emotion, development, and psychotherapy: A dialectical constructivist perspective. In J. Safran & L. S. Greenberg (Eds.), *Emotion, psychotherapy and change* (pp. 302–335). New York: Guilford Press.

Pascual-Leone, J. (2002). *Lectures on developmental constructivism*. Unpublished manuscript, York University, Toronto, Ontario, Canada.

Pascual-Leone, J., & Irwin, R. R. (1998). Abstraction, the will, the self and modes of learning in adulthood. In M. C. Smith & T. Pourchot (Eds.), *Adult learning and development* (pp. 35–66). Mahwah, NJ: Erlbaum.

Perls, F. S. (1969). *Gestalt therapy verbatim*. Lafayette, CA: Real People Press.

Perls, F. S., Hefferline, R. F., & Goodman, P. (1951). *Gestalt therapy*. New York: Julian Press.

Pos, A. E., & Greenberg, L. S. (2005). *Early differences in alliance building and emotional processing affecting therapy progress and outcome*. Panel discussion at the annual conference of the Society for Psychotherapy Research , Montreal, Canada.

Pos, A. E., Greenberg, L. S., Goldman, R. N., & Korman, L. M. (2003). Emotional processing during experiential treatment of depression. *Journal of Consulting and Clinical Psychology*, 6, 1007–1016.

Raskin, N. J., & Rogers, C. R. (1989). Person-centered therapy. In R. J. Corsini & D. Wedding (Eds.), *Current psychotherapies* (4th ed., pp. 155–194). Itasca, IL: F. E. Peacock Publishers.

Rennie, D. L. (1998). *Person-centered counseling: An experiential approach*. London: Sage.

Rice, L. N. (1974). The evocative function of the therapist. In L. N. Rice & D. A. Wexler (Eds.), *Psychotherapy and patient relationships* (pp. 36–60). Homewood, IL: Dow Jones-Irwin.

Rogers, C. R. (1942). *Counseling and psychotherapy: Newer concepts in practice*. Boston: Houghton Mifflin.

Rogers, C. R. (1951). *Client-centered therapy: Its current practice, implications, and theory*. Boston: Houghton Mifflin.

Rogers, C. R. (1959). The essence of psychotherapy: A client-centered view. *Annals of Psychotherapy*, 1, 51–57.

Rogers, C. R., Gendlin, E. T., Kiesler, D. J., & Truax, C. B. (1967). *The therapeutic relationship and its impact: A study of psychotherapy with schizophrenics*. Madison: University of Wisconsin Press.

Sartre, J. P. (1956). *Being and nothingness* (H. Barnes, Trans.). New York: Philosophical Library. (Original work published 1943)

Schneider, K. J., & May, R. (1995). *The psychology of existence: An integrative, clinical perspective*. New York: McGraw-Hill.

Silberschatz, G., Fretter, P. B., & Curtis, J. T. (1986). How do interpretations influence the process of psychotherapy? *Journal of Consulting and Clinical Psychology*, 54, 646–652.

Singer, E. (1970). *Key concepts in psychotherapy* (2nd ed.). New York: Basic Books.

Stevens, J. O. (1971). *Awareness: Exploring, experimenting, experiencing*. Lafayette, CA: Real People Press.

Toukmanian, S. G. (1986). A measure of client perceptual processing. In L. S. Greenberg & W. Pinsof (Eds.), *The psychotherapeutic process* (pp. 107–130). New York: Guilford Press.

Warwar, S. H., & Greenberg, L. S. (2003). *Emotional injuries and forgiveness*. Panel discussion at the annual conference of the Society for Psychotherapy Research, Weimar, Germany.

Watson, J. C., & Rennie, D. L. (1994). Qualitative analysis of clients' subjective experience of significant moments during the exploration of problematic reactions. *Journal of Counseling Psychology, 41*, 500–509.

Yalom, I. D. (1981). *Existential psychotherapy*. New York: Basic Books.

Yontef, G. M., & Simkin, J. S. (1989). Gestalt therapy. In R. J. Corsini & D. Wedding (Eds.), *Current psychotherapies* (4th ed., pp. 323–361). Itasca, IL: F. E. Peacock Publishers.

3

INSIGHT IN
COGNITIVE–BEHAVIORAL THERAPY

MARTIN GROSSE HOLTFORTH, LOUIS G. CASTONGUAY,
JAMES F. BOSWELL, LESLIE A. WILSON, APHRODITE A. KAKOUROS,
AND THOMAS D. BORKOVEC

Why should cognitive–behavioral therapists care about insight? At first glance, many of them might view it as a foreign concept, an *ego-alien* construct that belongs to psychoanalytically oriented therapists. In fact, if one invited mental health professionals of any orientation to "free associate" to the word *insight*, few would utter the words *behavior theory* or *cognitive–behavioral therapy* (CBT). This, we believe, is because many confuse the definition of insight with a restricted number of techniques or processes that may foster it (e.g., client's free association, therapist interpretations). Insight, however, can and should be defined independently of what may facilitate it. It should also be defined by using a jargon-free vernacular, as opposed to a set of terms tied to a particular theoretical orientation.

In this chapter, insight is defined as the acquisition of new understanding. It is our contention that when defined this way, insight is highly compatible with how cognitive–behavioral therapies are currently practiced. We argue that most of today's cognitive–behavioral therapists help (systematically and intentionally) their clients gain new perspectives on the origins, determinants, meanings, or consequences of their (or others') behaviors, thoughts, intentions, or feelings.

In this chapter we examine the importance of the construct of insight in the cognitive–behavioral tradition by highlighting its usage, definition, and associated empirical research. The first section of this chapter addresses theoretical considerations. We show that although insight was at first dismissed within this tradition, influential leaders of the cognitive–behavioral orientation later emphasized it. We also argue that a careful consideration of recent contributions of cognitive–behavioral therapists can lead to a multidimensional (schema-focused) conceptualization of insight that might further clarify this construct. This conceptualization is based on the construct of *schema*, which can be defined as an individual's view or representation of self and others. In the second section, we review empirical and clinical literature to assess whether insight really occurs in CBT, if such insight fits the dimensions emphasized in our schema-focused perspective, if these insights differ from those achieved in other orientations, and if they are beneficial to clients. We conclude the chapter by offering directions for future research about insight that might be of particular interest for cognitive–behavioral therapists and researchers.

THEORETICAL CONSIDERATIONS

From Rejection to Understanding: A Brief Historical Perspective on Insight in CBT

Early behaviorally oriented writers avoided the concept of insight because it implied the involvement of unconscious processes (Cautela, 1993). In fact, some authors explicitly discounted any value for insight for behavioral treatment. For Bandura (1969), *insight* or *awareness* were seen as phenomena of "social conversion," in which the client learns and adopts the therapist's point of view. Far from seeing insight (at least when involving psychodynamic hypotheses) as a legitimate goal in behavior modification, Bandura argued that the pursuit of such social conversion raises ethical questions.

Other historical figures of behavioral therapy assigned only a minor role to insight in therapeutic change. Shoben (1960) recognized that insight might contribute to psychological recovery, but he also stated that in anxiety disorders, "extinction or counter-conditioning is still necessary" (p. 69). Cautela (1965) reported cases of "insight-like events" during desensitization training. Although in these cases "no attempt was made by the therapist to make the patient aware of etiological factors concerning the symptom complex, the patient gave insightful-like comments as the desensitization procedure became effective" (p. 59). However, Cautela explained utterances such as

"Oh, I see it!" merely as verbal statements that express changes in the symptomatic behavior (p. 63). Insight-like events, therefore, were seen as epiphenomenal by-products of symptom change rather than as causal agents.

The introduction of a cognitive perspective within the behavioral orientation, however, paved the way for a different view of insight. Beginning in the late 1960s, behavioral therapists imported the concepts of encoding, storing, and retrieving information from the information processing model in cognitive psychology (Goldfried, 2003). Cognition as an *organismic variable* became a determinant or causal event in the sequence of factors involved in functional analyses of behaviors: stimuli, organismic variables, reactions, and consequences (S-O-R-C). Despite differences among the various cognitive–behavioral therapies (CBTs), agreement existed on the components of cognitions, their role in human functioning, and their relationship to change in psychotherapy. Specifically, cognition was seen as consisting of general ideas, beliefs, and assumptions that mediated operant and classical conditioning and thus the relationship between stimuli and behavioral reactions. Especially relevant to the issue of insight, cognitive–behavioral therapists also agreed that self-understanding can lead directly to therapeutic change (see Westerman, 1989).

A major proponent of cognitive–behavioral therapy who explicitly used the concept of insight was Albert Ellis. As psychodynamic therapists did before him (see chap. 1, this volume), he proposed a distinction between intellectual and emotional insights in rational–emotional behavioral therapy. In both types of insights the client acknowledges that particular beliefs are erroneous, recognizes that particular behaviors are self-defeating, and experiences a wish to change these beliefs and behaviors. However, intellectual and emotional insights differ in terms of intensity, that is, the number or kinds of behaviors affected, the force of the pursuit, the effectiveness, and the commitment (Ellis, 1963). Although Ellis characterized intellectual insight as "nothing but an idle New Year's resolution (or fond dream) that one will alter effortlessly" (p. 125), he noted that emotional insight "involves seeing and believing; thinking and acting; wishing and practicing" (p. 126).

In other classical references to cognitive–behavioral therapy the phenomenon of insight seemed to be implied but was termed *cognitive change, cognitive restructuring, rational restructuring, cognitive realignment, rational reevaluation,* or *discovery of irrationality.* For Beck (1976), the process of cognitive change consisted of becoming aware of one's thoughts, recognizing which thoughts are inaccurate, and substituting more accurate thoughts. Insight, one could argue, is involved in recognizing the irrationality of automatic thoughts and becoming aware of alternative cognitions. On the basis of Beck's view, one could also argue that a more significant cognitive change (or a deeper insight) takes place with the identification of assumptions underlying cognitive distortions.

Mahoney (1974) saw the change of cognitive contingencies (CCs) as an important goal of cognitive behavior modification (e.g., to allow myself to watch football on Sunday nights, I need to work all weekend). For Mahoney, CCs were mediational symbolic products of stimulus–response–consequence relationships that made up our assumptive worlds (cognitive schemas). If CCs are maladaptive, the therapist's job is to "detect and communicate (adaptive) contingencies in a manner which will enhance therapeutic cognitive realignment" (p. 163). The process of *belief modification*, according to Mahoney, can be an incremental and gradual alteration, or it may be "all-or-none" in the form of a "cognitive click." In addition, Mahoney adopted Ellis' distinction between intellectual and emotional insights and supported Ellis' conviction that purely intellectual insight is ineffective or inadequate and rarely leads to significant change.

Meichenbaum (1977) also defined cognitive restructuring as a central concept for behavior change and viewed it as a means as well as the end of the process. Cognitive structure was presented as "a meaning system . . . a kind of 'executive processor,' which 'holds the blueprints of thinking,' . . . the source of the scripts from which all such dialogues borrow" (pp. 212–213). Cognitive restructuring, therefore, represents a schema change. Meichenbaum stressed the distinction between cognitive change as schema change involving multiple dimensions of functioning and "purely intellectual insights." Change in cognitive structure was necessary but not sufficient for behavioral change.

Goldfried and Davison (1976) argued that clients' frequent expectation of insight as the vehicle of change is incompatible with a behavioral model. However, they also acknowledged having observed insight in their clinical practice and the therapeutic changes it seemed to produce. These insights "may have entailed personal revelations that we provided to our clients, vaguely articulated hunches that we followed up, or therapeutic moves that we blindly stumbled upon, but which yielded therapeutic benefits well beyond our hard-headed comprehension" (p. 16). These authors proposed the systematic pursuit of *cognitive relabeling* or *rational restructuring* in which the client becomes aware of inaccuracies in thinking, evaluates beliefs more rationally, and substitutes a more realistic appraisal.

It seems clear that although insight is not a concept that most mental health professionals associate with CBT, it is regarded as a core process of change in this orientation, at least when defined as gaining a new understanding of self or others. Although it would be fair to assume that most cognitive–behavioral therapists would refuse to be described as "insight-oriented," one might agree with Paul Wachtel (1977) when he argued that

> on the basis of both clinical experience and the findings of research on perceptual learning, cognitive restructuring, and so on, I believe behavior therapists have underestimated the therapeutic value of insight into or clarification of the issues in one's life. . . . (p. 144)

We go one step further by arguing that the careful consideration of several constructs that have recently emerged in the CBT literature can offer a helpful conceptualization of insight.

Integrating New Directions: A Schema-Focused View of Insight

Over the last decades, authors associated with the cognitive–behavioral tradition have provided sophisticated analyses of internal dimensions of human functioning, which reflect potential determinants of behaviors. We attempt to integrate some of these contributions into a schema-focused perspective of insight. This perspective formulates insight as a change of knowledge structures, that is, schemas about self and others. The concept of schema is not a new addition to the cognitive–behavioral tradition. This construct, however, allows us to tie together recent developments that can inform a multidimensional view of insight. Specifically, we argue that change in self-schemas involves different levels of mental representation. In addition, we postulate that such change is associated with varying levels of emotional activation. Finally, we argue that rather than representing a departure from CBT tradition, the schema-focused perspective of insight reflects a learning process that is consistent with other major CBT constructs.

Schemas

Schemas can be described as mental representations in long-term memory or as a "cognitive representation of individuals, past experiences with other people, situations, and themselves, which helps them to construe events within that particular aspect of their life" (Goldfried, 2003, p. 56). For example, as a result of having been bullied and teased by his peers as he began elementary school, a client of one this chapter's authors developed a view of himself as weak and pitiful, as well as interpersonally inept and unacceptable. Throughout his life he became vigilant about (and avoided when possible) any cues of social threat or dismissal, perceived others (especially in unfamiliar social and career situations) as making fun of him or rejecting or marginalizing him, and felt not only like an outcast but also like a coward for not confronting them. Now a divorced 50-year-old, he came to therapy with social anxiety that intensified after moving to a new state to begin a job as an interior designer in a relatively large office. It is not surprising that such a life change provided a fertile ground for repeated triggering of his maladaptive schema.

At a biological level, schemas can be described as neuronal activation tendencies organized into cell assemblies (Hebb, 1949) or neuronal groups (Edelman, 1987). The Hebbian cell assembly is a classic, empirically supported neurophysiological example of brain organization in which neurons are associated with each other via repeated joint activation. The joining together of a multitude of specialized neurons into a neural group is a result of hierarchical organization (Hubel & Wiesel, 1968) and of synchronous activation. As do all forms of knowledge, schemas reflect networks of connections, which are stored in different memory systems.

Schemas influence the encoding and retrieval of information and thereby regulate which information reaches conscious awareness. Consistency with the content of the self-schemas (an obvious form of connection) influences what the person expects and retains from new experiences (Goldfried, 2003; Grawe, 2004). Self-schemas are "cognitive generalizations about the self, derived from past experience, that organize and guide the processing of the self-related information contained in an individual's social experience" (Markus, 1977, p. 63). Through this partially selective process of perceiving and encoding, the self and the world are perceived as coherent and organized (Goldfried & Robins, 1983). Thus, in the case previously described, new situations are perceived and interpreted in ways consistent with the client's engrained view of self and others. As he enters a new social interaction he feels inept and anxious; he is also convinced that others think he looks pitiful (like a "loser") and that he does not belong with them. He also scans for, often detects, and then ruminates about cues that indicate people are talking about and making fun of him.

In recent efforts to refine the concept of schema that has traditionally been adopted in cognitive therapy (e.g., Beck, 1976), Safran (1990; Safran & Segal, 1990) argued that self-schemas are interpersonal in nature—our views of self are intrinsically linked with our views of others and our relationships with them. This is clearly illustrated in the case described, as the client's representation of who he is (inept, pitiful, unacceptable) is fully embedded in his understanding of the world (as a threatening, rejecting, and humiliating place). It is interesting to note that Safran also argued that these schemas are based on early interactions with attachment figures, allowing the person to encode information that will "increase . . . the probability of maintaining relatedness with these figures" (Safran, 1990, p. 93). It is possible that the foundation of the client's perception of himself and others rested on earlier and consistent representations that he developed from his interaction with his parents. It may also be that the events with others that took place after infancy created a new template for defining who he is, how people perceive him, and what he should expect from others (peers and friends, after all, are important attachment figures!).

Objects and Complexity of Schematic Change

A change in self-schemas necessarily reflects a person's new understanding, a different view of who he or she is (or was) and a new comprehension of his or her relationships (past, present, future) with others. As such, this type of change fits the cognitive–behaviorally oriented definition of insight that we present early in this chapter.

It is important to consider that insight, from a schema-focused perspective, can reflect different types of changes. Changes in self-schemas (or insight) can vary in terms of the object of understanding. Clients, in other words, can acquire a new perspective about different aspects of their functioning. As we mentioned previously, a client can gain a new understanding of the origins, determinants, meanings, or consequences of his or her (or others') behaviors, thoughts, intentions, or feelings. Schematic changes can also vary in terms of complexity. New understandings can reflect a more or less extensive set of new connections among numerous objects of understanding. In addition, they may reflect broad (encapsulating) integration of themes and patterns in a person's life across different aspects of the self or different types of interpersonal relationships, or different phases of life.

In the case discussed earlier, the new understanding that the client developed during therapy encompassed different components of his functioning (e.g., thoughts, feelings, behaviors) and reflects a significant level of complexity, in terms of both breadth and depth. Through the exploration of his views of self and others (which seemed to have been facilitated by empathic listening and gentle exploration of core dysfunctional attitudes), the client realized that what made sense then is not true now—and has not been valid for a long time. He was helpless when facing repeated humiliations and rejections. The fact is that he was not strong enough (psychologically and physically) to rebuff the attacks on him (and he realized that it would have been difficult for anyone in his situation at this emotionally delicate developmental period of his life). Although the conclusions he drew from this experience might have appeared logical (e.g., people cannot be trusted, I am so intrinsically inept that I can't belong to any group and my work can't be of any worth or value), he understands that these conclusions cannot be generalized to the relationships he has now and to the tasks he is asked to perform. He is competent at what he does, what he does is important and praised, and there are people who care about him and appreciate who he is (friends, customers, therapist).

Levels of Representation

In addition to involving different objects and reflecting diverse levels of complexity, change in cognitive generalization about the self and others can take place at different levels of the self-representation. In other words, insight can vary in depth.

A self-schema can obviously be conscious. Individuals are able to recognize, articulate, and verbalize some aspects of who they are (or who they believe they are). However, not all knowledge (including self-schemas) is accessible to awareness. These different levels of knowledge representation have been associated with different modes of psychological functioning and different memory systems, that is, the *explicit* and the *implicit* modes/memory systems (Epstein, 1990; Grawe, 2004). Whereas schemas in the explicit mode are associated with conscious awareness and can be accessed voluntarily (top-down activation), memory contents in the implicit mode are preattentive, nonconscious, and only accessible via situational stimuli (bottom-up activation; Grawe, 2004). Teasdale (1993) made a similar distinction by describing two different kinds of meaning, the specific–explicit and the generic–implicit codes. These two kinds of meaning relate to two different kinds of mental codes that process information within the human memory. Explicit meaning is coded in propositional code, which deals with specific meanings, discrete concepts, and relationships between the concepts and can be expressed in language. In contrast, implicit meaning is coded in implicational code that is more holistic–generic and is not directly translatable into language.

These distinct levels of representation and memory systems suggest that different types of insight, or self-schematic change, can take place. One can achieve a new understanding of self and others by changing explicit knowledge structures, for example, by making new connections between consciously experienced information. One can also modify his or her perception or interpretation of self by becoming conscious of and verbalizing previously implicit memories or nonconscious links between memories. In the case described earlier, some insights that the client made during therapy involved the connection and the cause and effect relationship that seems to exist between the early victimization from his peers and the difficulties he has experienced later in life. He seems to have become aware of the extensive and pervasive impact (in terms of the domains of his life that have been affected, from childhood through adulthood) of the conclusions that he derived about himself and others from being attacked, humiliated, and rejected. By expressing these conclusions in session, he appeared to gain clearer awareness or felt with more intensity some feelings that he experienced then and now. As described in the next section, the experience of emotion (which is intrinsically linked to the distinction between explicit and implicit meaning) may be particularly conducive for the transformation of nonconscious processes to conscious ones.

Insight and Emotion

Among the most important questions regarding insight are whether it always involves emotion and whether emotion is necessary for insights to lead to change. In contrast with humanistic and psychodynamic orientations, the cognitive–behavioral tradition has mostly viewed emotion as a phenomenon to be controlled rather than experienced or deepened (Mahoney, 1980, Messer, 1986; Samoilov & Goldfried, 2000). This has been the case even though a number of its luminaries (Ellis, Mahoney, Meichenbaum) have recognized the importance of emotional insight. More recently, however, a number of cognitive–behaviorally oriented therapists have formulated sophisticated and multidimensional views of emotion, which might allow a schema-focused view of insight to recognize more adequately the role of emotion.

The Interacting Cognitive Systems (ICS) approach by Teasdale (1993), for example, provided constructs that can be helpful in distinguishing between intellectual and emotional insights. Using the explicit–implicit distinction, Teasdale proposed that although implicit meanings are directly linked to emotion, "propositional representations of emotion-related information cannot, alone, elicit emotion" (p. 346). As such, the former are viewed as *hot cognitions* whereas the latter are referred to as *cold cognitions*. Teasdale argued, "'Intellectual' belief or knowing with the head is agreement with specific propositional meanings, whereas 'emotional' or 'intuitive belief,' 'knowing with the heart', is related to the state of holistic implicational representations" (p. 346). In accordance with this theory, intellectual insight can be described as making new connections only at an explicit (propositional) level. Emotional insight, however, would require that in addition to intellectual insight, an integration of the person's implicit representations (patterns of implicational code) takes place.

Using closely related concepts, Safran (1989) proposed that insight needs to involve an integration of two modes of functioning to be conducive to change. He described two ways of acquiring knowledge about the "real world," that is, perception and conceptual thought, that parallel the implicit–explicit distinction previously discussed. Whereas perception is concerned with the acquisition of currently transpiring knowledge and is more closely connected to emotion and action, conceptual thought involves making connections between abstract concepts, a process that distances the individual from immediate perceptions and emotional reactions. Similar to Teasdale's implicit meaning, perception is related to an ongoing bodily processing of current situations that give rise to *bodily sentience* (Gendlin, 1991) that only later becomes integrated with higher level cognitions to form emotions (Greenberg & Safran, 1987; Leventhal, 1984). Safran argued that the most powerful insights are those that integrate perception and conceptual thoughts.

> A conceptual understanding of the way in which one constructs one's own reality can never bring about real change. Ultimately, one must experience what one is doing at a bodily felt level. Ultimately, new behavior can only flow out of new bodily felt experience, and this can only take place in the present. . . . The required insight, however, is a bodily felt awareness. In that very moment of awareness, there is a change in bodily sentience. This, I believe, is what we are referring to when we talk about emotional insight. . . . Therefore, insight that is associated with emotion is considered to be more conducive to change because it links implicit and explicit meaning and leads to a reappraisal of an event or situation that tells the person 'what this means to me now.' (p. 237)

The intrinsic connection between emotion and implicit meaning is also emphasized in Safran's (1990) view of schemas. As previously mentioned, he postulated that our views of self are based on early interaction with attachment figures. He also assumed that some of the information related to such attachment behavior is affective in nature and is therefore coded, at least in part, in expressive-motor form. As such, he argued that although "some aspects of an individual's interpersonal schemas may be readily accessible in conceptual/linguistic form, other aspects may be more difficult to access symbolically" (p. 94). It is interesting to note that the experience of emotion can then become a way to facilitate the transformation of a previously implicit memory into an explicit one. Because some emotional experiences are intrinsically connected to core views of self, access to such emotions can trigger past memories and associated meanings. Safran (1990) argued that working with clients in an emotionally alive or immediate way can allow for the transformation of information coded at the expressive-motor level into conceptual representation. In the case described earlier, the client's reexperience and expression in the therapy room of his shame, anger, and fear seemed to facilitate his connection (at an intellectual and experiential level) between the past and the present; it also appeared to lead to his reorganization of his view of self (to one of being more competent and acceptable) and the world (as having trustworthy and meaningful others, as well as those less decent but ultimately less dangerous and therefore unworthy of any thoughts or concerns).

In line with Teasdale's and Safran's work, we hypothesize that insight (or change in self-schemas) is likely to lead to stronger and longer lasting therapeutic improvement if it involves emotional experience associated with the activation and modification of previously implicit meaning. However, we do not believe that intense or deep emotional processes or activation is absolutely necessary for self-schematic change. As mentioned earlier, we believe that insight can occur at the level of explicit memory—in other words, making conscious what was unconscious is not a condition for insight. In the same way, we believe that intellectual (or mostly intellectual) insight can also be helpful. Briefly said, deep (in terms of representation level) and emotional insight is not the only type of insight. When insight combines both depth and intensity of emotion, however, it is likely to have greater therapeutic impact.

Although we propose that emotion is not necessary for insight to take place or be helpful, we also suggest that the experience of joy is one emotion that is a frequent consequence of insight. The experience of joy is not typically associated with the psychodynamic view of insight but its activation is consistent with learning mechanisms emphasized in the cognitive–behavioral tradition. Specifically, we argue that the experience of joy derives from one or both of two sources inherent to psychotherapy change process. Some insights solve or give the promise of solving the emotional problem (negative reinforcement), and some insights create or give the promise of the creation of positive opportunities (positive reinforcement). The intensity of joy experienced after an insight will be a function of the degree of the problem, the degree of perceived solution or possibility of solution for the problem, or the degree of the positive possibilities or realities that it creates.

Insight Experiences as Learning

Although a schema-focused perspective allows the consideration of a number of dimensions frequently linked to insight, there is the question of whether it belongs alongside other CBT constructs. Within this theoretical tradition, all therapeutic change can be conceived of as *learning*, that is, the forming of new connections. Classical conditioning creates the learning of new connections by perceptions that one stimulus is consistently followed by another stimulus. Operant conditioning creates new learning by strengthening connections between stimuli and voluntary action and by stimulus and response generalizations of those connections. Vicarious learning does the same through mere observation. Etymologically speaking, all words are artificially created symbols and derive meaning from their connection to concrete objects or actions; they may later acquire more abstract meanings through subsequent associations. Like all other stimuli and responses, abstract concepts such as self-representations acquire further meaning (or modifications in meaning) through new connections with other concepts or through experiences that build additional associations. As such, change in self-schemas can be seen as a modification of the associative networks regarding oneself and therefore as a form of learning.

Closely related to the concept of learning, insight can also be defined as a form of corrective experience. Grawe (2004) argued that corrective experiences can be generated by triggering the schemas underlying the patient's problematic experiences and behavior and then by overlaying them with new schemas. Grawe (1997) also identified two types of corrective experiences: *clarification of meaning* and *mastery/coping*. In this context and related to Wachtel's observation that we noted earlier in the chapter, insight can be viewed as a clarification experience. It is a specific corrective experience in which new connections are made between pieces of knowledge (schemas) involving the self that were previously unconnected—such as the cause and effect connections the client previously discussed made between traumatic events and later difficulties.

In terms of therapeutic interventions, schema activation and corrective experiences can be achieved by traditional cognitive–behavioral techniques as well as by interventions that are in line with Safran's contribution described earlier. For example, schemas can be activated by the identification or monitoring of conscious thoughts or the triggering of previously implicit meaning and memories, which is more likely to take place when clients are working in an emotionally immediate way. Corrective experiences can be facilitated by the challenge of conscious thoughts and the behavioral disconfirmation of explicit self-perceptions. As illustrated in the case described earlier, a corrective experience can also be fostered by the transformation (into consciousness) and modification of previously implicit (emotionally laden) experiences associated with dysfunctional attitudes that are at the core of the client self-schemas.

It is important to stress that schema change is a necessary but insufficient condition for insight. For a schema change to be considered an insight, the perspective shift has to be consciously experienced and therefore able to be verbalized. Thus going back to the notion of levels of representations, although the object of insight might refer to previously implicit meaning or memory content, such an object must become explicit for insight to take place. Insight, however, is not restricted to the transformation of implicit information into explicit, as it can also reflect new associations between conscious meanings about self (or modifications of conscious self-representation). Insight varies in depth but ultimately requires conscious awareness of the self-schemas.

The description of a schema-focused perspective allows a fuller definition of insight as a new understanding of oneself or others. Essentially, insight is a learning process (a corrective experience of clarification) in which one consciously perceives connections between two or more mental representations (schemas) that one had not previously viewed as connected or connected in a particular way. This definition contrasts with mere awareness, which only implies recognition of some components of functioning. In both awareness and insight, consciousness is involved. However, the former can be described as schema activation but only the latter refers to schematic change. The schema-focused perspective described also suggests that the insight is multifaceted, involving the following dimensions: *object (or content)*, *complexity*, *level of representation*, *intensity of feelings*, and *acceleration* (see Table 3.1).

We purposely included a wide array of content in the object dimension in Table 3.1 because our earlier description in this chapter of insight in CBT (i.e., "a new perspective on the origins, determinants, meanings or consequences of their (or others') behaviors, thoughts, intentions, or feelings") allows an integration of various topics that therapists of different orientations focus on when fostering self-understanding. Our dimension of acceleration was not derived from the constructs presented in our schema-focused perspective on insight. Rather, it captures Mahoney's (1974) distinction of *belief modification* in terms of incremental–gradual alteration, or change in an all-or-none fashion.

EMPIRICAL AND CLINICAL OBSERVATIONS

Having offered a cognitive–behaviorally based view of insight, we now turn to a number of important questions: Does insight occur in CBT? If so, do these insights fit into our schema-focused conceptualization? Do insights in

TABLE 3.1
Dimensions of Insight

Dimension	Explanation
Object(s)	The target(s) of the new understanding (e.g., emotions, cognitions, wishes and fears, behaviors, interpersonal relationships, situational contingencies, individual development).
Complexity	The number of connections–links (meaning bridges) or integration (e.g., identification of themes or patterns) involved in a new understanding.
Level of representation	The level of explicitness of the object(s) previous to the insight.
Intensity of feelings	The level of bodily experiences and emotions that are associated with the insight.
Acceleration	The degree of suddenness of the understanding (ranging from continuous–cumulative to *Aha!*– cognitive click).

CBT differ from insights that occur in other forms of therapy? Is insight beneficial in CBT outcome? To answer these questions we surveyed empirical studies as well as case reports of insight events in CBT.

Does Insight Occur in CBT?—Empirical Studies

A number of studies examined the occurrence or intensity of insight in CBT alone or as compared with other orientations. Clarke, Rees, and Hardy (2004) provided evidence that insight occurs in CBT by analyzing posttherapy interviews with five successfully treated clients who received CBT for depression, each of whom was seen by a different therapist. The authors used grounded-theory methods to infer 10 categories of important experiences during the course of therapy. One of these categories was "Understanding/ Patterns/Core Beliefs." Among the events coded in this category were "comments about how the therapy had prompted them to revise their views of depression, therapy, or themselves" (p. 77).

In another study, Gershefski, Arnkoff, Glass, and Elkin (1996) examined the helpful aspects of treatment using the posttreatment data from the National Institute of Mental Health (NIMH) Treatment of Depression Collaborative Research Program (Elkin, Parloff, Hadley, & Autry, 1985; Elkin et al., 1989) in which CBT, interpersonal therapy (IPT), drug treatment, and placebo were compared. Clients reported the particular helpful aspects of their treatment, which were then coded in terms of specific or common helpful aspects of therapy. "Insights" was one of the subcategories in the common category of "Learned Something New." Overall, 36% of the clients of all treatment conditions showed responses that were coded into this common category. It is interesting to note that the differences between the conditions (CBT, IPT, drug, and placebo) in the percentage of completers with responses coded into this category were not significant. In another study on important (helpful and unhelpful) events, Llewelyn, Elliott, Shapiro, Hardy, and Firth-Cozens (1988) found that *personal insight* (a helpful event defined as "client sees something new about self, sees links; a sense of 'newness' experienced" [p. 108]) did occur in CBT treatment but with significantly lower frequency than in psychodynamic therapy.

The client's experience of insight (assessed through one self-reported item, i.e., "Today I clearly realized connections that I had not seen before") was also measured in the three conditions of the Berne Comparative Treatment Study (BCTS; Grawe, Caspar, & Ambühl, 1990): broad-spectrum behavioral therapy (BSBT), interactional behavioral therapy (IBT), and client-centered therapy. Although both BSBT and IBT are based on Lazarus's (1973) multimodal therapy, the choice of interventions in IBT is guided by an assessment of the client's approach and avoidance motivation (based on Caspar's [1995] Plan Analysis case formulation). Results indicated that clients in broad-spectrum behavioral therapy experienced a higher mean intensity of insights than clients in client-centered therapy.

These studies provide support for the conclusion that insight occurs in CBT. Although some evidence suggests that it may not be as prevalent as in psychodynamic–interpersonal therapy, other findings suggest that it happens as frequently as in interpersonal therapy and that it is rated higher than in client-centered therapy. These results should be viewed with caution, however, because different operational definitions of insight were used across studies. Furthermore, each study involved different comparison conditions (e.g., CBT vs. psychodynamic therapy; CBT vs. client-centered therapy) and no replications of such comparisons have been reported. Finally, insight-like experiences were reported with similar frequencies in placebo and drug therapies, which raises interesting questions about the nature or measurement of insight (see chap. 6, this volume).

Does Insight Occur in CBT?—Case Reports

Insight events have also been reported in clinical descriptions of single cases in CBT. A number of case reports describe the occurrence of insight events in the midst of traditional behavioral techniques not specifically designed to generate them. Powell (1996) reported that "about 15% of patients treated behaviorally for physical or emotional disorders in a university-based clinic showed evidence of behavior therapy-generated insights" (p. 303). Examples of such insights have been reported by Cautela (1965, 1993), Powell (1987, 1988, 1996), and Sedlacek (1979). These insights cover a wide range of objects and complexity. Their contents involved issues such as client's symptoms, emotions (e.g., linking anger and guilt to vascular spasms), cognitions (e.g., reevaluation of danger associated with feared object), wishes (e.g., linking occupational and marital problems to unfulfilled wishes for children), interpersonal problems (e.g., change of disrespectful attitude toward alcoholic husband), situational contingencies (e.g., linking fear of trembling in interpersonal situations to a fear of negative evaluation by others related to parents' divorce), and individual development (e.g., linking overly high expectations for performance to previous attempts at receiving love of overly demanding father). Some insights reflected a fairly simple acquisition of new meaning, such as the client's reassessment of the real danger of a traffic accident, although others reflected complex, emotionally laden connections that involved previously implicit memories about the self and significant others. One client, for example, linked newly accessed memories of sexual abuse by the client's brother to problems of overeating, alcohol abuse, guilt feelings, and suppressing her sexuality. Another client linked having cold hands to a lack of attention from parents after the client's brother had a nervous breakdown. The interventions that preceded these and other insights during behavioral therapy were relaxation techniques, biofeedback, constructing a hierarchy within systematic desensitization, desensitization per se, self-monitoring, or exploring feelings related to the client's symptoms and distress.

Other insights have been reported to occur in the context of cognitive interventions explicitly designed to help clients gain a new understanding of self and others. Examples of this are reported by the five clients in CBT in Clarke et al.'s (2004) study. The object of clients' reports of new understanding concerned cognitions (e.g., learning a new way of thinking about self, knowing what changes to work on), symptoms (e.g., better understanding of anxiety, reattribution of reasons for depression), and individual development (e.g., recognition that going through certain hardships changes you as a person). Interesting issues about insight also emerged in Rees et al.'s (2001) comprehensive process analysis of a problem clarification event in CBT with a depressed female client. In the discussion of the gap between the client and her husband, the problem was identified as the fact that she avoids confrontation with him by shrugging off and dismissing her own desires. The therapist first assisted the client in recognizing and clarifying the problem, which led the client to confirm the therapist's suggestion that she might not know exactly what she wants or how to express that she felt "stuck." The therapist then offered steps toward a possible solution in a Socratic dialogue. The therapist modeled the client's dysfunctional thinking as well as possible assertive behaviors in relation to her "wants" in the relationship. During the session in which the insight occurred, the client showed no signs (verbal, behavioral, or emotional) that an insight had taken place. After the session, while filling out material on immediate session impact, it was clear that the session material did produce insight. She described her insight experience with the following words:

> And this actually hadn't struck me before. The dawning of realization—
> good heavens! . . . I felt so stupid. It seems so obvious, doesn't it? Inad-

equacy that I hadn't spotted it for myself a long time ago. For somebody who's supposed to be intelligent, I can be really stupid at times. . . . It's high time after 20 years that I started to say what I wanted, and that it perhaps won't be the end of the world if I do. (Rees et al., p. 340)

This example illustrates several important points. First, insight is sometimes the result of a lot of work. In this case, the client gained a new understanding of self following many CBT interventions. Second, it shows that insights can be delayed: They may not be observable in the session itself but might emerge afterwards. As noted by Schottenbauer, Glass, and Arnkoff (see chap. 15, this volume), new understanding can take place during homework that cognitive–behavioral therapists frequently assign between sessions (as also noted by Schottenbauer and her colleagues, as well as by Gelso and Harbin, chap. 14 of this volume, the influence of between-session activities on insight takes place in different forms of therapy). Third, as far as can be gathered from the client's report, an insight can be accelerated and may sometimes need a trigger (such as completing a postsession report).

Insights also seem to occur in cognitive–behavioral therapy as a result of nonbehavioral interventions. Kuhlman (1982), for example, described beneficial impacts of a therapist's interpretation and the client insight that followed. The client came to therapy to deal with a blockage he experienced when taking tests in college. The insight occurred after the construction of a fear hierarchy in the context of systematic desensitization. The therapist noticed a negative allusion from the client to his wife and fed it back to the client. The client first reacted defensively but in the next session expressed that the marital situation had relevance for the test-taking problems. After the therapist made an interpretation about the symbolic significance of his test-taking problems as a displaced expression of his anger toward his spouse, the client realized that he had negative feelings toward his wife for controlling his actions. Following this new, emotionally laden understanding of self, he was able to do well on his exams and started confronting his wife.

On the basis of the empirical studies and case reports, it appears that our definition of insight as a new understanding of self and others fits a specific type of events that occur in CBT, events that at least some clients receiving this form of therapy perceive as helpful. The description of several cases suggests that our schema-focused perspective captures important dimensions along which insight events may vary (wide range of objects, complexity of connection between these objects, level of representations of the same objects, intensity of emotion experienced during making connections) and degree of acceleration or suddenness of these new connections (or learning).

Are There CBT-Specific Insights?

Although empirical studies point to potential differences in the frequency of insights in different treatments, the question remains whether insights in CBT differ from those in other treatments. At least one study has addressed this important question. Using Comprehensive Process Analysis (CPA), Elliott et al. (1994) compared insight events of three clients in CBT with insight events of three clients in psychodynamic–interpersonal therapy. The authors defined insight as consisting of four elements (Elliott, 1984): (a) metaphorical vision or seeing with figurative eyes, (b) perception of patterns and links, (c) suddenness, and (d) newness. All insight events were taken from successful phases in the respective therapies. Although all insight events involved a meaning bridge, insight events in CBT did not involve painful awareness as an emotional effect, a feature that the events in psychodynamic therapy showed. In addition, insight events in CBT were "primarily reattributional in nature," whereas insight events in psychodynamic therapy involved "cross-session linking of core interpersonal conflict themes." The authors concluded that "it is thus important not to assume that insight is the same in the two treatments" (p. 460).

A case example reported by Elliott et al. (1994) illustrates these results. A female teacher reported an insight in the fifth session of therapy after she had been instructed in relaxation procedures, keeping a diary, and assertion strategies. The insight involved a reattribution of an interpersonal problem at work as the fault of a colleague, not the client:

> We went over a situation which happened today, where I had thought I'd let myself down and made a fool of myself, and when the therapist pointed out that it was [a] fairly common situation and quite funny, I suddenly saw another side to it and felt much better. (p. 455)

On the basis of the dimensions of our schema-focused view, this insight experience would be described as fairly sudden but not very complex, apparently associated with neither intense emotions nor previously implicit memory.

One important question future research should address, however, is whether this is the only type of insight occurring in CBT, especially when this treatment is conducted in a natural setting, as opposed to a clinical trial context (as in Elliott et al.'s [1994] study). Some examples described in the case reports section, as well as the clinical case briefly described earlier in this chapter (albeit derived from an integrative or assimilative form of CBT [see Castonguay, 2000]) suggest that this may not be the case.

Is Insight Beneficial in CBT?

In a previous section we showed that insight has been described by clients as a helpful event that occurs in CBT. Knowing how many clients find insight beneficial or how helpful it is compared with other therapy events would provide a more specific assessment of its potential impact.

Cadbury, Childs-Clark, and Sandhu (1990) examined helpful aspects of CBT with 29 anxiety clients participating in an anxiety management group. After treatment was completed, participants rated the helpfulness of several specific techniques. They also ranked nonspecific therapy factors in terms of helpfulness. Results indicated that 66% of the participants gave the technique *explanation of anxiety* the highest helpfulness rating. In addition, two insight-related nonspecific factors were given the two highest ranks for helpfulness: *universality* (realization that they are not alone with problems) and *self-understanding*. O'Leary and Rathus (1993) analyzed reports clients gave after termination about the most helpful aspects of therapy for depressed women experiencing marital discord. Twenty women participated in marital therapy, and 11 women in cognitive therapy. Their reports were coded into 12 response categories, one of which was "Insight into Own Problems." Thirty-six percent of cognitive-therapy clients reported insight as one of the most helpful aspects of therapy. In contrast, none of the clients in marital therapy did.

Another way of assessing the potential impact of insight is to measure its relationship with outcome. In the study by Gershefski et al. (1996) discussed earlier in this chapter, client statements coded as *Learning Something New* did not relate to outcome. Insight did not predict symptom change in CBT or psychodynamic therapy in the study by Llewelyn et al. (1988).

Using related constructs, other studies have yielded more promising results. Muran et al. (1995) studied the capacity of cognitive shift and other suboutcome measures to predict outcome of cognitive therapy for 53 depressed and/or anxious outpatients. They operationalized cognitive shift by one item. After a qualitative description ("Please describe the belief, thought, attitude, or expectation that was worked on during the session"), clients rated cognitive shift using the item "How much did this belief, thought, attitude, or expectation change during the session?". Using this single item, the authors found cognitive shift to have a strong predictive relationship to patient-rated outcome. However, although cognitive shift predicted change in interpersonal problems, in automatic thoughts, in target complaints, and success as rated by the client, it did not significantly predict symptom change, global adjustment, or therapist-rated success. These results indicate that the relationship between the degree of insight and treatment outcome might depend on the types of outcome measure used.

Although the authors did not explicitly measure insight, the results of Tang and DeRubeis's (1999) study of sudden gains in CBT might be indicative of the positive role of insight in symptom change. The authors compared the level of cognitive change achieved by clients in sessions before and after a sudden gain occurred. Cognitive changes were measured by the Patient Cognitive Change Scale (PCCS), which includes seven categories: (a) *bringing a belief into awareness*, (b) *identifying an error in cognitive process or belief*, (c) *arriving at a new belief on a specific issue*, (d) *bringing a schema into aware-*

ness, (e) *identifying an error in a schema*, (f) *arriving at a new schema*, and (g) *accepting a new cognitive technique*. Results showed that there were significantly greater cognitive changes in sessions immediately before the sudden gain than in previous sessions. Clients who experienced sudden gains were less depressed at the end of treatment and at follow-up. Which of the cognitive changes assessed in this study fulfill our definition of insights awaits further analysis. However, the results suggest a causal role of cognitive changes in (rapid) symptom improvement, which might also include cognitive changes that can be classified as insights.

As a whole, studies relating insight and outcome in CBT have led to mixed results. Developing instruments that would capture the different dimensions of insight suggested by our schema-focused model may allow researchers to better capture outcome variance. It should also be mentioned that process-outcome studies are not without pitfalls and that many variables that are assumed to play a role in client improvement have failed to be linked with posttreatment change (Stiles, 1988). Thus, it is possible that most of the effect of insight on outcome is not direct. As such, future studies should also investigate the relationship between insight and less distal outcomes (during or after specific sessions).

·CONCLUDING COMMENTS

At the outset of our inquiry on the role of insight in cognitive–behavioral therapy (CBT), we were convinced that CBT has not paid enough systematic attention to the change process. We reviewed classic literature in CBT and found that until the cognitive revolution, behavioral therapy ignored, paid lip service to, or dismissed the importance of insight. However, the concept of schema and the recognition of cognitive mediation as a determinant of behavior allowed reconsiderations of the potential role of insight in therapeutic change. We reviewed different lines of research and theory from cognitive psychology and CBT that highlighted different aspects of insight as a schematic change. After delineating dimensions of insight on the basis of these contributions, we surveyed empirical studies and clinical case reports to examine the evidence for the role of insight in CBT and to determine if some support could be found for our definition and schema-focused perspective on insight. At the end of this effort, it seems fair to return to the question we stated at the onset of the chapter: Why should cognitive–behavioral therapists care about insight?

As the previous survey of empirical literature and published case reports showed, insight obviously occurs in CBT. Although various types of insights (e.g., referring to different objects, reflecting diverse levels of representation, involving more or less emotion) were observed in CBT, it may be that this approach (at least when conducted within the context of clinical trials) differs from other orientations in terms of frequency and quality of insight events. Finally, although neither conclusive nor unambiguous, there are indications that insight might be beneficial in CBT. As research in conditioning suggests that conscious awareness of contingencies increases learning and performance (Bandura, 1969), it is reasonable to assume that the subjective experience of schema change is likely to facilitate therapeutic change. In other words, we believe that insight can have causal influences on cognition, emotion, behavior, and thus change in psychotherapy. More specifically, insight can in our view increase the client's self-efficacy (sense of control or mastery) and enable him or her to experience greater freedom over past and current determinants of functioning (i.e., increase his or her ability to choose or enlarge his or her repertoire of behaviors toward self and others). Taken together, these results and considerations should trigger the curiosity of CBT researchers and practitioners about the exact role of insight in CBT, as well as about the ways it might be used to increase the therapeutic efficacy of CBT. With this in mind, we suggest a number of questions that could guide future investigations on insight.

The question of utmost importance for scientifically minded therapists—cognitive–behavioralists and others—is whether insight is causal or epiphenomenal. Although Skinnerians would argue that it is not causal, we believe it can have a causal effect. This, however, is not likely to be an all-or-none issue. Rather, we assume that insight is an epiphenomenon in some cases and a causal antecedent in others. Only sophisticated research will be able to address this issue. An example of such research is the longitudinal study by Kivlighan, Multon, and Patton (2000) on psychoanalytic counseling. Using time-series analyses of client-reported insight events, the authors demonstrated that increases in insight across sessions led to reductions in target complaints. Similar studies should be conducted in CBT. Studies should also investigate whether richer (in terms of breadth and complexity), deeper (in terms of implicit memories), or more emotional insights contribute to greater therapeutic change. Ultimately, however, experimental single case designs and between-groups additive designs in which interventions are manipulated to increase insight should be conducted to directly answer the question of causality.

Further investigations should also pay attention to the antecedents and consequences of insight. In time-series analyses, Hoffart and Sexton (2002) showed that an increase in optimism predicted the occurrence of insights in inpatients with panic disorder and *Diagnostic and Statistical Manual of Mental Disorders* (4th ed.; American Psychiatric Association, 1994)–Cluster C personality traits receiving CBT. Client, therapist, technical, and relationship factors providing the best conditions to foster insight should be examined with longitudinal designs. Analyses of the consequences of insight need not be restricted to symptomatic outcomes but should also include other indicators of favorable change. For example, Grosse Holtforth, Grawe, and

Castonguay (in press) showed that the level of clarification (a concept similar to insight) predicts reduction of avoidance motivation, especially when occurring in early phases of treatment and with depressed clients.

Another question of particular interest is whether insight is necessary for change to occur. Being cognitive–behaviorally oriented, we strongly agree with Westerman's (1989) statement that "it might be possible to accomplish meaningful change in therapy by means of purely active interventions and without patients arriving at new insights" (p. 208). However, on the basis of our schema-theoretical conception, we argue that verbalizing and making schema changes conscious is likely to increase the therapeutic potential of purely action-oriented interventions. Consequently, we are convinced that one way of improving the effectiveness of CBT (when working with some clients) would be to enlarge or refine its techniques to foster insight. Whether this would best be achieved by further developing cognitive–behavioral interventions or integrating procedures associated with other traditions is a fascinating empirical question.

REFERENCES

American Psychiatric Association. (1994). *Diagnostic and statistical manual of mental disorders* (4th ed.). Washington, DC: Author.

Bandura, A. (1969). *Principles of behavior modification.* New York: Holt, Rinehart & Winston.

Beck, A. T. (1976). *Cognitive therapy and emotional disorders.* New York: International Universities Press.

Cadbury, S., Childs-Clark, A., & Sandhu, S. (1990). Group anxiety management: Effectiveness, perceived helpfulness and follow-up. *British Journal of Clinical Psychology, 29*(2), 245–247.

Caspar, F. (1995). *Plan analysis: Toward optimizing psychotherapy.* Seattle, WA: Hogrefe & Huber.

Castonguay, L. G. (2000). A common factors approach to psychotherapy training. *Journal of Psychotherapy Integration, 10,* 263–282.

Cautela, J. R. (1965). Desensitization and insight. *Behaviour Research and Therapy, 3,* 59–64.

Cautela, J. R. (1993). Insight in behavior therapy. *Journal of Behavior Therapy and Experimental Psychiatry, 24,* 155–159.

Clarke, H., Rees, A., & Hardy, G. E. (2004). The big idea: Clients' perspectives of change processes in cognitive therapy. *Psychology and Psychotherapy: Theory, Research and Practice, 77*(1), 67–89.

Edelman, G. (1987). *Neural Darwinism: The theory of neuronal group selection.* New York: Basic Books.

Elkin, I., Parloff, M. B., Hadley, S. W., & Autry, J. H. (1985). NIMH Treatment of Depression Collaborative Research Program: Background and research plan. *Archives of General Psychiatry, 42*, 305–316

Elkin, I., Shea, M. T., Watkins, J. T., Imber, S. D., Sotsky, S. M., Collins, J. F., et al. (1989). National Institute of Mental Health Treatment of Depression Collaborative Research Program: General effectiveness of treatments. *Archives of General Psychiatry, 46*, 971–982.

Elliott, R. (1984). A discovery-oriented approach to significant events in psychotherapy: Interpersonal process recall and comprehensive process analysis. In L. N. Rice & L. S. Greenberg (Eds.), *Patterns of change* (pp. 249–286). New York: Guilford Press.

Elliott, R., Shapiro, D. A., Firth-Cozens, J., Stiles, W. B., Hardy, G. E., Llewelyn, S. P., & Margison, F. R. (1994). Comprehensive process analysis of insight events in cognitive–behavioral and psychodynamic–interpersonal psychotherapies. *Journal of Counseling Psychology, 41*, 449–463.

Ellis, A. (1963). Toward a more precise definition of "emotional" and "intellectual" insight. *Psychological Reports, 13*, 125–126.

Epstein, S. (1990). Cognitive–experiential self-theory. In L. Pervin (Ed.), *Handbook of personality theory and research: Theory and research* (pp. 165–192). New York: Guilford Press.

Gendlin, E. T. (1991). On emotion in therapy. In J. D. Safran & L. S. Greenberg (Eds.), *Emotion, psychotherapy and change* (pp. 255–279). New York: Guilford Press.

Gershefski, J. J., Arnkoff, D. B., Glass, C. R., & Elkin, I. (1996). Clients' perceptions of treatment for depression: I. Helpful aspects. *Psychotherapy Research, 6*, 233–247.

Goldfried, M. R. (2003). Cognitive–behavioral therapy: Reflections on the evolution of a therapeutic orientation. *Cognitive Therapy and Research, 27*(1), 53–69.

Goldfried, M. R., & Davison, G. C. (1976). *Clinical behavior therapy.* New York: Holt, Rinehart & Winston.

Goldfried, M. R., & Robins, C. (1983). Self-schemata, cognitive bias, and the processing of therapeutic experiences. In P. C. Kendall (Ed.), *Advances in cognitive–behavioral research and therapy* (Vol. 2, pp. 33–80). San Diego, CA: Academic Press.

Grawe, K. (1997). Research-informed psychotherapy. *Psychotherapy Research, 7*, 1–19.

Grawe, K. (2004). *Psychological therapy.* Seattle, WA: Hogrefe & Huber.

Grawe, K., Caspar, F., & Ambühl, H. R. (1990). Die Berner Therapievergleichsstudie: Wirkungsvergleich und differentielle Indikation. In Differentielle Psychotherapieforschung: Vier Therapieformen im Vergleich [The Bern therapy comparison study: Comparison of effectiveness and differential indication]. *Zeitschrift für Klinische Psychologie, 4*(19), 338–361.

Greenberg, L. S., & Safran, J. D. (1987). *Emotion in psychotherapy: Affect, cognition and the process of change.* New York: Guilford Press.

Grosse Holtforth, M., Grawe, K., & Castonguay, L. G. (in press). Predicting a reduction of avoidance motivation in psychotherapy: Toward the delineation of differential processes of change operating at different phases of treatment. *Psychotherapy Research*.

Hebb, D. O. (1949). *The organization of behavior: A neuropsychological theory*. New York: Wiley.

Hoffart, A., & Sexton, H. (2002). The role of optimism in the process of schema-focused cognitive therapy of personality problems. *Behavior Research and Therapy*, 40, 611–623.

Hubel, D. H., & Wiesel, T. N. (1968). Receptive fields of single neurons in the cat's striate cortex. *Journal of Physiology*, 148, 574–591.

Kivlighan, D. M., Jr., Multon, K. D., & Patton, M. J. (2000). Insight and symptom reduction in time-limited psychoanalytic counseling. *Journal of Counseling Psychology*, 47, 50–58.

Kuhlman, T. L. (1982). Symptom relief through insight during systematic desensitization: A case study. *Psychotherapy: Theory, Research and Practice*, 19(1), 88–94.

Lazarus, A. A. (1973). Multimodal behavior therapy: Treating the "BASIC ID." *Journal of Nervous and Mental Disease*, 156, 404–411.

Leventhal, H. (1984). A perceptual-motor theory of emotion. In L. Berkowitz (Ed.), *Advances in experimental social psychology* (Vol. 17, pp. 117–182). New York: Academic Press.

Llewelyn, S. P., Elliott, R., Shapiro, D. A., Hardy, G., & Firth-Cozens, J. (1988). Clients' perceptions of significant events in prescriptive and exploratory phases of individual therapy. *British Journal of Clinical Psychology*, 27, 105–114.

Mahoney, M. J. (1974). *Cognition and behavior modification*. Cambridge, MA: Ballinger.

Mahoney, M. J. (1980). Psychotherapy and the structure of personal revolutions. In M. J. Mahoney (Ed.), *Psychotherapy process* (pp. 157–180). New York: Plenum Press.

Markus, H. (1977). Self-schemas and processing information about the self. *Journal of Personality and Social Psychology*, 35, 63–78.

Meichenbaum, D. (1977). *Cognitive–behavioral modification: An integrative approach*. New York: Plenum Press.

Messer, S. B. (1986). Behavioral and psychoanalytic perspectives at therapeutic choice points. *American Psychologist*, 41, 1261–1272.

Muran, J. C., Gorman, B. S., Safran, J. D., Twining, L., Samstag, L. W., & Winston, A. (1995). Linking in-session change to overall outcome in short-term cognitive therapy. *Journal of Consulting and Clinical Psychology*, 63, 651–657.

O'Leary, K. D., & Rathus, J. H. (1993). Clients' perceptions of therapeutic helpfulness in cognitive and marital therapy for depression. *Cognitive Therapy and Research*, 17(3), 225–233.

Powell, D. R. (1987). Spontaneous insight associated with behavior therapy: The case of Rex. In J. C. Norcross (Ed.), *Casebook of eclectic psychotherapy* (pp. 325–349). Philadelphia: Brunner/Mazel.

Powell, D. R. (1988). Spontaneous insights and the process of behavior therapy: Cases in support of integrative psychotherapy. *Psychiatric Annals, 18*(5), 288–294.

Powell, D. R. (1996). Behavior therapy-generated insight. In W. Ishaq & J. R. Cautela (Eds.), *Contemporary issues in behavior therapy: Improving the human condition* (pp. 301–314). New York: Plenum Press.

Rees, A., Hardy, G. E., Barkham, M., Elliott, R., Smith, J. A., & Reynolds, S. (2001). 'It's like catching a desire before it flies away': A comprehensive process analysis of a problem clarification event in cognitive–behavioral therapy for depression. *Psychotherapy Research, 11,* 331–351.

Safran, J. D. (1989). Insight and action in psychotherapy. *Journal of Integrative and Eclectic Psychotherapy, 8*(3), 3–19.

Safran, J. D. (1990). Towards a refinement of cognitive therapy in light of interpersonal theory: I. Theory. *Clinical Psychology Review, 10,* 87–105.

Safran, J. D., & Segal, Z. V. (1990). *Interpersonal process in cognitive therapy.* New York: Basic Books.

Samoilov, A., & Goldfried, M. R. (2000). Role of emotion in cognitive-behavior therapy. *Clinical-Psychology: Science and Practice, 7,* 373–385.

Sedlacek, K. (1979). Biofeedback for Raynaud's disease. *Psychosomatics, 20*(8), 535–541.

Shoben, E. J. (1960). Psychotherapy as a problem in learning theory. In H. J. Eysenck (Ed.), *Behavior therapy and the neuroses* (pp. 52–78). New York: Pergamon Press.

Stiles, W. B. (1988). Psychotherapy process-outcome correlations may be misleading. *Psychotherapy: Theory, Research, Practice, Training, 25,* 27–35.

Tang, T. Z., & DeRubeis, R. J. (1999). Sudden gains and critical sessions in cognitive–behavioral therapy for depression. *Journal of Consulting and Clinical Psychology, 67,* 894–904.

Teasdale, J. (1993). Emotion and two kinds of meaning: Cognitive therapy and applied cognitive science. *Behaviour Research and Therapy, 31,* 339–354.

Wachtel, P. (1977). *Psychoanalysis and behavior therapy: Toward an integration.* New York: Basic Books.

Westerman, M. A. (1989). A naturalized view of the role played by insight in psychotherapy. *Journal of Integrative and Eclectic Psychotherapy, 8,* 19–22.

4

MANIFESTATIONS AND FACILITATION OF INSIGHT IN COUPLE AND FAMILY THERAPY

LAURIE HEATHERINGTON AND MYRNA L. FRIEDLANDER

As Messer and McWilliams noted in chapter 1 of this volume, the concept of insight historically has been associated with psychoanalytic psychotherapy. It has taken time for other approaches, couple and family therapies included, to address the role of insight and define it conceptually. In couple and family therapy, the domain of *insight* encompasses not only understandings about the self (how I am) but also understandings about others (how you are) and the multiperson system (how we are together). Moreover, clients in conjoint therapy often make connections among these elements and these cognitive understandings are—in successful therapy—closely related to emotional experience, emotional expression, and interpersonal change. Thus we define insight as a new or changed understanding of how one's own or others' behavior, emotions, or cognitions play a role in couple and family processes.[1] This understanding is typically, but not always, about making connections between these elements.

---

[1]We note the compatibility of this definition of insight and that offered by Grosse Holtforth et al. (see chap. 3, this volume) from the perspective of cognitive–behavioral therapy.

How do we know that insight does, in fact, occur in couple and family therapy? First, our clients teach us. They do so *directly*—both spontaneously within therapy sessions or in response to systematic studies in which they are the informants, specifically qualitative and self-report studies. And they do so *indirectly*—when we study the process of change in the therapy and systematically observe the ways in which insight, emotional, and interpersonal processes change in coordination with each other. In this chapter we consider all these sources of information and discuss clinical and research material that illustrates the manifestations of insight in couple and family therapy. We then discuss several means of facilitating insight, with examples drawn from our professional experience as clinicians and family therapy researchers.[2]

MANIFESTATIONS OF INSIGHT IN CONJOINT TREATMENT

In this section we highlight two specific ways that insight, broadly defined, can be experienced in family therapy. The first, arguably the simplest, manifestation is the client's recognition of similarities between his or her own behavioral or socioemotional issues and those of others in the nuclear or extended family, for example, "I just figured out that, like me, you and all the other females in our family get depressed; the men just get drunk." We refer to this as *insight into similarities and reciprocals*.

The second manifestation is an *insight into causality*—how one's behavior influences the behavior of another family member ("So I'm pushing you too hard and then you withdraw?") or vice versa ("Now I see that when you come home late, I overeat"). In these examples, the causal insight is linear. In its more complex form, the insight can be a rich understanding of how one's own cognitions, emotions, and behaviors are reciprocally influenced by the cognitions, emotions, and behaviors of others in the family, for example,

> When I stopped fighting with you about your homework and told you to go to bed, you argued that you couldn't—you had to finish your report! Now I realize the homework struggle we're locked into is a vicious cycle between us.

Insight Into Similarities and Reciprocals

According to Bowen (1976; Kerr & Bowen, 1988), an important route to improved differentiation of self is insight into the multigenerational transmission of psychopathology. Emotional patterns within the nuclear family,

---

[2]Clinical case examples and vignettes are either from actual cases (with identifying material and characteristics heavily disguised) or are composites of cases from our personal professional experiences.

for example, attack–defend or pursue–withdraw, are passed down from one generation to the next, sometimes in obvious ways (physical or sexual abuse) or more subtly. In therapy, a father realized that his 19-year-old son's compulsive exercising paralleled his own compulsive gambling, which also began in late adolescence. A mother who was distraught that her 16-year-old daughter was involved with a gang leader realized there was a pattern in the behavior of women in her family. Her grandmother flouted the prevailing social norms of her time (the 1930s) by getting divorced and remarried, her mother did so by marrying interracially (in the 1960s), and she herself did the same by leaving her husband and declaring herself a lesbian (in 2002). The client explained that in each generation, the women were under the heavy thumbs of autocratic fathers and were rebelling by choosing partners of whom their parents disapproved.

In another case, a couple was struggling with traditional gender-role misunderstandings. The wife complained that her husband had no interest in her personal life or in emotional intimacy of any kind, and the husband was baffled by his wife's expectations and frustrated at being described as a failure when, in his eyes, he was "a good provider and a concerned father." After four relatively unproductive sessions focused on communication, everyone—the therapist included—was unsure how to move forward. The wife, Rochelle, wanted a "soul mate," which her husband Frank wasn't and presumably never would be. Yet both were committed to their marriage and to raising their four children. Divorce was out of the question.

At the beginning of the fifth session, Rochelle made a startling comment. She said,

> We've been talking about communication, and although we do okay in here, there's just nothing by way of conversation when we get home. So I don't think this topic is going to get us anywhere. I figure if I want to stay married (and I do), I need to stop looking for meaningful discussions with Frank. I get that from my friends instead.

By asking to redirect the therapy, Rochelle was making a bold statement. Frank listened quietly, with no visible reaction. Clearly he too had become tired of trying to force something that didn't come naturally.

The therapist was more than willing to go in another direction but thought it might be helpful to understand how Rochelle came to her conclusion. Rochelle related the following story:

> Our daughter, who's 10, is really interested in astronomy. She asked me to get up at three in the morning with her to look at some comet or something through the telescope, so I did. As we were standing there on the porch, she was so very excited, and I was . . . well, frankly, I was bored to tears. I just wanted to be back in bed! I was going through the motions for her, though, not getting anything out of it for myself. I only did it because I love her, that's what parents do. So then I thought, 'This is

how Frank feels when I talk about my career or anything else I'm doing that's not related to the family. He's just not interested—period.' And then I thought that if I want to stay married, I need to 'move on' and accept that he's just not interested in anything I have to say that's personal about myself.

Although he was listening, Frank remained silent and unmoved. When asked by the therapist for his reaction, he merely said, "I think it'd be a good idea for us to talk about something different."

Here, then, is an example of insight into similarities and reciprocals. Rochelle came to see that despite her husband's disinterest in her personal life, he would "go through the motions" for her sake, just as she would for their daughter. Although she did not state it explicitly, Rochelle's acceptance of the same attitude that she complained her husband had adopted was freeing. The couple had two more sessions before terminating therapy. Although Rochelle did not have the husband she longed for, she appreciated Frank for what he did offer and made a conscious choice to put her frustrations aside.

In this example, a client came to accept a problematic attitude and behavior in her partner when she recognized it in herself. In another case, one member of a lesbian couple became aware that their dysfunctional pattern of interaction mirrored the pattern of her partner's parents. Stacy had been complaining bitterly about Allison's mistreatment of her, with little understanding of (or interest in) the origins of her partner's behavior. Allison would harp on Stacy over any minor issue, and their struggle at times escalated to screaming and name calling. During a week's visit with Allison's parents, however, Stacy noticed that Allison's mother did the same thing to Allison's father.

In the therapy session following this visit, Stacy explained that Allison behaved like her mother by putting Stacy in the father's role. This insight made perfect sense to Allison too, who until that point had been unaware of the similarity between her mother's behavior and her own. As the conversation continued, the therapist asked the couple to consider whether their interactions might also mirror something in Stacy's family of origin. Without missing a beat, Stacy remarked that, "At least with Allison criticizing me all the time over every little thing, I don't feel invisible like I did when I was a kid." Stacy described at some length the total lack of emotional contact in her family of origin. These insights led to a more powerful insight—her understanding, on a feeling level, of why she stayed with Allison despite the heartache and perpetual drama.

This last awareness is an example of what is called an *insight into reciprocals*, that is, one in which a person comes to see that her or his behavior or reaction in one relationship is the opposite of what it is (or was) in another relationship. In the earlier case of Rochelle and Frank, Rochelle also recognized a pattern in the family—feigning interest for another's sake. With her husband, Rochelle was the individual trying to win the other's interest; with her daughter, Rochelle was the one going through the motions.

Insight Into Causality, Linear and Circular

Sometimes an insight simply emerges in a therapy conversation, although often, as in Rochelle's case, a new awareness comes about at home and is set in motion by something that took place in session. Of course, this experience occurs in individual therapy as well as conjoint treatment. What is unique to conjoint therapy, however, is that insight about how one's behavior, cognitions, and emotions influence and are influenced by others is stimulated not by introspection but by having a new experience of other family members right in the therapist's office. A husband was asked by a friend why his marriage had improved. The husband replied that he had been surprised to see the couple's (male) therapist take his wife so seriously. This observation made him realize that he had always treated his wife like a petulant child, which angered her tremendously. Now he was trying to turn it around, apparently successfully. In this case the insight was unidirectional, or linear; the recognition of the influence of one cause (the husband's patronizing treatment of his wife) on one effect (the wife's angry response). In other couple and family cases, clients' insights involve circular causal patterns; for example, the husband realizes that his patronizing causes his wife's angry outbursts and that her outbursts in turn increase his patronizing.

Whereas in this case the husband's insight came about spontaneously, in some family therapy approaches it is the result of the therapist's planned strategy. Strategizing is often necessary because it is difficult for clients to see themselves as others do, and patterns of interaction with significant others can become so entrenched over time that their dysfunctional features become invisible. Dad only sees that the kids misbehave when he's around; the kids see themselves as trying to get the attention of their often-absent father; Mom feels overworked and burdened, unaware that she treats her husband like a guest in their home, expecting little and requesting nothing; one partner only sees the other withdrawing but not his or her own nagging. Not getting satisfaction, they try harder, with "more of the same" behavior.

How do therapists get clients to take a metaperspective, to see what they see? Later in this chapter we discuss various interventions designed to illuminate for clients the ways in which the solution can become the problem. However it comes about, an understanding of this simple phenomenon helps clients punctuate a sequence of events differently ("I see that my patronizing makes you angry") and promotes second-order change (Watzlawick, Weakland, & Fisch, 1974). As we discuss in this chapter, family therapies differ in substantial and interesting ways in how they make insights explicit to clients or whether it is even necessary to do so.

Insights into causality can be profound, particularly when they prompt behavior change. In an emotional session, a couple comes to understand that they both have sexual fears—he about impotence, she because of her childhood abuse history. They discover that avoidance of sexuality allows them to protect each other without acknowledging their own anxiety about sexual intimacy.

Another couple came for help to "get over" the wife's affair. Profoundly regretful, apologetic, and guilt-ridden, Jan had become a "doormat" for her husband Ron after the affair had been revealed 6 months earlier. For his part, Ron used his wife's transgression to get his way whenever they had a difference of opinion. Jan became increasingly depressed, Ron increasingly angry. For several sessions neither husband nor wife could see a way out of this destructive pattern. After all, she was the guilty party, and he was the righteous victim.

The therapist decided to push the couple toward a new experience in light of the fact that the therapeutic alliance was strong and balanced and both clients were open to help in therapy and motivated to keep their marriage from failing. The therapist first asked Jan to voice her anger about what Ron was putting her through, while Ron was instructed to listen but not comment. The therapist then asked Ron to express the hurt and pain he felt over Jan's infidelity while she remained silent. Although it took coaxing for each spouse to express the reciprocal emotion, they did eventually and with strong feeling. Afterward, Ron commented spontaneously, "Whoa! I can see how my being so angry at Jan protects me from being mad at how much I've fucked up, too!" Jan quickly interjected,

> And if you stay mad at me, then I can feel like a victim instead of really trying to figure out why I had the affair and if I want to stay married to you! As long as you keep blaming me, I feel like I have to hold onto you, but maybe I don't even want to!

Although this comment implied that Jan might flee the marriage, her insight had precisely the opposite effect. She made a decision to fight for herself and for an equal partnership with Ron. Ron, who was disgusted with the narrow, angry place he'd been in for so many months, was more than willing to meet his wife's challenge.

FACILITATING INSIGHT

As shown in the previous examples, therapists can promote insight in any number of ways, even unintentionally. Sometimes merely eliciting each client's side of the story allows insights to emerge spontaneously because the others are active observers and not objects of another's story, as in individual therapy. Sometimes family members need to be pushed to experience each other differently before new understandings occur, and sometimes insights occur between sessions when clients begin behaving differently or (as in Rochelle's case) start interpreting each other's behavior differently. In this section we discuss ways to facilitate insight through three points of access: behavior, cognition, and emotion.

Promoting Insight Through Behavior Change

Couple therapy originated from a behavioral tradition, and the earliest couples approaches focused on helping partners identify and modify dysfunctional patterns of communication. It was clear early on that clients' cognitions (underlying beliefs, expectancies, assumptions, attributions) as well as their behavior needed to be addressed, and that behavior change and insight influence one another reciprocally. In one case (Friedlander, Escudero, & Heatherington, 2006) a husband had the insight that he'd abandoned his wife and newborn child out of fear that he would become a neglectful, distant father like his own. In couple therapy this man was motivated but passive and inexpressive, despite the fact that he'd been the one to suggest getting professional help to save the marriage. After weeks of attempts to influence the couple's relationship through verbal exploration, the therapist suggested that they begin "dating," with all discussion about the fate of their marriage off limits. When this intervention sparked a positive change, the therapist suggested family outings with the baby. As the coupled inched toward reconciliation, the therapist asked the wife to tell her husband how she saw him as a father. When she spontaneously and enthusiastically praised her husband's parenting, he burst into tears. Although choked up, he explained the terror he'd felt about duplicating the relationship he had with his own father.

Insight can emerge spontaneously when a therapist disrupts problem-maintaining sequences. This kind of intervention, the staple of strategic and problem-focused theorists such as Haley (1973), Madanes (1981), and Watzlawick et al. (1974), involves breaking up rigid interactions that keep people in confining roles. Many clients come to a new awareness when they see family members behaving differently. Charlene, for example, was directed to refrain from her hovering mother behavior for 2 weeks. She was not to remind her 13-year-old daughter about homework or chores nor comment on Ashley's friends, bedtime, eating habits, and so on. Ashley, suddenly freed from her mother's control, began behaving more responsibly than she ever had. Astounded by the change, Charlene remarked, "To my amazement, everything that I was doing to keep her on track was actually working against what I intended!"

We should note, however, that the purpose of strategic interventions is not cognitive change. Indeed, a hallmark of some of these therapies is dramatic interventions (e.g., the invariant prescription, paradoxical interventions), deliberately delivered without explanation or rationale (Haley, 1973). Although such interventions can have dramatic results, they have not been studied extensively, and there is no empirical knowledge of how well they work to break up rigid interactional patterns and help family members develop more functional ones. Important questions for future research include how family members understand these interventions, whether and how they lead to new insights, and whether those insights are indeed critical to successful outcomes.

Promoting Insight Through Cognitive Change

In contrast, there are couple and family approaches and techniques that target cognitions explicitly. Working with clients' cognitive constructions is a straightforward way to facilitate insight. Three common interventions are reframing (or relabelling), differentiating intents and effects, and focusing on reciprocals.

In structural family therapy (Minuchin, 1974), one of the earliest models of family therapy, families are enjoined to see the problem behavior in a new light, for example, to see anorexia not as an uncontrollable illness but as a quest for autonomy, conduct disorder as a means of protecting mom and dad from their marital tension, and so on. Various strategies, most notably provocative questioning ("Ask your mother what she would do all day if you were not a 'bad' kid"), are used to prime family members to accept a new, less blaming construction of the problem ("Your misbehavior is a selfless act to keep your parents from fighting"), if not to arrive at it themselves. Strategies include simple relabeling ("That behavior is 'bad,' not 'mad'"), redefining ("This problem is not just about your skipping school—it's about your mom's letting you manipulate her"), or reattribution of motives (M. Goldfried, personal communication, March 30, 2004), as in the selfless act example described previously.

Reframing is popular clinically and several sophisticated variations of this intervention are typically used in treatments for delinquent adolescents, notably functional family therapy (FFT; see, e.g., Sexton & Alexander, 2003). In FFT, reframing is not simply the act of finding a positive connotation of problematic behavior but is a series of ongoing exchanges between and among family members and the therapist that set in motion "alternative cognitive and attributional perspectives that help redefine meaning events and thus reduce the negativity and redirect the emotionality surrounding events" (Sexton & Alexander, 2003, p. 334). Behavior change follows from these alternative perspectives. To illustrate the process, when a family member makes a negative, blaming statement ("Your selfish attitude causes all our arguing"), the therapist begins by accepting and validating the speaker's underlying emotion or central issue ("You seem really angry with your son"). The therapist then introduces a reframe, essentially an alternative meaning. FFT offers three recommended strategies: *meaning change* (e.g., reframing the child's anger as a fear that his or her parent won't be strong enough to parent him), *challenge* (suggesting some goal or direction, e.g., "Your challenge will be to show him that you can"), and *linking* (essentially offering a systemic or family construction of the problem, e.g., "Your behavior and his feed off each other and become larger than either of you"). Linking is a particularly good strategy for promoting insight. Listening carefully to clients' responses to reframing interventions allows the therapist to build and modify the responses using the clients' own words and feelings, so that over time the reframe becomes a theme that they have constructed together and jointly own (Sexton & Alexander, 2003).

Intensive process research shows how reframing is linked to emotion and behavior. For example, in therapy with 37 two-parent families of delinquent adolescents, Robbins, Alexander, and Turner (2000) studied what happens immediately after a family member makes a defensive (negative) communication. The authors categorized the therapist interventions as reframe, reflection, or elicit-structure and family members' subsequent responses as supportive or defensive communications. Results showed positive effects for therapist reframes in reducing defensive communications. It is important to note that the adolescents' responses to reframes were particularly positive. Overall the findings showed that therapist reframes can successfully interrupt dysfunctional family interactions. The effects, the authors suggested, may be related to the benefits of a conjoint treatment: When family members witness reframes that do not involve them directly, they are less resistant than they are to more direct interventions.

In this kind of work, reattributions of motives (e.g., selfless as opposed to selfish) can be made as well as reattributions of causes (e.g., an illness as opposed to a developmental choice). Some therapists make the motivation part of reframes explicit by differentiating intents and effects. That is, the therapist goes further than a simple reframe (essentially, "You could think about it this way instead of that way") to point out the consequences of automatically concluding that another's motives are mean-spirited or uncaring. One person interprets another's behavior as retaliation and responds in anger, but the other person had no intent to harm the first. When they argue, the struggle about "what you did to me" can quickly degenerate. The therapist's role in such conflicts is to help each person see the futility of zero-sum thinking, that is, "I'm right, you're wrong." The intention may well have been harmless, even benevolent, although its effect on the other person was harmful.

The path to insight does not have to be didactic. When the therapist sees a vicious cycle he or she can promote a change through enactment rather than try to explain circular causality. Insight often occurs as a by-product. For example, one middle-age couple, Ted and Donna, was trying to keep their new marriage safe from the problems in Ted's extended family. The couple came for help to stop bickering over how Ted's parents and siblings were "constantly taking unfair advantage of him" (Donna's words). Donna would rant about the issue, becoming red in the face. Ted would sit stiffly, seemingly unmoved. Disconnected from his anger, Ted was letting Donna carry the emotional burden for them. As homework between sessions, the therapist asked Ted to make a list of everything he was annoyed about. He was instructed to compose the list alone and then read it to Donna, who was not to comment until she'd heard the entire list. The therapist offered no explanation for this unusual assignment.

In the following session, both spouses were lighthearted, affectionate, and relaxed, a tremendous difference from their previous demeanor. They explained that halfway through reading his list to Donna, Ted began getting angry and expressed it with great feeling. The two started joking about "what a piece of work" his brother was and indulged in playful revenge fantasies about those who were driving them crazy. Donna explained, "Once I saw that Ted was mad too, I wasn't alone in the way I felt about his family. I'd been doing the work for him!"

In another strategy, *focusing on reciprocals*, therapists guide clients toward understanding their part in an interpersonal struggle by asking them to observe or think about another relationship, one of their own or someone else's. In two of our earlier examples, Rochelle saw herself in Frank's role when she interacted with her daughter, and Stacy saw her abusive relationship with Allison as paralleling the struggle between Allison's parents.

Another woman, Deirdre, reported being "turned off" whenever she tried to tell her husband about her problems at work. He would make suggestions and tried to be supportive through problem solving. Deirdre rejected each suggestion and became increasingly frustrated with him. Although it was clear to the therapist that Deirdre's husband was trying his best to help, Deirdre saw him as unsupportive and critical. The therapist asked Deirdre to think about how she responded when her youngest child was bullied at school. Deirdre quickly replied that she sometimes became frustrated with him out of despair that he wouldn't stand up to the bullies or get help from a teacher. Then she said, "I probably get mad at him, but it's because I hate to see him hurt like that." The therapist replied, "And that may be why Don sounds frustrated when you two are talking about your job—he loves you, and hates to see you hurting." As Don nodded vigorously, Deirdre cried out, "Is that right, Don? I just never thought it might be out of love!" When Don said, "Of course it's out of love," Deirdre's eyes filled with tears. Softly, she said, "I thought you'd stopped loving me."

Although they developed separately from family therapies, the cognitive–behavioral marital therapies (Dattilio & Epstein, 2003) also offer an effective approach to facilitating insight. In cognitive–behavioral couple therapy traditional behavioral techniques such as communication training and problem-solving techniques are delivered in tandem with insight-facilitating interventions, which are deemed jointly facilitative of change. Insight-facilitating interventions are familiar to cognitive therapists. For example, family members are told about automatic thoughts and cognitive distortions (e.g., if one's partner finds fault with a specific habit, the thought "He hates me, why did I marry him?" may occur). Clients are coached to recognize these thoughts and distortions and to make the connection with negative emotional and behavioral responses. Assessing and modifying other cognitions such as unrealistic expectancies about marriage and attributions (especially attributions about the causes of the partner's negative behaviors) are also used. These strategies rest on a solid base of research on basic processes in marriage. As Fincham (2001) noted, "The evidence for an association between attribution and marital satisfaction is overwhelming, making it possibly the most robust, replicable phenomenon in the study of marriage" (p. 8).

These types of insights are not limited to the structural family or cognitive–behavioral approaches to therapy in which they originated; the kinds of interventions described also have parallels in the narrative and constructivist approaches. In constructivist family therapy (Sluzki, 1992), for example, an important task is transforming family members' constructions of the problem from an intrapersonal one ("He's a smart mouth, no respect") to an interpersonal one ("We need a little more respect all around in this family"). Using intensive task analysis of four successful and four unsuccessful transformation events, Coulehan, Friedlander, and Heatherington (1998) mapped the therapist interventions and client performances that seemed to result in successful transformations. In the first phase of the event, the old story is retold: Constructions of the problems and solutions are aired, interpersonal aspects are highlighted by the therapist (e.g., the therapist asks questions of parents that elicit statements of how their behavior may be affecting their daughters' depression), and exceptions and distinctions are highlighted. If the therapist can successfully persuade the clients to do some of these actions, it is all the better for the therapy. In one successful event case, the grandfather remarked to the grandson at the end of a questioning sequence, "This, I got to give you credit. Before, you used to be very abusive, say, violent to your grandmother."

In the second phase of the event, the affect of family members shifts as the new story is jointly constructed and emerges: Family members begin to acknowledge positive characteristics of the problem person, references to family structure or family history emerge that help defuse the blaming, and family strengths or shared values are identified. Finally, and perhaps most important, the possibility of change or hope emerges. If therapy is successful, family members' statements are markedly less intrapersonal and blaming by the end of the session compared with the beginning. In another treatment approach known as *attachment-based family therapy* (Diamond, Siqueland, & Diamond, 2003), research has shown that parents tended to begin the first session with attributions that blamed the child; however, over time parents voiced more interpersonal or relational constructions of the problem. Sequential analyses demonstrated that the latter followed therapists' reframes and that the interpersonal cognitive set persisted over time in the session.

Again the correlation of cognitive insights and shifts in affect can be seen. Although she initially thought her 17-year-old daughter, Brenda, was depressed over her social life and poor grades, Tonya (a single mother) was astounded when Brenda—with the therapist's help—tearfully explained that she felt neglected at home and out of touch with her mother. Taken aback, Tonya exclaimed, "I thought you wanted more freedom and to break away from me!" As Tonya looked at her tearful, vulnerable daughter, her heart ached for the little girl inside the sad young woman. Later in the session Tonya admitted pulling away from her daughter, as she misinterpreted Brenda's self-imposed isolation as rejection. In the following session Tonya explained that by distancing herself from Brenda, she had been protecting herself. She couldn't bear the idea that her only child would soon be moving out.

We end this section with a simple observation and question. The observation is this: At times an insight works to facilitate change even though it is unclear whether the insight is accurate. For example, a father, mother, and 13-year-old daughter were locked in an escalating argument about whether the daughter should be allowed to attend a rock concert on a school night in a town an hour away. The daughter challenged the parents to specify their objections and mounted counterarguments for each. The negativity of the discussion mounted and the mother voiced her interpretation of the daughter's behavior as spoiled, petulant, and entitled. The father remarked, "Boy, is she going to be a good lawyer when she grows up." This reframe from spoiled behavior to assertive, lawyer-like behavior; from trait attribution ("she's spoiled rotten") to situational use of an influence strategy ("she's doing her best to convince us"); from a negative to a positive cast broke the tension. Everyone laughed, and the family successfully negotiated the conditions under which the daughter could attend concerts in the future. Which construction ("spoiled" vs. "just a good negotiator") was accurate? In this relatively benign situation, it didn't seem to matter.

The question is, does accuracy ever matter? This question highlights fundamental philosophical differences between the cognitive versus constructivist underpinnings of various treatment approaches. Both cognitive and constructivist approaches speak to the issue of insight and inform several current, popular models of family therapy. On the one hand, in the cognitive therapy tradition, beliefs, explanations, and cognitions are held to be accurate or inaccurate, realistic or distorted, or at the very least, functional or dysfunctional in a pragmatic sense. This reality assumption is fundamental both to the rationale presented to clients and to the interventions themselves—challenging automatic thoughts, changing schemas, providing dramatic and authoritative reframes. Cognitive–behavioral couple and family therapy, structural family therapy, and various hybrid approaches implicitly or explicitly assume that the truth or accuracy of clients' insights matter.

On the other hand, in approaches based on constructivist–narrative (Niemeyer, 2002) and postmodern social constructionism (Anderson, 2003), the veridicality of insights or cognitive constructions cannot be ascertained and is not critical. In this epistemological tradition, "beliefs or insights are not a straightforward matter of developing realistic 'mental maps' of an external world." Rather, constructivists "emphasize the personal and collective processes by which people organize their experience and coordinate their relationships with one another" and therapy focuses on helping clients to adequately or usefully construe and "interpret their past, negotiate their present, and anticipate the future." (Neimeyer & Stewart, 2000, p. 338). In various family therapy approaches based on this philosophical stance, therapists attempt to facilitate changes in family constructions and new insights not from a "truth" position, but from a "not knowing" position through collaborative inquiry. As Anderson (2003) said,

> In this inquiry, the client's story is told in such a way that it clarifies, expands, and shifts. Whatever newness is created is co-constructed from within the conversation, in contrast to being imported from outside of it. (p. 131)

Or, as articulated by narrative couple therapists Freedman and Combs (2002), therapy involves not trying to solve problems or promote more accurate insights, but "collaborating with people to change their lives through enriching the narratives they and others tell concerning their lives" (p. 308).

The question whether insights need to be accurate to be therapeutic is one of practical as well as philosophical importance. The answer determines not only the therapists' stance in regard to the clients' constructions of the problem but also which specific interventions to use and which to eschew. The answer is also important theoretically as the foundation for propositions and research about the mechanisms of change depend on how one answers it.

Promoting Insight Through Emotional Experiencing

Although it may be artificial to distinguish emotions and cognitions, and in some cases cognitive change can produce emotional shifts, it is important to recognize that insight can spontaneously accompany heightened emotional experiencing. Using the *definitive intervention* (Bradley & Furrow, 2004, p. 243) in emotion-focused couple therapy (Greenberg & Johnson, 1988), the therapist challenges the blamer until hurt, pain, and longing are released. Although insight is not necessarily the goal of this intervention, it can come about when the recipient of the blame witnesses a dramatic change in the blamer's emotional state. Joanna, for example, had come to see her husband Dick as a bully—and only as a bully. When Dick was urged to express his neediness and fear of losing his wife, Joanna realized that she wanted to see herself as Dick's victim to rationalize her decision to leave him. Emotion-focused therapists (Greenberg & Johnson, 1988) have produced strong theoretical and empirical support for the utility of these *softening events*.

Elements of the softening event are also seen in the *reattachment* task in attachment-based family therapy for depressed adolescents (Diamond et al., 2003). The therapist first builds a foundation by reframing the presenting problem (the adolescent's depression) and the goals of treatment relationally while making strong alliances with all family members. The therapist then guides the adolescent to share his or her specific grievances with the parents. These often include themes of anger and vengeance, which give way to loss, sadness, and fear. Parents are coached to listen nondefensively; if the task is successful, parents gain a deeper understanding of their child's emotional experiencing, which in turn helps to lessen tension and promote different attributions about the child's behavior. This change sets the stage for bringing parent and child closer and for parents to provide support and connection that protect against depression.

Promoting insight through cognitive change and promoting insight through emotional experiencing are clearly interconnected in practice and theory. For example, in discussing *acceptance*, a popular concept in marital therapy, Snyder and Wills (1991) noted,

> Acceptance may be a primary (direct) consequence of interventions promoting spousal intimacy through self-disclosure or "joining" against the relationship conflict, or a secondary (indirect) consequence of interventions along a cognitive dimension facilitating a more functional understanding of the basis of the conflict. Similarly, more traditional learning-based interventions directed at behavior change may facilitate secondary positive affective consequences, particularly when spouses' cognitions regarding their partner's desired behaviors involve attributions of caring and commitment of their partner to them and their relationship. (pp. 434–435)

The earlier case of Rochelle and Frank is an illustration of the kind of acceptance born of insights gained in therapy. Moreover, insights in the cognitive and emotional domains may potentiate the effects of the other, and in some therapies (e.g., emotion-focused couple therapy), emotional processing is fundamental.

STUDYING INSIGHT IN FAMILY THERAPY: METHODOLOGICAL CONSIDERATIONS

As noted earlier, acceptance and other insight-related phenomena are connected in practice and theory; thus, the actual ways in which couple and family therapists work with insight within their sessions will differ according to their theoretical orientations. In addition to understanding theory and practice, empirical questions about how insight is related to change processes need to be answered. Although a full discussion of research methods for studying insight in couple and family therapy is beyond the scope of this chapter, we offer the following considerations as a starting point.

The many methodological considerations in studying insight in family therapy may be loosely grouped as (a) measurement strategies, that is, how to assess insight in family therapy, and (b) analytic strategies, that is, how to study change processes that involve insight. Assessing insight in family therapy is as difficult as in any form of psychotherapy. As our definition of insight suggests, insight involves some kind of change—a new state of understanding or a new connection between elements. Thus, therapists might consider asking clients to try to reflect directly on such change using postsession questionnaires or interviews. In one study (Coulehan et al., 1998) this kind of reflection proved to be almost impossible for the average adult client at an outpatient family therapy clinic. As clear as they seemed to the therapist–researchers, questions such as, "Right now, how do you view the problem for which you came to therapy?" and "If you are now thinking about the problem differently than you did earlier, in what way is your thinking different?" confused most family members. Indeed, it may be more obvious to therapists than to clients how the clients came to new understandings; while therapists are busy facilitating and watching for new understandings, their clients' attention may be more focused on experiencing them.

However, it does not seem unreasonable to ask clients about their new understandings, for therapists know that clients sometimes spontaneously report such changes during sessions. Another possible strategy is to use observational coding systems that tap articulations of insight, marked by statements such as "Now I can see . . . ," "I'm beginning to understand that . . . ," or "I never realized until now that . . . ." As far as we know, this strategy has not yet been devised but it may be quite feasible. A limitation of this strategy, however, is that clients do not always voice their insights. For this reason, insights that are not observable might be elicited using strategies such as structured Interpersonal Process Recall (IPR; Elliott, 1986; Elliott & Shapiro, 1988). Although primarily used in experiential therapy, this strategy could be used to ask family members to watch videotapes of their just-completed sessions and note the points at which they came to some new understandings or insights. Tape-assisted reflection of this kind might prove more viable than a simple postsession written questionnaire.

The second set of considerations involves how to study the change processes that facilitate or follow insight. In addition to appropriate assessment strategies, there are two key ingredients: (a) a clearly articulated model of insight change processes and (b) analytic strategies that are appropriate for conjoint therapy, that is, multiple participants whose affective experiencing, cognitions, and behaviors have reciprocal influences. Further, these ingredients need to be linked. For example, if the model suggests that a parent's insight into the child's attachment needs facilitates softening behavior toward the child, this process must be tested by analyzing those elements in sequential relation to each other, both within and across individuals.

As an illustration, Dattilio (2005) provided a model for restructuring family members' schemas that links automatic thoughts and schemas to interpersonal behavior between subsystem dyads (mother–child, mother–father). The model specifies the presumed relationships between the family schemas and interpersonal behaviors as well as clinical strategies for helping clients achieve insights about their beliefs and schemas. Family members are coached to challenge their beliefs (e.g., "all signs of weakness lead to a threat to one's welfare" [p. 27]) and experiment with them ("allow myself to cry on one occasion in front of my family" to "see if a display of negative emotion is necessarily 'deadly'" [p. 27]).

A handful of therapeutic approaches other than the cognitive–behavioral couple therapies provide good models for studying insight and insight-related phenomena. These approaches include emotion focused therapy for couples (Greenberg & Johnson, 1988; Johnson, 1996), functional family therapy (Sexton & Alexander, 2003), and attachment-based family therapy for depressed adolescents (ABFT; Diamond et al., 2003), each of which offers a clearly articulated, empirically tested model of the change process that uses strategies that preserve the complexity of conjoint treatments. In successful ABFT, for example, therapists help the adolescent identify family conflicts or events that have challenged the attachment bond; the parents listen and acknowledge these as their child discusses them and find ways to apologize for their contributions to the damaged trust. When successful, this process leads to forgiveness by the adolescent and a renewed commitment by all parties to repair their relationships. Insights about one's own and others' behaviors are thus integrally related to the process of change. Other approaches that also concern themselves with insight, for example, constructionist therapies, are relatively understudied, but there is no reason why research on these approaches could not be undertaken. There are many systems-friendly analytic tools, such as sequential analysis techniques (e.g., Bakeman & Casey, 1995), that permit the study of short-term contingencies or patterns of behaviors, affects, and cognitions across multiple participants (see Heatherington, Escudero, & Friedlander, 2005), and the actor–partner interdependence model (APIM; Cook & Snyder, 2005), which permits the study of longer-term interpersonal influence and the study of partners' effects on each other's behavior in relation to treatment outcome, as well as others (see Kazak, Howe, Kaslow, & Snyder, 2005). Although these data-analytic strategies are not focused on insight per se, insight can and should be studied as one element within a web of other therapy change processes as it can shed light on how these elements work together in sessions with multiple participants. Knowledge of these contingencies is the progress needed for understanding the manifestations and facilitation of insight in couple and family therapy.

CONCLUDING COMMENTS

The term *insight* is rarely encountered in the writings of systemic thinkers and therapists. Because of its association with intrapsychic, psychodynamic models, it may originally have been considered a distraction, or even a detraction, from the focus on problematic interpersonal behaviors. In addition, like their behavioral therapy contemporaries, early family therapists sought to avoid the so-called black box phenomena of cognitions and emotion. However, the cognitive revolution, the constructivist challenges, new research strategies and findings on the process of change in couple and family therapy, and most important our clients themselves have highlighted the importance of insight in systemic change. Indeed, there is a robust and growing body of evidence that suggests insights of the kind we describe are a critical, if not common, factor in successful family therapy.

Fundamentally, insight in family therapy is about making connections—connections across domains (interactional behavior, affective, cognitive) and across subsystems (the self, partner, children, past generations). As we hope our examples illustrate, conjoint couple and family sessions are rich with opportunities for promoting insight.

REFERENCES

Anderson, H. (2003). Postmodern social construction therapies. In T. L. Sexton, G. R. Weeks, & M. S. Robbins (Eds.), *Handbook of family therapy* (pp. 125–146). New York: Brunner-Routledge.

Bakeman, R., & Casey, R. L. (1995). Analyzing family interaction using SDIS & GSEQ. *Journal of Family Psychology, 9,* 131–143.

Bowen, M. (1976). Theory in the practice of psychotherapy. In P. Guerin (Ed.), *Family therapy: Theory and practice* (pp. 42–91). New York: Gardner Press.

Bradley, B., & Furrow, J. L. (2004). Toward a mini-theory of the blamer softening event: Tracking the moment-by-moment process. *Journal of Marital and Family Therapy, 30,* 1–12.

Cook, W. L., & Snyder, D. K. (2005). Analyzing nonindependent data in couple therapy using the actor–partner interdependence model. *Journal of Family Psychology, 19,* 133–141.

Coulehan, R., Friedlander, M. L., & Heatherington, L. (1998). Transforming narratives: A change event in constructivist family therapy. *Family Process, 37,* 17–33.

Dattilio, F. (2005). The restructuring of family schemas: A cognitive behavior perspective. *Journal of Marital and Family Therapy, 31,* 15–30.

Dattilio, F., & Epstein, N. B. (2003). Cognitive–behavioral couple and family therapy. In T. L. Sexton, G. R. Weeks, & M. S. Robbins (Eds.), *Handbook of family therapy* (pp. 146–176). New York: Brunner-Routledge.

Diamond, G., Siqueland, L., & Diamond, G. (2003). Attachment-based family therapy for depressed adolescents: Programmatic treatment development. *Clinical Child and Family Psychology Review, 6,* 107–127.

Elliot, R. (1986). Interpersonal process recall (IPR) as a psychotherapy process research method. In L. S. Greenberg & W. M. Pinsof (Eds.), *The psychotherapeutic process: A research handbook* (pp. 503–527). New York: Guilford Press.

Elliot, R., & Shapiro, D. A. (1988). Brief structured recall: A more efficient method for studying significant therapy events. *British Journal of Medical Psychology, 61,* 141–153.

Fincham, F. D. (2001). Attributions in close relationships: From Balkanization to integration. In G. J. O. Fletcher (Ed.), *Blackwell handbook of social psychology* (pp. 3–31). Oxford, England: Blackwell.

Freedman, J. H., & Combs, G. (2002). Narrative couple therapy. In A. S. Gurman & N. S. Jacobson (Eds.), *Clinical handbook of couple therapy* (pp. 308–334). New York: Guilford Press.

Friedlander, M. L., Escudero, V., & Heatherington, L. (2006). *Therapeutic alliances in couple and family therapy: An empirically informed guide to practice.* Washington, DC: American Psychological Association.

Greenberg, L. S., & Johnson, S. M. (1988). *Emotionally focused couples therapy.* New York: Guilford Press.

Haley, J. (1973). *Uncommon therapy.* New York: Norton.

Heatherington, L., Escudero, V., & Friedlander, M. L. (2005). Couple interaction during problem discussions: An integrative methodology. *Journal of Family Communication, 5,* 191–207.

Johnson, S. M. (1996). *The practice of emotionally focused marital therapy: Creating connection.* New York: Brunner/Mazel.

Kazak, A. E., Howe, G. W., Kaslow, N. J., & Snyder, D. K. (2005). Methodology in family science [Special issue]. *Journal of Family Psychology, 19*(1).

Kerr, M., & Bowen, M. (1988). *Family evaluation.* New York: Norton.

Madanes, C. (1981). *Strategic family therapy.* San Francisco: Jossey-Bass.

Minuchin, S. (1974). *Families and family therapy.* Cambridge, MA: Harvard University Press.

Neimeyer, R. A. (2002). Constructivism and the cognitive psychotherapies: Conceptual and strategic contrasts. In R. L. Leahy, E. Dowd, & E. Thomas (Eds.), *Clinical advances in cognitive psychotherapy: Theory and application* (pp. 110–126). New York: Springer Publishing Company.

Neimeyer, R. A., & Stewart, A. (2000). Constructivist and narrative psychotherapies. In C. R. Snyder & R. C. Ingram (Eds.), *Handbook of psychological change* (pp. 337–357). New York: Wiley.

Robbins, M., Alexander, J., & Turner, C. W. (2000). Disrupting defensive family interactions in family therapy with delinquent adolescents. *Journal of Family Psychology, 14*, 688–701.

Sexton, T. L., & Alexander, J. F. (2003). Functional family therapy: A mature model for working with at-risk adolescents and their families. In T. L. Sexton, G. R. Weeks, & M. S. Robbins (Eds.), *Handbook of family therapy* (pp. 323–350). New York: Brunner-Routledge.

Sluzki, C. (1992). Transformations: A blueprint for narrative change in therapy. *Family Process, 31*, 217–230.

Snyder, D. K., & Wills, R. M. (1991). Facilitating change in marital therapy and research. *Journal of Family Psychology, 4*, 426–435.

Watzlawick, P., Weakland, J. H., & Fisch, R. (1974). *Change.* New York: Norton.

5

INSIGHT AS A STAGE
OF ASSIMILATION:
A THEORETICAL PERSPECTIVE

WILLIAM B. STILES AND MEREDITH GLICK BRINEGAR

This chapter describes a theoretical conception of insight within the *assimilation model*, which is a theory about the process of psychological change (Stiles, 2002; Stiles et al., 1990). According to this conception, insight is a middle stage in a developmental sequence that clients follow in successful psychotherapy. In the sequence, insight or understanding follows the emergence and formulation of a problem and precedes the working through and application of the understanding.

The assimilation model suggests that psychologically traces of experiences can be considered as agentic internal voices. Insight is understood as a manifestation of the formation of a meaning bridge or mutual understanding between the voice of a problematic experience and the larger community of voices within the person.

In this chapter, we first offer a brief summary of the assimilation model and the concept of internal voices. Next, we summarize a sequence of developmental stages that has emerged from case study research on the model, paying particular attention to the stages leading to insight. Finally, we offer some examples of research on the model, drawing particularly on the case studies.

THE ASSIMILATION MODEL AND THE VOICES METAPHOR

The assimilation model is an evolving description of how people change. Its core strategy is tracking clients' problems across sessions in psychotherapy. This strategy has shaped its basic concepts. The model analytically divides personality into trackable parts, described as *traces of experience* or *voices*. Problems are construed as experiences whose traces are partly or completely disconnected from the rest of the person. The model takes a longitudinal or developmental perspective on psychotherapeutic change, which is described as the *assimilation of problematic experiences*. In successful therapy, the traces of the problematic experiences are assimilated so that they become an integrated part of the person. This process of assimilation inevitably entails a degree of accommodation (change) in both the problematic traces and other parts of the person.

Traces and Voices

The model suggests that experiences leave traces that can be reactivated. When the traces are reactivated, triggered by related meanings, they respond by speaking and taking action. That is, in the assimilation model information is not passive, acted on by some central agency within the person. Instead, the traces of experience themselves have agency. The metaphor of *voice* underlines this agentic quality.

The model suggests that personality can be construed as *communities of voices* that represent the person's diverse life experiences. Normally, the voices are accepted, welcomed, and integrated into the community. Their integration is shown by their being smoothly accessible from each other. That is, a person can move easily and comfortably from speaking out of one set of experiences to speaking out of the other. Voices emerge when they are needed, called forth by circumstances. Cooking skills emerge in the kitchen; teaching skills emerge in the classroom; appropriate answers emerge and speak when questions are asked. In this sense, the community of voices represents a repertoire of resources available to the person.

Problematic Voices

Some voices represent traces of experiences that are discrepant, foreign, disturbing, or traumatic and hence have been suppressed or dissociated. The traces are kept separate by intense negative emotion (Stiles, Osatuke, Glick, & Mackay, 2004). Such problematic voices may be constructed from experiences of traumatic or distressing events or dysfunctional primary relationships. When such a problematic voice is addressed by circumstances (i.e., when some event triggers it), it wants to speak, but this intrusion is experienced as painful and unwanted and the problematic voice may be quickly avoided. In the course of successful therapy, problematic voices emerge, are recognized and named, confront and engage with the community, reach mutual understandings with the community, and apply these understandings in everyday life.

Psychotherapy as Building Meaning Bridges

According to the assimilation model, psychotherapy can be seen as the process of literally coming to terms with problematic voices. In the safety of therapy and with facilitation by the therapist (Leiman & Stiles, 2001), the problem emerges and is recognized, named, formulated, understood, worked through, and eventually mastered. The recognition, naming, formulating, understanding, and so forth are semiotic or sign-mediated processes conducted through verbal and nonverbal signs.

The work toward insight can be described as building a *meaning bridge*. A meaning bridge is a sign or system of signs that has the same meaning to both author and addressee. For example, to the extent that you understand what you are reading, the words on this page are meaning bridges between you, the reader, and us, this chapter's authors. In psychotherapeutic insight, the meaning bridge is between internal voices and comprises signs that have the same meaning to the problematic voice as to the dominant community of voices.

A meaning bridge that constitutes a therapeutic insight can be understood as an expression or characterization of the problematic experience that is acceptable and understandable to both the problematic and dominant voices. It is a way of accurately encompassing both the problematic and nonproblematic aspects in one coherent expression. It is a sign or a set of signs that conveys the content of the shared understanding.

A meaning bridge between two internal voices makes one smoothly accessible to the other. The person can volitionally take a position on either side of the bridge as circumstances demand. For example, in one case, Debbie's formerly disconnected experiences that were once expressed as uncontrolled and humiliating verbal outbursts and triggered by signs of rejection became a smoothly accessible assertiveness, used appropriately when circumstances required self-assertion (Stiles, 1999). To accomplish this, Debbie, with the therapist's help, developed an understanding of an angry, defiant, rejecting part of herself that emerged and lashed out uncontrollably when she felt rejected. The words *rejecting* and *rejected* were signs that both parts of Debbie considered as embodying crucial aspects of the problematic experience. Through these (along with other) signs, both parts could name, recognize, and understand each other. Her understanding or insight (which incorporated the words *rejecting* and *rejected*) was elaborated and applied, allowing Debbie to make contact with her defiant voice so she could express it with moderation and control. In this way, psychotherapy uses sign mediation to turn problems into resources.

THE ASSIMILATION SEQUENCE AND
THE PLACE OF INSIGHT ON THE FEELINGS CURVE

The Assimilation of Problematic Experiences Sequence (APES; see Table 5.1) represents a current theoretical understanding of the sequence through which a problematic voice passes as it is assimilated into the dominant community of voices. The APES summarizes observations made primarily in a series of intensive case studies on the assimilation model (Brinegar, Salvi, Stiles, & Greenberg, 2006; Honos-Webb, Stiles, & Greenberg, 2003; Honos-Webb, Stiles, Greenberg, & Goldman, 1998, 2006; Honos-Webb, Surko, Stiles, & Greenberg, 1999; Knobloch, Endres, Stiles, & Silberschatz, 2001; Leiman & Stiles, 2001; Osatuke et al., 2005; Osatuke, Gray, Glick, Stiles, & Barkham, 2004; Shapiro, Barkham, Reynolds, Hardy, & Stiles, 1992; Stiles & Angus, 2001; Stiles et al., in press; Stiles, Meshot, Anderson, & Sloan, 1992; Stiles et al., 1991; Stiles, Shapiro, & Harper, 1994; Stiles, Shapiro, Harper, & Morrison, 1995; Varvin & Stiles, 1999). Thus, the theoretical understanding embodied in the APES is not an abstract hypothesis about developmental processes in therapy but is a clinically informed and evolving account of the therapeutic process (i.e., the assimilation model). The process and logic by which the case observations have been incorporated into the assimilation model in general and the APES in particular has been described elsewhere (Stiles, 2003). In short, the theory grows and changes to accurately describe detailed observations made in each new case as well as previous cases.

The theory suggests that emotion varies systematically across APES stages. The S-shaped feelings curve, shown as the solid line in Figure 5.1, gives a schematic description (Stiles et al., 1991, 2004). The curve represents the *feeling level*, that is, the overall direction and intensity of emotion in relation to a particular problematic voice as a function of its assimilation stage. At the earliest stages, when the problematic voice is *warded off* or *avoided* (APES Stages 0–1), the client may experience transient distress but the average feeling level is only mildly negative. Feelings are most negative as the problematic voice emerges at APES Stage 2; this stage is sometimes marked by intense moments of emotionally painful breakthrough, in which previously avoided problematic experiences are acknowledged and confronted. The distress then moderates as the problem is named and stated (APES Stage 3). The feeling level rises rapidly across APES Stages 3 to 5 as the problem is

TABLE 5.1
Assimilation of Problematic Experiences Sequence

Stage	Stage name	Description
0	*Warded off/dissociated*	Client is unaware of the problem; the problematic voice is silent or dissociated. Affect may be minimal, reflecting successful avoidance. The problematic voice may express itself through somatic symptoms, acting out, or state switches.
1	*Unwanted thoughts/active avoidance*	Client actively avoids facing the experience. Problematic voices emerge in response to therapist interventions or external circumstances but are then suppressed or avoided. Affect is intensely negative but episodic and unfocused; the connection with the content may be unclear.
2	*Vague awareness/ emergence*	Client is aware of a problematic experience but cannot formulate the problem clearly. Problematic voice emerges into sustained awareness. Affect includes intense psychological pain associated with the problematic material.
3	*Problem statement/ clarification*	Content includes a clear statement of a problem—something that can be worked on. Opposing voices are differentiated and can name and talk about each other. Affect is negative but manageable, not panicky.
4	*Understanding/insight*	The problematic experience is formulated and understood in some way. Voices reach an understanding with each other (a meaning bridge). Affect may be mixed, with positive and negative periods.
5	*Application/working through*	The understanding is used to work on a problem. Voices work together to apply the understanding to problematic situations. Affective tone is positive, optimistic.
6	*Resourcefulness/problem solution*	The formerly problematic experience has become a resource, used for solving problems. Voices can be used flexibly. Affect is positive, satisfied.
7	*Integration/mastery*	Client automatically generalizes solutions; the formerly problematic voice is fully integrated, serving as a resource. Affect is positive or neutral (i.e., this is no longer something to get excited about).

Note. Assimilation is considered as a continuum, and intermediate levels are allowed; for example, 2.5 represents a level of assimilation halfway between *vague awareness/emergence* (2.0) and *problem statement/clarification* (3.0).

clarified, discussed, and understood and the understanding is applied. It is important to note the moderate average feeling level in this segment of the APES does not represent the absence of strong emotion, but rather an alternation of positive and negative moments. The peak of positive feelings comes

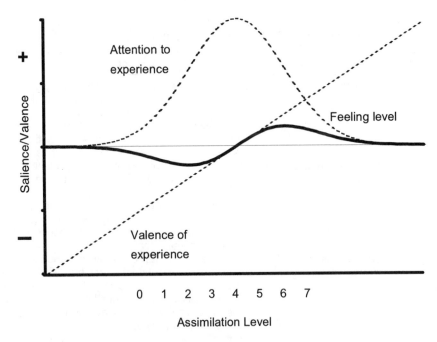

Figure 5.1. Assimilation curves.

at APES Stage 6, when the problem is resolved and the formerly problematic experiences are recognized as resources. Feelings then return to neutral as the material is mastered and is no longer an issue.

Figure 5.1 depicts the theoretical suggestion that a client's feeling level in relation to a problem can be understood as the product of two simpler theoretical quantities. One is the valence of the community's encounters with the problematic voice. The other is the salience of the problematic voice, which may be understood as the attention paid to the problematic voice or the degree to which it is in awareness. The dotted lines in Figure 5.1 plot these two hypothetical underlying processes as a function of assimilation. The ascending diagonal *valence curve* represents the degree to which the affect on encountering a particular experience is negative (at low assimilation levels) or positive (at high assimilation levels). The normal *salience curve* represents the amount of attention paid to the experience, which is low if the experience is *warded off* or *avoided* (APES Stages 0–1) or if it is integrated and therefore unremarkable (APES Stage 7) and highest in the middle range (APES Stages 3–5) when the problem is being clarified and understanding is being achieved and applied.

In principle, problems may be brought to therapy at any APES stage and any progress along the continuum could be considered as improvement. In practice, however, problems tend to be brought to treatment in the range of APES Stages 1 to 3 (Stiles, Shankland, Wright, & Field, 1997), presumably because this is the range in which the problems are most distressing (see Figure 5.1). Theoretically, problems must progress through stages in sequence in any therapy. In case material, however, stages may appear out of sequence for a variety of reasons (Brinegar et al., 2006; Stiles, 2005b). For example, different strands of a problem may progress at different rates, so that different strands may be at different stages; a particular experience may appear at different stages from the perspective of different internal voices; or a client may appear more advanced along the APES continuum while working with the therapist than while working alone (Leiman & Stiles, 2001). Furthermore, different theoretical approaches (psychodynamic, cognitive–behavioral, experiential, etc.) may give different emphasis to insight (APES Stage 4) and other APES stages (Elliott et al., 1994; Stiles, Barkham, Shapiro, & Firth-Cozens, 1992; Stiles et al., 1997), and insight may look different from the perspective of different theoretical approaches, as illustrated by other chapters in this volume (e.g., Messer & McWilliams, chap.1; Pascual-Leone & Greenberg, chap. 2; Grosse Holtforth et al., chap. 3; Heatherington & Friedlander, chap. 4).

The APES stages and the curves underline the main point of this chapter: Insight is a middle stage (i.e., Stage 4) in a developmental therapeutic process. It is a particularly interesting and rewarding stage. APES Stage 4 is at the point of fastest improvement in the feeling level and the point at which the balance shifts from negative to positive (Figure 5.1). Theoretically, the content of the insight—the meaning bridge—integrates the expressions of the problematic experience with the expressions of the perspective from which it was formerly problematic. This mutual view or encompassing formulation—this coming to terms—shows a way forward, a possible path toward joint action involving these formerly opposed parts of the person. There is positive emotion (e.g., pride at making progress or understanding something in a new way) but also frustration and feelings of being overwhelmed at the thought of making changes. The person must still work through the formulation by applying it in daily life and seeing how well the meaning actually performs. The formulation may not fit as well as hoped and many adjustments may be necessary.

RESEARCH ON INSIGHT IN THE ASSIMILATION MODEL

Consistent with its pivotal position in the APES sequence, the insight stage has been of particular interest to assimilation investigators, as it has been to so many other clinicians and researchers (e.g., see chap. 7, this volume). In this section, we review two qualitative assimilation analyses that focused on insight in single cases and a quantitative contrasting groups study in which APES-rated insight distinguished good- from poor-outcome cases.

Substages Leading to Insight: The Case of Margaret

Taking advantage of a case in which the transition from APES Stage 3 to Stage 4 was prolonged and explicit, Brinegar et al. (2006) identified a series of intervening substages and checked these in a second case. The first case in this double case study concerned Margaret (a pseudonym). The study focused on the developing relations between her problematic, demanding *care-for-me* voice and her dominant community's representative, a hyper-responsible *caretaker* voice. For a narrative account of Margaret's insight, see chapter 9, this volume.

Margaret, a 58-year-old Caucasian woman, was treated for depression in 17 sessions of client-centered therapy as part of the York Depression Project (Greenberg & Watson, 1998). She was one of the most successful cases in that project by standard measures. The assimilation process was tracked from the point at which the problem was clearly recognized and stated (APES Stage 3) to the point at which a mutual understanding was successfully negotiated, constituting the insight (APES Stage 4; see Table 5.1 for stage descriptions). A listing of the names of these substages (numbered 3.2–3.8) and descriptions of manifestations in this case illustrates the fine-grained developmental process.

- APES 3.2—*Rapid cross fire*. Opposing voices fought for the floor. The care-for-me voice triggered contradictions from the caretaker voice and vice versa.
- APES 3.4—*Entitlement*. The care-for-me voice became bolder, acted entitled to speak, spoke for longer periods, was demanding and aggressive. The caretaker voice was slower to qualify or object, which offered more openings for the care-for-me voice.
- APES 3.6—*Mutual respect and attention*. The care-for-me voice could hold the floor, speak without interruption, seemed to expect respect, was worthy of esteem. The caretaker voice had greater empathy for opposing experiences.
- APES 3.8—*Active search for understanding*. Explicit efforts to understand the problem. Both voices listened intently and offered tentative shared understandings.

The process of moving from *problem statement* (APES Stage 3) to *insight* (APES Stage 4), was judged as taking 9 of Margaret's 17 sessions. At the beginning of therapy, Margaret's problematic care-for-me voice was entering awareness, and her dominant caretaker voice were both evident in Margaret's speech. They seemed to alternate, as if answering each other in a conflictual dialogue. In the following passage from Session 1, the caretaker voice (in boldface) and the care-for-me voice (in italics) seemed to alternate in a sort of intrapersonal dialogue within Margaret's speech, expressing diametrically opposed views of her husband. (Ellipses [. . .] indicate omitted speech within passages; dashes [—] indicate hesitations and pauses.)

Margaret: **You know, my husband is a very nice person.**
He's a very easygoing person, you know.
But I mean, he's wrapped up in his job
and its just that I—I know I don't understand it enough you know.
Like I just sort of feel like
hey, I've been giving giving, giving to kids and the husband for
*   30-odd years;*
when is it going to be my turn?
And that sounds awfully selfish, I know,
but maybe [laughs]. . .

As therapy progressed, the relationship between these voices could be traced. In the *rapid cross fire* stage (APES Stage 3.2), the care-for-me voice expressed longing for help and support from her husband. Speaking from this voice within the intrapersonal dialogue, Margaret would communicate frustration over giving so much without getting anything in return: "You know I've been nurturing people for thirty odd years; isn't it about damn time someone started nurturing me?" Speaking from her caretaker voice, Margaret would quickly retort that a good wife should focus on her family's needs, not her own. For example, the caretaker voice made the following statement immediately after the care-for-me voice expressed some frustration over taking care of her husband's frail aunt: "I felt guilty because I felt I should be more understanding because she was an old lady."

As the voices expressed themselves more extensively, they stopped interrupting and began listening to each other; Margaret's intrapersonal dialogue became less fragmented, with fewer directly contradictory expressions. Gradually, each voice listened to what the other had to say. In so doing, the caretaker and care-for-me voices seemed able to look jointly at the problem and offer tentative understandings that captured both their experiences. In Session 11, an understanding came about; that is, insight was reached. Both of Margaret's voices realized their role in maintaining the problem. The meaning bridge was a view that encompassed both the caretaker and care-for-me positions. Caretaker acknowledged pushing her husband away, refusing to let him help for fear of losing her identity and sense of self worth. Care-for-me hadn't expressed her needs, assuming that her husband should be able to read her mind. In light of this, both voices recognized that Margaret's husband probably felt left out and didn't know how to help.

Margaret: *Yeah, you know, I never looked at it that way before.*
I just always . . . had this feeling of resentment
that my, my sole support [slight laugh] wasn't there.

Therapist: *Uh-huh, like he should have supported you more.*

Margaret:	Yeah,
	and maybe he just felt left out, you know, that
	as I say, I was so consumed with my parents,
	that maybe I pushed him out of my life? . . .
Therapist:	Maybe he didn't know how to help or— ?
Margaret:	**Yeah.**
Therapist:	Maybe he didn't know what you needed at the time.
Margaret:	. . . *Yeah, you know, I never thought of it that way,*
	isn't that strange
	. . . *I guess maybe I was just so angry*
	and so let down and, you know—.

Incorporating her husband's perspective allowed Margaret to see her role in her unhappy marriage. Brinegar et al. (2006) concluded that the meaning bridge between care-for-me and caretaker involved a characterization of how caretaker's need to be caring had led Margaret to hide care-for-me's needs for care from her husband—to push him away when he tried to respond to her neediness. In the insight passage quoted previously, Margaret first broached a shared understanding, "I was so consumed with my parents that I just pushed him out of my life," which emotionally connected the two previously separate realms of experience. It allowed care-for-me access to the experiences represented by caretaker and formed a basis for subsequent joint action.

Building a Meaning Bridge: The Case of Jan

Jan, a 42-year-old Caucasian woman, was treated for depression with 16 sessions of process–experiential psychotherapy. Jan, like Margaret, was a participant in the York Depression Project and was considered one of the most successful cases (Greenberg & Watson, 1998). The assimilation of several themes in Jan's therapy has been previously reported (Honos-Webb et al., 1999). For the purpose of this chapter we review one of the themes described there, the superwoman theme, by focusing on the insight Jan reached and framing it in terms of a meaning bridge between two conflicting voices.

According to the assimilation analysis, Jan's dominant voice was strong and independent and could capably care for herself and others in a variety of capacities. In contrast, Jan's problematic voice seemed weak and dependent, expressing neediness and the desire to be taken care of by others. At times in therapy, Jan referred to these parts of herself as *superwoman* and *little girl*, respectively. The problematic little girl voice was *warded off* (APES Stage 0) at the start of therapy but was gradually assimilated into Jan's community over the course of therapy, eventually glimpsing APES Stage 7 (*integration/mastery*).

During Sessions 4 through 9, the little girl voice was judged at APES Stage 3 with respect to the superwoman voice. That is, Jan's conflicting voices were clearly in awareness and openly opposing each other in the sort of intrapersonal dialogue illustrated earlier in the Margaret passages. Jan's voices were sparring and seemed incompatible. For example, superwoman stated, "I don't want to give up my independence and being strong and being able to cope on my own." Little girl quickly responded "yet, I still want to be protected." Superwoman felt as though little girl should stand up for herself, although little girl felt that superwoman was overly controlled, especially in regard to emotions.

As the moment of insight approached, Jan's voices began listening to each other instead of immediately making a counterargument within the intrapersonal dialogue, as Margaret did in APES Stage 3.6, *mutual respect and attention*. The following passage occurred in Session 10 in the context of an empty-chair task for a self-evaluative split. From an assimilation perspective, the split was between superwoman (in boldface) and little girl (in italics).

> Jan: [sigh]—*You're always pushing—and ah—*
> *to get hold of yourself*
> *and to keep—your emotions in control and uh,*
> *your feelings in control*
> *and you always watch what you say.*
>
> Therapist: Mm-hmm.
>
> Jan: *—Ah—*
> *I don't know if I could be as strong as that.*
>
> Therapist: Mm-hmm. Is there any—anything that you want from her? You said she's always pushing.
>
> Jan: *I guess I want to be more like her.*
>
> Therapist: Mm-hmm.
>
> Jan: *and I want to sort of like to [be] swept up—you know just taken over.*

It appears that an important shift in perspective occurred when the therapist asked little girl to consider what she wanted from superwoman.

After little girl admitted that she admired superwoman's strength and wanted to be like her, Jan temporarily experienced inner turmoil and a sense of being torn; she felt confusion over distinguishing between the two voices, as they started to share some common ground.

> Therapist: What are you feeling like?
>
> Jan: Very mixed—messages
>
> Therapist: Mm-hmm.

Jan:	[*sniff*] like I can't distinguish one
Therapist:	Mm-hmm.
Jan:	—one personality [*sniff*]
Therapist:	Kind of all—
Jan:	from the other.
Therapist:	Kind of all kind of muddled
Jan:	Yeah.
Therapist:	—OK.
Jan:	It's always like I see myself as— two split personalities,
Therapist:	Mm-hmm, OK.
Jan:	as two altogether different people and

Immediately after Jan voiced her confusion, superwoman responded to little girl's desire for strength. Superwoman appeared to want to help, to fulfill the opposing voice's wish to be taken over.

Jan:	[*sigh—sniff*] **I feel like the stronger part of me now is thinking** **go over** **and coming together—** **and it's overpowering. . .** **and overpowering the weaker person.**

It seemed that the voices jointly construed the event as superwoman lending strength, which little girl appreciatively accepted. The following passage seemed to capture the moment of insight and Jan's reaction to it:

Jan:	It's almost as though the stronger person sitting there just, came over, took over [*sniff*] . . . to be supportive and lend strength . . . I was feeling so vulnerable and weak, and then it seemed like this—[*sniff*]—um— coming together. as two things coming together, you know, two people coming together is like, and one. And all of a sudden I felt like—a lot stronger.

Passages from the subsequent intrapersonal empty-chair dialogue elaborated the nature of the coming together. Speaking as superwoman, Jan gave reassurance:

> Jan: **You don't have to be afraid,**
> **we're all here to help you,**

> Therapist: Mm-hmm.

> Jan: **and you'll get stronger**
> **and you don't have to be a little girl**
> **and that little girl can grow up to be a strong per—**
> **you know, a strong woman—**

> Therapist: Mm-hmm.

> Jan: **who can ah, look after herself too.**

Speaking a few moments later as little girl, Jan described feeling reassured:

> Jan: *I'm not so scared anymore [now] that I know that you're there*
> *and that you're strong*
> *and you're going to—protect me I guess.*

> Therapist: Mm-hmm.

And a bit later she said,

> Jan: *You're going to—*
> *protect me I guess . . .*
> *I know it's difficult—[sniff]—*
> *and I keep falling down.*
> *But I really appreciate you being there.*

Thus, little girl asked for and received help from superwoman. Superwoman seemed to have lost her defensive, controlling quality and rather than chastising little girl for needing help and instantly taking over, agreed to lend strength.

Jan's meaning bridge involved the recognition by both voices that each had something to offer. Superwoman and little girl seemed to agree that the stronger part could be supportive and lend strength when the weaker part (who was more attuned to emotional needs) needed and asked for it. Superwoman could accept little girl's emotional needs as her own and perhaps, paradoxically, gain some self-esteem from helping her own weak and dependent side. The joint nature of this understanding was evident in Jan's comments about feeling as if two things, or people, had come together as one. This marked the expression as a new meaning bridge, signaling insight. Using this bridge, the two voices could begin to work together on fulfilling Jan's needs.

Insight Associated With Positive Treatment Outcome

The assimilation model links psychotherapy's process with its outcome by suggesting that movement to higher levels of assimilation represents improvement. As indicated in the case examples of Margaret and Jan, insight is only one stage along the journey toward positive outcome, but it is an important one. Insight can be considered a turning point, as described earlier in relation to the feelings curve plotted in Figure 5.1. The figure shows how attaining the APES insight stage might be distinctively associated with decreases in distress. Theoretically, APES Stage 4 is characterized by a rapid rate of change in the average feeling level and its crossing from negative to positive valence.

One manifestation of this rapid change and positive transition is a tendency to respond more positively than previous responses given on an inventory of depressive symptoms. In support of this suggestion, a study by Detert, Llewelyn, Hardy, Barkham, and Stiles (in press) found that assimilation-defined insight was statistically associated with symptomatic improvement in very brief treatment for depression.

The Detert et al. (in press) study assessed outcome as improvement on the Beck Depression Inventory (BDI; Beck, Steer, & Garbin, 1988), which can be understood as an index of emotional distress. In four good-outcome cases and four poor-outcome cases, clients' central problems were consensually formulated by the investigators. Transcribed passages concerning these problems were rated on the APES by trained raters. All of the good outcome cases reached APES Stage 4 in these passages, but none of the poor outcome cases did so, a result that was significant by Fisher's exact test, $p = 0.029$. That is, APES-measured insight with respect to the client's central problem was consistently associated with positive outcome, as measured by the BDI.

Although achieving an insight is associated with reductions in distress, the developmental process of assimilation does not stop with insight. Theoretically, the understanding achieved at APES Stage 4 is applied, modified, and elaborated in subsequent assimilation stages during successful therapy.

The *intrapersonal* change represented by the insight (the meaning bridge linking an initially unwanted voice to the dominant community of voices) led to much needed *interpersonal* changes in Margaret's and Jan's lives. After Margaret understood why and how she had contributed to her husband's failure to meet her needs she was able to make changes; for example, speaking up when she needed something and letting her husband help. Conversely, she was able to relax and allow herself to be cared for. For example, she described not feeling responsible for every detail of her daughter's wedding, allowing others to take care of things; care-for-me had become an ability to enjoy an important occasion—a resource, rather than a problem (Brinegar et al., 2006).

In a similar fashion, after reaching her insight Jan started asking her husband for help. Little girl realized that she couldn't and shouldn't be responsible for all domestic tasks; superwoman lent strength by demanding help from her husband ("You're going to be doing a lot more cooking") and was also able to relax:

> Jan: It's okay. I don't have to be superwoman
>   and it's okay to ask for help,

that if I can't manage it or can't do it um, [*cough*]
people are not going to think any less of me because of that.

Note that in both cases accommodation occurred alongside assimilation. Little girl, for example, became stronger and more confident in expressing her needs and superwoman softened, losing her harsh edge while remaining strong and capable.

CONCLUDING COMMENTS

In summary, the assimilation model regards insight as a middle stage in a continuous developmental process that underlies therapeutic progress. According to this model, insight can be described as mutual understanding between internal voices (understood as active, agentic traces of experience). Through achieving this mutual understanding, the problematic voice joins the community of voices and the community is changed, both by the addition itself and by the accommodation needed to assimilate it. The assimilation of the problematic voice opens the possibility of joint action, thus turning the problem into a resource.

The assimilation model's account of insight has grown mainly by case study (Stiles, 2002, 2003; Stiles & Angus, 2001). Every case has something to teach, though investigators typically don't know what they will learn when they begin to study it. A case study's focus and direction depends on the investigator's attention as much as on the project's design. Attention to the development and application of insight within cases will inevitably improve our theoretical understanding of these processes in future work.

Case study demands attention to the complexity and richness of the case material. No single case can prove an isolated hypothesis, but observations of a case that match a theory in rich and elaborate detail can lend the theory some confidence (Campbell, 1979; Stiles, 2005a). Each observation of a case either fits the theory (thus strengthening it), contradicts the theory (thus demanding modifications), or has not been addressed by the theory (thus suggesting directions for extending it). The assimilation model's understanding of insight is growing by incorporating new clinical observations in each of these ways. The model is still young, however, addressing very limited aspects of the insight process, and there is great scope for extension.

REFERENCES

Beck, A. T., Steer, R. A., & Garbin, M. G. (1988). Psychometric properties of the Beck Depression Inventory: Twenty-five years of evaluation. *Clinical Psychology Review, 8*, 77–100.

Brinegar, M. G., Salvi, L. M., Stiles, W. B., & Greenberg, L. S. (2006). Building a meaning bridge: Therapeutic progress from problem formulation to understanding. *Journal of Counseling Psychology, 53,* 165–180.

Campbell, D. T. (1979). "Degrees of freedom" and the case study. In T. D. Cook & C. S. Reichardt (Eds.), *Qualitative and quantitative methods in evaluation research* (pp. 49–67). Beverley Hills, CA: Sage.

Detert, N. E., Llewelyn, S. P., Hardy, G. E., Barkham, M., & Stiles, W. B. (in press). Assimilation in good- and poor-outcome cases of very brief psychotherapy for mild depression. *Psychotherapy Research.*

Elliott, R., Shapiro, D. A., Firth-Cozens, J., Stiles, W. B., Hardy, G. E., Llewelyn, S. P., & Margison, F. R. (1994). Comprehensive process analysis of insight events in cognitive–behavioral and psychodynamic–interpersonal psychotherapies. *Journal of Counseling Psychology, 41,* 449–463.

Field, S. D., Barkham, M., Shapiro, D. A., & Stiles, W. B. (1994). Assessment of assimilation in psychotherapy: A quantitative case study of problematic experiences with a significant other. *Journal of Counseling Psychology, 41,* 397–406.

Greenberg, L. S., & Watson, J. (1998). Experiential therapy of depression: Differential effects of client-centered relationship conditions and active experiential interventions. *Psychotherapy Research, 8,* 210–224.

Honos-Webb, L., Stiles, W. B., & Greenberg, L. S. (2003). A method of rating assimilation in psychotherapy based on markers of change. *Journal of Counseling Psychology, 50,* 189–198.

Honos-Webb, L., Stiles, W. B., Greenberg, L. S., & Goldman, R. (1998). Assimilation analysis of process–experiential psychotherapy: A comparison of two cases. *Psychotherapy Research, 8,* 264–286.

Honos-Webb, L., Stiles, W. B., Greenberg, L. S., & Goldman, R. (2006). An assimilation analysis of psychotherapy: Responsibility for "being there." In C. T. Fischer (Ed.), *Qualitative research methods for psychologists: Introduction through empirical studies* (pp. 3–21). New York: Academic Press.

Honos-Webb, L., Surko, M., Stiles, W. B., & Greenberg, L. S. (1999). Assimilation of voices in psychotherapy: The case of Jan. *Journal of Counseling Psychology, 46,* 448–460.

Knobloch, L. M., Endres, L. M., Stiles, W. B., & Silberschatz, G. (2001). Convergence and divergence of themes in successful psychotherapy: An assimilation analysis. *Psychotherapy, 38,* 31–39.

Leiman, M., & Stiles, W. B. (2001). Dialogical sequence analysis and the zone of proximal development as conceptual enhancements to the assimilation model: The case of Jan revisited. *Psychotherapy Research, 11,* 311–330.

Osatuke, K., Gray, M. A., Glick, M. J., Stiles, W. B., & Barkham, M. (2004). Hearing voices: Methodological issues in measuring internal multiplicity. In H. H. Hermans & G. Dimaggio (Eds.), *The dialogical self in psychotherapy* (pp. 237–254). New York: Brunner-Routledge.

Osatuke, K., Humphreys, C. L., Glick, M. J., Graff-Reed, R. L., Mack, L. M., & Stiles, W. B. (2005). Vocal manifestations of internal multiplicity: Mary's voices. *Psychology and Psychotherapy: Theory, Research and Practice, 75,* 21–44.

Shapiro, D. A., Barkham, M., Reynolds, S., Hardy, G., & Stiles, W. B. (1992). Prescriptive and exploratory psychotherapies: Toward an integration based on the assimilation model. *Journal of Psychotherapy Integration, 2,* 253–272.

Stiles, W. B. (1999). Signs, voices, meaning bridges, and shared experience: How talking helps. *Visiting Scholar Series, 10.* New Zealand: School of Psychology, Massey University.

Stiles, W. B. (2002). Assimilation of problematic experiences. In J. C. Norcross (Ed.), *Psychotherapy relationships that work: Therapist contributions and responsiveness to patients* (pp. 357–365). New York: Oxford University Press.

Stiles, W. B. (2003). When is a case study scientific research? *Psychotherapy Bulletin, 38,* 6–11.

Stiles, W. B. (2005a). Case studies. In J. C. Norcross, L. E. Beutler, & R. F. Levant (Eds.), *Evidence-based practices in mental health: Debate and dialogue on the fundamental questions* (pp. 57–64). Washington, DC: American Psychological Association.

Stiles, W. B. (2005b). Extending the Assimilation of Problematic Experiences Scale: Commentary on the special issue. *Counselling Psychology Quarterly, 18,* 85–93.

Stiles, W. B., & Angus, L. (2001). Qualitative research on clients' assimilation of problematic experiences in psychotherapy. In J. Frommer & D. L. Rennie (Eds.), *Qualitative psychotherapy research: Methods and methodology* (pp. 112–127). Lengerich, Germany: Pabst Science Publishers.

Stiles, W. B., Barkham, M., Shapiro, D. A., & Firth-Cozens, J. (1992). Treatment order and thematic continuity between contrasting psychotherapies: Exploring an implication of the assimilation model. *Psychotherapy Research, 2,* 112–124.

Stiles, W. B., Elliott, R., Llewelyn, S. P., Firth-Cozens, J. A., Margison, F. R., Shapiro, D. A., & Hardy, G. (1990). Assimilation of problematic experiences by clients in psychotherapy. *Psychotherapy, 27,* 411–420.

Stiles, W. B., Leiman, M., Shapiro, D. A., Hardy, G. E., Barkham, M., Detert, N. E., & Llewelyn, S. P. (in press). What does the first exchange tell? Dialogical sequence analysis and assimilation in very brief therapy. *Psychotherapy Research.*

Stiles, W. B., Meshot, C. M., Anderson, T. M., & Sloan, W. W., Jr. (1992). Assimilation of problematic experiences: The case of John Jones. *Psychotherapy Research, 2,* 81–101.

Stiles, W. B., Morrison, L. A., Haw, S. K., Harper, H., Shapiro, D. A., & Firth-Cozens, J. (1991). Longitudinal study of assimilation in exploratory psychotherapy. *Psychotherapy, 28,* 195–206.

Stiles, W. B., Osatuke, K., Glick, M. J., & Mackay, H. C. (2004). Encounters between internal voices generate emotion: An elaboration of the assimilation model. In H. H. Hermans & G. Dimaggio (Eds.), *The dialogical self in psychotherapy* (pp. 91–107). New York: Brunner-Routledge.

Stiles, W. B., Shankland, M. C., Wright, J., & Field, S. D. (1997). Aptitude-treatment interactions based on clients' assimilation of their presenting problems. *Journal of Consulting and Clinical Psychology, 65,* 889–893.

Stiles, W. B., Shapiro, D. A., & Harper, H. (1994). Finding the way from process to outcome: Blind alleys and unmarked trails. In R. L. Russell (Ed.), *Reassessing psychotherapy research* (pp. 36–64). New York: Guilford Press.

Stiles, W. B., Shapiro, D. A., Harper, H., & Morrison, L. A. (1995). Therapist contributions to psychotherapeutic assimilation: An alternative to the drug metaphor. *British Journal of Medical Psychology, 68,* 1–13.

Varvin, S., & Stiles, W. B. (1999). Emergence of severe traumatic experiences: An assimilation analysis of psychoanalytic therapy with a political refugee. *Psychotherapy Research, 9,* 381–404.

6

INSIGHT AS A COMMON FACTOR

BRUCE E. WAMPOLD, ZAC E. IMEL, KULDHIR S. BHATI,
AND MICHELLE D. JOHNSON-JENNINGS

The *Random House College Dictionary* (1984) defines *insight* as "an instance of apprehending the true nature of a thing, esp. through intuitive understanding." Two aspects of this definition may be altered to fit the context of psychotherapy as we conceptualize it. First, the *truth* of the understanding may be unimportant. Second, the dictionary definition of insight highlights the involvement of intuition; in psychotherapy, the *Aha!* phenomenon might be construed as being based on intuition. For our purposes, the manner by which the explanation is acquired, as well as the form and content of the explanation, are unimportant. It does not matter whether the understanding is invoked by a well-timed interpretation, stimulated by emotional experiencing, or explicitly provided by the therapist. What is important is that the patient attains an explanation and that the explanation is strategic to the process and outcome of psychotherapy (i.e., it is adaptive). Thus, we propose that insight involves obtaining a functional understanding of one's problem, complaint, or disorder through the process of psychotherapy and that insight is a beneficial common factor present in and critical to all psychotherapeutic orientations. Our definition and conceptualization builds on the pioneering work of Jerome Frank (e.g., Frank & Frank, 1991), Judd

Marmor (e.g., 1962), Sol Garfield (e.g., 1995), and E. Fuller Torrey (e.g., 1972).

In this chapter we present several vignettes to show insight is a common factor in different therapeutic contexts and approaches in the treatment of adult depression. We then offer a pantheoretical model of how insight involves a process of acquiring an adaptive explanation for one's problems, complaint, or disorder. Finally, we end by describing the various ways in which insight is central to the therapeutic process and how it affects therapy in a positive manner.

FOUR CLIENTS WHO ACQUIRE DIVERSE EXPLANATIONS FOR THEIR DEPRESSION

To illustrate insight as a common factor, we present four vignettes involving adults with depression.

Vignette 1

John is European American, age 42, and married with two children. He has a bachelor's degree in mechanical engineering. He is dissatisfied with his current employment and is beginning a master's degree program in engineering, because he believes that an advanced degree is the best path to a more rewarding career. His academic progress in the first 5 weeks of the semester has been difficult, as he commutes a long distance to school, works full time, has some marital discord, and has performed poorly on the initial assignments and examinations. John reports feeling quite depressed and anxious.

John believes his experience in graduate school demonstrates that he no longer has the academic ability to compete with the younger students in his program. He describes his depression mathematically—a system in which at a local extreme feedback no longer affects the process (he draws a curve to illustrate this to the therapist).

The therapist decides to treat John using cognitive–behavioral therapy (CBT). The therapist engages John and helps him realize that he overgeneralizes in that one poor score on a single test leads him to think that he cannot cognitively compete at the graduate level. Furthermore, the therapist helps John understand that he makes attributions about his abilities when the cause may be due to circumstances (e.g., he did not have time to study for an exam). CBT for John's depression was successful.

Vignette 2

Susan is African American, age 40, and divorced with one daughter. Susan is a professor of literature at a prestigious liberal arts college in a rural New England town. She exhibits symptoms of depression, which she expresses primarily as loneliness. She is also socially anxious, which compounds her loneliness. Susan's father died in an accident when she was 5 years old. Her mother, who was unemotional and withdrawn, had a series of relatively short relationships with men after the death of Susan's father. Susan's mother expected Susan to treat each of these men as an authority figure.

Susan's therapist takes an experiential approach, focusing on the loss of her father and her relationships with the male figures in her life. Through the course of therapy, Susan realizes that she has not grieved the loss of her father and that her insecurity stems from the transitory nature of men in her life. The therapist emphasizes not only that Susan is valued for her sensitivity and gentleness (positive traits derived from her experience) but also that Susan's traits can ultimately lead to submission. As Susan works through the losses in her life, the therapist helps her translate her insights into changes in her current romantic relationship. The insight-oriented therapy was successful in treating Susan's depression.

Vignette 3

Victoria is a 64-year-old European American woman. She and her husband, a preacher, raised two sons. Victoria's husband died 10 years prior to her therapy, and she no longer sees her sons more than once a year, purportedly because of geographic separation. She maintained the highly religious and conventional values that she gained from her parents. Victoria experienced dysphoria throughout her life, originating with an episode of postpartum depression after the birth of her first son. Victoria's depression presents primarily somatically (i.e., fatigue, melancholy, and hypochondrias), and she presents these physical symptoms to her family physician.

After the physician assures Victoria that she is in good health and explains that her symptoms seem to originate from depression, Victoria confides to the physician that before her marriage she had a premarital affair, and became pregnant but miscarried. Victoria informs her doctor that she believed the miscarriage was her punishment for lack of faith at that time; she has not told anyone about this and believes her depression must be God's punishment for her immoral behavior.

Victoria's physician explains that depression is due to a chemical imbalance and is not related to moral deficiencies. The physician explains that postpartum depression is normal and that her brain simply did not regain its appropriate chemical balance, which he illustrated with an animated diagram of the brain that was similar to television commercials Victoria had seen. The physician prescribes a selective serotonin reuptake inhibitor (SSRI), which Victoria takes; her depression remits.

Vignette 4

Peter is a single, 35-year-old Native American man who resides in an urban environment. Peter has a bachelor's degree in computer science but has had little job stability because of his depression. Peter was raised on a reservation until he was 13, at which time his single mother moved to the city in search of employment. Peter reportedly did not give being Native American "much thought" until he was confronted with racism and discrimination during high school. Peter attended a predominately White local university and felt he needed to succeed in an academically rigorous field (computer science) to avoid being labeled an "affirmative action student." Since graduating, Peter has worked as an entry-level programmer, but he feels he is denied career opportunities because of racism and discrimination. Peter's job performance begins to deteriorate, and he experiences increasing feelings of depression. He begins to drink to numb feelings of worthlessness and extreme loneliness. Peter tells his friends that he drinks because everyone expects him to be a "drunk" due to his ethnic heritage.

One day Peter runs into a childhood friend. It is evident to this friend that Peter is ill, so the friend invites Peter to visit him on the reservation, where his friends and family hold a *sweat* for Peter. During his stay, Peter seeks out and works with a traditional healer and begins to understand that his feelings of being lost, lonely, and depressed are the result of being away from his community and tradition; he begins to see that he needs to regain balance and heal within the community by its traditional methods.

The traditional healer encourages the community to support Peter and prescribes herbal medicine for 1 month. Peter also seeks employment through his tribe. Peter's depression remits along with his self-destructive drinking.

Four Diverse Cases and a Healing Practice Commonality

Seemingly, these four vignettes have little in common. One therapy is a widely used treatment for depression (i.e., CBT), one might be labeled as traditional psychotherapy (i.e., insight-oriented psychotherapy), and the other two would not be considered psychotherapies at all (i.e., psychopharmacological and indigenous healing practices). Yet these approaches share a component that is central to all healing practices.

To identify this common factor and to illustrate its importance, the following thought experiment is proposed. Imagine you have had a pain in your gut for several days that varies in intensity and is not responding to over-the-counter remedies. The pain is now beginning to interfere with sleep. Your anxiety increases as you realize that your uncle died of colon cancer. Your partner insists you see your physician and despite your reluctance you agree. The physician takes a short history, inquires about symptoms, physically examines you, and has several laboratory tests conducted. At the end of the consultation, the physician indicates that you need to take medication three times a day for 2 weeks, and that he expects that at the end of this regimen the symptoms will disappear. The physician indicates that you should call if (a) the symptoms worsen or (b) you are not better after 2 weeks. However, you find something quite unsatisfying about this consultation, which immediately becomes apparent when your partner asks, "So, what is wrong with you?" and you respond, "I don't know."

The missing aspect of the consultation is that you were not given an explanation for your problem. Acquiring an understanding of one's problems remains not only an expectation of the patient but also serves as a critical element in the process and outcome of all healing practices, including psychotherapy. In each vignette the specified healer (psychotherapist, physician, and traditional healer) presented the affected individual with a framework for understanding the nature of his or her malady and how it interfered with his or her life. In this chapter we present a model of insight that involves the acquisition of an explanation and explicate the theory and research on which it is based.

THEORETICAL MODEL: ACQUIRING AN ACCEPTABLE AND ADAPTIVE EXPLANATION

In this section we propose a theoretical model of insight as a common factor. This model emphasizes the dysfunctional explanations the patients possess when they enter therapy and the adaptive explanations that are acquired in the process of therapy.

Dysfunctional Explanation and Therapeutic Provision of an Alternative

Patients often enter therapy with either no explanation for their problem, complaint, or disorder or with an explanation that is not functional. John believes he is depressed because his age and lack of aptitude are responsible for his poor performance in school. Victoria believes her fatigue and melancholy stem from moral inadequacies and lack of faith. Susan believes she is depressed because she does not have a loving and close relationship with a man. Peter may have no cogent explanation of his depression or even recognize that he is depressed. In all the vignettes, the individual's explanations and beliefs (or lack thereof) about their depression lead either to inaction or action that is not remedial for their depression (e.g., Peter's drinking). Frank and Frank (1991) would say that the client is *demoralized*.

Every therapeutic approach provides an explanation for the client's disorder and this explanation is communicated to the client through the process of therapy (Frank & Frank, 1991). In some instances the client receives an explicit explanation, as is the case for CBT:

> In their first session Sally's therapist educates her about the nature and course of her disorder, about the process of cognitive therapy, and about the cognitive model (i.e., how her thoughts influence her emotions and

behavior). He not only helps her to set goals, identify and evaluate thoughts and beliefs, and plan behavioral change, but also teaches her how to do so. (Beck, 1995, p. 7)

John's therapist offered a similar explanation about the nature of depression and helped John realize that his negative self-attributions led to feelings of hopelessness (for a more complete description of insight in CBT, see chap. 3, this volume). Susan's understanding about the ways her childhood experiences were affecting her led to more adaptive choices about current relationships (see chaps. 1 and 2 on insight in dynamic and experiential therapies, this volume). Victoria was influenced by the power of a biological explanation of her depression, and the explanation Peter was given promoted a renewed connection to family and cultural ties. In these examples, the clients attained explanations that were not only different from the ones held prior to therapy but also furthered the process of therapy toward a positive outcome. The idea that the theoretical rationale is a factor common to all psychotherapies (and for that matter, all healing practices) is not new (Frank & Frank, 1991; Marmor, 1962; Torrey, 1972). Indeed, Frank and Frank discussed a "rational, conceptual scheme, or myth that provides a plausible explanation for the patients' symptoms" (p. 42) as one of four components of all psychotherapies that are useful in combating demoralization.

The thought experiment presented earlier illustrates that patients expect that an explanation for one's disorder will be provided. Yalom (1995) discussed the basic need to have an explanation:

> The unexplained—especially the fearful unexplained—cannot be tolerated for long. All cultures, through either a scientific or a religious explanation, attempt to make sense of chaotic and threatening situations . . . One of our chief methods of control is through language. Giving a name to chaotic, unruly forces provides us with a sense of mastery or control. (p. 84)

Indeed, it has been suggested that humans have evolved to make explanations: "Our most analytic brain functions appear to have been designed through evolutionary selection, to discern causal relationships in the external world" (Averill, Ekman, & Panksepp, 1994, p. 21). By discerning causal relationships, humans create order and gain a sense of their world. Gardner (1998), drawing implications from evolution for clinical practices, explains that storytelling, with its roots in our primal curiosity, may be the core feature of humanity, ultimately leading to many of our cultural myths. The imperative to understand our environment and construct explanations may have given rise to religion, metaphysics, and ultimately science (Gardner, 1998). From the most universal concepts of human life to the most mundane, humans create explanations to guide their daily interactions.

Factors Related to the Potency of an Explanation: Context, Cultural Proximity, and "Truth"

The vignettes illustrate that when it comes to explanations, one size does not fit all. According to the model presented in this chapter, the explanation must be accepted by the client and lead to demonstrable outcomes through certain pathways to be effective, as shown in Figure 6.1. In this section we discuss context, cultural proximity, and the "truth" of the explanation as important considerations related to the efficacy of the explanation provided to the client.

Context is vital to an explanation's legitimacy (Frank & Frank, 1991; Torrey, 1972). The thought experiment in which the patient expected and desired an explanation for the pain in his or her gut shows that not every explanation would be sufficient. Because the patient presented to a practitioner of modern medicine (i.e., medical doctor), it is likely the patient would find only explanations of a physiochemical nature acceptable. An explanation for the pain that involved an imbalance of *chi* would not have been acceptable as it is contradictory to the cultural expectation for the healing practice of Western medicine. Thus the following principle is offered: To be effective and acceptable, the explanation provided to the client must lie within the expected cultural frame in which the healing practice is most often conducted, should be proximal to the client's currently held explanation or expectation, and should not create dissonance with the attitudes and values of the client that would cause the client to reject the explanation outright (see Frank & Frank, 1991; Torrey, 1972). This principle becomes more difficult to adhere to in an increasingly pluralistic, postmodern world in which one can make fewer assumptions about an individual's belief systems and cultural background (Downing, 2004).

Cultural proximity is critical in each of the vignettes. John, who is analytic and rational, responded to a cognitive explanation for his depression, whereas Susan, who is introspective and emotional, responded to a therapy that allowed the explanation to emanate from her emotional experience (guided by the therapist). Victoria and Peter did not present to a psychotherapist and may not have found traditional psychological explanations for their disorders persuasive. Victoria presented to a physician and her understanding was shaped in part by advertisements of antidepressants; she also tended to think of life in moral and religious rather than psychological terms. In a psychological framework, Peter's cultural alienation and social isolation were addressed by his reintegration into the native community; in an indigenous framework, the Native American rituals attended to his spiritual needs. To Peter, sweat lodges and herbal medicine were acceptable and comforting in the context of his experience.

Every healing paradigm has institutions that legitimize certain explanations as valid. For example, medical explanations and treatments are le-

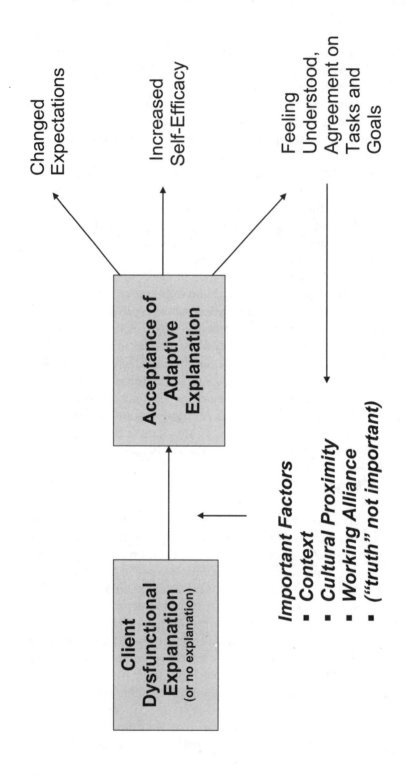

Changed
Expectations

Increased
Self-Efficacy

Feeling
Understood,
Agreement on
Tasks and
Goals

Acceptance of
Adaptive
Explanation

Client
Dysfunctional
Explanation
(or no explanation)

Important Factors
- *Context*
- *Cultural Proximity*
- *Working Alliance*
- *("truth" not important)*

Figure 6.1. Theoretical model: acquiring an acceptable and adaptive explanation.

gitimized by the Food and Drug Administration, which symbolizes legitimacy through governmental authority. Pharmaceutical industry advertisements further influence beliefs about the causes and treatment of disorders. An extensive and thorough examination of these processes is provided by Latour (1999), who used the discovery of pasteurization as a referent and detailed the processes of legitimization and "coming-into-existence" of an explanation. Further, different cultures may be more accepting of explanations that fit within and are sensitive to their cultural norms and belief systems (Sue, 2004; Sue & Sue, 1999). Thus, explanations may be imbedded in the culture, but institutions and processes influence the culture's core beliefs about disease and healing—that is, cultural beliefs about healing are not static but are constantly evolving.

There is research evidence to support the notion that the explanation provided must take into account the client's worldview, culture, attitudes, and values. Client ratings of perceived-etiology similarity with the counselor were found to be predictive of satisfaction with counseling (Atkinson, Worthington, & Dana, 1991). Furthermore, the therapist's ability to understand and respond to the salient aspects of the client's cultural milieu may be more important to the client than similarity of race or gender alone (e.g., Ito & Maramba, 2002; Pikus & Heavey, 1996). Clients who offer existential reasons for depression do better in a cognitive therapy than in a behavioral activation treatment for depression (Addis & Jacobson, 1996). Individuals who ruminate about their depressed mood tend to have more negative reactions to psychotherapies with more active and challenging interactive orientations and do better with insight-oriented rationales (Addis & Carpenter, 1999). Clients who endorse a cognitive model of depression do better in CBT than clients who do not (Simons, Lustman, Wetzel, & Murphy, 1985). Elkin, Yamaguchi, and Arnkoff (1999) found that congruence between predilections for a treatment and receipt of the treatment predicted engagement in therapy, although several studies failed to find a relationship between preference for therapy and outcome (Arnkoff, Glass, & Shapiro, 2002). Finally, Lyddon (1991) found that clients' epistemic styles predicted preferences for treatments.

It appears that the truth of the explanation is not necessary for the acquisition of an explanation or its efficacy. Note that this discussion cannot be addressed satisfactorily here, given the tricky epistemological considerations related to the concept of truth. Nevertheless, we take the position that there is no compelling argument that one explanation is closer to the truth than another or that the truth value of the explanation is related to outcome. This is an argument proposed by Frank and Frank (1991), who referred to the explanation as a "myth" and emphasized that scientific truth of the explanation is not the curative factor.

The argument for myth rather than truth rests on several observations. For most disorders, all treatments intended to be therapeutic are equally effective (Wampold, 2001), which suggests that one explanatory system is not superior to another. Moreover, treatments matched to purported etiological aspects (e.g., CBT for clients with dysfunctional attitudes) do not produce better outcomes than treatments mismatched to these aspects (Wampold, 2001). There is no reason to believe that John, who benefited from CBT for his depression, exhibited more dysfunctional thoughts than Victoria, Peter, or Susan; similarly, there is no reason to believe that Victoria has a greater chemical imbalance in her brain than John, Peter, or Susan. Furthermore, the explanations for the benefits of a treatment have frequently been shown to be untrue, as has been the case for systematic desensitization (e.g., Kirsch & Henry, 1977). There are many examples of therapies that presented convincing explanations and had efficacious therapeutic outcomes even though later research showed the explanations to be invalid (e.g., eye movement desensitization and reprocessing, Mesmer's animal magnetism therapy). Many psychologists would object to referring Peter to a Native American healer because such treatment does not rest on traditional psychological explanations. The important point is that many therapies are efficacious not because of the purported truth of the explanation but because clients accepted the explanation and the explanation provided therapeutic actions and changed expectations (Wampold & Bhati, 2004). Moreover, congruence between therapist interventions and case conceptualization appears more important than the content of the conceptualization (Castonguay, 2000). One notable exception can be found in the context of brief dynamic therapy. Specifically, it has been found that "accuracy" of interpretation is related to outcome (Crits-Christoph, Cooper, & Luborsky, 1988); however, it is difficult to discriminate accuracy as truth from accuracy as correspondence with therapist case formulation (Piper, Joyce, McCallum, & Azim, 1993).

An interesting issue is whether truth of explanation is more important for some approaches than others (see chap. 1, this volume, for a discussion of truth in psychodynamic therapies). Jopling (2001) criticized insight-oriented therapies for creating "adaptive self-misunderstanding," as the insight comes at the end of a nondeterministic process (i.e., many different and conflicting insights could result from the process of therapy) and therefore client improvement is merely contentment based on a false premise (or ignorant bliss). Susan comes to the realization that her depression is related to unresolved grief for her father's death. However, she may have come to other insights, for example, that her depression was related to alienation from her African American community and her immersion in the academy of scholars at her rural, predominately European American college. It is noteworthy that cognitive and behavioral therapists have yet to establish that their explanations for disorders are any more truthful than are the insights gleaned from experiential or insight-oriented therapies. For example, the explanation that underlies Barlow's panic control therapy (2002) is not more scientifically established than several other explanations for panic, despite the efficacy of the treatment (Roth, Wilhelm, & Pettit, 2005). What is important is that the explanation is acceptable and benefits the client, an observation conceded by Meichenbaum (1986), an advocate of cognitive–behavioral therapy:

> As part of the therapy rational, the therapist conceptualized each client's anxiety in terms of Schacter's model of emotional arousal (Schacter, 1996) . . . . After laying this groundwork, the therapist noted that the client's fear seemed to fit Schacter's theory that an emotional state such as fear is in large part determined by the thoughts in which the client engages when physically aroused. . . . Although the theory and research upon which it is based have been criticized . . . the theory has an aura of plausibility that the clients tend to accept: The logic of the treatment plan is clear to clients in light of this conceptualization. (p. 370)

Leykin and DeRubeis (2006) conducted a study that investigated how successful treatment affects one's preexisting beliefs about the causes of depression; this provided additional evidence for the importance, but not uniqueness, of explanation in psychotherapy. They found that client explanations for their depression that were not consistent with the respective treatment rationale (either cognitive or biological) decreased as a result of treatment (although explanations that were concordant with the respective treatments did not increase). This result lends support to the conclusions that (a) the particular explanatory system is not critical and (b) change in one's explanations is associated with treatment benefits.

Garfield (1995) summarized the important aspects of insight:

> It seems reasonable to hypothesize that the *precise* nature of the insights and understandings provided by the therapist are of relatively minor importance. What does appear to be of importance is whether or not the client accepts the rationale offered by the therapist. (p. 97)

HOW INSIGHT FURTHERS THE PROCESS OF PSYCHOTHERAPY AND LEADS TO BENEFITS

We contend that insight assists in the process and is beneficial to the patient in three ways. First, the newly acquired explanation may instill belief and change the response expectancies of the client. Second, the process of acquiring the explanation is critical to the formation of the working alliance. Finally, insight should lead to action and a renewed sense of mastery by increasing the self-efficacy of the client with regard to solving his or her problems.

Change in Response Expectancy

Response expectancies are personal estimates regarding the likelihood that a nonvolitional response will occur (Kirsch, 1985). Response expectations differ from outcome expectations in that response expectancies refer to internal, subjective experience, such as anxiety, depression, and pain, rather than external events. Kirsch (1985) argued that response expectancies exert strong control over whether or not a nonvolitional response will occur. For example, the activating effects of caffeine (a nonvolitional response) can be experimentally induced in participants who are drinking decaffeinated coffee but who believe they are drinking nondecaffeinated coffee. The nonvolitional nature of many psychological disorders can be the most debilitating aspect of the condition; for example, the anxiety about having a panic attack at any moment may lead to the client's avoidance of public spaces, a result that may be more debilitating than the actual experience of the attack. Kirsch (1999) discussed examples in which changing an individual's perception of pain, depression, or anxiety is synonymous with changing the states themselves. Thus, "the perception is not just of the experience, it is the experience" (Kirsch, 1999, p. 7).

Kirsch (e.g., 1997) argued that changes in response expectancies are responsible for much of the benefits of psychotherapy. For example, the benefits of systematic desensitization have been shown to be due to the expectancies created rather than by the specific protocol delivered (Kazdin & Wilcoxon, 1976; Kirsch & Henry, 1977). Moreover, a likely explanation for the benefits of many established psychotherapies (such as CBT for depression) in the first few sessions before specific ingredients of the treatments have been delivered (Wampold, 2001), is that clients' response expectancies have changed (Kirsch, 1997). The explanation for the problem, complaint, or disorder provided by therapist and accepted by the client may be the primary means by which response expectations are altered.

In the medical context, placebo effects are induced by the patient's belief in the benefits of the sham drug or procedure administered; decaffeinated coffee has an activating effect because the participant *believes* that he or she is ingesting caffeine. The client in therapy typically believes that he or she has no control over his or her problems or that various nonvolitional states are highly likely, if not inevitable. The therapeutic explanation provides an alternative that suggests the patient has control or that various internal states are not inevitable. In this context, Frank and Frank's (1991) *remoralization* may be synonymous with changing response expectancies.

Victoria, for example, is induced by her therapist and drug advertisements to believe that an antidepressant will correct her chemical imbalance, which causes her depression to remit; these beliefs and a subsequent change in response expectancies may explain the remission of her depression (this argument is enhanced by evidence that suggests that much of the benefits of SSRIs is due to the placebo effect; Kirsch, Scoboria, & Thomas, 2002). John's CBT therapist carefully explains that CBT will be helpful because John's way of thinking about himself, others, and the world contributes to his depression and anxiety; however, before John's cognitions change, he believes his depression and anxiety are not inevitable and he feels better. It has been noted that there is a strong correlation between placebo effects and treatment effects (Moerman, 2002; Moerman & Jones, 2002; Walach & Maidhof, 1999). This result suggests that belief in the effectiveness of a treatment is connected to the effectiveness of the placebo, whose benefits are due to the belief in and expectations of the sham treatment.

Working Alliance

The working alliance is one of the most critical aspects of therapy (Gelso & Carter, 1994). It has been found that there is a relatively strong relationship between working alliance and outcome (Horvath & Bedi, 2002), a result than seems to apply across theoretical orientations (e.g., Krupnick et al., 1996). As generally conceptualized, the working alliance is composed of three components: bond, agreement on tasks, and agreement on goals (Bordin, 1979). Psychotherapy involves an empathic therapist who listens to the client's description of his or her problem or complaints. Providing an explanation to the client that is constructed in a manner acceptable to the client's framework and is culturally imbedded communicates a deep understanding of the client and thus facilitates the bond. The client's acceptance of the therapist's explanation facilitates a collaborative relationship within therapy (Frank & Frank, 1991). This mutual acceptance of an explanation for one's problems, complaint, or disorder facilitates agreement about the tasks and goals of therapy, as we discuss in the next section. As the alliance is related to outcome, the extent to which providing clients an explanation for their problems, complaints, or disorder assists in the formation of the alliance should be considered beneficial.

The relationship between insight and alliance may be viewed as a process that involves numerous reciprocal iterations throughout the course of therapy in that the alliance facilitates acceptance of the explanation *and* an explanation that communicates understanding and hope to the patient, which augments the alliance (see chap. 14, this volume, for a discussion of insight and therapeutic relationship). Because Susan has a trusting relationship with her therapist, she is able to examine her life in a safe environment. As she comes to believe that her depression is related to unresolved grief and poor models for male relationships, the alliance is furthered by her therapist, who empathizes with the difficulty caused by events in her childhood and who links Susan's insights with action. Thus, Susan feels understood and is willing to agree on the tasks and goals of therapy. However, providing an explanation that is unacceptable to the client would communicate misunderstanding. Had John's therapist provided a psychodynamic explanation (e.g., a successful father who disapproved of John's lack of ambition) that John felt was unscientific and typical "shrink" thinking, John may have felt alienated from the therapist (particularly if the therapist interpreted John's reluctance as resistance or transference). Bohart (see chap. 12, this volume) discusses the fact that the client's understanding is critical to the success of therapy.

Although an explanation may not be conveniently extracted from the interpersonal context in which it is given, Binder and Strupp (1997) noted that most links between techniques and outcomes failed to consider interpersonal context or tone. For example, therapists using similar techniques with similar clients may demonstrate vastly different outcomes, depending on interpersonal style. Specifically, a therapist's positive outcome cases demonstrated more affiliative modes of communication and negative outcomes cases involved more negative interpersonal contexts (Henry, Schacht, & Strupp, 1986, 1990). Thus, providing more opportunities for the client to acquire the therapeutically provided explanation for the disorder does not necessarily lead to better results (Hoglend, 1993; Piper et al., 1993). Indeed, more interpretation may actually harm the client if therapists are not mindful of the manner in which such interventions are offered (Schut & Castonguay, 2001).

Self-Efficacy and Action

A compelling explanation disambiguates a healing process that may at best seem opaque to many clients and at worst incomprehensible, thus increasing the likelihood that clients will become more actively involved in therapy. To reiterate Miechenbaum's (1986) emphasis on the link between conceptualization and treatment actions: "The logic of the treatment plan is clear to clients in light of this conceptualization" (p. 370). Providing treatment without providing an explanation renders the treatment a mystery and most likely attenuates the effectiveness of the treatment. As discussed previously, clients desire an explanation and are unlikely to adhere to the treatment regimen without one. There is persuasive evidence that patients' awareness of whether or not they are receiving medical treatment (i.e., open vs. hidden treatments) dramatically affects treatment outcome (Benedetti et al., 2003). Further, after reviewing the literature related to homework in psychotherapy, Scheel, Hanson, and Razzhavaikina (2004), came to a similar conclusion about treatment rationale and recommended that therapists "provide a rationale for how the homework activity will benefit the client that matches client's beliefs about his or her problem and how change may occur" (p. 51). Therefore, by providing an explanation and clear conceptualization of a treatment plan congruent with the client's beliefs, the client is more likely to engage in the treatment and more likely to exhibit positive treatment outcomes.

An understanding of the importance of acquiring an explanation in psychotherapy can be seen in the context of self-efficacy. Bandura (1986) differentiated self-efficacy from outcome expectations in the following ways: Self-efficacy encompasses one's self-appraisal of personal capabilities within a particular context, whereas outcome expectation is the assessment of the consequences of completing that task. It has been shown that self-efficacy affects daily choice, efforts, persistence, thought patterns, and affective reactions (Bandura, 1986, 2004).

Explanations help clients believe that therapy will be successful (i.e., increases outcome expectancy) and reinforces their belief that they can complete the tasks (i.e., follow the treatment protocol) to achieve those outcomes. The resulting increase in self-efficacy, according to Bandura (1986, 2004), leads to action—in the therapy (participating in the therapeutic process) and outside of therapy (completing homework and making changes).

There is a body of evidence suggesting that outcome expectations predict outcome in psychotherapy. An interesting result found in the NIMH Treatment of Depression Collaborative Research Program study is that client pretherapy responses to a one-item expectancy measure significantly predicted outcome (Sotsky et al., 1991). In a reanalysis of these data, alliance measures were found to mediate the effect of expectancy on outcome, and it was suggested that patients who expect treatment to be effective are more likely to engage effectively in the therapeutic process, which in turn brings about greater symptom reduction (Meyer, Pilkonis, & Krupnick, 2002), as predicted by self-efficacy theory.

FUTURE RESEARCH ON INSIGHT AS A COMMON FACTOR

Future research needs to investigate the relationship between acquisition of an explanation and the process and outcome of therapy (see chap. 7, this volume, for a review of the research on insight). Unfortunately, it is difficult to experimentally manipulate the explanation variable, although under some conditions this might be possible. In a structured therapy in which the explanation for one's disorder is explicitly provided to the client, two conditions could be considered: In one condition clients receive the explanation and in the other they do not. This design could be blinded vis-à-vis the therapist by having the explanation provided to the clients outside of therapy (e.g., written handouts or video presentations)—of course, the reciprocal nature of insight and alliance discussed previously, as well as the cultural context, are ignored in this design. Moreover, to be a bona fide common factor, the role of insight must be established across therapies.

More naturalistic research might investigate how explanations are provided by therapists. This endeavor would be a natural extension of the work of Addis and Jacobson (1996) and Addis and Carpenter (1999) and would have the added benefit of increased generalizability, a quality sorely missed in the preponderance of psychotherapy research (Westen, Novotny, & Thompson-Brenner, 2004). Furthermore, researchers might be guided by the theory of cultural proximity offered by Torrey (1972) and Frank and Frank (1991) in that explanations judged to be more proximal to the client's culture may demonstrate enhanced outcomes. Specifically, researchers could measure pretherapy explanations clients give for their difficulties as well as the explanations offered to them once in therapy, noting how the relationship of these two factors and the client's culture relate to outcome and other process variables. Recent research demonstrated the variability among therapists in terms of outcomes within treatments in clinical trials as well as in actual practice (Huppert et al., 2001; Kim, Wampold, & Bolt, 2006; Wampold & Brown, 2005). Thus research might focus on the ways in which therapists practicing the same therapies offer explanations and the reasons clients accept them.

One issue in any study of the role of insight is that there is a need for reliable and valid measures of the explanations that clients hold for their problems before therapy and after explanations have been provided or insights have occurred. Although there is not much work in this area, a viable beginning in the area of depression is the Reasons for Depression Questionnaire (Addis, Truax, & Jacobson, 1995; Thwaites, Dagnan, Huey, & Addis, 2004).

Understanding insight as a common factor has implications for the design of clinical trials. One variation of clinical trials involves a comparison of an active treatment to a common factor control in which the common factor control is intended to act as a placebo-type design to establish the specificity of the active treatment (Baskin, Tierney, Minami, & Wampold, 2003; Wampold, 2001). To accomplish this goal, the common factor control must adequately provide *all* common factors. These controls are described as providing a relationship with an empathic healer, as if the relationship is the only or the primary common factor to be controlled. These common factor controls rarely provide a cogent rationale for the treatment (because one does not exist), or a believable explanation for the client's disorder, problem, or complaint. That is, common factor controls do not control for insight, something all psychotherapies provide in one way or another.

CONCLUDING COMMENTS

Acquiring an acceptable and adaptive explanation is an integral and critical part of the therapeutic process. The truth of the insight is not as important as whether the explanation acquired makes sense to the client, fits within his or her worldview, and most important, is accepted by him or her. When clients acquire and acknowledge an explanation they may feel a renewed sense of hope (i.e., change in response expectations) that for some clients may be a sufficient curative factor. The process of acquiring a contextually appropriate explanation develops and strengthens the working alliance, and the alliance in turn increases the likelihood that the explanation will be accepted and will further the process of therapy. Further, the newly acquired explanatory system instills belief and increases the self-efficacy of the client. Thus, insight as we have defined and conceptualized it is fundamental both to the therapeutic process across orientations and to the benefits that result. The notion of insight as a common factor across psychotherapeutic orientations is not new. Indeed, as Marmor (1962) noted almost 40 years ago,

> Each school gives its own particular brand of insight. Whose are the correct insights? The fact is that patients treated by analysts of all these schools may not only respond favorably, but also believe strongly in the insights which they have been given. (p. 289)

Nevertheless, the importance of acquiring an explanation through insight for the process and outcome of therapy is largely unknown. It is clear that this is an area in need of increased attention by those interested in the common factors of therapy.

REFERENCES

Addis, M. E., & Carpenter, K. M. (1999). Why, why, why?: Reason-giving and rumination as predictors of response to activation- and insight-oriented treatment rationales. *Journal of Clinical Psychology, 55*, 881–894.

Addis, M. E., & Jacobson, N. S. (1996). Reasons for depression and the process and outcome of cognitive–behavioral psychotherapies. *Journal of Consulting and Clinical Psychology, 6*, 1417–1424.

Addis, M. E., Truax, P., & Jacobson, N. S. (1995). Why do people think they are depressed? The Reasons for Depression Questionnaire. *Psychotherapy: Theory, Research, Practice, Training, 32*, 476–483.

Arnkoff, D. B., Glass, C. R., & Shapiro, S. J. (2002). Expectations and preferences. In J. C. Norcross (Ed.), *Psychotherapy relationships that work: Therapist contributions and responsiveness to patients* (pp. 335–356). New York: Oxford University Press.

Atkinson, D. R., Worthington, R. L., & Dana, D. M. (1991). Etiology beliefs, preferences for counseling orientations, and counseling effectiveness. *Journal of Counseling Psychology, 38*, 258–264.

Averill, J. R., Ekman, P., & Panksepp, J. (1994). Are there basic emotions? In P. Ekman & R. J. Davidson (Eds.), *The nature of emotion: Fundamental questions* (pp. 5–47). New York: Oxford University Press.

Bandura, A. (1986). *Social foundations of thought & action: A social cognitive theory.* Englewood Cliffs, NJ: Prentice Hall.

Bandura, A. (2004). Health promotion by social cognitive means. *Health Education & Behavior, 31*(2), 143–164.

Barlow, D. H. (2002). *Anxiety and its disorders: The nature and treatment of anxiety and panic* (2nd ed.). New York: Guilford Press.

Baskin, T. W., Tierney, S. C., Minami, T., & Wampold, B. E. (2003). Establishing specificity in psychotherapy: A meta-analysis of structural equivalence of placebo controls. *Journal of Consulting and Clinical Psychology, 71,* 973–979.

Beck, J. S. (1995). *Cognitive therapy: Basics and beyond.* New York: Guilford Press.

Benedetti, F., Maggi, G., Lopiano, L., Lanotte, M., Rainero, I., Vighetti, S., & Pollo, A. (2003). Open versus hidden medical treatments: The patient's knowledge about therapy affects the therapy outcome. *Prevention & Treatment, 6,* Article 1. Retrieved April 5, 2006, from http://content.apa.org/journals/pre/6/1/1

Binder, J. L., & Strupp, H. H. (1997). "Negative Process": A recurrently discovered and underestimated facet of therapeutic process and outcome in the individual psychotherapy of adults. *Clinical Psychology: Science and Practice, 4,* 121–139.

Bordin, E. S. (1979). The generalizability of the psychoanalytic concept of the working alliance. *Psychotherapy: Theory, Research and Practice, 16,* 252–260.

Brady, J. P. (1967). Psychotherapy, learning theory, and insight. *Archives of General Psychiatry, 16,* 304–311.

Castonguay, L. G. (2000). A common factors approach to psychotherapy training. *Journal of Psychotherapy Integration, 10,* 236–282.

Crits-Christoph, P., Cooper, A., & Luborsky, L. (1988). The accuracy of therapists' interpretations and the outcome of dynamic psychotherapy. *Journal of Consulting and Clinical Psychology, 56,* 490–495.

Downing, J. N. (2004). Psychotherapy practice in a pluralistic world: Philosophical and moral dilemmas. *Journal of Psychotherapy Integration, 14,* 123–148.

Elkin, I., Yamaguchi, J. L., & Arnkoff, D. B. (1999). "Patient-treatment fit" and early engagement in therapy. *Psychotherapy Research, 9,* 437–451.

Frank, J. D., & Frank, J. B. (1991). *Persuasion and healing: A comparative study of psychotherapy* (3rd ed.). Baltimore: Johns Hopkins University Press.

Gardner, R. (1998). The brain and communication are basic for clinical human sciences. *British Journal of Medical Psychology, 71,* 493–508.

Garfield, S. (1995). *Psychotherapy: An eclectic–integrative approach* (2nd ed.). New York: Wiley.

Gelso, C. J., & Carter, J. A. (1994). Components of the psychotherapy relationship: Their interaction and unfolding during treatment. *Journal of Counseling Psychology, 41,* 296–306.

Goldfried, M. R. (1980). Toward the delineation of therapeutic change principles. *American Psychologist, 35,* 991–999.

Henry, W. P., Schacht, T. E., & Strupp, H. H. (1986). Structural analysis of social behavior: Application to a study of interpersonal process in differential psychotherapeutic outcome. *Journal of Consulting and Clinical Psychology, 54,* 27–31.

Henry, W. P., Schacht, T. E., & Strupp, H. H. (1990). Patient and therapist introject, interpersonal process, and differential psychotherapy outcome. *Journal of Consulting and Clinical Psychology, 58,* 768–774.

Hoglend, P. (1993). Transference interpretations and long-term change after dynamic psychotherapy of brief to moderate length. *American Journal of Psychotherapy, 47*, 494–507.

Horvath, A. O., & Bedi, R. P. (2002). The alliance. In J. C. Norcross (Ed.), *Psychotherapy relationships that work: Therapist contributions and responsiveness to patients* (pp. 37–70). New York: Oxford University Press.

Huppert, J. D., Bufka, L. F., Barlow, D. H., Gorman, J. M., Shear, M. K., & Woods, S. W. (2001). Therapists, therapist variables, and cognitive–behavioral therapy outcomes in a multicenter trial for panic disorder. *Journal of Consulting and Clinical Psychology, 69*, 747–755.

Ito, K. L., & Maramba, G. G. (2002). Therapeutic beliefs of Asian American therapists: Views from an ethnic-specific clinic. *Transcultural Psychiatry, 39*(1), 33–73.

Jopling, D. A. (2001). Placebo insight: The rationality of insight-oriented psychotherapy. *Journal of Clinical Psychology, 57*, 19–36.

Kazdin, A. E., & Wilcoxin, L. A. (1976). Systematic desensitization and nonspecific treatment effects: A methodological evaluation. *Psychological Bulletin, 83*, 729–758.

Kim, D. M., Wampold, B. E., & Bolt, D. M. (2006). Therapist effects in psychotherapy: A random effects modeling of the NIMH TDCRP data. *Psychotherapy Research, 16*, 161–172

Kirsch, I. (1985). Response expectancy as a determinant of experience and behavior. *American Psychologist, 40*, 1189–1202.

Kirsch, I. (1997). Response expectancy theory and application: A decennial review. *Applied and Preventive Psychology, 6*, 69–97.

Kirsch, I. (1999). *How expectancies shape experience*. Washington, DC: American Psychological Association.

Kirsch, I., & Henry, D. (1977). Extinction versus credibility in the desensitization of speech anxiety. *Journal of Consulting and Clinical Psychology, 45*, 1052–1059.

Kirsch, I., Scoboria, A., & Thomas, J. (2002). The emperor's new drugs: An analysis of antidepressant medication data submitted to the U.S. Food and Drug Administration. *Prevention & Treatment, 5*, Article 23. Retrieved April 5, 2006, from http://content.apa.org/journals/pre/5/1/23

Krupnick, J. L., Sotsky, S. M., Simmens, S., Moyer, J., Elkin, I., Watkins, J., & Pilkonis, P. A. (1996). The role of the therapeutic alliance in psychotherapy and pharmacotherapy outcome: Findings in the National Institute of Mental Health treatment of depression collaborative research program. *Journal of Consulting and Clinical Psychology, 64*, 532–539.

Latour, B. (1999). *Pandora's hope*. Cambridge, MA: Harvard University Press.

Leykin, Y., & DeRubeis, R. J. (2006). *Changes in patients' beliefs about the causes of their depression following successful treatment*. Manuscript submitted for publication.

Lyddon, W. J. (1991). Epistemic style: Implications for cognitive psychotherapy. *Psychotherapy, 28*, 588–597.

Marmor, J. (1962). Psychoanalytic therapy as an educational process. In J. H. Masserman (Ed.), *Science and psychoanalysis* (Vol. 5, pp. 286–299). New York: Grune & Stratton.

Meichenbaum, D. (1986). Cognitive–behavior modification. In F. H. Kanfer & A. P. Goldstein (Eds.), *Helping people change: A textbook of methods* (3rd ed., pp. 346–380). New York: Pergamon Press.

Meyer, B., Pilkonis, P. A., & Krupnick, J. L. (2002). Treatment expectancies, patient alliance, and outcome: Further analyses from the National Institute of Mental Health Treatment of Depression Collaborative Research Program. *Journal of Consulting and Clinical Psychology, 70,* 1051–1055.

Moerman, D. E. (2002). "The loaves and the fishes": A comment on "The emperor's new drugs: An analysis of antidepressant medication data submitted to the U.S. Food and Drug Administration." *Prevention & Treatment,* Article 5. Retrieved May 4, 2006, from http://content.apa.org/journals/pre/5/1/29

Moerman, D. E., & Jones, W. B. (2002). Deconstructing the placebo effect and finding the meaning response. *Annals of Internal Medicine, 136,* 471–476.

Panksepp, J. (1994). Are there basic emotions? In P. Ekman & R. J. Davidson (Eds.), *Nature of emotion: Fundamental questions* (pp. 5–47). New York: Oxford University Press.

Pikus, C. F., & Heavey, C. L. (1996). Client preferences for therapist gender. *Journal of College Student Personnel, 10,* 35–43.

Piper, W. E., Joyce, A. S., McCallum, M., & Azim, H. F. A. (1993). Concentration and correspondence of transference in short-term psychotherapy. *Journal of Consulting and Clinical Psychology, 61,* 586–595.

Random House college dictionary (Rev. ed.). (1984). New York: Random House.

Roth, W. T., Wilhelm, F. H., & Pettit, D. (2005). Are current theories of panic falsifiable? *Psychological Bulletin, 131,* 171–192.

Scheel, M. J., Hanson, W. E., & Razzhavaikina, T. I. (2004). The process of recommending homework in psychotherapy: A review of therapist delivery methods, client acceptability, and factors that affect compliance. *Psychotherapy: Theory, Research, Practice, Training, 41,* 38–55.

Schut, A. J., & Castonguay, L. G. (2001). Reviving Freud's vision of a psychoanalytic science: Implications for clinical training and education. *Psychotherapy: Theory, Research, Practice, Training, 38,* 40–48.

Simons, A. D., Lustman, P. J., Wetzel, R. D., & Murphy, G. E. (1985). Predicting response to cognitive therapy of depression: The role of learned resourcefulness. *Cognitive Therapy and Research, 9,* 79–89.

Sotsky, S. M., Glass, D. R., Shea, M. T., Pilkonis, P. A., Collins, J. F., Elkin, I., et al. (1991). Patient predictors of response to psychotherapy and pharmacotherapy: Findings in the NIMH Treatment of Depression Collaborative Research Program. *American Journal of Psychiatry, 148,* 997–1008.

Sue, D. W. (2004). Whiteness and ethnocentric monoculturalism: Making the "invisible" visible. *American Psychologist, 59,* 761–769.

Sue, D. W., & Sue, D. (1999). *Counseling the culturally different*. New York: Wiley.

Thwaites, R., Dagnan, D., Huey, D., & Addis, M. E. (2004). The Reasons for Depression Questionnaire (RFD): UK standardization for clinical and nonclinical populations. *Psychology and Psychotherapy: Theory, Research and Practice, 77*, 363–374.

Torrey, E. F. (1972). What Western psychotherapists can learn from witchdoctors. *American Journal of Orthpsychiatry, 42*, 69–76.

Walach, H., & Maidhof, C. (1999). Is the placebo effect dependent on time? A meta-analysis. In I. Kirsch (Ed.), *How expectancies shape experience* (pp. 321–332). Washington, DC: American Psychological Association.

Wampold, B. E. (2001). *The great psychotherapy debate: Model, methods, and findings*. Mahwah, NJ: Erlbaum.

Wampold, B. E., & Bhati, K. S. (2004). Attending to the omissions: A historical examination of evidence-based practice movements. *Professional Psychology: Research and Practice, 35*, 563–570.

Wampold, B. E., & Brown, G. S. (2005). Estimating therapist variability: A naturalistic study of outcomes in managed care. *Journal of Consulting and Clinical Psychology, 73*, 914–923.

Westen, D., Novotny, C. M., & Thompson-Brenner, H. (2004). The empirical status of empirically supported psychotherapies: Assumptions, findings, and reporting in controlled clinical trials. *Psychological Bulletin, 130*, 631–663.

Yalom, I. D. (1995). *The theory and practice of group psychotherapy* (4th ed.). New York: Basic Books.

II

RESEARCH

7

INSIGHT IN PSYCHOTHERAPY: A REVIEW OF EMPIRICAL LITERATURE

MARY BETH CONNOLLY GIBBONS,
PAUL CRITS-CHRISTOPH, JACQUES P. BARBER,
AND MEGAN SCHAMBERGER

Perhaps one of the most important, though elusive, constructs in the psychotherapy literature is insight. The term *insight* means different things to different people and has been referred to in psychotherapy research and clinical literatures by various terms. Other chapters in this volume discuss in depth the definitional and conceptual issues surrounding insight as an important construct for psychotherapy; for example, chapter 3 provides a cognitive–behavioral perspective on insight, chapter 4 examines insight from couples and family therapy orientations, and chapter 6 discusses insight as a common factor across therapeutic orientations. In this chapter, our goal is to review the empirical literature on insight. To accomplish this, we provide a working definition of the term that guided our selection of studies. However, we recognize that a number of issues and questions arise in defining the concept of insight and that these definitional questions hinder the integration of research results from the empirical literature on insight. Thus, we see the present review as a preliminary attempt to make sense of the limited empirical work in this domain.

WORKING DEFINITION OF INSIGHT

Although the models of psychotherapy available today vary widely in their proposed mechanisms of change, almost all share one important component. This component is that psychotherapy is viewed as an educational experience. Patients, through various techniques, come to understand something new about themselves. Within insight-oriented models, this gain in understanding has traditionally been referred to as insight. However, even among the insight-oriented theorists the term *insight* has various meanings. In classical analysis, patients gain insight into repressed traumatic experiences. In analytically oriented approaches, patients gain understanding, intellectually and emotionally, of general maladaptive relationship patterns without attempts to uncover specific traumatic origins. Nevertheless, all analytic approaches share the premise that patients' gains in understanding lead to eventual symptom alleviation through the implementation of new, more adaptive beliefs or behaviors.

What is common in the various uses of the term *insight* is that a connection is made. Such a connection can be between past and present experiences, or between thoughts, feelings, desires, or behaviors. The connection is a new understanding of such elements that was not previously recognized. *Insight* can refer to the event of obtaining such new understanding (e.g., an *Aha!* experience) or to the tendency to be able to achieve such understanding (insightfulness). This general definition of insight is the one used for the current review. Whereas some authors labeled this construct *insight* (Luborsky, 1962), others used the term *self-understanding* (Connolly et al., 1999; Crits-Christoph, 1984) to refer to the same concept. Thus, for this chapter we identified any empirical studies using either term to capture the learning of new connections.

EMPIRICAL STUDIES OF INSIGHT

We located studies for the current chapter through a MEDLINE and PsycINFO search using the terms *insight* and *self-understanding*. We then identified and reviewed studies that met our working definition. Our review focuses on five types of studies: (a) studies of the tendency to be insightful (i.e., a patient personality dimension) as a predictor of the outcome of psychotherapy, (b) studies of gains in insight or self-understanding over the course of therapy in relation to outcome, (c) studies of insight in therapy in relation to other aspects of psychotherapy process, (d) studies of therapist interventions in relation to the development of insight, and (e) methodological studies of insight (reliability and validity studies). We include a detailed description of each of the studies, and at the end of each section, we provide a summary of research findings and limitations. Our conclusion section provides a summary of the major trends apparent across the research review.

Patient Insightfulness as Predictor of Therapy Outcome

A variety of studies have tested the hypothesis that more insightful patients fare better in psychotherapy, particularly psychodynamic (insight-oriented) therapy. Results of these studies have been mixed. A summary of studies of patient insightfulness in relation to outcome is provided in Table 7.1. Included in the table is the definition of insight used, the methodology used to assess the construct, and the general findings of each study.

Rosenbaum, Friedlander, and Kaplan (1956) asked psychiatry residents to rate patient pretreatment insight, which they defined as the degree to which the patient demonstrated awareness of the factors influencing his or her illness. Patients were divided into three groups on the basis of their level of improvement. Results revealed that the groups did not differ significantly regarding level of insight at pretreatment.

Kelman and Parloff (1957) studied self-awareness as a dimension of change as it was assumed that self-awareness constituted a value shared by many therapeutic approaches. Two measures of self-awareness were included, and in both cases, self-awareness was defined as "the extent to which a patient sees himself as others see him" (p. 283). A self-awareness Q-sort, a methodology in which patients sort self-descriptors to represent perceived self and ideal self, was used to determine the degree of congruence between the patient's perceived behavior and his or her behavior as observed by a trained observer. The second measure of self-awareness consisted of the discrepancy between the ratings the patient expected and the ratings he or she actually received from fellow group members on each of three dimensions: respect, leadership, and friendship. Results indicated that the self-awareness Q-sort correlated significantly with the symptom checklist indicating that self-awareness was associated with symptom level. However, the authors noted that this result could have been a chance phenomenon as they calculated a large number of correlations.

Luborsky (1962) assessed insight on 24 patients before treatment, at the end of treatment, and 2 years later. Insight was described as comprising "awareness, ability to compare actual state of functioning with desired state of functioning, and concern about the discrepancy" (Burstein, Coyne, Kernberg, & Voth, 1972, p. 22). Results indicated that insight, rated pretreatment, did not correlate significantly with change in the therapist's health–sickness ratings across treatment (Luborsky, 1962). The investigator concluded that the initial position of the patient on personality variables has little to do with the amount of change he or she will make in psychotherapy.

Luborsky et al. (1980) used the Patient Insight Scale, consisting of seven items and rated by two independent clinical raters from session transcripts,

TABLE 7.1
Summary of Empirical Findings on Insight

		Patient insightfulness as predictor of therapy outcome		
Study	Construct	Definition	Methods	Findings
Rosenbaum (1956)	IN	Awareness of factors influencing illness	Single-item rating	Pretreatment IN not related to improvement.
Kelman (1957)	SA	Extent patient sees self as others see patient	Self Q-sort versus Q-sort of observer	Change in SA not significantly correlated with outcome.
Luborsky (1962)	IN	Awareness, ability to compare actual to desired state	Single-item rating	Pretreatment IN not related to outcome.
Luborsky (1980)	IN	NP	Seven items rated from transcripts of patient attractiveness as psychotherapy client	Early IN not correlated with outcome.
Crits-Christoph (1984)	SU	Understanding of interpersonal patterns	Ratings of verbalized understanding of CCRT	Average SU correlated with outcome.
Hoglend (1994)	IN	Recognition of wishes, defenses, patterns, in relation to symptoms	Single-item rating	Pretreatment IN related to treatment length, attrition, and pursuit of additional treatment.
Gelso (1997)	IN	Connection of affect with intellectual understanding	Single-item rating	High levels of insight with high transference predict better outcome.
Hoffart (2002)	SU	NP	Single-item rating	Greater patient SU early in therapy was related to a reduction in emotional distress.

Gains in insight over the course of therapy in relation to outcome

Study	Construct	Definition	Methods	Findings
Vargas (1954)	SA	Increase in self-thought; more aware of new self patterns	Ratings of self-statements from sessions	SA increased across successful psychotherapy.
Mann (1959)	IN	Degree of congruence between self view and other view	Two items rated	No relation between change IN and change individual adjustment.
Crits-Christoph (1984)	SU	Understanding of interpersonal patterns	Ratings of verbalized understanding of CCRT	No significant change in SU.
Hoglend (1994)	IN	Recognition of wishes, defenses, patterns, in relation to symptoms	Single-item rating	Change in IN positively related to 2-year outcome.
Diemer (1996)	IN	Understanding something about the self	Single-item rating	Event insight improved significantly across treatment; No correlation between insight and outcome provided.
Connolly (1999)	SU	Understanding of interpersonal patterns	Self-report SUIP	Change in SU not related to change in symptoms.
Kivlighan (2000)	IN	Conscious awareness of thoughts and feelings that may be contributing to emotional distress	Patient responses on Important Events Questionnaire were rated using the Insight Rating Scale	Increases in IN related to decrease in symptom distress.
Grande (2003)	IN	Hierarchical scale achieved through different levels of awareness	Observational ratings on the Heidleberg Structural Change Scale	Patients who had gained definitive insight by the end of treatment were more able to cope with daily struggles after treatment.

Note. All studies cited in the first column list the first author only. Full authorship for each study is listed in the reference list. IN = insight, SU = self-understanding, SA = self-awareness, NP = not provided, CCRT = core-conflictual relationship theme, SUIP = self-understanding of interpersonal patterns scale.

as a predictor of treatment outcome in the Penn Psychotherapy Project. The insight score was included in a factor representing the patient's attractiveness as a psychotherapy patient. The scale demonstrated good interrater reliability and internal consistency. The results indicated that insight did not correlate significantly with outcome as assessed by a composite score (Morgan, Luborsky, Crits-Christoph, Curtis, & Solomon, 1982). A further study using the same sample of patients used a guided clinical rating of self-understanding (Crits-Christoph, 1984; Luborsky, Crits-Christoph, Mintz, & Auerbach, 1988). In this investigation, the patient's core-conflictual relationship theme (CCRT) was derived from a composite of three independent judges' ratings of the content of the patient's main wishes or needs, the patient's responses to others, and responses of others to the patient from the psychotherapy transcripts of Sessions 3 and 5. Next, independent judges rated the patient's in-session expression of self-understanding on the basis of the patient's understanding of the CCRT components. Interjudge reliability for the self-understanding ratings was quite good. Results indicated that patients' average levels of self-understanding did correlate significantly with outcome, correcting for initial level.

Hoglend, Engelstad, Sorbye, Heyerdahl, and Amlo (1994) defined insight as the patient's ability to recognize wishes, defenses, and interpersonal patterns and to relate these components to the presenting symptoms. The authors argued that in the absence of a standard test to assess insight, expert clinical ratings were the best choice for measuring this construct. A sample of 43 patients was rated by experts using a single-item rating of insight on the basis of a clinical interview that was audiotaped. The expert raters in this investigation were also the therapists for these patients. Interrater reliability was unsatisfactory for the pretreatment assessment of insight and marginally acceptable when assessed at a 2-year follow-up interview. The results indicated that pretreatment level of insight was related to treatment length, attrition, and pursuit of additional treatment.

Gelso, Kivlighan, Wine, Jones, and Friedman (1997) evaluated the interaction of transference and insight in the prediction of outcome for 33 clients treated with 12 sessions of counseling for personal problems. Insight was represented by two counselor-rated items for intellectual insight and emotional insight. *Intellectual insight* was defined as the cognitive understanding of cause–effect relationships, whereas *emotional insight* was defined as the connection of affect with intellectual understanding. Neither intellectual nor emotional insight was significantly correlated with treatment outcome. However, there was a significant interaction between transference and emotional insight in that high levels of transference together with high levels of emotional insight predicted better outcome.

Hoffart, Versland, and Sexton (2002) evaluated 35 patients who participated in an 11-week inpatient treatment program that was designed to understand the impact of self-understanding, empathy, and guided discovery on schema belief and emotional distress. The three process variables were assessed by the therapist and an expert observer. To assess the three process variables, the experimenter used questions such as, "To what extent did you feel that the therapist understood you and realized how you felt?" and "To what extent did you find promising ways to see your difficulties?" Answers to these items were rated on a scale ranging from 0 to 100. The investigators found that self-understanding was highly correlated with the Task Impact subscale of the Session Impact Scale, which measures insight into self, other, or problem solution. Results showed that greater patient self-understanding early in therapy was related to a reduction in schema belief and emotional distress.

In summary, only marginal support was evident for the hypothesis that more insightful patients have better treatment outcomes. Although two studies found that insight early in treatment was associated with outcomes of inpatient treatment, three outpatient studies failed to find a relation between pretreatment or early-in-treatment insightfulness and various measures of outcome. However, one study did find a relation between insightfulness and retention in treatment. Moreover, one study found that patient level of emotional insight was associated with better outcome when transference levels were also high. It may be that initial levels of insightfulness are important to psychotherapy, but this variable only indirectly affects treatment outcome through its effects on other variables. Thus, having the capacity for insight might lead to better engagement in psychotherapy (particularly insight-oriented therapy) or greater openness to examining aspects of the self when such aspects are hindering progress in therapy (e.g., negative transference reactions). Furthermore, assessment of insightfulness as actually displayed in early psychotherapy sessions appears to be related to outcome, but pretreatment assessments of insightfulness are not.

Gains in Insight Over the Course of Therapy in Relation to Outcome

More important than a patient's preexisting level of insightfulness might be the amount of new insight acquired during therapy. Unfortunately, relatively few empirical investigations have attempted to assess precisely what the patient comes to understand about him- or herself in psychotherapy and whether the acquisition of such insight is associated with better treatment outcome. A summary of studies on gains in insight in relation to outcome is provided in Table 7.1. Included in the table is the definition of insight used, the methodology used to assess the construct, and the general findings of each study. We briefly discuss each of these studies in this chapter.

As part of an investigation of the effectiveness of client-centered psychotherapy, Vargas (1954) examined the role of self-awareness in relation to success in treatment. The investigators defined self-awareness as a threefold process in which the patient begins to think about him- or herself more often, becomes less aware of previous self-perceptions and more aware of other previously undescribed patterns of behavior, then finally discovers new aspects of him- or herself. The transcripts of 10 psychotherapy cases were analyzed using a self-description instrument, revealing good interrater reliability. The results indicated that successful psychotherapy was characterized by an increase in discussion of the self, an increase in discussion of original aspects of the self, and an increase in discussion of emergent aspects of the self. This investigation used a broad definition of self-awareness. As operationalized in this investigation, the content of the client's awareness was not defined. It is not clear from this experiment whether the clients increased their awareness of their interpersonal patterns, cognitive distortions, or simply behavioral characteristics.

In 1959, Mann and Mann examined the relative efficacy of three kinds of group experience: group discussion, task-oriented study group activity, and group-centered role playing. The authors noted that one criterion useful in assessing personality change is insight: "the degree of congruence between an individual's view of himself and the view which others have of him" (p. 91). Ninety-six participants were recruited from a graduate course and assigned to one of the three types of groups. Two items were used to rate insight at the beginning and the end of each group session. Results indicated that all group members showed increases in insight over the course of the group experience and that the three kinds of group experience did not differ in the degree to which they increased insight. Finally, no relation was found between change in insight and change in individual adjustment.

Data from the Penn Psychotherapy Project cited previously (Crits-Christoph, 1984; Luborsky et al., 1988) also examined change in insight from Sessions 3 to 5 in relation to outcome. Patients did not show significant change in self-understanding from Session 3 to Session 5. Consequently, change in self-understanding did not correlate significantly with outcome.

In the Hoglend et al. (1994) study that examined initial insightfulness in relation to outcome, the authors also tested whether change in insight levels over a 2-year period of therapy was related to change in psychodynamic outcome measures. A significant association between change in insight and overall dynamic change was found.

Diemer, Lobell, Vivino, and Hill (1996) evaluated 25 clients who completed 12 sessions of counseling that included unstructured sessions, dream interpretation sessions, and event interpretation sessions. Insight was assessed on a 9-point scale by trained judges on the basis of the client's written interpretation of the dream or event. For the investigation, insight was defined as understanding something about the self, including the client's ability to "articulate patterns or reasons for behaviors, thoughts, or feelings" (p. 103). Interrater reliability for the insight rating across 4 judges was good. Clients improved significantly across counseling on measures of symptomatology, interpersonal functioning, and event insight. However, no correlation between change in insight and other outcome measures was given in this report.

Connolly, Crits-Christoph, Shelton, et al. (1999) defined *self-understanding* as "the understanding of maladaptive interpersonal patterns" (p. 473). To measure the construct, Connolly and colleagues developed and tested a measure of self-understanding called the Self-Understanding of Interpersonal Patterns Scale (SUIP). The problematic relationship patterns that one might experience are represented in each of the 19 items of the SUIP. Patients rate both whether they recognize a particular pattern as relevant to their own relationships and their level of understanding (0 to 4) about that particular problem. For each client, two scores are derived from the items: (a) a recognition score and (b) the average level of self-understanding the patient has across those problematic areas. The SUIP was tested in five different patient populations to assess internal consistency, test–retest reliability, discriminant validity, convergent validity, and content validity. The SUIP demonstrated good internal consistency and test–retest reliability for both the recognition score and the self-understanding score across both clinical and control populations. The SUIP converged with measures of similar constructs, including the degree to which one is reflective in thinking. The SUIP did not correlate significantly with divergent constructs, such as symptom measures and measures of interpersonal distress. In a sample of patients with generalized anxiety disorder who were treated with either supportive expressive psychotherapy or medication, self-understanding was more significantly changed in the psychotherapy group compared with the medication group, despite comparable symptom change across treatments. However, change in self-understanding across psychotherapy was not significantly associated with change in symptoms.

Kivlighan, Multon, and Patton (2000) examined whether gains in insight are related to symptom reduction by evaluating 12 patients who had received 20 sessions of psychotherapy. After each session patients completed the Important Events Questionnaire (IEQ), a 5-item self-report questionnaire. The items on the IEQ are open-ended and refer to the therapy session that has just taken place. Responses on the IEQ are then classified into different categories on the basis of the therapeutic mechanisms to which they refer. The IEQs were rated by three judges using the Insight Rating Scale (IRS), a 9-item scale on the degree of insightfulness displayed by each patient in their open-ended responses. Interrater reliability for the IRS was good for both the total score and for the emotional insight items. Results indicated that a linear increase in insight across treatment was related to a decrease in symptom distress.

Grande, Rudolf, Oberbracht, and Pauli-Magnus (2003) evaluated 49 clients after the conclusion of a 12-week inpatient psychotherapy treatment to assess the endurance of psychotherapeutic effects. Insight was measured through observational raters using the Heidleberg Structural Change Scale, a scale used to identify patients' approaches to dealing with individually defined problem areas such as internal conflicts, structural vulnerabilities, and maladaptive relationship patterns. For the investigation insight was seen as hierarchical, with levels of awareness ranging from the problem being unconscious to dealing with the problem in a naturalistic fashion. Results showed that those patients who gained definitive insight into their problems during psychotherapy were more competent in dealing with the daily struggles of life after treatment had ended.

In summary, there are mixed results for studies examining gains in insight in relation to treatment outcome. Four investigations found that increases in insight across treatment were related to positive treatment outcomes, whereas four other investigations found no significant relationship. With the diversity of insight measures, outcome measures, treatment types, timing of assessments, and treatment lengths, it is difficult to draw conclusions from the review of these eight studies. Of the investigations that found no statistically significant effects, one study evaluated only nonpatient student groups, and one study evaluated change in insight only across 3 early treatment sessions. The other two studies (Connolly et al., 1999; Diemer et al., 1996) found that insight changed significantly across treatment, but both found no relation to symptom change. However, both investigations looked across relatively short time periods, ranging from 12 to 20 sessions. Three studies with positive findings evaluated the relation of insight to outcome over a greater number of treatment hours. Kivlighan et al. (2000) evaluated change across 20 weeks, and Hoglend et al. (1994) evaluated change across 2 years. In addition, Grande et al. (2003) evaluated change over 12 inpatient weeks of treatment. It may be that gains in insight have greater influence on long-term outcomes, and other factors, such as the positive supportive relationship, are responsible for shorter-term treatment gains.

The results of some studies provide some empirical support for one of the main theories of psychotherapy: Improvements in symptoms and life functioning are possible if insight is gained, at least when longer term outcomes are examined. However, several caveats should be noted. First, none of the studies ruled out reverse causation. (Insight markers follow from improvements in psychotherapy.) Second, the studies did not isolate the specific types of insights that are responsible for improvement in psychotherapy. A third caveat is that the limits on generalizability of these findings across different types of treatment and patient presenting problems are not clear. Nevertheless, these findings are encouraging about the potential role of insight in psychotherapy and suggest that further research on this dimension may be crucial to understanding how certain psychotherapies work.

Insight in Relation to the Therapeutic Process

Early in the history of psychotherapy research, Dymond (1948) stressed the need to define the concept of insight, given its prominent role in many types of psychotherapy. In an attempt to clarify the term, Dymond defined insight as the patient's ability to understand "the self–other patterns or roles which the individual has incorporated and which form the basis for his expectations of others, his structuring of his life situations and the place he feels he occupies in them" (p. 229). Dymond had 20 university students complete the Wechsler-Bellevue Adult Intelligence Scale, the Thematic Apperception Test (TAT), and a brief interview regarding familial relationships. A blind analysis of the TAT was conducted, which produced a personality profile in terms of interpersonal relationships for each participant. This profile was then read aloud, and the participant was given the opportunity to confirm or deny each statement. Verbally denied material was checked against the interview material to determine if denial was a result of the shortcomings of the test or a lack of insight. The investigator then computed insight as the degree of agreement between the blind TAT analysis and the participant's perceptions of the resultant personality profile. Empathy was further estimated from the TAT responses by rating the degree to which each participant "took the role" of the characters introduced into their stories. The results indicated that individuals low on empathy seemed to lack insight into their interpersonal relationships. The investigator concluded that empathy is a necessary mechanism for building well developed self–other patterns. The reliability of these measures was not reported.

Unlike other attempts to measure insight, Dymond (1948) addressed the complexity of insight by accounting for the interpersonal aspects of self-understanding in the construct definition. Criterion measurement was not restricted to the ability to understand the behaviors and views of others; rather, the participant's ability to assess interpersonal patterns, including acts of the self and acts of others, was measured. One might argue with the validity of using TAT responses as a criterion, yet the investigator compared these profiles with the participant's own account of his or her own interpersonal relationships. At the same time, the methodology might be improved by including multiple independent judges so that reliability estimates could be computed. Finally, the method seems both time consuming and costly and in fact has not been used since its introduction in 1948.

To understand the differences in therapeutic factors in the treatment of young children, Shechtman and Ben-David (1999) conducted a study comparing individual and group treatments for aggressive boys. Shechtman (2003) followed up on the results and looked at the differences in process variables, such as insight occurring in both individual and group counseling sessions. Therapeutic factors were examined by rating audiotaped transcripts of the sessions using the Group Counseling Helpful Impact Scale. This scale consists of four major subscales: emotional-awareness–insight, relationship–climate, other versus self-focus, and problem identification–change. Results showed that patients tended to have a higher rating of insight or emotional awareness in group sessions compared with individual sessions.

Smith (1959) asked students in peer groups to rate the individuals in their group who took each of three roles: aggressing, blocking, and withdrawing. An insight score was computed by comparing the number of roles the student assigned to himself with the average number assigned by fellow group members. Thus, in this experiment, insight was operationalized as one's perceptions of his or her own behavior within a group. The results revealed that insight was significantly negatively associated with defensiveness.

Raingruber (2000) asserted that recognition from another is a key component in the development of self-understanding. Clients develop self-understanding when their therapist recognizes the importance of their thoughts, feelings, and behaviors. The investigator videotaped psychotherapy sessions between 8 patients and nurse therapists to test his hypothesis. The footage was shown to both patient and therapist after the session, and they were asked to describe significant interactions and identify helpful therapeutic tools. A panel of investigators reviewed the audiotaped interviews to identify consistent themes in the sessions. Results showed that clients tended to develop self-understanding when their therapists were attentive to emotional issues and recognized the relevance these issues had to their lives and presenting problems.

In the investigation by Connolly et al. (1999) that implemented the SUIP to evaluate self-understanding of interpersonal patterns, there was significantly greater self-understanding in the dynamic psychotherapy group compared with the medication group. Although this finding seems to support the unique contribution of therapist dynamic interpretations in the therapeutic process, future studies are needed to evaluate this finding as random assignment to treatment groups was not used.

Multiple qualitative investigations also evaluated the relation of insight to the therapeutic process. Elliott (1984) used a discovery-oriented method to evaluate insight events in the therapeutic process (see chap. 8, this volume, for a full description). Comprehensive process analysis (CPA) revealed that clients' indirect requests for help may indicate a readiness for interpretive work and that insight events serve an alliance-building function. Elliott et al. (1994) used the CPA to evaluate six insight events in two treatments. The investigators found that insight events were related to interpretations of recent life events.

In summary, there is a lack of studies evaluating the relation of insight to other important psychotherapy process variables. Although there is evidence suggesting that greater insight is attained in the therapeutic process when there is greater empathy, less defensiveness, and greater therapist attention to relevant emotional material, each of these relations is supported by a single study. There are a number of investigations that evaluate the patient's perspective of important therapeutic events. Although these studies do not directly measure insight, many provide evidence of the impact of insight on the therapeutic process. For a complete review see Elliott and James (1989).

Therapist Interventions That Facilitate Insight

How do therapists foster insight in therapy? In classic psychoanalysis as well as modern theories of brief or focal psychodynamic therapy, interpretation is the central therapist intervention designed to increase insight. For example, the interpretation of problematic relationships within a patient's life is often seen as a key technique in promoting patient insight within modern dynamic psychotherapies such as Luborsky's (1984) supportive–expressive therapy (SE) and Strupp and Binder's (1984) time-limited dynamic psychotherapy. These therapeutic models promote techniques that enable patients to see maladaptive relationship patterns, to understand the development of the pattern, and to see ways in which the pattern is related to their present symptoms. Within these therapies, therapists help patients understand their relationship patterns outside of therapy through interpretations and help patients understand their relationship patterns within the therapeutic relationship through transference interpretations.

Several studies have looked at the frequency of such therapist interpretative statements within the context of modern interpersonal–psychodynamic therapies. However, results across these studies have varied, most likely because of differences in the definition and measurement of interpretations. For example, Stiles (1979) classified 30% of therapist statements as interpretations based on content and 40% of therapist utterances as interpretations based on therapist intent. Hill, Helms, Tichenor, and Speigel (1988) found a much lower rate of 8%. Manual-guided dynamically oriented therapies are expected to be more explicit in defining and implementing therapist interpretations; however, there is still a high degree of variability in rates of interpretations within the literature. Stiles, Shapiro, and Firth-Cozens (1988) found that based on intent, more than 20% of therapist statements were classified as interpretations within interpersonal dynamic psychotherapy. Piper, Debbane, de Carufel, and Bienvenu (1987) reported that 14% of therapist speaking turns within a dynamic therapy, or an average of 5 statements per session, could be classified as interpretations; Connolly, Crits-Christoph, Shappell, Barber, and Luborsky (1998) found that 4% of therapist statements were interpretative. These results suggest that interpretations of maladaptive relationship patterns, often the key to fostering insight, vary among different psychodynamic approaches.

The frequency and accuracy of both interpretations and transference interpretations have been investigated in terms of the relation of these insight-fostering interventions to process variables and outcome. Foreman and Marmar (1985) investigated the frequency of interpretation among six patients who had poor alliances early in therapy. Of those cases, three improved their alliances across treatment. Compared with the group of patients who did not exhibit a significant improvement in alliance, patients who did progress were more likely to be in a treatment that addressed patient defenses. Piper et al. (1987) defined interpretation as addressing at least one dynamic component (impulses, anxiety, defenses, and dynamic expressions) and at least one nondynamic component (objects and resultant expressions). The investigators found that patients who received higher ratings on the therapists' overall usefulness of therapy were more likely to be involved in interventions that addressed two or three of the dynamic components. Hill et al. (1988) did not find a relation between number of interpretations offered in 12 to 20 sessions of therapy and outcome; however, the investigators did find an association between self-concept and interpretations. Studies such as these indicate the importance of formulating interpretations for patients to gain self-understanding into maladaptive relationship patterns.

A similar importance can be placed on interpretations of interpersonal patterns between the patient and therapist. Several investigations have also looked at the relationship between outcome and transference interpretation. Malan (1976) found that a greater proportion of transference interpretations related to the parental or sibling relationship predicted positive treatment outcome. More recent studies incorporated the quality of patients' interpersonal functioning. For example, investigations found that patients who had a high quality of object relations, defined as the patient's lifelong pattern of relationships, and who had a high proportion of transference interpretations tended to have poor treatment outcome (Hoglend, 1993; Piper, Azim, Joyce, & McCallum, 1991). Conversely, Connolly et al. (1999) found that patients with low quality of interpersonal relationships who receive a high amount of transference interpretations within sessions tend to have poor outcomes. Although these three studies seem inconsistent with one another, Connolly et al. (1999) noted that the investigators evaluated different treatments that included very different frequencies of interpretation. The Piper et al. (1991) study used more interpretations per session than the investigation by Connolly et al. Thus, the investigations evaluated the relation between the use of interpretations and outcome across very different ranges of frequency of interpretation. The studies could be complementary and suggest that even patients with a high quality of object relations can benefit from low levels of transference interpretation within psychotherapy sessions. These studies clearly raise a central concern about insight: More is not always better. Some patients, particularly lower functioning patients, might be overwhelmed by psychological material that is emotionally difficult for them. Part of the art of therapy may be in the timing of interventions. Patients might need to be ready to hear and process potential insight-oriented interventions. For example, if a therapist interprets a deep transference theme (such as a patient having erotic feelings toward the therapist) at the wrong time in therapy, this insight, even if acknowledged by the patient, might lead the patient to drop out of therapy or avoid material (e.g., dreams, fantasies, memories) that is connected to these feelings.

Other facets of insight-producing interventions beyond frequency or timing need to be considered. One good interpretation may produce lasting insight, and therefore the quality or accuracy of interpretations might be more important to outcome than raw frequency. Several studies have investigated the accuracy of interpretations and transference interpretations in relation to therapy outcome. After investigating the plan compatibility of three psychotherapy cases, Silberschatz, Fretter, and Curtis (1986) found that transference interpretations that were consistent with a patient's case formulation produced the best outcome. Norville, Sampson, and Weiss (1996) elaborated on this study with the addition of four cases and found a significant correlation between the average plan compatibility of interpretations and the patient's plan attainment ratings. Investigations by Crits-Christoph, Cooper, and Luborsky (1988) of 43 patients engaged in dynamically oriented therapy showed that accuracy in interpreting a patient's wish and response of other were significantly associated with treatment outcome. Barber, Crits-Christoph, and Luborsky (1996) showed that highly competently delivered expressive interventions predicted subsequent outcome beyond the contribution of supportive interventions, therapeutic alliance, and earlier symptomatic improvement. They also showed that the competent delivery of these techniques, rather than their frequency, resulted in better outcome. Although that study did not directly assess insight, it assessed therapeutic interventions intended to promote self-understanding into patients' core conflictual relationship themes.

In terms of transference interpretations, Piper, Joyce, McCallum, and Azim (1993) found that patients with a low quality of object relations had poor 6-month follow-up outcome with greater correspondence of transference interpretations, and patients with a greater quality of object relationships tended to have better outcome with greater correspondence of transference interpretations. Although the empirical literature on interpretation and transference interpretation seems to suggest that greater frequencies and greater accuracy predict symptom change, the relationship is often complex. It is important for therapists to learn how to formulate accurate interpretations and therapeutic interpretations to promote patient insight.

The relative balance of an interpretative (insight-oriented) focus by therapist versus a supportive focus was examined in an investigation by Buckley, Conte, Plutchik, Wild, and Karasu (1984). Using a one-item scale, the authors found that greater emphasis on supportiveness was associated with a positive psychotherapy outcome. However, it is likely that a therapy can be both supportive and interpretative, and the scale used did not allow for this. One might assume that a therapeutic focus on insight should predict outcome, if insight is in fact a necessary component. However, a small quantity of insight relative to support may be all that is needed for therapy to be successful. In conclusion, this design does not provide information regarding the unique contributions to psychotherapy outcome of either insight-oriented or supportive techniques.

In summary, a number of studies that evaluated interventions intended to produce insight, rather than directly assessing the construct of insight, point to the importance of gains in insight in the therapeutic process. Results were mixed for studies evaluating the relation between the frequency of interpretation and treatment outcome. Although two investigations found that a higher frequency of interpretation was related to improvement in the alliance and higher usefulness scores, Hill et al. (1988) found no direct relation between frequency of interpretation and treatment outcome. Regarding transference interpretations, three investigations found it was important to consider a patient moderating variable, quality of object relations, in investigations of the relation between the frequency of transference interpretations and treatment outcome. These investigations (Connolly et al., 1999; Hoglend, 1993; Piper et al., 1991) found that higher levels of transference interpretation were problematic for at least some patients, suggesting that it is the quality of the insight gained rather than the quantity that is important to a successful psychotherapy. All four investigations that evaluated the quality of therapist interpretations found that high accuracy or competence in interpreting maladaptive interpersonal problems predicted a positive symptom course. These investigations suggest that high quality interpretations produce greater gains in insight during psychotherapy, which lead to a positive symptom course.

Methodological Studies of Insight

A few studies have focused purely on methodological issues in regard to the measurement of insight. This section includes studies that focused only on the reliability and convergent validity of instruments for assessing insight. Husby et al. (1985) attempted to develop a brief follow-up form to evaluate the effects of psychotherapy that would address multiple outcome criteria including symptom relief, social functioning, and self-understanding. For this investigation, the construct of self-understanding was defined globally as the patient's ability to learn more about him- or herself. Each item was rated by three independent judges. The follow-up form developed by Husby et al. indicated that the outcome criteria could be reliably assessed in a short period of time, although reliability for the self-understanding item alone was not reported.

Tolor and Reznikoff (1960) based their investigation on the premise that insight can be measured by "determining the degree to which the subject accurately interprets a number of hypothetical constructs" (p. 287). Participants were asked to choose from among four explanatory statements representing different levels of insight for each of 27 hypothetical situations. The authors report adequate test–retest reliability for this instrument. Furthermore, validity was assessed by comparing test scores for 68 patients with a single-item insight rating obtained from their treating psychiatrist and psychologist. Results indicated a significant relation between patients' test scores and insight as judged independently by psychologists and psychiatrists. The authors recognized that their definition of insight deviated from the traditional interpretation that defines insight as awareness of one's own behavioral patterns. Here, insight was defined as the ability to understand impersonal hypothetical situations.

Tolor and Reznikoff (1960) suggested an interesting approach to the assessment of insight, yet it is unclear whether their instrument assessed the intended construct of insight. It is possible that one's ability to understand the views of others has little bearing on one's ability to introspect. As analytic theorists have pointed out, one's ability to understand one's interpersonal patterns depends to a large extent on the resistances to change evident in the therapeutic process. Therefore, one could easily imagine a patient who is able to objectively assess the defense mechanisms portrayed by another, but because of his or her own resistances, is unable to have personal insight. Although the ability to understand the views of others seems important to healthy interpersonal interactions, and may in fact be an important component of self-understanding as defined by modern dynamic theorists, this ability alone fails to do justice to the complexity of the construct of self-understanding.

CONCLUDING COMMENTS

Given the importance of insight in the theoretical literature, it is surprising that so little effort has been made over the past 40 years to operationalize the construct and test its relevance to psychotherapy outcome. Among the investigations undertaken, methodological problems abound. Many investigations failed to establish content validity in the instruments implemented, including several studies that did not explicitly define the construct (Buckley et al., 1984; Luborsky et al., 1980; Sifneos, 1984).

Furthermore, Mann and Mann (1959), Kelman and Parloff (1957), Raingruber (2000), Smith (1959), and Tolor and Reznikoff (1960) did not use definitions that adequately captured the domain of insight. Whereas Tolor and Reznikoff defined self-understanding as the ability to understand the views of others, the other three investigations defined self-understanding as the degree of congruence between self-concept and how others view the individual. In the case of Kelman and Parloff, it is not clear whether group members' ratings were influenced by their own interpersonal problems and thus fell short of being an objective assessment. Mann and Mann did not specify to whose view the patient's self-concept was being compared. Raingruber asserted that self-understanding can only develop if the patient believes that the therapist is economizing the importance of his or her emotional issues. In either case, the criterion against which the patient's view is compared seems suspect. Clearly, such assessments do not adequately assess the patient's understanding of his or her own interpersonal patterns. Of those investigations that provided adequate construct definitions, many methodological problems exist. Many investigations have failed to establish instrument reliability or have relied on single-item ratings (Buckley et al., 1984; Hoffart et al., 2002; Husby et al., 1985; Luborsky, 1962; Rosenbaum et al., 1956; Sifneos, 1984).

Our examination of the empirical literature reveals that, consistent with the variability and ambiguity found in the theoretical literature on insight, few empirical studies have adequately defined or operationalized the construct of insight. Many studies failed to achieve content validity as described by Cronbach and Meehl (1955). Specifically, many investigations attempted to explore the construct of insight yet failed to explicitly define the construct of interest. In addition, the lack of an adequate definition in each of these investigations is evident by the implementation of measures that fail to do justice to the full complexity of the construct suggested by the clinical and theoretical literature.

The diversity of the definitions of the construct used in these investigations, along with the methodological flaws discussed, make it difficult to draw any firm conclusions regarding the role of insight in psychotherapy. It is noteworthy that a review of the insight literature published over 30 years ago arrived at the same conclusion (Roback, 1974), namely that efforts are needed to more precisely define and operationalize the construct. However, despite the methodological problems in the measurement of insight, inconsistencies across studies, and lack of studies providing definitive tests of clinical theories about insight, we can offer the following tentative conclusions from the research literature.

First, it appears that pretreatment levels of patient insightfulness are not particularly relevant to the outcome of psychotherapy. In contrast, the amount of gain in insight over the course of treatment, regardless of where one begins, is associated with improvement in psychotherapy. Although clinical lore has held that insightful patients are good candidates for psychodynamic psychotherapy in particular, perhaps such insightful patients are simply more satisfying to have as patients. It may be that such preexisting insightfulness can be used to facilitate intellectualization as a defense, effectively avoiding the real issues and keeping the therapist off track.

The studies documenting that change in insight is associated with longer-term treatment outcome (Hoglend et al., 1994; Kivilighan et al., 2000; Vargas, 1954) are encouraging in terms of validating the general clinical belief about the role of insight in psychotherapy. Indeed, entire schools of psychotherapy have been based on the importance of insight as a curative factor. Despite findings that are generally supportive of the value of insight in psychotherapy, research has only begun to scratch the surface in understanding how and to what degree insight is a primary mechanism of therapeutic change.

One central question that has not been addressed is whether the task of therapy is to make patients generally more insightful, or whether what is crucial is obtaining insight about one or a few central issues. Arguments could be made for both types of gains in insight. Psychotherapy may function, in part, by teaching the skills of acquiring insight—questioning one's motives, searching for connections between the past and present or between different people or events, and exploring the meaning of emotionally significant dreams, interpersonal interactions, and memories. To the extent that such skills are acquired, there is a greater likelihood that an important specific insight is obtained, leading to improvements in symptoms and functioning. Thus, both gains in general insight (reflecting increased skills at obtaining insight) and specific insights about emotionally charged issues may lead to therapeutic change.

Further, more research is needed to evaluate interventions designed to facilitate insight within psychotherapy. Although studies evaluating the frequency of interpretation report mixed findings, studies evaluating the accuracy (Crits-Cristoph et al., 1988; Piper et al., 1993; Silberschatz et al., 1986) and competence (Barber et al., 1996) of interpreting interpersonal patterns consistently show a relation between the quality of dynamic interpretations and treatment outcome. Theoretically, these studies suggest that well-timed competent interpretations within dynamic psychotherapies lead to gains in patient insight. These gains in insight lead patients to new, more adaptive behaviors that result in symptom alleviation. Although these investigations are promising in suggesting the importance of gains in insight within psychotherapy, further research is needed to validate the mechanism through which high quality interpretations lead to symptom reduction.

In the scientific study of insight, little progress has been made in measuring the types of specific insights about emotionally relevant interpersonal themes. The scale developed by Connolly, Crits-Christoph, and Shelton, et al. (1999) that assesses self-understanding of interpersonal patterns appears to be a promising step in this direction. Even with this scale, patients receive scores based on their insight about a range of interpersonal themes. It may be necessary to tailor the assessment of insight directly to the most salient issues for each patient. However, there are practical difficulties in designing such a highly patient-specific assessment approach. Questionnaire methods that by design cannot be highly ideographic will continue to have a place in research on insight on the basis of their convenience and ease of use.

In addition to better assessment methods, future research on insight would benefit from research designs that allow for stronger tests of whether achieving insight is causally related to improvements in symptoms and functioning. At the least, it would be important to determine the direction of potential causation. This would involve ensuring that the changes in insight precede change in symptoms and functioning. None of the reviewed studies attended to this issue directly. Part of the problem is knowing the ideal time points for sampling changes in insight and changes in symptoms and functioning. It may be that insights occurring over several months of therapy have their greatest impact years into the future, when patients reencounter similar circumstances (e.g., similar relationships or traumas). Alternatively, it may be that the lag between achieving an insight and positive impact on symptoms is a matter of hours or days. Without assessing the correct time course for these events, it is difficult to sort out the possible causal effects between insight and other outcomes.

In addition to time precedence, a major problem with correlational studies, of course, is the possibility of third variables that might explain apparent correlational findings. Investigators should attempt to measure potential third variables such as early improvement (which leads to both insight and final change, thereby potentially introducing a spurious correlation between insight and final change), degree of involvement in therapy, catharsis, persuasion by the therapist, and other process variables. The relation of gains in insight to outcome could then be examined by statistically controlling for the influence of these third variables. Ideally, if more could be learned about how best to assess insight and the types of outcomes that are most affected when insights are achieved, experimental tests could be performed to more effectively rule out third variables. Until then, it will be difficult for research on insight to advance at a faster pace. Nevertheless, the literature that exists has provided us with a roadmap and some insight about how best to investigate this elusive yet crucial facet of psychotherapy.

REFERENCES

Barber, J., Crits-Christoph, P., & Luborsky, L. (1996). Effects of therapist adherence on patient outcome in brief dynamic therapy. *Journal of Consulting and Clinical Psychology, 64,* 619–622.

Buckley, P., Conte, H. R., Plutchik, R., Wild, K. W., & Karasu, T. B. (1984). Psychodynamic variables as predictors of psychotherapy outcome. *American Journal of Psychiatry, 141,* 742–748.

Burstein, E. D., Coyne, L., Kernberg, O. F., & Voth, H. (1972). The quantitative study: Psychotherapy outcome. *Bulletin of the Menninger Clinic, 36,* 1–59.

Connolly, M. B., Crits-Christoph, P., Shappell, S., Barber, J. P., & Luborsky, L. (1998). Therapist interventions in early sessions of brief supportive–expressive psychotherapy for depression. *Journal of Psychotherapy Practice and Research, 7,* 290–300.

Connolly, M. B., Crits-Christoph, P., Shelton, R. C., Hollon, S., Kurtz, J., & Barber, J. P. (1999). The reliability and validity of a measure of self-understanding of interpersonal patterns. *Journal of Counseling Psychology, 46,* 472–482.

Connolly, M. B., Crits-Christoph, P., Shappell, S., Barber, J. P., Luborsky, L., & Shaffer, C. (1999). Relation of transference interpretations to outcome in the early sessions of brief supportive–expressive psychotherapy. *Psychotherapy Research, 9,* 485–495.

Crits-Christoph, P. (1984). *The development of a measure of self-understanding of core relationship themes.* Paper presented at NIMH workshop on methodological challenges in psychodynamic research, Washington, DC.

Crits-Christoph, P., Cooper, A., & Luborsky, L. (1988). The accuracy of therapists' interpretations and the outcome of dynamic psychotherapy. *Journal of Consulting and Clinical Psychology, 56,* 490–495.

Cronbach, L., & Meehl, P. (1955). Construct validity in psychological tests. *Psychological Bulletin, 52,* 281–302.

Diemer, R. A., Lobell, L. K., Vivino, B. L., & Hill, C. E. (1996). Comparison of dream interpretation, event interpretation, and unstructured sessions in brief therapy. *Journal of Counseling Psychology, 43,* 99–112.

Dymond, R. F. (1948). A preliminary investigation of the relation of insight and empathy. *Journal of Consulting Psychology, 12,* 228–233.

Elliott, R. (1984). A discovery-oriented approach to significant change events in psychotherapy: Interpersonal process recall and comprehensive process analysis. In L. Rice & L. Greenberg (Eds.), *Patterns of change: Intensive analysis of psychotherapy process* (pp. 249–286). New York: Guilford Press.

Elliott, R., & James, E. (1989). Varieties of client experience in psychotherapy: An analysis of the literature. *Clinical Psychology Review, 9,* 443–467.

Elliott, R., Shapiro, D. A., Firth-Cozens, J., Stiles, W. B., Hardy, G. E., Llewelyn, S. P., & Margison, F. R. (1994). Comprehensive process analysis of insight events in cognitive–behavioral and psychodynamic–interpersonal psychotherapies. *Journal of Counseling Psychology, 41,* 449–463.

Foreman, S. A., & Marmar, C. R. (1985). Therapist actions that address initially poor therapeutic alliances in psychotherapy. *American Journal of Psychiatry, 142,* 922–926.

Gelso, C. J., Kivlighan, D. M., Wine, B., Jones, A., & Friedman, S. C. (1997). Transference, insight, and the course of time-limited therapy. *Journal of Counseling Psychology, 44,* 209–217.

Grande, T., Rudolf, G., Oberbracht, C., & Pauli-Magnus, C. (2003). Progressive changes in patients' lives after psychotherapy: Which treatment effects support them? *Psychotherapy Research, 13,* 43–58.

Hill, C. E., Helms, J. E., Tichenor, V., & Spiegel, S. B. (1988). Effects of the therapist response modes in brief psychotherapy. *Journal of Counseling Psychology, 35,* 222–233.

Hoffart, A., Versland, S., & Sexton, H. (2002). Self-understanding, empathy, guided discovery, and schema belief in schema-focused cognitive therapy of personality problems: A process-outcome study. *Cognitive Therapy and Research, 26*, 199–219.

Hoglend, P. (1993). Transference interpretations and long-term change after dynamic psychotherapy of brief to moderate length. *American Journal of Psychotherapy, 47*, 494–507.

Hoglend, P., Engelstad, V., Sorbye, O., Heyerdahl, O., & Amlo, S. (1994). The role of insight in exploratory psychodynamic psychotherapy. *British Journal of Medical Psychology, 67*, 305–317.

Husby, R., Dahl, A. A., Dahl, C. I., Heiberg, A. N., Olafsen, O. M., & Weisarth, L. (1985). Short-term dynamic psychotherapy: The Oslo group's form to score outcome, the reliability testing of this form and observer characteristics. *Psychotherapy & Psychosomatics, 43*, 1–7.

Kelman, H. C., & Parloff, M. B. (1957). Interrelations among three criteria of improvement in group therapy: Comfort, effectiveness, and self-awareness. *Journal of Abnormal and Social Psychology, 54*, 281–288.

Kivlighan, D. M., Multon, K. D., & Patton, M. J. (2000). Insight and symptom reduction in time-limited psychoanalytic counseling. *Journal of Counseling Psychology, 47*, 50–58.

Luborsky, L. (1962). The patient's personality and psycho-therapeutic change. In H. Strupp & L. Luborsky (Eds.) *Research in psychotherapy* (Vol. 2, pp. 115–133). Washington, DC: American Psychological Association.

Luborsky, L. (1984). *Principles of psychoanalytic psychotherapy: A manual for supportive–expressive treatment.* New York: Basic Books.

Luborsky, L., Crits-Christoph, P., Mintz, J., & Auerbach, A. (1988). *Who will benefit from psychotherapy?* New York: Basic Books.

Luborsky, L., Mintz, J., Auerbach, A., Christoph P., Bachrach, H., Todd, T., et al. (1980). Predicting the outcome of psychotherapy: Findings of the Penn psychotherapy project. *Archives of General Psychiatry, 37*, 471–481.

Malan, D. H. (1976). *Towards the validation of dynamic psychotherapy: Replication.* New York: Plenum Press.

Mann, J. H., & Mann, C. H. (1959). Insight as a measure of adjustment in three kinds of group experience. *Journal of Consulting Psychology, 23*, 91.

Morgan, R., Luborsky, L., Crits-Christoph, P., Curtis, H., & Solomon, J. (1982). Predicting the outcomes of psychotherapy by the Penn Helping Alliance rating method. *Archives of General Psychiatry, 39*, 397–402.

Norville, R., Sampson, H., & Weiss, J. (1996). Accurate interpretations and brief psychotherapy outcome. *Psychotherapy Research, 6*(1), 16–29.

Piper, W. E., Azim, H. F., Joyce, A. S., & McCallum, M. (1991). Transference interpretations, therapeutic alliance, and outcome in short-term individual psychotherapy. *Archives of General Psychiatry, 48*, 946–953.

Piper, W. E., Debbane, E. G., de Carufel, F. L., & Bienvenu, J. P. (1987). A system for differentiating therapist interpretations from other interventions. *Bulletin of the Menninger Clinic, 51,* 532–550.

Piper, W. E., Joyce, A. S., McCallum, M., & Azim, H. F. (1993). Concentration and correspondence of transference interpretations in short-term psychotherapy. *Journal of Consulting and Clinical Psychology, 61,* 586–595.

Raingruber, B. (2000). Being with feelings as a recognition practice: Developing clients' self-understanding. *Perspectives in Psychiatric Care, 36,* 41–50.

Roback, H. R. (1974). Insight: A bridge of the theoretical and research literatures. *The Canadian Psychologist, 15*(1), 61–88.

Rosenbaum, M., Friedlander, J., & Kaplan, S. M. (1956). Evaluation of results of psychotherapy. *Psychosomatic Medicine, 18,* 113–132.

Shechtman, Z. (2003). Therapeutic factors and outcomes in group and individual therapy of aggressive boys. *Group Dynamics: Theory, Research, and Practice, 7,* 225–237.

Shechtman, Z., & Ben-David, M. (1999). Individual and group psychotherapy of childhood aggression: A comparison of outcomes and processes. *Group Dynamics: Theory, Research, and Practice, 3,* 263–274.

Sifneos, P. E. (1984). Short-term dynamic psychotherapy for patients with physical symptomatology. *Psychotherapy and Psychosomatics, 42,* 48–51.

Silberschatz, G., Fretter, P. B., & Curtis, J. T. (1986). How do interpretations influence the process of psychotherapy? *Journal of Consulting and Clinical Psychology, 54,* 646–652.

Smith, E. E. (1959). Defensiveness, insight, and the K scale. *Journal of Consulting Psychology, 23,* 275–277.

Stiles, W. B. (1979). Verbal response modes and psychotherapeutic technique. *Psychiatry, 42,* 49–62.

Stiles, W. B., Shapiro, D. A., & Firth-Cozens, J. A. (1988). Verbal response mode use in contrasting psychotherapies: A within-subject comparison. *Journal of Consulting and Clinical Psychology, 54,* 646–652.

Strupp, H. H., & Binder, J. L. (1984). *Psychotherapy in a new key: A guide to time-limited psychotherapy.* New York: Basic Books.

Tolor, A., & Reznikoff, M. (1960). A new approach to insight: A preliminary report. *The Journal of Nervous and Mental Disease, 130,* 286–296.

Vargas, M. J. (1954). Changes in self-awareness during client-centered therapy. In C. R. Rogers & R. F. Dymond (Eds.), *Psychotherapy and personality change* (pp. 145–166). Chicago: University of Chicago Press.

8

DECODING INSIGHT TALK: DISCOURSE ANALYSES OF INSIGHT IN ORDINARY LANGUAGE AND IN PSYCHOTHERAPY

ROBERT ELLIOTT

Many linguists, from Whorf (1956) to more recent social construction-ists such as Gergen (1999), have persistently argued that language powerfully constrains human experience. It does this largely through the words and metaphors available to speakers in a particular culture for representing and communicating their experiences. The purpose of this chapter is to describe some of the linguistic resources available to people in our culture (with a few examples from other cultures) for discussing experiences of self-related in-sight. These resources include a stock of words for insight and related experi-ences, the syntax in which those words are embedded, and the underlying metaphors implicit in the stock of words. A close analysis of insight discourse should pay dividends in two ways: First, it will reduce conceptual confusion, thus fostering better theories and research. Second, it will further the under-standing of people's experience of insight, which will facilitate the ability to track what clients get out of therapy.

In modern Western societies, the concept of insight is central to shared cultural understandings of the institution of psychotherapy. The cultural script, fed by more a century of media presentations of therapy (cf. Brandell, 2004), emphasizes insight into connections between past trauma and current problems as the central change process in psychotherapy. But what is insight? And how do speakers in our culture accomplish discourses that recognizably exemplify this cultural script? Using the methods of discourse analysis (DA), these questions can be approached from different angles, including deconstruction of general language usage (standard dictionary definitions, etymology, and synonyms) and examination of texts in which clients describe specific insights in their treatments. I offer examples of both of these in this chapter.

DA (van Dijk, 1997a, 1997b) is a family of related analytic methods that involve close examination of texts to clarify their structures, the strategies used to construct them, and the implicit assumptions embedded in them. In this chapter I apply DA to very different sorts of data. First, I use *lexical–metaphor analysis*, commonly associated with Lakoff and Johnson (1980, 1999), to identify the implicit metaphors embedded in the vocabulary used to talk about insight in ordinary language. Second, I use a slightly broader set of tools to analyze clients' accounts of particular insight events in their therapies. Overall, these analyses are intended to clarify the cultural resources used by clients to construct talk about important experiences in therapy. Deriving as they do from linguistics, these methods typically use a single analyst, but offer proof by example, encouraging readers to critically evaluate the author's interpretations for themselves.

To more fully appreciate the results of the analyses reported, it is important to review what I brought to this investigation. Most important, over several earlier studies my colleagues and I investigated clients' experiences of insight events in therapy, developing an event-based definition of therapeutic insight. In Elliott (1984), I used an analysis of how four clients spoke about important moments of insight in their therapy to describe the four major elements that appeared to be part of prototypical insight: (a) *metaphorical vision*, referring to seeing with figurative eyes (e.g., "It made me see I have a tremendous conflict there"); (b) *connection*, or perceiving patterns or links (e.g., "He really put together all the pieces"); (c) *suddenness* (e.g., "I was sort of amazed. Wow!"), often with a sensation of something "clicking"; and (d) *newness*, the sense of discovering something not previously known (e.g., "It was just something I never thought about that she presented"). This last element, *newness*, was salient in client accounts (see Elliott, 1985), but appears to have been slighted in dictionary and scientific definitions (e.g., Morris, 1981).

An important issue identified in this study (see Elliott, 1985) was the distinction between insight and awareness. I argued that the four elements of insight described contrast neatly with features of the closely related phenomenon of awareness. In this formulation, awareness events are typically described using tactile or *somesthetic* metaphors (getting in touch with feelings); they appear generally to involve an increase in the *salience* (presence or accessibility) of discrete elements of experience (memories, feelings, images). Awareness usually involves *gradual* assimilation of *old* (often avoided or ignored) elements of experience. Thus, although recognizing that insight and awareness are to some extent fuzzy categories organized around prototypes and partially overlapping in meaning, on the basis of my previous research I approached the present analyses with the assumption that they would be distinguishable using these four features.

METAPHOR ANALYSIS OF ORDINARY INSIGHT LANGUAGE

An important and underappreciated approach to DA is the analysis of general language use, including dictionary definitions, synonyms, slang, and etymology. The idea is that ordinary language embeds millennia of attempts by speakers to symbolize particular experiences, especially using metaphors (Austin, 1970; Elliott, in press; Lakoff & Johnson, 1999). Thus, my first approach to understanding insight discourse was to look at the range of ordinary language that people have used to talk about it. After all, this is what therapy clients draw on in constructing accounts of their therapy experiences. The method is closely related to conceptual analysis methods described by Lakoff and Johnson (1980, 1999). It begins by creating a corpus of language used to discuss an abstract concept such as *self* or *morality*. Synonym lists, thesauruses, and slang dictionaries are used to generate a list of words or phrases that mean roughly the same thing. Each word or phrase is analyzed for its current metaphoric content; its etymology is then analyzed, tracing it back whenever possible to its earliest roots in Proto–Indo–European, a reconstructed language spoken 6,000 to 7,000 years ago (Watkins, 1981) to determine the concrete metaphor on which the term was originally based. As is the case with other forms of DA, a single analyst was used; however, the reader is urged to consult the examples given as well as the primary data (available in the sources cited).

The Insight Metaphor

Today, the word *insight* is commonly understood as the act or ability to see into oneself or others. Thus, the person is viewed as similar to a dark or opaque container (Lakoff & Johnson, 1980) to be illumined and visually probed. However, the original meaning of the word, dating from around 1200 CE, appears to have been the possession of a metaphorical *internal sight*, that is, the ability see "with the eyes of the mind or understanding" (*Oxford English Dictionary* [OED], 1989). Thus, it was conceived of as a kind of second sight and had spiritual or even magical connotations. It was much later, around 1600 CE, that the word came to refer to seeing the inner character or nature of things, the usage that was eventually adopted by psychology in the early 20th century. However, it may be that some of our continuing fascination with the concept of insight derives from its former connection to religion and magic.

Synonyms and Etymologies in English and Other Languages

Common English language synonyms for insight as a state or capacity include *wisdom, profundity, sagaciousness, sagacity, sageness,* and *sapience,* which refer to "deep, thorough, or mature understanding"; or *intuition, instinct, intuitiveness,* which refer to the "power to discern the true nature of a person or situation" (Morris, 1981). A longer list adds a mixture of state–capacity and event words (e.g., *click, understanding, acumen*).

Similarly, the main index words for insight in other languages commonly refer to either seeing into or through something (e.g., German *Einsicht,* Spanish *perspicacia*) or penetrating into something (e.g., French *penetration,* Russian *pronitsatyelnost*). An exception is the Hebrew *binah,* which derives from *build* (Mechon Mamre, 2004; see Elliott, in press, for construction metaphors in verbs of knowing). Most of these words refer to the state or capacity sense of insight. Words in other languages referring specifically to insight as an event are rarer, but include the French *aperçu* (from *perceive + to*), a revealing glimpse of something (Corréard & Grundy, 1995); the Russian *prozreniye* (from *to see through*), which refers to insight as a sudden regaining of one's vision (Katzner, 1994); the classical Greek, *epiphaneia,* originally a sudden manifestation or shining forth (Morris, 1981) but now used to refer to a moment of sudden illumination; and the Japanese *dousatsu,* which originally referred to a conjecture about what is hidden in a cave (Haig, 1997). All four of these insight event words rely directly or indirectly on visual metaphor.

After assembling a list of 34 English synonyms and slang terms for insight and 14 non-English or computer jargon (e.g., *grok*) words, I analyzed the origins of each and organized their root metaphors into open categories. This analysis is shown in Exhibit 8.1, which organizes the metaphoric insight terms in this collection into categories corresponding to the different types of primary sensory-motor experience found in their etymologies (cf. Lakoff & Johnson, 1999). There appear to be three main root metaphors: Perceiving/Sensing, Entering/Penetrating, and Coming Into Possession. The three main categories roughly correspond to insight as a special kind of perceptual process, as a psychological movement, and as a mental object. (For an additional small group of miscellaneous unrelated terms, see Exhibit 8.1.)

Insight as a Special Kind of Perceptual Process

Perceiving/Sensing is the most common category of insight language, with subcategories of Being Conscious/Watching. Perceiving/Sensing meta-

EXHIBIT 8.1
Insight-Related Language: Root Metaphors and Examples

A. Perceiving/Sensing: in general: *sagacity, sageness, sapience, savvy* (slang), *awareness, satori* (perceive, wake up)
   1. Being Conscious/Watching
      a. Waking Up: *satori* (spoken Japanese), *buddha*
      b. Guarding/Protecting: *awareness, observation*
   2. Sensing
      a. Seeing/Looking/Observing: *wise/wisdom, intuition, enlightenment, hip/hip to* (slang), *perspicacity, vision, zen* (jargon), *see the light* (slang), *flash on it* (slang), *second sight, have one's eyes opened, insight, Einsicht* (German), *perspicacia* (Spanish), *aperçu* (French), *prozreniye* (Russian), *zen* (computer jargon)
      b. Shining/Showing: *epiphany/epiphaneia* [classical Greek]
      c. Tasting/Drinking: *sage/sageness, sapience, savvy, grok* (invented/jargon)
      d. Poking/Prodding (with a stick or sharp object): *instinct, acumen*
      e. Picking Out/Discriminating: *discernment*
B. Entering/Penetrating
   1. Proximity/Into-ness/Similarity: *understand* (1: to stand under another), *intuition, instinct, insight, satori* (Japanese kanji: to know in your heart), *Einsicht* (German), *dousatsu* (Japanese), *astute* (from practicing a craft learned from living in a town), *on the same wavelength* (slang), *be with it* (slang)
   2. Penetration/Through-ness: *penetration* (also French), *pronitsatyelnost* (Russian), *aperçu* (French: current meaning)
   3. Depth/Bottom-ness: *Profundity, understand* (2: to know what stands under something, i.e., its foundation)
C. Coming Into Possession
   1. Seizing/Taking: *comprehension, apprehension, grasp, perception/perceptivity/perceptiveness, aperçu* (French: etymology), *I got it* (slang), *it just came to me* (slang)
   2. Being Pushed/Hit From Outside: *get one's drift* (slang), *it hit me* (slang)
      a. From the Sky/God: *divination* (divine influence)
D. Miscellaneous Unrelated Terms: *Aha!* reaction (imitative, slang: surprise expression), *click* (imitative, slang: sound of something falling into place); *judgment* (legal: from showing/pronouncing); *shrewdness* (animal folklore: a small evil animal); *binah* (Hebrew: to build)

Note. Most of the words in this table were collected from the *American Heritage Dictionary* (AHD, Morris, 1981), *Roget's New Millennium Thesaurus* (2006), *Roget's International Thesaurus* (Chapman, 1977), or *The Random House Thesaurus of Slang* (Lewin & Lewin, 1988). Root metaphors were mostly obtained from the AHD, including the Indo–European Roots Index. Some words appear in multiple places, reflecting different stages of word history or derivation.

phors are most common, with visual forms of sensing most common: Seeing/Looking/Observing (e.g., *wise, see the light*). Less expected sensing metaphors are the tactile Poking/Prodding, as with a sharp stick (*instinct*), and the gustatory Tasting/Drinking. The most unusual example of the latter is the invented word *grok*, from Heinlein's 1961 science fiction novel, *Stranger in a Strange Land*, supposedly derived from a Martian word that originally meant *to drink*. More conventionally, a smaller number of words exemplify the subcategory Being Conscious/Watching (including *awareness* and the spoken Japanese *satori*).

Insight as a Psychological Movement

The second main category is Entering/Penetrating, made up of various ways of expressing the idea that insight is analogous to moving toward, into the midst of, or to the bottom of something (e.g., the *in* in *insight*; also both possible original meanings of *understand*; see Elliott, in press). Entering/Penetrating can also be semantically linked to Perceiving/Sensing because it is often the route or result of Perceiving/Sensing; that is, what is perceived in insight is not on the surface but rather hidden inside, in the middle, or at the bottom. In this way, insight can be viewed as a destination arrived at through some kind of journey (cf. Pieracci, 1990).

Insight as a Mental Object

The third main category is Coming Into Possession, most commonly by an active process of Seizing/Taking (e.g., *comprehension, it just came to me*). However, there are also examples of a more passive process of Being Pushed/Hit From Outside, best exemplified by the slang *it hit me*. Interestingly, Coming Into Possession is a common metaphor for Perceiving/Sensing (e.g., *perception*, from *through* + *seize*), thus linking the two categories together. In other words, insight can be metaphorically expressed as Coming Into Possession. What is possessed is an insight, which the client can then put into words and figuratively carry out of the session. This is an example of Lakoff and Johnson's (1980) *ontological metaphor*, that is, the conversion of processes or qualities into metaphoric things to make them easier to handle.

Thus, most insight words analyzed can be organized around the core concept of Perceiving/Sensing and two complementary visions of what it means to perceive or sense something. The sensing involved in insight can be seen as originating from a state in which the person is separated from something they seek to know; they are metaphorically outside what they want to know, and so they do not own it and they cannot sense it (Lakoff & Johnson, 1999). Being metaphorically blind or asleep, they lack possession or contact with what they do not understand. At the same time, they cannot get past the surface of what they do not know and are blind to its inner nature. Insight occurs when individuals open their eyes (or other senses) or awake from sleep, and thus enter into what they seek to know, getting below the surface and at the same time possessing the knowledge that had eluded them. In its most culturally general sense, this is a version of the Quest archetype (Pieracci, 1990): a process of exploring outer and inner worlds, passing through obstacles until one finally penetrates the mystery and comes into possession of something special and transforming. This is the general process pointed to by the implicit metaphors in this collection of insight language.

AN ANALYSIS OF CLIENT ACCOUNTS OF INSIGHT EVENTS

How do clients in therapy make use of the cultural resources found in the stock of insight words and metaphors? How do they use these materials to construct accounts of actual insight events? I now turn to a different form of DA, one that examines a corpus of client-derived accounts of significant therapy events. An interesting feature of this collection is that they are derived from process–experiential (PE) therapy (Greenberg, Rice, & Elliott, 1993), a treatment that typically views insight with some distrust. Like other experiential–humanistic therapies (e.g., Gestalt; Perls, 1969), PE therapy distinguishes between awareness and insight and favors the former. In addition to being to a certain extent anti-insight, PE is a noninterpretive therapy. This means that PE therapists do not talk about insight and do not try to encourage it in their clients by offering interpretations. In this way, the therapy offers excellent conditions for studying the spontaneous emergence of insight accounts from the clients themselves with little or no direct therapist encouragement.

This analysis draws on a collection of 100 significant therapy events identified and described by clients in the University of Toledo Experiential Therapy of Depression Project (1986–1991). Forty-nine clients were diagnosed with major depressive disorder, were seen for 12 to 24 sessions of PE therapy, and produced one or more significant therapy events for this study. They were seen by seven graduate students in clinical psychology as well as a postdoctoral fellow and the author. In the following paragraphs I describe the method used to study a collection of client-described insight events, offer examples of these events, and present analyses of the insight words and more general insight metaphors used, which leads to a comparison of insight versus awareness discourse in this collection of events.

Helpful Aspects of Therapy Form

After each session, clients completed the Helpful Aspects of Therapy Form (HAT; Elliott, Slatick, & Urman, 2001), in which they were asked to describe in their own words (a) the event in the session that they felt was the most *helpful* and (b) what made it helpful. This self-report form typically produces brief accounts of specific within-session significant therapy events (Elliott & Shapiro, 1988).

Selection of Insight Events

Every four sessions, a researcher interviewed the client by playing a video of the session so he or she could identify a significant event (*brief structured recall*; Elliott & Shapiro, 1988). As part of this interview, the client rated the presence of 16 therapeutic reactions including personal insight using a 5-point scale; after this, she or he selected the most important reaction. Next, the therapist viewed the client-selected event and rated the client's likely reactions on the same instrument, again selecting the most important reaction. One month later, client and therapist each reviewed the event and once again rated the client's reactions and selected the most important reaction. To qualify as having had an insight event, the client had to have selected personal insight as the most important reaction, either right after the session or a month later; furthermore, the insight classification had to be confirmed either by its being (a) selected most important on a second measurement (client at a different time, or therapist at either time) or (b) rated as at least moderately present (rating of 3 or greater) in at least two other measurements (Elliott & Shapiro, 1988).

This procedure identified 19 insight events, involving 13 clients. However, when I read the clients' HAT descriptions of these events, it seemed clear from my perspective as an experiential therapist and from my previous research that only 7 were clearly and recognizably accounts of insight events. Although they did not include all four features of visual metaphor, newness, suddenness, and connection (presented at the beginning of this chapter), these events felt similar to descriptions of the prototypical insight events. The other 12 events were less clear but from their descriptions sounded like awareness events (see Elliott, 1989), even though the clients and therapists rated insight as the most important client reaction. Exhibit 8.2 (text sections) presents two examples; one is a description of a clearly marked insight event, the other an awareness-marked insight event. (The full set of event descriptions may be obtained by writing to the author.)

My first finding was that many of these clients had a broader definition than mine in that they perceived insight in situations that did not necessarily involve newness, suddenness, connection, or visual metaphor. This result raises several questions that I address in the rest of this chapter: (a) What linguistic markers was I using to distinguish between insight and awareness in these event descriptions; (b) what did the clients see in common in these two sets of events that led them to rate both as insight events; and (c) should I (and my experientially oriented colleagues) adopt a broader definition of insight?

Examples of Insight- and Awareness-Marked Insight Events

To illustrate the analysis, two examples are presented in Exhibit 8.2: an insight-marked insight event and an awareness-marked insight event. Client 59 (Exhibit 8.2, Part A) is a woman with depression who had the best overall outcome in the study, and this clearly marked insight event tied together two of her main issues—her unresolved grief over her mother's death and conflicts with her adolescent daughter. The analyses of her significant event

EXHIBIT 8.2
Examples of Discourse Analysis of Two Client Descriptions
of Insight Events

A. Insight-marked insight event, Client 59, Session 6:
   1. Text: *(Question: Which event was most helpful?)* "When we were talking about my mother and myself, and about my daughter, J., & myself." *(Question: What made this event helpful?)* "It made me realize that after my mother died, I put all my energy into my relationship with J. That I passed from a daughter–mother relationship to a mother–daughter relationship."
   2. Lexical markers/metaphors (words used to describe reaction):
      a. *It made me*: external force as origin of experience
      b. *realize*: to make real, bring into being
      c. "that I *passed* from X relationship to Y relationship": relationships are sequential locations on the same journey through life (relationship parallel/transition; layperson's transference account)
B. Awareness-marked insight event, Client 70, Session 23 (includes material added during recall session):
   1. Text: "During the session we got in touch with my core, and allowed it to surface. There is a side of my personality I never let anybody see. We let it come out. It allowed me to see what my basic self is really like and how it felt, how it felt about the world in general."
   2. Lexical markers–metaphors:
      a. *We allowed, we let it*: collective action, permission/approval
      b. *Got in touch + with my core*: possession, tactile, depth metaphors
      c. "Allowed it to *surface*," "let it *come out*": containment/visual metaphor: in/hiding versus out/showing
      d. "Allowed me to *see what* my *basic* self is really like": visual metaphor, nature/kind, depth metaphor: base versus top

from Session 6 can be summarized by the following explication of the client's description: "Our discussion acted as an outside force that brought into being a helpful insight in the form of an understanding of an important life transition sequence involving parallel relationship patterns."

The second example comes from Client 70, a man with depression who initially had one of the poorest outcomes after his therapist had to leave to go on internship. (He was given 8 sessions by another therapist, after which he improved substantially; the example event derives from this additional treatment.) His insight-event account (Exhibit 8.2, Part B, from Session 23) contains a mixture of different insight and awareness markers:

> During the session we got in touch with my core, and allowed it to surface. [*added in recall*] There is a side of my personality I never let anybody see. We let it come out. It allowed me to see what my basic self is really like and how it felt, [*added in recall*] how it felt about the world in general.

What distinguishes these two descriptions? First, Client 59 describes her event in more passive, less participatory terms, as something that happened to her; Client 70 used more active, collective language ("we"). Second, Client 59's insight was described as newly emerging into being, whereas Client 70 described an aspect that had been present but hidden (awareness, in my view). Third, Client 59 locates her event in the session by specifically referring to the content of the insight; Client 70 never specifies exactly what it was that he became aware of. Client 59 uses an ontological metaphor (*realize*), but Client 70 uses many different metaphors, some more characteristic of the insight words described earlier (possession, visual, tactile, and depth metaphors), others from a more liberatory discourse of permission and overcoming barriers. Client 59 describes newness and connection and implies suddenness by referring to a specific moment in the session, but visual metaphor is absent. Client 70's description is the opposite: He uses visual metaphor (among others), but there is no connection, newness, or suddenness. If his event is insight, then it is a different kind than hers, bringing the "inside out" rather than making new connections.

Lexical Markers: Insight Words

Using the same methods of lexical and metaphor analysis used earlier in this chapter, I examined the specific words the clients used to describe their insights. I started with the seven insight-marked insight events as these provide easier access to insight discourse and then moved on to the awareness-marked events. (Unless noted, the definitions and etymologies were taken from the *American Heritage Dictionary*, Morris, 1981.) Because the corpus is so small and because I was interested in identifying linguistic *possibilities* used by clients, rather than *typical* usage, words used in even a single event are presented and analyzed.) This corpus yielded more insight than awareness words, which is not surprising given the focus of this study (see also Table 8.1, Part A).

1. *Realize* (+ *that* or *why*)–*really*–*real*. Almost all the insight descriptions (6 out of 7) used the word *realize*. Client 31 (Session 10), gave a typical description: "[The event was] where I realized why it is so hard for me to apologize." Etymologically, the word *realize* comes from *real* plus *-ize*. *Real* refers to the quality of being a fact or genuine and derives from the Latin *res*, meaning *thing* or *matter*. The *-ize* in the word is a suffix used to turn nouns or adjectives into verbs and often refers to the action by which the named thing, process, or state comes into being. Thus, *realizing* is making something real; that is, factual or genuine. Interestingly, the original meaning of *realize* appears to have been converting an idea into external, public existence; however, in the 19th century, American writers began to use the word in the sense of "apprehend[ing] with the clearness or detail of reality; . . . understand[ing] or grasp[ing] clearly" (OED, 1989). This last meaning is close to the definition of awareness used in Elliott (1984, 1985); thus, it is not surprising that *realize* does not uniquely mark insight descriptions. In fact, it was used in 4 of the 12 awareness-discourse insight events. The difference may have to do with whether *realize* is followed by *why* versus *that* or *how* (e.g., Client 117, Session 11: "*Realizing that* I'm beginning to believe in myself").

TABLE 8.1
Discourse Features in Insight-Marked Versus
Awareness-Marked Insight Events

	Insight-marked (*n* = 7)	Awareness-marked (*n* = 12)	Total (*n* = 19)
A. Insight words (lexical markers):			
Realize	6	4	10
Really/reality	2	3	5
(Be)cause	2	5	7
Understand	2	2	4
Find out	1	0	1
Insight (also *new*)	1	0	1
Reason	1	0	1
Aware	0	2	2
B. Insight metaphors (content)			
External force	2	3	5
Spatial movement	1	2	3
Visual	0	2	2
Barrier	1	1	2
Possession	0	1	1
Depth	0	1	1
Tactile	0	1	1
Unburdening	0	1	1
C. Content themes			
Client described interpersonal patterns	5	0	5
Gave a reason/goal	4	0	4
Specific emotions	0	6	6
Presence of type/kind of experience	1	5	6
Responsibility/attribution	0	3	3

The words *really* and *reality*, which share the root *real* with *realize*, also appeared in the accounts, as in "choosing to do what I really want to do" (Client 31, Session 7), and *reality* (Client 3, Session 5, pointed to her mother's approval that "in reality I know I'll never get"). These words occurred in two insight-marked events and in three awareness-marked events.

2. *Why*. Two of the seven descriptions used the conjunction *why*, as in " . . . we were discussing why I seem to procrastinate so badly" (Client 31, Session 7). Used this way, *why* means "the reason, cause or purpose for which," and derives ultimately from the Proto–Indo–European *kwo-*, the source of most of the interrogative forms in Western languages. In this small corpus, *why* is an uncommon but clear insight discourse marker that does not occur in any of the awareness-marked events.

3. *(Be)cause*. Similarly, 2 of the 7 descriptions used the word *cause* to refer to insights. For example, Client 31 (Session 7) used forms of the word twice in a row: " . . . it might be *caused* because in the back of my mind I'm 'rebelling' . . . ." The word *because* is a contraction of *by cause of*. *Cause* originally referred to a *thing* or *matter* in the sense of a side in a dispute (cf. *cause célèbre*). As with *realize*, *because* was found in several awareness descriptions,

but 4 of the 5 were used to explain why the event was important rather than to describe the content of an insight.

4. *Understand.* The phrase *understand*, as in "it made me understand my feelings toward my supervisor" (Client 70, Session 14), was used in 2 insight-marked and 2 awareness-marked descriptions. The origin of the word *understand* and the source of its underlying metaphor (to *stand under*) are obscure, dating back at least to the 9th century CE (Quinion, 2002); in general, it can be said to refer to a way of knowing that relies on active, nonimposing, experience-near interaction with its object, seeking to find its implicit but underlying nature (Elliott, in press).

5. *Find out.* To *find out* is to come upon information after a search, or an example of Lakoff and Johnson's (1999) *knowledge is hunting* metaphor. One insight description (and no awareness descriptions) used this term to portray an insight: "I found out that I 'learned' it [problematic behavior] from both my mom and dad" (Client 31, Session 10). It is a clearly recognizable metaphor for discovering something new and uses the inside-out image illustrated by Client 70's event described earlier.

6. *Insight.* Only one insight description (and no awareness descriptions) referred explicitly to the subject of this chapter, *insight:* "It gives me new insights into [my] relationship with others" (Client 67, Session 6). Perhaps it was too obvious!

7. *Reason.* The word *reason* was also used in a single insight description (and no awareness descriptions): " . . . the reason I had trouble telling employees what to do was that I didn't trust them" (Client 70, Session 14). The word *reason* comes from the Old French *raison*, which in turn derives from the Latin *ratus*, meaning *thought out or considered*; this can be traced back to the Proto–Indo–European *ar-*, *meaning to fit together* (Morris, 1981). The underlying meaning of *reason* is thus *to consider or put together*, which exemplifies the metaphor *knowledge is completing a puzzle*, clearly exemplifying the element of connection I proposed earlier as prototypical of insight. In fact, three other insight-marked events contained descriptions of reasons (see Table 8.1, Part C), but only one actually contained the word.

8. *Aware.* None of the insight-marked accounts used the word *aware*, but 2 awareness-marked accounts did (e.g., Client 9, Session 5: "I became aware of posturing" [in the session]). Today, *aware* means "having knowledge of something"; however, in both its Old English (*gewaer*) and Proto–Indo–European (*wer-*) forms it originally meant *to watch out for*, with the implication of possible danger (the modern English word *guard* comes from the same root).

Summary: Primary Metaphors in Insight Words

This analysis suggests that there is a rich vocabulary for insight. (A more complete analysis of awareness words awaits the investigation of the larger set of awareness events.) The words used to mark insight discourse in these descriptions can be summarized in terms of a set of possible metaphors:

1. Insight Is Answering a Question (*why*).
2. Insight Is Successfully Searching/Seeing (*insight, find out*); in contrast, Lack of Insight Is Being Lost or Blind.
3. Insight Is Entering (*understand*); in contrast, Lack of Insight Is Being Outside.
4. Insight Is Piecing Together/Connecting (*reason*); Lack of Insight Is Disconnectedness.
5. An Insight Is a Thing / Matter (*realize, cause*).
6. Awareness Is Being on Guard (*aware*).

Some of these metaphors correspond to those uncovered in the lexical analysis summarized in Exhibit 8.1: Searching/Seeing, Entering, and Thing/Matter (insight as a Possession). However, the analysis identified three metaphors not found in that analysis: Answering a Question, Piecing Together/Connecting, and Being on Guard. (Given the small size of the corpus, it would be good to try to replicate these.)

Content Markers in Insight and Awareness Accounts

Not all the insight discourse markers in this collection of events took the form of specific words; many took the form of implicit metaphors or themes in the events' content. To identify these I searched through the event texts, looking specifically for instances of the root metaphors in Exhibit 8.1 but also searching for all metaphoric constructions. The results of this analysis are summarized in Table 8.1, Part B.

Insight Metaphors

The most common metaphor was External Force, corresponding to the root metaphor Being Pushed/Hit From Outside (Exhibit 8.1, Part C; e.g., Client 117, Session 11: "*It* makes me feel really good"). This occurred in 5 of the 19 events in the corpus (2 insight-marked and 3 awareness-marked). This metaphor implies that the client is the passive recipient of something that originated outside of him or her.

Clients used a Spatial Movement metaphor in 3 events (1 insight-marked, 2 awareness-marked). As Lakoff and Johnson (1999) noted, this is a common metaphor for time, for intentional action, and for change. Client 59 (Session 6) provided an example of this metaphor when she described her insight into a key pattern in her relationships with her mother and her daughter: "I *passed from* a daughter–mother relationship *to* a mother–daughter relationship." This metaphor was not found in the root metaphor collection extracted from insight synonyms; its closest cousin is the Entering/Penetrating metaphor, which describes a different kind of movement (deeper rather than from one thing to a similar neighbor).

Of the other root metaphors in Exhibit 8.1, only the Visual metaphor occurred in more than one event (2 awareness-marked, but no insight-marked events; see Exhibit 8.2, Part B). One metaphor not uncovered in the earlier analysis, *barrier*, occurred in multiple events (one event in each set; e.g., Client 67, Session 6: "I have built an anti-emotion *wall* around myself," an insight-marked event). Thus, the analysis of this corpus of insight events replicated some of the common stock of word-based insight metaphors in Exhibit 8.1 and added a couple of others.

Insight Versus Awareness Content

Finally, I looked at content markers or themes, the different kinds of event content described by clients (see Table 8.1, Part C). Two content themes clearly distinguished insight-marked events: Five insight-marked events—but none of the awareness-marked events—contained client descriptions of interpersonal patterns (e.g., Client 31, Session 10: "I found out that *I 'learned' it from both my mom and dad*"). In addition, in 4 insight-marked events (vs. no awareness-marked events), clients explained actions or feelings by citing reasons or goals (e.g., Client 70, Session 7: "Realized that the reason I had trouble telling employees what to do was that *I didn't trust them*").

On the other hand, three themes were distinctive of awareness-marked events: First, in six of these events (and no insight-marked events) clients referred to specific emotions (e.g., happiness, guilt, disgust). Second, 5 awareness-marked events (and only one insight-marked event) simply referred to the presence of types of experience, often as part of a *realize that* construction (e.g., Client 103, Session 15: "It made me realize that *I don't like some of my feelings*"). Third, 3 awareness-marked events (and none of the insight-marked events) contained references to responsibility/attribution of blame for events (e.g., Client 128, Session 5: "I have *no control or being responsible* for ownership of my brother's feelings"). In all, 9 of 12 awareness-marked events contained at least one of these three content markers.

DISCUSSION AND IMPLICATIONS

In this chapter, I follow Lakoff and Johnson's (1999) recommended strategy of using multiple methods for identifying the underlying conceptual structure of important cultural categories of experience, in this case the concept of insight. The analysis of culturally preserved metaphors embedded in standard words for insight revealed three main interlocking metaphors: perceiving, entering, and coming into possession. Some client descriptions of insight events contained what sounded like clear insight markers, including the words *realize* or causal language such as *because* (both based on the metaphor *insight is a thing*); moreover, these descriptions included clear content markers (themes), mainly interpersonal patterns and reasons or goals. Many other descriptions, however, sounded more like awareness; these awareness-marked insight events also had distinctive content markers, including references to the presence of specific emotions or other experiences, or attribution of blame. What are the implications of these analyses for the definition of insight, for the understanding of its nature, for further research, and for clinical practice?

Event Discourse Analysis: Broadening the Definition of Insight

In the second part of this chapter I raise three questions. First, what linguistic markers distinguish what appeared to be insight from what sounds (at least to me) more like awareness in this collection of client insight event descriptions? In the analyses, I examine various discourse features in search of the implicit cues I used in my initial, intuitive sorting of insight events into insight- and awareness-marked subtypes. These analyses, summarized in the previous paragraph, suggest that my intuitions were most likely based on a combination of lexical (e.g., *realize*) and content themes, with content themes being most distinctive (e.g., patterns or reasons vs. specific emotions or other experiences).

Second, what did clients see in common in these two sets of events that led them to rate both as insight events? A likely answer lies in the emphasis on newness in the item clients used to rate insight [italics added]: "Realized something *new* about self. I got an insight about myself or understood something *new* about me. I saw a *new* connection or saw why I did or felt something. (Note: There must be a sense of *newness* about the self.)"

This definition, based as it is on earlier work on client insight (Elliott, 1984, 1985), includes the previously noted lexical markers *realize, insight, understand,* and *why*. In addition, *connection* is referred to. However, *newness about self* is the central defining feature. Thus, I think the insight awareness-marked insight events have in common some sense of newness about themselves. For the clients who reported insight-marked insight events, this most often took the form of interpersonal patterns and reasons/goals, content associated with prototypical insights emphasizing connection and explanation (Elliott, 1984). This can be referred to as insight in a narrow sense (Insight-1).

However, in the awareness-marked events, clients also described newness, especially (a) becoming newly aware of the presence of specific experiences, (b) accessing specific emotions they either did not know they had or did not know they had so strongly, or (c) coming to new conclusions about who was responsible for unfortunate situations in their lives (reattribution).

If newness is central and shared across insight events, then this suggests an answer to my third question, whether my definition of insight should be broadened. Although experiential therapists might prefer to call these phenomena awareness, it is clear that clients did not care about such fine distinctions and had no trouble referring to a wider range of experiences as insight (Insight-2)—especially given that we had reminded them to look for newness! The situation is analogous to the common finding in cross-cultural research that apparently similar categories often have significantly different ranges in different cultures. For example, the Hopi folk concept of depression is much broader than the corresponding *Diagnostic and Statistical Manual of Mental Disorders* (4th ed.; American Psychiatric Association, 1994) category (Rogler, 1999). My tentative conclusion is that the narrow definition of insight held by experiential therapists may refer to prototypical instances of insight (Insight-1), but that their clients, and possibly the general population, appear to use a substantially broader definition (Insight-2).

The Nature and Construction of Insight Events

What do the analyses tell about the nature of insight events and their social construction? First, both the general stock of insight words (analyzed for root metaphors) and the client texts (analyzed for root metaphors and content themes) offer a broader range of metaphors for insight than had been previously apparent. Earlier research in this program emphasized the visual metaphor so obvious in the word *insight*; beyond this, these clients and the general population of speakers also implicitly compared insight with perceiving/sensing more broadly, entering/penetrating, coming into possession, answering, connecting, and guarding. It is clear that, as Lakoff and Johnson (1999) noted, speakers have a variety of systems of metaphoric language available for describing experiences of therapeutic insight.

Second, taking metaphors as attempts by people to capture particular experiences in language, it is possible to construct a discourse-based model of the insight event process, approximately along the following lines:

1. Insight starts from a state of being outside a problem or dealing with disconnected problematic elements. This state motivates a question and a process of searching for an answer (while perhaps guarding against danger).
2. This search results in overcoming a barrier or connecting disparate elements together, and thus sensing (seeing, touching) or entering into a new understanding of the problematic experience.
3. The effect is a thing-like answer or possession that the person can work with (store, use, build on).

Although intended primarily as a map of the culturally available possibilities for understanding and describing the experience of insight, this model bears a striking resemblance to the process model in Elliott (1984), which consisted of the three phases of processing, insight, and elaboration. This suggests the possibility that it may also capture something important about clients' process of change in insight events.

Researching Insight Events

The present study (like Elliott, 1984, and Elliott et al., 1994) is based on a small sample of insight events and thus requires further research and replication. However, it comes with the advantage of a baseline of the metaphors available in our stock of insight words. This analysis of a wide range of common synonyms, slang, and translations for the word *insight* complements the analysis of a small set of more intensively analyzed insight texts.

Nevertheless, it would be interesting to examine insight event descriptions in behavioral and psychodynamic therapies to see if there are differences in discourse markers. This would help to overcome the limitation that this study was largely based on my intuitions about what counts as insight discourse. Other English language speakers with different theoretical orientations might come up with different discourse markers. To a certain extent, readers of this chapter can consult the examples in Exhibits 8.1 and 8.2 and judge for themselves, but a more thorough audit would require study of the primary texts (available from the author). In addition, it would be important to investigate the awareness events in the present data set to see how they compare with the insight events. Nevertheless, I hope that I have at least illustrated the potential utility of the various forms of DA for studying significant therapy events.

CONCLUDING COMMENTS

The array of insight discourse presented provides a preliminary map that therapists can use to recognize client insights and also to help clients encode their insights into language. Unfortunately, experiential and humanistic therapists have traditionally viewed insight with skepticism, as not central and possibly even counterproductive. In contrast, the insight events studied here demonstrate that insight does occur in these treatments and can be productive: Some of these events came from the best outcome cases in the study. Nevertheless, it is clear that these clients highly valued the sense of newness they developed in these events. It is also clear that these were not mere intellectual insights but instead were emotionally tinged, personally significant new connections and newly perceived emotional experiences.

Finally, from the point of view of therapist intervention, it is interesting that none of the insight event descriptions analyzed here mentioned therapist contributions. This was very different from the client event descriptions in Elliott et al.'s (1994) study, in which clients in 4 of the 6 insight events in psychodynamic or cognitive–behavioral therapies referred explicitly to specific therapist comments. Although this does not prove that the therapists in this study did not directly contribute to their clients' insights or even interpret them, it clearly raises the possibility that clients in PE therapy can derive important insights on the strength of their own self-exploration process without explicit interpretation or obvious input from therapists. How is this possible? The events analyzed here are consistent with the central model of the change process in PE therapy (Elliott & Greenberg, 1997), which holds that experiential therapies help clients generate new experiences by facilitating a vivid and deeply explored interplay of internal opposites, such as situation and reaction, critic and experiencer, and most fundamentally, reason and feeling.

REFERENCES

American Psychiatric Association. (1994). *Diagnostic and statistical manual of mental disorders* (4th ed.). Washington, DC: Author.

Austin, J. L. (1970). *Philosophical papers* (2nd ed.). New York: Oxford University Press.

Brandell, J. R. (2004). *Celluloid couches, cinematic clients: Psychoanalysis and psychotherapy in the movies.* Albany, NY: SUNY Press.

Chapman, R. L. (1977). *Roget's international thesaurus* (4th ed.). New York: HarperCollins.

Corréard, M. H., & Grundy, V. (Eds.). (1995). *The Oxford–Hachette concise French dictionary.* New York: Oxford University Press.

Elliott, R. (1984). A discovery-oriented approach to significant events in psychotherapy: Interpersonal process recall and comprehensive process analysis. In L. Rice & L. Greenberg (Eds.), *Patterns of change* (pp. 249–286). New York: Guilford Press.

Elliott, R. (1985). Helpful and nonhelpful events in brief counseling interviews: An empirical taxonomy. *Journal of Counseling Psychology, 32,* 307–322.

Elliott, R. (1989). Comprehensive process analysis: Understanding the change process in significant therapy events. In M. Packer & R. B. Addison (Eds.), *Entering the circle: Hermeneutic investigation in psychology* (pp. 165–184). Albany, NY: SUNY Press.

Elliott, R. (in press). A linguistic phenomenology of ways of knowing and its implications for psychotherapy research and psychotherapy integration. *Journal of Psychotherapy Integration.*

Elliott, R., & Greenberg, L. S. (1997). Multiple voices in process–experiential therapy: Dialogues between aspects of the self. *Journal of Psychotherapy Integration, 7,* 225–239.

Elliott, R., & Shapiro, D. A. (1988). Brief structured recall: A more efficient method for identifying and describing significant therapy events. *British Journal of Medical Psychology, 61,* 141–153.

Elliott, R., Shapiro, D. A., Firth-Cozens, J., Stiles, W. B., Hardy, G., Llewelyn, S. P., & Margison, F. (1994). Comprehensive process analysis of insight events in cognitive–behavioral and psychodynamic–interpersonal therapies. *Journal of Counseling Psychology, 41*, 449–463.

Elliott, R., Slatick, E., & Urman, M. (2001). Qualitative change process research on psychotherapy: Alternative strategies. In J. Frommer & D. L. Rennie (Eds.), *Qualitative psychotherapy research: Methods and methodology* (pp. 69–111). Lengerich, Germany: Pabst Science.

Gergen, K. J. (1999). *Invitation to social construction.* Newbury Park, CA: Sage.

Greenberg, L. S., Rice, L. N., & Elliott, R. (1993). *Facilitating emotional change: The moment-by-moment process.* New York: Guilford Press.

Haig, J. H. (1997). *The new Nelson Japanese–English character dictionary.* Rutland, VT: Charles E. Tuttle.

Katzner, K. (1994). *English–Russian, Russian–English dictionary* (Rev. expanded ed.). New York: Wiley.

Kipfer, B. A. (Ed.). (2006). *Roget's new millenium thesaurus.* Los Angeles: Lexico Publishing Group.

Lakoff, G., & Johnson, M. (1980). *Metaphors we live by.* Chicago: University of Chicago Press.

Lakoff, G., & Johnson, M. (1999). *Philosophy in the flesh: The embodied mind and its challenge to Western thought.* New York: Basic Books.

Lewin, E., & Lewin, A. E. (1988). *The Random House thesaurus of slang.* New York: Random House.

Mechon Mamre. (2004). *Hebrew language: Root words.* Retrieved December 17, 2004, from http://www.mechon-mamre.org/jewfaq/root.htm

Morris, W. (Ed.). (1981). *The American Heritage dictionary of the English language.* Boston: Houghton Mifflin.

Oxford English Dictionary (2nd ed.). (1989). New York: Oxford University Press.

Perls, F. S. (1969). *Gestalt therapy verbatim.* Moab, UT: Real People Press.

Pieracci, M. (1990). The mythopoesis of psychotherapy. *Humanistic Psychologist, 18*, 208–224.

Quinion, M. (2002, June 1). *Understand.* Retrieved July 25, 2004, from http://www.worldwidewords.org/qa/qa-und1.htm

Rogler, L. H. (1999). Methodological sources of cultural insensitivity in mental health research. *American Psychologist, 54*, 424–433.

van Dijk, T. A. (Ed.). (1997a). *Discourse as social interaction.* London: Sage.

van Dijk, T. A. (Ed.). (1997b). *Discourse as structure and process.* London: Sage.

Watkins, E. (1981). Indo–European and the Indo–Europeans. In W. Morris (Ed.), *The American Heritage dictionary of the English language* (pp. 1496–1504). Boston: Houghton Mifflin.

Whorf, B. L. (1956). *Language, thought, and reality: Selected writings.* Cambridge, MA: MIT Press.

9

MARGARET'S STORY: AN INTENSIVE CASE ANALYSIS OF INSIGHT AND NARRATIVE PROCESS CHANGE IN CLIENT-CENTERED PSYCHOTHERAPY

LYNNE ANGUS AND KAREN HARDTKE

From a narrative-informed therapy perspective, it is the sudden awareness of new ways of experiencing and understanding the connections between actions, emotions, and intentions of self and others, expressed in personal stories, that is definitive of client insight and narrative story change in psychotherapy. One's stories of self and others are made meaningful when one can construct a coherent, causal account that provides a cogent explanation of factors that enhance or impede significant relationships with others. Accordingly, it is not surprising that psychotherapy researchers have begun to empirically investigate the relationship between narrative coherence and psychological well-being in a variety of clinical populations (Angus & Bouffard, 2004; Dimaggio & Semerari, 2004; Gonçalves & Machado, 2004; Gonçalves, Machado, Korman, & Angus, 2002; Pennebaker & Seagal, 1999; Russell & Bryant, 2004). Narrative coherence markers identified in these studies have included: (a) a clear sense of the beginning, middle, and end of the story; (b) descriptions of the internal subjective experiences of protagonists and antagonists; (c) an explicit understanding of causes or factors that contributed to conflicting emotions, actions, and intentions of self and others; and (d) an inner-felt sense of resolution in which an old problem is seen and experienced in a new, often more positive light that promotes a heightened sense of self-coherence, personal agency, and hopefulness. Despite these research initiatives, the relationship between client insight, problem resolution, and heightened narrative coherence has not been investigated in the psychotherapy research literature.

To address this gap, this chapter reports findings from an intensive, narrative analysis of story coherence and insight that emerged in the context of one client's struggle to address unresolved feelings of anger and resentment toward her husband. The major aim of this exploratory study will be to identify key stages of narrative change that contribute to the emergence of new ways of seeing, experiencing, and understanding self and others—insight—in the context of one good-outcome, client-centered therapy dyad. Specifically, the contributions of client storytelling, emotional differentiation, and new meaning-making will be assessed in light of the emergence of insight, problem resolution, and enhanced story coherence.

Angus and Bouffard (2004) argued that in the case of emotionally traumatizing personal memories, overpowering and often contradictory emotions can interfere with the narrator's attempts to organize the experience as a coherent narrative that can be subsequently shared with others and reflected on for further self-understanding. In psychotherapy, a client's inability to successfully organize and integrate the conflicting emotions and actions experienced in the context of troubling events is an indicator of what gestalt therapists refer to as *unfinished business* (Greenberg, 2002). From a narrative perspective, unfinished business represents the definitive "broken story" (Angus & Bouffard, 2004) in which the client's thoughts and feelings about a distressing or traumatic event have remained fragmented, disconnected, and "not understood." As such, distressing memories of loss, shame, and humiliation may resist assimilation to a client's preexisting self-narrative (Brinegar, Salvi, Stiles, & Greenberg, 2006). Angus and Bouffard (2004) viewed this broken story as an ideal focus for the identification of client and therapist strategies that contribute to the emergence of client insights, emotional integration, story coherence, and behavior change.

Specifically, Angus, Levitt, and Hardtke (1999) stated that moments of therapeutic change—and insight—are likely to emerge from dialectical shifts between autobiographical memory narrative disclosure (*external narrative processes*), emotional differentiation (*internal narrative processes*), and meaning-making (*reflexive narrative processes*) modes of inquiry in therapy sessions. The external narrative process mode entails personal storytelling that addresses the description and elaboration of emotionally salient autobiographical memories in which the question of what happened is addressed. The internal narrative process mode entails emotional differentiation that addresses the description and elaboration of painful emotions and bodily experiences connected with personal memory narratives and addresses the question of what was felt during an event, as well as what is experienced during the retelling of the memory in therapy session. Finally, the reflexive narrative process mode entails new meaning-making that addresses understanding what happened in an event (*external storytelling*) and what was felt (*internal subjective feelings*) in which the questions "why did this happen?" and "what does it mean to me?" are addressed. It is in the context of the reflexive narrative process mode that a new insight regarding connections between intentions and actions of self and others and a new awareness of the meanings of emotional experiences are most likely to occur. Greenberg and Angus (2004) suggested it is the emergence of new ways of experiencing, symbolizing, organizing, and understanding troubling emotions in the context of problematic life stories that is often the first step toward the articulation of a more coherent, understandable self-narrative in psychotherapy. As such, the articulation of a more coherent life story may be an important narrative outcome of successful psychotherapy.

Findings that emerged from the intensive case analysis of 18 experiential therapy dyads (Angus, Lewin, Bouffard, & Rotondi-Trevisan, 2004) at the York Psychotherapy Center provide a measure of empirical support for narrative processes model. Specifically, the Narrative Processes Coding System (NPCS; Angus et al., 1999) sequence analyses have established that clients consistently prioritize shifts to storytelling (external narrative process mode) and reflexive meaning-making (reflexive narrative process) in both good- and poor-outcome therapy sessions. In contrast, good-outcome experiential therapists were more likely to shift clients from a reflexive meaning-making to the identification and differentiation of new emotional experiences (internal narrative mode). The transition from storytelling to emotional differentiation was found to be most successful when it was first preceded by the client's active exploration of her or his experiential responses to a narrative, in the context of a reflexive inquiry mode. On the basis of the NPCS research findings (Angus et al., 2004), it is proposed that client insights into long-standing relationship conflicts and the construction of an emotionally coherent memory narrative will be enhanced by the strategic engagement in all three narrative process modes.

The purpose of the study discussed in this chapter was to conduct an exploratory, qualitative analysis of the interrelationship between client narrative expression (Angus & McLeod, 2004) and personal insight in the context of an intensive case analysis of one good-outcome client-centered psychotherapy dyad selected from the York I Depression Study (Greenberg & Watson, 1998). First, findings that emerged from the sequential analyses of NPCS topic segments (Hardtke, 1996) are presented in this chapter and used as a guide for the selection of key sessions and within-session episodes, associated with a client-generated insight event. Next, the selected sessions and topic segments are subjected to an intensive, microanalytic application of the second stage of the NPCS procedures that entails the identification of external, internal, and reflexive mode shifts. Finally, client stories are assessed for the degree of narrative coherence. Although generalizations are necessarily constrained by the limited sample size, this intensive case analysis of micronarrative change processes and story coherence is an important first step for the development of an empirically validated model of narrative processes and client insight. With further testing and evaluation, we hope that this research initiative will provide an in-depth understanding of how client insight and narrative change can be facilitated in the context of brief therapy treatments for depression.

THE CLIENT

At the time of the study, Margaret—a pseudonym—was a 58-year-old, Caucasian, married, full-time homemaker who was the mother of two adult children. She met criteria for major depressive disorder (Spitzer, Williams, Gibbon, & First, 1995) and completed a battery of standardized measures including the Beck Depression Inventory (BDI; Beck, Steer, & Garbin, 1987) and a client consent form. After completion of the assessment measures, Margaret was one of 18 clients randomly assigned to the Brief Client-Centered Therapy treatment arm of the York I Depression Study (Greenberg & Watson, 1998). Her treatment program consisted of 17 one-hour audio- and videotaped therapy sessions that were transcribed for intensive process analyses (Brinegar et al., 2006; McLeod, 2004; McLeod & Lynch, 2000).

In the York I Depression Study (Greenberg & Watson, 1998), clients were considered to have achieved good outcomes if at termination they evidenced a clinically significant drop in depressive symptomatology—as measured by the BDI—and no longer met criteria for major depressive disorder. As reported in that study, Margaret's BDI scores (range 0 to 63) dropped from 21 (moderate-level depression) at the start of the study to 12 (nondepressed) at the conclusion of her therapy sessions. Additionally, Margaret no longer met criteria for major depressive disorder (Spitzer et al., 1995) at therapy termination.

Margaret was selected as the focus of this intensive analysis of narrative change and insight for three specific reasons: (a) she reported that a significant shift event occurred in Session 11, (b) she reported long-standing feelings of resentment and anger toward her husband that stemmed from troubling experiences in her past and she met criteria for unfinished business (Greenberg, 2002), and (c) she was identified as having met criteria for clinically significant, positive outcomes at therapy termination.

THE THERAPIST AND THERAPY APPROACH

The therapist was a 30-year-old, Caucasian doctoral student in clinical psychology at York University in Toronto, Ontario, Canada. She had 2 years of clinical experience prior to completing a 24-week therapy training program supervised by specialists in both client-centered and process experiential psychotherapy. On the basis of adherence ratings (Greenberg & Watson, 1998) completed by raters for the York I Depression Study, Margaret and her therapist were assessed as adhering closely to a client-centered mode of therapy practice.

NARRATIVE PROCESSES CODING SYSTEM

The NPCS is designed for application to therapy session transcripts and entails a two-step procedure. The first step enables trained raters to reliably subdivide and characterize therapy session transcripts into topic segments according to content shifts in the verbal exchange between client and therapist. Each topic segment is characterized in terms of key issue, relationship focus, and whether or not the shift was initiated by the client or the therapist. When identifying key issues, raters provide a gist of the therapy session discourse that draws on the client's or therapist's words. Relationship focus reflects the primary relationship that is addressed in the topic segment. For example, a primary focus of *husband* would be characterized as *self in relation to husband*, whereas the client's focus on self-exploration and intrapersonal issues would be characterized *self in relation to self*.

The second step of the NPCS coding procedures entails the identification of three narrative process mode types: (a) external narrative process sequences that provide autobiographical memory narratives (past and present) or information; (b) internal narrative process sequences that provide a description of experiential subjective feelings and emotions; and (c) reflexive narrative process sequences that entail recursive questioning and meaning-making processes in relation to beliefs, actions, and emotions represented in current and past events, within the context of the previously identified topic segments. Additionally, raters also identify who initiates the narrative sequence subtype—therapist or client—in the context of the therapy session dialogue. The NPCS has demonstrated construct validity and good levels of interrater agreement in a series of recent psychotherapy process studies (Angus & Hardtke, 1994; Angus et al., 1999; Hardtke, Levitt, & Angus, 2003; Levitt & Angus, 2000; Levitt, Korman, & Angus, 2000; Levitt, Korman, Angus, & Hardtke, 1997).

RESULTS

Relational Focus and Topic Segment Analyses

All therapy sessions that made up Margaret's brief client-centered therapy treatment were fully transcribed and then analyzed for the occurrence of NPCS topic segments. Raters coded each topic segment in terms of primary relationship focus and key issue. Using a sample of two early and three late therapy sessions, two trained raters were able to establish an interrater agreement level of 84% for identifying topic segment shifts in the therapy sessions and 91% for identifying primary relational focus for the identified topic segments.

A total of 584 topic segments were identified in the 17 therapy sessions. Margaret initiated 87% of all topic shifts in her therapy sessions, and her therapist was responsible for 13% of topic turns. Consistent with the tenets of a client-centered therapeutic model (Rogers, 1959), it appears Margaret was a highly active contributor to the topic focus of her therapy sessions.

In terms of relational themes, self in relation to husband (35%) was the most predominant relational focus across all sessions. The second most frequently occurring relational focus was self in relation to self (18%). This relational theme represented topic segments in which the client's active self-exploration of key issues—an important goal of client-centered therapy—was the predominant focus of inquiry. Prior to Session 11, the relational focus of self in relation to self was identified as occurring in only 3 sessions: Session 3, 17%; Session 5, 28%; Session 9, 15%. In contrast, following Session 11 a significant shift to heightened client self-exploration was evidenced. The theme of self in relation to self was consistently present in all 6 remaining therapy sessions at significantly higher levels of frequency than in earlier sessions: Session 12, 32%; Session 13, 35%; Session 14, 32%; Session 15, 43%; Session 16, 65%; and Session 17, 19%. Accordingly, the analysis of topic segment relational foci across sessions appeared to indicate that a significant shift to self-focus had emerged subsequent to Session 11.

In addition to the topic segment findings, Margaret also reported a significant shift in her understanding of a key issue or problem after the completion of Session 11 (Hardtke, 1996). On the basis of the topic segment relational-focus analyses, as well as Margaret's own self-report, Session 11 was chosen for the selection of key topic segments pertaining to the client's core concern—her relationship with her husband. Additionally, to provide a baseline representation of Margaret's story of depression prior to therapeutic reconstruction, Session 1 was selected for inclusion in this study of narrative process mode change and client insight.

A Qualitative Analysis of Narrative Process Modes and Client Insight

To identify stages of narrative process change, coherence, and insight, topic segments addressing Margaret's primary relationship focus—her relationship with her husband—were selected from Sessions 1 and 11. Each selected topic segment was then rated for narrative processes mode shifts: storytelling, emotional differentiation, and meaning-making modes. The initiator of each narrative mode shift—client or therapist—was also identified. For the purposes of the study, a fine-grained, intensive application of the second stage of the Narrative Processes Coding System (Angus & Bouffard, 2004; Laitila, Altonen, Wahlstrom, & Angus, 2001) was adopted. As such, narrative mode shifts of less than 4 transcript lines were identified in this analysis. Lynne Angus completed the initial analysis of selected topic segments drawn from Session 1 and Session 11, and Karen Hardtke served as an auditor for the narrative process sequence ratings.

The intensive narrative process mode analysis of selected topic segments in Sessions 1 and 11 resulted in the emergence of a three-stage model of insight generation and narrative change. The first stage—*setting the scene*—represented findings emerging from the analysis of Session 1. The second stage—*narrative self-disclosure and emotional differentiation*—and third stage—*emotional meaning-making, insight, and story reconstruction*—emerged from the intensive analysis of selected topic segments and narrative process shifts identified in Session 11.

Setting the Scene

At the time of her participation in the York I Depression Study (Greenberg & Watson, 1998), Margaret lived with her husband, Carl (pseudonym) and daughter, Dahlia (pseudonym). Although she took pride in her role as a full-time caregiver for both her immediate family and aging parents, she also noted that recent events had led to many changes in her daily life. Specifically, her father had recently died and her elderly mother required constant nursing home care for a debilitating neurological disorder. Additionally, her daughter was about to be married and would be moving out of the family home. Her son, Bill (pseudonym) was already living out of town to complete his university studies. Margaret and her husband were about to become empty nesters and her role as a full-time mother was about to undergo a significant change.

In her initial therapy session, Margaret linked the onset of her feelings of depression to distressing events that had occurred in one particular year in the context of an external narrative mode:

> Client: But um—no, basically, um—my depression . . . . I like I think is being sort of over the—last 5 years, um—it just seemed that there was 1 year in my life that everything happened. Well first of all my son moved out to city . . . . then I have a daughter too but you know she was going to university at that point, so she wasn't really at home either . . . and then, um—I started having problems with my parents in that, um, my mother had arthritis has arthritis and um—I was like; I come from a fairly big family

but I was the only one who didn't go to business and I ended up looking after my parents.

In this autobiographical narrative, Margaret recounts events in a disconnected, truncated manner that lacks an explicit temporal structure and provides limited contextual elaboration. Moreover, in terms of narrative coherence the lack of narrative elaboration detailing what happened in each event and the impact on her makes it difficult to understand how the disparate experiences are interconnected and the meaning they have for Margaret in the context of her struggle with depression.

Margaret also tells her therapist that during the same period of time, her husband Carl had become increasingly engaged in various work responsibilities; as a result, she feels neglected and resentful.

> Client: I look back on it. At the time I was very resentful because, you know, I felt all the responsibility was falling on me and the result was that it came to a point that when our children left home—he started in on this job—and he didn't have time to support me and I felt very neglected . . . I mean he's wrapped up in his job and it's just—I know *I don't understand it enough* like I just sort of feel like, 'Hey, I've been giving, giving, giving to the kids and the husband for 30-odd years; when is it going to be my turn?'

In this initial session Margaret gives expression to her long-standing feelings of resentment and bitterness toward her husband. She feels that her selfless devotion to the nurturance of others has not been reciprocated and she is angry and resentful about this turn of events. However, it is not yet clear how the events of that year and her current feelings of emotional neglect, resentments, and depression are interconnected. Although Margaret seems to link her husband's increased job responsibilities with feelings of emotional neglect, she also says, "I don't understand it enough." She thus provides her therapist with a clear marker of self-incoherence and client unfinished business.

In the context of a reflexive narrative sequence, the therapist responds to Margaret's expression of confusion by connecting "the 1 year in my life that everything happened" with her feelings of resentment and bitterness toward her husband:

> Therapist: Well I'm not sure. . . your sense that you have been giving especially in that year that everything happened all at once . . .

> Client: Mm-hm . . .

> Therapist: and kind of now waiting to get something back and not just getting it.

With this empathic response, the therapist sets the stage for a narrative framing of Margaret's bitter resentments as an understandable outcome of feeling neglected by others, especially her husband, "in that year that everything happened." In essence, the therapist supplies a connection between Margaret's inner desires, emotions, and actions that draws on the narrative plotline of unfinished business. In so doing, a plausible retelling of Margaret's story of depression emerges that provides a causal connection between emotions felt and actions taken and in turn enhances the development of story coherence.

Margaret furthers elaborates the therapist's narrative framing of her emotional problems as unfinished business when she connects her experience of "feeling let down" with her feelings of anger and resentment in her marriage. A key marker of client unfinished business (Greenberg, 2002) is the feeling of being stuck in a repetitive cycle of resentment, bitterness, and complaint that is highly resistant to change. In the following, Margaret describes a vicious emotional cycle of fear, hurt, and anger that she finds herself "caught in":

> *Client:* I find it particularly with Carl . . . that's my husband, I know I can sort of let myself relax to a certain extent and things go along and then I think, uh-uh, no one's going to do that to me again, and I think deep down I'm thinking . . . you're not going to hurt me . . . my way of expressing fear is that I get angry and I yell and I know I am not being a nice person . . . it bothers me somehow, you know, I think, "Why can't I be a nice person?"

It is clear that Margaret is truly puzzled by her own emotions and actions and cannot understand why she just cannot stop feeling angry and resentful toward her husband.

During Session 1, both therapist and client contribute to the co-elaboration of a new narrative context of meaning—unfinished business—to supply a coherent understanding of long-standing feelings of resentment and anger toward her husband. It is also evident, however, that Margaret has yet to achieve a full understanding about how events in the past led to or caused her current feelings of resentment and mistrust toward her husband. According to Hill and O'Brien's (1999) three-stage model of helping, an extended exploratory phase of therapy typically precedes a shift to new self-awareness, insight, and understanding. At the conclusion of Session 1, the stage is set for an extended accounting of current concerns regarding her son, problems arising in the planning of her daughter's wedding, and continuing feelings of anger and resentment toward her husband, in the context of addressing current family issues. It is not until Session 11, during which Margaret discloses a series of emotionally distressing memories from "that year that everything happened," that a new way of seeing and understanding her husband's lack of responsiveness—in essence, insight—is achieved.

Narrative Self-Disclosure and Emotional Differentiation

At the outset of Session 11, it is clear that Margaret and her therapist agree that feelings of anger and resentment toward her husband are the most important issues to address in her therapy sessions:

Client: You know how we were talking last week, like being important, the biggest thing in my life seems to be my problem with Carl. And that seems to be what I could resolve, actually if we could resolve—um, if we could be together, I think I could handle all the other tensions better.

As she begins to reflect on her marriage in the session and encounters past memories, Margaret seeks reassurance from her therapist that returning to the past will indeed help her achieve her most important therapeutic goal:

Client: I don't know whether it is good to go back like this or not, is it?

Therapist: I think it is because it sounds like you're still holding feelings from back then.

Client: If I could just let go of some of these feelings, I think I would be an awful lot happier.

With this interchange Margaret sought out and received reassurance from her therapist that (a) returning to memories of the past is of key importance for understanding where her current problematic emotions "come from," and (b) her feelings of resentment and anger toward her husband are important and point to a personally salient experience that has not yet been fully storied or understood.

In pursuit of her goal, Margaret recalls the point in time—"the year when everything seemed to happen"—when she first started to feel tensions in her marriage and a growing estrangement from her husband. In the context of a secure therapeutic alliance, she then discloses a series of emotionally distressing memories (external narrative mode) about her disabled parents and her attempts to care for them during that year:

Client: Yeah it really, it was very bad . . . I was spending more and more time over there (at my parents' apartment) and of course then I think there was the resentment too, of—I come from a fairly big family, like I have two sisters and three brothers, but I was doing all the work . . . like I was, over cleaning the apartment and making meals and they started getting like, particularly my Dad started getting terribly confused.

Margaret moves to a reflexive meaning-making stance to provide an overall assessment of that time in her life—"it really was horrendous;" then, spontaneously, a specific new emotional awareness—internal narrative process mode—emerges for Margaret in the sessions:

Client: . . . and I think [deep breath] the part that hurt the most [crying] was that, it was my mother's reaction to me . . . at times, you know [still crying], it would really hurt.

It is in the context of this new emotional awareness that Margaret shifts back to an external narrative process mode to disclose a specific, detailed autobiographical memory of her mother that provides a context for her acute feelings of hurt:

Client: One time in the apartment, they got cockroaches, oh—and of course, I had to go over, and my mother, all my life I, my mother was the fussiest housekeeper, I mean she kept her house immaculate . . . and um, I had to go over and empty out all the cupboards for them to come in and spray. . .I mean it was just horrible, you know, they, and I mean I, I figured I kept the apartment as clean as I could possibly clean it. . . . But um, as I say, this time with the cockroaches, so I went over the night before, I emptied all the cupboards, and my Mother [*sigh*], it was just horrendous, saying, "I don't have cockroaches, it's only dirty people that have those," and oh, she just went on and on and on and on . . . and she went down the hall to the superintendent's door, and I was in the apartment when it was happening [*sniffs*] and she was telling them that, I was forcing her to do this, that sort of thing. And then I went in the elevator to try and bring her back upstairs again . . . she hit me and [*crying*] I think that was the most horrible thing, you know, to stand there in that elevator and your mother hits you, at my age?

In contrast to Margaret's vague, rather incoherent, and overgeneral representation in Session 1, this narrative account in Session 11 of her mother's assault is highly specific and emotionally charged. In terms of narrative coherence markers there is evidence of a clear beginning, middle, and end, with actions coherently organized along an unfolding, linear time line. It is important to note that Margaret includes a representation of the intentions, emotions, and perceptions that she experienced while the event unfolded. As a result, during the session her therapist is better able to empathically enter into her moment-to-moment experiencing of the painful event.

In the case of emotionally traumatizing memories, painful and disturbing emotions may resist assimilation to preexisting views and beliefs about self and others. Especially in the context of a child's relationship with his or her parents, unexpected breaches of safety and trust may call into question the loving intentions of the other. Additionally, primary emotions such as feelings of humiliation, disgust, shame, or fear are often accompanied by withdrawal from others (Greenberg, 2002) that further impedes the disclosure of trauma experiences to friends or family. Finally, a further sense of betrayal, isolation, anger, and resentment may ensue if attempts to tell others about these events are minimized, ignored, or rebuffed. As discussed later in this chapter, it is this scenario—unfinished business—that forms the basis of Margaret's feelings of resentment and hurt toward her husband.

Emotional Meaning-Making, Insight, and Story Reconstruction

To help Margaret access a fuller experiential awareness of her emotional distress in relation to the memories of her mother, the therapist shifts to a reflexive narrative process mode in the session:

> *Therapist:*   I wonder if you have really ever allowed yourself to realize how awful it was?

> *Client:*   I think what you said is really true, people would say, 'Oh, it must have been horrible.' And I think, huh, it wasn't that bad [*flippantly*]. But then, maybe my mind's just shutting it out because it was horrible . . . because when I think, like that situation when my mother hit me? [*tearful*] . . . it was almost like, um, I'm so ashamed, you know that?

Rogers (1959) suggested that experiencing a feeling "denotes an emotionally tinged experience, together with its personal meaning. Thus it includes the emotion but also the cognitive content or the meaning of the emotion in its experiential context" (p. 198). Accordingly, it is important that therapists accurately capture both the internal feeling and the external context—in essence, what the feeling is about—in their empathic reflections. The therapist demonstrates this form of empathic response when she combines the narrative action of the scene ("here she is hitting you") with Margaret's internal world of emotions and intentions ("and you're trying to do what's best for her") in response to Margaret's disclosure of feeling shame. This empathic response evocatively highlights the disjunction between Margaret's caring intentions and the angry assault she experienced at the hands of her confused mother. It is precisely this confusing—incoherent—disjunction between good intentions and unexpected bad outcomes, along with overpowering feelings of anger, shame, and humiliation, that contributed to Margaret's shutting out her own emotional experiences of "that horrible year."

In response to her therapist's evocative, empathic reflection, Margaret suddenly experiences a new appreciation of her husband's actions and his intentions during "that horrible year." In essence, Margaret experiences a moment of insight. She begins by stating,

> *Client:*   And, but you know, to give Carl credit, and I guess, I have blamed him for this, but actually, I guess in a way to give him credit, he has never brought that up to me . . . the confusion that it cost with our family . . . he has never once referred to it.

In this moment, Margaret begins to reevaluate the intentions she attributed to her husband and his seeming disinterest in her family problems. In particular, Margaret begins to consider if Carl's lack of interest in her past troubles may have arisen out of caring intentions and a desire to protect her from remembering troubling memories and reliving painful emotions. She then recalls the following memory (external narrative mode):

> *Client:*   He used to get mad at my sisters, he would get furious and then it got to the point that I wouldn't, if I were mad, was mad at them, I wouldn't say anything to Carl because I know, you know,

and then I'd say to him, 'Don't you dare talk about my sisters like that!' So it got to the point that he said nothing and then it got to the point that I withdrew even more because he wouldn't say anything against my sisters, so, and I wouldn't get any action from him, so I just didn't talk about it.

Margaret's disclosure of this generic autobiographical memory narrative provides a new, more comprehensive narrative account of the respective role each partner played in the inception of the communication rupture in their marriage. After focusing on the elaboration of Margaret's subjective feelings and needs, the therapist offers the following conjecture in the context of a reflexive narrative mode:

Therapist: So somehow you wanted support, and yet what he, when he said something and it was against your family, it kind of hurt you and so you kind of pushed him away a bit.

For the first time in her therapy sessions, Margaret begins to consider the idea that she may have had a part to play in her husband's emotional withdrawal from her:

Client: I mean as I say, I'll admit like, it really was a bad time and as I say, part of it was my fault too, I guess maybe I pushed Carl away in a lot of ways. . . .

Margaret is then able to empathically articulate what Carl might have felt when she pushed him away:

Client: So that he got to the point he thought, 'okay, that's the way she feels, she can, I'm not gonna, you know, try any more.'

It is in the context of this extended, reflexive inquiry that a moment of insight occurs for Margaret:

Client: Maybe Carl felt . . . I never thought about it this way until now but maybe he felt so left out too, maybe he just felt left out . . . you know I have never looked at it this way before . . . isn't that strange . . . I just had this feeling of resentment that my sole support wasn't there and maybe he just felt left out you know that as I say, I was so consumed with my parents . . . so angry, so let down . . . that maybe I pushed him out of my life.

In this moment of insight Margaret begins to challenge her belief that her husband abandoned her emotionally at a time of acute distress. She begins to consider whether Carl may have in fact felt "pushed out" by (a) her intolerance of his criticisms of her siblings, despite her own feelings of anger and resentment toward them, and (b) her own emotional withdrawal in the face of painful memories of humiliation and shame. Moreover, the therapist helps coconstruct a new, more coherent narrative account that provides a causal link between her current feelings of anger and resentment and past events with her disabled parents. It is in the context of this reconstructed narrative that the therapist identifies Margaret's powerful feelings of hurt and shame—felt in relation to her mother—as setting the stage for her strong feelings of resentment and anger toward her husband.

> Therapist: It is important to remember how tough it was back then and maybe some of those feelings spilled over to the marriage, when really a lot of the turmoil was from other things.

In terms of story reconstruction, Margaret discovered that some of her own actions may have contributed to the problems in her marriage; as such, she may be able to change her behavior to secure better outcomes in the future. Additionally, a caring and skilled therapist validated her expression of painful emotions and her need for nurturance and care. Margaret may now be willing to see if her needs can be seriously addressed in her relationship with her husband. It is important to note that the therapist's sustained empathic engagement with her in the therapy relationship is a lived instantiation of the possibility of achieving this important goal.

Summary

In summary, the intensive narrative process analysis resulted in the identification of a three-stage model of client narrative expression and insight. The first stage, entitled *setting the scene*, entailed a narrative process mode analysis of Margaret's initial representation of her story of depression. The initial story disclosed to her therapist in Session 1 lacked a sense of temporal structuring and a clear sense of beginning, middle, or end. Also, the internal responses or experiences of significant others were only minimally described in her narrative. Margaret explicitly stated that she did not understand the actions and intentions of significant others—especially her husband—and had trouble identifying the specific reasons for her current emotional distress. On the basis of the coherence criteria noted in the introduction, Margaret's narrative expression was viewed as conveying low narrative coherence.

In response to Margaret's narrative disclosure, the therapist scaffolds a plausible connection between Margaret's inner hopes, emotions, and actions that draws on the narrative plotline of unfinished business. In so doing, the therapist helps to coconstruct a plausible retelling of Margaret's story of depression that provides a causal connection between emotions felt and actions taken and in so doing, facilitates the development of story coherence. As discussed by Angus and Bouffard (2004), addressing the source of longstanding feelings of resentment and anger toward significant others is the important first step toward resolving conflicting emotions and achieving self-narrative story coherence.

The second stage was entitled *narrative self-disclosure and emotional differentiation* and emerged from the intensive narrative process mode analysis of Session 11. Specifically, Stage 2 represented a detailed unfolding of Margaret's disclosure of an emotionally salient autobiographical memory narrative that set the stage for the emergence of a new insight and the development of enhanced story coherence in Stage 3. First, by establishing a strong therapeutic alliance in which Margaret felt safe and secure to tell her stories (external narrative mode), the therapist supported and encouraged her to disclose an emotionally salient, personal memory of her mother that occurred before the onset of her long-standing relationship problems with her husband. As noted in the RESULTS section, and in contrast to Session 1, Margaret's narrative description of this personal memory met three of four criteria of narrative coherence. This form of narrative change was evidenced in the context of an external narrative process mode.

Once externalized as a spoken narrative, Margaret was able to reflexively look back on her own lived experience of the event and symbolize and differentiate her internal world of intense emotions and feelings (internal narrative mode) that were evoked by and connected with the told story. In the context of an internal narrative mode, Margaret was able to access and symbolize her intense feelings of shame, humiliation, and emotional pain evoked by the memory of her mother hitting her. In so doing, she transformed a *lived story* into an externalized *told story* (Stern, 2004) that could now be shared with caring others and reflected on for further understanding and meaning-making in the therapy session. For example, as she emerged from her intense emotional response to remembering the story of her mother hitting her, Margaret seemed to gain a new appreciation of how intensely distressing this period of her life was. In doing this she begins to reassess the impact it may have had on her family, especially her husband. Experiencing and symbolizing the intense, painful emotions evoked by this memory appeared to prepare the ground for new narrative meaning reconstruction and the emergence of insight (reflexive narrative mode).

The third and final stage—*emotional meaning-making, insight and story reconstruction*—emerged from an intensive narrative process analysis of the topic segments that followed Margaret's disclosure of her emotionally salient memory of her mother in Session 11. In the context of a reflexive narrative mode and in response to her new awareness of feelings of shame, humiliation, and desire to shut off these distressing emotions, Margaret begins to consider whether Carl may have felt pushed out of her emotional life. It is in the context of fully experiencing and accepting the tremendous impact of her own feelings and actions that a new awareness of, or insight into, Carl's actions and intentions emerges for Margaret in the session.

A new, more coherent narrative account begins to take shape to provide an explanation for her long-standing but rarely acknowledged feelings of humiliation and shame in relation to the care of her disabled parents. Additionally, a temporal ordering of events emerges that highlights a new connection between emotionally harrowing experiences with her mother and the onset of feelings of anger and resentment toward her husband. Now located as understandable outcomes of her shameful and hurtful experiences with her mother, these feelings provide a context of understanding and a resolution of unfinished business with her husband.

CONCLUDING COMMENTS

The purpose of this study was to intensively explore the relationship between narrative change and client insight in the context of one good-outcome, client-centered dyad drawn from the York I Depression Study. Specifically, the narrative process model was used as a heuristic for both the selection of transcript segments and the characterization of storytelling, emotional differentiation, and new meaning-making modes of inquiry. In particular, this exploratory, intensive, case analytic approach to narrative process change was designed to assess the unique contributions that therapists and clients make to the narrative reconstruction of core client concerns that occur before, during, and after an insight event in brief client-centered therapy sessions for depression.

In terms of the present intensive case analysis, it appears that it was Margaret's active reflective awareness (reflexive narrative mode) of her intense emotional distress (internal narrative mode) in the context of a specific memory narrative (external narrative mode) that set the stage for the emergence of a new, compassionate understanding of her husband's intentions and actions in relation to her own unmet needs. Margaret's new insight specifically addressed the narrative coherence of her story of depression in which her husband's hurtful actions are now understood as unintended outcomes of caring intentions. It is important to note that Margaret develops a new appreciation of her emotional needs and the role she may have played in the development of a communication breakdown with her husband. As such, she gains a new appreciation of her own agency and the hopeful possibility that she may be able to make positive differences in her marriage. Furthermore, the significant rise in topic segment self–self relational focus that occurs after Session 11—and is sustained to Session 16—may be an empirical marker of this important new discovery.

Finally, although the qualitative findings that emerge from this study provide preliminary support for the contributions of narrative process modes to the emergence of client insight and story coherence change, it remains for future studies to establish the generalizability of these findings to specific treatment populations and treatment approaches. Additionally, it will be important to draw on the firsthand accounts of therapists and clients engaged in the development of insight experiences to further assess the validity of findings reported in this chapter.

REFERENCES

Angus, L., & Bouffard, B. (2004). The search for emotional meaning and self-coherence in the face of traumatic loss in childhood: A narrative process perspective. In J. Raskin & S. Bridges (Eds.), *Studies in meaning* (Vol. 2, pp. 137–156). New York: Pace University Press.

Angus, L., & Bouffard-Bowes, B. (2002). "No lo entiendo": La busqueda de sentido emocional y coherencia personalante una perdida traumatica durante la infancia [I do not understand it: The search for emotional sense and personal understanding when faced with a traumatic loss during childhood]. *Revista de Psicoterapia, 13*(49), 25–46.

Angus, L., & Hardtke, K. (1994). Narrative processes in psychotherapy. *Canadian Psychology, 35,* 190–203.

Angus, L., Hardtke, K., & Levitt, H. (1996). *Narrative Processes Coding System training manual.* Unpublished manuscript, York University, North York, Ontario, Canada.

Angus, L., Levitt, H., & Hardtke, K. (1999). The Narrative Processing Coding System: Research applications and implications for psychotherapy practice. *Journal of Clinical Psychology, 55,* 1255–1270.

Angus, L., Lewin, J., Bouffard, B., & Rotondi-Trevisan, D. (2004). What's the story? Working with narrative in experiential psychotherapy. In L. Angus & J. McLeod (Eds.), *Handbook of narrative and psychotherapy: Practice, theory and research* (pp. 87–102). Thousand Oaks, CA: Sage.

Angus, L., & McLeod, J. (Eds.). (2004). *Handbook of narrative and psychotherapy: Practice, theory and research.* Thousand Oaks, CA: Sage.

Bachman, J., & O'Malley, P. (1977). Self-esteem in young men: A longitudinal analysis of the impact of educational and occupational attainment. *Journal of Personality and Social Psychology, 35,* 365–380.

Beck, A. T., Steer, R. A., & Garbin, M. G. (1987). Psychometric properties of the Beck Depression Inventory: Twenty-five years of evaluation. *Clinical Psychology Review, 8,* 77–100.

Brinegar, M. G., Salvi, L. M., Stiles, W. B., & Greenberg, L. S. (2006). Building a meaning bridge: Therapeutic progress from problem formulation to understanding. *Journal of Counseling Psychology, 53,* 165–180.

Dimaggio, G., & Semerari, A. (2004) Disorganized narratives: The psychological condition and its treatment. In L. Angus & J. McLeod (Eds.), *Handbook of narrative and psychotherapy: Practice, theory and research* (pp. 263–282). Thousand Oaks, CA: Sage.

Elliott, R., Shapiro, D., Firth-Cozens, J., Stiles, W., Hardy, G., Llewelyn, S. & Margison, R. (1994). Comprehensive process analysis of insight events in cognitive–behavioral and psychodynamic–interpersonal psychotherapies. *Journal of Counseling Psychology, 41,* 449–463.

Gonçalves, O. F., & Machado, P. P. P. (2004). Nurturing nature: Cognitive narrative strategies. In L. Angus & J. McLeod (Eds.), *Handbook of narrative and psychotherapy: Practice, theory and research* (pp. 103–118). Thousand Oaks, CA: Sage.

Gonçalves, O. F., Machado, P. P. P., Korman, Y., & Angus, L. (2002). Assessing psychopathology: A narrative approach. In L. E. Beutler & M. L. Malik (Eds.), *Rethinking the DSM: A psychological perspective* (pp. 149–176). Washington, DC: American Psychological Association.

Greenberg, L. S. (2002). *Emotion-focused therapy: Coaching clients to work through their feelings.* Washington, DC: American Psychological Association.

Greenberg, L. S., & Angus, L. (2004). The contribution of emotion processes to narrative change: A dialectical-constructivist approach. In L. Angus & J. McLeod (Eds.), *Handbook of narrative and psychotherapy: practice, theory and research* (pp. 331–350). Thousand Oaks, CA: Sage.

Greenberg, L. S., & Watson, J. (1998). Experiential therapy of depression: Differential effects of client-centred relationship conditions and process experiential interventions. *Psychotherapy Research, 8,* 210–224.

Hardtke, K. (1996). *Characterizing therapy focus and exploring client process: Investigating therapeutic modalities from a narrative approach.* Unpublished master's thesis, York University, Toronto, Ontario, Canada.

Hardtke, K., Levitt, H., & Angus, L. (2003). Narrative Prozesse im Beratungs- und Psychotherapiediskurs: Das Narrative Processes Coding System (NPCS) [Narrative processes in the consulting and psychotherapy discourse: The Narrative Processes Coding System]. *Zeitschrift fuer Qualitative Bildungs-, Beratungs- und Sozialforschung, 3*(1), 123–141.

Hill, C., & O'Brien, K. (1999). *Helping skills: Facilitating exploration, insight, and action.* Washington, DC: American Psychological Association.

Laitila, A., Altonen, J., Wahlstrom, J., & Angus, L. (2001). Narrative Process Coding System in marital and family therapy: An intensive case analysis of the formation of a therapeutic system. *Contemporary Family Therapy, 23*(3), 309–322.

Levitt, H., & Angus, L. (2000). Psychotherapy process measure research and the evaluation of psychotherapy orientation: A narrative analysis. *Psychotherapy Integration, 9*(3), 279–300.

Levitt, H., Korman, Y., & Angus, L. (2000). A metaphor analysis in the treatment of depression: Metaphor as a marker of change. *Counseling Psychology Quarterly, 13,* 23–36.

Levitt, H., Korman, Y., Angus, L., & Hardtke, K. (1997). Metaphor analyses in good- and poor-outcome psychotherapy: Unloading a burden vs. being burdened. *Psicologia: Teoria, Investigao e Practica, 2,* 329–346.

Lewin, J. K. (2001). *Both sides of the coin: Comparative analyses of narrative process patterns in poor- and good-outcome dyads engaged in brief experiential psychotherapy for depression*. Unpublished master's thesis, York University, Toronto, Ontario, Canada.

McLeod, J. (2004). Social constructionism, narrative, and psychotherapy. In L. Angus & J. McLeod (Eds.), *Handbook of narrative and psychotherapy: Practice, theory and research* (pp. 351–366). Thousand Oaks, CA: Sage.

McLeod, J., & Lynch. G. (2000). "This is our life": Strong evaluation in psychotherapy narrative. *European Journal of Psychotherapy, Counselling and Health, 3*, 389–406.

Pennebaker, J., & Seagal, J. (1999). Forming a story: The health benefits of narrative. *Journal of Clinical Psychology, 55*, 1243–1254.

Rogers, C. R. (1959). A theory of therapy, personality, and interpersonal relationships, as developed in the client-centered framework. In S. Koch (Ed.), *Psychology: A study of a science, Vol. 3. Formulations of the person and the social context* (pp. 184–256). New York: McGraw-Hill.

Russell, R., & Bryant, F. (2004). Minding our therapeutic tales: Treatments in perspectivism. In L. Angus & J. McLeod (Eds.), *Handbook of narrative and psychotherapy: Practice, theory and research* (pp. 211–226). Thousand Oaks, CA: Sage.

Spitzer, R., Williams, J., Gibbon, M., & First, M. (1995). *Structured clinical interview for DSM–IV*. New York: American Psychiatric Press.

Stern, D. (2004). *The present moment in psychotherapy and everyday life*. New York: Norton.

10

THE ATTAINMENT OF INSIGHT IN THE HILL DREAM MODEL: A CASE STUDY

CLARA E. HILL, SARAH KNOX, SHIRLEY A. HESS,
RACHEL E. CROOK-LYON, MELISSA K. GOATES-JONES,
AND WONJIN SIM

The search for meaning in dreams has occupied people since their earliest days, with evidence of some type of dream dictionary found in every culture (see Van de Castle, 1994). In more recent times, people have turned to psychotherapists (e.g., Freud, Jung, Adler) to help them achieve insight into their dreams. Although most theories of dream interpretation focus on uncovering meaning in the dream (i.e., gaining insight), dream theorists differ about the role of therapists in giving interpretations of the dream to the client versus encouraging clients to arrive at their own interpretations.

Among the various approaches to understanding dreams, the Hill (1996, 2004a) dream model is particularly well-suited for examining the process of insight development because insight is a key goal of this approach. The Hill model involves three stages. During the exploration stage, the therapist assists the client in exploring several major images of her or his dreams using the four relatively structured, client-centered, DRAW steps (description,

We thank the therapist and client for their participation in this study, Jessica Stahl and Missy Roffman for data collection for the larger study, the undergraduate judges for coding insight and action ideas related to the dream, and Kai Pantin for transcribing the session. We thank James Gormally for the metaphor about gold dust.

reexperiencing, associations, and identifying waking-life triggers). In the insight stage, the therapist builds on the foundation established in the exploration stage to help the client gain insight into the dream. Using the understanding of the dream acquired through these first two stages, the therapist and client work together in the action stage to formulate ideas about changes the client might make in her or his waking life.

Several findings related to insight have emerged in studies that have been conducted on the Hill model (see review in Hill & Goates, 2004). First, clients in 3 (out of 3) studies identified gaining awareness or insight as the most helpful component of their dream sessions. Second, in 7 of 8 studies clients indicated on self-report measures that they had gained insight; in fact, the level of this insight was consistently more than a standard deviation higher than that reported by clients in regular therapy (i.e., not using the Hill dream model). Third, in 6 studies of brief (2–20 sessions) individual therapy involving dream work, judges rated that client insight reflected in the written interpretations of their presenting dreams increased dramatically as a result of dream work (average effect size = 1.06, where anything over .80 is considered to be large; Cohen, 1988). Fourth, Hill, Rochlen, Zack, McCready, and Dematatis (2003) found no differences in judge-rated client insight into dreams in sessions in which therapists probed for insight compared with sessions in which therapists probed for insight and also offered at least one interpretation during the insight stage; this suggests that therapist use of interpretation may not yield additional insight beyond what is gained through probing for insight. Finally, in their most recent study, Hill et al. (in press) found that clients who gained the most insight during dream sessions had low levels of insight prior to the session and high levels of client involvement and therapist competence and adherence in the session itself.

Thus, using a variety of different measurement methods, it has been shown that clients valued insight in dream sessions and that they gained insight into their dreams as a result of sessions. However, very little is known about the mechanisms through which insight is attained in dream sessions, other than the fact that client involvement and therapist adherence and competence are related to insight gains and that therapist interpretation may not be necessary for insight gains. Knowledge about how client insight develops in dream sessions might provide clues about how insight develops in therapy more generally, a useful pursuit given that insight is a major goal of many therapies (see Messer & McWilliams, chap. 1; Pascual-Leone & Greenberg, chap. 2; Grosse Holtforth et al., chap. 3, this volume).

The purpose of the present study, then, was to investigate the development of insight within a single case of dream work. We used Hill et al.'s (1992) definition of insight:

The client expresses an understanding of something about him/herself and can articulate patterns or reasons for behaviors, thoughts, or feelings. Insight usually involves an "aha" experience, in which the client perceives self or world in a new way. The client takes appropriate responsibility rather than blaming others, using "shoulds" imposed from the outside world, or rationalizing. (pp. 548–549)

Because we currently know little about how insight develops in dream sessions and because insight might develop differently across clients, we studied one case of a client who developed insight during a dream session. We used a combination of quantitative and qualitative methods to maximize our ability to highlight the development of insight in this case and relied on consensus among six researchers (all of whom are authors of this chap.) before we felt confident in any of our assertions.

In the remainder of the chapter we first describe the process and outcomes of the session, documenting that insight did occur. We then explore factors suggested from psychotherapy process research (Hill & Lambert, 2004; Hill & Williams, 2000); dream work research (Hill & Goates, 2004); and our clinical experiences that may have facilitated or inhibited insight gains. The factors were dream salience, the therapeutic relationship, client characteristics (readiness or eagerness for insight, involvement in the session, and psychological-mindedness), and therapist factors (adherence and competence with the model, lack of countertransference, and therapist skills—specifically, probes for insight and interpretations). In addition, we remained open to evidence for other factors that arose from our immersion in the session.

METHOD

In this section, we describe the procedures of the larger study from which the case was selected and then discuss the selection of the specific case. In addition, we provide information about the chosen client and the research team for this case study. Finally, we describe the procedures for the analysis of this case.

Selection of a Case From Archival Data

We selected a case from the data set of a larger study (Hill et al., in press). Hill et al. examined the effects of client predictor variables (attitudes toward dreams, dream salience, insight into dream, action ideas related to dream, and initial level of functioning on the target problem reflected in the dream) and the process of the three stages (exploration, insight, action) of the Hill dream model on session outcome, using single 60 to 90 minute sessions conducted by 42 trained therapists with 157 recruited clients. Prior to sessions, clients completed measures of attitudes toward dreams and dream salience; they also wrote an interpretation of their dream and indicated action ideas related to the dream. After each of the three stages of the session, clients and therapists completed measures of client involvement and therapist adherence and competence. Following the session, clients completed measures of the therapy relationship, quality of the session, functioning related to the target problem (both current and retrospectively for presession), and intention to act; therapists evaluated the therapy relationship and the quality of the session. At a 2-week follow-up, clients indicated the degree to which they had implemented their action plan and rated their functioning on their target problem. Judges (trained undergraduate students) rated the level of client insight in the presession written dream interpretations, in spoken interpretations at the end of the exploration and insight stages, and in written interpretations at the 2-week follow-up; they also rated therapist competence and client involvement in each stage in the session. See Hill et al. (in press) for more information about these measures.

To select a case, we reviewed the data for the first 50 of the 157 sessions (all that had been conducted at the time). We chose a session for which there was a large gain in judge-rated client insight into the dream from presession to the 2-week follow-up; high within-session ratings of therapist competence and client involvement as assessed by the client, therapist, and trained judges; high client perceptions of session quality and therapeutic relationship; and large client-rated reductions (i.e., improved functioning) on the target problem. Hence, from the quantitative ratings we knew that the client, therapist, and judges all perceived this to be a good session and that the client was judged as achieving insight and making therapeutic gains.

Shari (pseudonym) was a 23-year-old college senior of Arabic descent. At the time of the session she was not in therapy, nor had she ever been in therapy. She was about average in terms of her attitudes toward dreams compared with the rest of the sample (see Table 10.1). The therapist was a 29-year-old White, female, counseling psychology doctoral student with 4 years of experience as a therapist. She had conducted 20 dream sessions using the Hill model and had high self-efficacy for using the model (she rated herself 8 on a scale ranging from 0–9, in which 9 = *high self-efficacy*). Her theoretical orientation was an integration of interpersonal, client-centered, psychodynamic, and existential theories.

Research Team

Two White women (one 55-year-old professor, one 42-year-old assistant professor) served as the primary team in analyzing the data. Four women (one White 53-year-old assistant professor, one White 31-year-old assistant professor, one White 24-year-old graduate student, one Asian 22-year-old graduate student) served as auditors, checking the conclusions reached by the primary team. Regarding theoretical orientation, using three 5-point scales (5 = *high*), the six researchers rated themselves 4.50 (*SD* = .55) on humanistic–experiential, 3.33 (*SD* = .52) on psychoanalytic–psychodynamic, and 2.50 (*SD* = .84) on behavioral–cognitive orientations.

TABLE 10.1
Scores for the Session Compared With Data From the Larger Sample

	Shari	Larger sample (N = 159)	
Measure	Score	M	SD
Judge-related client insight			
Initial	5.33+	4.31	1.58
Postexploration stage	6.67++	5.37	1.51
Postinsight stage	8.00++	5.99	1.61
Follow-up	9.00++	6.21	1.93
Judge-related client action ideas			
Initial	4.00+	3.06	1.58
Postaction stage	6.33++	5.25	1.31
Follow-up	5.33	4.89	1.93
Client dream salience	3.60+	3.18	0.77
Client dream attitudes	3.78	3.74	0.66
Client involvement			
Client-rated	9.00+	8.35	0.98
Therapist-rated	7.00	6.99	1.24
Judge-rated	7.44++	6.50	1.02
Therapist competence			
Client-rated	9.00++	8.39	0.63
Therapist-rated	6.33	6.56	1.34
Judge-rated	7.33++	6.02	1.19
Client-rated RS	5.00+	4.57	0.60
Therapist-rated RS	4.25	4.09	0.64
Client-rated SES	5.00+	4.57	0.67
Therapist-rated SES	4.50+	4.10	0.67
Client target problem			
Presession	6.00	6.52	2.72
Postsession	10.00	9.86	2.17
Follow-up	11.00+	9.13	2.09
Intent to act	2.00	1.79	0.86
Implementation	4.00	3.50	1.15

Note. Effect size (ES) = (sample mean – client's score)/sample standard deviation; + = medium ES; ++ = large ES. Insight and action ideas were rated by trained undergraduate judges for the Hill et al. (in press) study using 9-point scales (1 = low, 9 = high). Dream Salience and Attitude Toward Dreams were completed by the client prior to the session using 5-point scales (1 = low, 5 = high). Client Involvement and Therapist Competence were rated using 9-point scales (9 = high) and are averaged across the exploration, insight, and action stages. Relationship Scale (RS) and Session Evaluation Scale (SES) used 5-point scales (5 = high). Target Problem ("anxiety about moving in with fiancé and discussing this issue with him; working collaboratively with him to solve issues") used a 13-point scale (1 = worst possible, 13 = best possible functioning). Intent to Act used a 6-point scale (1 = high intent). Implementation used a 5-point scale (5 = high).

Procedures

The first two authors read the transcript and listened to the audiotape of the session independently. They then read the transcript aloud together, looking for evidence of contributors to insight that emerged from being immersed in the session. Next, they reviewed the session again, looking for evidence of the influence of factors listed earlier in this chapter (e.g., the therapeutic relationship, dream salience). They made a list of the evidence for all of the facilitating and inhibiting factors for this specific case, using consensus for each decision.

The first two authors suspected (on the basis of hearing the audiotape of the session) that therapist skills were a factor in facilitating client insight; therefore, they asked the whole team to code therapist skills used in each therapist speaking turn and client insight in the immediate next client speaking turn. Thus, the team used Hill's (2004b) Helping Skills System to code (by consensus) the predominant therapist skill (e.g., restatement, interpretation) in each therapist speaking turn (note that the category of *open questions* was further divided into *general open questions* and *probes for insight* because previous data, e.g., Hill et al., 2003, had suggested that the more narrowly defined probes seemed helpful in the insight stage); they also rated (by consensus) each client statement for level of insight using a 5-point scale ranging from *none* (1) to *very high* (5) based on Hill et al.'s (1992) definition of insight cited earlier.

The four auditors then listened to the tape, read the transcript carefully, and indicated their level of agreement or disagreement with each judgment made by the first two authors. In addition, they looked for factors and evidence that had been overlooked and offered other conclusions. The first two authors then considered the auditors' comments and made considerable changes through a process of discussion and consensus. This audit–reconsideration process continued several times until all researchers were confident in the conclusions.

THE DREAM, INITIAL CLIENT INTERPRETATION, AND ACTION IDEAS

Shari presented a recurrent dream she had three times in the previous few months:

> I'm in an unfamiliar house. I've never been in the house before, but I feel very comfortable in it. I'm in the kitchen with my fiancé. He's never been in the house, either. It seems as if I'm in the Midwest. We're conversing and there's background noise, like a machine going on, a blender or something. We're just talking. I don't know exactly what we're talking about. Then all of a sudden, everything just is still, quiet, almost as if you're watching like a still frame or something. We look outside and there's a huge tornado coming our way.

Prior to the session, Shari wrote the following interpretation:

> The dream probably means that there is some perceived turbulence in my life or my relationship with my significant other. The tornado prob-

ably symbolizes this turbulence. Or, the dream may signify my fear of turbulence to come because the dream takes place in an unknown environment/house.

In terms of action ideas, she said,

> Based on my current understanding of the dream, I would probably want to reevaluate my relationship or current life circumstances and identify and work on any problem areas. For example, if I find a problem in my relationship, I can discuss the problem with my significant other and take measures to alleviate the problem. Or, if I see a problem in my current life circumstances such as my career choice, I can search for other careers that will better suit my interests.

PROCESS AND OUTCOME OF THE SESSION

We provide information about the process of the 75-minute session (about 40 minutes in exploration, 20 minutes in insight, and 15 minutes in action) so readers have a context within which to evaluate our findings. Client speech has been edited slightly (e.g., deleted "you know," "like") throughout the chapter for readability.

The Exploration Stage

After retelling the dream, Shari said (in response to the therapist's query) that she did not feel scared when she woke up from the dream but felt "confused," that the dream was "weird," and that her breath had "been taken away for a brief second right when I see the tornado."

The therapist then guided the client through an exploration of four major images using the DRAW steps. First, she asked Shari to "paint me a picture of that house in your dream." Shari described the kitchen as small and indicated where the window, sink, and appliances were; described the paint and wallpaper as having a dark yellowish tint but that the room was bright; and stated that the house as a whole was small and confining. She described feeling "comfortable" and said that the house "makes me feel kind of old . . . like I've been living there for a long time." Associations (abbreviated) to the house were that it was old, cozy, and friendly. Waking-life triggers included driving home and seeing a little shack by the roadside, living in a small house when she was a child, moving to a larger house, living in a confined space in the university dormitory, and now living in a bigger apartment.

Moving to the image of the fiancé, Shari noted that he was debating with her in the dream. She described him as taller and "always looking down on me," older, and having a "really nice demeanor in the dream." She felt "happy and comfortable" with him, like "it's natural to be there with him," and noted that they were teasing each other. Her associations were that her fiancé is grumpy in the morning, sensitive and sweet, opinionated, stubborn, intelligent, a "just perfect person," but she also said that she was frustrated with him because he was "not a go-getter." She noted that "we've been engaged for a while" and "don't have the money right now to sustain a marriage" and that she was "getting frustrated with that."

With the image of the Midwest, Shari said she went to school in the Midwest, where everything was "slower" and "people were nicer," although she also said it was "tornado valley [sic]." She felt that she "belonged there" and that it was a place she'd "want to be when I'm older." When asked what prompted the image of the Midwest, she said that she was "graduating this August" and thinking about applying to graduate schools there.

In the last image, Shari described the tornado as very huge, gray, turbulent, and coming slowly toward the house. At that point, "time stood still," everything other than the tornado receded, and she didn't know what to do. She did not turn to her fiancé in the dream, but rather felt that she was on her own and knew that she "should take action right away." She associated tornadoes with disasters, chaos, the unexpected, and a forced change. For waking-life triggers, she mentioned recent tornado warnings, being worried about sudden changes in her life that could be disasters, and wanting control over what was going on in her life.

After summarizing what they had covered in the exploration stage, the therapist asked Shari about her current thoughts about the meaning of the dream. Shari responded,

> There's some kind of conflict in my life or something I'm worrying about, whether it pertains to my fiancé or just my general life right now. I'm worried about a change that might be occurring, and I see some kind of turbulence, some kind of negative associations that I might be having to this change. Or maybe I'm feeling kind of negative feelings toward the environment that I'm in now or the relationship I'm in now, and I want to fix it. I basically want to solve it. It might mean that I want to move on to the next stage of my life or that I need or want change and see comfort in change, but at the same time I see a negative aspect to change as well, meaning that change is basically moving. I feel comfortable in that environment, but all of a sudden I see disaster coming. So maybe I feel negative and positive feelings about doing this change or moving. Or maybe I see some kind of conflict in my own relationship with my fiancé. I want everything to change, meaning that if I want to go away to school or if I want to choose a different career, I want something else to happen in my life, I want to get married.

Insight Stage

Given that Shari's interpretation at the end of the exploration stage focused on current conflicts in her life, the therapist encouraged Shari to work on understanding the dream at the waking life level in this stage. The therapist first asked Shari to clarify what she wanted in life. Shari responded that she wanted a career, to go to graduate school, to get married and move in with her fiancé, and to change environments. However, she also seemed ambivalent about making changes (e.g., she said that she wanted to make "multiple changes all at once" but doing so "burns me out"; she said that she usually feels good after accomplishing a lot of things but then "I just want to lie down on the couch or go for a walk and like not to think of anything").

The therapist encouraged Shari to think about aspects of her dream that she had not incorporated into her interpretation. Specifically, she asked Shari to speculate about why everything in the dream disappeared when the tornado arrived. Shari suggested that the dream indicated that when problems came up, she had to deal with them on her own. Having to deal with problems on her own led Shari to recall that she had focused on trying to make her fiancé happy at the beginning of their relationship, but her studies recently had become a greater priority and so she was less focused on her fiancé. She also said that she and her fiancé had lived together for a while near the beginning of their relationship, but it did not work out because "our lives were so different" and she "is more of a control freak than he is."

At the end of the insight stage, the therapist asked Shari about her current thoughts regarding the meaning of the dream. Shari responded,

> It probably deals with my relationship. I'm very comfortable with him and we're really good for each other, but at the same time I feel all of these stressors coming up. I don't know exactly how to deal with them, what should I do, or what we can do as a team together. Maybe I'm thinking the dream means that the tornado comes and I want to handle it all myself. Maybe for me maybe that's not the way it should be. Maybe it should be both of us handling it together rather than me trying to handle everything myself. Maybe that's a sign to me telling me it's both of us, not just me working at it.

The Action Stage

When asked how she would change the dream, Shari said she would like to work with her fiancé to cope with the tornado, and she would like to have the tornado farther in the distance so they "could still see it" but have "more time to have fun." When asked to translate these changes to waking life, Shari said she wanted to "change how I go about dealing with certain circumstances that come up," and she wanted to talk with her fiancé when there is a problem so they "see each other's points of view." Specifically, she said she wanted to include her fiancé more in her activities, discuss her fears with him, and talk to him about wanting to move in together. The therapist asked if there was a specific time that she could plan such a talk, and Shari said, "I can ask him to take a walk with me and maybe discuss what's bothering me." In summarizing her action plan, Shari said, "I'm going to be more aware of how I'm feeling and what kinds of problems are arising in my life," "see how that relates to my relationship," and "discuss problems more often with my fiancé so things don't build up."

Outcome of the Session

In comparison to the average client (see Table 10.1), Shari and the therapist evaluated the relationship and the session highly. In addition, Shari gained more insight and action ideas than the average client, rated herself as functioning higher than average on her target problem at follow-up, but was about average in terms of intention to act and implementation. Hence, from this evidence we assert that this was a very helpful session and that the client made therapeutic progress, particularly in terms of insight gains.

Two-Week Follow-Up

Shari indicated that she had spent 5 to 10 minutes a day on average after the session thinking about her dream. Her written interpretation at follow-up was,

> The dream may represent my desire to share responsibility and decisions with my fiancé since I feel like I deal with many issues independently, which in turn induces overwhelming feelings. The tornado may represent these overwhelming feelings that get amplified when I feel like I am facing an issue alone. Or the dream may represent my feelings that my fiancé sometimes doesn't work collaboratively with me to resolve relationship issues but rather avoids them. This avoidance may be represented by his fading away in the dream as the tornado approached. Therefore, the tornado may represent my feelings of frustration towards him, which only get more amplified as he avoids the issue.

In terms of action, Shari wrote that, "We went for a walk and discussed the desire to become more of a unit with regard to activities and life decisions; we briefly mentioned moving in together."

FACTORS ASSOCIATED WITH INSIGHT

We now discuss the dream, relationship, client, and therapist factors that seemed to be associated with these insight gains. We provide evidence for our speculations by referring to specific statements from the session. We remind readers that because this was not an experimental manipulation, we cannot be certain that these factors actually did or did not lead to insight gains. Replication will be necessary to confirm our speculations.

Dream Factors Related to Insight Gains

Shari's score on the Dream Salience measure was above average (see Table 10.1), which indicates that this was a salient dream for her. Relatedly, the therapist asked, "Can you maybe talk a little more about what it was about this dream that prompted you to bring it in?" Shari replied,

> It's just that I never had a dream with a natural disaster in it. I usually have dreams where I'm interacting with people I know. I didn't know what it meant to have a disastrous thing happen in the dream, so I brought it in. And since this has happened three times, it's just kind of weird to me that it just keeps popping up.

In fact, Shari used the word *weird* 19 times in reference to the dream, all during the exploration stage; this suggests that she thought the dream was unusual and puzzling. In addition, in several instances Shari indicated confusion about what the dream meant (e.g., "I just feel confused, like I don't feel threatened or anything like that. You would think that you would be scared, but I feel confused, like what the hell happened right now?").

Furthermore, the dream seemed salient because it was directly related to pressing issues in Shari's waking life. In her presession interpretation, Shari clearly linked the dream to her waking life, although the referents were vague ("perceived turbulence in my life or relationship with my fiancé . . . or fear of turbulence to come"). In the session as well, she suggested that the dream was related to her relationship with her fiancé, graduating and making decisions about graduate school and a career, and needing a change in general. Shari was graduating soon and preparing to move on to the next phase of her life, but nothing was settled in terms of her romantic relationship or her career.

However, the dream was surprisingly devoid of affect; the only feeling word that Shari used, in fact, was *comfortable*. Furthermore, the first part of the dream was relatively mundane, as the client and her fiancé were simply talking in the kitchen. Even with the coming of the tornado Shari reported there was stillness and a vague sense of anticipation, but the tornado stayed in the distance and did not seem to be a direct threat. Perhaps it was easier for Shari to talk about a dream that was not *too* salient. This dream seems ideal to explore in a single session because it was not too negative, overwhelming, or threatening to the client.

Overall, then, the dream seemed salient to the client. Shari was puzzled but not overwhelmed by the dream, was concerned because it was recurrent, and related it directly to her waking life. In the literature there is evidence that emotional arousal is necessary for therapeutic change (Festinger, 1957; Levy, 1963), and we suggest that this dream was indeed arousing for this client. Thus, we postulate that the dream itself was a contributor to the insight gains—it motivated Shari to want to understand it.

The Therapeutic Relationship

At postsession, both Shari and the therapist evaluated the therapeutic relationship highly (see Table 10.1). The strength of the relationship was also reflected in the therapist's and client's ability to move smoothly through all steps of the model. In addition, there were no obvious markers of client resistance to therapist influence (e.g., "Yes, but"), nor any indication of ruptures in the relationship. Furthermore, with regard to Bordin's (1979) three components of the therapeutic relationship, there seemed to be a good bond in the dyad (their ratings suggested that they liked working together), agreement on tasks (the therapist explained the model completely at the beginning and they progressed smoothly through the session), and agreement on goals (both tacitly agreed to work on a dream in the session).

Thus, if we apply Rogers's (1957) theory that a good relationship is a necessary condition for client change (if the therapist accepts the client, the client comes to accept herself, and thus her self-actualizing tendencies are unblocked), we can speculate that the relationship in this case had an indirect influence on insight gains. We assert, then, that the therapeutic relationship formed the foundation on which client involvement and therapist skills could be built.

CLIENT FACTORS RELATED TO INSIGHT GAINS

We identified both facilitating and limiting client factors that seemed to be related to insight gains. More specifically, client readiness, motivation, and involvement seemed to be facilitating factors, whereas the client's emotional mutedness, lack of self-reflectiveness, contradictions, giggling, and tentative style seemed to be limiting factors.

Facilitating Client Factors

Client Readiness and Motivation

Shari clearly had been thinking about and trying to figure out the meaning of the dream on her own, as evidenced by the initial moderate amount of insight and action ideas related to her dream (see Table 10.1). Furthermore, in a presession measure, Shari agreed with the statement (giving a rating of 4 on a 5-point scale, 5 = high), "I am eager to learn more about what this particular dream means," providing another indication that she was ready to gain more insight. Given the evidence in the literature about client readiness being a contributing influence on therapeutic change (Prochaska & Norcross, 2002), we speculate that Shari's readiness and eagerness laid the foundation for her insight gains. Specifically, we postulate that her readiness contributed to her becoming involved in the session and allowed her to be open to therapist influence.

Client Involvement

The therapist, client, and judges all rated the client as having been moderately to extremely involved in the session (see Table 10.1). We note, as well, that Shari was a very cooperative client: She complied with everything the therapist asked her to do (e.g., explored the images, actively struggled to understand the dream, and came up with action ideas), did not resist the therapist's gentle structuring of the session in any way, and did not try to change the course of the session.

On the basis of the theory that clients are the ones who make the changes through their direct involvement, or are the "self-healers" (Bohart & Tallman, 1999), we speculate that client involvement thus directly contributed to insight gains. We caution, however, that client involvement cannot be separated from therapist competence (i.e., had the therapist been less competent in using the model, Shari likely would have been less involved).

Limiting Client Factors

Although Shari was in many ways an ideal client and was obviously very motivated and engaged in the session, in our study we observed some behaviors that seemed to limit her ability to gain insight. First, her affect was flat, her manner muted, and she did not exhibit any strong emotions (e.g., laughter, crying).

Second, Shari did not seem particularly psychologically minded or self-reflective. The closest she came to being aware of the reasons for her behavior was a statement that, "My personality is all or nothing. I just go out and I either do it or I don't . . . that's just how I am. I'm always very much all or none." This statement seemed more a description of her personality than an exploration of how she became that way. Similarly, she seemed aware that she sometimes took out her frustrations on her fiancé when she was "stressed out" because of her having to study when he had free time, but she went no deeper than this recognition of a behavioral pattern. Likewise, she expressed curiosity as to why her fiancé appeared in her dreams, but her explanation extended no further than that they were "used to being around each other."

Third, Shari contradicted herself several times. She said that the kitchen had a "dark yellowish tint" that was "a little weird," but it felt "comfortable to be there," and "it's bright even though the wallpaper is kind of yellowish, dark yellowish." When asked what was appealing about the Midwest, Shari replied,

> It's just away from here, because I mean I love it here, and I grew up here, but I just need a change, and I think that when I make a change, I want

a total change. I want everything to be different, so it probably has to do with moving as far away as I can, but for some reason I don't want to go too far away.

As another example, Shari described the tornado as 5 times the size of a 13-story building, whereas later she said it was 3 times the size of an apartment building. Similarly, she said the tornado was "a mile away or so, a half a mile, a mile away, I mean pretty much a couple miles away."

Fourth, Shari giggled 74 times during the session, particularly when she seemed anxious (e.g., she giggled when describing her fiancé: "He's so sensitive and sweet, and like, he's opinionated and a little stubborn."). Similarly, Shari used the phrases "I don't know," "you know," and "like" frequently, which gave a sense of tentativeness or indecisiveness to her presentation style.

The muted affect, lack of self-reflectiveness, contradictions, giggling, and tentative style could reflect guardedness or defensiveness, anxiety, confusion about the dream, or underlying unconscious conflicts blocking her path to understanding the dream. We also wondered as we reviewed the session about the influence of Shari's culture, specifically whether her being of Arabic descent influenced these behaviors in the session. Unfortunately, the topic of culture was never addressed, so we do not have any data from which to draw conclusions about its potential influence. Thus, despite the evident gains Shari received from the session, it is possible that some factors (e.g., personality, culture) blocked her from delving even more deeply into her dream and thus achieving greater insight.

Summary of Client Factors

On the facilitating side, Shari was a "dream" client who was ready for dream work and involved in the process of collaborating with the therapist to understand her dream. On the limiting side, Shari had flat affect, was not psychologically minded, contradicted herself, giggled, and used tentative phraseology. On balance, however, the facilitating factors outweighed the inhibiting factors and seemed to help Shari gain insight.

THERAPIST FACTORS ASSOCIATED WITH INSIGHT GAINS

Several therapist factors appeared to be related to client insight gains. More specifically, therapist adherence and competence in applying the model, positive countertransference reactions, and skills all seemed to be associated with insight gains.

Therapist Adherence and Competence in Applying the Model

In this analysis we judged that the therapist adhered closely to the model, following the steps almost exactly and moving smoothly between the stages.

In fact, the session could be viewed as an example of how to implement this model. Furthermore, the therapist, client, and trained judges all rated the therapist as having been moderately to extremely competent in the session (see Table 10.1). In addition, it seems that the therapist was very responsive to the client's needs as she gave Shari a lot of room to respond and did not rush or push her (e.g., she allowed the client to describe fully the images in her dream).

The session might have been even more productive, however, had the therapist been more curious and probed for more exploration. For example, when Shari described the house in the dream as small and confining, it may have been beneficial had the therapist helped Shari explore her other experiences with houses (e.g., was her childhood home also small and confining?) and other functions of houses (e.g., for what other purposes are houses used?). Similarly, Shari mentioned that she had attended college for a year or two in the Midwest and then returned to complete her degree in her home state. We were curious as to why she chose to return and what, if any, relevance this decision may have had to her dream. Likewise, when Shari stated that she and her fiancé had earlier lived together for a short time, but that it hadn't "worked out," we wondered what had happened and how that event may have been connected to her dream. In another example, at the end of the exploration stage the therapist summarized the dream (as called for in the dream model) but then did not ask the client for her reactions to the summary. Furthermore, more insight might have been attained had the therapist guided Shari to work with the dream at levels of insight other than just connecting the dream to her waking life (e.g., to parts of self).

Countertransference Reactions

At postsession, the therapist reported only "slight" countertransference in working with this client. She indicated, "I felt very comfortable with the client, as she [client] was quite involved in the session from the beginning. I also felt I could relate to some of her experiences, particularly in the area of change." Furthermore, the therapist indicated that her own unresolved issues were evoked by the client only "slightly" in that

> I am facing similar issues in my desire for change. I am at a point where I am eager for change in my life, but I am also comfortable with the way my life has been for years. I am fearful of what change might bring, but I feel like doing the same old same old is getting me down. I just don't want to change for the sake of change and then regret it, which is what the client seems concerned about.

Thus, the therapist's positive feelings about the client and identification with her probably helped create a bond that allowed the client to feel safe enough to pursue insight (and certainly did not appear to impede insight acquisition). We wondered, though, whether the reason the therapist did not press Shari to go deeper (see section on competence in this chap.) arose from her identification with Shari (e.g., perhaps the therapist was reluctant to push Shari to explore an area about which the therapist felt unresolved in her own life).

Therapist Skills

Because probes for insight directly ask the client to think about insight, and interpretations offer some possible insights, we hypothesized that these two skills would facilitate immediate insight. Hence, as indicated previously, we coded therapist skills in each therapist speaking turn and client insight in the subsequent client speaking turn. A repeated measures analysis of variance (ANOVA), however, found that probes for insight and reflection of feeling led to more immediate client insight than did the other therapist skills (see Table 10.2). In this section we discuss examples from the session to illustrate these results.

Probes for Insight

Therapist probes for insight (e.g., "What do you think the dream means?") typically were associated with insight in the subsequent client response. In one example the therapist said,

> In the dream one of the things that struck me was the fact that you said when you realized that this tornado was coming at you, everything else, even your fiancé, kind of disappear and that you're thinking about you. I'm wondering if anything comes up for you about what that's about?

Shari responded,

> A lot of the times in the beginning of my relationship with my fiancé, I was very much always wanting him to be happy and pleased. And he was like, 'hey, that's not how it works, we're both supposed to be taken care of.' So I was like, 'okay,' so I eased down. But as time went on, I kind of eased down too much. I kind of felt like I don't think my stuff is more important than his but sometimes I put it in front of him. But at the same time I think he's more important, but at the same time I want to get this done so I can spend time with him. So maybe with the dream when that problem came up maybe I thought I was just, hey, it's my problem, it's not your problem, so I don't want you to deal with it, just go do your own thing and I'll deal with it and come back to you after I'm done.

Probes for insight thus seemed to allow the therapist to function as a coach who facilitated and even empowered Shari in coming to her own understanding of the dream. Probes for insight may also have been more effective than the other skills because they instructed the client in exactly what the therapist wanted her to do (e.g., "tell me what the dream means"). In

TABLE 10.2
Frequency of Predominant Skills Used by the Therapist and Average Client Insight in the Following Speaking Turn

Predominant skills	N	M	SD
Minimal encourages	1	1.00	—
Closed question	10	1.00$_c$	0.00
Open question	41	1.05$_c$	0.31
Restatement	37	1.22$_{bc}$	0.58
Reflection	5	1.60$_{ab}$	0.89
Probe for insight	19	2.11$_a$	0.88
Interpretation	2	1.00	—
Information	6	1.00$_{bc}$	0.00
Direct guidance	0	—	—

Note. The predominant skill in each therapist speaking turn was coded by consensus using Hill's (2004b) Helping Skills System. *Insight* was rated using a 5-point scale ranging from *none* (1) to *very high* (5) based on Hill et al.'s (1992) definition of insight. A repeated measures ANOVA conducted on those skills that occurred more than three times was significant, $F(5,117) = 11.51$, $p < .001$. Post hoc analyses contrasted the skills using a least-squares differences method; subscripts that share any of the same letters were not significantly different from one another ($p < .05$).

addition, probes may have indicated a genuine curiosity on the therapist's part that allowed the client to feel that the therapist was really interested in her. These findings support previous literature on the helpfulness of probes (Hill & Gormally, 1977; Hill et al., 2003) but refine our understanding that it is probes for insight rather than generic probes that lead to insight.

It is interesting to note that several probes for insight occurred in the exploration stage, whereas Hill (1996, 2004a) implied that most insight is gained in the insight stage. Some exploration stage probes asked about triggers for the images in waking life (e.g., "What might have triggered the image of . . . ?"), whereas others were *why* questions that asked the client to search inward for her thoughts ("Why are you doing that?," "What is it about being older . . . ?," and "What is it that is appealing . . . ?"). In contrast, the probes used in the insight stage inquired about the meaning of the parts of the dream (e.g. "What is it about change . . . ?," "What might that mean?") or encouraged the client to integrate different parts of the dream into her interpretation (e.g., "I'm wondering if that ties in here?"). Thus, the therapist modified the probes to fit the stage (i.e., exploration stage probes focused on specific images, whereas insight stage probes focused on the dream as a whole), which probably enhanced their effectiveness.

Reflections of Feelings

Of the four reflections of feelings used, two led to minimal or moderate insight. For example, toward the end of the session the therapist reflected, "But it [problems in the relationship with her fiancé] still sounds like something that's a little worrying to you." Shari replied,

> Yeah, yeah, I know our relationship is going to work if everything stays the same because we've had our ups and downs, and we know what it

feels like to have our ups and downs, but at the same time I want to be able to know if something happens in the future, will I be able to deal with it and will you be able to deal with it and we can, can we both deal with it together.

Interpretations

Because we had hypothesized that interpretations would lead to insight, we examined qualitative evidence for delayed effects of this skill on insight development that might not have been found using the analysis of the immediate effects (i.e., the ratings of insight immediately following interpretations). The therapist gave two interpretations of what the dream might mean. In the first, the therapist said, "So [the] tornado is change happening. That's change coming at you." The client responded only minimally, "Probably yeah, that makes sense." The therapist continued, "So it sounds like there's a struggle for you about wanting things to change, wanting to have this relationship on your terms and have things settled, but also feeling that pull, you're not ready, he's not ready, the two of you still have stuff to work out." Again, the client responded minimally, "That's true, yeah." The therapist then went on to ask the client what she thought the dream meant now that they had gone through the insight stage. The client's interpretation expanded on her own initial interpretation by including material from the insight stage, primarily related to understanding more about how she did not turn to her fiancé for help.

The therapist, then, used interpretations at the end of the insight stage as a way of summarizing and pulling together what the client had been discussing. They were close to the surface (more like restatements) and did not delve into deep material. Shari passively agreed with the therapist's interpretations but did not enthusiastically endorse them or add new material (the latter is often seen as a sign of the effectiveness of an interpretation; see Basch, 1980). These interpretations thus did not seem to be particularly helpful for Shari to expand on what she had already gained from the insight stage.

We wonder if even more insight would have been gained, however, had the therapist given an interpretation related to Shari's contradictions about her fiancé (e.g., "You seem to have an approach–withdrawal dance going on with your fiancé in which you demand more closeness and he withdraws," or "I wonder if you are afraid of making a commitment to your fiancé because you are worried that you will lose your identity"). Such interpretations may have deepened Shari's affect and encouraged her to examine these issues. However, Shari might not have been ready or open in this single session to pursue deeper interpretations. In addition, such interpretations might have been counterproductive for this particular client because she might have become passive or learned not to trust her own interpretive powers.

In our analysis we were struck by how few interpretations were used in the session and speculated that there was something about the client that caused the therapist to use a more probing, rather than interpretive, style. The therapist, however, indicated during questioning that she rarely uses interpretations and that this session was typical of her style. We can assume, then, that the low number of interpretations was due to the therapist's orientation, although the therapist may also have been responsive to the client's need to come up with her own interpretation.

Other Skills

We also qualitatively examined restatements and open questions for any evidence that they might have led to client insight. Both skills seemed to be helpful in supporting the client and helping her explore and both were used in the same or nearby speaking turns as probes for insight and reflections of feelings. We found minimal evidence, however, that restatements and open questions were directly associated with insight gains for this client. Of course, these other interventions may have been more indirect in their influence on promoting insight by setting the stage for the other skills to work. Had the therapist only probed for insight, for example, Shari might not have felt understood nor perceived that the therapist was working collaboratively to help her explore the dream. We noted that the therapist often restated first to set the stage and then used a probe for insight in the same speaking turn. Thus, the combination of skills may have helped Shari feel understood and then more able to gain insight.

Summary of Therapist Factors

The therapist, who had conducted a number of dream sessions previously, adhered closely to the model and was competent in its implementation (which was facilitated by and facilitated client involvement). We conclude that therapist adherence and competence contributed to client involvement and thus to insight development, which is consistent with Hill's (2004a) suggestion that successful implementation of the exploration and insight stages can lead to insight.

Furthermore, we conclude that the therapist was able to be adherent and competent because she was relatively unfettered by debilitating countertransference. In fact, the therapist identified with the client, which seemed to help create a bond between them. Thus, we judge that the lack of countertransference was indirectly associated with insight gains.

In terms of skills, we found that probes for insight and reflection of feelings were the most effective in directly facilitating immediate client insight. Furthermore, we noted that the combination of skills seemed helpful, with restatements and general open questions setting the stage for the probes for insight and reflections of feelings to work.

CONSEQUENCES OF INSIGHT

Shari's interpretation and action ideas (presented earlier in this chapter) before the session were vague and diffuse: She said that the dream could be related to some unidentified turbulence in her life, her relationship with her fiancé, or her fear of some future problem. Likewise, her initial action ideas were to reevaluate her relationships or current life circumstances and fix any identified problems. By the end of the insight stage, however, she had narrowed her interpretation down to problems in her relationship with her fiancé, which then seemed to allow her to formulate specific action ideas and develop the motivation to carry them out. Having the clear action plan and an intention to act seemed to enable Shari to implement the action ideas. We speculate, then, that gaining insight in the exploration and insight stages enabled Shari to formulate a good action plan and develop an intention to act during the action stage, which in turn helped her implement her action ideas after the session and begin to resolve her target problems. Hence, because the client likely could not have formulated a clear action plan without having some understanding of the dream, we assert that insight led to action.

We cannot make any assertions about changes in other typical therapy outcomes (e.g., self-esteem, symptomatology, interpersonal functioning) as these variables were not measured in this study. We guess that making changes in this specific interpersonal problem led to enhanced self-esteem, improved interpersonal communication, and a better relationship with her fiancé, but we simply have no evidence to make these assertions.

CONCLUDING COMMENTS

Although insight is often discussed as a sudden *Aha!* experience (Elliott et al., 1994), it is important to note that there was no moment in this session when the client suddenly "got" the meaning of the dream. Indeed, there was also no moment in which the therapist (or any of us reviewing the session) acquired a brilliant new insight into the dream. Instead, the client seemed to know roughly what the dream was about prior to the session and then sharpened and deepened her understanding as a result of the dream session. Rather than viewing her insight as a *gold nugget* dropped on her by the therapist or revealed suddenly, a better metaphor for her acquisition of insight may be *gold dust* that was gradually sifted and gathered. Thus, Shari seemed to have a fairly good initial grasp of the meaning of her dream in relation to her waking life and just needed help to nurture it into a deeper understanding. We are curious to know whether this metaphor of gold dust would apply to other cases. If so, we recommend that suddenness is not necessary in the definition of insight.

Furthermore, we are intrigued that Shari continued to gain insight even after the session. We speculate that Shari's continuing to work on the dream after the session reflected her keen desire to understand the dream, which can also be seen by the fact that she thought about the dream before the session. In addition, we speculate that her continued work after the session was partially due to the therapist's encouragement of Shari's ability to actively derive her own insight rather than waiting for the therapist to deliver *the* interpretation, a technique that might have rendered Shari passive in the insight process. Interestingly, it may also be that the lack of a definitive or complete insight at the end of the session stimulated Shari to continue to speculate about the dream on her own. Similarly, Wilson, Centerbar, Kermer, and Gilbert (2005) found that people prefer not knowing the exact end of a movie or story because not knowing prompts them to continue thinking about alternative endings. Thus, it may actually be better for therapists not to deliver *the* interpretations of dreams completely (even if that were possible), because our goal as therapists is often to encourage clients to keep working on their own. In the case of dreams, such a premise suggests that therapists offer clients tools with which they can work to understand their own dreams, rather than giving clients *the* interpretation of the dream.

Factors Leading to Insight

On the basis of our careful observation of this case, it seems that the following factors were associated with Shari's attainment of insight: dream salience, the therapeutic relationship, client factors (readiness, involvement in the tasks of the session), and therapist factors (adherence and competence, lack of countertransference, and skills—specifically, probes for insight and reflections of feeling). Furthermore, we found evidence that client factors (flat affect, lack of psychological-mindedness, possible guardedness or anxiety) and therapist factors (overidentification with the client) may have limited insight gains. Finally, we suggest that the insight gained in the session led directly to action and to problem resolution.

With regard to how these factors may fit together in this case, we think that the dream provided the initial motivation for the client, given that she felt some pressure to understand its meaning. When the client began the session, she was ready to work and the therapist was competent at approaching the session, both of which helped to build the therapeutic relationship. This in turn fostered the client's involvement and the therapist's ability to adhere to and be competent at implementing the model. Because of the relationship, client involvement, and therapist adherence and competence, the client was able to engage in the tasks of dream work. According to Hill (1996, 2004a), these tasks involve accessing and activating the cognitive schema (memory structures) related to her dream images and organizing the elements in a new way. By articulating her new cognitive organization (i.e., insight), the client was able to expand on her understanding of the meaning of her dream. Because the insight was salient for the client, she was able to use it to develop an action plan, which she implemented after the session. Implementation of her action ideas likely helped her to further consolidate the insight and thus work on her target problem. We suggest that it would be useful to examine such schema changes further and compare changes in insight in therapy with findings about schemas and schema change from cognitive psychology (Barile-Spears, Booher, & Durso, 2004; Durso, Rea, & Dayton, 1994).

Implications for Theory and Practice

These results suggest that the exploration stage may be more important than was previously thought. Hill (1996, 2004a) conceptualized the exploration stage as a time that primarily set the foundation for later insight but assumed that insight was attained in the insight stage. It is clear from this session and from the larger study from which this session was drawn (Hill et al., in press), however, that clients gain at least as much insight during the exploration stage as they do in the insight stage. Specifically, the therapist's queries to Shari about triggers in her waking life directed Shari to think about why a particular image occurred, thus stimulating an insight process. It may make sense, then, to think of the exploration stage as stimulating pieces of insight that then are consolidated in the insight stage into a coherent narrative about the meaning of the whole dream.

Implications for Research

As we look to future research directions we urge investigators to replicate these findings with new cases of dream work, those that are both similar and dissimilar to this client. Furthermore, we encourage additional examination of how probes for insight and reflections of feelings affect insight development with different types of clients. We remain curious about the finding that interpretations did not stimulate client insight and encourage researchers to examine this question as well. Finally, it would be interesting to trace the relationship between insight acquisition and other therapy outcomes (e.g., symptom reduction) to investigate the role of insight in behavioral change and improved client functioning.

REFERENCES

Barile-Spears, A. L., Booher, S., & Durso, F. T. (2004). The effect of computer-mediated communication of knowledge structures in problem-solving situations. *Cognitive Technology, 9*, 43–48.

Basch, M. F. (1980). *Doing psychotherapy.* New York: Basic Books.

Bohart, A. C., & Tallman, K. (1999). *How clients make therapy work: The process of active self-healing.* Washington, DC: American Psychological Association.

Bordin, E. S. (1979). The generalizability of the psychoanalytic concept of the working alliance. *Psychotherapy: Theory, Research and Practice, 16,* 252–260.

Cohen, J. (1988). *Statistical power analysis for the behavioral sciences* (2nd ed.). Hillsdale, NJ: Erlbaum.

Durso, F. T., Rea, C. B., & Dayton, T. (1994). Graph-theoretic confirmation of restructuring during insight. *Psychological Science, 5,* 94–98.

Elliott, R., Shapiro, D. A., Firth-Cozens, J., Stiles, W. B., Hardy, G. E., Llewelyn, S. P., & Margison, F. R. (1994). Comprehensive process analysis of insight events in cognitive–behavioral and psychodynamic–interpersonal psychotherapies. *Journal of Counseling Psychology, 41,* 449–463.

Festinger, L. (1957). *A theory of cognitive dissonance.* Evanston, IL: Row, Peterson.

Hill, C. E. (1996). *Working with dreams in psychotherapy.* New York: Guilford Press.

Hill, C. E. (Ed.). (2004a). *Dream work in therapy: Facilitating exploration, insight, and action.* Washington, DC: American Psychological Association.

Hill, C. E. (2004b). *Helping skills: Facilitating exploration, insight, and action* (2nd ed.). Washington, DC: American Psychological Association.

Hill, C. E., Corbett, M. M., Kanitz, B., Rios, P., Lightsey, R., & Gomez, M. (1992). Client behavior in counseling and therapy sessions: Development of a pantheoretical measure. *Journal of Counseling Psychology, 39,* 539–549.

Hill, C. E., Crook-Lyon, R. E., Goates-Jones, M. K., Roffman, M., Stahl, J., Sim, W., & Johnson, M. (in press). Prediction of the session process and outcome in the Hill dream model: Contributions of client characteristics and the process of the three stages. *Dreaming.*

Hill, C. E., & Goates, M. K. (2004). Research on the Hill cognitive–experiential dream model. In C. E. Hill (Ed.), *Dream work in therapy: Facilitating exploration, insight, and action* (pp. 245–288). Washington, DC: American Psychological Association.

Hill, C. E., & Gormally, J. (1977). Effect of reflection, restatement, probe, and non-verbal behavior on client affect. *Journal of Counseling Psychology, 24,* 92–97.

Hill, C. E., & Lambert, M. J. (2004). Methodological issues in studying psychotherapy processes and outcomes. In M. J. Lambert (Ed.), *Handbook of psychotherapy and behavior change* (5th ed., pp. 84–136). New York: Wiley.

Hill, C. E., Rochlen, A. B., Zack, J. S., McCready, T., & Dematatis, A. (2003). Working with dreams using the Hill cognitive–experiential model: A comparison of computer-assisted, therapist empathy, and therapist empathy + input conditions. *Journal of Counseling Psychology, 50,* 211–220.

Hill, C. E., & Williams, E. N. (2000). The process of individual therapy. In R. W. Lent & S. D. Brown (Eds.), *Handbook of counseling psychology* (pp. 670–710). New York: Wiley.

Levy, L. H. (1963). *Psychological interpretation.* New York: Holt, Rinehart & Winston.

Prochaska, J. O., & Norcross, J. C. (2002). Stages of change. In J. C. Norcross (Ed.), *Psychotherapy relationships that work: Therapist contributions and responsiveness to patients* (pp. 303–314). New York: Oxford University Press.

Rogers, C. R. (1957). The necessary and sufficient conditions of therapeutic personality change. *Journal of Consulting Psychology, 21,* 95–103.

Van de Castle, R. L. (1994). *The dreaming mind.* New York: Ballantine Books.

Wilson, T. D., Centerbar, D. B., Kermer, D. A., & Gilbert, D. T. (2005). The pleasure of uncertainty: Prolonging positive moods in ways people do not anticipate. *Journal of Personality and Social Psychology, 88,* 5–21.

11

THE CHANGE AND GROWTH EXPERIENCES SCALE: A MEASURE OF INSIGHT AND EMOTIONAL PROCESSING

ADELE M. HAYES, GREG C. FELDMAN, AND MARVIN R. GOLDFRIED

Psychotherapy can facilitate change in that it provides a safe environment in which clients can learn to manage overwhelming distress, approach previously avoided material, express and experience negative emotions, and gain insight (Greenberg, 2002a; Greenberg & Safran, 1987). Insight is the process of developing understanding and constructing new meaning. Insight is a critical component of what has been labeled self-understanding, cognitive processing, assimilation–accommodation, meaning-making, emotional processing, and experiencing. Although different terms have been used, theorists across theoretical orientations hypothesize that gaining insight in an affectively charged context is a central process of change in psychotherapy (Brewin, Dalgleish, & Joseph, 1996; Foa & Kozak, 1986; Greenberg, 2002b;

This project was supported by National Institute of Mental Health grant R21 MH62662 awarded to the first author. We thank William Galyardt, David Greenawalt, Melanie Harris, Jose Sandoval, Jamie Lewis Smith, Jennifer Strauss, and Barbara Wolfsdorf, and our research and therapist teams. We also thank all of the participants in this study.

Samoilov & Goldfried, 2000; Stiles et al., 1990; Teasdale, 1999; Whelton, 2004).

In most of these theories insight is conceptualized as a dynamic variable that can range from fleeting or superficial realizations to more elaborated and substantial understandings and perspective shifts. Emotion-related material can be processed in different ways to yield these different levels of insight. Greenberg (2002b) reviewed literature on two systems that interact in the construction of personal meaning—a conscious, conceptual system and a tacit, experiential processing system. Teasdale (1999) described two similar systems—one that operates at the propositional level and another that operates at the implicational level. The propositional level is described as *conceptualizing/doing*, which involves thinking about thoughts, emotions, and goals in a relatively detached way. The implicational level is described as *mindful experiencing/being*. This involves integrated cognitive–affective exploration, awareness, and experiencing of feelings directly rather than as objects of conceptual thought. It is important at this level to also take a nonevaluative stance to facilitate insight and processing. Theorists from a number of perspectives agree that the most substantial and transformative insights occur in an affectively charged environment and at the experiential level of processing. Insight at this level is thought to promote broad, therapeutic changes in one's view of self and others, hope, and behavior (for reviews see Greenberg, 2002b; Pascual-Leone & Greenberg, chap. 2, this volume; Samoilov & Goldfried, 2000; Whelton, 2004).

Theories on recovery from trauma and adversity describe a process that is strikingly similar to what happens in psychotherapy and provide further support for insight as an important change process. For example, expressive writing about traumatic events has been found to have a range of beneficial effects on psychological and physical health, and insight in the context of affective arousal is hypothesized to be one of the mechanisms of change (Hunt, 1998; Pennebaker & Seagal, 1999; Sloan & Marx, 2004; Smyth, True, & Souto, 2001). In their theory of posttraumatic growth, Tedeschi and Calhoun (2004) described the natural processing of trauma and also noted how this is similar to the process of change in psychotherapy. A trauma can disturb one's core sense of self, the future, and the world. This disturbance is associated with initial distress and intrusive thoughts that can be overwhelming and can also be avoided. In a supportive environment, the person can move from recurrent, intrusive thoughts and avoidance to more deliberate exploration and insight, which includes meaning-making and schema change. The new, positive meanings that emerge can result in broad changes, including a reprioritization of goals and a greater appreciation for one's personal strengths, life circumstances, relationships, and spiritual life (see also Linley & Joseph, 2004).

Thus, research on psychotherapy, expressive writing, and recovery from trauma and adversity suggests that insight in the context of affective arousal is associated with a variety of positive outcomes. An assumption of this emphasis on affective arousal is that there will be a transient period of distress and destabilization during the processing of emotions and transformative insight (A. M. Hayes & Harris, 2000; A. M. Hayes & Strauss, 1998; Mahoney, 1991). In an initial study on the process of change in cognitive therapy for depression (A. M. Hayes & Strauss, 1998), we found that more affective arousal and variability in the cognitive, affective, behavioral, and somatic domains of functioning (destabilization) predicted more improvement in depression at the end of therapy. However, we did not have a measure of insight at that time to examine whether insight was occurring during this period of turbulence.

In this chapter, we describe a more recent study from a trial of integrative therapy for depression (A. M. Hayes, Beevers, Feldman, Laurenceau, & Perlman, 2005), in which we apply a new measure that we have developed to code therapy sessions and narratives for therapeutic insight and processing. With this measure we examine whether insight was associated with affective arousal and whether insight predicted posttreatment symptom improvement. We also examine whether insight was associated with positive changes in one's view of self and future, as predicted by theories of insight in psychotherapy and processing of trauma and adversity. The measure can also be used to study client processes that inhibit insight.

FACTORS THAT INHIBIT INSIGHT

When studying the process of developing insight, it is important to also consider factors that can interfere with insight, such as ruminative analysis and avoidance. Insight-seeking can stall out in a repetitive and unproductive loop of questioning and analyzing, as is the case with rumination, worry, obsession, and other forms of perseverative thought. If attempts to understand one's experiences persist over time without leading to some insight or clarity, it is useful to disengage and perhaps reinitiate the process at a later time. Chronic questioning and insight-seeking characterize a variety of forms of psychopathology, especially depression and anxiety disorders (Borkovec, 2002; Brewin et al., 1996; Lyubomirsky & Nolen-Hoeksema, 1993; Nolen-Hoeksema, 2000; Segerstrom, Stanton, Alden, & Shortridge, 2003; Watkins & Baracaia, 2001). Teasdale (1999) called this level of processing "mindless emoting," in which an individual is immersed in and identified with his or her affective reactions with little self-awareness or productive internal exploration or reflection. Therapeutic insight in its early stages can look like rumination in that it can involve questioning, analyzing, intrusive thoughts, and distress, but these two types of insight-seeking are associated with very different outcomes. These two inhibiting factors are important to consider when studying the process of change.

A way to disengage from recurrent insight-seeking and to decrease distress is to avoid the disturbing material. This avoidance can take many forms, including distraction, denial, cognitive distortion, suppression, repression, substance abuse, self-harm, disengagement, dissociation, and even suicide (S. C. Hayes, Wilson, Gifford, Follette, & Strosahl, 1996; Ottenbreit & Dobson, 2004). Ruminative processes can also serve the function of avoidance in that excessive thinking and emotionality can block deep experiencing (Borkovec, 2002). Those prone to intrusive thoughts, rumination, and worry might also avoid experiences that will trigger the recurrent thoughts because they are aware of this vulnerability (Borkovec, 2002; Segal, Williams, & Teasdale, 2002). There is evidence that avoidance is not associated with productive insight, but rather with a rebound of the avoided material and perpetuation of an avoidance–intrusion–rumination cycle (Beevers, Wenzlaff, Hayes, & Scott, 1999; Brewin et al., 1996; Wenzlaff & Luxton, 2003). There is also substantial evidence that both chronic insight-seeking and avoidance are associated with poor psychological and health outcomes (Gross, 2002; S. C. Hayes et al., 1996; Kiecolt-Glaser, McGuire, Robles, & Glaser, 2002; Nolen-Hoeksema & Davis, 2004; Salovey, Rothman, Detweiler, & Steward, 2000; Segerstrom et al., 2003). Therefore, it might be useful to study these two inhibiting factors when studying the process of gaining insight.

MEASURES OF INSIGHT AND EMOTIONAL PROCESSING

The primary goal of this chapter is to describe a coding system that we developed to study insight and processing in the context of therapy and in narratives from those undergoing difficult life circumstances, such as individuals with a chronic illness (e.g., HIV/AIDS). To illustrate how the coding system can be used, we present findings from an integrative therapy for depression in which clients wrote weekly essays about their depression over the course of therapy. We also present an individual case to elaborate on the process of gaining insight and the factors that inhibit insight.

Most measures that assess insight in psychotherapy describe stages of processing that range from avoidance to awareness, superficial understanding and insights, elaborated insights and working through, shifts in meaning, and problem resolution or completion–integration (e.g., Angus, Levitt, & Hardtke, 1999; Greenberg, 2002b; Klein, Mathieu-Coughlan, & Kiesler, 1986; Stiles et al., 1990). Because of the importance of focusing on emotion-related material and affective arousal in the development of insight and meaning-making, the label *emotional processing* is often used to describe this type of therapeutic change. As the scale that we developed is based on an integration of ideas across the literature in psychotherapy change, expressive writing, and recovery and growth after adversity, we use the term *insight–processing* so that the construct is recognizable across research areas.

Because insight–processing, rumination, and avoidance can co-occur, have different time courses, and be associated with different outcomes, it is sometimes useful to study these three insight-related variables separately. Some measures of insight and processing, such as the Experiencing Scale (Klein et al., 1986) and Assimilation of Problematic Experiences Scale (Stiles et al., 1990), place insight–processing, rumination, and avoidance on the same continuum as a single variable. Another related scale, the Narrative Processes Coding System (Angus et al., 1999), does not include categories that directly assess avoidance or ruminative insight-seeking.

The scale that we developed, the Change and Growth Experiences Scale (CHANGE; A. M. Hayes & Feldman, 2005), can complement these other measures as it is designed to code the extent of *insight–processing, rumination, and avoidance* so they can be studied as separate variables, with perhaps different relations with outcome and different correlates. It can also be used to examine whether insight–processing is associated with changes in one's sense of self and future. The scale includes categories to assess negative and positive affect, behavior, somatic functioning, and relationship quality, but for the purposes of this chapter we focus only on the variables that relate directly to insight–processing. We also present an interesting methodology for studying the process of change as we had clients write essays about their depression over the entire course of therapy. This provides a rich source of data and a unique window into the change process from the client's perspective. Although the process of gaining insight involves therapist interventions, the therapeutic relationship, and client processes, the CHANGE focuses only on client processes. We are developing a companion measure for coding therapist interventions, but in this chapter we focus only on the client version of the CHANGE.

CHANGE AND GROWTH EXPERIENCES SCALE

The CHANGE is a rating system that can be used to describe client processes related to therapeutic progress. It can be used to rate session tapes and transcripts from therapy as well as essays and expressive writing tasks. We have used the scale to study the process of recovery in an integrative therapy for depression (A. M. Hayes et al., 2005), and we are using it to study the process of change in cognitive therapy for personality disorders. We are also using the scale outside of the context of therapy to study the processing of negative life events in a group of HIV-positive long-term survivors, who wrote essays about stressful experiences over a 7-year follow-up period.

The unit of analysis for the CHANGE is a full session or essay. Raters read or listen to the session or essay and then rate the categories. Training involves approximately 10 to 15 hours, and it is best if the raters have some clinical experience. Raters are trained to criterion on a set of practice essays that were used to develop the scale.

In this chapter we illustrate how the CHANGE can be used to study insight, rumination, and avoidance in an integrative therapy for depression (A. M. Hayes et al., 2005; A. M. Hayes & Harris, 2000). The categories from the CHANGE that were coded were as follows: *insight–processing, avoidance, positive view of self, negative view of self, positive hope,* and *negative hope.* We coded the *view of self* and *hope* to examine whether insight–processing was associated with the course of change on these variables, as well as with overall symptom change. *Rumination* is a category that is calculated from the insight–processing scores. The highest or peak values were used to study insight–processing, whereas rumination scores were the number of essays after the midpoint of therapy that were rated as having low levels of insight–processing. The rumination score thus includes a time dimension of the number of essays with exploration and questioning but without progress or significant insight. Each item of the CHANGE is rated on a scale of 0 (*not present or very low*), 1 (*low*), 2 (*medium*), and 3 (*high*). Categories are not mutually exclusive and can co-occur. For example, it is not uncommon for essays to reflect ambivalence. One could write about both positive hope and negative hope in the same essay. All examples of the coding categories are drawn from the essays in the clinical trial of the integrative therapy for depression that we describe in a later section.

CHANGE Coding Categories

Insight–processing is exploring and questioning issues and material with some new connections, meaning, or perspective shift. We conceptualize insight on a continuum ranging from few, fleeting, or superficial connections to a more elaborated understanding that represents a perspective shift. A high level of insight–processing is often accompanied by high levels of affect. However, affective arousal without some insight or perspective shift is not considered insight–processing. This category is designed to capture concepts that have been labeled in the literature as emotional processing, meaning-making, benefit-finding, assimilation–accommodation, and schema change. Thus, it contains aspects of both cognitive and affective change. An example of a Level 3 insight–processing is as follows:

> I have been through a lot. I realize that I have been spending so much time trying to run away from myself that I have lost my compass. I have ended up with a man who is not good for me and in a job that is below me. I put up with the hurt because I thought I did not deserve better. It had eroded my spirit. I felt like a dead person. That realization makes me feel nauseous and disgusted, but I am now discovering my strength and potential. I had no idea what I was capable of. I deserve better! It is terrifying how self-esteem can affect the course of your life.

Rumination scores are derived from the ratings on the insight–processing category. We considered rumination to be the number of sessions rated as low after the midpoint of therapy, when clients were to move to the processing of core issues. More specifically, the rumination score is the number of essays after the midpoint of therapy that were rated as having a low level (1) of insight–processing divided by the total number of essays available for that client after the midpoint. The mean number of essays over the second phase of therapy was 14.23 ($SD = 2.85$), and the mean number of essays that were rated as having low levels of insight–processing was 5.29 ($SD = 3.76$). An example from the depression trial (identifying information removed) of unproductive insight-seeking across several weeks is,

> I am sitting in my apartment again reviewing all of my failures. I can't turn my head off. Over and over and over it goes. I piss everyone off and then I lose everything . . . here I go again. What the hell is wrong with me? Why can't I get out of this cycle? I have to stop spinning. It just makes things worse . . . Why can't get out [sic] of my head? I've got to stop.

In this example the client is questioning and trying to understand his situation, but he is caught in a perseverative loop that does not yield new understanding or a perspective shift. This example reflects unproductive rather than productive attempts at gaining insight.

Avoidance is defined as difficulty facing disturbing emotions, thoughts, or circumstances. Avoidance often involves attempts to block or move away from disturbing experiences and can include drinking or using other drugs to numb oneself, discontinuing and avoiding therapeutic tasks, shifting topics abruptly or maintaining a superficial focus, and isolating and withdrawing from external stimulation. An example from the depression trial of a Level 3 avoidance is, "I can't stand myself any more. I need to shut my brain off. This weekend I sat home, drank, and listened to loud music over and over. I can't write about this stuff anymore. It is making me sick."

To examine whether insight–processing influenced the course of change on *view of self* and one's *sense of hope*, we coded both positive and negative sense of self and hope. Positive self and hope are not coded if there is simply an absence of their negative counterparts; there must be evidence of positive descriptions that are at least somewhat elaborated. *Positive self* is the extent to which the person writes about him- or herself as worthwhile, competent, deserving of respect, and otherwise acceptable (Example Level 3: "For the first time in a long time, I felt strong. I went to a community activism event, and I felt so open and was able to connect with others again. With all that I have been through, I think I have something to offer to the group."). *Negative self* is the extent to which the person writes about feeling like a failure, incompetent, undesirable, inadequate, or otherwise flawed (Example Level 3: "Well, I sat around all day yesterday and thought about all the people I have let down. I was supposed to be the family success, and here I am sitting in a beat-up, old rental barely able to hold down a slacker job. This is not how I imagined middle age. I have failed at everything I have touched.").

Positive hope is the extent to which the person expects that the future will be better and that progress can be made on problem areas. This includes a commitment to change (Example Level 3: "I am beginning to see a way out of this black hole. I think I will make it. I am going to try."). *Negative hope* is the extent to which the person sees a disturbing and negative future, feels overwhelmed and stuck, sees few options, and has little motivation for change (Example Level 3: "Whatever . . . what's the point in trying? Things just keep piling up and nothing makes any difference. Why bother?").

BRIEF OVERVIEW OF THE INTEGRATIVE THERAPY FOR DEPRESSION

We now present data from the first open trial of an integrative therapy for depression developed by A. M. Hayes, and we use that study to illustrate how the CHANGE can identify points of insight, avoidance, and rumination. The findings and the therapy are presented in detail in A. M. Hayes et al. (2005), so we review them only briefly here. Depression provides an interesting context in which to study the process of developing insight because the disorder is characterized by hopelessness and a vacillation between rumination and avoidance, which are factors that inhibit the development of insight and change. Clients wrote essays about their depression each week over the course of therapy, which provides a way of capturing the process of change from the clients' perspectives. We coded these essays and could track different aspects and correlates of insight–processing across sessions.

This integrative therapy was designed to address the cognitive, interpersonal, and behavioral factors in recent psychopathology models of depression as well as factors associated with wellness and mental health. The first phase of therapy (Sessions 1–8) focuses on decreasing rumination and avoidance and teaching more adaptive emotion regulation skills. This includes teaching mindfulness meditation, coping skills, and healthy lifestyle habits related to sleep, diet, and exercise. These skills help to reduce the symptoms of depression, stabilize the client, and prepare the person to undergo the more difficult second phase of therapy (Sessions 9–18).

In the second phase of therapy, clients are asked to describe in session the negative view of self that occurs when they are most depressed. Clients then explore the historical antecedents of this negative view of self. They also reread the essays they wrote about their depression in the early sessions of therapy. These are somewhat like exposure exercises in that they are designed to fully activate the depressive network of negative thoughts, affect, behavior, and even somatic responses. In this historical and affectively charged context, and without avoiding or ruminating, therapists help participants move toward processing difficult material and emotions and to formulate strategies to address problematic circumstances. The strategies used in this *activation phase* combine elements of Greenberg's (2002a) experiential therapy for depression, schema-focused therapies (Beck, Freeman, Davis, et al., 2004; Young, Klosko, & Weishaar, 2003), and exposure-based therapies for post-traumatic stress disorder (Foa & Rothbaum, 1998; Resick & Schnicke, 1993).

Phase 3 (Sessions 19–24) is designed to help the client restabilize, solidify new perspectives, practice new ways of interacting and regulating emotions, and set goals and begin to hope again. After depression, clients often fear hope, positive affect, and positive experiences, so the third phase includes exposure to these experiences to reduce tendencies to avoid and sabotage positive changes.

CHANGE IN DEPRESSION AND TRANSIENT AFFECTIVE AROUSAL

Thirty-three clients who met *Diagnostic and Statistical Manual of Mental Disorders* (4th ed.; American Psychiatric Association, 1994) criteria for major depression enrolled in this open trial. The sample was 66% female and 34% male and was ethnically diverse, as 39% of participants were White, 51% were Hispanic/Latino, 2% were Asian American, 2% were African American, and 6% described themselves as of other or mixed heritage. The mean age was 36.76 (range 16 to 58). Twenty-nine clients completed at least 4 sessions past the midpoint of therapy and were considered completers.

Depression decreased significantly over the course of therapy on the Beck Depression Scale (BDI–II; Beck, Steer, & Brown, 1996) and the Modified Hamilton Rating Scale for Depression (MHRSD; Miller, Bishop, Norman, & Maddever, 1985) in both the intent-to-treat and the completer samples, and the effect sizes were large (A. M. Hayes et al., 2005). To study the process of change, we focused on the MHRSD because it is interview-based and it includes somatic and anxious symptoms that might capture better than the BDI the hypothesized period of symptom exacerbation (affective arousal) in the second phase of therapy. The MHRSD was assessed biweekly, so we were able to examine the trajectory of change in the completer sample using individual growth curve analysis of hierarchical linear modeling (HLM; Raudenbush & Bryk, 2002).

There was a significant linear decrease in depression over the course of therapy. It is interesting to note that there was also a significant cubic pattern of change in that there was a linear decrease in depression symptoms in the first half of therapy, a transient period of worsening as the core issues of depression were addressed in the second half of therapy, and then an additional decrease in symptoms (A. M. Hayes, Laurenceau, & Feldman, in press; A. M. Hayes et al., 2004). This suggests that there was a period of affective arousal during the schema change phase of therapy, as predicted.

To study the process of change, we coded the weekly essays that clients wrote about their depression across the course of therapy. Following the methodology used by Pennebaker (1997), clients were asked to write essays about their depression for 20 minutes each week. They were asked to write about their deepest thoughts and feelings related to their depression. These essays were designed to capture the impact of the therapy sessions over the week and also to facilitate insight and processing over the course of therapy.

The coders were three doctoral-level clinical psychology graduate students and one bachelor's-level research assistant. Coders were trained to criterion for approximately 10 hours, with approximately 5 hours of practice coding. After reaching criterion agreement (intraclass correlation of at least .80), coders rated the essays in pairs, and they were paired with each other coder an equal number of times. Weekly to biweekly meetings were held to review discrepancies and to prevent rater drift. Interrater agreement on all coding categories was good to excellent (intraclass correlation = .73 to .84). Because agreement was good, the ratings of coders were averaged and the averaged ratings were used in the analyses.

We focused on three variables coded in the weekly essays—*insight–processing, avoidance*, and *rumination*—as predictors of the course of change in depression. An examination of the individual plots of these variables over the course of therapy revealed that both insight–processing and avoidance scores tended to peak and then return to a low score. We therefore examined the peak (highest level) processing and peak avoidance scores in Phases I and II of therapy as predictors of the trajectory of change in depression (MHRSD), using HLM analyses. For this chapter, we also computed rumination scores and conducted analyses with those scores. Pretreatment depression severity did not significantly predict the rumination, avoidance, or insight–processing scores. Peak insight–processing and avoidance scores and the rumination scores were also examined as predictors of the trajectories of *positive view of self, negative view of self, positive hope*, and *negative hope* across the course of therapy, using HLM.

On the basis of the literatures reviewed earlier on the process of change in therapy, expressive writing, and adversarial growth, we hypothesized that more insight–processing would be associated with better outcomes, whereas more avoidance would be associated with worse outcomes. Peak insight–processing scores were higher during the second phase of therapy when there was a period of heightened emotionality, as indicated by the transient exacerbation of depression symptoms. Peak processing scores during the second phase (but not during the first phase) were associated with improvement in depression (MHRSD). Moreover, there was a significant reduction in depression immediately after the session in which the second phase peak insight–processing score occurred. Depression levels immediately before the peak did not predict the level of insight–processing, which suggests that insight–processing is not a function of symptom improvement that has already occurred.

Our findings suggest that insight–processing was associated with affective arousal and with clinical improvement. These findings are similar to recent work by Pos, Greenberg, Goldman, and Korman (2003), who found that higher levels of emotional processing (as measured by the Experiencing Scale) in the later phase of experiential therapy predicted more change in depression at the end of treatment. Castonguay, Goldfried, Wiser, Raue, and Hayes (1996) also found that higher experiencing scores predicted more improvement in cognitive therapy for depression.

In addition, HLM analyses revealed that peak insight–processing was significantly correlated with an increase in the expression of hope and a positive view of self in the weekly essays. It is interesting that peak insight–processing was also associated with the expression of a negative view of self across the essays. Therapeutic processing and insight can involve the exploration of one's depressive view of the self as well as the exploration and emergence of a more positive sense of self in the same essay, as is illustrated in the case example presented in the next section. Related to this, it is possible for a more positive sense of self, identity, and sense of purpose to emerge in the midst of destabilization and suffering, as can be the case in adversarial growth (Baumeister, 1991; Linley & Joseph, 2004; Tedeschi & Calhoun, 2004). We discuss in other sources the idea that a period of destabilization, during which the old distressing patterns are activated and new patterns are developing, can precede change in depression (A. M. Hayes & Harris, 2000; A. M. Hayes & Strauss, 1998).

In contrast, more rumination in the second phase of therapy (but not in the first phase) predicted worse outcomes. Because we conducted the analyses of rumination for this chapter and they are not presented elsewhere, we provide the statistical results rather than a summary of the findings. HLM analyses revealed that more rumination in the second phase of therapy predicted less improvement in depression over the course of therapy ($B = 6.15$, $SE = 2.47$, $t = 2.49$, $n = 26$, $p = .02$). HLM analyses also revealed that rumination during this period was associated specifically with hopelessness ($B = 1.25$, $SE = .45$, $t = 2.77$, $n = 28$, $p = .01$) in the essays and not with positive self, negative self, or positive hope.

Peak avoidance scores during the second phase of therapy (but not in the first phase) were associated with less change in depression and with more statements of hopelessness and negative view of self in the essays. As expected, avoidance also was not associated with the emergence of hope and a positive view of self. Clients' levels of depression in the session immediately before their peak value of avoidance did not significantly predict the levels (0–3) of the peak value. This suggests that those with higher peak levels of avoidance were not simply those who were more depressed. Avoidance is likely to interfere with the insight–processing work of therapy and may further inhibit change because, ironically, it can promote the intrusion of unwanted material and rumination. As reviewed earlier, there is a large body of research on the psychological and health consequences of avoiding and suppressing emotions.

The findings from this study on an integrative therapy for depression suggest that the CHANGE might be a useful measure of the stages of insight, from exploration to working directly with therapeutic material and coming to a new perspective. The scale can also capture attempts to move away from and avoid difficult material as well as ruminative insight-seeking, both of which were associated with worse outcomes. Findings suggest that higher levels of insight–processing are associated with transient affective arousal and also with positive changes in one's view of self and hope, which are thought to be consequences of gaining deeper levels of insight (Greenberg, 2002b; Samoilov & Goldfried, 2000; Whelton, 2004).

Because this is the first study using the CHANGE, the findings must be interpreted cautiously, and there are a number of limitations to be addressed in subsequent studies. This was an open trial of an integrative therapy for depression, so there is no control group with which to compare the CHANGE variables and their associations with outcome. We designed the study so the first phase of therapy could serve as a within-client control in that insight–processing was predicted to be low in that phase and higher in the activation phase of therapy. This method, however, does not obviate the need for a control group. It will be important to demonstrate more clearly that the changes in insight–processing and avoidance are related to therapist interventions and not to external life events and other nontherapy variables. A control condition would help in this regard, as would a measure of the therapist interventions used and their timing. We are currently developing such a measure as a companion to the CHANGE. It is also critical to tease apart insight–processing, rumination, and avoidance from symptom levels because it is possible that those who are experiencing symptom relief are more able to move to higher levels of insight–processing, whereas those who are more distressed get stuck in rumination or avoidance. We did examine the depression scores immediately before the peak insight–processing and avoidance scores and found that symptom level in the prepeak sessions did not predict subsequent levels of insight–processing or avoidance. This is a step in the right direction, but with the collection of more data points it would be possible to examine the associations between the preceding symptom trajectory (rather than a single time point) and the peak scores using piecewise growth curve modeling (Collins, 2006). Related to this, we chose to examine peak values of avoidance and insight–processing, which do not reveal the course of these variables over time. The variables can be examined as trajectories over time, but in this dataset the variables were episodic as they increased quickly and then rapidly decreased to zero. The pattern of these variables might differ in other datasets. The rumination variable is problematic, but it was an attempt to capture exploration and questioning that persists over time with little movement. In the most recent version of the CHANGE we have constructed a variable that is separate from the insight–processing variable, called *unproductive processing*. Although we have attempted to examine the temporal sequencing of variables, it is important to remember that these analyses are correlational in nature and causality has not yet been examined.

CASE EXAMPLE

We now illustrate how the CHANGE can be used at the level of a case rather than at the level of group data summarized across individuals. This example will show how the client vacillates between avoiding difficult material and becoming overwhelmed and stuck in repetitive cycles of insight-seeking. We contrast this pattern with insight that leads to productive processing of negative thoughts and emotions and the emergence of a more positive view of self, hope, and behavior change. The CHANGE was used to code essays that the client wrote over the course of therapy, so the focus of our description is on the process of gaining insight from the client's perspective. Therapist interventions were not coded nor was the content of the therapy sessions.

The client, whom we call S.F., was a divorced, 45-year-old, Caucasian man who went through a period of heroin addiction approximately 10 years ago; his history also included one suicide attempt after the divorce from his first wife. Since his divorce he had a series of relationships with "interesting, but emotionally abusive women who needed him" and who were similar to his first wife. When S.F. presented for treatment, he had been in a relationship for 4 years with a woman with a chronic substance abuse problem who was unemployed and emotionally "needy and draining." The level of conflict in the relationship was severe and chronic. As with his parents, S. F. felt that he was not allowed to express his feelings or needs and that the only reason the girlfriend kept him around was to care for her. He reported feeling chronically unfulfilled and empty. Although he was successful in his job as a screenwriter, he felt worthless and like a failure. S. F. was chronically flooded with ruminative thoughts related to this sense of failure. He had an avoidant style of coping that involved withdrawing from others, picking arguments with others to "tune out," and denying the chronic problems in his relationship.

S.F. had three previous episodes of depression and had received psychotherapy for one of the episodes, with little improvement. He enrolled in our treatment program for an integrative psychotherapy for depression (A. M. Hayes et al., 2005; A. M. Hayes & Harris, 2000). At intake, he met SCID criteria for major depression and endorsed a moderate to severe level of symptom severity (BDI = 30; MHRSD = 18). We have altered identifying information in the case description and sample codings to protect the identity of the client.

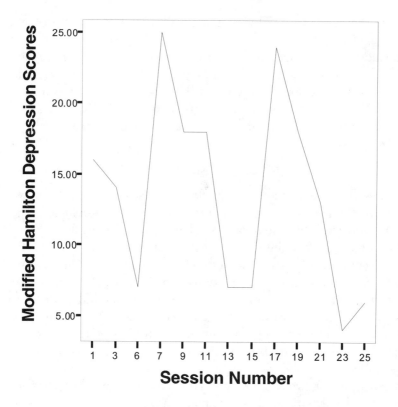

Figure 11.1. Modified Hamilton Rating Scale for Depression (MHRSD) scores for case example administered biweekly across the course of therapy.

Change in Depression Symptoms

Every other week, S.F.'s depression symptoms were assessed using the MHRSD (Miller et al., 1985). As shown in Figure 11.1, S.F.'s pattern of symptom change was characterized by periods of worsening followed by improvement, as we reported on the full sample of study participants. The second phase of therapy was characterized by an increase in depression symptoms but then by a rapid decrease in symptoms and improvement in his general quality of life. These positive gains were maintained at the 1-year follow-up assessment.

The Course of Therapy

The weekly written essays were coded using the CHANGE. Figure 11.2 shows the ratings of insight–processing in the essays that matched the MHRSD assessments. Because of space constraints, we did not plot the scores on the other variables coded, but we do note the scores in the essay segments. The

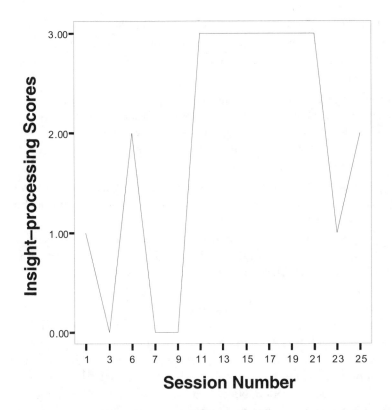

Figure 11.2. Insight–processing ratings for case example across sessions. Weekly essays were coded by two raters using the Change and Growth Experiences Scale (CHANGE). Ratings were averaged. Scores are plotted for essays that matched the week that the Modified Hamilton Rating Scale for Depression (MHRSD) was administered. Rumination is a variable constructed from the coding of insight–processing. The variable is captured by the number of essays with low levels of processing in the weeks after the midpoint of therapy divided by the number of essays that were written during that period.

early essays by S.F. capture high levels of avoidance (Level 3) and unproductive questioning and insight-seeking that did not progress (Level 1). This rumination occurred frequently in the first five essays. These essays also illustrate high levels of negative view of self and hopelessness (Level 3). A sample of an essay with themes that repeated over several weeks is as follows:

> I am simply not dealing with my problems. I don't have the strength to look at things. It reminds me of how I got addicted to heroin years ago. Once you are stoned, the house could fall down, and you don't give a damn. My own brain has become that drug. How did I get here? What is the matter with me? Why am I so weak? I have wasted my life. Will I ever get out of this hell? I can't stop thinking!

By Session 8, which occurred at the end of the stress management phase of therapy, S.F. began to avoid less and started to explore his relationship with his girlfriend. At this point in the therapy he had learned to recognize avoidance and rumination and had been taught emotion regulation and mindfulness meditation skills. These skills helped him to open and begin to tolerate difficult and avoided emotions. His essay for that week read,

> I woke up terrified on Sunday morning. For the first time, I allowed myself to feel scared about my situation. I read over the mindfulness literature and made a concerted effort to stay with the feelings of fear, even though they made me physically ill. I am beginning to realize that my girlfriend is incapable of a healthy relationship.

S.F. was more able to tolerate the distress associated his situation and was becoming more aware of the unhealthy nature of his current relationship (insight–processing, Level 2).

At the next session, he wrote very little and had shut down (avoidance, Level 3): "What is the point of all of this? I feel as if I am back where I started. I can't write." The therapist noted this avoidance and encouraged the client to use the emotion regulation skills he had learned to stay with the difficult material. In Session 10 the therapy focused on activating and exploring his negative view of self and avoided emotions. The therapist focused on exploring S. F.'s feelings of failure and worthlessness and had S.F. reread his early essays from the period when he was most depressed. As S.F. began to examine examples of his failure, he realized that he was actually quite successful at work. He had not failed, but instead was feeling bored and unchallenged. After that session, S.F. wrote about feeling unimportant and that he did not have an identity. He was also able to recognize that he does receive praise and recognition at work, but he does not attend to or trust it:

> Well, I won an award at work, but once again my boss mispronounced my name. It is so clear to me that whatever identity I brought with me to this job has evaporated. I am reminded of this day to day. If I turned to stone, I'm not sure anyone would notice. I am so numb and tuned out. On the other hand, I won this award. I have won a number of them, but I don't seem to notice. It is frightening to see how I allow rejection to outweigh the praise I get at work and from other places.

There is avoidance (Level 3) in this essay but also some awareness (insight–processing, Level 2) of his tendency to attend to or perceive rejection and ignore or ridicule praise. There is a focus both on negative view of self (Level 3) and on positive view of self (Level 2).

In the next session, the focus of therapy shifted to his core sense of self. The session was more affectively charged than in previous sessions as S.F. explored the roots of his sense of failure and worthlessness. He realized that his negative views had a long history, and as he looked back he saw that he had wasted his potential, avoided opportunities, and continually disappointed his parents. His parents had viewed him as special, and he remembered vividly numerous instances of "seeing the disappointment in their faces."

During that week S.F. went to a funeral of a close friend, which triggered his own life review. S.F. wrote,

> [My friend] was described as so "well-defined." I am so far from that . . . so undefined, amorphous. Something happened that goes to the core of my depression. I've been caught in the rumination 'buzz saw' all week thinking about what I have become. I have been talking about this in therapy, and life seems to come right behind that and hit the themes again. Waking, sleeping all day, waking. This morning I went into a quiet room to do my breathing exercises. The buzz saw attacked. I tried to ignore it. It attacked again. I told it to go away. It attacked again. I restarted the breathing six or seven times. Then I started to hyperventilate. I couldn't keep it out. I cried and cried and cried. I couldn't get a grip. I felt the sadness, loneliness, protection, and pain. I cried and cried, but I felt alive. I think in all of the mess, I am finding my self. I consider this a victory.

S.F. was wrestling with rumination by trying to avoid (Level 3), but then he let himself feel the emotions fully. In the context of the work he had been doing in therapy, he realized that at the core of his depression was his loneliness, fear of getting close to others, and moving forward (insight–processing, Level 3). In the next session, he reported feeling that "the veil had lifted," and he felt "clearheaded." After a visit to his parents, he reported that the visit brought "moments of great tenderness and closeness with both parents." There was a sense of openness.

In Sessions 14 and 15, S.F. reported that his depression was receding:

> I am scared to say it, but there is no doubt that my depression is receding. I feel less lonely because I am letting others penetrate my walls. I am more aware than ever that the walls are so dense and forbidding. So much of me is in the shadows. I'm thinking that's why I get involved with women who cannot decode the secret. That way I stay safe. Why am I hiding? From whom? Why? On another topic, I applied for another job. I took a risk . . . I am sick of avoiding. I have nothing to lose; possibly a lot to gain.

S.F. was not avoiding (Level 0) and continued to open. He was beginning to realize how his sense of self relates to themes in his problematic relationships (insight–processing, Level 3), and he was taking risks. He was engaging in positive interactions with friends and family and was feeling hopeful (Level 3).

During Week 17, he had an argument with his girlfriend that escalated into a break up. He reported that something just "snapped." He was no longer afraid. The next week, he hit a turning point and a high level of insight–processing:

> I passed a point of no return with my girlfriend. I went from guilt and obligation of having to carry her to hot, bubbling rage, and it kicked me into action. Enough! There is no escaping the truth. My need to feel loved and wanted led me to be taken by a psychological con woman. For

so long I let her convince me that loving her was more important than living for myself. Look at the price I paid: loss of identity, loss of spark, loss of intimate friendships, loss of opportunity. All for what? To save someone who can't be saved and is like a human virus. I became saturated with a diseased way of thinking. Why? That is the hard part that I must answer so that it does not happen again. We broke up. I changed the locks.

His MHRSD scores spiked from below 10 for several weeks to 24 and then to 18. There is a high level of focus on negative view of self, but it is also associated with significant insight, empowerment, and behavioral changes. The result was that S.F. ended the relationship and his girlfriend moved out.

Our theoretical model and recent empirical investigation (A. M. Hayes et al., 2005; A. M. Hayes & Strauss, 1998) suggest that the period before change would be associated with transient symptom exacerbation. In the case of S.F., the turning point that began at Session 17 was indeed associated with a high level of negative affect and a worsening of the depression symptoms. The therapist explained to the client that this period of destabilization was important to shake loose the old ways of thinking and produce more permanent changes in his depression. The therapist encouraged S.F. to try to fully engage emotionally in session but to give himself permission to not think too much about the sessions at home. The therapist also encouraged S.F. to engage in pleasant activities and use his mindfulness exercises to help so he would not be overcome with rumination or avoidance.

Therapy then focused on encouraging S.F. to continue to engage in positive connections with others and supporting him in his attempts to extract himself from his relationship with his girlfriend. He was still afraid of positive emotions and taking risks, so he was encouraged to engage in and process these types of experiences. He also reported a discomfort associated with moving out of the caretaker role as he fostered and developed more reciprocal relationships. Over the next couple of weeks, he connected deeply with friends at a charity event and reported feeling that people cared about him and that he was part of a larger community. At Session 22, his former girlfriend had been repeatedly calling him for help with a crisis; for the first time, he felt a distance from her "chaos" and felt as though something had changed and there was no going back. Yet he also felt

empty and alone, as if I am going through the motions. I am off to see family and friends who care so much about me and are so proud of me for taking this step. I am proud of me too. I know I am going in the right direction, away from a harmful person and toward a more enriching life. But, there are so many disconnects. I am scared. Depression, being so familiar, almost seems like a place where I can feel comfortable.

There is a low level of avoidance (1) and also a high level (3) of hope and positive view of self. This essay captures the ambivalence and distress associated with change and the positive consequences of insight and emotional processing.

By the next session, S.F.'s depression score had dropped to 4. He was receiving support from family and friends and began to set goals for his "new life, without the cloud of depression." The depression remained at low levels, and he continued to focus on "the practicalities of my new life, which are both exhilarating and daunting. I am ready to participate in life." There is a high level of hope. He maintained the gains that he made in the acute phase of therapy, and over the continuation phase he struggled with his ex-girlfriend's attempts to resume the relationship and her threats of suicide. In the year after therapy, S.F. found out that his father had cancer, and he was able to grieve after his father's death without becoming depressed. He had begun a healthy relationship and was able to work through the anxiety that this produced. He did not engage in his previous attempts to regulate the fear, such as avoidance and relationship sabotage. He also started a new job in which he felt more challenged, appreciated, and fulfilled. These gains were maintained at the 1-year follow-up interview.

This case illustrates how different aspects of insight—insight–processing, rumination, and avoidance—unfold and interact over the course of a therapy for depression. The problems of depression illustrate the roles of chronic and unproductive insight-seeking (rumination) as well as disengagement and avoidance, which are processes that can interfere with the development of insight. In the case example, periods of avoidance and rumination are apparent, but the client was also able to process difficult emotions and thoughts and develop new connections, understanding, and shifts in perspective. The essays with high levels of insight–processing seemed to involve the activation of depressive schemas and the exploration of his negative view of self and sense of hopelessness. There were high levels of distress and depression during these periods, which is consistent with the idea of activation of the depressive network, insight and processing in this context, and significant decreases in depression (cf. Foa & Kozak, 1986; A. M. Hayes & Strauss, 1998; Pos et al., 2003; Teasdale, 1999). A more positive sense of self and hope seemed to emerge from this process. This case and the full sample analyses suggest that the CHANGE can be useful to differentiate productive and unproductive insight-seeking and avoidance. The findings also suggest that it can be useful to examine these different variables separately rather than as part of a single continuum.

CONCLUDING COMMENTS

The findings from our initial research suggest that coders can be trained to use the CHANGE in a brief period of time and can reach and maintain good levels of interrater agreement. This study also provides initial evidence of predictive validity in that the variables were associated in the expected direction with symptom outcome and with changes in clients' views of self and hope. The CHANGE categories do overlap with measures of experiencing (Klein et al., 1986) and assimilation (Stiles et al., 1990), but the CHANGE includes categories that are not included in those scales and provides a way to study multiple variables over time. In addition to the variables described in this chapter, the CHANGE includes variables to assess negative and positive affect, behavior, somatic responses, and relationship quality and it includes a focus on the historical roots of current problems. This breadth of coverage allows for the examination of multiple variables and their interactions over time but there is some sacrifice of detail when compared with measures designed to assess a single construct (e.g., experiencing, assimilation).

The measure presented focuses only on client responses in essays or in therapy sessions, but we are developing a companion version that assesses the focus of therapist interventions (therapist focus on positive and negative thoughts, affect, behavior, somatic functioning, and relationships), and on support, the therapeutic relationship, historical roots of current problems, corrective information, and homework. The measure of rumination described in this chapter has also been improved. The method of calculating the number of ratings of low level (1) insight–processing in the second half of therapy is rather crude and is derived, redundantly, from the insight–processing variable. In the new version of the CHANGE we include a separate variable called unproductive questioning and perseverative analysis to capture rumination, worry, obsessions, and other forms of recurrent and repetitive analysis.

Although the initial interrater agreement estimates and predictive validity are promising, the CHANGE will need to be examined in other samples and compared with other measures to examine concurrent and discriminant validity. We are now using the CHANGE to code therapy sessions from a clinical trial of cognitive therapy for obsessive–compulsive and avoidant personality disorders. The study of the roles of rumination, avoidance, and insight–processing will be particularly interesting in problems characterized by rigid and deeply entrenched, maladaptive patterns. We expect to find again that rumination and avoidance inhibit change and that insight–processing is associated with transient affective arousal and then with symptom reduction. The CHANGE is in the early stages of development, but we hope that it will be a useful measure of insight–processing and of those variables that inhibit change across a variety of therapies and clinical problems.

REFERENCES

American Psychiatric Association. (1994). *Diagnostic and statistical manual of mental disorders* (4th ed.). Washington, DC: Author.

Angus, L., Levitt, H., & Hardtke, K. (1999). The Narrative Processes Coding System: Research applications and implications for psychotherapy practice. *Journal of Clinical Psychology, 55*, 1255–1270.

Baumeister, R. F. (1991). *Meanings of life.* New York: Guilford Press.

Beck, A. T., Freeman, A., Davis, D. D., & Associates (2004). *Cognitive therapy of personality disorders.* New York: Guilford Press.

Beck, A. T., Steer, R. A., & Brown, G. K. (1996). *Beck Depression Inventory manual* (2nd ed.). San Antonio, TX: Psychological Corporation.

Beevers, C. G., Wenzlaff, R. M., Hayes, A. M., & Scott, W. D. (1999). Depression and the ironic effects of thought suppression: Therapeutic strategies for improving mental control. *Clinical Psychology: Science and Practice, 6*, 133–148.

Borkovec, T. D. (2002). Life in the future versus life in the present. *Clinical Psychology: Science and Practice, 9*, 76–80.

Brewin, C. R., Dalgleish, T., & Joseph, S. (1996). A dual representation theory of posttraumatic stress disorder. *Psychological Review, 103*, 670–686.

Castonguay, L. G., Goldfried, M. R., Wiser, S., Raue, P. J., & Hayes, A. M. (1996). Predicting the effect of cognitive therapy for depression: A study of unique and common factors. *Journal of Consulting and Clinical Psychology, 64*, 1–8.

Collins, L. M. (2006). Analysis of longitudinal data: The integration of theoretical model, temporal design, and statistical model. *Annual Review of Psychology, 57*, 505–528.

Foa, E. B., & Kozak, M. J. (1986). Emotional processing of fear: Exposure to corrective information. *Psychological Bulletin, 99*, 20–35.

Foa, E. B., & Rothbaum, B. O. (1998). *Treating the trauma of rape: Cognitive–behavioral therapy for PTSD.* New York: Guilford Press.

Greenberg, L. S. (2002a). *Emotion-focused therapy: Coaching clients to work through feelings.* Washington, DC: American Psychological Association.

Greenberg, L. S. (2002b). Integrating an emotion-focused approach to treatment in psychotherapy integration. *Journal of Psychotherapy Integration, 12*, 154–189.

Greenberg, L. S., & Safran, J. D. (1987). *Emotion in psychotherapy: Affect, cognition, and the process of change.* New York: Guilford Press.

Gross, J. J. (2002). Emotion regulation: Affective, cognitive, and social consequences. *Psychophysiology, 39*, 281–291.

Hayes, A. M., Beevers, C., Feldman, G., Laurenceau, J. P., & Perlman, C. A. (2005). Avoidance and insight–processing as predictors of symptom change and positive growth in an integrative therapy for depression. *International Journal of Behavioral Medicine, 12*, 111–122.

Hayes, A. M., & Feldman, G. C. (2005). *The Change and Growth Experiences Scale (CHANGE).* Unpublished manuscript.

Hayes, A. M., & Harris, M. S. (2000). The development of an integrative treatment for depression. In S. Johnson, A. M. Hayes, T. Field, N. Schneiderman, & P. McCabe (Eds.), *Stress, coping, and depression* (pp. 291–306). Mahwah, NJ: Erlbaum.

Hayes, A. M., Laurenceau, J. P., & Feldman, G. C. (in press). Discontinuities and nonlinearities in the study of change in psychotherapy. *Clinical Psychology Review.*

Hayes, A. M., Laurenceau, J. P., Feldman, G. C., Beevers, C. G., Perlman, C., & Galyardt, M. (2004, November). Do the principles of exposure apply to depression? In S. A. Hayes (Chair), *New advances in emotional processing and exposure-based treatments.* Symposium conducted at the annual convention of the Association for the Advancement of Behavior Therapy, New Orleans, LA.

Hayes, A. M., & Strauss, J. L. (1998). Dynamic systems theory as a paradigm for the study of change in psychotherapy: An application to cognitive therapy for depression. *Journal of Consulting and Clinical Psychology, 66,* 939–947.

Hayes, S. C., Wilson, K. W., Gifford, E. V., Follette, V. M., & Strosahl, K. (1996). Emotional avoidance and behavioral disorders: A functional dimensional approach to diagnosis and treatment. *Journal of Consulting and Clinical Psychology, 64,* 1152–1168.

Hunt, M. G. (1998). The only way out is through: Emotional processing and recovery after a depressing life event. *Behaviour Research and Therapy, 36,* 361–384.

Kiecolt-Glaser, J. K., McGuire, L., Robles, T. F., & Glaser, R. (2002). Emotions, morbidity, and mortality: New perspectives from psychoneuroimmunology. *Annual Review of Psychology, 53,* 83–107.

Klein, M. H., Mathieu-Coughlan, P., & Kiesler, D. J. (1986). The Experiencing Scales. In L. S. Greenberg & W. M. Pinsof (Eds.), *The psychotherapeutic process: A research handbook* (pp. 21–71). New York: Guilford Press.

Linley, P. A., & Joseph, S. (2004). Positive change following trauma and adversity: A review. *Journal of Traumatic Stress, 17,* 11–21.

Lyubomirsky, S., & Nolen-Hoeksema, S. (1993). Self-perpetuating properties of dysphoric rumination. *Journal of Personality and Social Psychology, 65,* 339–349.

Mahoney, M. (1991). *Human change processes.* New York: Basic Books.

Martin, L. T., & Tesser, A. (1996). Some ruminative thoughts. In R. S. Wyer Jr. (Ed.), *Ruminative thoughts* (pp. 1–47). Hillsdale, NJ: Erlbaum.

Miller, I. W., Bishop, S. B., Norman, W. H., & Maddever, H. (1985). Modified Hamilton Rating Scale for Depression: Reliability and validity. *Psychiatry Research, 14,* 131–142.

Nolen-Hoeksema, S. (2000). The role of rumination in depressive disorders and mixed anxiety/depressive symptoms. *Journal of Abnormal Psychology, 109,* 504–511.

Nolen-Hoeksema, S., & Davis, C. G. (2004). Theoretical and methodological issues in the assessment and interpretation of posttraumatic growth. *Psychological Inquiry, 15,* 60–64.

Ottenbreit, N. D., & Dobson, K. S. (2004). Avoidance and depression: The construction of the cognitive–behavioral avoidance scale. *Behaviour Research and Therapy, 42,* 293–313.

Pennebaker, J. W. (1997). Writing about emotional experiences as a therapeutic process. *Psychological Science, 8,* 162–166.

Pennebaker, J. W., & Seagal, J. D. (1999). Forming a story: The health benefits of narrative. *Journal of Clinical Psychology, 55,* 1243–1254.

Pos, A. E., Greenberg, L. S, Goldman, R. N., & Korman, L. M. (2003). Emotional processing during experiential treatment of depression. *Journal of Consulting and Clinical Psychology, 71,* 1007–1016.

Raudenbush, S. W., & Bryk, A. S. (2002). *Hierarchical linear models: Applications and data analysis methods* (2nd ed.). Thousand Oaks, CA: Sage.

Resick, P. A., & Schnicke, M. K. (1993). *Cognitive processing therapy for rape victims: A treatment manual.* Thousand Oaks, CA: Sage.

Salovey, P., Rothman, A. J., Detweiler, J. B., & Steward, W. T. (2000). Emotional states and physical health. *American Psychologist, 55,* 110–121.

Samoilov, A., & Goldfried, M. R. (2000). Role of emotion in cognitive–behavior therapy. *Clinical Psychology: Science and Practice, 7,* 373–385.

Segal, Z. V., Williams, J. M. G., & Teasdale, J. D. (2002). *Mindfulness-based cognitive therapy for depression: A new approach to preventing relapse.* New York: Guildford Press.

Segerstrom, S. C., Stanton, A. L., Alden, L. E., & Shortridge, B. E. (2003). Multidimensional structure for repetitive thought: What's on your mind, and how, and how much? *Journal of Personality and Social Psychology, 85,* 909–921.

Sloan, D. M., & Marx, B. P. (2004). Taking pen to hand: Evaluating theories underlying the written disclosure paradigm. *Clinical Psychology: Science and Practice, 11,* 121–137.

Smyth, J. M., True, N., & Souto, J. (2001). Effects of writing about traumatic experiences: The necessity for narrative restructuring. *Journal of Social and Clinical Psychology, 20,* 161–172.

Stiles, W. B., Elliott, R., Llewelyn, S. P., Firth-Cozens, J. A., Margison, F. R., Shapiro, D. A., & Hardy, G. (1990). Assimilation of problematic experiences by clients in psychotherapy. *Psychotherapy: Theory, Research, Practice, Training, 27,* 411–420.

Teasdale, J. D. (1999). Emotional processing, three modes of mind, and the prevention of relapse in depression. *Behaviour Research and Therapy, 37,* S53–S78.

Tedeschi, R. G., & Calhoun, L. G. (2004). Posttraumatic growth: Conceptual foundations and empirical evidence. *Psychological Inquiry, 15,* 1–18.

Watkins, E., & Baracaia, S. (2001). Why do people ruminate in dysphoric moods? *Personality and Individual Differences, 30,* 723–734.

Wenzlaff, R. M., & Luxton, D. D. (2003). The role of thought suppression in depressive rumination. *Cognitive Therapy and Research, 27,* 293–308.

Whelton, W. J. (2004). Emotional processes in psychotherapy: Evidence across therapeutic modalities. *Clinical Psychology and Psychotherapy, 11,* 58–71.

Young, J. E., Klosko, J. S., & Weishaar, M. E. (2003). *Schema therapy: A practitioner's guide.* New York: Guilford Press.

III

CLINICAL ISSUES

12

INSIGHT AND THE ACTIVE CLIENT

ARTHUR C. BOHART

At the conclusion of the beloved film *The Wizard of Oz* (Langley, Ryerson, & Woolf, 1939), the good witch Glinda advises Dorothy that she's "always had the power to go back to Kansas." But, Glinda adds, this ability is something Dorothy needed to discover for herself by examining her own experiences. Reflecting on this, Dorothy realizes, "if I ever go looking for my heart's desire again, I won't look any further than my own backyard. Because if it isn't there, I never really lost it to begin with."

Thus, before Dorothy can return to Kansas, she needs to acquire *insight*. Can Glinda (the expert) find the answers for her? No. She must discover it for herself through her experience of engaging in a search to get back home. I believe that clients in psychotherapy are similar to Dorothy. Ultimately, though therapists (Glinda, in this example) can help guide clients to productive insights, it is clients who must discover the insights or their meanings for themselves.

I have argued that it is clients who make therapy work (Bohart, 2006; Bohart & Tallman, 1999). Although therapists generally acknowledge that clients are active self-healers, theoretical descriptions of how therapy works rarely include clients' active contributions. I have described what I mean by the client as an active self-healer:

all clients have the capacity to be actively involved in generatively learning about their lives and making changes. They may enter therapy demoralized or discouraged and so not take initiative. However, in their everyday lives they have generally been at least partially successful as active problem solvers. . . . To be an active self-healer in therapy means: (a) to actively involve oneself in the process; (b) actively try on, learn from, or "inhabit" whatever interventions or interactions constitute the therapy process; (c) actively contribute through one's generative capacity to think dialectically, make inferences, and extract meaning; (d) use one's capacities for logical thinking; (e) creatively misinterpret therapists' interventions; (f) use therapists' interventions as tools in one's own way; (g) learn through an iterative process of trying ideas from therapy out and then shaping them on the basis of feedback from life; (h) experience the interventions and draw inferences from that experience; and (i) apply what is being learned in everyday life. (Bohart, 2006, pp. 219–220)

In this chapter I look at client characteristics and client states that may promote or inhibit attaining insight. I then explore what clients may do to promote the attainment of insight. Finally, given insight attainment, I briefly consider how clients may use it to change. There is little research on most of the variables I consider; this chapter is a map for future research.

DEFINITION AND NATURE OF INSIGHT

I define insight as "gaining a new perspective or a new understanding." Defined this way, insight can be a sudden event (an *Aha!*) or something that develops gradually over time. Phenomenologically speaking, the following appear characteristic of insight, particularly of specific *Aha!* insight events. First, the metaphors people use to describe insights are primarily perceptual ("Oh, I see!"). Second, there is a sense of recognition or discovery, or "dawning." Third, insights are not things that one can typically make happen by will. They are experienced as happening to one. Fourth, the experience may be beyond words. Often, in fact, people feel they know the answer before they can say it.

CLIENT CHARACTERISTICS THAT MAY
FACILITATE OR IMPEDE INSIGHT

Some client dispositions may be more likely to facilitate or impede the attainment of insight than others. On the basis of a recent search of the literature, as well as my 4 decades of reading the professional literature, I have decided to address the client characteristics outlined in the following sections.

Psychological Mindedness

In psychoanalytic therapy it was assumed that good candidates for therapy already possessed insight. This meant that (a) they already had some self-understanding, and (b) they possessed the kind of reflective capacity needed to generate further insight. A current version of this idea is *psychological mindedness* (PM; McCallum & Piper, 1997). There are several conceptual and operational definitions of PM. One commonality is that a person high in PM has a propensity to turn inward and to search for psychological explanations. Some definitions emphasize psychodynamic explanations.

There are different measures of PM (McCallum & Piper, 1997). Research by McCallum, Piper, and colleagues (McCallum & Piper, 1999; Piper, McCallum, Joyce, Azim, & Ogrodniczuk, 1999) found that PM relates to improvement in both interpretive and supportive therapy. It also relates to engaging in productive work in insight-oriented therapy. In an attempt to look at PM in another way, Beutler, Harwood, Alimohamed, and Malik (2004) reviewed 19 studies. They found that clients who are self-reflective, introverted, and introspective benefited from insight-oriented therapy, whereas impulsive, aggressive, undercontrolled, and symptom-focused clients did not. Using self-report measures of PM, several studies (summarized in Conte & Ratto, 1997) found no relationship between PM and global functioning, but it was related to likelihood of staying in therapy. Conte and Ratto also summarized findings relating self-report measures of PM to personality variables. These included assertiveness; sociability; being accepting of rather than rejecting of others; ego strength; mastery and competence; a capacity to reconcile discrepancies in behavior, attitudes, and feelings; autonomous functioning; and less authoritarianism.

Although these studies suggest that clients high in PM may work harder, stay longer, and do better in insight-oriented therapy, there is little evidence that PM specifically leads to a greater capacity to attain insight. In fact, Diemer, Lobell, Vivino, and Hill (1996) found no correlations between measures of PM and insight.

A related concept is alexithymia, which is a lack of awareness of feeling life and an inability to verbalize feelings (Taylor & Taylor, 1997). Theorists have suggested that people with alexithymia may not benefit from insight-oriented therapy, and there is some evidence to that effect (Taylor & Taylor, 1997). Alexithymia correlates negatively with PM.

Experiencing

Experiencing (Bohart, 1993), broadly defined, refers to a form of learning: learning through experience. Later in this chapter I discuss different forms this type of learning can take. One particular meaning comes from Gendlin (1968). According to his theory of experiencing, the process of developing useful insights is a process of tuning into feelings and bodily felt meanings, reflecting on them, and putting them into words (a process called *focusing*). Early research by Gendlin and colleagues (Gendlin, Beebe, Cassens, Klein, & Oberlander, 1968) found that some clients were dispositionally higher in ability to focus than others. These clients achieved better results in therapy.

The Experiencing Scale (EXP; Klein, Mathieu-Coughlan, & Kiesler, 1986) was developed as a measure of the degree to which clients engage in productive experiential focusing. It specified the types of client thinking and self-exploration processes that should be likely to lead to productive insight. On the EXP, clients in Stages 1 to 3 talk in relatively impersonal, nonreflective, nonemotional ways. There is a shift at Stage 4 to focusing on internal experience and exploration. Supporting earlier research, Hendricks (2002) concluded that high levels of experiencing are associated with better outcomes in therapy. In other work, Klein et al. (1986) summarized research on correlates of focusing ability. Presumably these would also be correlates of a capacity for developing insight. These included introspective style, cognitive complexity and differentiation, reflectiveness, expressive capacity, obsessiveness, self-consciousness, and attraction to psychotherapy. Focusing ability also correlates with creativity. Klein et al. concluded that the EXP is a measure of reflective style.

Although the theory of experiencing was developed in part to explain which kinds of insights are therapeutic, I could locate only one study (Hill et al., 1992) that specifically found that high levels of experiencing were related to insight.

Client Ability to Participate in the Therapy Interpersonal Relationship

There is reason to believe that participation in interpersonal dialogue, such as dialogue that occurs in therapy, can facilitate insight. Staudinger and Baltes (1996) found that individuals who discussed their dilemmas with friends came up with "more wise" solutions than those who merely thought about their problems by themselves. Martin and Stelmaczonek (1988) found that events that clients identified as important were those that involved expressions of insight and understanding as well as those that contained dialogue indicative of deep, elaborative, and conclusion-oriented information processing. The implication of these studies is that a facilitative dialogical context, such as that used in therapy, can support effective self-reflection, which leads to insight.

However, not all clients may be able to use such a context to generate insight. There is evidence that clients with good interpersonal relationships and object relations work better in insight-oriented therapy than in supportive therapy (Clarkin & Levy, 2004). The fact that these clients work better in insight-oriented therapy does not mean that they will be more likely to attain useful insights, but it does suggest this as a hypothesis.

Similarly, individuals low in another interpersonal skill, social perspective taking, may not have the self-reflective capacities to engage in productive insight work in therapy (Menna & Cohen, 1997). Social perspective taking is the capacity to hold multiple dimensions and perspectives in mind in an interpersonal context. There is little direct evidence relating social perspective taking to insight.

Openness

One might expect openness to correlate with a capacity for insight because research generally finds that variables such as openness and curiosity correlate with better learning and problem-solving ability (Peterson & Seligman, 2004). Orlinsky, Grawe, and Parks (1994) concluded that there is a relationship between patient self-relatedness, which includes being open and accepting toward oneself, and outcome in therapy. Winter (2003), using the Repertory Grid technique, found that "tight construing" predicted poor results in group therapy for a variety of disorders, but not in individual therapy. However, Diemer et al. (1996) found no evidence of a correlation between a trait measure of openness and insight in psychotherapy.

One might, conversely, expect that variables representing the opposite of openness, such as repression or a need for self-consistency, might mitigate against insight attainment. Wickramasekera (1998) postulated a high risk model of threat perception. In his model he argued that certain people are less likely to be aware of internal conflicts (repression), and it is those individuals who are more likely to develop somatization disorders. These individuals will also not obtain insight as readily in therapy through typical verbal means. Wickramasekera gave an example of a man who had serious psychosomatic symptomatology who had not been helped by other methods. However, when repression was overcome and insight facilitated by showing the patient his physiological responses to discussions about his wife, he finally began to use therapy productively.

A related idea is self-consistency (Andrews, 1991). There is considerable literature suggesting that people strive to assimilate discrepant information to preserve the way they view themselves. It could be expected that those high in the need to preserve self-consistency might have greater difficulty attaining insight. However, this hypothesis awaits research.

Creativity

Of all the characteristics that should relate to insight, creativity is one of the most obvious. Descriptions of insight events and creative experiences are almost identical. Consider the story about Bohr discovering the wave-particle theory of light (Bruner, 1986):

> Let me say now what Niels Bohr told *me*. The idea of complementarity in quantum theory, he said, came to him as he thought about the impossibility of considering his son simultaneously in the light of love and in the light of justice, the son just having voluntarily confessed that he had stolen a pipe from a local shop. His brooding set him to thinking about the vases and the faces in the trick figure-ground pictures: you can see only one at a time. And then the impossibility of thinking simultaneously about the position and the velocity of a particle occurred to him. (p. 51)

Is this discovery an insight? Or is it creative, or both? It is clearly both. Wallas's (1926) four-stage model of the creative process is also a description of the insight process: (a) preparation—initial sensing and exploring of a problem; (b) incubation—problem is not consciously pursued and unconscious mental process are involved; (c) illumination—sudden flash of insight when a new idea, solution, or relationship emerges; and (d) verification—the incomplete product of the illumination stage is revised, refined, and corrected.

There is extensive literature on personality correlates of creativity. These correlates include tolerance of ambiguity, flexibility, risk taking, preference for disorder, delay of gratification, freedom from sex-role stereotyping, perseverance, courage, independence, nonconformism, unconventionality, wide interests, greater openness to experiences, behavioral and cognitive flexibility, and risk-taking boldness (Peterson & Seligman, 2004; Selby, 2004). We might therefore expect these characteristics, as well as a capacity for creativity itself, to correlate with a likelihood of attaining insight in psychotherapy. Selby's (2004) grounded theory study found some evidence to support this; however, other than this study there is little research on this topic.

Levels of Cognitive Development

Levels of cognitive development (Basseches, 1994) may influence both the likelihood that a client will attain insight and the type of insight the client achieves. Clients at a higher level of cognitive development, for example, might be able to achieve sophisticated insights. However, insight may lead to moving to a higher level of cognitive development. Research on major personal (quantum) change (Miller & C'de Baca, 2001) found that quantum change often results from insight and that such changes often include moving to a higher level in moral functioning. As far as I know, the role of cognitive development has rarely been studied in psychotherapy.

Goal Orientation

There is an extensive literature in the area of education on the relationship of students' goal orientations to their abilities to cope insightfully with challenging learning situations. There are several conceptions of goal orientation, but in this chapter I focus on the research of Dweck (Dweck & Leggett, 1988; Tallman, 1996). Dweck found that children who felt helpless in school or failed at a task tended to either give up or perseverate, using the same strategy that had not worked in the past. In addition, they exhibited defensiveness and drew their attention away from the task (they were not task-focused). In contrast, mastery-oriented children begin to creatively search to find new solutions when they failed. They kept their eye on the task (they were task-focused).

Further research found that being mastery-oriented or helpless was associated with (a) different goal orientations toward learning situations and (b) different fundamental beliefs about the nature of intelligence. Children who were mastery-oriented believed that intelligence is incremental and focused on the *process* of learning. They treated failure as information. In contrast, helpless children focused on what success or failure meant about them. Tallman (Bohart & Tallman, 1999; Tallman, 1996) has suggested that having a process or task focus is important in therapy and has argued that therapists of different orientations should attempt to encourage mastery-oriented behavior in clients.

Summary

In general, with the possible exception of experiencing, there is minimal evidence that different client characteristics increase or decrease the probability of attaining insight. Several variables have been shown to increase the probability of clients doing well in insight-oriented therapy, but this does not mean that they increase the probability of attaining insights per se. Most variables considered, including various personality correlates, can be plausibly related to a capacity to attain insight; however, further research is needed on this subject.

CLIENT PSYCHOLOGICAL STATES

Clients' psychological states may also affect their readiness to learn and their capacity to attain insight.

Stress and Levels of Thinking

Pennebaker (1989) developed a "levels of thinking" scale and has used it to study journaling. He found that participants under stress exhibited a narrower perspective, were less likely to reflect on causes, and were less aware of emotion. This suggests that when individuals are under stress they may not be as likely to think in ways that could lead to productive insight. This implies that one major function of therapy may be to help clients reduce stress to foster productive thinking.

Involvement

Given the importance of client involvement in making therapy work (see summary of research in Orlinsky et al., 1994), it is reasonable to assume that clients who are involved are more likely to attain insight. Involvement includes a willingness to participate in therapeutic assignments, to invest effort in the process, and to participate in the therapeutic relationship.

Client Readiness

Clients must be ready to attain insight in two ways. First, they will be more likely to work to achieve insight if they are aware of the need for change. Such awareness may occur when answers to lingering problems have not been forthcoming. Studies of the process of change (Baumeister, 1994; Marris, 1974; Miller & C' De Baca, 2001) suggest that insights leading to major personal transformations occur along the lines of Kuhn's (1962) *paradigm shift*. Individuals (a) become aware of discrepancies between what they want or how they see themselves or the world and how their life actually is; (b) initially try to assimilate the discrepancies to old views or paradigms; (c) when that doesn't work, there eventually is a perspective or paradigm shift; (d) which is a new way of seeing and can be a major reorganization of world view. Two models of the change process in psychotherapy, those of Prochaska, Norcross, and DiClemente (1994) and Stiles (1999), start with initial stages in which clients are unaware of problems and move toward dawning awareness and contemplation of the need for change. Dawning awareness is followed by exploration, insight, and then by application and action (see Hill, 2004).

Second, as in any learning process client readiness depends on where the client is in the exploring–learning process (see Vygotsky, 1978, for his concept of the *zone of proximal development*). The implication is that learning will usually be stepwise. Clients will be more likely to attain insight after having done sufficient preliminary work exploring the components of the problem. Hill's (2004) stepwise model of the therapy process, for example, includes exploration as the first step before understanding. Furthermore, deep insights will depend on clients' having attained earlier, *preparatory* insights. These models suggest that the ability of therapists' responses to help the client attain insight depend on where the client is in his or her stage of development.

There is reason to believe that insight attainment in therapy has such a stepwise property. In psychodynamic theory it has long been argued that clients attain useful insights only at a certain point in their process of development. That is, insights are useful only if they are just under the surface of consciousness. Things that are too deep will not be understood. In general, evidence has supported the hypothesis that moderate interpretations are best. Interpretations that are too superficial will make clients stop working toward insight; those that are too deep will make clients stop or resist (Bohart, 1970). In experiential therapy, Sachse (1991) found that if therapists used meaning constructions of medium complexity (relative to the client's place in the process of development), clients were more likely to use them.

Summary

In general, it can be hypothesized that the attainment of insight by clients will depend on how far they have come in the self-change process. This can be generally encompassed within the concept of their zone of proximal development. Additionally, clients who are under stress may be less likely to engage in the kind of higher level thinking needed to foster insight. Clients who are not involved will be less likely to attain insight.

HOW MAY CLIENTS CONTRIBUTE TO FOSTERING INSIGHT?

I have previously synthesized theory and research to suggest a model of the activities of productive client thinking in therapy (Bohart, 2001a). Productive thinking includes exploration of factors involved in problems, clarification and identification of goals, evaluation of prior attempts to solve problems, generation of new conceptions of the problem, generation of possible solutions, and evaluation and testing of new conceptions and possible solutions. Insight is a part of this process. I described the process of productive thinking as follows:

1. The client is reflective.
2. The client adopts a preaffirmative position (adopts a phenomenological orientation—meaning an open, receptive, nonjudgmental orientation).
3. The client stands back to see things in a broader perspective.
4. The client thinks dialectically.
5. The client is personally involved.
6. The client deals with personal meaning.
7. The level of meaning lies between too detailed and too abstract (e.g., middle-level categorization).
8. The client's process is experiential: Insights need to arise in the context of direct experience, accessing experiential referents of past experiences, or present experiences in therapy, or experiences created through exercises and homework.

9. The client's reflective process includes emotion.

10. The client is in a process-focused, task-oriented state of mind.

In this section I examine elements from this model that may contribute to the attainment of insight. Two variables from the model (5 and 10) have been considered in previous sections. One (7) I do not include in the discussion because it is not clear how it specifically facilitates insight. I include additional elements that are not listed that have come to my attention through the process of preparing this chapter.

To attain insight, Dorothy had to engage in a lengthy search that consisted of having many experiences in the world. She attained insight after a question by Glinda stimulated her to reflect. Overall, I suggest these may be the two overarching activities that contribute to insight attainment: learning through searching and having experiences, and productive reflection. These two activities may occur sequentially, with one following the other (as with Dorothy); however, they are more commonly intertwined.

Learning Through Experience

In a previous part of this chapter I considered the ability to focus on internal experience as a dispositional variable. In a broader sense, learning through experience is a therapeutic commonality (Bohart, 1993). Since Freud's work it has been recognized that sheer intellectual insight does not appear to be effective in psychotherapy. I have argued that insights need to arise in the context of experiencing (Bohart, 1993). Arising in the context of experiencing can mean different things. First, it can mean the activation of relevant emotion. Second, it may mean tuning into bodily felt meanings (Gendlin, 1996). Third, it may mean testing out dysfunctional beliefs in the context of everyday life, in the context of the therapeutic relationship, or in the context of relevant concrete examples (Beck, Rush, Shaw, & Emery, 1979). Fourth, it may mean recreating the bodily symptoms and experiences associated with a particular problem to gain a new perspective on them (what Grawe, 1997, called "problem actuation"), as in cognitive–behavioral therapy. And finally, it may mean gaining insights through behavioral experimentation.

These different forms of learning through experience can be subsumed under two general categories: learning by searching internal experience and learning by having experiences in the world. An example of attaining insight through a search of internal experience is Clarke's (1996) "creation of meaning" procedure. Clarke's procedure helps clients create meaning when they have experienced a trauma or loss that challenges a cherished belief. Her meaning creation process involves symbolizing the discrepancy between the cherished belief and the experience, symbolizing the emotional reaction to this discrepancy, condensing feelings into words and symbols, and synthesizing the relationship between thoughts and feelings. An example of attaining insight through having experiences in the world is given by Goldfried

(1979). In learning how to ski, one is told to "bend the knees." One can understand this intellectually, but it is a different matter to practice until one gets an experiential insight into what this means: "Oh! Bend the *knees!*" (p. 366). Many cognitive–behavioral activities involve learning by having experiences in the world, such as trying out new behaviors. Trying new behaviors may provide new perspectives and lead to insight.

In terms of searching internal experience, I have been particularly influenced by Gendlin's (1996, 1997) theory of experiencing. I noted earlier that this was developed in part to identify the conditions under which productive insight develops. To understand Gendlin we need to go beyond the standard Western dichotomy between thoughts and feelings (feelings meaning emotions). For Gendlin, meanings are not only thoughts. There are also meanings that are experienced in the body, which he called "bodily felt" meanings. I will not explicate this further here, but see Bohart (1993, 2001b).

From Gendlin's (1996, 1997) point of view we understand more at the experiential level than we do at the level of explicitly conceptualized knowledge. If one were to diagram these two, a broader circle would represent experiential knowing, and a smaller circle inside would represent knowledge that has been articulated into language. Gendlin's level of experiential knowing is in a class of related concepts, including tacit knowing. What is different about Gendlin's view is that although typical views of tacit knowing reserve sophistication for explicit conceptual knowing, and see tacit knowing as automatized, for Gendlin, experiential knowing is more finely textured and more complex than what has been incorporated into verbal knowledge structures. Effective insights are those that arise from a process of tuning into felt experience and finding the right words to articulate it. The process of finding the right words leads to a *felt shift*. The new understanding is not just a discrete piece of knowledge. Rather, the process of attaining it already changes how the person experiences self and world. Gendlin called the process "focusing" and developed a procedure for fostering it (Gendlin, 1996). Focusing, which can be seen as an insight-generating procedure, has been found to be associated with positive therapeutic outcomes (Hendricks, 2002).

Gendlin's (1996) focusing procedure is a specific procedure that individuals can use on their own to generate productive insights. It is a back and forth process of connecting thoughts and feelings (Bohart, 2001b). Watson and Rennie (1994) found that when clients "attempted to match the words . . . against the visual images and felt-senses . . . [they] came to new realizations about themselves" (p. 133). There is evidence supporting the importance of connecting thoughts and feelings (Clarke, 1996; Klein et al., 1986; Pennebaker, 1990).

Productive Reflection

Productive reflection appears to be the second key element in attaining insight. Rennie's (2002) tape-assisted recall studies of clients' experience found clients to be highly active in reflective thinking. Clients often got insights that were not shared with therapists. Watson and Rennie (1994) studied what clients were doing during the use of an experiential therapy procedure. Once again, it was found that clients were highly active in reflecting on their problems and that this reflection was the key to gaining insights. The process, as they described it, involved symbolic representation of experience, reflexive self-examination, making new realizations, and revisioning the self.

In the following paragraphs I briefly consider a laundry list of activities that may contribute to productive reflection and insight attainment:

1. *Adopting a preaffirmative position.* Adopting a preaffirmative position involves suspending judgment and prior conceptions to take a fresh look at a problem. This has been identified as a factor in fostering both creativity (Selby, 2004) and insight (Sternberg & Davidson, 1995). It particularly involves suspension of self-criticism to more openly evaluate information.

2. *Standing back to see things in a broader perspective.* Gaining insight is fostered by seeing things in a broader perspective and becoming aware of elements and connections one had not noticed before. This is also referred to as gaining distance. Gonçalves, Henriques, and Machado (2004) argued that the skill of distancing oneself is important in productive narrative processing in therapy. They believe human flexibility rests in the ability to reflect on the thinking process and create multiple meanings. Pennebaker (1990) noted that part of the productive process of journaling is to become more detached as one writes about a trauma. The writer stands back and considers the causes of the event and his or her own emotional reactions. This leads to a gradual change in perspective. A key concept in therapy, in and of itself, is that "I am not my problem" (White, 2004).

At the same time, the person must not get too distant from experience and lost in abstractions. Neither should the person be too up close and not able to see the forest for the trees. Going back and forth from a close, experiential examination of experience to a more distanced perspective and back again seems to be optimal.

3. *Being receptive (i.e., to temporarily adopt a stance of receptive listening).* This includes adopting a preaffirmative position, suspending self-criticism, and then tracking experience—listening and attending, like one is watching a movie or meditating (Martin, 1997)—in contrast to critically analyzing. Active analysis and interpretation may come later. Conclusions may be reached inductively, emerging from this attending process and involving synthesis, rather than through logical deduction. Receptivity is a component of the focusing procedure (Gendlin, 1996). I have argued that it is the mindstate encouraged by the eye movement desensitization and reprocessing procedure (Bohart, 2001b), a process that can lead to insight.

4. *Systematic observation.* Systematic observation, such as that used in behavioral therapy, may facilitate insight. For example, keeping track of one's

diet may provide insight into how one has gained weight and may provide insight into how to reverse the trend. In cognitive therapy, keeping track of dysfunctional cognitions may provide insight into how one generates them.

Systematic observation may include the processes described previously: adopting a preaffirmative position and suspending judgment, standing back and gaining distance, and receptive listening in the form of simple observation and keeping track, rather than analysis.

5. *Paying attention to internal information.* The kind of creative problem solving that occurs in psychotherapy appears to necessitate that clients be aware of, attend to, and incorporate internal information into their activities. Previously in this chapter, I mentioned paying attention to internal experience. Experience can include felt meanings, emotion, and dreams, as well as thoughts. An internal focus is particularly emphasized by psychodynamic and experiential therapists, but cognitive–behavioral therapists also focus clients on their inner thoughts and feeling processes. It makes sense that a client must reflect on his or her personal construals and experiences to modify them (and must also reflect on external events). Several scales of productive information processing, such as the EXP scale, have at the unproductive end of information processing an external focus and at the productive end a focus that includes internal information. Research by experiential therapists (e.g., Greenberg & Angus, 2004) has shown that an internal focus is important in leading to productive information processing.

6. *Thinking dialectically.* Thinking dialectically involves considering the opposites of a particular issue until a new synthesis emerges. Rychlak (1994) noted that a key part of how people learn is by posing dialectical challenges to themselves. Humans do not only think *a*; when they think *a*, they often think *not a*. Engaging in a juxtaposition of opposites is a characteristic of creative thinking (Selby, 2004). Techniques such as the two-chair procedure in gestalt and experiential psychotherapy give the client a chance to play with different perspectives. The client could be said to be engaging in an experiment in perspective-taking, which may promote insight.

7. *Logical analysis.* Clients may also attain insight through the logical analysis of beliefs, as in cognitive therapy. However, using cognitive therapy as a model, logical analysis appears to work best when combined with elements previously mentioned, such as adopting a preaffirmative position and gaining distance. In addition, it appears to be more effective when it is not abstract but is grounded in concrete experiential examples, including live examples in the therapy session. These are all encouraged by cognitive therapists, who do not simply diagram to the client new, more logical ways to see things. The therapists' activity of appealing to logic rests on clients' preexisting capacities for recognizing and following logical arguments.

8. *Client narrative activity.* Levitt and Rennie (2004), using tape-assisted recall in their research, reported that clients got insights just from telling their story, even if they kept the insights to themselves. Pennebaker's (1990)

studies of journaling—a narrative form of processing—have shown that insight attainment is a major result of journaling.

9. *Rumination.* Rumination has a negative connotation. However, going over and over an experience may be useful to help understand and assimilate it. Researchers who study the processing of traumatic experiences have found that ruminating over the trauma is a key part in successful processing (Tedeschi, Park, & Calhoun, 1998). However, not all rumination is helpful. Tedeschi et al. report that rumination that involves negative self-criticism is not useful.

10. *Use of metaphors and analogies.* I earlier gave the example of Neils Bohr, who used the metaphor of not being able to both love his child and hold him to justice. Angus and Rennie (1989) documented the use of metaphor in furthering productive therapeutic processing. Clarke (1996) found that metaphor was useful in her study of creation of meaning events. There is a cognitive psychology literature on the use of metaphor and analogy for fostering insight (e.g., Dominowski & Dallob, 1995).

11. *Searching for the right word.* In the literature on both cognitive psychology (Schooler, Fallshore, & Fiore, 1995) and on psychotherapy (Elliott et al., 1994; Watson & Rennie, 1994) there are repeated findings that finding the exact word is important in facilitating insights and cognitive shifts.

12. *Active interpretation.* Clients create meaning and find insights in part by interpreting what happens to them in therapy. Elliott et al. (1994) analyzed insight events in therapy and found that

> clients actively and selectively process therapeutic material. For example, during the session the client rejected the therapist's attempts to link the client's feelings to the therapeutic relationship . . . and to the client's relationship with his son . . . In addition, the event itself also was a selection by the client of what he regarded as most helpful in the session. (p. 461)

They also found that some of the events that clients considered significant were seemingly minor occurrences. Why? Because the client may be aware of important themes in them. Talmon (1990) interviewed former clients and found that

> I had taken my interventions and my words much too seriously. Patients reported following suggestions that I could not remember having made. They created their own interpretations, which were sometimes quite different from what I recollected and sometimes more creative and suitable versions of my suggestions. . . . (p. 60)

We have found in qualitative studies (e.g., Bohart & Byock, 2003) that clients interpreted empathy responses as either providing insight or support, depending on what the client needed.

13. *Interpersonal dialogue.* Talking about one's problems with other people is a time-honored procedure for gaining new understanding, in everyday life

and business as well as in psychotherapy. Many of the processes already described may happen when talking over problems with other people: trying out new perspectives, narrating, searching for the right word, logical analysis, and examination of both internal and external experience. In addition, in a dialectical fashion, one can compare one's ideas and perspectives to that of others.

14. *Other activities.* I briefly note other components that may contribute to productive reflection and insight attainment. Schooler et al. (1995) mention improving recognition of new elements and hence insight by changing context, which can lead to seeing the problem from a new angle. Another strategy is to represent the problem differently. Perseverance, risk-taking, and playfulness all can play a role in enhancing insight. Other techniques that may foster creativity and therefore insight include the use of expressive arts (Selby, 2004). For example, Jung used active imagination (writing, drawing, and painting). Selby also mentions the importance of feeling that one is in a safe interpersonal environment.

HOW DO CLIENTS USE AND BENEFIT FROM INSIGHT?

Assuming that clients have attained insights, how do they use them? A first question is, does the insight change the person, or must the person use the insight for change to ensue? In some instances, insight may be transformative. Gendlin's (1996) theory of experiencing holds that insights that are arrived at by a certain process (focusing) lead to bodily felt shifts, so that a person who experienced insight now experiences the world differently. At a more molar level, descriptions of quantum changes that followed insight (Miller & C'de Baca, 2001) suggest the possibility of persons being transformed by insight.

However, most therapists know of instances in which clients achieve insight but do not magically change. Stage models of therapy, such as those of Prochaska et al. (1994) and Hill (2004), imply that insight is not useful unless it leads to action. In their study of encounter groups, Lieberman, Yalom, and Miles (1973) found that clients needed to actively apply insights for the insights to be useful. Elliott et al. (1994) found that an insight was followed by the client's engaging in further cognitive elaboration. The client then used the insight to test out new perceptions. Grande, Rudolf, Oberbracht, and Pauli-Magnus (2003) found that insights helped clients treat external demands in their everyday lives as opportunities for productive, concrete change.

However, little is known about how insights actually promote change. Following are speculations on how insight might help. First, insight brings new knowledge. This new knowledge may imply new actions and new behaviors for the client to try out. Second, insight may lead to increased coherence. Clients often come into therapy feeling demoralized and anxious because things don't make sense—there is incoherence in their worldviews. Finding a useful explanation that brings coherence may reduce anxiety and increase feelings of hope (Fingarette, 1963). This in turn may lead to new productive thinking or behavioral exploration. Third, insight may lead to acceptance. For example, one may be able to let go of a cherished belief (Clarke, 1996) or an impossible hope (e.g., that one's father will ever love one), so that the person can move on. Fourth, gaining insight may lead to a shift in how the individual understands the world, from either–or thinking to realizing that the world has shades of gray.

It is unlikely that it will turn out that there is a simple linear causal relationship between insight and change. Insights may lead directly to change (e.g., Gendlin and quantum change) or lead to change through application of new behaviors, which in turn may lead to further insight. Engaging in new behaviors may lead to the development of new insight, which in turn may imply still other new behaviors. For a complex living system such as a human being, embedded in other complex living systems (families, neighborhoods, cultures, countries), it is likely that insight will be one of many factors that can play a role in change.

CONCLUDING COMMENTS

To bring together ideas from the this chapter, I hypothesize that the following are factors that increase the probability of gaining insight. First, the client engages in a reflective examination of the problem or solution space. This includes an exploration of both external experience and internal experience. This exploratory activity is facilitated by the client's adopting a preaffirmative or phenomenological position. The client tries looking at problems and solutions from various new angles or new perspectives, which can be helped along by exercises. Exploration can also include testing out alternative perspectives through new behavior. Reflectivity would include some degree of nonjudgmental, open listening or tracking, not unlike a meditative mindset in which conclusions are reached inductively rather than deductively. It may include dialectical thinking of developing opposites and comparing and contrasting them. All these activities may increase a productive sense of distance from the problem and the experience. This may lead to the insight that "I am not my problem," which may in turn lead to further insights.

Insights will be grounded in experience, either in concrete external experience gained through behavioral exercises, keeping track of dysfunctional cognitions in concrete situations in life, or through accessing internal experience. The person will also adopt a task, or process focus, in which failure feedback is treated as information. Other factors such as using metaphor, searching for the right word, systematic observation, ruminating over experiences until they are assimilated, and creating narratives may be helpful. Clients will have a better chance of attaining insight if they go step by step. The kinds of understandings they achieve in any given moment will depend on their zone of proximal development. Clients may creatively interpret (or even misinterpret) feedback to generate new insights. The simple act of talking over their problems with another person (the therapist) may function as an experiment in perspective-taking and may stimulate insight.

Clients will be more likely to engage in these processes if there is an emerging awareness of a discrepancy between their goals and values in life and the actualities of their life. They may also be more likely to engage in these activities if they are psychologically minded and possess other personality characteristics that appear to facilitate the attainment of insight. Some insights may be life-changing, creating quantum changes. More likely and more often, insights need to be assimilated through work, including repeated practice (such as in cognitive–behavioral therapy), or through application and testing out in life.

I am not commenting extensively here on what therapists can do to facilitate client insight, because this topic is covered in many chapters in this book. However, I briefly note that to encourage clients' active involvement in the insight process, therapists should listen empathically to promote a nondefensive stance, mindfulness, and stepping back and perspective-taking. They should promote emotional awareness and receptive internal listening. They should promote a process orientation (such as both cognitive and client-centered therapists do). They should promote behavioral experimentation. Finally, they should promote noncritical evaluation of logical thinking.

In fact, many of the processes I list are processes that therapists try to facilitate (e.g., logical thinking, awareness of internal experiencing). Understanding how these hypothesized client processes intersect with what therapists do, particularly in terms of different therapy approaches and different therapy relationships, will be important in understanding how clients contribute to the insight process.

Most of my conclusions are hypotheses based on inferences from theory and research. Research is needed to see how well, or even if, this schematization matches up with reality. Quantitative studies relating frequency of insights to personality characteristics and client activities, as well as qualitative studies on how clients experience the process leading up to an insight and how they subsequently use insights, are needed.

REFERENCES

Andrews, J. D. W. (1991). *The active self in psychotherapy*. New York: Allyn & Bacon.

Angus, L. E., & Rennie, D. L. (1989). Envisioning the representational world: The client's experience of metaphoric expressiveness in psychotherapy. *Psychotherapy: Theory, Research, Practice, Training, 26*, 373–379.

Basseches, M. (1994). *Dialectical thinking and adult development*. Norwood, NJ: Ablex Publishing.

Baumeister, R. F. (1994). The crystallization of the discontent in the process of major life change. In T. F. Heatherton & J. L. Weinberger (Eds.), *Can personality change?* (pp. 281–297). Washington, DC: American Psychological Association.

Beck, A. T., Rush, A. J., Shaw, B. F., & Emery, G. (1979). *Cognitive therapy of depression*. New York: Guilford Press.

Beutler, L. E., Harwood, T. M., Alimohamed, S., & Malik, S. (2004). Therapist variables. In M. Lambert (Ed.), *Bergin and Garfield's handbook of psychotherapy and behavior change* (5th ed., pp. 227–306). New York: Wiley.

Bohart, A. (1970). *Insight and interpretation in psychotherapy*. Unpublished specialized comprehensive exam paper, University of California, Los Angeles.

Bohart, A. (1993). Experiencing: The basis of psychotherapy. *Journal of Psychotherapy Integration, 3*, 51–67.

Bohart, A. (2001a). How can expression in psychotherapy be constructive? In A. Bohart & D. Stipek (Eds.), *Constructive and destructive behavior* (pp. 337–364). Washington, DC: American Psychological Association.

Bohart, A. (2001b). A meditation on the nature of self-healing and personality change in psychotherapy based on Gendlin's theory of experiencing. *The Humanistic Psychologist, 29*, 249–279.

Bohart, A. (2006). The client as active self-healer. In J. C. Norcross, L. E. Beutler, & R. F. Levant (Eds.), *Evidence-based practices in mental health: Debate and dialogue on the fundamental questions* (pp. 218–226). Washington, DC: American Psychological Association.

Bohart, A., & Byock, G. (2003, July). *How does empathy facilitate?* Paper presented at the World Conference for Person-Centered and Experiential Psychotherapy and Counseling, Egmond aan Zee, The Netherlands.

Bohart, A., & Tallman, K. (1999). *How clients make therapy work: The process of active self-healing*. Washington, DC: American Psychological Association.

Bruner, J. (1986). *Actual minds, possible worlds*. Cambridge, MA: Harvard University Press.

Clarke, K. M. (1996). Change process in a creation of meaning event. *Journal of Consulting and Clinical Psychology, 64*, 465–470.

Clarkin, J. F., & Levy, K. N. (2004). The influence of client variables on psychotherapy. In M. Lambert (Ed.), *Bergin and Garfield's handbook of psychotherapy and behavior change* (5th ed., pp. 194–226). New York: Wiley.

Conte, H. R., & Ratto, R. (1997). Self-report measures of psychological mindedness. In M. McCallum & W. E. Piper (Eds.), *Psychological mindedness: A contemporary understanding* (pp. 1–26). Mahwah, NJ: Erlbaum.

Diemer, R. A., Lobell, L. K., Vivino, B. L., & Hill, C. E. (1996). Comparison of dream interpretation, event interpretation, and unstructured sessions in brief therapy. *Journal of Counseling Psychology, 43,* 99–112.

Dominowski, R. L., & Dallob, P. (1995). Insight and problem solving. In R. J. Sternberg & J. E. Davidson (Eds.), *The nature of insight* (pp. 33–62). Cambridge, MA: MIT Press.

Dweck, C. S., & Leggett, E. L. (1988). A social–cognitive approach to motivation and personality. *Psychological Review, 95,* 644–656.

Elliott, R., Shapiro, D. A., Firth-Cozens, J., Stiles, W. B., Hardy, G. E., Llewelyn, S. P., & Margison, F. R. (1994). Comprehensive process analysis of insight events in cognitive–behavioral and psychodynamic–interpersonal psychotherapies. *Journal of Counseling Psychology, 41,* 449–463.

Fingarette, H. (1963). *The self in transformation.* New York: HarperCollins.

Gendlin, E. T. (1968). The experiential response. In E. H. Hammer (Ed.), *Use of interpretation in treatment.* New York: Grune & Stratton.

Gendlin, E. T. (1996). *Focusing-oriented psychotherapy.* New York: Guilford Press.

Gendlin, E. T. (1997). *Experiencing and the creation of meaning: A philosophical and psychological approach to the subjective.* Evanston, IL: Northwestern University Press.

Gendlin, E. T., Beebe, J., III, Cassens, J., Klein, M., & Oberlander, M. (1968). Focusing ability in psychotherapy, personality, and creativity. In J. M. Shlien (Ed.), *Research in psychotherapy* (Vol. III, pp. 217–241). Washington, DC: American Psychological Association.

Goldfried, M. R. (1979). Cognition and experience. In P. C. Kendall & S. D. Hollon (Eds.), *Cognitive–behavioral interventions: Theory, research, and procedures* (pp. 141–146). New York: Academic Press.

Gonçalves, O. F., Henriques, M. R., & Machado, P. P. P. (2004). Nurturing nature: Cognitive narrative strategies. In L. E. Angus & J. McLeod (Eds.), *The handbook of narrative and psychotherapy* (pp. 103–118). Thousand Oaks, CA: Sage.

Grande, T., Rudolf, G., Oberbracht, C., & Pauli-Magnus, C. (2003). Progressive changes in patients' lives after psychotherapy: Which treatment effects support them? *Psychotherapy Research, 13,* 43–58.

Grawe, K. (1997). Research-informed psychotherapy. *Psychotherapy Research, 7,* 1–20.

Greenberg, L. S., & Angus, L. E. (2004). The contributions of emotion processes to narrative change in psychotherapy: A dialectical constructivist approach. In L. E. Angus & J. McLeod (Eds.), *The handbook of narrative and psychotherapy* (pp. 331–350). Thousand Oaks, CA: Sage.

Hendricks, M. N. (2002). Focusing-oriented–experiential psychotherapy. In D. J. Cain & J. Seeman (Eds.), *Humanistic psychotherapies: Handbook of research and practice* (pp. 221–252). Washington, DC: American Psychological Association.

Hill, C. (2004). *Helping skills: facilitating exploration, insight, and action* (2nd ed.). Washington, DC: American Psychological Association.

Hill, C., Corbett, M. M., Kanitz, B., Rios, P., Lightsey, R., & Gomez, M. (1992). Client behavior in counseling and therapy sessions: Development of a pantheoretical measure. *Journal of Counseling Psychology, 39,* 539–549.

Klein, M. H., Mathieu-Coughlan, P., & Kiesler, D. (1986). The Experiencing Scales. In L. S. Greenberg & W. Pinsof (Eds.), *The psychotherapeutic process: A research handbook* (pp. 21–72). New York: Guilford Press.

Kuhn, T. S. (1962). *The structure of scientific revolutions.* Chicago: University of Chicago Press.

Langley, N., Ryerson, F., & Woolf, E. A. (Writers). (1939). *The Wizard of OZ* [Screenplay]. Retrieved July 6, 2006, from http://sfy.ru/sfy.html?script=wizard_of_oz_1939

Levitt, H. M., & Rennie, D. L. (2004). Narrative activity: Clients' and therapists' intentions in the process of narration. In L. E. Angus & J. McLeod (Eds.), *The handbook of narrative and psychotherapy* (pp. 299–314). Thousand Oaks, CA: Sage.

Lieberman, M. A., Yalom, I. D., & Miles, M. B. (1973). *Encounter groups: First facts.* New York: Basic Books.

Marris, P. (1974). *Loss and change.* Garden City, NY: Doubleday.

Martin, J. (1997). Mindfulness: A proposed common factor. *Journal of Psychotherapy Integration, 7,* 291–312.

Martin, J., & Stelmaczonek, K. (1988). Participant identification and recall of important events in counseling. *Journal of Counseling Psychology, 35,* 385–390.

McCallum, M., & Piper, W. E. (Eds.). (1997). *Psychological mindedness: A contemporary understanding.* Mahwah, NJ: Erlbaum.

McCallum, M., & Piper, W. E. (1999). Personality disorders and response to group-oriented evening treatment. *Group dynamics: Theory, Research, and Practice, 3,* 3–14.

Menna, R., & Cohen, N. J. (1997). Social perspective taking. In M. McCallum & W. E. Piper (Eds.), *Psychological mindedness: A contemporary understanding* (pp. 189–210). Mahwah, NJ: Erlbaum.

Miller, W. R., & C'de Baca, J. (2001). *Quantum change.* New York: Guilford Press.

Orlinsky, D. E., Grawe, K., & Parks, B. K. (1994). Process and outcome in psychotherapy. In A. E. Bergin & S. L. Garfield (Eds.), *Handbook of psychotherapy and behavior change* (4th ed., pp. 270–376). New York: Wiley.

Pennebaker, J. W. (1989). Stream of consciousness and stress: Levels of thinking. In J. S. Uleman & J. A. Bargh (Eds.), *Unintended thought* (pp. 327–350). New York: Guilford Press.

Pennebaker, J. W. (1990). *Opening up.* New York: Morrow.

Peterson, C., & Seligman, M. E. P. (2004). *Character strength and virtues.* New York: Oxford University Press.

Piper, W. E., McCallum, M., Joyce, A. S., Azim, H. F., & Ogrodniczuk, J. S. (1999). Follow-up findings for interpretive and supportive forms of psychotherapy and patient personality variables. *Journal of Consulting and Clinical Psychology, 67,* 267–273.

Prochaska, J. O., Norcross, J. C., & DiClemente, C. C. (1994). *Changing for good.* New York: Morrow.

Rennie, D. L. (2002). Experiencing psychotherapy: Grounded theory studies. In D. J. Cain & J. Seeman (Eds.), *Humanistic psychotherapies: Handbook of research and practice* (pp. 117–144). Washington, DC: American Psychological Association.

Rychlak, J. F. (1994). *Logical learning theory.* Lincoln: University of Nebraska Press.

Sachse, R. (1991). *Clients must understand their therapists. The phrasing of interventions determines their effect.* Unpublished manuscript, University of Ruhr, Bochum, Germany.

Schooler, J. W., Fallshore, M., & Fiore, S. M. (1995). Epilogue: Putting insight into perspective. In R. J. Sternberg & J. E. Davidson (Eds.), *The nature of insight* (pp. 559–588). Cambridge, MA: MIT Press.

Selby, C. E. (2004). *Psychotherapy as a creative process: A grounded theory exploration.* Unpublished doctoral dissertation, Saybrook Graduate School, San Francisco.

Staudinger, U. M., & Baltes, P. B. (1996). Interactive minds: A facilitative setting for wisdom-related performances? *Journal of Personality and Social Psychology, 71,* 746–762.

Sternberg, R. J., & Davidson, J. E. (Eds.). (1995). *The nature of insight.* Cambridge, MA: MIT Press.

Stiles, W. B. (1999). Signs and voices in psychotherapy. *Psychotherapy Research, 9,* 1–21.

Tallman, K. (1996). *The state of mind theory: Goal orientation concepts applied to clinical psychology.* Unpublished master's thesis, California State University Dominguez Hills, Carson, CA.

Talmon, M. (1990). *Single session therapy.* San Francisco: Jossey-Bass.

Taylor, G. J., & Taylor, H. L. (1997). Alexithymia. In M. McCallum & W. E. Piper (Eds.), *Psychological mindedness: A contemporary understanding* (pp. 77–104). Mahwah, NJ: Erlbaum.

Tedeschi, R. G., Park, C. L., & Calhoun, L. G. (Eds.). (1998). *Posttraumatic growth.* Mahwah, NJ: Erlbaum.

Vygotsky, L. S. (1978). *Mind in society: The development of higher psychological processes.* Cambridge, MA: MIT Press.

Wallas, G. (1926). *The art of thought.* Orlando, FL: Harcourt, Brace.

Watson, J. C., & Rennie, D. L. (1994). A qualitative analysis of clients' subjective experience of significant moments in therapy during the exploration of problematic reactions. *Journal of Counseling Psychology, 41,* 500–509.

White, M. (2004). Folk psychology and narrative practices. In L. E. Angus & J. McLeod (Eds.), *The handbook of narrative and psychotherapy* (pp. 15–52). Thousand Oaks, CA: Sage.

Wickramasekera, I. (1998). Secrets kept from the mind but not the body or behavior: The unsolved problems of identifying and treating somatization and psychophysiological disease. *Advances in Mind–Body Medicine, 14,* 81–132.

Winter, D. A. (2003). Repertory grid technique as a psychotherapy research measure. *Psychotherapy Research, 13,* 25–42.

13

ON LEADING A HORSE TO WATER: THERAPIST INSIGHT, COUNTERTRANSFERENCE, AND CLIENT INSIGHT

JEFFREY A. HAYES AND JOSLYN M. CRUZ

How do therapists derive insight into their clients? That is the primary question addressed in this chapter. To what extent is therapist insight a necessary precondition to client insight? What is the role of therapist countertransference in inhibiting or fostering client insight? In considering these questions, we draw from existing research and theory as well as from our own clinical and supervisory experiences, and we also offer new ideas designed to stimulate further thinking and research on insight.

DEFINING INSIGHT

Colloquial expressions reveal much about the word *insight*. For example, when a person wishes to communicate that she or he comprehends what another is saying, she or he might say, "I see," as if conveying, "I have *sight into* what you are saying." Understanding is thus linked metaphorically to seeing. Other metaphors similarly convey the notion that insight is linked to vision, which itself requires light, as reflected in phrases such as *to see the light, to be enlightened,* or *to shed light on a problem.* Alternatively, when one is *in the dark* about something, one lacks knowledge of or understanding about it. And as we discuss later in this chapter, all people possess "blind spots" of which they are by definition unaware. Also of interest is the fact that prior to the 13th century origins of the word *insight,* according to poet Robert Bly (1988) there was a prevalent belief that "darkness contains intelligence and nourishment and even information" (p. 42).

In this chapter, we take a rather conventional approach to defining insight as *deep understanding.* Convention notwithstanding, it bears mentioning that the point at which understanding is sufficiently deep to qualify as insight is inherently subjective. As therapy is also subjective, the lack of definitional precision does not pose much of an obstacle in terms of clinical relevance. After all, it is up to the therapist and the client to decide when insights have been acquired. At a minimum, one can safely say that when a therapist possesses insight into a client, he or she understands the client at a qualitatively deeper level than when the client first walked into his or her office. Although insights typically are tied to patterns of behavior in the client (Marmor, 1980), in general, client insight is equivalent to new and meaningful discoveries of self.

On one level, this definition of insight is simple and straightforward. However, because in this chapter we deal with insight from the therapist's perspective, the term must be distinguished from a similar construct, namely empathy. Empathic understanding occurs when the therapist comprehends on an intellectual or emotional level what the client conveys (Bohart & Greenberg, 1997; Duan & Hill, 1996). In this regard empathy and therapist insight are overlapping constructs; both are related to understanding. However, there are occasions when the therapist understands something that the client has not revealed and may even attempt to conceal. These are instances of therapist insight that are distinct from empathy. For example, the therapist may connect previously disparate pieces of information about a client, perceive the latent meaning associated with a client's verbalizations, or interpret a personality inventory, all of which may yield a new understanding of the client. We consider insight to be a broader construct than empathy, therefore, in that it pertains to the therapist's understanding of what the client has communicated, intentionally or not, in virtually any form.

LEADING A HORSE TO WATER

A familiar proverb coined in 1546 by English dramatist John Heywood suggests "you can lead a horse to water but you cannot make it drink." This colloquial expression serves as a useful heuristic for framing the central questions of this chapter. We might consider the horse—with all due respect—to be the client, the person leading the horse to be the therapist, and the water to be insight. Three questions pertinent to this axiom arise: Is it necessary for the therapist to know where the water is located for clients to drink from it? Is it helpful for the therapist to know where the water is located? What facilitates or hinders the therapist from knowing where the water is located? (This chapter does not address the issue of making the horse drink water, i.e., clients' resistance to insight).

We return to the adage, "you can lead a horse to water . . . " to be clear about several assumptions. First, there is no single source of water, just as there is no sole piece of insight in therapy. The process of understanding in therapeutic work is one of continual unfolding and deepening, so insight may come at different times and from various wells, streams, or oases. Second, in this chapter we work on the assumption that drinking water is a good thing. Assuming water is pure, no one would argue with the literal, life-sustaining value of imbibing it. Finally, the idea that the person directing the horse knows where the water is located is implicit in the expression. Similarly, in psychotherapy it may be assumed that the therapist possesses insight toward which the client is lead. However, this assumption requires closer inspection. Is it possible for clients to find their own way to water, either in the absence of a therapist or in the presence of a therapist who does not know the location of water? We begin our discussion with a review of the first part of this question.

FINDING WATER ON ONE'S OWN

At the risk of stating the obvious, it is possible for individuals to acquire insight without ever entering therapy. A well-known example is the self-analysis that Freud undertook throughout his life, dedicating time each day toward gaining self-insight. In addition, the large market for self-help books is testimony to the number of people interested in gaining self-awareness, often without the aid of psychotherapy (Scogin, 2003). Self-examination is no easy task, however; as Thoreau observed, it is as difficult to perceive oneself accurately as it is to see behind oneself without turning around. One obstacle to acquiring insight on one's own is the human tendency to project unacceptable aspects of the self onto others. Until a person recognizes that he or she is engaged in this process, projection interferes with taking responsibility for integrating disowned parts of the self. However, as soon as an individual realizes she or he is projecting, she or he can use this realization to serve as a cue to aspects of the self that she or he finds undesirable or unacceptable. "What does it say about me that I find this person, or some particular attribute of this person, so repulsive?" Consider, for example, the man who tends to be critical of overweight individuals. When his critical focus is directed back to himself he can explore what it is about himself that makes him critical of people who are overweight. He may discover that he is uncomfortable with his own body image and that he projects this discomfort outwardly onto others. "On the path of self-study, [one] learns that he himself possesses all the faults that he finds in others" (Ouspensky, 1949, p. 223).

Of course, a host of defense mechanisms such as repression, intellectualization, and denial play similar roles in obscuring and, if recognized, potentially facilitating insight. According to Maslow (1968), one of the chief obstacles to overcoming these barriers is a fear of self-knowledge. In fact, Maslow believed that Freud's greatest discovery was that most psychological illness results from individuals' fear of truly knowing their "emotions, impulses, memories, capacities and potentialities" (p. 60). Freud (1916/1989) proposed that fear of the consequences of insight can stimulate self-preserving defense mechanisms. This fear of the unknown may cause difficulties when a person strives to gain insight without the presence of a therapist who can provide assistance in working through resistances. (For additional discussion on this topic, please refer to chap. 1, this volume.)

Maslow (1968) also noted that the acquisition of insight often leads to the challenging awareness that one must act differently. Ouspensky emphasized this point (1949, p. 145) as well: "Self-observation brings man to the realization of the necessity for self-change." Ouspensky then made the point that the very process of observing oneself, which he viewed as critical to acquiring insight, is a powerful mechanism of transformation:

> In observing himself a man notices that self-observation itself brings about certain changes in his inner processes. He begins to understand that self-observation is an instrument of self-change, a means of awakening. By observing himself he throws, as it were, a ray of light onto his inner processes, which have hitherto worked in complete darkness. And under the influence of this light the processes themselves begin to change. (pp. 145–146)

Horney (1942/1962) provided additional support for the notion that individuals can benefit from attempts to acquire insight on their own. She pointed out that the gains made in self-analysis can be attributed, at least in part, to the increased inner strength that results from solo expeditions to explore often uninviting inner terrain. Further accentuating the capacity of human beings for self-insight, Rogers (1951) suggested that individuals invariably tend toward self-actualization. When a person begins to uncover internalized conditions of worth, the discrepancy between one's real and ideal selves widens. The larger the discrepancy between one's real and ideal selves, the more threatening the experience of gaining insight becomes. Thus, the process of gaining insight engenders an internal battle between fear and courage. Tillich (1958) spoke profoundly to this tension and to the consequences of avoiding such a struggle:

Anxiety turns us toward courage, because the other alternative is despair. Courage resists despair by taking anxiety into itself. This analysis gives the key to understanding pathological anxiety. He who does not succeed in taking his anxiety courageously upon himself can succeed in avoiding the extreme situation of despair by escaping into neurosis . . . in the neurotic state self-affirmation is not lacking; it can indeed be very strong and emphasized. But the self which is affirmed is a reduced one. Some or many of its potentialities are not admitted to actualization, because actualization of being implies the acceptance of nonbeing and its anxiety . . . This limited extensiveness of self-affirmation can be balanced by greater intensity, but by an intensity which is narrowed to a special point accompanied by a distorted relation to reality as a whole. (p. 66)

Before bringing this section to a close we comment on attitudinal and technical aspects of seeking insight on one's own. In our estimation, it would be hard to overstate the importance of self-knowledge. Gurdjieff (1973) expressed the significance of self-understanding in the following passage:

If a man reasons and thinks soundly, no matter what path he follows . . . he must inevitably arrive back at himself, and begin with the solution of the problem of what he is himself and what his place is in the world around him. For without this knowledge, he will have no focal point in his search. Socrates' words "Know thyself" remain for all those who seek true knowledge. (p. 43)

In a simpler but no less profound fashion, the 8-year-old daughter of one of us was being tucked into bed one night and asked, "Mom, who am I? I've really been wondering about this a lot. I mean I can see you and Dad. I know what you look like and who you are, but *who am I?*" Her mother lovingly reassured her that she was asking good questions whose answers would reveal themselves if she continued to explore. Attitudinally, then, self-exploration is a serious endeavor and should be approached as such (although this does not preclude moments of deep laughter, joy, or wonderment at seeing oneself anew). We believe that one needs to be deeply invested in becoming self-aware for the process of self-observation to yield fruits. Given the difficulty of the task, half-hearted attempts are likely to produce few gains.

From a technical as opposed to attitudinal point of view, Ouspensky (1949) suggested wiping the slate clean when committing oneself to the task of self-discovery: "A man must begin observing himself as though he did not know himself at all, as though he had never observed himself" (p. 106). In this way, it is possible to see oneself freshly and more objectively, rather than distorting information to fit preconceived notions of the self. After wiping the slate clean, Ouspensky suggested activities such as observing the contents of one's daydreams and imaginings, as well as studying and struggling against ingrained habits. For example, one of us found that the practice of intentionally opening doors with his nondominant hand for short periods of time has been beneficial in terms of yielding self-insight. This exercise in going against the grain generated self-insights related to mindfulness, self-criticism, automatic behavior, having his hands full, transitioning, and the pace at which his life is lived. Gestalt therapy techniques also can be effective aides in generating insight on one's own. Identifying polarities, focusing awareness, and empty chair techniques all can further a person's self-understanding. Insight also may be gained by journaling and reviewing previous journal entries. Finally, individuals may acquire insight outside of therapy through self-administered personality inventories, guided fantasies, vicarious observation, introspection, feedback from others, meditation, catharsis, reflecting on early memories, and dream analysis. In fact, the self-analysis that Freud began through dream interpretation has an ancient history and continues to be widely practiced today. Through the process of exploration, experiencing affect, and recollection of associated memories, clients may gain insight into the meaning behind their dreams without the direct assistance of a therapist (Hill, 2004a).

In conclusion, it seems quite possible for individuals to gain self-insight without being in therapy. However, finding water on one's own and summoning the courage to drink from it are extremely difficult tasks, and these tasks may be made easier by the assistance of a therapist. In the next section, we address the situation in which an individual seeks self-insight through therapy, but the therapist lacks insight into the client.

WHEN THE THERAPIST DOES NOT KNOW WHERE THE WATER IS LOCATED

Because a person can acquire insight without being in therapy, it must be possible for a client to gain insight in the presence of a therapist who lacks insight. The only logical condition that would preclude this from being true would be the presence of a therapist who lacks insight and prevents a client from gaining insight. We cannot persuade ourselves to accept such a statement—too many of our own clients have found water when we were convinced we were in the middle of the Sahara. Thus, the pertinent issue is how the therapist who lacks insight might nonetheless facilitate the client's acquisition of insight.

To begin, it may be useful to point out one distinction. There are therapists who lack insight as a temporary state and those whose lack of insight seems to be nearly a trait. More attention will be devoted here to therapists' situational lack of insight, as we believe this to be the more common of the two. Fortunately, from our clinical and supervisory experience we can postulate that when the therapist temporarily lacks insight into the client, all is not lost. At these times therapists can journey alongside their clients, rather than feeling responsible for leading them to water. Using basic counseling skills, the therapist can provide an environment in which the client can take primary responsibility for obtaining insight. For example, the therapist may offer support as the client works to understand repressed events and feelings. Through the therapist's active display of interest the client may develop more interest in him- or herself. A therapist may ask questions in an attempt to gain new information about the client, and as a result the client may come to a new understanding of him- or herself (see chap. 10, this volume). In a safe therapeutic environment, the client may be more willing to risk experiencing a variety of affective reactions that can lead to insight (Miller, 1984). The initial stages of therapy are facilitated by establishing rapport and creating a safe therapy environment, helping clients to expand on their personal narratives, assisting clients in being able to experience uncomfortable affect, and empathizing with clients (Hill, 2004b). All these initial aspects of therapy can be conducted alongside the client and do not require that the therapist possess insight into the client. These goals can be met through the therapist's attending, listening, reflecting, and open-ended questioning. In short, a collaborative therapeutic environment may activate the client's inner healing capacities, including the potential for acquiring self-insight (Bohart & Tallman, 1999; Hayes, 2002).

WHEN THE THERAPIST KNOWS WHERE THE WATER IS LOCATED

How might therapist insight facilitate client insight? One way a client may benefit from a therapist's insight is when the therapist connects the client's past experiences to present conflicts. In these situations the therapist may do well to tie new information to self-knowledge the client already has, as learning tends to occur more easily when new information is connected to existing knowledge. The insightful and skilled therapist may offer connections between past experiences and present issues in the form of a well-timed, thoughtful interpretation. The therapist must carefully choose the timing and presentation of statements meant to facilitate insight so the client can receive them. In the experience one of us had working with a client who had been a perpetrator as well as a victim of abuse, the therapist needed to carefully balance the client's experience as both abuser and abused. Although it was important for the client to gain insight into the consequences of his actions on his victims, declarative statements to this effect would not have been internalized by the client in a helpful manner. Instead, it was critical that the therapist acknowledge the client's conflictual state as both victim and perpetrator. Early in therapy the client began to justify his actions by stating that his victims had enjoyed the abuse. The therapist knew that at some level the client did not believe this to be true, nor did the therapist believe that it was. Again, however, a mere statement of the therapist's beliefs about the client's actions probably would have precluded subsequent disclosure on the client's part, which would have prevented his gaining further insight and strengthened his defenses. The therapist needed to maintain an empathic resonance with the client's self-presentation as well as with his underlying guilt, rage, and remorse.

Therapists can also help clients derive insight into themselves by identifying themes in the clients' lives of which clients are unaware. Metaphorically, this requires a shift from working alongside the client to being at least a half step ahead of the client so the therapist can truly lead the client to water. Here it is important not to get too far ahead of the client; helpful guides need to maintain enough, but not too much, distance. Along these lines, Hill (2004b) suggested that insightful therapists are able to engage in advanced interventions such as challenging, interpreting, sharing insights, and responding in the moment even as they anticipate the consequences of their behaviors. Other methods the therapist can use to help facilitate client insight include shedding light on environmental circumstances, encouraging self-observation and evaluation, and focusing on the client's emotions, intentions, and self-expectations (Goldfried, 1995). Because the insightful therapist is capable of uncovering unconscious conflicts within the client, it is more likely that the client will gain a deeper level of self-insight when working with such a therapist. Similarly, clients may need the guidance of a therapist to gain insight into the meaning of their dreams. Hill (2004a) cautioned, however, that for therapists to use insight-oriented dream interventions effectively, the working alliance must be firmly established, and the client must be ready to receive the therapist's interpretations. Given the inherent mystery of the dream world, neither the therapist nor the client can lay claim to possessing objective insight into dreams, but together they may nonetheless work to enhance client self-understanding. An insightful therapist is able to conceptualize a dream using knowledge gained from a variety of external methods, absent the biases and defenses inherent to the dreamer. By contrast, a person engaging in self-analysis through dreams may shy away from material that is threatening; in doing so, he or she may avoid addressing potentially meaningful aspects of the dream. The differentiated stance of the therapist allows the client's dream to be conceptualized by taking into account all aspects of the client. However, even a therapist who possesses insight must be aware that interpretations may be influenced by their own motives, personal symbols, and experiences.

HOW DOES THE THERAPIST FIND WATER?

The question that naturally arises is, how does the therapist gain insight into the client? Again, a word or two about attitude may be in order at the outset of this discussion. On the basis of our clinical and supervisory experience we believe it is important that new therapist insights be held lightly and viewed speculatively. As with any search for truth, it is helpful to obtain multiple sources of confirmation as the rush to judgment can lead one over a cliff. As therapists we have found that the process of understanding one's clients requires an attitude of constant curiosity, as well as an openness to being wrong about one's current insights. Perhaps most clinicians' natural curiosity contributes to their ability to tolerate or even appreciate the ambiguities and complexities of searching for truth in human beings. Furthermore, in the process of navigating their own internal landscape introspective therapists develop sensitivity to the difficulties of such exploration and likely respect others for their willingness to engage in such a journey. Finally, we have found it helpful for therapists to have a genuine passion for inquiry and a healthy reverence for the unknown.

Rollo May, like many existential therapists, downplayed the role of technique in the therapist's quest for insight into the client. He wrote,

> Our Western tendency has been to believe that *understanding follows technique*; if we get the right technique, then we can penetrate the riddle of the patient. . . .The existential approach holds the exact opposite approach—namely, that *technique follows understanding*. The central task and responsibility of the therapist is to seek to understand the patient as a being and as being in his world. (May, 1983, pp. 151–152)

How does the therapist come to understand the client? To begin, information must be gathered and organized before it can be understood. As virtually all novice therapists know, one of the main challenges in any session is deciding what information to attend to. Clients constantly bombard therapists with information. The most important information is often conveyed nonverbally—the client covers her lap with a pillow, avoids eye contact when discussing her feelings, or interrupts the therapist when he mentions her infidelity. Therapists have to attend to what clients are saying, but not so much that they miss what clients do not say and not so closely that they lose the capacity to retain and perhaps offer their own perspective. The therapist's theory and experience are invaluable in providing direction about what to attend to, as well as how to organize information gathered from clients. Rather than expound on this topic, which is addressed in other chapters in this volume, we direct our focus to the matter of clinical epistemology—how therapists know what they know about clients.

Knowledge may emanate from many sources, including authority figures, reason, science, faith, and experience. Although all these bases for knowledge are applicable to the general domain of psychotherapy, they are not all equally relevant to a therapist's attempts to understand a specific client. For example, science is geared toward identifying nomothetic laws, but in the 50-minute hour, therapists are interested in idiographic truths—what is true for this client at this moment. These idiographic truths may be a function of what an authority figure has said (e.g., a supervisor), or they may result from some combination of faith, reason, and experience. Experience can be divided further into at least two kinds: professional and personal. Professional experience is useful in providing therapists with a framework for recognizing similarities between clients. The client presenting with irritability and pressured speech, for example, may remind the therapist of a former client with bipolar disorder. In this way, professional experience serves as a potential source of insight. Of course, the new client may not have bipolar disorder, and generalizations from previous clinical experience need to be exercised cautiously. As Kluckhohn and Murray (1949) prudently observed, "Every man is in certain respects a) like all other men, b) like some other men, and c) like no other man" (p. 35).

In terms of therapists' personal experiences serving as a source of insight into clients, we suspect that this is more common than the relative absence of literature on this topic suggests. The therapeutic value of one's own historical data is captured nicely by Palmer (2000), who wrote, "The story of my journey is no more or less important than anyone else's. It is simply the best source of data I have on a subject where generalizations often fail but truth may be found in the details" (p. 90). One area in which the therapist's personal background has received attention as a potential source of insight into clients is in the area of drug and alcohol use. Although many therapists who are in recovery believe that having overcome a history of substance abuse is helpful, data indicate that outcomes are generally comparable for therapists who are and are not in recovery (Culbreth, 2000; Najavits & Weiss, 1994). A common problem with many studies that have been conducted in this area, however, is that therapists in recovery tend to be less educated than therapists who are not in recovery, and education has not been controlled for as a confounding factor (Culbreth, 2000). Thus, it could be that therapists in recovery are more effective than equally educated therapists who are not in recovery. Alternatively, therapists in recovery may use different therapeutic processes than therapists who are not in recovery, but may arrive at similar outcomes. It also is possible that therapists who have long resolved a particular difficulty may have moved so far beyond the experience that they can no longer draw profitably from it to gain insight into the client. In essence, an issue that is fairly resolved but dormant is of little therapeutic value. It is also true that therapists who have worked through particular issues run the risk of overgeneralizing from their own processes of gaining insight, believing that what was helpful for them will necessarily be helpful for clients. Therapists' recognition of distinctions between self and client is critical to not making this kind of mistake.

The possibility that the therapist's personal history can serve as a type of *inner well* from which insight might be drunk is consistent with the ancient notion of the wounded healer, which posits that sufficient resolution of one's own issues facilitates the healing of another's wounds (Hayes, 2002). In the words of Jung (1963), "Only the wounded physician heals" (p. 134). Jung went on to write, "The patient's treatment begins with the doctor, so to speak. Only if the doctor knows how to cope with himself and his own problems will he be able to teach the patient to do the same" (p. 132). Rogers (1951) echoed a similar sentiment in an interview conducted toward the end of his life. In a rather remarkable statement, he said,

> The therapist needs to recognize very clearly the fact that he or she is an imperfect person with flaws which make him vulnerable. I think it is only as the therapist views himself as imperfect and flawed that he can see himself as helping another person. Some people who call themselves therapists are not healers because they are too busy defending themselves. (Baldwin, 1987, p. 48)

Despite the clinical relevance of the notion of the wounded healer, little research has been devoted to this area. It seems possible, for example, to empirically examine the idea that clients might derive more insight when paired with a therapist who has experienced and sufficiently worked through issues similar to those of the client than when paired with a therapist who has not experienced such issues. Might therapists understand clients' experiences better if therapists have been there themselves? The sentiment that clients might have such a preference was expressed by a young soldier from a small Pennsylvania town who had returned home after being injured in battle in Iraq. He was experiencing symptoms of posttraumatic stress disorder, and his mother encouraged him to seek therapy. His response reflected his apprehension: "The people I'd be talking to, they weren't there and they don't know what it's like" (Brenckle, 2003, p. A1).

COUNTERTRANSFERENCE AND THE THERAPIST'S SEARCH FOR WATER

The flip side of the idealistic notion of the wounded healer is the therapist who has been wounded but who has not healed sufficiently to be of help to others. This represents the classical notion of countertransference of which Freud (1910/1959) warned when he wrote, "No psycho-analyst goes further than his own complexes and internal resistances permit" (p. 289). Furthermore, "You can understand people only as much as you understand yourself" (Ouspensky, 1971, p. 30). Thus, if one's inner well is toxic or does not hold much water, it cannot serve as a helpful source of insight for clients. Research attests to the fact that the therapist's unresolved personal issues can cause the therapist to miss or distort important information about a client (Cutler, 1958; Fiedler, 1951; McClure & Hodge, 1987; Rosenberger & Hayes, 2002). Therapists also display a tendency not to maintain an appropriate therapeutic distance from clients when their countertransference issues are provoked (Hayes & Gelso, 1991, 1993; Hayes, McCracken, et al., 1998; Latts & Gelso, 1995; Robbins & Jolkovski, 1987; Rosenberger & Hayes, 2002). When therapists move too close to clients, or too far away, therapists are less likely to see their clients accurately and therefore are in a compromised position in regard to facilitating client insight. Fortunately, research also has documented that therapist qualities such as self-awareness, anxiety management, conceptual skills, empathy, and self-integration can help therapists successfully manage countertransference (Hayes, Riker, & Ingram, 1997; Van Wagoner, Gelso, Hayes, & Diemer, 1991).

CONCLUDING COMMENTS

In conclusion, we posit that therapist insight into the client is not a necessary precondition for clients to obtain self-insight. In fact, individuals can acquire insight on their own as well as in the presence of a therapist who lacks insight. However, limited therapist insight probably sets a ceiling on helpfulness: Therapists who lack insight can only set facilitative conditions for clients to *discover water*, whereas therapists who possess insight can actively direct clients toward becoming aware of that which clients do not know about themselves. The role of the therapist needs to be kept in proper perspective. Although client insight is not strictly a function of the therapist, a therapist who possesses insight can help the client gain insight. Therapists can draw from their professional and personal experiences to assist in the process, although countertransference issues need to be attended to and managed.

REFERENCES

Baldwin, M. (1987). Interview with Carl Rogers on the use of the self in therapy. *Journal of Psychotherapy and the Family, 3,* 45–52.

Bly, R. (1988). *A little book on the human shadow.* New York: HarperCollins.

Bohart, A. C., & Greenberg, L. S. (Eds.). (1997). *Empathy reconsidered.* Washington, DC: American Psychological Association.

Bohart, A. C., & Tallman, K. (1999). *How clients make therapy work: The process of active self-healing.* Washington, DC: American Psychological Association.

Brenckle, L. (2003, May 15). Memories of war in Iraq stay with local Marine. *Centre Daily Times,* pp. A1, A13.

Culbreth, J. R. (2000). Substance abuse counselors with and without a personal history of chemical dependency: A review of the literature. *Alcoholism Treatment Quarterly, 18,* 67–82.

Cutler, R. L. (1958). Countertransference effects in psychotherapy. *Journal of Consulting Psychology, 22,* 349–356.

Duan, C., & Hill, C. E. (1996). The current state of empathy research. *Journal of Counseling Psychology, 43,* 261–274.

Fiedler, F. E. (1951). On different types of countertransference. *Journal of Clinical Psychology, 7,* 101–107.

Freud, S. (1959). Future prospects of psychoanalytic psychotherapy. In J. Strachey (Ed. & Trans.), *The standard edition of the complete psychological works of Sigmund Freud* (Vol. 11, pp. 139–151). London: Hogarth Press. (Original work published 1910)

Freud, S. (1989). *Introductory lectures on psychoanalysis.* New York: Norton. (Original work published 1916)

Goldfried, M. R. (1995). Toward a common language for case formulation. *Journal of Psychotherapy Integration, 5,* 221–244.

Gurdjieff, G. I. (1973). *Views from the real world.* New York: Penguin.

Hayes, J. A. (2002). Playing with fire: Countertransference and clinical epistemology. *Journal of Contemporary Psychotherapy, 32,* 93–100.

Hayes, J. A., & Gelso, C. J. (1991). Effects of therapist-trainees' anxiety and empathy on countertransference behavior. *Journal of Clinical Psychology, 47,* 284–290.

Hayes, J. A., & Gelso, C. J. (1993). Male counselors' discomfort with gay and HIV-infected clients. *Journal of Counseling Psychology, 40,* 86–93.

Hayes, J. A., McCracken, J. E., McClanahan, M. K., Hill, C. E., Harp, J. S., & Carozzoni, P. (1998). Therapist perspectives on countertransference: Qualitative data in search of a theory. *Journal of Counseling Psychology, 45,* 468–482.

Hayes, J. A., Riker, J. R., & Ingram, K. M. (1997). Countertransference behavior and management in brief counseling: A field study. *Psychotherapy Research, 7,* 145–153.

Hill, C. E. (2004a). *Dream work in therapy.* Washington, DC: American Psychological Association.

Hill, C. E. (2004b). *Helpings skills: Facilitating exploration, insight, and action* (2nd ed.). Washington, DC: American Psychological Association.

Horney, K. (1962). *Self-analysis.* London: Routledge & Kegan Paul. (Original work published 1942)

Jung, C. G. (1963). *Memories, dreams, reflections.* New York: Random House.

Kluckhohn, C., & Murray, H. A. (1949). *Personality in nature, society, and culture.* New York: Knopf.

Latts, M. G., & Gelso, C. J. (1995). Countertransference behavior and management with survivors of sexual assault. *Psychotherapy: Theory, Research, Practice, Training, 32,* 405–415.

Marmor, J. (1980). *The interface between the psychodynamic and behavioral therapies.* New York: Plenum Press.

Maslow, A. H. (1968). *Toward a psychology of being.* New York: Van Nostrand.

May, R. (1983). *The discovery of being*. New York: Norton.

McClure, B. A., & Hodge, R. W. (1987). Measuring countertransference and attitude in therapeutic relationships. *Psychotherapy, 24*, 325–335.

Miller, A. (1984). *Thou shalt not be aware: Society's betrayal of the child*. New York: Penguin.

Najavits, L. M., & Weiss, R. D. (1994). Variations in therapist effectiveness in the treatment of patients with substance use disorders: An empirical review. *Addiction, 89*, 679–688.

Ouspensky, P. D. (1949). *In search of the miraculous*. New York: Random House.

Ouspensky, P. D. (1971). *The fourth way*. New York: Random House.

Palmer, P. J. (2000). *Let your life speak*. San Francisco: Jossey-Bass.

Robbins, S. B., & Jolkovski, M. P. (1987). Managing countertransference feelings: An interactional model using awareness of feelings and theoretical framework. *Journal of Counseling Psychology, 34*, 276–282.

Rogers, C. R. (1951). *Client-centered therapy*. Cambridge, MA: Riverside Press.

Rosenberger, E. W., & Hayes, J. A. (2002). Origins, consequences, and management of countertransference: A case study. *Journal of Counseling Psychology, 49*, 221–232.

Scogin, F. R. (2003). The status of self-administered treatments. *Journal of Clinical Psychology, 59*, 247–249.

Tillich, P. (1958). *The courage to be*. New Haven, CT: Yale University Press.

Van Wagoner, S., Gelso, C. J., Hayes, J. A., & Diemer, R. (1991). Countertransference and the reputedly excellent therapist. *Psychotherapy: Theory, Research, Practice, Training, 28*, 411–421.

14

INSIGHT, ACTION, AND THE THERAPEUTIC RELATIONSHIP

CHARLES J. GELSO AND JAMES HARBIN

Fundamental questions about the presence of patient insight in psychotherapy pertain to the relation of insight to action. Specifically, does patient insight instigate effective action, and thus ameliorate symptoms? Alternatively, does insight accompany or actually result from changes in behavior? Also, what is the frequency with which each of these causal sequences occurs? For example, in regard to the impact of insight, it would be extremely helpful to know the extent to which insight leads to change. Is appropriate change an inevitable, common, or infrequent result of patient insight? This chapter seeks to address these concerns and questions. We examine the ways in which insight and action are interconnected; in doing so, we offer the view that insight most readily occurs and leads to behavior change in the context of a strong therapeutic relationship, especially when insight pertains directly to that relationship. We offer seven propositions about the connection of insight to action. Our aim is to develop propositions that are capable of being translated into testable hypotheses and are also useful to practitioners.

In reflecting on the connection of insight to action, we begin with a quote from the great therapist–theoretician and founder of interpersonal psychotherapy, Harry Stack Sullivan (1954), who had this to say about the relation of insight and action:

> It is almost uncanny how things fade out of the picture when their *raison d'etre* is revealed. The brute fact is that man is so extraordinarily adaptive that, given any chance of making a reasonably adequate analysis of the situation, he is quite likely to stumble into a series of experiments which will gradually approximate more successful living . . . .[The role of both patient and therapist is] uncovering those factors which are concerned in the person's recurrent mistakes, and which lead to his taking ineffective and inappropriate action. *There is no necessity to do more* [italics added]. (p. 226)

It is our contention that Sullivan (1954) was both right and wrong in this theoretically audacious statement. He was right in that at least certain kinds of insight usually lead to action changes. In fact, empirical support for this assertion was uncovered by Kivlighan, Multon, and Patton (2000), who found that during brief therapy (20 sessions), symptom reduction followed sessions in which high patient insight occurred. However, Sullivan's contention was also wrong in viewing insight as invariably (or nearly so) sufficient to induce such change. Also, although he seemed to hint at it, Sullivan did not directly address the view that the causal line between insight and action was more circular than unidirectional, as we shall discuss. Finally, Sullivan seemed to ignore the inherent interaction between insight and action that actually appears in his statement. His "series of experiments" likely included changes in action that both resulted from and led to insight.

BASIC WORKING DEFINITIONS AND CONCEPTIONS

Definitions and conceptions of insight are offered in various chapters of this volume. Here we offer working definitions that are needed to make our subsequent thinking clear to the reader. We offer these for both key constructs in this chapter, insight and action.

Insight and Its Two Sides—Intellect and Affect

The concept of insight is usually thought of as a fundamental element of psychoanalytic and, more broadly, psychodynamic conceptions of therapy. In these systems insight typically reflects patients' understanding of material that previously had been unconscious, usually embedded in the distant past where the original trauma or traumata reside. This understanding usually pertains to thoughts and affects that had been defensively hidden from consciousness as a result of anxiety. Our working definition is similar to but broader than those emanating from psychoanalytic theory. We define *insight* as awareness and understanding of (a) underlying feelings, thoughts, and actions; (b) the interconnection of these and their connection to earlier events; and (c) the relation of internal events (thoughts and feelings) to external events (what are usually labeled *actions* or *behaviors*, which we use interchangeably). In our conception, insight need not directly pertain to one's distant past (e.g., early childhood) and need not directly reflect unconscious processes, although it often does. Its fundamental feature is the awareness and understanding of feelings, thoughts, or actions about which the patient had been previously unaware. The more inclusive and pervasive the insights, however, the more they will be linked to and instigative of change in behavior. We have more to say about inclusiveness and pervasiveness in this chapter.

Many theoreticians have sought to make differentiations within the more general definitions of insight that we have described (including our definition). One key distinction has been that between intellectual and emotional insight (Crits-Christoph, Barber, Miller, & Beebe, 1993). Intellectual insight may be considered a cognitive process in which the patient grasps the cause–effect sequences in his or her conflicts. Emotional understanding, however, is thought to involve affect, such that the patient both grasps certain internal events intellectually and experiences feelings related to those events that previously had been unavailable or not experienced. For clinicians who make such a distinction, it is emotional insight that is considered the most effective in promoting behavior change (see Wachtel, 1997, for a review of this distinction).

First offered many years ago by Strachey (1934) and given great impetus by Alexander and French (1946), this distinction between intellectual and emotional insight has been a controversial one over the years. Criticisms of the distinction are captured by Wachtel (1997), who noted that clinicians have persistently observed that emotionless remembering and understanding tend to have little therapeutic value. Wachtel noted that

> The way of dealing with the problem traditionally has been to distinguish between intellectual and emotional insight. This seems to me a rather unsatisfactory solution. Precisely why emotional insight is therapeutic and intellectual insight is not cannot be addressed by means of this conceptual strategy. It provides a *name*, which helps point to an important distinction, but it gives little help in providing an explanation. Moreover, the decision about whether an insight is real insight or only an intellectual one is not always easy to make at the time. Often, the decision is made retrospectively, when the patient does not change after voicing it. (p. 93)

We agree with Wachtel that it is often difficult to differentiate intellectual from emotional insight and that post hoc decisions are unsatisfactory. We also agree that the distinction simply names the process rather explaining why one form of insight "works" (e.g., leads to behavior change) and the other does not. We maintain, however, that therapists can and do effectively differentiate the two (see Gelso, Kivlighan, Wine, Jones, & Friedman, 1997) and that naming a key distinction is an important and useful thing. Further, as to why one works and the other does not, Wachtel (1997) himself went on to offer the explanation that

> intellectual and emotional insight appears as a distinction whose impor-
> tance derives from whether, or how thoroughly, the patient is exposed to
> those cues that really make him anxious. Since in most instances, anxi-
> ety is most strongly attached to a complex configuration of cues in which
> verbal, affective, cognitive, and motoric elements are all prominent, ver-
> balizing without the other cues being present is unlikely to have much
> therapeutic value. Thus, "intellectual insight" is ineffective. (p. 94)

The point in this complex statement is that anxiety, the presumed core problem, is often attached to the complex configuration of cues noted in this quote and these cues represent, for example, feelings and thoughts that are the source of the patient's basic anxiety. According to Wachtel (1997), for the insight to be effective, its verbal expression must connect to those cues (e.g., feelings and thoughts). When it does connect, anxiety abates and be-havior change is likely to occur. We suggest that Wachtel's explanation, which seems to us to be learning-based, is but one explanation of why intel-lectual insight has limited change-inducing capability, whereas emotional insight is more impactful. There are other plausible explanations, and subse-quently we offer one such explanation.

In sum, we suggest that what is often called emotional insight is the most effective kind of insight, that it is indeed observable by clinicians and raters, and that it can be reliably rated (see empirical efforts of Gelso, Hill, & Kivlighan, 1991; Gelso et al., 1997). At the same time, we think the term itself is problematic. To begin with, the term emotional insight, is too readily confused with emotional catharsis or abreaction, which probably has limited value in promoting change beyond temporary relief. Also, the term is mis-leading because it does not imply the cognitive element that is necessary for insight. Because of these problems, we suggest the term *integrative insight*, and we define this as the integration of cognitive understanding and emotional experience. When patients experience integrative insight, they are able to grasp cognitively the causes of their conflict and problems and simultaneously experience feelings that had not previously been in awareness and attached to this cognitive understanding. The integration of cognition and affect al-lows the patient to take a step toward solving internal conflicts and behaving differently. In other words, integrative insight precipitates helpful action. However, at times such insight is not enough to promote sufficient and du-rable behavior change. Later in this chapter we discuss what allows for such change.

The Meaning of Action

Our working definition of action encompasses overt behavior, both at the motoric and verbal level. Of course, one can refer to internal events as behavior, but we believe this stretches the concept to the point that it is no longer useful. Probably all therapists, including the most behaviorally oriented, acknowledge the importance of internal events such as cognitions, emotions, feelings, and physiological states. What people feel and experience internally, in fact, may be the essence of their humanness. However, when referring to *action*, the outward verbal or motoric expression of internal events is what is implied. Indeed, for internal events to be most meaningful to the person, we expect them to also appear externally. For example, the socially anxious patient usually exhibits anxiety externally in a wide range of ways. And although at times it may be more important for the patient to feel less anxious than to behave less anxiously, the fact is that the lessened anxiety does show itself in changed actions. It is important to underscore, however, that these actions may be very subtle and difficult for an observer to detect, no less measure. They are exhibited externally, nonetheless.

Throughout this chapter, we use the terms behavior and action synonymously and both refer to external events at the motoric and verbal levels. Also, most indications of symptom change reflect, at least partly, overt behavior or action, as symptoms are generally considered to be outward expressions of underlying conflicts and complex states.

THEORETICAL PROPOSITIONS ABOUT INSIGHT AND ACTION

We offer seven theoretical propositions about the relationship of insight to action in diverse psychotherapies. The interplay of insight and action is underscored, as is the role of the therapeutic relationship in this interplay.

Proposition 1: It Is Largely Integrative Insight That Instigates Behavioral Change

In regard to intellectual insight, Wachtel (1997) had this to say:

> Some patients, in fact, particularly obsessional individuals, have learned a discrimination such that verbalizing *almost anything* can occur without anxiety, *so long as it is not in the context of emotional arousal and of an inclination to act on what is being said.* Thus, for such a patient, verbalizing even seemingly "significant" things is likely to be therapeutically fruitless unless the other cues to which anxiety is attached are produced along with the verbal cues. (p. 94)

Patients such as those described by Wachtel readily experience intellectual insight without any accompanying change in behavior. This phenomenon is by no means restricted to persons with obsessional disorders, however, and we would add that for most people, intellectual insight can have positive consequences. The person who cognitively understands (i.e., intellectual insight) for the first time how her present conflicts have been determined by a long string of childhood experiences will feel relieved and saner because of this understanding. She will see, perhaps for the first time, that what may have seemed like capricious behavior on her part indeed had causes. The person who comes to understand intellectually how he damages promising relationships because of his fears and gets an intellectual glimpse of what those fears are will have moved a step forward. This intellectual insight may serve as a road map for the person as to where she or he must head in the therapeutic exploration.

At the same time, insights that are restricted to intellectual understanding are limited in their change-inducing potential. Furthermore, for patients such as those to whom Wachtel refers, intellectual understanding has a defensive function. In presenting the appearance of genuine understanding, it unconsciously allows the patient to avoid experiencing threatening affects. As we have suggested, integrative insight is more likely to stimulate change in behavior and result in symptom reduction. An example is the case of a person treated by the first author. (Note that identifying information in the cases we present has been modified.)

> The patient, Sandra, was a 21-year-old college junior seen in twice-a-week therapy. She had a history of depression accompanied by cutting her wrists and arms. Sandra's key maladaptive pattern was to be extremely pleasing to others—to use her great sensitivity as a means of figuring out what others wanted from her and then providing that. Her own needs never seemed to figure into the equation. As her therapy progressed, Sandra gained increasing integrative insight into how this pattern began in her relationship with her emotionally labile father, whose feelings she constantly had to be attentive to for fear that if she displeased him he would withdraw affection from her. This fear was exacerbated by the fact that Sandra essentially had no positive connection with her mother, a deeply narcissistic woman whose attention to others' needs, including Sandra's, rarely seemed to go beyond public show. Although Sandra's relationship with her father and mother was explored over the course of many weeks and months, it appeared that the "lightbulb" went on during a certain phase of the work. She seemed to grasp deeply the role of the daughter–father–mother triangle in her need to constantly give others what they wanted at her own expense. As she described understanding this for the first time, she appeared deeply connected emotionally to this understanding. Following this insight, Sandra was clearly more able to tell her father what was on her mind and what she needed, and she was able to exhibit this self-expression in her other relationships as well. The

changes in action were not dramatic or continuous; however, they were clearly noticeable and they persisted. Although the exploration surrounding the insight was very painful, and although Sandra felt sad as she emotionally and cognitively grasped the things she did not get in her earlier and current life with her parents, she did not become clinically depressed. She also never attempted to cut herself.

What is it about integrative insight that facilitates change? This vexing question may be addressed theoretically at many levels, ranging from highly reductive (physiological–biological) explanations to constructive explanations (themselves ranging from psychological to metaphysical). Fruitful explanations may be offered at any and all levels on this reductive–constructive continuum. The recent work of Schore (2003), for example, allows for explanations in terms of brain physiology (reductive). Although such work is promising, our inclination is toward more constructive explanations. For us, the process through which integrative insight creates behavior change revolves around its tendency to increase the believability of, for example, how childhood relationships cause certain maladaptive feelings. To exemplify further, with integrative insight the patient comes to really believe that he or she is worthwhile, but that he or she has felt a deeply embedded sense of worthlessness over many years because of certain interpersonal experiences while growing up. Until one truly feels what may be intellectually understood, the understanding is experienced as highly tentative, perhaps only conjectural. Another way of saying this is that one cannot fully believe one's intellectual understandings and connections until one is able to emotionally experience them. Additionally, the affective component of an integrative insight is part of the patient's reexperiencing what was once damaging in the present context of a safe therapeutic relationship. Within this context, reexperiencing tends to be healing. After an integrative insight increases the believability of an understanding and begins such healing, the patient is better able to discriminate between the pain of beliefs tied to the past and the reality of the present. Patients then are able to diminish the tendency to overgeneralize maladaptive feelings, perceptions, and cognitions from the past into the present. These internal shifts tend to facilitate new actions or behavior change in the patient.

Proposition 2: Action Itself May Instigate Insight

In the same way that insight appears to facilitate action, we offer that action or behavior change tends to further patients' understanding of themselves and their emotional conflicts. To return to the quote by Sullivan, the key phrase regarding action affecting insight is that "man is so extraordinarily adaptive that given any chance of making a reasonably adequate analysis of the situation, *he is likely to stumble into a series of experiments which will gradually approximate more successful living* [italics added]" (1954, p. 226).

We take this statement to mean that after sizing up the situation and the problem (not necessarily experiencing insight), patients try out actions or behaviors that tend to be an improvement over prior actions. Thus, the great psychodynamicist Sullivan (1954) was implying action without insight. We go a step further and suggest that when adaptive behavior change occurs, it often creates self-understanding or insight. In the case of Sandra reported earlier, behaving in ways that revealed what she wanted and felt with her father and friends allowed the patient to gain the insight that people would not stop caring about her if she acted more like herself. Indeed, this behavior change created greater intimacy. The patient's action change also reduced her anxiety about rejection, which in turn allowed for more insights about her present defensive patterns and their link to past traumata.

In discussing their three-stage model of therapeutic change (exploration, insight, and action), Hill and O'Brien (1999) made a further point about how action affects insight. They stated that

> Taking action is crucial for consolidating the new thinking patterns learned in the insight stage. Action concretizes the abstract insights for clients into more permanent schemas. Moreover, new understandings can be fleeting unless something is done to help the client consolidate them. Old thinking patterns and behaviors easily resurface unless new thinking and behaviors are practiced and incorporated. (p. 64)

Thus, actions not only may create conditions for insight to occur, but they fortify insights and allow them to become part of the patient's conceptual system. Similarly, behavior therapists have examined how treatment aimed at behavior change may instigate insight (e.g., Cautela, 1993; Powell, 1988, 1996). Powell (1988), for example, noted that in about 15% of the cases treated behaviorally in his clinic for problems ranging from migraines and Raynaud's phenomena to performance anxiety, there is clear evidence of behavior therapy stimulating insights that appear to be an important part of the change process. What is most notable about such a finding is that in many cases work on behavior change alone, using behavioral methods, stimulates important insights. We infer from this that actual behavior change in many of these individuals also promotes insight.

Proposition 3: In Therapies of All Orientations, There Exists a Feedback Process in Which Insight and Action Are Mutually Influential

Up to this point we have suggested that integrative insight tends to instigate behavior change, and that behavior change tends to stimulate insight. Further, insight and action often mutually influence each other in a circular fashion. Thus, in any given therapy integrative insights allow some change in behavior, which in turn allows for a deepening or broadening of insight, which then instigates more behavior change. In effective therapy this interactive process continues throughout the work. This process may begin with either insight or action changes; which one it begins with does not especially matter. The point is that for at least some patterns, there is an unending synergy between insight and action. We hasten to add that insight and behavior change do not always lead to changes in each other, but each does have some degree of influence on the other. For example, in the case of Sandra, understanding deeply how her absence of attachment to her mother made her need for attachment to her father an almost life and death matter did not appear to create substantial action changes. Instead, this insight seemed to create a kind of readiness for change, a change that would occur when she felt sufficiently strengthened internally to allow her to behave differently with, for example, her father. In turn, her behaving differently with father did not create major insights, but instead moved her in the direction of further insights when she was emotionally ready for them.

A key phenomenon in this insight–action cycle is what is referred to in psychoanalysis as *working through*. In his seminal writings on classical psychoanalysis, Greenson (1967, 1978) described working through as "the analysis of those resistances and other factors which prevent insight from leading to significant and lasting changes in the patient" (1978, p. 232). The process of working through occurs after the patient has attained an insight. The essence of working through in classical analysis is repeatedly helping the analysand understand and change the internal resistances that prevent insights from stimulating change. Although we are not accustomed to thinking of classical analysis as focusing on behavior change, one cannot read Greenson's theoretical statements or cases without appreciating that he was deeply concerned with action or behavior change. For example, in one of his central writings he told us that "Only rarely does insight lead very quickly to behavior change; and then it is usually transitory or remains isolated and unintegrated" (Greenson, 1967, p. 44). Further, he said that "In order for an insight to be effective it is necessary for it to be repeated many times; single interpretations do not produce lasting change" (Greenson, 1978, p. 244). And, most to the point of this chapter, he asserted that "A variety of circular processes are set in motion by working through *in which insight, memory, and behavior change influence each other* [italics added]" (1967, p. 42). This kind of thinking is reminiscent of Freud's (1919/1958) comment that in the analytic treatment of agoraphobia "One succeeds only when one can induce [people with agoraphobia] by the influence of analysis . . . to go into the street and to struggle with their anxiety while they make the attempt" (p. 166).

Our understanding of working through is essentially the same as Greenson's (1978), with some minor modifications that reflect our departure from his classical position. In the working through phase, the therapist helps the patient see how a particular pattern into which the patient has already gained insight occurs in manifold situations. As this occurs, the patient in effect gains repeated insights, which is usually necessary for change to occur.

These insights aid the patient in trying out new behaviors, for example, in his or her relationships. And as previously noted, the behaviors and their consequences lead to further insights. Some of these insights and behaviors occur in the therapeutic relationship, others occur between sessions, and still others connect insight and behavior change within and pertaining to the therapeutic relationship to changes outside the session. We have more to say about insight, action, and the therapeutic relationship in subsequent sections of this chapter.

The interplay of insight and action occurs over time and their mutual effect on each other takes time. Greenson (1978) commented wisely on this time dimension when he stated that

> Repetition is necessary in order to overcome the patient's tendency to ward off painful affects, impulses, and fantasies. Finally, the reiteration of an insight gives the patient a further opportunity for mastery of anxiety and a chance to try out new modes of response. All these facts explain why working through takes a long time. The old was painful and yet familiar and safe; in this way it resembled an old love object. Repetition offers opportunities to part with the old, and to become acquainted with the new. (p. 244)

Although the depth and breadth of working through may be less substantial in brief therapy than in the classical analysis to which Greenson (1978) referred, working through does indeed occur in briefer work, and the insight and action changes unfolding in brief treatment are well-known and documented (e.g., Lambert & Ogles, 2004). A case example from the work of the second author helps illuminate the feedback process between insight and action—the working through process—in a time-limited therapy that lasted 12 sessions.

> Elizabeth was a 30-year-old graduate student in vocal performance who sought therapy for concerns related to performance and general anxiety. She felt highly anxious singing in front of others, was quite self-critical, and felt others were constantly judging her. Elizabeth's parents also displayed constant worries about judgments from others. For example, when Elizabeth was growing up, her mother would tell her to never change clothes with the lights on (even when the blinds were closed) because neighbors might see her. As treatment began, she still changed with the lights off, even as her husband teased her about it. Elizabeth's parents were also critical of her decision to become a singer and wanted her instead to be more practical in her career choice. However, during the first several sessions Elizabeth resisted attempts to explore how her past family experiences may have influenced her present anxiety. During sessions, Elizabeth's speech was so rapid that there was little or no space or time to think through her conflicts and examine their underlying meanings. Despite that, a "good enough alliance" formed. The shallowness of her early sessions soon became a source of frustration to her and her thera-

pist. After discussing this frustration, as well as her frustration with speaking so quickly, she slowed down her speaking at her therapist's request and subsequently his gentle reminding. (Note that this speech change is considered a behavior change.) As she processed this change, Elizabeth noted that it was difficult because she suddenly became aware of how focused she was on people around her and how concerned she was with trying to predict what the therapist was thinking. Through this exploration she gained some insight into the reason for her rapid speech. This insight enabled her to tolerate her self-consciousness in therapy and to explore it more deeply. Also, she began to make links between her parents' "shoulds" and her anxiety and fear that others were constantly judging her. She explored how she feared and expected such judgment from her therapist, which helped her see the therapeutic relationship more realistically.

Toward the latter part of the 12 sessions Elizabeth began exhibiting greater changes outside the sessions. Her supervisors noted her improved singing performance and that she seemed more relaxed in performances. For the first time, she began to test her expectations and perceptions of what others thought of her by asking them. Elizabeth learned to her surprise that others responded positively toward both her singing and her interpersonal skills. As this was occurring outside of therapy Elizabeth explored her reactions during the sessions. By this process of working through, she experienced a substantial decline in anxiety and worry about others' reactions.

Proposition 4: Insight Learned in the Context of a Good Therapeutic Relationship Is Most Likely to Lead to Constructive Action Change

Gaining integrative insight into feelings and thoughts that were previously hidden from awareness is a daunting task. It requires that the patient allow painful and at times frightening feelings and thoughts to come into awareness. Changing maladaptive patterns, too, is a daunting task, especially when these patterns are long-standing and durable. As the Greenson (1978, p. 244) quote noted earlier indicates, such change entails giving up the old and familiar for, we would add, the unknown and often frightening. A strong therapeutic relationship provides support and encouragement for the patient to accomplish these tasks of insight and behavior change. By a strong therapeutic relationship, we mean a working alliance marked by sufficient trust, emotional connection, and collaborativeness. As Proposition 4 indicates, such a relationship also aids the patient in transforming integrative insight into behavior change. In attachment terms, the good therapeutic relationship provides the patient with a secure base and a safe haven as he or she seeks to try out new behaviors and give up old ones.

In a strong therapeutic relationship trust usually outweighs doubt and fear. In one part of the patient's mind (e.g., the observing side, or ego), he or she is able to trust the therapist's good intentions and skill, even as the patient harbors doubts and fears about the therapist in another part of his or her psyche. This trust allows the patient to consciously open up, and it permits material that had been unavailable to awareness to become available. An attachment for the purpose of the work can develop between the two, and both are able to enact their roles—to do their share of the work.

In addition to a sound working alliance, the good therapeutic relationship includes what we consider a sound real relationship. This element includes genuineness on the part of each participant, as well as experiencing each other in a way that befits the other, rather than deeply misperceiving the other because of, for example, the patient's wishes and fears. Within the good real relationship participants experience a sufficient degree of liking and caring for each other. In other words, the valence of the mutual affect is mostly positive, although there will be negative elements (see Gelso, 2002, 2003, 2004).

A qualitative study on successful long-term, dynamic therapy by the first author and his collaborators (Gelso, Hill, Mohr, Rochlen, & Zack, 1999) underscores the importance of the therapeutic relationship in fostering the emergence of threatening affects and cognitions into awareness, that is, insight. After interviewing 11 dynamically oriented therapists about a successful case, Gelso et al. concluded that almost everything the therapists said suggested that the working alliance and real relationship, characterized by mutual trust and liking, served as crucial buffers that allowed difficult feelings (i.e., transference feelings) to emerge into the open and become resolved. From an attachment perspective, Gelso et al. noted that sound working alliances and real relationships among the 11 therapists and their clients appeared to provide clients with a safe haven and secure base from which they could venture inward to explore what might otherwise be threatening feelings. Although it was not examined in this study, we expect that such a relationship also facilitated patient transformations of inner explorations (i.e., insights) into action.

Proposition 5: Insight Acquired About the Experienced Therapeutic Relationship Between Therapist and Patient Has the Greatest Potential for Leading to Behavior Change

Integrative insight that is acquired about one's inner world and its connection to earlier conflict, as well as to current life outside of therapy, is important for behavior change. However, we maintain that it is insight into the dynamics of the therapeutic relationship itself that is the most powerfully mutative.

To specify the ways in which insight into the therapeutic relationship leads to behavior change, we must first clarify what is meant by the relationship and its elements. The first author and his collaborators (Gelso & Carter,

1985, 1994; Gelso & Hayes, 1998) have defined the therapeutic relationship in general terms as the attitudes and feelings the patient and therapist experience toward each other and the manner in which these are expressed. The relationship is best seen as consisting of certain elements or components. In this chapter, we discuss the central components of those articulated by the first author and his collaborators : the working alliance, the real relationship, and client transference. Patient insight into transference and the real relationship, in particular, is significant in facilitating behavior change, and we briefly delineate the *why* and *how* of these interconnections. The working alliance, however, is essential in fostering insight into the other two components.

The working alliance may be seen as the foundation of the psychotherapy relationship in the sense that it must be strong if the work of therapy is to be engaged in at all and if treatment is to continue productively. Further, there is clear empirical support for the importance of a sound working alliance in successful treatment across theoretical orientations (Constantino, Castonguay, & Schut, 2002; Horvath & Bedi, 2002). As we describe in this chapter, a sound working alliance allows the patient to experience the sense of safety and confidence in the therapist that is needed to gain insight into transference and the real relationship, which in turn fosters adaptive behavior change. Following we briefly summarize our view of how and why insight into transference and real relationship may instigate action.

Combining traditional with postmodern conceptions, transference may be seen as the patient's experience of the therapist reflecting that patient's internal world and history. It also reflects a projection onto the therapist of thoughts, feelings, and actions that tend to not befit the therapist, but are more fitting of figures from the patient's earlier life. Transference may be seen as a part of virtually all psychotherapies, a contention for which there is emerging empirical support (see reviews by Gelso & Hayes, 1998; Kivlighan 2002). There is evidence that as therapy progresses, patients gain insight into this transference, even when they are not involved in insight-based therapies (Gelso et al., 1997). Because of the immediacy of the therapy relationship, the patient's here-and-now grasp of how and what he or she does in this relationship can be deeply powerful learning. Further, this *first-hand learning* provides a powerful basis for further and perhaps more significant learning or insight. That is, patients' insight into how they construct and distort the therapy relationship allow them to see in an experientially present and clear way how they construct and distort close relationships in the rest of their lives. This vividly experienced personal learning (i.e., integrative insight) fosters behavior change in these outside relationships, although not in a one-trial learning sense. Consistent with Proposition 3, the repeated learning and trying out in the real world is usually needed for durable change to occur.

We suggest that the dynamics of learning about the real relationship with one's therapist are similar to that of transference, although much less theorized about and empirically examined. As the patient comes to experience the therapist as a person and to see and understand how each feels toward the other, this understanding generalizes to the world outside of therapy and fosters changes in how the patient responds to and experiences others. For example, the patient who comes to understand that the therapist likes her as a person will begin to behave differently toward the therapist as a result of this insight and will also behave differently with others. The patient who comes to trust his therapist deeply (and accurately) as a person and to understand the basis for this trust is more likely to take the risk of trusting others who are trustworthy "on the outside" and behave accordingly.

Again, what makes insight into transference and the real relationship in psychotherapy powerful learning and capable of being transformed into behavior change outside of therapy is the first-hand, immediate nature of the learning in the context of a safe and secure relational situation. From a learning perspective (Kohlenberg & Tsai, 1995; Wachtel, 1987), therapist reinforcement of client insight and change within the hour quickly follows that change and thus more powerfully reinforces it.

Proposition 6: Therapies That Focus on Insight Are Most Likely to Produce Changes in Insight; Therapies That Focus on Action Are Most Likely to Produce Changes in Action; and Therapies That Pay Attention to Both Insight and Action Are Most Likely to Produce Changes in Both

Although evidence amassed over many years suggests that insight therapies may affect behavior as well as insight and behavior therapies may affect insight as well as behavior, experience suggests that therapies will effect the greatest change in the domains in which they exert the greatest attention. Given this expectation, it follows that therapies and therapists who pay attention to both insight and action will produce the greatest changes in both. This is not to say that all therapists should be eclectic or even integrative. One can have strong theoretical leanings and still pay attention to the domain that is not most central to the preferred theory. For example, Greenson (1967, 1978), as noted earlier in this chapter, was a classical psychoanalyst who certainly paid attention to and valued behavioral change in the analytic work. Powell (1996) is clearly a behaviorally oriented therapist who values insight. These are just a couple of examples but there are numerous others, appearing particularly in the literature of the integrative therapy movement. In essence, practitioners of vastly different theoretical orientations, such as psychodynamic and behavioral therapies, can learn to make use of the interaction between insight and action and still maintain their theoretical integrity (see Anchin, 2002; Frank, 2002; Horowitz, 2002; Wachtel, 1987).

How can a therapist maintain his or her theoretical position and also attend to alternative views with respect to insight and action? As dynamically oriented therapists, one of our major aims is to foster integrative insight (and intellectual insight at times) in our patients. We use techniques revolving around exploration, reflection, and interpretation in our work, and we pay close attention to the dynamics of the therapy relationship. We believe each patient has a core set of issues that may be labeled core conflictual relationship themes (Luborsky, Popp, Luborsky, & Mark, 1994) or cyclical maladaptive patterns (Strupp & Binder, 1984). We seek to help our patients gain insight into those themes or patterns—where they come from, their meanings and aims, and how they manifest themselves in both the therapeutic relationship and the world outside of therapy. However, as we seek such insights we are also attentive to what the patient does and says, in his or her relationship with us as well as in his or her "outside" life. Further, when it evolves from and is consistent with the patient's dynamics and the dynamics of the therapeutic relationship, we offer suggestions about behavior in the patient's outside life. Moreover, even as insight therapists we expect to see behavioral changes in our patients and we occasionally help patients work toward those directly. A brief case example from Gelso's work may clarify this:

> During a phase of long-term therapy with a 51-year-old, White female patient, the patient's eating difficulties were discussed. Exploration revolved around the patient's disgust for food and for people who enjoy eating. The patient explored fantasies of being a starving child who placed herself in a cocoon in a fetal position. She knew that no one would be there to nurture her, so being walled off from everyone seemed safer than facing how they (e.g., parents) "starve" her. Through exploration of this material, the patient gained integrative insight into how food and emotional nourishment were connected and how her revulsion at the thought of enjoying food was tied to a lack of emotional nourishment and empathy throughout childhood. Her insights about these issues helped her feel less disgust about eating. Given the longstanding nature of this problem, however, her therapist helped her examine the specifics of her eating behavior and her reactions to her husband and children eating; he offered occasional behavioral suggestions in this area. These seemed to further aid the facilitative effects of insight and fortify changes that were occurring in the patient's eating behavior, her feelings about enjoying food, and her behavior with her family.

From the vantage point of the behavior therapist, the case of Linda, reported by Powell (1996), nicely exemplifies insight during behavior therapy. Linda was a 40-year-old human resources manager with Raynaud's disease and was referred to behavior therapy for treatment. The Raynaud's was quite pronounced, as the patient's hands were blue and very painful. She wore gloves even in the summer. Linda had profited from psychotherapy on two prior occasions, although it never addressed her Raynaud's disease. As Powell reported,

> After one evaluation session, Linda was referred for autogenic training. She was monitored by me at 2- and 3-week intervals after starting be-

havioral treatment. Linda was seen a total of four times. While practicing hand warming with autogenic training and thermal biofeedback, she found herself suddenly very sad and wanting to cry. As Linda thought about it she recognized that she was angry about her brother's nervous breakdown when she was 16. This resulted in her parents focusing all of their attention on him, leaving Linda feeling uncared for. She had previously been the star of the family and the favorite. Though she was stoic at the time, repressing her anger and loss she felt, Linda recognized that her cold hands began around that period. After she vented these feelings, Linda reported that she felt much better. Coincidentally, her Raynaud's disease gradually abated. (pp. 303–304)

Although this behavioral therapist did not work toward insight deliberately, he did create a climate that allowed it, and we assume that as the patient expressed her feelings, the therapist sought to facilitate this exploration. In fact, he suggested that the patient might profit from further sessions exploring her feelings about her parents and brother. She declined, and a 7-month follow-up revealed that her Raynaud's was still improved.

Proposition 7: Therapy Outcomes Are Most Durable When Changes in Insight and Action Both Occur to High Degrees

In reflecting on the six previous propositions, it appears that they clearly lead to this assertion. Changes in both insight and action are expected to reinforce and facilitate each other. When both insight and behavior change occur, that in itself implies some internal resolution of the patient's core issues. In addition, it is by now well-known that when behavior changes are reinforced by others and by the patient's internal world they are most likely to become fortified. These factors point to the likelihood that constructive change in therapy will be long lasting when both insight and action changes are made to a high degree. Little more needs to be said about this proposition. It awaits empirical scrutiny.

CONCLUDING COMMENTS

Insight and action tend to be synergistic processes. We suggest that each affects the other, and that there exists an ongoing mutuality between the two in the process of psychotherapy. Although we propose that integrative insight in itself leads to action or behavior change, the greatest and most durable overall change is predicted to occur when the therapist pays attention to both insight and action.

Our seven propositions about the interplay of insight and action are offered with the hope of both aiding practice and fostering research. The latter has been notably lacking. Emerging research by Kivlighan et al. (2000) on insight and the therapeutic relationship and Wonnell and Hill (2000) in the area of dream interpretation represent promising lines of inquiry. A small cluster of studies now relate insight to various aspects of outcome (e.g., Gelso et al., 1997; Grenyer & Luborsky, 1996; Hoglend, Engelstad, & Sorbye, 1994; Kivlighan et al., 2000; Luborsky, Crits-Christoph, Mintz, & Auerbach, 1988; O'Connor, Edelstein, Berry, & Weiss, 1994), and at least one of these demonstrates an interaction effect between what we term *integrative insight* and another variable (transference) in affecting outcome (Gelso et al., 1997). At least some aspects of the outcome measures in these studies incorporate action or behavior changes as defined here. However, we did not find any studies that directly examined the interplay of insight and action. Such studies would contribute substantially to the basic psychology of psychotherapy—to understanding the fundamental processes involved in change among and within therapies of diverse orientations.

REFERENCES

Alexander, F., & French, T. M. (1946). *Psychoanalytic therapy: Principles and application.* New York: Ronald Press.

Anchin, J. C. (2002). Relational psychoanalytic enactments and psychotherapy integration: Dualities, dialectics, and directions: Comment on Frank. *Journal of Psychotherapy Integration, 12,* 302–346.

Cautela, J. R. (1993). Insight in behavior therapy. *Journal of Behavior Therapy and Experimental Psychiatry, 24,* 155–159.

Constantino, M. J., Castonguay, L. G., & Schut, A. J. (2002). The working alliance: A flagship for the "scientist–practitioner" model in psychotherapy. In G. S. Tryon (Ed.), *Counseling based on process research: Applying what we know* (pp. 132–165). Boston: Allyn & Bacon.

Crits-Christoph, P., Barber, J. P., Miller, N. E., & Beebe, K. (1993). Evaluating insight. In N. E. Miller and L. Luborsky (Eds.), *Psychodynamic treatment research: A handbook for clinical practice* (pp. 407–422). New York: Basic Books.

Frank, K. A. (2002). The "ins and outs" of enactment: A relational bridge for psychotherapy integration. *Journal of Psychotherapy Integration, 12,* 267–286.

Freud, S. (1958). Lines of advance in psycho-analytic therapy. In J. Strachey (Ed. & Trans.), *The standard edition of the complete psychological works of Sigmund Freud* (Vol. 17, pp. 159–168). London: Hogarth Press. (Original work published 1919)

Gelso, C. J. (2002). Real relationship: The "something more" of psychotherapy. *Journal of Contemporary Psychotherapy, 32,* 35–40.

Gelso, C. J. (2003). *Measuring the real relationship: Theoretical foundation.* Paper presented at the 111th annual convention of the American Psychological Association, Toronto, Ontario, Canada.

Gelso, C. J. (2004). *A theory of the real relationship in psychotherapy.* Paper presented at the annual conference of the Society for Psychotherapy Research, Rome, Italy.

Gelso, C. J., & Carter, J. A. (1985). The relationship in counseling and psychotherapy: Components, consequences, and theoretical antecedents. *The Counseling Psychologist, 13*, 155–244.

Gelso, C. J., & Carter, J. A. (1994). Components of psychotherapy relationship: Their interaction and unfolding during treatment. *Journal of Counseling Psychology, 41*, 296–306.

Gelso, C. J., & Hayes, J. A. (1998). *The psychotherapy relationship: Theory, research, and practice.* New York: Wiley.

Gelso, C. J., Hill, C. E., & Kivlighan, D. M. (1991). Transference, insight, and the counselor's intentions during a counseling hour. *Journal of Counseling & Development, 69*, 428–433.

Gelso, C. J., Hill, C. E., Mohr, J. J., Rochlen, A. B., & Zack, J. (1999). Describing the face of transference: Psychodynamic therapists' recollections about transference in cases of successful long-term therapy. *Journal of Counseling Psychology, 46*, 257–267.

Gelso, C. J., Kivlighan, D. M., Wine, B., Jones, A., & Friedman, S. (1997). Transference, insight, and the course of time-limited therapy. *Journal of Counseling Psychology, 44*, 209–217.

Greenson, R. R. (1967). *The technique and practice of psychoanalysis.* New York: International Universities Press.

Greenson, R. R. (1978). *Explorations in psychoanalysis.* New York: International Universities Press.

Grenyer, B. F. S., & Luborsky, L. L. (1996). Dynamic change in psychotherapy: Mastery of interpersonal conflicts. *Journal of Consulting and Clinical Psychology, 64*, 411–416.

Hill, C. E., & O'Brien, K. M. (1999). *Helping skills: Facilitating exploration, insight, and action.* Washington, DC: American Psychological Association.

Hoglend, P., Engelstad, V., & Sorbye, O. (1994). The role of insight in exploratory psychodynamic psychotherapy. *British Journal of Medical Psychology, 67*, 305–317.

Horowitz, M. J. (2002). Self- and relational observation. *Journal of Psychotherapy Integration, 12*, 115–127.

Horvath, A. O., & Bedi, R. P. (2002). The alliance. In J. C. Norcross (Ed.), *Psychotherapy relationships that work: Therapist contributions and responsiveness to patients* (pp. 37–69). London: Oxford University Press.

Kivlighan, D. M. (2002). Transference, interpretation, and insight: A research–practice model. In G. S. Tryon (Ed.), *Counseling based on process research: Applying what we know* (pp. 166–196). Boston: Allyn & Bacon.

Kivlighan, D. M., Multon, K. D., & Patton, M. J. (2000). Insight and symptom reduction in psychoanalytic counseling. *Journal of Counseling Psychology, 47*, 50–58.

Kohlenberg, R. J., & Tsai, M. (1995). Functional analytic psychotherapy: A behavioral approach to intensive treatment. In W. T. O'Donohue & L. Krasner (Eds.),

Theories of behavior therapy: Exploring behavior change (pp. 637–658). Washington, DC: American Psychological Association.

Lambert, M. J., & Ogles, B. M. (2004). Efficacy and effectiveness of psychotherapy. In M. J. Lambert (Ed.), *Handbook of psychotherapy and behavior change* (5th ed., pp. 139–190). New York: Wiley.

Luborsky, L., Crits-Christoph, P., Mintz, J., & Auerbach, A. (1988). *Who will benefit from psychotherapy: Predicting therapeutic outcome.* New York: Basic Books.

Luborsky, L., Popp, C., Luborsky, E., & Mark, D. (1994). The core conflictual relationship theme. *Psychotherapy Research, 4,* 172–183.

O'Connor, L. E., Edelstein, S., Berry, J. W., & Weiss, J. (1994). Changes in the patient's level of insight in brief psychotherapy: Two pilot studies. *Psychotherapy: Theory, Research, Practice, Training, 31,* 533–544.

Powell, D. H. (1988). Spontaneous insights and the process of behavior therapy: Cases in support of integrative psychotherapy. *Psychiatric Annals, 18,* 288–295.

Powell, D. H. (1996). Behavior therapy-generated insight. In J. R. Cautela & W. Ishaq (Eds.), *Contemporary issues in behavior therapy: Improving the human condition* (pp. 301–314). New York: Plenum Press.

Schore, A. N. (2003). *Affect disregulation and the disorders of the self.* New York: Norton.

Strachey, J. (1934). The nature of the therapeutic action of psycho-analysis. *International Journal of Psycho-Analysis, 15,* 127–159.

Strupp, H., & Binder, J. (1984). *Psychotherapy in a new key.* New York: Basic Books.

Sullivan, H. S. (1954). *The psychiatric interview.* New York: Norton.

Wachtel, P. L. (1987). *Action and insight.* New York: Guilford Press.

Wachtel, P. L. (1997). *Psychoanalysis, behavior therapy, and the relational world.* Washington, DC: American Psychological Association.

Wonnell, T. L., & Hill, C. E. (2000). Effects of including the action stage in dream interpretation. *Journal of Counseling Psychology, 47,* 372–379.

15

HOW INSIGHT IS DEVELOPED, CONSOLIDATED, OR DESTROYED BETWEEN SESSIONS

MICHELE A. SCHOTTENBAUER, CAROL R. GLASS,
AND DIANE B. ARNKOFF

Although an abundance of literature has been written on the development of insight in psychotherapy, almost all of it has focused on insight within the therapy session. Less well-understood is the process by which therapy clients develop, consolidate, or lose insight between sessions. The near lack of investigation in this area reflects the emphasis of research on the mechanisms by which psychotherapy can effect change and is based on the assumption that it is the therapy session that causes such change. However, if one shifts focus and considers that psychotherapy is just a small portion of the client's weekly life, it becomes evident that there may be many more factors influencing the client's transformation. In this chapter we have collected the extant literature and research that explore the formation of insight outside of therapy sessions from a variety of theoretical perspectives: psychodynamic, cognitive and behavioral, humanistic and experiential, integrative and eclectic psychotherapy, family systems, and group therapy. We follow this with a discussion of directions for further research.

THEORETICAL PERSPECTIVES AND
ACCOMPANYING RESEARCH EVIDENCE

While the concept of insight is relevant to a variety of theoretical orientations, it has primarily been associated with psychodynamic psychotherapy. We thus begin by considering the psychodynamic perspective, and then broaden the discussion to other theories.

Psychodynamic Theories

There are a variety of psychodynamic and psychoanalytic theories, starting with Freud and including various object relational and self-psychological perspectives (for a review, see St. Clair, 2000). In general, these psychodynamic and psychoanalytic theories conceptualize insight as one of the primary agents of psychotherapeutic change (Crits-Christoph, Barber, Miller, & Beebe, 1993). "Valid insight, 'seeing into' the deep structure of one's formerly repressed conflict motives, was said to yield a significantly better integrated, more flexible, and more maturely functioning ego" (Crits-Cristoph et al., 1993, p. 408). There is some evidence that this may be the case; for example, a large-scale, longitudinal study found that psychoanalysis and psychodynamic psychotherapy were associated with improvements in functioning not only concurrently with therapy but also for years after the end of treatment (Blomberg, Lazar, & Sandell, 2001). Although this suggests that patients either possess or develop the ability to make progress independent of the therapeutic hour, the precise role of insight between sessions has not been the topic of much discussion in the psychodynamic literature. This chapter presents a variety of psychodynamic concepts that are relevant to this issue, along with any available research that supports the theories. The ideas discussed include the role of defenses, reflective functioning, working through, and object relations.

Defenses

Starting with the work of Freud (1894/1953), the concept of defenses has had a central role in psychoanalytic psychotherapies. Although the theory of the role and nature of defenses in psychological functioning has evolved over time (Greenberg & Mitchell, 1983), defenses can be generally conceptualized as psychological mechanisms used to manage feelings or maintain self-esteem (McWilliams, 1994). Defense mechanisms are often construed as maladaptive ways of avoiding strong and threatening feelings; however, they are in fact used by everyone and it is the type of defenses employed, rather than the use itself, that leads to pathology (McWilliams, 1994). Defenses have been categorized into higher or more adaptive mechanisms, as well as lower or less adaptive mechanisms (e.g., McWilliams, 1994; Perry, 1993).

In psychoanalytic theory it is believed that the development of insight into and change in defense mechanisms can lead to enduring change in psychological structure and improvement in symptoms (e.g., Crits-Cristoph et al., 1993). Indeed, increased adaptation in the level of defensive functioning has been linked to symptomatic change in long-term follow-up studies of intensive psychodynamic psychotherapy for treatment-refractory individuals and those with personality disorders (e.g., Bond & Perry, 2004; Speanburg et al., 2004). Improvement in defenses following short-term treatment has been less marked (Perry et al., 2004).

The implications that changes in defense mechanisms have for clients' development of insight outside of sessions have not been clearly delineated in the literature. Nevertheless, several links can be hypothesized. First, changes in defensive functioning could impact client development of insight both between sessions and after psychotherapy has ended, so clients with more adaptive defenses would have more tolerance of psychological material and could deal with it in more adaptive ways. Second, it is plausible that insight would not be maintained between sessions if maladaptive defenses are strong enough or if the insight is related to material that is too anxiety-provoking. In this case, if defenses are lessened first, insight may be retained and expanded on between sessions. Third, patients who rely heavily on maladaptive defenses such as projective identification may tend to recreate interpersonal situations that help them lose insight between sessions. These specific hypotheses, however, are in need of research.

Development of Reflective Functioning

One concept that has appeared repeatedly in the psychoanalytic literature under many different names is the idea that patients can develop the ability to gain their own insight or to analyze themselves over time. This notion has its roots in the work of Freud (1911/1953, 1914/1953) and his notions of binding (*Bindung*), or an ability to link mental sensations and representations, a precursor to developing insight (Lecours & Bouchard, 1997). It has reappeared numerous times in the literature under different nomenclature. Whether it has been called *self-reflexivity* (e.g., Aron, 2000; Auerbach & Blatt, 1996), *mentalization* or *reflective functioning* (e.g., Fonagy, Gergely, Jurist, & Target, 2002), *self-analysis* (e.g., Krantrowitz, Katz, & Paolitto, 1990), or the ability to examine one's own experience using a constructivist perspective (I. Z. Hoffman, 1991), the basic idea is that clients can build the capacity to reflect on their own affective and lived experience as they retain connection with that experience, thereby developing insights on their own, independent of the therapist. Whatever name it goes by, this ability is thought to promote adjustment on a day-to-day level and to be retained by patients long after therapy has been completed. Originally, this ability was considered the prerequisite for psychoanalysis; contemporary authors have come to believe that it can be developed through psychotherapy (Aron, 2000) and research has supported this (Levy & Clarkin, 2003).

In recent years, a great deal of both theoretical work and research has been done around the concepts of mentalization or reflective functioning, which emphasize the importance of both cognitive and affective components of the ability to reflect on interpersonal relationships. Fonagy, Target, Steele, and Steele (1998) have operationalized mentalization as reflective function and have developed a measure for research. This measure rates participants on the quality of their ability to use reflective functioning when discussing themselves, their family, and their relationships during an adult attachment interview. It has been applied in a number of studies, primarily among patients with borderline personality disorder (BPD), as BPD has been theorized to be related to problems with attachment and mentalization (for a review, see Bateman & Fonagy, 2003). Treatments that target mentalization and reflective functioning aim to improve the stability of object relations, self-concept, and relationships.

Several randomized controlled trials have examined the efficacy of psychoanalytically based treatments that aim to improve mentalization and reflective functioning among patients with BPD. One treatment was shown to be more effective at termination and 18-month follow-up than standard psychiatric care; in fact, patients continued to make significant gains in social and interpersonal functioning after the treatment had ended (Bateman & Fonagy, 1999, 2001). Symptoms such as frequency of suicide attempts and acts of self-harm; number and duration of inpatient admissions; and self-reported measures of depression, anxiety, general symptom distress, and interpersonal functioning were significantly decreased among the group that received psychoanalytic treatment compared with standard psychiatric care. This study did not directly measure reflective functioning but hypothesized that it was related to the improvements in the client's functioning. Currently, a randomized controlled trial of mentalization-based treatment of borderline personality disorder is being conducted that investigates this relationship (Bateman & Fonagy, 2004). Preliminary findings from a separate study conducted on psychodynamic treatment for BPD found that a psychodynamic psychotherapy called *transference-focused psychotherapy* resulted in significantly increased reflective functioning when compared with dialectical behavior therapy or supportive psychotherapy (Levy & Clarkin, 2003).

Some research on mentalization and reflective functioning has also been conducted with children. Ensink, Normandin, and Kernberg (2004) found that compared with a waiting list control group, a reflective functioning treatment was effective for decreasing behavioral problems, dissociation, play disruption, and sexualized behaviors among young sexually abused children who had experienced extrafamilial abuse. For children who had experienced intrafamilial abuse, hypervigilance decreased significantly, and their ability to relate to the therapist increased significantly but change on other measures was not significant.

In general, these studies on psychodynamically oriented treatments targeting reflective functioning seem to support the notion that increased reflective functioning (e.g., the ability to generate one's own insight) is related to improved behavioral and affective functioning between sessions and after therapy has ended. One study, however, suggests the relationship might not be so clear. Krantrowitz et al. (1990) conducted a long-term (5 to 10-year) follow-up of 17 patients who had received psychoanalytic treatment. In semistructured interviews, 13 patients reported an increased self-analytic function; however, there was not a clear relationship between this function and maintenance of treatment gains. Although the specific content of the treatment they received was not well-defined and the measurement of self-analytic function was different from the reflective functioning measure used in the other research cited here, this study suggests that further research is necessary.

Some research has been conducted on concepts that are somewhat similar to reflective functioning. For example, psychological mindedness has been defined as the capacity to achieve insight. Psychological mindedness has been operationalized in several scales (e.g., Conte & Ratto, 1997; Shill & Lumley, 2002) and a variety of research has attempted to link this concept to improvement in therapy. Although it was originally thought of as a stable trait that predicted the amount of change that was possible in therapy, several outcome studies have shown that psychological mindedness can improve as a result of therapy (for a review, see McCallum & Piper, 1997). Research on this area, however, has not been applied to progress between sessions or after termination of therapy.

Working Through

Another psychoanalytic concept closely associated with insight between sessions is that of working through. This concept has been discussed by many authors, beginning with Freud (1914/1953). Working through is considered to be a process over time in which repeated, elaborated interpretations by the therapist result in insight that the client tries out in his or her life between sessions. The client then brings new experiences into the therapeutic relationship and the cycle is repeated. Working through is thought to be related to lasting changes (Greenson, 1978).

Psychoanalysis has traditionally placed emphasis on the therapeutic relationship as the agent of change and has tended to dismiss actions on the part of the patient outside therapy as "acting out" (Frank, 1992; Gelso & Harbin, see chap. 14, this volume). However, a number of psychoanalytic theorists, including Alexander and French (1946), Atkins (1970), Gill (1983), and Sandler (1976), have developed the opinion that there is a cyclical relationship between the development of insight and adaptive action (Frank,

1992). Thus, the progress a client makes in the session is hypothesized over time to lead to adaptive actions between sessions. Adaptive actions are hypothesized to solidify and lead to more insight, both within and between sessions. Galatzer-Levy (1988) described working through in analysis as a reactivation of a natural process of finding adaptive solutions in a person who has come to maladaptive solutions in the past (e.g., in highly stressful or traumatic situations that did not allow for a more adaptive range of solutions to be considered).

Rosenblatt (2004) discussed working through in terms of changing procedural memory and knowledge, which are difficult to change and need repeated practice. *Declarative* memory (directly recalled factual knowledge) may be contrasted with *nondeclarative* memory (implicit or procedural knowledge that underlies skills, is not easily linked to language, and is hard to change; Squire & Schater, 2002). Knowledge of how to interact with people relies heavily on nondeclarative knowledge and tends to be changed with both insight and practice, rather than through insight alone (Rosenblatt, 2004). According to Rosenblatt, insight does not always lead to immediate behavior change; practice in similar and different situations is necessary before change can take place. He suggested that a therapist should be encouraging of the patient's attempts to change and help the patient through the difficult process of creating change.

Wallerstein and Dewitt's (1997) classification of psychodynamic psychotherapies into two forms, expressive and supportive, suggests that the role of insight varies according to the type of therapy. Expressive therapy emphasizes within-session insight-oriented techniques, with the aim of creating an ego that can function better between sessions (which, as we have seen, may be related to the development of insight between sessions); however, supportive psychotherapy includes techniques such as actively arranging interventions between sessions, and development of insight has a less central role.

Object Relations

One well-researched area with respect to insight between sessions is the theory of object relations. Internalized representations of self and other have played a central role in psychoanalytic theory, dating back to Freud (for a review, see Orlinsky & Geller, 1993). Most notably, they have been featured in object relational models such as the writings of Mahler (1971), Klein (1932/1975), and Kernberg (1976), but also have been present in self-psychological, attachment, and other theories (Orlinsky & Geller, 1993). The internalized representations of self and other have been thought to arise from early interaction with parents, in which either underformed or malevolent representations can cause a variety of psychopathology (Greenberg & Mitchell, 1983). Research has shown both that patients with healthier levels of object relations make more progress during psychotherapy and that object relations become more coherent and adaptive through the process of psychodynamic psychotherapy (Blatt, Auerbach, & Aryan, 1998). Recent research has shown that internalized representations of self and other are thought to be essential to the discussion of the development, maintenance, or loss of insight between sessions, and to maintenance of gains and continuation of improvement after psychotherapy ends. Several excellent articles include a review of the relevant literature (for reviews see Knox, 2003; Knox, Goldberg, Woodhouse, & Hill, 1999; Orlinsky & Geller, 1993; Orlinsky, Geller, Tarragona, & Farber, 1993).

Most research on therapist representations has been conducted with two instruments, the Therapist Representation Inventory (TRI; Geller, Cooley, & Hartley, 1981) and the Intersession Experience Questionnaire (IEQ; Orlinsky & Lundy, 1986; Orlinsky & Tarragona, 1986). The TRI consists of three parts: a free response section; the Therapist Embodiment scale (which measures thoughts about the therapist that relate to the senses, such as pictures, sounds, and bodily sensations); and the Therapist Involvement scale (which measures themes in thoughts, feelings, wishes, and fantasies about the therapist). The IEQ includes questions about the frequency and incidence of experienced representations, their psychological circumstances, their contexts and contents, the feelings evoked by them, and whether they were discussed. One study (Knox et al., 1999) used a qualitative research method called Consensual Qualitative Research (Hill, Thompson, & Williams, 1997) to analyze interviews regarding therapist representations with 13 patients.

Orlinsky et al. (1993) found that, most often, patients' representations included "I would like my therapist to be proud of me," "I try to solve my problems in the way my therapist and I worked on them in psychotherapy," and "In a sense, I feel as though my therapist has become a part of me." Between sessions, clients showed two tendencies with regard to their therapist representations. *Supportive–guiding representations* included invoking the image of the therapist in a problem-solving dialogue about distressing situations, as well as positive feelings and thoughts about the therapist. Although attainment of insight as a result of these internal dialogues was not directly measured, it is plausible that insight into a specific situation could have been the result of such experiences. The second tendency, called *conflict-containing representations*, consisted of thinking or daydreaming about the therapist (especially during distressing moments) and having negative feelings about the therapist or therapy.

Use of therapist representations is quite frequent. Research suggests that most patients (90%) invoke representations of their therapists between sessions, with most occurring directly before and after sessions (Orlinsky et al., 1993). Types of representations invoked are related to therapeutic sessions; more positive in-session experiences are related to supportive or guiding representations, whereas negative in-session experiences are related to conflict-containing representations (for a review, see Orlinsky et al., 1993).

Therapist representations appear to be used mostly in stressful situations and are associated with positive outcome. Geller et al. (1981) found that patients tend to use therapist representations more frequently and invoke them more strongly in stressful conditions. Intersession experience of supportive–guiding representations was significantly related to improvement in therapy (Geller & Farber, 1993; Knox et al., 1999; Tarragona, 1989).

After termination of therapy, former patients have been shown to keep representations of their therapists and refer to them to continue the work of therapy (M. Epstein, 1989; Geller et al., 1981; Wzontek, Geller, & Farber, 1995; for a review, see Orlinsky et al., 1993).

Cognitive and Behavioral Perspectives

Although *insight* is not a concept directly addressed by many cognitive–behavioral therapists, this approach to psychotherapy is extremely important when considering the issue of insight that arises between sessions. Homework assignments, which by definition are completed by clients outside the therapy hour (Shelton & Ackerman, 1974), are an "integral part of behavior therapy" (Spiegler & Guevremont, 2003, p. 6). In fact, Spiegler and Guevremont suggested that clients frequently do the majority of the therapeutic work in behavioral therapy outside of the therapy sessions. Cognitive therapy has also always incorporated homework assignments (e.g., recording cognitions to discover the relationships between thoughts, behavior, and feelings; testing the validity of assumptions and thoughts), and Beck, Rush, Shaw, and Emery (1979) devoted an entire chapter to this "integral, vital component of treatment" (p. 272).

In their review of the psychotherapy process literature comparing the activities that make cognitive–behavioral therapy (CBT) different from short-term psychodynamic–interpersonal therapy, Blagys and Hilsenroth (2002) found that the item that most differentiated the two approaches was the frequency with which outside-of-session activities and homework were used. Although a survey of practicing psychologists in New Zealand revealed that 98% reported the use of homework assignments, cognitive–behavioral therapists used homework activities more systematically and in a significantly greater percentage of sessions (Kazantzis & Deane, 1999).

Results from a meta-analysis of homework in cognitive and behavioral therapy (Kazantzis, Deane, & Ronan, 2000) show that psychotherapy with homework assignments leads to better treatment outcome and that homework compliance is a strong predictor of treatment success (e.g., Burns & Spangler, 2000). In addition to being a chance to practice new skills, behavior, or cognitive principles that were imparted during the session, completion of homework assignments can serve to generate new understandings, awareness, exploration, and insight into factors associated with the presenting problem. The change process begun during the therapy session thus continues during the week through client action (Gelso & Harbin, chap. 14, this volume; Scheel, Hanson, & Razzhavaikina, 2004). Tompkins (2004) described the use of homework to increase understanding and awareness, stressing both self-monitoring and psychoeducational tasks. In addition, postsession assignments can include behaving in more adaptive ways, deliberately engaging in the problematic behavior, performing a behavior that prevents the problem behavior, replacing dysfunctional thoughts with problem-reduced ones, and self-reinforcement or self-punishment (Mahrer, Nordin, & Miller, 1995).

Insight Through Practice of Cognitive and Behavioral Techniques

The most frequent form of homework used during the cognitive–behavioral intervention in the Second Sheffield Psychotherapy Project was practicing alternative behaviors (30%), with an additional 5% categorized as practicing cognitive techniques that had been taught in therapy (Startup & Edmonds, 1994). These between-session activities can lead to what Powell, who has written most on the topic of insight and behavioral therapy, referred to as *behavior therapy-generated insight* (BGI; Powell, 1996) or *behavior therapy aroused insights*, occurring in perhaps 15% of clients (Powell, 1988). He described several ways in which BGI occurs as a function of between-session experiences during the time clients are receiving behavioral therapy. Clients may spontaneously recognize factors associated with their symptoms or gain awareness of events linked to the etiology of the symptom, which is then enhanced through discussions with the therapist. The occurrence of insight may be enhanced by specifically telling clients they could experience insights, feelings, and thoughts that they should share with the therapist and encouraging them to look for relationships between past conflicts and current symptoms (Powell, 1996). Similarly, Powell (1988) suggested that therapists should watch for unexpected feelings and thoughts that may arise from the practice of muscle relaxation and other behavioral interventions.

Kuhlman (1982) gave an excellent example of how insight can arise during the process of systematic desensitization. The client, an undergraduate who was going blank during tests, was taught muscle relaxation and given homework to develop a fear hierarchy. At the next session, as he was elaborating on one scene by adding more feelings and thoughts, the client saw himself feeling more anxious when his wife told him to do well "or else," but claimed the problem was not related to his marriage. At the following session, however, he reported having thought about the issue and decided it was relevant to his problem taking tests; he followed this by confronting his wife and by taking an exam the next week. Kuhlman saw this symptom reduction, which occurred between sessions, to be a direct result of the insight acquired.

Powell provided other examples of spontaneous insights generated by the use of behavioral therapy. While practicing systematic desensitization, one medical student realized he felt like an imposter who did not deserve to be in medical school and that the exam he feared would show him to be a phony (Powell, 2004). A client anxious about public speaking who practiced a modified form of systematic desensitization improved substantially (Powell, 1986), with insights into his high ambitions, the relationship with his father, and his own behavior surfacing as a result of the behavioral practice and further discussion with the therapist. Another client practicing progressive muscle relaxation became aware of several times when his body tensed up; he then realized his problem stemmed from his choice of career and long work hours (Powell, 1988).

Finally, spontaneous insight need not be related to symptom reduction. Powell (1995) reported a case in which the insights aroused led to negative outcomes. While practicing behavioral self-hypnosis for migraine headaches, the client felt as though someone was standing behind him in his head; this led to the realization that this was his father and led to an upsetting memory of a traumatic event that occurred the year before the headaches began. Powell (1988) also suggested that relaxation-induced anxiety (Heide & Borkovec, 1983), depression, or obsessive thinking may "signal the presence of buried conflicts and foreshadow a beginning awareness of them" (p. 293).

Powell (1996) provided a number of interesting explanations as to why behavioral therapy arouses such spontaneous insights. Those relevant to insight between sessions include (a) relaxation allows greater awareness of the client's physical state and thus recognition of contributing thoughts and feelings; (b) relaxation and other behavioral interventions lower defenses and lead to awareness of suppressed feelings and insight into conflicts; (c) reduction in symptom distress frees the client to think about why the problems exist; and (d) techniques such as relaxation and desensitization have physiological effects on the brain, affecting both thoughts and mood. Research is needed, however, to test these hypotheses.

Insight Through Self-Monitoring or Self-Recording

Self-monitoring refers to clients observing and recording their behavior between sessions (Spiegler & Guevremont, 2003). This approach can help clients increase their awareness of the duration or frequency of a problem, the intensity and type of emotion experienced, and the circumstances that accompany a problem (Tompkins, 2004).

Self-monitoring, or keeping records of feelings, moods, activities, or events, was the second most frequent category of homework assignments (22%) given to CBT clients in the Second Sheffield Psychotherapy Project, and an additional 8% dealt with recording thoughts (Startup & Edmonds, 1994). Cautela (1993) considered behavioral insight to be "awareness of the antecedents that control target behavior, awareness of what the target behavior is or should be (e.g., assertiveness), and awareness of the consequences that influence the strength and rate of the target behavior" (p. 155). He presented several clinical examples, one of which is especially relevant because behavioral insight appeared to be due primarily to the way the client interpreted the findings of his recordkeeping homework. The client, a man with agoraphobia whose job was in jeopardy, was assigned to listen to tapes of covert reinforcement and to drive further distances each day; during this time he recorded his progress, thoughts, and feelings when he had to stop. This self-recording led him to become aware of why he developed his fear of driving far from home and his fear of being promoted when his boss retired, which was then addressed through other behavioral therapy interventions.

Insight Through Psychoeducation and Bibliotherapy

Reading assignments are often used as an adjunct to CBT. Startup and Edmonds (1994) found that 14% of the homework assigned in the cognitive–behavioral intervention in the Second Sheffield Psychotherapy Project fell into the category of developing a greater understanding of one's problems by increasing information. In his book on homework in psychotherapy, Tompkins (2004) stated that 60% to 80% of clinicians regularly assign self-help readings to at least some clients. When such books are actively incorporated into psychotherapy (in contrast to self-directed reading), this approach is referred to as *bibliotherapy* (Campbell & Smith, 2003). The most highly rated purpose of recommending bibliotherapy is to increase awareness and to generate insight, although reinforcing concepts and strategies from a session and helping to promote changes in lifestyle are also rated highly (Campbell & Smith, 2003). Frequently used in CBT (Pantalon, Lubetkin, & Fishman, 1995), bibliotherapy has also been suggested as a way of promoting insight in Adlerian psychotherapy (Jackson, 2001). A recent meta-analysis of 29 outcome studies incorporating cognitive bibliotherapy for depression yielded positive effects (Gregory, Canning, Lee, & Wise, 2004).

Humanistic and Experiential Perspectives

Between-session activities are not a highlight of humanistic and experiential approaches to psychotherapy, with *emotional restructuring* (Greenberg & Paivio, 1997) and *experiencing* (Mahrer, 1986) emphasized, rather than insight. However, it is notable that Carl Rogers (1951), in his classic book on client-centered therapy, presented numerous examples of client material written after the session and describes how "here, as so often, the significant insights occur between interviews, and while the insight appears simple enough, it is the fact that it comes to have emotional and operational *meaning*, which gives it its newness and vividness" (p. 119).

Gendlin (1981, 1996) described an experiential technique called *focusing*, in which the client is taught to experience bodily *felt sense* and express it with a label, image, or metaphor in order to get in touch with and work through emotional material by achieving insight, or a *felt shift*, and emotional resolution. The technique is taught within sessions, but clients are encouraged to use it between sessions. Focusing can be considered a skill similar to the reflective functioning discussed in the section on psychoanalytic psychotherapy.

Greenberg, Rice, and Elliott's process–experiential therapy (1993) includes awareness homework based on discoveries in the session. Clients may be directed to pay attention to the process accompanying certain experiences and become aware of self-evaluations, needs, feelings, and internal criticisms. For example, a client may be encouraged to become more aware of his or her experience and "explore what happens in you that leads to this feeling" (Greenberg & Paivio, 1997, p. 114).

Integrative and Eclectic Perspectives

Homework practice is an important part of several integrative or eclectic psychotherapies and may play a role in increasing awareness of thoughts and feelings. For example, mindfulness-based cognitive therapy stresses the importance of a minimum of 40 minutes a day of practice that becomes a part of clients' daily lives (Segal, Williams, & Teasdale, 2002). Segal et al.'s suggestion that observing and accepting will lead clients to see thought patterns as simply thoughts and not facts can be considered a form of between-session insight.

Eye movement desensitization and reprocessing (EMDR) is an integrative treatment (Shapiro, 2002) that incorporates journaling between sessions into the eight-phase process of change (Shapiro, 1995). In the closure phase, clients are instructed to keep a journal or log of any disturbances (e.g., negative thoughts, memories, images, situations, dreams, and past events) that arise during the week as additional processing continues to occur. The log helps identify material that needs to be dealt with in later sessions. Shapiro (1995) noted that clients who may be more resistant to in-session treatment may process the material later. Clients are urged to see these between-session occurrences as a positive sign and to develop a sense of objectivity and acceptance. *Spontaneous insight* and the development of new positive beliefs is one possible outcome of the EMDR process (Shapiro & Forrest, 1997).

Wachtel's (1977, 1987) theory of cyclical psychodynamics is a major contribution to the integration of psychodynamic and behavioral therapy. In Wachtel's approach, working through is seen as a function of "repeated exposure to anxiety-provoking cues" (1977, p. 93), with insight both a cause and a consequence of therapeutic change. Anxiety reduction through exposure will help reduce repression and facilitate thinking, memory, understanding, and insights. He also proposed that assertiveness training can be important for facilitating insight, as encouraging new real-life actions (through both in-session and planned outside-of-session experiences) will lead to new understanding, and new understanding will generate new behavioral efforts.

Mahoney's (1991, 2003) work on human change processes and constructive psychotherapy emphasized the use of private diaries or journals to contribute to understanding and change and to help clients gain perspectives on their present and past life. He encouraged not only entries of current events, dreams, and memories but also a dual-entry format that adds a place for running commentary that is written after reflecting on the initial entries. He believed in the importance of action and practice and saw psychotherapy as something done by clients, not to them, with the goal of finding meaning and patterns in personal experiences. Bibliotherapy, unsent letters, and life-review exercises are additional examples of activities between sessions that Mahoney suggested can be used to help provide meaning, increase awareness of private experience, and create new possibilities.

Finally, cognitive–analytic therapy (CAT; Ryle & Kerr, 2002) is a synthesis of cognitive–behavioral and psychoanalytic object relational theory that prescribes a specific series of interventions to be conducted in a time-limited format. The main emphasis is on the process of reformulating the client's problems; the reformulation culminates at the end of therapy by the therapist writing a letter to the client that summarizes what he or she has learned about the client. This procedure is an attempt to help solidify the insight after the termination of therapy and to provide a mechanism for sustaining the insight. Ryle and Kerr (2002) offered an excellent review of research on CAT.

Family Systems Perspectives

Although insight is an important concept in several types of family therapy (for a review see Heatherington and Friedlander, chap. 4, this volume), the role of insight between family therapy sessions is less often discussed. Several exceptions are mentioned here.

Cognitive–behavioral family therapists focus on increased awareness and understanding of the role of cognitions in maintaining problematic situations and on changing these thoughts and behaviors. At least one therapist insisted that "understanding or insight is paramount" (Leslie, 1988, p. 77). As with other cognitive–behavioral approaches, homework assignments are used to monitor thoughts to increase awareness of cognitions (Bedrosian, 1988). Other between-session assignments can consist of behavioral experiments designed to test and change distorted thoughts and beliefs, as well as keeping diaries or logs of home interactions to provide data to either support or challenge particular expectations and attributions (N. Epstein, Schlesinger, & Dryden, 1988). Dattilio (2002) listed a number of homework assignments including the use of bibliotherapy, videotaping interactions, activity scheduling, self-monitoring, behavioral tasks, and cognitive restructuring to provide better understanding, awareness, and the chance to turn new insights for coping behaviors into action.

One form of family therapy particularly amenable to the idea of insight between sessions is Bowen family systems therapy (Bowen, 1976). Bowenian therapy melds insight obtained during the session with a focus on changes that will take place at home. Equal emphasis is placed on insight and action, with insight thought to lead to action (Nichols & Schwartz, 1998). The process of differentiation from other family members is an essential element of Bowenian therapy that includes both intrapersonal and interpersonal elements. Through a broad assessment of the extended family and developing personal relationships with those members, additional insight may be obtained (Nichols & Schwartz, 1998). The bulk of this work takes place between sessions.

One other type of family therapy is worth noting in this discussion. Narrative therapy (White & Epston, 1990) rejects the concept of insight because of a postmodernistic emphasis on lack of objective knowledge. However, it does place importance on *narrative reconstruction*, which can be viewed as a constructivist analogy to insight. Although change in narrative therapy is thought to occur in sessions, there is a shift toward the end of therapy on emphasizing support structures outside therapy. This can be considered an attempt to promote the preservation of the narrative reconstruction (e.g., insight) after therapy has ended.

In types of family therapy that are similar to particular "brands" of individual therapy, our previous discussion of the use of insight between sessions in individual therapy could be easily applied. For example, the discussion of insight between sessions in psychodynamic psychotherapy is relevant to object-relations family therapy (e.g., Scharff & Scharff, 1987) or to family therapy based on reflective functioning models (Safier, 2003), although there is little discussion to this regard in the literature.

One concept from family systems therapy that is relevant to the development, maintenance, or loss of insight between sessions is that the family system profoundly affects an individual within the system who is attempting to change (L. Hoffman, 1981). A maladaptive family may facilitate loss of insight in an individual through rigid, maladaptive family patterns or through actively or implicitly discouraging change, whereas a family open to change may help facilitate insight. Within family therapy specifically, it is possible that insight between sessions could be related to intersession family discussion of the session or the issue that was the topic of the session. Research on these topics is necessary, however.

DIRECTIONS FOR FUTURE RESEARCH

We note that a number of overarching questions for research are suggested from this review of the literature. For example, theoretical and empirical writings on insight between sessions are a small but growing part of the psychotherapy literature. More research is needed on whether the ability to develop and sustain insight between sessions is related to psychotherapy outcome. In addition, is the ability to develop and sustain insight between sessions a stable characteristic or one that can be changed through intervention? If so, what interventions are most effective in this regard? What patient diagnoses, personality factors, or environmental factors are related to the development of insight between sessions? Research is also needed to assess whether the ability to develop and sustain insight between sessions is related to continued improvement after termination; however, better methods of assessment of insight and changes between sessions must be developed to conduct this research.

To date, most research on insight between sessions in psychodynamic psychotherapy has been conducted on therapist representations. Research, however, has primarily focused on conscious use of representations (self-report or interview questions directly inquiring about representations). It might be helpful to develop measures or research tools to assess unconscious internalization or use of representations of the therapist; attachment interviews might be a helpful way of exploring this area. Another area in need of exploration is the process by which internalization happens in group and family therapy. For example, are group members internalized in representations? How might these be used between group sessions and after group therapy has ended? In family therapy, how might internalizations of the therapist(s) vary between family members? How does this affect relationships between family members? It would also be helpful to explore the utility of bringing the topic of therapist internalizations directly into treatment. Knox (2003) suggested that therapists might explicitly discuss representations with clients to help normalize the process and to facilitate their use to generalize treatment gains. In this regard, she also suggested that it might be beneficial to study therapist perspectives on clients' internal representations.

There already exists a promising body of research on the role of reflective functioning. More research, however, is needed to explore whether reflective functioning as a construct is causally linked to specific insights between therapy sessions and to improvement in client behavior and social–emotional functioning between sessions and after termination. It would be helpful to determine whether reflective functioning is uniquely fostered in certain types of treatment (e.g., psychoanalytic), or whether it is a common factor to many therapies, including CBT and humanistic therapy. It would be interesting to compare the types of insights generated between sessions in CBT and psychodynamic therapy. For example, are insights between sessions in psychodynamic therapy more complex and do insights in CBT lead more readily to action? Additionally, Powell's (1996) hypotheses about the conditions under which insight arises between sessions in behavioral therapy could be investigated not only in behavioral therapy but also in other types of therapy. His hypotheses deal with the freeing effects of relaxation, which can be likened to a change in defensive functioning.

Research pertaining to the loss of insight between sessions would be helpful. Specifically, it would help to know which specific defenses are related to loss of insight between sessions and how interactions with family members, friends, or specific events erode insight. It would also be beneficial to determine if specific techniques, such as homework or journaling, tend to prevent the loss of insight between sessions.

Finally, more research is needed on which factors help sustain insight and generate new insight after therapy is terminated. For example, in CAT (Ryle & Kerr, 2002) the therapist writes a letter to the client at termination that summarizes the client's primary psychological issues and gains to help preserve insight. It would be interesting to find out whether this technique is helpful in other types of therapy. Other areas for exploration involve the continued use of journaling after therapy termination and the effect of booster sessions on the maintenance of insight after therapy has ended.

CONCLUDING COMMENTS

Although addressed in many schools of therapy, the topic of insight between sessions is a relatively neglected aspect of the psychotherapy literature. It is not surprising that the two major schools of therapy that have addressed it most extensively have approached it in contrasting ways. The psychodynamic literature has focused in a theoretical fashion primarily on the structural personality change that occurs in therapy, with the implication that it will lead the way for improved functioning in general, during and outside of therapy. Thus, change in defense mechanisms, the development of reflective functioning, working through, and improvements in object relations have all been hypothesized to lead to more adaptive functioning in everyday life, which presumably is accompanied by the ability to develop one's own insight. Within object relations, the area of therapist representations has relevance to the topic of insight between sessions and research findings suggesting its importance and utility. Nevertheless, little research directly addresses the topic of insight between sessions, in spite of its obvious importance for progress in psychodynamic therapy and following termination.

In contrast, cognitive and behavioral approaches have directly addressed the issue of progress between sessions and how it can be systematically fostered, but with little theoretical backing that could help in a further understanding of the specific role of insight between sessions. Homework assignments are a hallmark of such therapy approaches, with varying goals of psychoeducation, practicing new behavior, and increasing awareness of and modification of behavioral and cognitive processes. Only Powell (1996) addressed the topic of insight resulting from homework at length. His hypothesis about why behavioral therapy leads to insight primarily involves relaxation and a decrease in symptomatology that allow a greater allocation of attention to important issues. This interesting hypothesis deserves further study. Additionally, further theoretical understanding of insight from a cognitive–behavioral perspective could lead to progress in the design of adaptive changes outside of cognitive–behavioral sessions.

REFERENCES

Alexander, F., & French, T. M. (1946). *Psychoanalytic therapy: Principles and application*. New York: Ronald Press.

Aron, L. (2000). Self-reflexivity and the therapeutic action of psychoanalysis. *Psychoanalytic Psychology, 17*, 667–689.

Atkins, N. (1970). Action, acting out, and the symptomatic act. *Journal of the American Psychoanalytic Association, 33*, 521–535.

Auerbach, J. S., & Blatt, S. J. (1996). Self-representation in severe psychopathology: The role of reflexive self-awareness. *Psychoanalytic Psychology, 13*, 297–341.

Bateman, A. W., & Fonagy, P. (1999). The effectiveness of partial hospitalization in the treatment of borderline personality disorder: A randomized controlled trial. *American Journal of Psychiatry, 156*, 1563–1569.

Bateman, A. W., & Fonagy, P. (2001). Treatment of borderline personality disorder with psychoanalytically oriented partial hospitalization: An 18-month follow-up. *American Journal of Psychiatry, 158*, 36–42.

Bateman, A. W., & Fonagy, P. (2003). The development of an attachment-based treatment program for borderline personality disorder. *Bulletin of the Menninger Clinic, 67*, 187–211.

Bateman, A. W., & Fonagy, P. (2004). Mentalization-based treatment of BPD. *Journal of Personality Disorders, 18*, 36–51.

Beck, A. T., Rush, A. J., Shaw, B. F., & Emery, G. (1979). *Cognitive therapy of depression*. New York: Guilford Press.

Bedrosian, R. C. (1988). Treating depression and suicidal wishes within the family context. In N. Epstein, S. E. Schlesinger, & W. Dryden (Eds.), *Cognitive–behavioral therapy with families* (pp. 292–324). New York: Brunner/Mazel.

Blagys, M. D., & Hilsenroth, M. J. (2002). Distinctive activities of cognitive–behavioral therapy: A review of the comparative psychotherapy process literature. *Clinical Psychology Review, 22*, 671–706.

Blatt, S. J., Auerbach, J. S., & Aryan, M. (1998). Representational structures and the therapeutic process. In R. F. Bornstein & J. M. Masling (Eds.), *Empirical studies of the therapeutic hour* (pp. 63–108). Washington, DC: American Psychological Association.

Blomberg, J., Lazar, A., & Sandell, R. (2001). Long-term outcome of long-term psychoanalytically oriented therapies: First findings of the Stockholm Outcome of Psychotherapy and Psychoanalysis Study. *Psychotherapy Research, 11*, 361–382.

Bond, M., & Perry, J. C. (2004, June). Long-term changes in defense styles with psychodynamic psychotherapy for depressive, anxiety, and personality disorders. In J. C. Perry (Chair), *Change in defensive functioning with psychotherapy.* Symposium conducted at the meeting of the Society for Psychotherapy Research, Rome, Italy.

Bowen, M. (1976). Theory in the practice of psychotherapy. In P. J. Guerin (Ed.), *Family therapy: Theory and practice* (pp. 42–90). New York: Gardner Press.

Burns, D. D., & Spangler, D. L. (2000). Does psychotherapy homework lead to improvements in depression in cognitive–behavioral therapy or does improvement lead to increased homework compliance? *Journal of Consulting and Clinical Psychology, 68,* 46–56.

Campbell, L. F., & Smith, T. P. (2003). Integrating self-help books into psychotherapy. *Journal of Clinical Psychology, 59,* 177–186.

Cautela, J. R. (1993). Insight in behavior therapy. *Journal of Behavior Therapy and Experimental Psychiatry, 24,* 155–159.

Conte, H. R., & Ratto, R. (1997). Self-report measures of psychological mindedness. In M. McCallum & W. Piper (Eds.), *Psychological mindedness: A contemporary understanding* (pp. 1–26). Mahwah, NJ: Erlbaum.

Crits-Cristoph, P., Barber, J. P., Miller, N. E., & Beebe, K. (1993). Patients' representations of their therapists and therapy: New measures. In N. E. Miller, L. Luborsky, J. P. Barber, & J. P. Docherty (Eds.), *Psychodynamic treatment research: A handbook for clinical practice* (pp. 407–422). New York: Basic Books.

Dattilio, F. M. (2002). Homework assignments in couple and family therapy. *Journal of Clinical Psychology, 58,* 535–547.

Ensink, K., Normandin, L., & Kernberg, P. F. (2004, June). Efficacy of a reflective functioning treatment (RFT) for young sexually abused children. In L. Normanin (Chair), *Reflective functioning and its applications in psychotherapy.* Symposium conducted at the meeting of the Society for Psychotherapy Research, Rome, Italy.

Epstein, M. (1989). *Mental representations of the psychotherapeutic relationship during the post-termination period.* Unpublished doctoral dissertation, School of Social Service Administration, University of Chicago, Chicago, IL.

Epstein, N., Schlesinger, S. E., & Dryden, W. (1988). Concepts and methods of cognitive–behavioral family treatment. In N. Epstein, S. E. Schlesinger, & W. Dryden (Eds.), *Cognitive–behavioral therapy with families* (pp. 5–48). New York: Brunner/Mazel.

Fonagy, P., Gergely, G., Jurist, E. L., & Target, M. (2002). *Affect regulation, mentalization, and the development of the self.* New York: Other Press.

Fonagy, P., Target, M., Steele, H., & Steele, M. (1998). *Reflective-functioning manual, version 5.0, for application to adult attachment interviews.* London: UCL Press.

Frank, K. A. (1992). Combining action techniques with psychoanalytic therapy. *International Review of Psychoanalysis, 19,* 57–79.

Freud, S. (1953). The neuro-psychoses of defense. In J. Strachey (Ed. & Trans.), *The standard edition of the complete psychological works of Sigmund Freud* (Vol. 3, pp. 43–61). London: Hogarth Press. (Original work published 1894)

Freud, S. (1953). Formulations on the two principles of mental functioning. In J. Strachey (Ed. & Trans.), *The standard edition of the complete psychological works of Sigmund Freud* (Vol. 12, pp. 218–226). London: Hogarth Press. (Original work published 1911)

Freud, S. (1953). Remembering, repeating, and working through. In J. Strachey (Ed. & Trans.), *The standard edition of the complete psychological works of Sigmund Freud* (Vol. 12, pp. 147–156). London: Hogarth Press. (Original work published 1914)

Galatzer-Levy, R. M. (1988). On working through: A model from artificial intelligence. *Journal of the American Psychoanalytic Association, 36*, 125–151.

Geller, J. D., Cooley, R. S., & Hartley, D. (1981). Images of the psychotherapist: A theoretical and methodological perspective. *Imagination, Cognition and Personality, 1*, 123–146.

Geller, J. D., & Farber, B. A. (1993). Factors influencing the process of internalization in psychotherapy. *Psychotherapy Research, 3*, 166–180.

Gendlin, E. T. (1981). *Focusing* (2nd ed.). New York: Bantam Books.

Gendlin, E. T. (1996). *Focusing-oriented psychotherapy: A manual of the experiential method.* New York: Guilford Press.

Gill, M. M. (1983). *Analysis of transference: Theory and technique.* New York: International Universities Press.

Greenberg, J. R., & Mitchell, S. A. (1983). *Object relations in psychoanalytic theory.* Cambridge, MA: Harvard University Press.

Greenberg, L. S., & Paivio, S. C. (1997). *Working with emotions in psychotherapy.* New York: Guilford Press.

Greenberg, L. S., Rice, L. N., & Elliott, R. (1993). *Facilitating emotional change: The moment-by-moment processes.* New York: Guilford Press.

Greenson, R. R. (1978). *Explorations in psychoanalysis.* New York: International Universities Press.

Gregory, R. J., Canning, S. S., Lee, T. W., & Wise, J. C. (2004). Cognitive bibliotherapy for depression: A meta-analysis. *Professional Psychology: Research and Practice, 35*, 275–280.

Heide, F. J., & Borkovec, T. D. (1983). Relaxation-induced anxiety: Paradoxical anxiety enhancement due to relaxation training. *Journal of Consulting and Clinical Psychology, 51*, 171–182.

Hill, C. E., Thompson, B. J., & Williams, E. N. (1997). A guide to conducting consensual qualitative research. *The Counseling Psychologist, 25*, 517–572.

Hoffman, I. Z. (1991). Discussion: Toward a social–constructivist view of the psychoanalytic situation. *Psychoanalytic Dialogues, 1*, 74–105.

Hoffman, L. (1981). *Foundations of family therapy: A conceptual framework for systems change.* New York: Basic Books.

Jackson, S. A. (2001). Using bibliotherapy with clients. *The Journal of Individual Psychology, 57*, 289–297.

Kazantzis, N., & Deane, F. P. (1999). Psychologists' use of homework assignments in clinical practice. *Professional Psychology: Research and Practice, 30*, 581–585.

Kazantzis, N., Deane, F. P., & Ronan, K. R. (2000). Homework assignments in cognitive and behavioral therapy: A meta-analysis. *Clinical Psychology: Science and Practice, 7,* 189–202.

Kernberg, O. (1976). *Object relations theory and clinical psychoanalysis.* New York: Jason Aronson.

Klein, M. (1975). *The psychoanalysis of children.* New York: Delta. (Original work published in 1932)

Knox, S. (2003). I sensed you with me the other day: A review of the theoretical and empirical literature on clients' internal representations of therapists. *Psychotherapy Bulletin, 38,* 2–5.

Knox, S., Goldberg, J., Woodhouse, S., & Hill, C. E. (1999). Clients' internal representations of their therapists. *Journal of Counseling Psychology, 46,* 244–256.

Krantrowitz, J. L., Katz, A. L., & Paolitto, F. (1990). Follow-up of psychoanalysis five to ten years after termination: II. Development of the self-analytic function. *Journal of the American Psychoanalytic Association, 38,* 637–654.

Kuhlman, T. L. (1982). Symptom relief through insight during systematic desensitization: A case study. *Psychotherapy: Theory, Research and Practice, 29,* 88–94.

Lecours, S., & Bouchard, M. (1997). Dimensions of mentalization: Outlining levels of psychic transformation. *International Journal of Psychoanalysis, 78,* 855–875.

Leslie, L. A. (1988). Cognitive–behavioral and systems models of family therapy: How compatible are they? In N. Epstein, S. E. Schlesinger, & W. Dryden (Eds.), *Cognitive–behavioral therapy with families* (pp. 49–83). New York: Brunner/Mazel.

Levy, K. N., & Clarkin, J. F. (2003, November). *Change in attachment organization in patients with borderline personality disorder.* Paper presented at the meeting of the North American Society for Psychotherapy Research Annual Meeting, Newport, RI.

Mahoney, M. J. (1991). *Human change processes: The scientific foundations of psychotherapy.* New York: Basic Books.

Mahoney, M. J. (2003). *Constructive psychotherapy: A practical guide.* New York: Guilford Press.

Mahler, M. S. (1971). A study of the separation–individual process and its possible application to borderline phenomena in the psychoanalytic situation. *Psychoanalytic Study of the Child, 26,* 403–422.

Mahrer, A. R. (1986). *Therapeutic experiencing: The process of change.* New York: Norton.

Mahrer, A. R., Nordin, S., & Miller, L. S. (1995). If a client has this kind of problem, prescribe that kind of postsession behavior. *Psychotherapy: Theory, Research, Practice, Training, 32,* 194–203.

McCallum, M., & Piper, W. E. (Eds.). (1997). *Psychological mindedness: A contemporary understanding.* Mahwah, NJ: Erlbaum.

McWilliams, N. (1994). *Psychoanalytic diagnosis.* New York: Guilford Press.

Nichols, M. P., & Schwartz, R. C. (1998). *Family therapy: Concepts and methods* (4th ed.). Boston: Allyn & Bacon.

Orlinsky, D. E., & Geller, J. D. (1993). Patients' representations of their therapists and therapy: New measures. In N. E. Miller, L. Luborsky, J. P. Barber, & J. P. Docherty (Eds.), *Psychodynamic treatment research: A handbook for clinical practice* (pp. 423–466). New York: Basic Books.

Orlinsky, D. E., Geller, J. D., Tarragona, M., & Farber, B. (1993). Patients' representations of psychotherapy: A new focus for psychodynamic research. *Journal of Consulting and Clinical Psychology, 61,* 596–610.

Orlinsky, D. E., & Lundy, M. (1986). *Intersession Experience Questionnaire (Therapist Form).* Chicago: University of Chicago Committee on Human Development.

Orlinsky, D. E., & Tarragona, M. (1986). *Intersession Experience Questionnaire (Patient Form).* Chicago: University of Chicago Committee on Human Development.

Pantalon, M. V., Lubetkin, B. S., & Fishman, S. T. (1995). Use and effectiveness of self-help books in the practice of cognitive and behavioral therapy. *Cognitive and Behavioral Practice, 2,* 213–222.

Perry, J. C. (1993). Defenses and their effects. In N. E. Miller, L. Luborsky, J. P. Barber, & J. P. Docherty (Eds.), *Psychodynamic treatment research: A handbook for clinical practice* (pp. 274–307). New York: Basic Books.

Perry, J. C., Banon, E., Lecours, S., Semeniuk, T., Trijsburg, R. W., Henry, M., et al. (2004, June). Change in defensive functioning in a pilot study of antidepressive medications plus 20 sessions of either CBT or dynamic psychotherapy for acute recurrent major depression. In J. C. Perry (Chair), *Change in defensive functioning with psychotherapy.* Symposium conducted at the meeting of the Society for Psychotherapy Research, Rome, Italy.

Powell, D. H. (1986). Spontaneous insight associated with behavior therapy: The case of Rex. *International Journal of Eclectic Psychotherapy, 5,* 140–166.

Powell, D. H. (1988). Spontaneous insights and the process of behavior therapy: Cases in support of integrative psychotherapy. *Psychiatric Annals, 18,* 288–294.

Powell, D. H. (1995). What we can learn from negative outcome in therapy: The case of Roger. *Journal of Psychotherapy Integration, 5,* 133–144.

Powell, D. H. (1996). Behavior therapy-generated insight. In J. R. Cautela & W. Ishaq (Eds.), *Contemporary issues in behavior therapy: Improving the human condition* (pp. 301–314). New York: Plenum Press.

Powell, D. H. (2004). Behavioral treatment of debilitating test anxiety among medical students. *Journal of Clinical Psychology, 60,* 853–865.

Rogers, C. R. (1951). *Client-centered therapy.* Boston: Houghton Mifflin.

Rosenblatt, A. (2004). Insight, working through, and practice: The role of procedural knowledge. *Journal of the American Psychoanalytic Association, 52,* 189–207.

Ryle, A., & Kerr, I. B. (2002). *Introduction to cognitive–analytic therapy: Principles and practice.* New York: Wiley.

Safier, E. J. (2003). Seven ways that the concepts of attachment, mentalization and theory of mind transform family treatment. *Bulletin of the Menninger Clinic, 67,* 260–270.

Sandler, J. (1976). Dreams, unconscious fantasies, and 'identity of perceptions.' *International Journal of Psychoanalysis, 3*, 33–42.

Scharff, D. E., & Scharff, J. S. (1987). *Object relations family therapy.* Northvale, NJ: Jason Aronson.

Scheel, M. J., Hanson, W. E., & Razzhavaikina, T. I. (2004). The process of recommending homework in psychotherapy: A review of therapist delivery methods, client acceptability, and factors that affect compliance. *Psychotherapy: Theory, Research, Practice, Training, 41*, 38–55.

Segal, Z. V., Williams, J. M. G., & Teasdale, J. D. (2002). *Mindfulness-based cognitive therapy for depression: A new approach to preventing relapse.* New York: Guilford Press.

Shapiro, F. (1995). *Eye movement desensitization and reprocessing: Basic principles, protocols, and procedures.* New York: Guilford Press.

Shapiro, F. (Ed.). (2002). *EMDR as an integrative psychotherapy approach.* Washington, DC: American Psychological Association.

Shapiro, F., & Forrest, M. S. (1997). *EMDR: The breakthrough "eye movement" therapy for overcoming anxiety, stress, and trauma.* New York: Basic Books.

Shelton, J. L., & Ackerman, J. M. (1974). *Homework in counseling and psychotherapy.* Springfield, IL: Charles C Thomas.

Shill, M. A., & Lumley, M. A. (2002). The Psychological Mindedness Scale: Factor structure, convergent validity and gender in a nonpsychiatric sample. *Psychology and Psychotherapy: Theory, Research and Practice, 75*, 131–150.

Speanburg, S., Perry, J. C., Zheutlin, B., Beck, S., Meyer, S., McGlaughlin, E. Q., et al. (2004, June). Change in defensive functioning after 3 to 7 years among adults with treatment–refractory disorders in the Austen-Riggs-Follow-Along Study. In J. C. Perry (Chair), *Change in defensive functioning with psychotherapy.* Symposium conducted at the meeting of the Society for Psychotherapy Research, Rome, Italy.

Spiegler, M. D., & Guevremont, D. C. (2003). *Contemporary behavior therapy* (4th ed.). Belmont, CA: Wadsworth/Thomson Learning.

Squire, L., & Schater, D. (2002). *The neuropsychology of memory* (3rd ed.). New York: Guilford Press.

St. Clair, M. (2000). *Object relations and self-psychology: An introduction* (3rd ed.). Belmont, CA: Brooks/Cole Thomson Learning.

Startup, M., & Edmonds, J. (1994). Compliance with homework assignments in cognitive–behavioral psychotherapy for depression: Relation to outcome and methods of enhancement. *Cognitive Therapy and Research, 18*, 567–579

Tarragona, M. (1989). *Patients' experiences of psychotherapy between sessions: Their relationship to some input, process, and output variables of psychotherapy.* Unpublished doctoral dissertation, University of Chicago, Chicago, IL.

Tompkins, M. A. (2004). *Using homework in psychotherapy: Strategies, guidelines, and forms.* New York: Guilford Press.

Wachtel, P. L. (1977). *Psychoanalysis and behavior therapy.* New York: Basic Books.

Wachtel, P. L. (1987). *Action and insight*. New York: Guilford Press.

Wallerstein, R. S., & DeWitt, K. N. (1997). Intervention modes in psychoanalysis and in psychoanalytic psychotherapies: A revised classification. *Journal of Psychotherapy Integration, 7,* 129–150.

White, M., & Epston, D. (1990). *Narrative means to a therapeutic end*. New York: Norton.

Wzontek, N., Geller, J. D., & Farber, B. A. (1995). Patients' posttermination representations of their psychotherapists. *Journal of the American Academy of Psychoanalysis, 23,* 395–410.

16

A PROCESS MODEL FOR FACILITATING SUPERVISEE INSIGHT IN SUPERVISION

NICHOLAS LADANY

If we therapists expect our clients to embrace and gain insight into themselves, so too should we be open to embracing and gaining insight into ourselves. A primary means for therapists, particularly therapists-in-training, to gain insight is through supervision. To that end, the purpose of this chapter is to offer a model for supervisors to use in facilitating supervisee insight. First, a definition of supervisee insight is offered. Second, a general critical events-based model of supervision is described, from which a specific model for facilitating supervisee insight is discussed. This conceptual model is then illustrated by an annotated clinical example. Finally, special considerations in relation to facilitating and inhibiting factors related to supervisee insight are discussed and research implications are provided.

DEFINING SUPERVISEE INSIGHT

Similar to client insight in psychotherapy, so too, do supervisees develop and attain insight in supervision. Although there is some literature on client insight from which to draw a definition (e.g., Elliott, 1984; Gelso &

Hayes, 1998; Hill & Williams, 2000; see also chap. 8, this volume), the literature on supervisee insight seems nonexistent. With this in mind, I propose the following definitional components of supervisee insight for the purposes of this chapter. Specifically, supervisee insight includes a change in cognitive and emotional interconnections regarding oneself in relation to past and present thoughts and feelings and behaviors with others, as related to the supervisee's work in therapy or supervision. Rather than seeing insight as a discrete event, I propose that insight is a matter of degrees of interconnections. At a more superficial level, insight may involve a supervisee's cognitive understanding of how his or her therapy behaviors directly influence a client's reactions. For example, Sally, a beginning supervisee, may recognize that she overuses thought-based questions with her clients (e.g., "What do you think?"), that in turn leads her client to avoid expressing feelings."

A deeper level of insight would include the supervisee's cognitive and emotional understanding of where his or her *therapy style* originates, how this style directly influences the client's reaction, and how he or she can change his or her style to better meet the client's needs. For example, Sally may recognize that when she was a child her mother shamed her into being less emotional, which in turn leads her to avoid emotional reactions in others. In her therapy sessions, she realized that she plays a part in stifling her client's emotions by asking thought-based questions. In addition, whenever the client becomes emotional, Sally understands that her shameful feelings stem from the internalized voice of her mother. In a subsequent therapy session Sally is able to catch herself asking thought-based questions and change her approach to make it more feeling-based, thereby fitting better with the client's needs. Finally, Sally is also able to recognize how she tends to avoid emotionally laden discussion in supervision and works toward staying more present with her feelings in future supervision sessions.

Unlike client insight, supervisee insight is more focused on the supervisee in relation to his or her work in therapy or supervision. Supervisee insight may include personal revelations; however, this definition narrowly includes self-revelations as they are related to the work in therapy or supervision. Also, supervisee insight is related to case conceptualization ability, although they are not necessarily synonymous. Insight at a more superficial level would be like a simple case conceptualization. Insight in this circumstance is an intellectualized insight. As insight deepens, it analogously is more similar to an *empathic conceptualization* that extends a bit beyond the client's dynamics and issues.

A CRITICAL EVENTS-BASED MODEL OF PSYCHOTHERAPY SUPERVISION

How can a supervisor "cause" insight in a supervisee? To answer this question I turn to Ladany, Friedlander, and Nelson (2005), who developed a critical events-based model of psychotherapy supervision. Their model was largely based on the task-analytic approach literature to developing models of therapeutic change (e.g., Greenberg, 1986; Rice & Greenberg, 1984; Safran, Crocker, McMain, & Murray, 1990). In addition to taking into account the traditional inherent differences between psychotherapy and supervision (e.g., involuntary, evaluative, explicitly educative), Ladany et al. based their model on the following assumptions. First, the model was intended to be pantheoretical so practitioners and researchers from multiple theoretical perspectives would find it useful. Second, the model attends largely to the interpersonal nature of supervision, thereby recognizing the contributions of both the supervisor and supervisee. Third, it considers the primary role of supervision to be focused on the supervisee's growth and development, rather than solely on case management. Fourth, it is assumed that the supervision process can be viewed as a series of events, each of which has a beginning, middle, and end, that may take place within one session or across multiple sessions. The final assumption is that these events are integrally linked with supervision outcome.

The events-based model of psychotherapy supervision recognizes that a number of common *critical events* can occur in supervision (e.g., supervisee skill deficit, sexual attraction, supervisee lack of insight, role conflict, gender misunderstanding). The *task* is what the supervisor attempts to accomplish in each kind of event (e.g., remediating the skill deficit, managing sexual attraction, facilitating supervisee insight). The model itself identifies three primary phases for a critical event: the *marker*, *task environment*, and *resolution*, all of which are embedded in a *supervisory working alliance*.

The Supervisory Working Alliance

The supervisory working alliance is considered the foundation on which the event can either lead toward a resolution or not. Bordin's (1983) model of the supervisory working alliance is used as the formulation, which consists of a mutual agreement on the goals of supervision between the supervisee and supervisor (e.g., enhance conceptualization skills); a mutual agreement on the tasks of supervision between the supervisee and supervisor (e.g., listen to audiotapes of therapy sessions); and an emotional bond between the supervisee and supervisor (i.e., mutual caring, liking, trusting, and respecting). The supervisory alliance has been one of the most examined variables in the supervision literature and has been found to be related to a number of supervision process and outcome variables (Bernard & Goodyear, 2004; Bradley & Ladany, 2001; Ellis & Ladany, 1997). As the supervisee and supervisor negotiate what is to take place in supervision, the alliance can strengthen or weaken. Moreover, the alliance plays a figure-ground role in supervision. In the earlier supervisory sessions or when supervision becomes conflictual, the alliance is typically the figure or where the attention in supervision is directed. Conversely, when the alliance is stable and strong it becomes the ground or foundation on which other supervisory work is accomplished, and it provides the context for more emotionally intense supervisory experiences. As I discuss in this chapter, when a supervisor is facilitating insight in a supervisee who is lacking insight, the alliance has to be relatively strong to weather the emotionally laden content in supervision.

The Marker

The marker in a critical event is typically a statement or series of statements made by the supervisee that indicates a need for assistance. It could be as simple as the supervisee saying something like, "I really need help understanding why I can't get this client to move in therapy." However, at other times the marker may be more subtle, such as when a supervisee forgets key features about a client, consistently doesn't mention a particular client in supervision, or behaves in a defensive manner toward the supervisor. The search for what underlies these types of markers becomes the charge of the supervisor and should inform the supervisor about what to do next in supervision. In addition, the marker indicates what the critical event is and is what sets the stage for the task environment.

For a supervisee insight event, the marker may show up in the manner in which the supervisee discusses a client in supervision. In the earlier example in which the supervisee lacked insight into her overly cognitive approach toward working with her client, the marker could have been her telling her supervisor, "I can't figure out how to move this client along," in a frustrated manner. Or, the marker could have presented itself while the supervisor was reviewing the supervisee's tapes. In this context, the supervisor may have heard the client crying, but instead of attending to the pronounced client affect the supervisee bristles a little and then pushes a cognitive agenda. In both circumstances the supervisor may notice that the supervisee is missing a connection in the client's life that may be related to unrecognized connections in the supervisee's professional and personal life.

The Task Environment

Once the marker has been identified, the next phase of the event is the task environment (Ladany et al., 2005). The task environment consists of a number of interaction sequences that involve supervisor operations and supervisee reactions. Twelve of the most common interaction sequences were identified and include (a) focus on the supervisory working alliance, (b) focus on the therapeutic process, (c) exploration of feelings, (d) focus on countertransference, (e) attending to parallel process, (f) focus on self-efficacy, (g) normalizing experience, (h) focus on skill, (i) assessing knowledge, (j) focus on multicultural awareness, (k) focus on evaluation, and (l) case review. It is understood that the interaction sequences are not orthogonal, nor are they exhaustive. In addition, they may be recursive and exist in a segment of a session or across multiple sessions. However, for the purposes of this model, they will be used as a heuristic for a supervisor to understand what may be important to attend to in supervision.

In the case of a facilitating supervisee insight event, the marker may be the supervisee questioning what he or she is missing in his or her therapeutic work. The subsequent interaction sequences that are deemed typical for this type of event include *focus on the therapeutic process, exploration of feelings, focus on countertransference,* and *attend to parallel process* (see Figure 16.1). When focusing on the therapeutic process, it is important that the supervisor understand what may be happening beyond the initial report of the trainee. When possible, the best way to do this is to listen to the tape of the therapy session. In addition, thoroughly examining the supervisee's experience of the therapy work often leads to clues about which aspects of insight are lacking. The supervisor must also be sure to explore the supervisee's feelings to get at the emotional aspects of insight. In this process, the supervisor can do two things. First, he or she can link the supervisee's affect with the supervisee's cognitive understanding of what is happening in therapy. Second, the supervisor can use this emotional material to focus on possible sources of supervisee countertransference, the next interaction sequence. In the context of each of these interaction sequences, the supervisor should also pay close attention to how parallel processes may be playing out in supervision, either by the supervisee mimicking the client from therapy or the supervisor mimicking the supervisee in therapy (parallel process going up). When parallel processes are identified, the supervisor then has the opportunity to offer a corrective emotional experience that, in turn, can be used by the supervisee to offer a corrective emotional experience to the client (parallel process going down).

The Resolution

The outcome of a particular task is deemed the resolution. The resolution is not a dichotomous result. Rather, there are degrees of resolution, just as there are degrees of insight gained. Although the model posits four types of resolution (i.e., self-awareness, knowledge, skills, and the supervisory working alliance), the first, self-awareness, is most applicable to a facilitating insight event (see chap. 14, this volume, on the interplay of insight and action). Self-awareness pertains to changes in the supervisee's understanding regarding personal biases, feelings, beliefs, and behaviors in relation to his or her work with clients. In relation to insight, the more successfully an event is resolved, the greater the insight. Conversely, unresolved events, or those with little resolution, would involve little insight gained on the part of the supervisee. The following mock case example is used to illustrate a process model for a successfully resolved supervisee insight event.

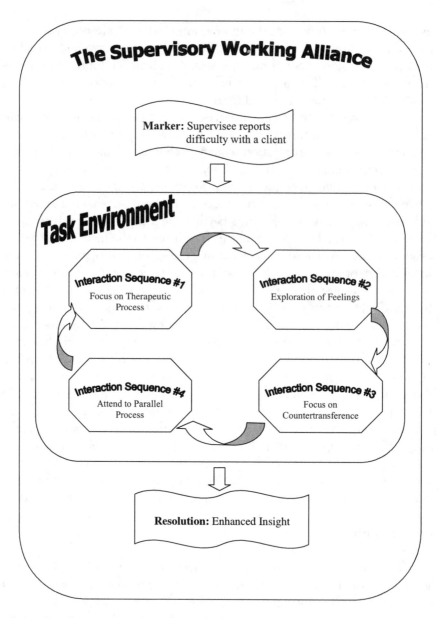

The Supervisory Working Alliance

Marker: Supervisee reports difficulty with a client

Task Environment

Interaction Sequence #1
Focus on Therapeutic Process

Interaction Sequence #2
Exploration of Feelings

Interaction Sequence #4
Attend to Parallel Process

Interaction Sequence #3
Focus on Countertransference

Resolution: Enhanced Insight

Figure 16.1. Facilitating a supervisee insight event.

A SUCCESSFULLY RESOLVED SUPERVISEE INSIGHT EVENT

The supervisory dyad consists of Debbie, a 42-year-old supervisor who has 15 years of clinical experience and 8 years of supervisor experience, and Melinda, a 32-year-old advanced practicum student in the 4th year of her psychotherapy training program. The setting is a university counseling center.

In their initial session, Debbie does well to discuss the structure of supervision (e.g., limits of confidentiality, supervision can be supervisee-focused and client-focused), thereby providing a role induction for Melinda. We find them in their sixth supervisory session. Their alliance to date has been relatively strong, and although Melinda came to the practicum with many skills, there were more she was able to gain in supervision and she has been comfortable talking, at points, about how her personal issues may influence her work with her clients. At this point in the session, they are talking about Charlie, a 19-year-old college sophomore who has a depressed mood largely because of difficulties with making friends, homesickness, and uncertainty about what major he should choose. In addition, he is in recovery for alcohol addiction and regularly attends weekly Alcoholics Anonymous meetings. Charlie and Melinda have met for five therapy sessions.

We join Debbie and Melinda at the beginning of their sixth supervisory session. In the following we see the supervisor and supervisee speaking, with comments in italics on the interactions taking place.

Marker

Supervisor: So what would you like to learn today?

Melinda: I definitely want to talk about this one client I have who is driving me crazy!

The marker is pretty clear and not very subtle. Any time a supervisee expresses concern with affect like this, the supervisor can be pretty sure that a marker has been offered.

Supervisor: Tell me more about what's happening.

Melinda: I have this client, Charlie. I like him overall, but he seems to ask me for things but never seems fully satisfied with what I tell him.

The marker seems adequate and offers the supervisor a glimpse into Melinda's work with this client. The supervisor has seen Melinda's work before and recognizes that she has not had this problem with other clients. She hypothesizes that there is something unique about this particular client interaction and sets out to explore what is happening in therapy. Specifically, the supervisor sets out to discover why she is stuck and if it has something to do with her lack of insight in relation to her client.

Focus on the Therapeutic Process

Supervisor: What kinds of things does he ask of you and how do you respond?

Melinda:	Well, he tells me he's sad and lonely so I suggest ways that he can meet other people, like joining clubs or seeking out people he meets in class.
Supervisor:	Okay.
Melinda:	He seems to like my ideas but when he comes back the following week, he hasn't done anything. And this happens week after week.
Supervisor:	Who notices in the therapy session that he hasn't done anything?
Melinda:	Me! If I left it up to him he would probably never mention it.
Supervisor:	So, it sounds like he requests your guidance and then passively sits back while you offer it to him. Then, although on the surface he seems to accept it, in the end he disregards it?

The supervisor summarizes the dance that goes on between the supervisee and the client, thereby offering one of the first pieces of insight.

Melinda:	Yes, that does seem to be the case. I hadn't thought of it that way.

Each accurate reflection should enhance and strengthen the bond component of the alliance.

The supervisor has explored what is happening in therapy and has been able to help the supervisee get a slightly better cognitive understanding of the situation with this client. She now moves to make an affective connection.

Exploration of Feelings

Supervisor:	So, what's that feel like when that happens?
Melinda:	Incredibly frustrating!
Supervisor:	I can imagine it must be like you are set up to fail?

The supervisor empathizes with supervisee's plight.

Melinda:	Exactly!
Supervisor:	He gets you to help him, but it's all a pretense because he never intends to follow though with what you offer him.
Melinda:	Yes!
Supervisor:	That would certainly frustrate me.

The supervisor self-discloses about her reactions, which likely strengthens the bond component of the alliance.

Melinda:	Well, I'm glad I'm not the only one!

Supervisor: I want you to try something for me if you are willing?

This ensures at least tacit agreement on the part of the supervisee.

Melinda: Okay.

Supervisor: If your interactions with Charlie could be portrayed in an image, what would it look like?

The supervisor uses imagery as a way to offer the supervisee some objective distance from her interactions.

Melinda: Hmm. That's a good question. It would probably look like a robin feeding her babies, constantly dropping worms to them; but instead of eating the worms, they take them in their beak and when she isn't looking, or is off getting more worms, they throw them out of the nest. Then she comes back with more worms and the same thing happens all over again.

Supervisor: Fascinating.

Melinda: Sounds pretty crazy, doesn't it?

Supervisor: No, not at all. So you can picture this mother robin working hard to give the babies something but these babies keep rejecting what is offered. And the rejection isn't direct. Rather, it's behind her back.

Melinda: Yup.

Supervisor: That's a great image. What's it feel like to be the mother robin?

The supervisor starts to bring it back to the task at hand. The supervisor also considers the metaphor as potentially reflective of parallel process to consider at some future point in time.

Melinda: Frustrating, as I said before, but there is some sadness as well.

Supervisor: Sadness. Say more about the sadness.

The supervisor points out another piece of insight, this time an emotional piece.

Melinda: Like a helplessness. No matter what she does, or gives, it's never enough or it's never right.

Through an exploration of feelings, Debbie has been able to expand the types of emotions Melinda experiences with this client. Now to deepen this experience, Debbie attempts to move Melinda into more personal areas.

Focus on Countertransference

Supervisor: Can you remember a time in your life when you felt like this before?

Melinda: I don't know. It's strange. The first thing that comes to mind is a birthday party I had when I was a kid. I don't remember much of the party, just the feeling of sadness that reminds me about how I'm feeling now.

Supervisor: Keep holding on to that feeling and see if any other specifics emerge.

Melinda: I was about 8 years old, I remember because we still had our dog at the time. And I remember some of my friends and my mom and other moms all around. There, of course, was cake, and we played outside. It was summertime.

Supervisor: Was your father around?

Melinda: No, he never made it to things like that. He was too busy at work or getting drunk at the bar. [*laughs*] No matter what I tried, he never was able to make it.

Supervisor: What kinds of things did you try?

Melinda: Well, I would always plead with him but that never worked. But I wouldn't have cared if he never came to any of my parties if he just was able to sober up. He finally did a few years ago, which I'm really happy about. Although, he's a mess physically.

Supervisor: Let's go back for a moment to what it was like to try to get him to come to the party. Or, maybe more to the point, did you ever try to get him or plead with him to stop drinking?

The supervisor pinpoints the dynamic that seems similar to the one between the supervisee and her client.

Melinda: Of course! But he never listened. Well, I should say he pretended to listen but he never did stop.

Supervisor: Kind of like how Charlie doesn't listen to things you tell him?

Melinda: Wow. [*looks sad and looks down at her feet*]

Supervisor: What's going on right now for you?

The supervisor attends to the here-and-now by making an immediacy comment

Melinda: I can't believe how similar it all feels. How could I have missed it?

Supervisor: Perhaps you missed it because you needed to miss it. But in your earnest search to help Charlie, you opened yourself up to find what you needed to.

The supervisor reinforces the supervisee's quest.

Melinda: Feels really overwhelming.

> *Supervisor:* I imagine it does.
>
> *Melinda:* So what do I do with all this?
>
> *Supervisor:* Well, one thing you can do is to work on your own personal stuff, in particular, your relationship with your father.

The supervisor misses an opportunity to empower the supervisee and instead offers a suggestion without exploring what the supervisee might come up with.

Although at the end of this segment Debbie misses an opportunity to explore what is happening in supervision, she does a very good job exploring Melinda's countertransference and facilitates the discovery of a link between her family and her behaviors with her client. As in therapy, important things that are missed in supervision often come back to be dealt with again. In this case, Debbie slowly catches on and will notice a pattern in supervision that seems to mimic a pattern in therapy between Melinda and Charlie.

Attend to Parallel Process

> *Melinda:* Yeah, maybe I could do that, but my father hasn't made it through many of the 12 steps and I don't like to play his therapist. Do you have any other suggestions?
>
> *Supervisor:* I suppose you could work on it in your own therapy.
>
> *Melinda:* [*hesitantly*] I suppose I could do that.

Although it is important for supervisors to encourage personal therapy for their supervisees, the timing of this suggestion is off.

> *Supervisor:* I get the feeling that this suggestion isn't going to make it to the top of your list.
>
> *Melinda:* I don't know.
>
> *Supervisor:* Melinda, I wonder if you have noticed that you have asked me for a couple of suggestions and each time I offer you some guidance, you seem to be hesitant about accepting it.

Supervisor makes a process comment.

> *Melinda:* I'm sorry. I shouldn't be doing that.
>
> *Supervisor:* Actually, it's okay because do you also notice that this is unlike you?
>
> *Melinda:* Yeah, that's true; usually I run out and work on most things we talk about in here.
>
> *Supervisor:* Yes, it does seem unlike you, but who does it seem more like?
>
> *Melinda:* [*smiles*] That does sound a lot like my client!

Supervisor: Good observation! So, what do you think you could do with all this new information?

Rather than continuing to take on the conflict, the supervisor turns the conflict back on the supervisee, thereby providing a corrective emotional experience for her.

Melinda: I suppose I could do what you are doing with me right now. Instead of giving him answers to all his questions, I could put it back on him.

Supervisor: Precisely. You can have him do more of the work in therapy.

Melinda: That certainly takes a lot of the pressure off me.

Debbie was able to demonstrate the parallel process (i.e., the client to therapist dependency that was mimicked in supervision) in vivo, which made it even more powerful. By the end of the interaction Melinda had gained another piece of insight, specifically, an idea of what it is like to be her client and how it feels to have a corrective emotional experience. Debbie hopes and believes that this corrective emotional experience can be passed down to the client through Melinda. The supervisor can now move on to the resolution phase, in which she can bring together all the pieces of insight with the intent of generalizing Melinda's newfound understanding.

Resolution

The supervisor supports supervisee's hard work and checks in with how she experienced doing this kind of work in supervision:

Supervisor: Melinda, you did really well with all of this today. I challenged you and had you attend to some painful things in your life. We worked on some heavy things today. How was that for you?

Melinda: Really hard, but really good.

Supervisor: How was it to do some of this work in supervision with me?

Melinda: It felt good. I feel safe in here. We've already done a lot this semester.

Supervisor: Yeah, we have. Maybe it would be helpful if we summarized what kinds of things you got out of this session?

Melinda: Well, I learned that things don't always seem as they appear! [*laughs*]

Supervisor: [*laughs with her*]

Melinda: But, I learned that my client asks for things and then rejects them and that makes me feel frustrated and sad.

Supervisor:	Good. So, the sadness or frustration can act as a cue to you that something else may be going on.
Melinda:	Yes, and in this case it had to do with my family. And then I essentially played my client here in supervision with you.
Supervisor:	Very good. Anything else?
Melinda:	I think that's it.
Supervisor:	What you can do with Charlie now that you know all this?
Melinda:	Oh, right. I could put the work back on him when we meet again.
Supervisor:	Exactly. And maybe that's what we can work on next, figuring out how to make that happen?
Melinda:	That sounds good.

At this point the supervisor recognizes that more work may need to be done in relation to Melinda's skills with working with this client; however, a lot has been accomplished and in particular, many cognitive and emotional pieces of the insight puzzle have been put together (i.e., interpersonal process between client and supervisee, supervisee's feelings of frustration and sadness, the affective link to childhood, and the parallel process). In the end, the resolution of the event was highly successful.

SPECIAL CONSIDERATIONS

Obstacles to Supervisee Insight

Clearly, this example shows a strong supervisory working alliance between a highly functional supervisee and a highly functional supervisor. Unfortunately, this scenario is not the most common one in supervision (Ladany, 2004). More likely, a number of intermediary variables come into play that disrupt or short-circuit this process.

First, there are supervisee-based insight obstacles, all of which are related to the supervisee's capacity for insight. In a case in which a supervisee has difficulty gaining insight, the supervisor must look for mitigating factors, such as a lack of foundational knowledge about psychotherapy, personal stressors, or ingrained interpersonal style problems (see chap. 13, this volume, for a discussion of therapist countertransference). In each circumstance, the supervisor must examine ways to help the supervisee work through these blocks to insight (e.g., personal therapy); in extreme cases in which the supervisee is profoundly unable to gain insight, the supervisor would need to consider removing her or him from the training site.

Supervisor-based insight obstacles can also influence the supervisee's ability to gain insight. Specifically, supervisor insight is likely the rate-limiting step in determining the extent to which supervisees gain insight. Supervisors must know how to gain insight into their own professional lives and must be comfortable with the process of facilitating supervisee insight to successfully assist supervisees. As seen in the example, part of the supervisor's role was to engage in therapy-like behaviors with the supervisee. This is not to suggest that supervision is the same as therapy. Rather, as the supervisee's personal issues influence his or her work as a therapist, the processes of supervision can look similar to the processes of therapy (e.g., exploration, looking at the past in relation to the present). To do all this, the supervisor must possess the skills necessary, must limit the amount of case review, and must have a strong enough alliance with the supervisee. Without these in place the work will likely not be productive, and in fact, the supervisee could be harmed.

Research Directions

Although the model is intended to be heuristically appealing to supervisor practitioners, empirical support is needed to validate its generalizability. Guidelines for investigating the applicability of this model of facilitating supervisee insight can be obtained from the validation of task analytic models for therapy (Greenberg, 1986; Greenberg, Heatherington, & Friedlander, 1996; Rice & Greenberg, 1984) and for supervision (Ladany et al., 2005). Using the current theoretical process model for facilitating supervisee insight as a starting point, the next step is for researchers to identify successfully and unsuccessfully resolved insight events in supervision (e.g., relying on videotapes of supervision). Then, applying qualitative and quantitative methodological approaches (using ratings from supervisors, supervisees, and others), these events can be compared and contrasted and a preliminary conceptual model created. In this new conceptual process model, types of markers could be identified and the types and order of interaction sequences could be noted. From this procedure a process model, or series of process models, could be formulated for successfully and unsuccessfully resolved insight events. Refinement of these models would then come from subsequent study with larger samples.

Of course, in developing these models the resolution of insight would need to be assessed in a reliable fashion. Preliminary work by Caspar, Berger, and Hautle (2004) may be a means of measuring insight. Caspar et al. have developed a computerized system of assessing a supervisee's case conceptualization. Although their work focuses more on the case conceptualization of the client, it seems possible to expand their work to include the range of emotional and cognitive interconnections that include the therapist to assess changes in supervisee insight.

CONCLUDING COMMENTS

Although the process model may look straightforward, it is clear that the complexities of real life supervision are never this neat. It should be recognized that the interaction sequences are not typically discrete units; rather, they likely overlap and blend into one another. In addition, they may occur in other orders, and for some insight events the ones identified may not be present. For example, it is certainly possible that no parallel process occurs and therefore would be seen as an interaction sequence. In a similar fashion, it could be the case that the supervision experience becomes quite intense and the supervisor has to attend more to the supervisory working alliance than expected. In addition, the present model looks as though it presumes that insight occurs in the context of a segment of one supervision session. In all likelihood, insight may also occur across multiple sessions, or long after supervision is completed. In essence, the process model is not intended as a one-size-fits-all model. Rather, it is hoped that it can be used as a conceptual template for supervisors and future researchers.

REFERENCES

Bernard, J. M., & Goodyear, R. K. (2004). *Fundamentals of clinical supervision* (3rd ed.). Needham Heights, MA: Allyn & Bacon.

Bordin, E. S. (1983). A working alliance based model of supervision. *The Counseling Psychologist, 11*(1), 35–41.

Bradley, L. J., & Ladany, N., (Eds.). (2001). *Counselor supervision: Principles, process, & practice* (3rd ed.). Philadelphia: Brunner-Routledge.

Caspar, F., Berger, T., & Hautle, I. (2004). The right view of your patient: A computer-assisted, individualized module for psychotherapy training. *Psychotherapy: Theory, Research, Practice, Training, 41*, 125–135.

Elliott, R. (1984). A discovery-oriented approach to significant events in psychotherapy: Interpersonal process recall and comprehensive process analysis. In L. N. Rice & L. S. Greenberg (Eds.), *Patterns of change: Intensive analysis of psychotherapy process* (pp. 249–286). New York: Guilford Press.

Ellis, M. V., & Ladany, N. (1997). Inferences concerning supervisees and clients in clinical supervision: An integrative review. In C. E. Watkins Jr. (Ed.), *Handbook of psychotherapy supervision* (pp. 567–607). New York: Wiley.

Gelso, C. J., & Hayes, J. A. (1998). *The psychotherapy relationship: Theory, research, and practice.* New York: Wiley.

Greenberg, L. S. (1986). Change process research. *Journal of Consulting and Clinical Psychology, 54*, 4–9.

Greenberg, L. S., Heatherington, L., & Friedlander, M. L. (1996). The events-based approach to couple and family therapy research. In D. H. Sprenkle & S. M.

Moon (Eds.), *Research methods in family therapy* (pp. 411–428). New York: Guilford Press.

Hill, C. E., & Williams, E. N. (2000). The process of individual therapy. In S. D. Brown & R. W. Lent (Eds.), *Handbook of counseling psychology* (pp. 670–710). Hoboken, NJ: Wiley.

Ladany, N. (2004). Psychotherapy supervision: What lies beneath. *Psychotherapy Research, 14,* 1–19.

Ladany, N., Friedlander, M. L., & Nelson, M. L. (2005). *Critical events in psychotherapy supervision: An interpersonal approach.* Washington, DC: American Psychological Association.

Rice, L., & Greenberg, L. S. (1984). *Patterns of change.* New York: Guildford Press.

Safran, J. D., Crocker, P., McMain, S., & Murray, P. (1990). Therapeutic alliance rupture as a therapy event for empirical investigation. *Psychotherapy: Theory, Research, Practice, Training, 27,* 154–165.

IV

PERSPECTIVIES FROM BASIC PSYCHOLOGY AND PHILOSOPHY

17

COGNITIVE STRUCTURES AND MOTIVES AS BARRIERS TO INSIGHT: CONTRIBUTIONS FROM SOCIAL COGNITION RESEARCH

BETH E. HAVERKAMP AND TY D. TASHIRO

The phenomenon of insight has been defined as "an elucidating glimpse" (Morris, 1969, p. 679). Within psychotherapy, this may be a glimpse into one's self, one's relationships, or one's circumstances. The relationship between self and circumstance and between person and environment is the core subject matter of social psychology and, as such, the discipline has much to contribute to the understanding of insight. Our understanding of insight, and the definition we use in the present work, is that it represents a cognitive change characterized by a sense of immediate understanding and discernment. Within a social–cognitive framework, insight can be viewed as the product of an information search set in motion by an experience of cognitive incongruence. Such an information search may occur largely outside awareness; if and when the search produces a sense of resolution, one experiences that resolution as insight.

Social psychologists have documented many events that set off extensive, energetic cognitive processing (e.g., violations of expectations, persuasion attempts, receiving discrepant information about a central trait) and have identified factors that facilitate shifts in attitudes, perceptions, and beliefs. These contributions are highly relevant to psychotherapy (for a discussion, see Heppner & Frazier, 1992) but, historically, have not targeted the sense of immediate understanding and resolution that is connoted by the term insight. However, social psychology research can illuminate the search process after it is underway.

Social psychology research on the self is particularly relevant to understanding what may facilitate or impede the experience of insight; in this chapter, we adopt a conceptualization of the self as the crucible of insight to organize our review of selected social psychological research. The chapter covers three areas of research on the self that we consider central to understanding insight. The first concerns the cognitive structures that are likely to be accessed during an information search, as they constitute the information available for a search. The second area of research examines how positive and negative affect influences which material enters self-awareness, and the third explores motives that propel and influence a self-relevant cognitive search after it is underway. Because much of the research we discuss has emerged from the field of social cognition, the chapter begins with a brief discussion of social cognition concepts and their potential relationship to insight.

As we explore the relevance of social psychology research for insight, we want to alert readers that current theory and research permits stronger conclusions about mechanisms that inhibit insight compared with mechanisms that might facilitate insight. Although we believe psychotherapy researchers and practitioners have much to learn from this body of research, our suggestions for facilitating insight must be regarded as tentative and sometimes speculative and await future empirical scrutiny.

SOCIAL COGNITION

Social psychological research relevant to insight is embedded within the cognitive paradigm that currently dominates the field. With the advent of the cognitive revolution, social psychologists adopted information processing models of person perception and self-awareness, giving rise to the field of *social cognition*. Today, most social psychological research builds on this tradition (Oschner & Lieberman, 2001). A core dimension of this cognitive perspective can be traced to Heider (1958), who described perception as a constructive process. For each of us, the vast amount of incoming information is first filtered and is then interpreted in the context of existing beliefs, motives, and ongoing external activity. As a result, our perceptions of people and events may have little objective resemblance to the original stimulus or to perceptions received by others. Perceivers in the same circumstances can differ in their focus of attention, their labeling or categorization of what is observed, and in the inferences they draw from the observed person, behavior, or situation (Schneider, Hastorf, & Ellsworth, 1979). Recently, social psychologists have described cognitive structures and processes that influence our perceptions, and their findings are described in the following sections of this chapter.

Schemas

Inferences are influenced by what have been termed *cognitive schemas*, organized knowledge structures that exert a powerful influence on what one notices, remembers, and concludes from a situation (Baldwin, 1992; Markus, 1977). Schemas are presumed to reflect an individual's prior experience and provide the means of structuring experience and perception, filling gaps in information and directing the search for new information. *Self-schemas* are organized cognitions about the self and, like other schemas, influence the way a person processes information (Markus, 1977). There is no single self-schema that corresponds to one's sense of self; every individual appears to posses multiple self-schemas that may have little relationship to each other (Markus & Nurius, 1986). Once established, schema-based interpretations are highly resistant to change and can lead to the disregard or discounting of contradictory information (Bierhoff, 1989). In considering the question of insight, it should be noted that the cognitive incongruity that sets an information search in motion could arise from a contradiction in schema content, from a limitation in a schema's explanatory ability, or from activation of contradictory self-schemas.

As an example of the way schemas may influence inference, imagine the manner in which a client with an attachment history characterized by betrayal might view a therapist's warmth with suspicion; a client with a secure attachment history could experience the same behavior as an affirmation. Similarly, clients whose self-schemas assign differing levels of importance to the attribute *breadwinner* are likely to experience a job loss differently. In both cases, the experience of insight might consist of recognizing alternative views of the situation.

Although the role of schemas in directing attention and influencing inference is well established (Baldwin, 1992), there are other attributes of cognitive processing that influence readiness to consider new information and the conclusions that are drawn from such information. To cite a few influences, it is known that perception can be altered by the vividness of a stimulus, the order in which information is received, the personal salience of an event, and the operation of cognitive shortcuts, or heuristics (Nisbett & Ross, 1980). What one may have considered a logical decision-making process turns out to be highly susceptible to inferential error and self-serving motives. Two specific areas of cognition, attitude change and human inference, provide further illustration of information processing.

Attitude Change

Research on attitudes and attitude change is a hallmark of social psychology, one that has particular relevance to psychotherapy. Clients often seek help in changing maladaptive attitudes toward themselves, others, or their situation. Research demonstrates that many attitudes are highly resistant to change and that maintenance of new attitudes is associated with factors such as depth of processing, message quality, and personal relevance (Petty & Cacioppo, 1986; Petty & Wegener, 1998). Stoltenberg and McNeill (1987) cautioned that many instances of insight in psychotherapy may be characterized by clients' acquiescent adoption of new ideas following minimal levels of thought. New evidence has challenged prevailing theories of attitude change in suggesting that conscious evaluation of alternatives is not a necessary component of the change process. Studies examining reductions in cognitive dissonance indicate that attitude change does not require conscious reasoning and may be an automatic process under some circumstances (for a review, see Ochsner & Lieberman, 2001).

Human Inference

As people attempt to make sense of their own and others' behavior, they must engage in a process of inference, taking available information and forming conclusions. As noted previously, perception and inference are not random or neutral. In addition to the effects of cognitive structures such as schemas, cognitive psychologists have documented the operation of cognitive heuristics and biases that affect inference (Kahneman, Slovic, & Tversky, 1982). The availability and representative heuristics, confirmatory bias, and reconstructive memory, discussed later in the chapter, may function as barriers to insight. We discuss self-serving bias, another potent influence on perception, in sections that consider self-knowledge.

Nisbett and Ross (1980) described heuristics as simple but powerful judgmental strategies that people use to process information in a rapid, effortless manner. They are applied automatically, without conscious intent. Although they are highly adaptive and accurate in the majority of cases, they can produce inferential errors and may operate as barriers to insight. The availability heuristic describes the fact that when people are called on to estimate the frequency or likelihood of an event, their estimates are influenced by the relative availability or accessibility of events in memory. For example, a therapist may encourage a socially anxious client to practice approaching strangers at a party. The client, in trying to imagine the response he or she will receive, is likely to be influenced by the relative accessibility of anxiety-provoking encounters remembered from prior social events.

The representativeness heuristic is used when people are faced with judgments involving categorization and is characterized by the application of basic "goodness of fit" criteria to determine the similarity of a new situation to one's existing categories of judgment. For example, our socially anxious client may try to judge whether a stranger at the party is open to conversation or not. Representativeness judgments often are prey to what is termed the *base rate fallacy* or a failure, in this case, to consider what proportion of people at a party are likely to be interested in meeting new people. With regard to insight, a client's appreciation of the automaticity of these heuristics and the possibility of error may help them generate alternate adaptive inferences.

Confirmatory Bias and Reconstructive Memory

Confirmatory bias is a form of active, selective attention for information that confirms one's existing judgments or perceptions and can exert significant influence after an information search is set in motion. After an impression is formed, the human mind typically seeks information consistent with the impression and ignores or actively discredits information that could contradict, or disconfirm, that impression (Snyder & Swann, 1976). This tendency is widespread and resistant to change and has been documented in depressed individuals (Dykman & Abramson, 1990) and in counselors (Haverkamp, 1993). Reconstructive memory is another process in which schemas direct an information search, in this case using current beliefs and feelings to fill gaps in memory (Ross & Buehler, 1994). Asked to recall an event, one may construct a seamless narrative that combines both experienced and imagined elements to produce a coherent whole.

The party-going, socially anxious client might exhibit both a confirmation bias and reconstructive memory. He is likely to perceive nonverbal signals that he is intruding on an existing conversation, as such cues fit his existing belief that he will not be welcomed. At the same time, he is likely to miss or dismiss a smile or verbal greeting that could be interpreted as welcoming him into a conversational group. Later in the evening, in response to a roommate's question about the party, he may even generate memories of a rude encounter or perceived slight, even though there is no objective evidence of such encounters.

To summarize, one's existing beliefs and expectations exert a powerful influence on what one notices, what one disregards, and even what one thinks one has noticed. To consider these tendencies relative to the question of what promotes insight, one must conclude that beliefs and expectations can operate as powerful barriers to viewing the self and one's situations in a new light. To provide a more explicit examination of this issue, we turn to social psychology's contributions in the realm of the self, the primary locus of psychotherapy's concerns with insight.

THE SELF AS THE CRUCIBLE OF INSIGHT

Social psychology's key contributions to understanding insight are based in the field's historical interest in the broad domain of self-knowledge and self-evaluation and can be traced back to William James's (1892) formulations of multiple social selves and his conception of the *me* (*what is known*) and the *I* (*the knower*). James described the *me* as the object of attention and reflection; it can be considered the *content* component of the self and includes multiple selves. The *I* is the *process* component and consists of the active, conscious, thinking aspect of self. The *I* is the self that reflects on and evaluates the *me*. With regard to insight, one could say that it is the *I* that experiences elucidating glimpses of the *me* and its hidden selves.

James's (1892) ideas continue to be influential. Building on these historical foundations, social psychological research on the self has ranged from descriptions of its structure and content to investigations of factors that motivate the encoding, retrieval, and construal of self-relevant material. Recently, social cognitive researchers have pursued a third domain of inquiry, that of automatic and unconscious processes that precede self-awareness. Although social psychologists have not provided a definitive answer to the question, "What is insight?" their findings can contribute to the understanding of which factors may facilitate or impede its emergence, and we discuss them in the following sections.

Cognitive Structures

Insight in psychotherapy is often concerned with making connections between aspects of the self that are in contradiction or with illuminating aspects that are hidden from awareness. Considering how self-concept and self-relevant memory are structured can provide clues to how such information may be accessed in the occurrence of insight. Social psychologists view the self-concept as arising from a broad and diverse family of self-schemas, cognitive structures that contain information about the self. Schemas direct our attention, memory, and evaluation with regard to self-relevant information and play an influential role in what enters self-awareness. For example, when one encounters information relevant to one's self-concept, the brain processes it more rapidly than other types of information and is more likely to store it in memory (Symons & Johnson, 1997). This suggests that if a therapist offers information that falls outside a client's current self-schemas, it is less likely to enter awareness or memory. Additionally, one's behavior is influenced by which self-schema is most accessible in memory. Fazio, Effrein, and Falender (1981) demonstrated that when alternate views of the self were activated (understood as activation of alternate self-schemas), people were induced to think and behave in new ways, which suggests that deliberate attention to less favored but more adaptive views of the self could be therapeutically useful.

Schematic formulations of the self are consistent with views of self-structure as a dynamic process that is characterized by continual reconstruction and reinterpretation of experience (Cantor & Kihlstrom, 1987). With increased experience, schemas grow in elaboration and complexity and can shift to accommodate new information, albeit slowly (Markus, 1983). Domains viewed as central to an individual's self-concept are associated with richly elaborated, well-organized, and highly accessible schemas (Markus, 1977), although such developed schemas are more resistant to change. A client whose insight produces a tentative shift toward a more positive self-concept might benefit from understanding that additional experience is required to solidify the new view and that integration of the new self-concept is likely to be a slow process.

The importance of social psychological models of self-structure rests in their implications for the accessibility of self-relevant information and, consequently, which material may be available for the emergence of insight. Markus (1977) and others have postulated the existence of numerous possible selves—past and future selves, desired and feared selves—and noted that the levels of association, interconnectedness, congruence, and accessibility of these subdomains of self-concept will vary across and within persons (Cantor & Kihlstrom, 1987). Although one's conscious perception of self may feel like a well-integrated and coherent whole, "the full stock of self-knowledge, however, is free to contain gaps, contradictions, inconsistencies, and plenty of material that is at best very loosely connected together" (Baumeister, 1999, p. 5).

Network theories of memory (Smith, 1996) have generated increasing interest in social psychology and provide a useful framework for thinking about the manner in which connections between divergent elements of the self are organized in cognitive structures. Although research has not linked this material to insight, it seems likely that learning more about the connections between self-relevant memories could inform our efforts to promote such connections. According to associative network theories, elements of different experiences are encoded into clusters or networks, rather than as discrete elements (Anderson, 1995). For example, perceptions made by a socially anxious client at a party may include various individual elements (e.g., music, people, anxiety) that are stored together in a memory network, not as separate elements. Because elements of a given experience are stored together in networks, recall of a few elements often activates entire networks. When new information is perceived (e.g., a crowded, new restaurant) elements stored in a given network may be activated (e.g., music, people).

The presence of some elements from a given memory network may then lower the threshold of accessibility to the entire cluster, including emotions (e.g., anxiety). Once the entire memory network is activated, it may assimilate new information into existing networks. Thus, our socially anxious client may find that anxiety symptoms begin to generalize to a broader range of social situations as new experiences are encoded into existing memory networks containing cognitions and emotions related to social anxiety. As we discuss next, the affective components of memory networks may be the "glue" that holds together memory networks (Isen, 1987).

Affect and Social Cognition

Although emotional reactions are implicated in the storage of experience in memory, a more compelling question concerns whether emotion facilitates or inhibits insight. Social psychological research on affect and social cognition typically focuses on the way emotion affects subsequent cognition (see Forgas, 2002; Aspinwall, 1998, for reviews). One theoretical approach in this area has been affect priming theory (Bower, 1981; Isen, 1987), which suggests that emotions are stored with other elements in memory networks. Of importance is the fact that particular memory networks do not have to be activated by cognition but can also be activated by experiencing emotion in the network (Isen, 1987), which appears relevant to questions of promoting insight.

Negative emotion typically serves the function of narrowing selective attention to the threatening aspects of the environment and activating physiological preparation for fight-or-flight behaviors (Fridja, 1994). Such selectivity can be adaptive because these cognitive and behavioral outcomes prepare individuals to cope with immediate threats. At the same time, a narrow cognitive focus could reduce the chance of forming links between previous cognitive structures and new information. This suggests that under conditions of negative emotion a narrowed cognitive focus could impede the emergence of insight.

Less is known about the function of positive emotion, but recent advances suggest that positive emotion may signal an absence of threat. This allows individuals the luxury of broadening cognitive focus and may even lead to memory recall of larger and more integrated memory networks (Isen, 1987). Furthermore, unlike the association between negative emotions and tendencies to engage in fight-or-flight behaviors, positive emotions seem to have no clear behavioral outcomes and in some cases may result in a decreased probability of action. Previous studies have found that compared with participants in neutral or negative affective states, participants experiencing positive emotion perform better on tests of creativity and engage in more unusual and adaptive negotiation behaviors, and children were able to solve complex tasks more quickly (Fredrickson, 1998). By implication, researchers may find that activation of positive emotion acts to facilitate insight when clients are motivated to engage complex problem-solving tasks. In the next section, we move from our review of cognitive structures to focusing on how motivated cognition can impede or foster insight.

Motivated Cognition

If cognitive structures approximate what is known (*me*), then motivated cognition most closely approximates the dimension of the self that actively searches for what is known (*I*). Social psychology research on motivated cognition provides valuable information about why some individuals are able to function with a chronic lack of insight and which situations may motivate individuals to achieve insight. Motivated cognition studies also introduce important theoretical and empirical questions concerning the quality of insight. That is, although achieving insight is one outcome, an entirely different question concerns whether the insight achieved is both accurate and useful. In the sections that follow we review motives for maintaining cognitive consistency and self-enhancing cognition, and the ways these seemingly competing motives illuminate questions concerning the accuracy and usefulness of insight. We conclude with a brief review of how relational contexts and affect can moderate when enhancement and consistency motives operate and review implications for insight in psychotherapy.

Maintaining Consistency

Why is a pattern of maladaptive thought or behavior obvious to an outside observer within minutes but unclear to the individual in question for years? In other words, why does insight not occur for such individuals? Part of this answer may lie in the robust finding that, under certain conditions, individuals prefer to have their world remain predictable and controllable rather than entertain information inconsistent with their current worldview. This desire for predictability can occur even though information inconsistent with one's current views is more accurate and useful. Self-verification theory is based on the notion that individuals are motivated to maintain consistency in their self-conceptions and do so in part by seeking feedback from others that is consistent with current self-conceptions (Swann, 1987). Because cognition about one's personality or beliefs is an abstract process, people often rely on social consensus from others to affirm abstract self-conceptions. Taken as a whole, self-verification processes are likely to serve as barriers to insight.

Numerous studies have found support for self-verification by demonstrating that individuals actively choose interaction partners who are most likely to confirm their self-conceptions and that individuals actively shape discussions in ways that lead others to provide self-verifying feedback. In addition, people selectively attend to self-verifying feedback, have better memory for self-verifying information, and perceive it as more credible than feedback that is inconsistent with self-conceptions (Swann, Pelham, & Krull, 1989). This tendency to seek self-verifying feedback not only applies to self-conceptions that are positive but also to self-conceptions that are negative. For example, depressed individuals are more likely than nondepressed individuals to seek out personal feedback that is negative and consistent with their negative view of themselves (Swann, 1997). Such individuals actively seek out interaction partners and selectively attend to information that will maintain their negative self-conceptions through self-verification.

We noted earlier that insight may result from an information search set in motion by an awareness of incongruity. However, even when people are forced to think about information from others that is inconsistent with current self-conceptions, people can regain cognitive consistency through dissonance reduction strategies (see Harmon-Jones & Mills, 1999, for a review). Cognitive dissonance occurs when individuals are faced with inconsistencies between two competing cognitions or when behavior and cognition are inconsistent. For example, a depressed client on the way to a party may have competing cognitions such as, "I want to make more friends," and "Nobody is going to like me." Because dissonance produces aversive negative affect (such as anxiety for the depressed client in this example), individuals are motivated to reduce the dissonance through changing their cognitions (e.g., "I will not want to be friends with anyone at this party anyway") or more rarely, by changing a behavior (e.g., going home). There is no evidence that dissonance on its own facilitates insight; instead, individuals are motivated to maintain cognitive consistency through dissonance reduction strategies, even when such rationalizations are not adaptive.

Although it is generally easier to modify cognitions, there are certainly instances when individuals change behavior to maintain consistency. Behavioral confirmation occurs when beliefs arising from one's own volition or the expectations of others lead to congruent behavioral realities (Snyder & Stukas, 1999). In other words, individuals' preexisting beliefs can shape the response they receive from others. For example, rejection-sensitive individuals tend to engage in maladaptive behaviors (e.g., jealous behaviors because they think they will be rejected) that actually serve to distance others from them (Downey & Feldman, 1996). Even when people try to change their behaviors they may encounter continued expectations from previous interaction partners to behave in a typical manner, which makes behavioral change difficult. Thus, consistency in beliefs and behavior can be maintained through a cycle of wanting to maintain consistency between personal expectations or the expectations of others and current behaviors, which may further decrease the chance that insight will emerge.

Although motivations to maintain cognitive consistency help explain why people can be resistant to insight, knowing how cognitive consistency operates can also provide a framework for devising strategies to facilitate insight. For example, adaptive insight can be produced through self-verification when individuals possess adequate cognitive resources and self-knowledge. In a series of experimental studies investigating insight and self-reflection, participants displayed more accurate self-understanding and more self-verifying interpersonal behaviors when they were given adequate time and freed of other cognitive responsibilities (e.g., holding a cognitive load; Hixon & Swann, 1993). In practice, this could translate into encouraging clients to create adequate pockets of time and freedom from other daily worries between sessions to increase opportunities for insight into their concerns. Although dissonance can impede progress by maintaining consistency in the face of incongruent information, dissonance inductions and providing well-thought-out routes for dissonance reduction can facilitate insight or change behavior in a positive manner (Aronson, 1999). For example, therapists use this strategy effectively when they use confrontation to point out contradictions between what clients believe (e.g., "I would like to make more friends") and how they are behaving (e.g., going back home instead of going to a party). When clients try to reduce the dissonance between beliefs and behavior by rationalizing (e.g., "No one will like me anyway"), therapists close off these cognitive routes to dissonance reduction (e.g., "You never went, so how do you know?"), which may force clients to consider behavioral change.

The behavioral confirmation framework could be applicable to establishing novel expectations in a therapeutic relationship that are more adaptive than the expectations held by those in the client's social networks. As Swann (1997) pointed out, however, a client's improved self-views that are achieved in therapy may be undone by individuals in the clients' social network whose expectations for familiar behavior activate a behavioral confirmation process. Future studies may investigate whether healthier expectations by a therapist may eventually lead to behavioral confirmation in response to these new, more adaptive expectations in therapy and whether these new behaviors may generalize to other social situations. The possibility that motivated cognition for consistency could provide a framework for facilitating insight, rather than primarily explaining why people have a lack of insight, is intriguing. However, the ideas listed are speculative at this point; future translational research is needed to bring these basic science findings into applied practice.

Self-Enhancement

Another line of motivated cognition research has examined the motive to inflate self-evaluations, a process generally labeled as *positive illusions* or *unrealistic optimism*. Given that many therapeutic insights involve awareness of less flattering aspects of the self, this well-established motive may serve as a tenacious barrier to insight. Across a broad range of domains, most people tend to see themselves as possessing better skills, personality traits, and abilities than the average person, and they also tend to inflate their self-ratings well above ratings provided by observers (see Taylor & Brown, 1988, for a review). By definition, self-enhancement is presumed to reflect a biased perspective, as not everyone can be above average. Mechanisms for self-enhancement include downward social comparison to others (e.g., "He's making less money than I am"), making internal attributions for successes (e.g., "I'm a great salesman!"), but making external attributions for failures (e.g., "No one will buy this lousy product"), and perceiving positive self-improvements over time when no objective improvement has occurred (e.g., "I'm putting in more time than my time sheet shows"; Taylor & Brown, 1988).

Although the data suggest that self-enhancement is inaccurate, research generally suggests that it is associated with higher self-esteem, more positive affect, better coping in the face of adversity, favorable life events, and better physiological responses to stress (e.g., Taylor, Lerner, Sherman, Sage, & McDowell, 2003a, 2003b). In further support of the usefulness of self-enhancement, studies have found that depressed people, one subset of individuals who appear not to engage in as much self-enhancement, are generally more accurate in their understanding of how others see them and in their expectations of future events. Some studies have found that high self-enhancers are susceptible to some negative outcomes, such as narcissistic features, foolish risk taking, and social exclusion (Sedikides, Herbst, Hardin, & Dardis, 2002); however, for most people self-enhancing is associated with favorable psychological and physiological outcomes.

The collective data suggest that self-enhancement is probably a barrier to insight for most individuals because it is by definition inaccurate, and the self-enhancer is probably motivated to continue inflating self-evaluations because they produce numerous psychological benefits (e.g., positive affect). Currently, the self-enhancement literature speaks indirectly to insight in psychotherapy; therefore, questions regarding insight and intervention await further empirical study.

Enhancement Versus Consistency and the Role of Accurate Cognition

At first glance it might appear that there is a contradiction between self-verification, (representing a desire for consistent accuracy) and self-enhancement (representing a desire for consistent, inaccurate, positive cognition). However, integrative studies pitting the two theories against each other have found that both motives can operate within the same person, as most people have both positive and negative self-conceptions that vary by different domains. When given free choice, individuals tend to self-enhance by selectively seeking positive feedback. However, when faced with both their best and worst attributes, they self-verify, seeking favorable feedback for their best attribute and negative feedback regarding their worst attribute

(Swann et al., 1989). It appears that people prefer to self-enhance when given free choice and self-verify those positive self-conceptions; however, when faced with negative personal attributes, individuals would rather self-verify than self-enhance. Studies have also examined how the relationship context (Reis, Collins, & Berscheid, 2000) can affect motivated cognition.

Studies investigating the moderating role of the relationship context found that cognitions regarding the self were more likely to change when participants engaged in behaviors publicly rather than privately (Tice, 1992). Participants randomly assigned to behave in an emotionally responsive manner were more likely to view themselves as possessing stable, emotionally responsive traits compared with those in an emotional stability or control group. However, these subsequent changes in self-concept were stronger when behaviors were performed in public rather than privately. This suggests that a client's adaptive insight (e.g., "I am likeable to others") will lead to a stronger change in self-concept if she or he is able to act on that insight in the presence of others. Other studies examining the moderating effects of the relationship context on self-enhancement found that being held accountable by having one's self-views become identifiable to another person significantly attenuated self-enhancement strategies. It appears that accountability reduces self-enhancement by increasing individuals' consideration of personal weaknesses in a given domain (Sedikides et al., 2002). Extending these findings to therapy, it may be that therapists could provide a source of accountability for clients or help them become accountable to others in their social network, thereby curtailing excessive self-enhancement.

Affect can also impact motivated cognition for self-enhancement versus accuracy. Negative feedback regarding the self can be useful because it conveys accurate diagnostic information that can be used to improve future life circumstances; however, it also carries the immediate cost of negative feelings. Research on self-verification suggests that most individuals seek negative feedback from others only when their choice of whether to consider negative self-attributes has been constrained. However, people can become self-motivated to seek out negative feedback in laboratory settings when randomly assigned to positive versus neutral or negative mood conditions (Raghunathan & Trope, 2002). Positive mood appears to serve as a resource that buffers individuals against the blow of negative feelings that accompanies negative feedback. Caffeine consumers in a positive mood demonstrated interest in negative feedback regarding caffeine consumption, displayed better memory recall of negative information about caffeine, and reported more intentions to change behaviors compared with consumers in negative moods. These differences were much stronger for participants who were high caffeine consumers compared with those who consumed less caffeine, suggesting that the preference for negative feedback in a positive mood operates when the negative feedback is self-relevant. Similar findings regarding more receptiveness to negative self-relevant feedback and accurate cognition have been reported for people high in optimism (Aspinwall & Richter, 1999). Thus, beyond broadening cognitive processes and encouraging creative problem-solving, positive emotion may reduce individuals' tendency to focus primarily on self-enhancing feedback and may motivate exploration for self-relevant negative feedback. This presents a challenge in the therapeutic domain, as negative affect is common in this context and clients experiencing sadness, anger, or fear may be less able to process negative information about the self. Alternately, these findings indirectly suggest that deliberate mood enhancement may facilitate self-exploration. Inviting clients to engage in activities that produce positive emotion (e.g., deep relaxation, positive imagery, or use of humor) prior to discussion of negative self-relevant information might facilitate client attention to difficult feedback.

In summary, recent findings in social psychology on motivated cognition suggest that individuals generally seek to self-enhance when freely choosing cognitive focus. However, there are certainly limits to self-enhancement, as most individuals will actually seek verification from others that is negative when contemplating a negative self-relevant domain. These effects can be strengthened or weakened by varying the relationship context or affective states. Although self-enhancement, self-verification, dissonance reduction, and behavioral confirmation can impede insight through maintaining consistency (self-verification) or inaccuracy (self-enhancement), these same frameworks may hold promise for facilitating insight. As noted in chapter 3 of this volume, cognitive therapists have developed a wide range of interventions to help clients challenge inaccurate self-perceptions. We encourage researchers to investigate whether coupling these techniques with mood enhancement and with varying relationship contexts may enhance their effectiveness in producing insight. The basic research in this area offers tantalizing hypotheses for psychotherapists, and we encourage future translational research to investigate their applicability to practice.

NEW DIRECTIONS: AUTOMATICITY AND ABSTRACTION

Whereas the self's efforts to exert control in managing emotion and thought are well established, recent research has emphasized automatic processes that do not appear to be associated with the self's conscious executive function. These issues are being addressed within the new, interdisciplinary field of social cognitive neuroscience. Its researchers are examining the interactions between social and motivational factors, information processing at the cognitive level, and neurological structures and brain mechanisms (Oschner & Lieberman, 2001).

Researchers investigating automatic, unconscious thought are pursuing issues that appear closely related to the process of insight, although this has not been their explicit target. They have learned that our minds have the capacity to process—and integrate—large amounts of information outside conscious awareness (Betsch, Plessner, Schwieren, & Gutig, 2001). Within this form of thinking, associations between cognitive categories or structures can occur rapidly and may lead to novel outcomes. This relates to our earlier discussion of network theories of memory (Smith, 1996), as it may be that unconscious thought is able to scan a larger number of network elements, thereby increasing the chance that creative associations and connections will be made. This description of goal-directed thought, occurring outside awareness, offers a tantalizing parallel to whatever events may precede the sudden *Aha!* that characterizes a moment of insight. In a similar vein, Dijksterhuis (2004) drew on research on *incubation*, a process in which the unconscious offers a solution to a problem that one has consciously ignored. He conducted a series of five experiments in which researchers elicited decisions from people who were either focused on or distracted from a decision task. In each case those engaged in unconscious decision making produced higher quality decisions, supporting a conclusion that unconscious thought can be effective in complex decision tasks.

Another area of recent research with implications for the production of insight is concerned with how mental representations are construed. Forster, Friedman and Liberman (2004) noted that solution of creativity tasks is enhanced when problem elements are construed at a high level of abstraction, as opposed to specific and concrete levels of representation. They designed a series of studies to test the proposition that thinking about a problem within a future time frame as opposed to the present "activates general processes of representational abstraction that facilitate subsequent attempts at insight problem solving and creative generation" (p. 179). Each of six experiments supported their contention that a distant future time perspective enhanced measured insight and creative performance. The authors interpreted their results as indicating a shift from concrete to abstract mental representation, and argue that such a shift enhances insight and creativity. One cannot help but wonder whether clients, if directed to think about their problems in a future time frame, would experience a similar increase in creativity and insight.

CONCLUDING COMMENTS

We began this chapter by describing the experience of insight as an elucidating glimpse, and in an attempt to characterize factors that may facilitate or impede such cognitive shifts we have drawn on social cognition research on cognitive structures and motives that may be implicated in this process. We close by taking a step back and asking, "What does social psychology offer the clinician or the psychotherapy process researcher with regard to insight?" Our primary conclusion is that insight is a process of self-perception; as such, we recommend attention to what social psychologists have learned about perceptual processes in general. This could involve exploring the role of cognitive schemas and heuristics, of cognitive structures associated with the self, and of motives such as self-verification and self-enhancement. Each has been shown to be highly influential in directing self-relevant cognition, and it would be surprising if such processes were not related to the phenomenon of insight.

We note that social psychological research has contributed more to identification of barriers to insight than to facilitating factors. At the same time, we believe that both clients and clinicians are likely to benefit from increased familiarity with the cognitive barriers identified. Explicit discussion of motives such as self-enhancement, for example, could increase a client's awareness of this largely automatic tendency and perhaps enhance his or her ability to monitor and resist its application. Similarly, clients who understand that they possess multiple self-schemas may find it easier to access alternative, more adaptive, views of the self.

Finally, recent research on creative problem solving that occurs largely outside of conscious awareness appears to be highly relevant to psychotherapeutic research and practice. Our primary conclusion after reviewing these studies is that therapists may be able to help clients access their innate, creative problem-solving abilities by adopting several basic practices. First, it appears that engendering positive emotion can help clients adopt a broader cognitive focus that in turn may facilitate more creative problem solving. Second, helping clients approach problems at high levels of abstraction, whether by construing decisions in a future time frame or by offering distractions from a linear, logical decision process, appears to help the mind access novel solutions. Schooler, Ohlsson, and Brooks (1993) found that conscious attention can actually reduce the likelihood of insight. They presented people with a series of insight puzzles, and those who were asked to report on how they were trying to solve the problem were able to solve 30% fewer puzzles. The authors concluded that the cognitive demand of focusing on one's thoughts interferes with the background "scanning" that is associated with the appearance of insight. To facilitate insight for clients, it may be more important to enhance the conscious desire for resolution than to enhance the conscious evaluation of content.

As we note at several points in this chapter, little social psychological research has targeted the therapeutic experience of insight directly; however, we maintain that this area of research has significant implications for understanding insight. In fact, the integrative approach that now characterizes social–cognitive research is producing results that may signal a new chapter in understanding the phenomenon of insight. Whereas most experimental insight research has employed linguistic and spatial puzzles, psychotherapy researchers can contribute their familiarity with insights that have high salience and personal relevance. We believe that the efforts of social–cognitive

basic science researchers can be enhanced by the contributions of psychotherapy researchers, and we look forward to their mutual collaboration.

REFERENCES

Anderson, J. A. (1995). Associative networks. In M. A. Arbib (Ed.), *Handbook of brain theory and neural networks* (pp. 102–107). Cambridge, MA: MIT Press.

Aronson, E. (1999). Dissonance, hypocrisy, and the self-concept. In E. Harmon-Jones and J. Mills (Eds.), *Cognitive dissonance: Progress on a pivotal theory in social psychology* (pp. 103–126). Washington, DC: American Psychological Association.

Aspinwall, L. G. (1998). Rethinking the role of positive affect in self-regulation. *Motivation and Emotion, 22*, 1–32.

Aspinwall, L. G., & Richter, L. (1999). Optimism and self-mastery predict more rapid disengagement from unsolvable tasks in the presence of alternatives. *Motivation and Cognition, 23*, 221–246.

Baldwin, M. W. (1992). Relational schemas and the processing of social information. *Psychological Bulletin, 112*, 461–484.

Baumeister, R. F. (1999). The nature and structure of the self: An overview. In R. F. Baumeister (Ed.), *The self in social psychology* (pp. 1–20). Levittown, PA: Psychology Press.

Betsch, T., Plessner, H., Schwieren, C., & Gutig, R. (2001). I like it but I don't know why: A value account approach to implicit attitude formation. *Personality and Social Psychology Bulletin, 27*, 242–253.

Bierhoff, H. W. (1989). *Person perception and attribution.* New York: Springer-Verlag.

Bower, G. H. (1981). Mood and memory. *American Psychologist, 36*, 129–148.

Cantor, N., & Kihlstrom, J. F. (1987). *Personality and social intelligence.* Englewood Cliffs, NJ: Prentice Hall.

Dijksterhuis, A. (2004). Think different: The merits of unconscious thought in preference development and decision making. *Journal of Personality and Social Psychology, 87*, 586–598.

Downey, G., & Feldman, S. I. (1996). Implications of rejection sensitivity for intimate relationships. *Journal of Personality and Social Psychology, 70*, 1327–1343.

Dykman, B., & Abramson, L. (1990). Contributions of basic research to cognitive theories of depression. *Personality and Social Psychology Bulletin, 16*, 42–57.

Fazio, R. H., Effrein, E. A., & Falender, V. J. (1981). Self-perceptions following social interaction. *Journal of Personality and Social Psychology, 41*, 232–242.

Forgas, J. P. (2002). Feeling and doing: Affective influences on interpersonal behavior. *Psychological Inquiry, 13*, 1–28.

Forster, J., Friedman, R. S., & Liberman, N. (2004). Temporal construal effects on abstract and concrete thinking: Consequences for insight and creative cognition. *Journal of Personality and Social Psychology, 87*, 177–189.

Fredrickson, B. L. (1998). What good are positive emotions? *Review of General Psychology, 2*, 300–319.

Frijda, N. H. (1994). Emotions are functional, most of the time. In P. Ekman & R. J. Davidson (Eds.), *The nature of emotion: Fundamental questions* (pp. 112–122). New York: Oxford University Press.

Harmon-Jones, E., & Mills, J. (1999). *Cognitive dissonance: Progress on a pivotal theory in social psychology.* Washington, DC: American Psychological Association.

Haverkamp, B. (1993). Confirmatory bias in hypothesis testing for client-identified and counselor self-generated hypotheses. *Journal of Counseling Psychology, 40,* 303–315.

Heider, F. (1958). *The psychology of interpersonal relations.* New York: Wiley.

Heppner, P. P., & Frazier, P. A. (1992). Social psychological processes in psychotherapy: Extrapolating basic research to counseling psychology. In S. D. Brown & R. W. Lent (Eds.), *Handbook of counseling psychology* (2nd ed., pp. 141–176). New York: Wiley.

Hixon, J. G., & Swann, W. B., Jr. (1993). When does introspection bear fruit? Self-reflection, self-insight, and interpersonal choices. *Journal of Personality and Social Psychology, 64,* 35–43.

Isen, A. M. (1987). Positive affect, cognitive processes, and social behavior. In L. Berkowitz (Ed.), *Advances in experimental and social psychology* (pp. 203–253). New York: Academic Press.

James, W. (1892). *Psychology: The briefer course.* New York: Holt.

Kahneman, D., Slovic, P., & Tversky, A. (Eds.). (1982). *Judgment under uncertainty: Heuristics and biases.* New York: Cambridge University Press.

Markus, H. (1977). Self-schemata and processing information about the self. *Journal of Personality and Social Psychology, 35,* 63–78.

Markus, H. (1983). Self-knowledge: An expanded view. *Journal of Personality, 51,* 543–565.

Markus, H., & Nurius, P. (1986). Possible selves. *American Psychologist, 41,* 954–969.

Morris, W. (Ed.). (1969). *American Heritage Dictionary of the English Language.* New York: American Heritage.

Nisbett, R., & Ross, L. (1980). *Human inference: Strategies and shortcomings of social judgment.* Englewood Cliffs, NJ: Prentice Hall.

Ochsner, K. N., & Lieberman, M. D. (2001). The emergence of social cognitive neuroscience. *American Psychologist, 56,* 717–734.

Petty, R. E., & Cacioppo, J. T. (1986). *Communication and persuasion: Central and peripheral routes to attitude change.* New York: Springer-Verlag.

Petty, R. E., & Wegener, D. T. (1998). Attitude change: Multiple roles for persuasion variables. In D. Gilbert, S. Fiske, & G. Lindzey (Eds.), *The handbook of social psychology* (4th ed., Vol. 1, pp. 323–390). New York: McGraw-Hill.

Raghunathan, R., & Trope, Y. (2002). Walking the tightrope between feeling good and being accurate: Mood as a resource in processing persuasive messages. *Journal of Personality and Social Psychology, 83*, 510–525.

Reis, H. T., Collins, W. A., & Berscheid, E. (2000). The relationship context of human behavior and development. *Psychological Bulletin, 126*, 844–872.

Ross, M., & Buehler, R. (1994). Creative remembering. In U. Neisser & R. Fivush (Eds.), *The remembering self* (pp. 205–235). New York: Cambridge University Press.

Schneider, D. J., Hastorf, A. H., & Ellsworth, P. C. (1979). *Person perception* (2nd ed.). Menlo Park, CA: Addison Wesley.

Schooler, J. W., Ohlsson, S., & Brooks, K. (1993). Thoughts beyond words: When language overshadows insight. *Journal of Experimental Psychology, 122*, 166–183.

Sedikides, C., Herbst, K. C., Hardin, D. P., & Dardis, G. J. (2002). Accountability as a deterrent to self-enhancement: The search for mechanisms. *Journal of Personality and Social Psychology, 83*, 592–605.

Smith, E. R. (1996). What do connectionism and social psychology offer each other? *Journal of Personality and Social Psychology, 70*, 893–912.

Snyder, M., & Stukas, A. A., Jr. (1999). Interpersonal processes: The interplay of cognitive, motivational, and behavioral activities in social interaction. *Annual Review of Psychology, 50*, 273–303.

Snyder, M., & Swann, W. B., Jr. (1976). When actions reflect attitudes: The politics of impression management. *Journal of Personality and Social Psychology, 34*, 1034–1042.

Stoltenberg, C. D., & McNeill, B. W. (1987). Counseling and persuasion: Extrapolating the elaboration likelihood model. In J. E. Maddux, C. D. Stoltenberg, & R. Rosenwein (Eds.), *Social processes in clinical and counseling psychology* (pp. 56–67). New York: Springer-Verlag.

Swann, W. B., Jr. (1987). Identity negotiation: Where two roads meet. *Journal of Personality and Social Psychology, 53*, 1038–1051.

Swann, W. B., Jr. (1997). The trouble with change: Self-verification and allegiance to the self. *Psychological Science, 8*, 177–180.

Swann, W. B., Jr., Pelham, B. W., & Krull, D. S. (1989). Agreeable fancy or disagreeable truth? How people reconcile their self-enhancement and self-verification needs. *Journal of Personality and Social Psychology, 57*, 782–791.

Symons, C. S., & Johnson, B. T. (1997). The self-reference effect in memory: A meta-analysis. *Psychological Bulletin, 121*, 371–394.

Taylor, A. E., & Brown, J. D. (1988). Illusion and well-being: A social psychological perspective on mental health. *Psychological Bulletin, 103*, 193–210.

Taylor, S. E., Lerner, J. S., Sherman, D. K., Sage, R. M., & McDowell, N. K. (2003a). Are self-enhancing cognitions associated with healthy or unhealthy biological profiles? *Journal of Personality and Social Psychology, 85*, 605–615.

Taylor, S. E., Lerner, J. S., Sherman, D. K., Sage, R. M., & McDowell, N. K. (2003b). Portrait of the self-enhancer: Well-adjusted and well-liked or maladjusted and friendless? *Journal of Personality and Social Psychology, 84,* 165–176.

Tice, D. M. (1992). Self-presentation and self-concept changes: The looking glass self as magnifying glass. *Journal of Personality and Social Psychology, 63,* 435–451.

18

INSIGHT AND COGNITIVE PSYCHOLOGY

FRANZ CASPAR AND THOMAS BERGER

During World War I, the German-American psychologist Wolfgang Köhler studied the behavior of an ape locked in a cage without food but with two wooden poles. At a distance out of the reach of either pole, Köhler placed bananas. After trying various methods for reaching the food, the ape suddenly seemed to hit on a solution. By connecting the poles (which had sockets at their ends) the ape reached the food. Because there was no observable process such as trial and error learning to reveal how the ape arrived at the solution, Köhler, one of the founders of gestalt psychology, used the term *Einsicht* (*insight*) to describe this sudden grasping of a useful relationship (Köhler, 1927). He and other gestalt psychologists dedicated the term *insight* to designate the sudden emergence of a solution to a problem, without apparent step-by-step evolution of the solution (Mayer, 1995). Köhler found that learning can take place by *Aha!* experiences or all-or-nothing ideas. One either knows it or one does not. Of course, the phenomenon of insight was a big challenge to behaviorists and their idea of a negatively accelerating learning curve.

At the interface of clinical and cognitive psychology it makes sense to make two distinctions: Insight can be seen as a state or as a process, and it

TABLE 18.1
Definition of Insight With Regard to a State or a Process and a More General or Specific Phenomenon

	State	Process
General	All a patient knows about him- or herself as opposed to ignorance, lack of awareness	All processes leading to insight, incremental and rational processes included
More narrow, involving novelty	Creative, higher-level views and solutions	Only creative, original processes, *Eureka!–Aha!* experience, meaning shift

can be seen as a more general phenomenon or as more specifically related to novelty. This is represented in Table 18.1.

For many cognitive scientists insight is seen as a special *state of knowledge* and, as a consequence, *a special process of its acquisition*: Insight in the meaning of *novel states* represents seeing into the essence of a situation, and such a clear view is not gained by a step-by-step process (Gredler, 2001; Schooler, Fallshore, & Fiore, 1995). The idea that insight is a one-step function rather than a steady, incremental process has led some scientists to characterize and operationalize insight by the absence of incremental *feeling of warmth* ratings before a solution is found (warmth is a measure of how close a person feels he or she is to reaching a solution; Metcalfe & Wiebe, 1987). When an individual attempts to solve a problem, the belief that she or he is approaching a solution generally increases gradually. In an insightful sudden *Aha!*-type solution process, people report no change in warmth until immediately before solving the problem (Metcalfe, 1986). The insight experience, a *Eureka!* or *Aha!* reaction, is associated with the sudden emergence of a solution.

In the clinical field, the term *insight* is often used in the broad sense. If a patient has insight into his or her functioning or a specific aspect of it (as subjective knowledge about properties, facts, and how they are related), the insight has not necessarily been gained within a short time nor was it accompanied by an *Aha!* experience. Insight includes a conscious understanding, which may have been gained in a continuous and maybe tedious, incremental process. The opposite of insight in this broader sense is not *incremental elaboration* but rather *lacking insight,* in the sense of not knowing or not understanding. In addition, insight refers to the process of how insight is gained, with a broader (possibly without sudden shifts) or a more narrow (only *Aha!* type of process) view.

This chapter concentrates on insight as a state and as a process involving novelty. When asking for cognitive psychological foundations for insight, we thus primarily have to look for contributions dealing with insight in this more narrow sense; however, as the broader view may be relevant for understanding how insight in the narrow sense comes about and whether or not it can be used, the broader view will also be addressed to some extent. To distinguish further, we designate the *acquisition* of insight, whenever specification seems necessary, as *Insight A* (A = acquisition). The *body of insights* that a person has acquired (the sum of knowledge independent of how it was gained) is designated *Insight B* (B = body of insight).

The task for us in this chapter is to convey insight-related concepts as well as methods from cognitive psychology and cognitive science that might be useful for the field of clinical psychology and psychotherapy. In comparison to the emphasis in chapter 3, this volume, on insight in cognitive–behavioral therapy (CBT), this chapter emphasizes underlying nonclinical theories. In comparison to chapter 17, this volume, which emphasizes insight and social psychology, this chapter concentrates on cognitive approaches; the overlap, social cognition, is also covered in chapter 17. The authors of chapter 17 also deal in part with similar phenomena and findings on a macro level, whereas our chapter deals with them on a micro level. It is logical to assume that cognitive–psychological approaches cannot provide a complete basis for understanding all theoretical and practical issues related to insight, but this chapter attempts to demonstrate that they can contribute important concepts. Throughout the chapter, cognitive is not defined in a narrow sense but as including emotional, motivational, and to some extent biological, aspects.

MODELS FOR THE UNDERSTANDING OF INSIGHT

How does insight develop? Why do people who reach a solution sometimes have the *Aha!* experience? Cognitive psychology offers several general approaches with the potential for conceptualizing insight. In this context, a traditional model, connectionist (neural network) models, and combined regulation models can be distinguished.

Limits of Traditional Cognitive Models

Traditional cognitive psychological models are defined as models using elements such as schemata, scripts, plans, and so forth (Bartlett, 1932). A common metaphor used to describe these models is that of the *computer*. In effect, such models hold that there is organized information, stored in units, and that this information is processed in some way by homunculus-like[1] entities, similar to the way information is stored in computer files, processed, and manipulated by programs.

---

[1] A *homunculus* is a metaphorical little man or woman or entity in our head who pulls the levers for our thoughts and behavior. There is a whole tradition of (usually implicitly) assuming such an instance, and the critique of it.

The value of traditional models, such as schema models, is apparent in chapters 3 and 17, this volume, and is therefore not reiterated here. Their limits are illustrated by comments in chapter 17 by Haverkamp and Tashiro that the models used throughout the chapter are more suitable for explaining how insight is inhibited than for how it comes about. The power of these models lies in their ability to capture some aspects of human information processing in a straightforward manner that is easily communicated. The limits lie in their static nature: They emphasize structures rather than processes. This makes it difficult to understand dynamic processes on a micro level. As insight is a dynamic phenomenon by nature, we dedicate the larger part of this chapter to alternative models.

Despite different emphases, the majority of cognitive psychologists recognize that insight involves some kind of unconscious or intuitive problem solving. People seem to experience insight when they suddenly overcome an impasse as a result of some unconscious processing (Dominowski & Dallob, 1995) and built-up tension is released.

For decades cognitive psychologists have conceptualized unconscious or intuitive problem solving as nothing but fast, automated, analytical problem solving (Simon & Simon, 1978). Recently, this position was challenged by concepts like implicit learning (Reber & Squire, 1994), parallel holistic processing (J. D. Smith & Shapiro, 1989), or Epstein's cognitive–experiential self-theory (Epstein, 1985, 1994; see also chap. 3, this volume, in regard to the distinction between implicit and explicit mode–memory). Epstein posited two systems of processing. The *rational* system operates consciously, slowly, and effortfully and uses logical rules of inference. In contrast, the *experiential* system is intuitive and works relatively automatically, relying on heuristics. In spite of such expansions, traditional information processing approaches notoriously have difficulty explaining nonconscious, implicit, intuitive processing, which is reflected in their reluctance to acknowledge intuitive processing as an important, scientifically interesting, and acceptable part of human information processing.

Connectionist or Neural Network Models

Connectionist or neural network models, an alternative family of information processing models, emphasize parallel, distributed, subsymbolic, self-organized, holistic processing (Holyoak & Spellman, 1993; Rumelhart & McClelland, 1986; E. R. Smith & DeCoster, 2000; Smolensky, 1988). Such models are based on precise mathematic formulas, an explicit architecture of the information processing structures; they can be used not only metaphorically but also in concrete simulations of psychological processes, including clinical problems. Computer models developed in connectionism contribute to our understanding of possible mechanisms underlying unconscious, intuitive processing (Rumelhart & McClelland, 1986). Implicit, unconscious, intuitive processing is—in the perspective of these models—the rule rather than the exception. As these models yield, in our view, a better understanding of insight phenomena than traditional cognitive models, and as they are not as well-known to most practicing therapists, we dedicate some space in this chapter to the introduction to connectionist models.

Connectionist models can be seen as a reformulation of early gestalt models (Read, Vanman, & Miller, 1997). In contrast to gestalt models, however, neural network approaches provide a better understanding of the processes underlying the development of insight. For example, although Köhler concluded on a macro level that when the ape was successful in problem solving it exhibited insightful behavior through the sudden reorganization of representations, connectionist models allow therapists to understand on a micro level how this reorganization takes place and to define parameters that promote reorganization.

These models represent a whole family of models that differ in detail but typically share some features. Comprehensive introductions to and accounts of these models were given by Caspar, Rothenfluh, and Segal (1992; entitled "The Appeal of Connectionism for Clinical Psychology"), Caspar (1997), Grawe (1998, 2004), Stein and Ludik (1998), or Stinson and Palmer (1991). We concentrate here on the most relevant features related to insight.

Typical connectionist models represent information (in contrast with traditional, "localist" semantic models) in a distributed manner in subsymbolic nodes (units that store and process information and represent artificial neurons) and their interconnections. This means that no meaning unit on a level of resolution common to normal language is represented in one single node; rather, the whole network reacts as though meaning units and the relations between them were represented (e.g., wetness is not an attribute of an individual water molecule, but of a huge number of molecules). If a concept is activated (e.g., a dog walking by is perceived), a partial network consisting of several nodes is activated. This indicates that the activated pattern of nodes in the network must represent something like a dog. Such a distributed representation reminds one of the fact that with lesions in the brain (as long as they are not too severe or located at highly sensitive spots), neither concrete memory content nor performance in general disappears, but phenomena of *graceful degradation* are observed.

Another crucial property of such models is their way of processing information. In contrast to traditional models, in which an instance is explicitly or implicitly required to change schemata or other elements of such models, neural network models do not require a homunculus. As we know from studies of the brain, information is processed by spreading (passing on) activation through synaptic connections from node to node, and learning entails the change of synaptic weights between the artificial neurons. For example, Einstein did not develop new neurons to find the relativity theory; old neurons connected in a new way.

As a consequence of the absence of a central information processor, processing can take place in a self-organized manner, parallel in the whole network or in several parts of it, and without conscious awareness. Learning can occur in a smooth and self-organized way. The dominant mechanism is to spread activation and to change connections in such a way that tension is minimized. If a comparison between the desired and the actual output is built in (e.g., the way it appears that English syllables should be pronounced and the way they actually are pronounced), a difference between the two creates tension that is reduced when a better solution is found. In this manner, systems can learn without a teacher. It is plausible that maternal language is learned in such a way.

As connectionist models are typically very good in the parallel satisfaction of multiple constraints, tension is best reduced in such a system when many (ideally, all) constraints are satisfied. *Connectionist problem solving* (Caspar et al., 1992) can take place in an effortless way, without conscious direction of attention or other deliberate processes. One can imagine it as moving around in a *tension landscape* (Figure 18.1). *Tension* is defined as the sum of unsatisfied constraints and is based on the simultaneous activation of negatively interconnected elements. A tension landscape can be calculated precisely on the basis of mathematic formulas, but in this context it is sufficient to understand it in a metaphoric way. Such a landscape represents the tension related to each possible state a system can take. A *state* is defined as a particular setting of activations and links. For example, a generalized negative perception of oneself and a feeling of pride are in contradiction. If the extent to which an individual can be proud is determined by the cognitions the person has about him- or herself, or by real life experiences he or she has, this represents a constraint in the system. The tendency to satisfy as many constraints as possible—leading to minimal tension—is a strong principle. This is illustrated by the idea that after many elements that are negative in content are activated (e.g., negative cognitions about oneself and the world), setting additional cognitive or emotional elements into a state that is negative in a common sense (e.g., "XY hates me"; "I have messed up things again"; despair) has a positive value from a connectionist point of view, as it reduces tension between the elements. Positive alternatives (e.g., "XY loves me"; "I have succeeded"; hope) would not fit the already strongly activated elements (constraints are not satisfied) and would increase the tension. Patterns (states) in which constraints can be satisfied (only elements that fit together well are activated at the same time) are preferred to patterns (states) in which many constraints remain unsatisfied. Tension can also be decreased by deactivation of entire conflictual patterns. For example, a depressed person would withdraw from domains in which a solution of conflictual activations seems impossible.

In a tension landscape there is a *global minimum* (absolutely deepest point in Figure 18.1), an ideal state in which the tension is overall minimal

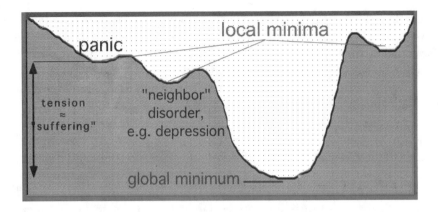

Figure 18.1. Tension landscape representing a neural network.

by satisfaction of a maximum of constraints. Whereas such a state is hardly ever reached, local minima are more typical. These are states in which the tension (*altitude* in Figure 18.1) is relatively low in comparison to the neighborhood (comparing peaks and valleys in the figure); as a consequence, the local minimum cannot be quit without a tension increase (*climbing* over a peak in Figure 18.1). However, the remaining tension is higher than in the ideal global minimum. It is more probable that the system settles in a local minimum *valley* than in an elevated state; it is relatively difficult to get out of such a state, at the same time it is not satisfactory to stay there because the remaining tension may be very high.

Local minima (also called *attractors*; Grawe, 1998) represent states in which many elements such as cognitions, emotions, behavior, biological states, and the environment fit together well. For example, a depression is a state in which many of these elements fit together, although the person at the same time suffers terribly because of the remaining tension. How this works is illustrated by the example of a therapist trying to introduce at least more positive cognitions, the most easily accessible elements: "Look at these beautiful spring flowers!" The depressed patient, in turn, responding through the lens of his depression, answers, "Last spring I could still enjoy them, but look at me now!" The attempt to introduce a seemingly positive element led to an increase of tension that was immediately "repaired" by the patient. To use the landscape metaphor, the therapist has moved him up the hill, limiting the local minimum a little; the patient has experienced the tension increase and made sure he can roll back in the old position.

The connectionist view can readily incorporate the concept of insight, as the following steps indicate:

1. When Insight A integrates many aspects relevant to a current problem, which is important (→ high tension) from a connectionist perspective, a huge reduction of tension is experienced. The *Aha!* experience can be seen

as an expression of such a tension reduction. The "addiction" of patients who have repeated insight experiences in long lasting therapies may partly be explained by the kick provided by the tension reduction, just as it is experienced in a elaborate joke with a startling but essential punch line.

2. Insight Bs can be seen as *solutions* a system may find by moving around in the landscape of possible states, without conscious effort.

3. Insight Bs can also be seen as local minima: They are patterns in which many elements fit well together, but they may still be far from the global *insight minimum* that would satisfy all relevant constraints in a perfectly coherent way. An insight, in contrast to the *repair of disturbance solution* of the depressed patient above, would allow a much larger tension decrease based on the satisfaction of a larger number of so far unsatisfied constraints. As an insight seldom leads to immediate real life solutions, the tension decrease may happen primarily in the part of the network in which the problem is represented cognitive–emotionally without all related elements fully activated. This is further illustrated by the fact that insight is often facilitated by the use of analogies (metaphors or stories) that contain the essence of the problem resolution without being immediately related to insight-hindering elements in the patient's real life. As an example (this example is unrelated to an individual high level insight but demonstrates the concept), if one tries to convey to an impatient person that the solution of his problem needs time, he may answer, "But I absolutely have to solve this problem by . . . ," or "I can't stand it even a day longer." The notion of having to be patient and to wait for a therapeutic effect (representing the insight desired by the therapist) is in obvious contrast to patient expectations, and negative connections are established immediately to the plain form of this potential insight. These represent unsatisfied constraints that render the acceptance and integration of such an insight difficult. In terms of the tension landscape, in this example tension has increased, and the ball has rolled back. In contrast, a therapist statement that "grass does not grow faster if one pulls on it" may lead to an integration of the concept of the necessity of patience and time, as the picture is in itself a strong pattern, supported by connections to ideas accepted by the patient since childhood (that grass needs time to grow); while through its distance (on the surface) from unbearable suffering, negative connections are not activated fast enough to prevent an integration of the idea.

4. How easy or difficult it is to develop a particular insight depends on the tension landscape (on specific local and global minima; e.g., are there maladaptive insights in which the patient can be caught?) and the current position of the system in the landscape (is the patient currently on the verge of a new insight or caught in an old view?) As a consequence, the therapist should know the individual landscape well as a prerequisite for stimulating insight in a successful and economical way.

5. The experience of coherence, considered important by several authors in this volume (e.g., those of chaps. 3, 17, and 21), is immediately evident from a neural network perspective as an expression of tension reduction when arriving in a new and lower local minimum.

6. Insight does not necessarily involve emotions but the development of a new, strong pattern is more probable if many elements—among them emotions—are involved. Insight is typically preceded by strong tension that may be experienced as any emotion, and it is probable that the shift in one's view of oneself or others goes along with positive (excitement, feeling in control, integrated) or negative (sadness, tension from contradictions to self-image) feelings.

Some of these points deserve further elaboration, as they suggest specific strategies or guidelines related to insight. Specifically, one consequence of Point 3 is that therapists need to develop a good understanding of why previous "insights" were developed and which advantages they have (i.e., in what way do they reduce tension). For example, a patient may have had the Insight B of being guilty, because his interactions with his family have developed a pattern of being useless and harmful. As the cognitive insight fits into a whole pattern and the family may even punish the attempt to move toward a more healthy view, the therapist may have to deal extensively with the old view (the pattern of being useless and harmful).

What determines the probability of finding insight? With respect to Point 4, the question is mainly about factors influencing the move of a system out of an old, relatively stable attractor state strengthened through past experiences into a reorganized, novel state. The process of finding insight can be seen as an antidote to getting stuck in an relatively stable attractor state, in a suboptimal local minimum.

A formulation by the cognitive scientist Norman (1986) can be directly related to insight:

> You have to shake up the system, heat up the temperature. Don't let it freeze into position. New interpretations suddenly arise, with no necessary conscious experience of how they came about; a moment of nothing and then clarity, as the system heats up, bounces out of one stable configuration and falls into a new configuration. (p. 538)

What *heating up* may mean can better be understood if we include neurobiological concepts. Connectionist models may provide a bridge between a psychological and a neurobiological view (Caspar, 2003; Caspar, Koch, & Schneider, 2005). A neurobiological perspective can also refine and enrich a connectionist perspective. A neurobiologically informed understanding of the factors influencing the movement of a system out of an attractor state is suggested by recent connectionist models simulating the effects of neuromodulators (Cohen, Braver, & Brown, 2002; Cohen & Servan-Schreiber, 1992). The following considerations use terms that are at first

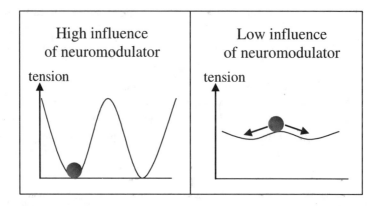

Figure 18.2. Changes in the tension landscape depending on the modulation. Data from Berger (2005).

somewhat remote from practice, but practical consequences should become clear later in this chapter.

In neurobiology it is well-known that the effects of *neuromodulators* such as dopamine are slower, longer lasting, and more spatially diffuse than the effects of *neurotransmitters* such as GABA (gamma-aminobutyric acid). Within the connectionist framework, the attractor model introduced earlier simulates the influence of neurotransmitters by spreading activation between directly connected nodes. In contrast, the effect of neuromodulators is simulated as a global change in the way the units process incoming information. In short, the presence of a neuromodulator potentiates the influences of afferent inputs (of neurotransmitters). Models implementing such a modulatory function proved useful for accounting for a wide range of phenomena, including the effects of disturbances of dopamine in schizophrenia (Cohen & Servan-Schreiber, 1992). It would be beyond the scope of this chapter to take a deeper look into the exact processes. However, with the help of the idea of a tension landscape it is possible to understand the effects of neuromodulation intuitively. Results of computational analyses that explore the influence of neuromodulation on the tension landscape are shown in Figure 18.2 (Berger, 2005).

Whereas the presence of a simulated neuromodulator deepens the valleys and heightens the hills of the tension landscape (Figure 18.2—high influence of neuromodulator), the absence of a neuromodulator flattens the landscape (Figure 18.2—low influence of neuromodulator). From this perspective, low modulatory influence allows the ball (which represents the present state of a system) to move freely in the landscape. Only if modulation is introduced again do valleys become deeper and the ball rolls into a new, stable state. In addition, computational analyses support the view that new attractors (or new valleys in the landscape) or novel configurations of old patterns can only be activated if the spreading of activation starts in an unstable, low modulation state (Berger, 2005). From this perspective, insight or the activation of a reorganized pattern can occur if—following an unstable, low modulatory state—increased modulation amplifies the activation of a novel configured pattern and strengthens new connections. Concordant with this assumption, Ohlsson (1992; see also Knoblich, Ohlsson, Haider, & Rhenius, 1999) proposed a "modern theory of insight" (Ansburg & Dominowksi, 2000) that includes mechanisms of elaboration and constraint relaxation. Whereas the elaboration mechanism involves adding information to a problem representation, constraint relaxation involves rejecting features of the solution that were previously thought necessary. From a connectionist perspective, broadening the view in an elaboration process relies on a low modulation state of the system. In this state, spreading activation over a network is much broader and not focused on strengthened patterns. In contrast, increased modulation promotes constraint relaxation in the sense of Ohlsson: Elements that are not coherent with the novel pattern are actively inhibited.

According to this view, Insight A involves at least two steps: (a) a low modulatory state of a system in which elaboration or adding new information is possible and (b) a high modulatory state in which new configurations or new coherent patterns are stabilized and strengthened. What determines the modulation of the neural system and the change process from a low to a high modulatory state and vice versa? To answer this question, it is helpful to introduce the theory of another famous gestaltist, Karl Duncker. According to Duncker (1945), mental blocks prevent people from finding insightful solutions. To investigate his concept, Duncker used an insight problem involving candles, tacks, and matchboxes. The goal was to mount candles at eye level on a wall. The solution is to melt wax on the top of a box, stick the candle in the wax, and tack the box on the wall. Most participants had problems finding a solution when the candles, tacks, and matches were in the boxes. In contrast, almost all participants solved the problem if they were given empty boxes next to candles, tacks, and matches. Participants apparently had difficulties devising a new use for the boxes when the boxes were used as containers. Duncker used the term *functional fixedness* to refer to situations in which people think of using a given object in its common way rather than in a more novel way. From a modern point of view, Duncker's term *functional* refers to situations in which neural patterns are boosted by neuromodulators. If a solution or neural pattern is functional in the sense of fitting together with goals, wishes, or needs, increased modulation occurs and stabilizes and strengthens the pattern. To be able to discuss how motivational variables like goals affect the probability to find insight through modulatory processes, we outline models of motivational regulation.

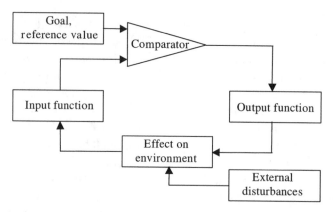

Figure 18.3. Negative feedback loop in a control model.

Models of Motivational Regulation

The Negative Feedback Loop

Ideas of self-regulatory, feedback control processes occurring in both living and artificial systems go back to Cannon's (1932) description of homeostatic processes and Wiener's (1948/1965) description of cybernetics. Other approaches were introduced by G. A. Miller, Galanter, and Pribram (1960), Powers (1973), or Carver and Scheier (1998). The feedback control process view holds that behavior is a continual process of moving toward representations of mental goals. People take steps to reduce the discrepancy between the goals and present states (Carver & Scheier, 1998; Caspar, 1995). The basic units of every control model are negative feedback loops with a reference value or goal, an output and an input function, and a comparator (Figure 18.3). In a negative feedback loop the input value, which is treated as equivalent to perception, and the reference value or goal are compared. Adjustments to shift the input closer to the reference value are made in the *output function* (which corresponds to behavior; Carver & Scheier, 1998). The crucial aspect of feedback control models is that they include the possibility of achieving goals or reference values regardless of the continual challenges by environmental disturbances because the perception is monitored. A thermostat, commonly used to illustrate feedback processes, measures the current air temperature (input) and does not turn on the heater (output) when a crowd of people (environment disturbances) heat the room to the thermostat's setting (reference value).

Subsystems Within the Feedback Loop

Recently, Carver and Scheier (2002) proposed a model that combines self-regulatory control-processes and self-organized, attractor model-like processes underlying connectionist models. They argued that self-organizing tendencies can be found in each component of a feedback control model (Figure 18.4).

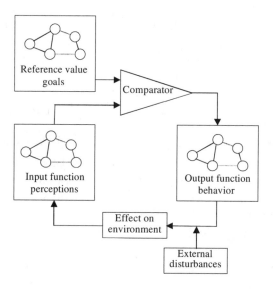

Figure 18.4. Self-organization embedded in a feedback-control model.

- Self-organization may take place within the perceptual *input function*. Carver and Scheier (2002) report a number of examples and findings supporting the view that multiple constraint satisfaction within the perceiving system serves to induce coherence within this part of a feedback loop (e.g., gestalt shifts). Observations were also made that actions "self-assemble" as they are realized, such that the action does not precisely correspond to what was initially intended (Kugler & Turvey, 1987). Such findings are in support of a self-organized *output function*.
- Finally, the active maintenance of goals in mind can be best explained by self-organized, attractor-like processes (E. K. Miller & Cohen, 2001).

An example illustrating the dual regulation model was given by Norman (1981). A professor comes home after work and goes into his bedroom to dress for the theater. His behavior is clearly regulated by a control process. He undresses and puts on pajamas without awareness and goes to sleep. Control processes have lost, self-organization has won! This could only happen because the goal "go to the theater" was not very strong. There is a divergence between goals and perception. Self-organization has won on three levels: On the perceptual level, entering the bedroom and undressing triggered the perception of a "go to bed" situation; on the behavioral level, undressing, putting on pajamas, and going to bed were a completely self-organized behavior that remained below the alarm threshold; and on the level of goals, the goal of getting a good night's sleep was formed bottom-up and competed successfully with the conscious goal of going to the theater. Gaining insight into such a process is not an easy endeavor and is more difficult in the absence of theoretical models capturing the collaboration of the two types of processes!

Modulatory Interaction Between Subsystems

In the model of Carver and Scheier (2002), the influences between the self-organized subsystems can be conceptualized as neuromodulatory processes. For example, in Cohen, Dunbar, and McClelland's (1990) connectionist model of Stroop task performance, a high-level module that specifies the relevant task or goal (in the case of a Stroop task color naming) modulates the flow of information processing in a low-level input–output module. Cohen et al. compared this model to the modulating effects of attention. The speed and stability of an appropriate neural pattern is governed by the modulatory top-down influence of attention (task demand or goal). The activation of goals in the *task* or *goal* subsystem deepens valleys and heightens hills in the input–output function.

Modulatory Interaction Between Subsystems and Insight

The idea of subsystems that modulate each other is complex, but it emphasizes an important point recent models in cognitive science offer toward a better understanding of insight. Imagine different subsystems, each consisting of a largely independent tension landscape. Then consider that there is a continuous alteration of each landscape promoted by a continuous interaction of subsystems. Whereas the landscape of a specific subsystem becomes flatter (modulation is decreased), hills mount up and valleys become deeper in the landscape of another subsystem (modulation is increased). The conditions for Insight A, defined earlier, must be considered. Finding an insightful solution involves two steps: (a) elaboration, which involves the ability to attend to new information, low modulation, or a flat tension landscape and (b) constraint relaxation, high modulation, or a stabilization of a new coherent pattern. Thus, insight is promoted if the subsystems are in a continuous modulatory interaction with each other that leads to ups and downs in the tension landscape of various subsystems. The system gets stuck in a tension minimum if the continuous interaction is interrupted. In Teasdale and Barnard's (1993) model of depression (which includes the idea of interacting cognitive subsystems), such a state is called *interlocked configuration*.

The crucial point related to insight is that the possibility of an emergence of new patterns is promoted by a dialectical process between subsystems. If in Duncker's matchbox problem matches are in the box, a participant may find the solution after she or he concretely manipulates the objects (e.g., opens the box) without a specific goal or subgoal in mind. While manipulating the objects, information processing takes part in the self-organized output function and frees up the mind in the goal subsystem (the tension in the goal subsystem is flat). This opens up the possibility that a new goal or subgoal will emerge that will change the modulatory influence on the output function again. In this case, it is the dialectical process of doing and thinking (finding a new goal) that can lead to the insightful solution.

If this dialectical process stops, the system works in a manner Watzlawick, Weakland, and Fisch (1974) described as *first order changes*. A first order change means that if a problem increases, the intensity of the solution increases as well (as in a simple feedback loop). For example, when it gets colder in the house, the solution is to turn up the heat. Or, when a car is moving too slowly, the solution is to step on the gas. Many problems can be solved by persisting in the attempt to reach a task or goal; a solution that has been functional in the past may work again (e.g., it is indeed quite functional to step on the gas to increase speed if the car is moving too slowly). However, when a problem requires a new solution, first order changes may prevent people from reaching a new solution (e.g., participants' inability to solve Duncker's matchbox problem). In terms of the described neural network model, a first order change is a process in which a goal representation increasingly modulates patterns in the self-organized output function and therefore increasingly activates behavioral patterns that have been strengthened through past experiences. As Watzlawick et al. summarized, first order changes lead to "more of the same" solutions, or as every psychotherapist should know, to a process in which the solution becomes the problem (e.g., a mother with obsessive–compulsive disorder may try to suppress or neutralize intrusive thoughts about stabbing her baby. This has the effect of increasing the frequency of the thoughts).

In contrast, a continuous modulatory interaction between subsystems (ups and downs in the tension landscape of each subsystem) allows second order changes (Watzlawick et al., 1974). A second order solution is defined as a change in the structure of a system (new connections) that requires a stepping out of the boundaries of a system or "moving out of the box" (Watzlawick et al., 1974, p. 99). The described neural network model moves out of the box if the modulation of the box or subsystem decreases. The tension landscape of this subsystem becomes flat, allowing the activation of new patterns (the system is no longer captured in a deep valley of the tension landscape). A common experience helps clarify this point: One does not usually have "flashes of illuminances" (Metcalfe & Wiebe, 1987) while one's mind is dominated (modulated) by a goal, and this rarely occurs while one is deliberately trying to find a solution. Often one has insightful experiences, for example, in the shower after stepping back or after disengaging from a goal, at least for a short time. As Wegner (2002) noted,

> The happiest inconsistency between intention and action occurs when a great idea pops into mind. The "action" in this case is the occurrence of the idea, and our tendency to say "Eureka!" or "Aha!" is our usual acknowledgment that this particular insight was not something we were planning in advance. Although most of us are quite willing to take credit

for our good ideas, it is still true that we do not experience them as voluntary. (p. 81)

Affective Modulation of Subsystems and Insight

The importance of a continuous interaction between subsystems becomes clear if we broaden our view on insight. Up to this point, we focused
on the contribution of cognitive psychology to understanding insight within
a problem-solving paradigm. Cognitive psychological approaches deal mainly
with questions such as how people actively solve insight problems with cognitive mechanisms that facilitate or hamper intended actions through insightful solutions. There are, however, approaches that include ideas about
subsystems and the interaction of subsystems that are more closely related to
emotions, needs, and an experiential system than to behavior and cognitive
behavior control. Kuhl's personality systems interactions theory (Kuhl, 2000,
2001) includes a subsystem called *extension memory*. According to Kuhl, the
extension memory consists of a large network of integrated representations
of experiences; internal states such as needs, emotions, and somatic feelings;
and values. This subsystem is necessary to achieve a deep understanding that
takes a great number of givens and self-aspects into account. The participation of the extension memory in information processing promotes insight in
the sense of creating meaning and understanding oneself. If one has an insightful experience on the basis of information processing in this subsystem,
one may think, "I just feel that my view is right" (Kuhl, 2000). This kind of
insight, which has received much interest by psychotherapists, is comparable
to states and processes described by humanistic (Rogers, 1961) and experiential approaches (Gendlin, 1996; Greenberg, Rice, & Elliott, 1993; Greenberg
& Safran, 1987).

Kuhl (2000, 2001) presented a huge range of findings in cognitive psychology and neurobiology in support of the existence of extension memory.
In terms of the described feedback control model, the extension memory can
be seen as a second high-level system instead of the subsystem, in which
explicit goals are represented. Following D. C. McClelland's (1985) distinction between implicit and explicit motives, Kuhl saw explicit motives, intentions, or goals represented in the *intention memory*, whereas he attributes
implicit motives to the extension memory. Comparably, representations in
the intention memory are related to explicit beliefs about the self, whereas
intuitive–holistic processing in the extension memory forms the basis of implicit self-representations. According to Kuhl, functional characteristics of
the intention memory include analytical thinking, verbal processing, and
other functions supporting analytical planning and volitional control of action. In contrast, the access to the extension memory and therefore to implicit self-representations, preferences, and needs finally enables self-
determined actions in the sense of the self-determination theory of Deci and
Ryan (1991; Ryan, Kuhl, & Deci, 1997).

One of the most important parts of Kuhl's (2000, 2001) complex theory includes the assumption that information processing in various subsystems can be energized or inhibited, which makes specific processes more or less likely. This is another way of saying that a subsystem can be modulated to a higher or lower degree, facilitating or hampering the spreading of activation within a specific subsystem (see previous discussion). In Kuhl's theory, variables determining the *energy* or modulation of specific subsystems are defined in so-called *modulation assumptions*.

What are the assumptions related to an increased modulation of the extension memory? The ability to gain insight in the broader sense of finding a deeper meaning in a difficult personal experience depends on the possibilities of constructing relationships between this experience and a variety of self-aspects. Therefore, insight depends on the modulation of the extension memory. In his second modulation assumption, Kuhl (2000, 2001) stated that critical levels of negative affect that cannot be downregulated inhibit access to the extension memory. *Downregulation* means reduction, but it is the preferred term as it encompasses the idea that the optimal level does not simply correspond to a minimal level but is reached through regulation processes. Downregulation of negative affect modulates and facilitates access to the large network of integrated self-representations and increases the probability of finding insightful meanings in line with individual needs.

In this concept the dialectical process can again be seen: Finding insight in this broader sense does not just include a modulation of the extension memory. Kuhl (2000, 2001) argued that the extension memory is in a continual exchange with another subsystem responsible for the detection of new, unexpected, and threatening perceptions. It stands in contact with the outer world. Contents or neural patterns in this memory are boosted or modulated through negative affect, often triggered through contact with the outer world (Kuhl, 2000, 2001). If negative affect cannot be downregulated (if the modulation of this subsystem cannot be decreased), the system gets stuck in a tension minimum, a self-organized neural pattern that is strongly related to negative affect. One can conceptualize symptoms of a panic attack or ruminations as a part of depression in this way. Grawe (1998) conceptualized this as *emotional attractors*. If negative affect can be downregulated, the modulation of negative patterns is decreased (the tension landscape in this subsystem is becoming flatter), which means that negative patterns are no longer as easily activated. At the same time, the extension memory is modulated (in the tension landscape of this subsystem, hills mount up and valleys become deeper). This allows the integration of negative experiences and the construction of meaning on the basis of a large network of experiences and internal states.

Kuhl (2000, 2001) gave many arguments for this idea and explained it with neurobiological findings. There is increasing evidence that a common aspect of various functions of the hippocampus, which is assumed to be part of the extension memory, relates to its capacity to form an enormous number of associations among sensations from the external and internal worlds (e.g., J. L. McClelland, McNaughton, & O'Reilly, 1995; Sutherland & Rudy, 1989). Findings demonstrating inhibition of hippocampal activity when stress levels exceed a critical threshold (Sapolsky, 1992), could indicate neurobiological mechanisms underlying the second modulation assumption. If the stress level is above the critical threshold, one is not able to access integrated self-representations. As a reversal of this hypothesis, Kuhl stated a self-relaxation assumption: Negative affect can be downregulated through the activation of the extension memory. From a neurobiological view, self-relaxation is mirrored in findings that the activation of the hippocampus causes a downregulation of cortisol concentration in response to stress (Sapolsky, 1992). Kuhl's assumption allows a reinterpretation of several findings in cognitive psychology. For example, it can explain why activation of self-representations facilitates the regulation of correlates of threatening and stressful experiences (Linville, 1987; Ryan, 1995; Showers & Kling, 1996).

According to Kuhl's (2000, 2001) theory, the inability to gain insight in a broader sense (not able to understand the relationship between experiences and self-aspects, or to find solutions that are in accordance with implicit motives, preferences, or needs) is as much the effect of stress as it is the cause of stress. Stress impairs access to the extension memory and increases the stress level again.

How does one break this vicious circle? Of course, the human system operates in the larger system of interpersonal relationships, which opens additional possibilities for breaking the circle (for a second order change of the human system). Adequate, accepting, and validating responses of others enhance the regulation of negative affects (e.g., Linehan, 1993) and therefore help to modulate the extension memory (see the concept of responsivity in attachment research, Bowlby, 1969). From this point of view, Kuhl's (2000, 2001) theory sheds new light on the role of interpersonal relationships in the process of finding insight. One can think that insight is facilitated through the content of communication. Another person (e.g., a psychotherapist) gives hints that allow the individual to see a problem from a different perspective. Specific contents of communication may be helpful to find insight. In addition, and more important, the view of a subsystem modulated in response to the regulation of negative affects suggests an unspecific influence of close interpersonal experiences on insight. A close relationship (including an attuned therapeutic relationship) energizes information processing related to insight in a broader sense.

USING COGNITIVE MODELS TO PROMOTE INSIGHT IN THERAPISTS AND PATIENTS

Professional psychotherapy should be based not only on empirical evidence for its effects but also on concepts soundly based in general psychology and other relevant domains. Unless one sees a therapist as a mere executor of algorithmically defined techniques, it is obvious that a therapist needs valid and sufficiently differentiated basic models of human functioning in the same way a medical doctor needs a good understanding of physical functioning. Although in a minority of simple cases if–then rules may lead to equally good success, in most cases the adaptation to the individual case needs to be informed by such models. For example, the procedure with a particular patient, the information the therapist picks up, the homework assignments he or she gives, and so forth, depend to a large extent on whether insight is seen as a mere cognitive issue or whether emotional and biological aspects are given more weight, and whether the therapist focuses solely on content or also on the modulation of subsystems.

As far as clients are concerned, the idea of helping them become their own therapist or scientist implies that relevant basic models should also be conveyed in an adequate form. For those who find some of the models presented earlier rather complex this may be hard to believe, but we have repeatedly experienced that patients understand, for example, the essence of a tension landscape easily, and more important, feel very much understood by such models.

The first function of cognitive models is thus to serve as a frame of reference for the development of an individual case conceptualization of the client. In addition, concrete consequences or principles can be derived from these models. We note this, however, with several caveats. Some strategies may already have been empirically evaluated in the context of a therapeutic approach into which they fit under one or another label, but they are presented here as ideas, not validated guidelines! In addition, such ideas should not be overgeneralized. A strategy that is therapeutic under one condition may be the opposite under other conditions. This is one of the values of (always hypothetical) individual case conceptualizations: They may tell the therapist whether a principle can work with a particular client in a particular situation. Needless to say, more independent research targeted on questions that are derived from psychological concepts is needed to make differential decisions on which of the sometimes contradictory principles to use in a specific situation.

Following are some heuristic rules and suggestions on the promotion of insight, which can be derived directly from cognitive psychological considerations:

1. Look for maladaptive patterns to which negative tensions should be established. A client's current situation may not be best characterized by the simple absence of useful insights: He may be stuck in the local minimum of a suboptimal Insight B. If one can find these, one should increase the tension related to them ("Has this insight helped you so far?"),

and lower the pass to better local minima by reducing the tension as the impact of hindering elements is decreased ("This is, in principle, a view that fits the way you are much better").

2. Decrease client irritation about a tension increase when an insight is approached ("When a new perspective is painful or hard to get at, this is perfectly compatible with the fact that it is valid and very useful in the long run"; "If there were no obstacles, no pass to climb over, you would have developed a better understanding of yourself a long time ago").

3. "Heat up the system" by stimulating motives and enhancing emotions. However, limit your heating up interventions to specific contents while at the same time calming the system by optimizing motivational and interpersonal variables (e.g., safe context and therapeutic relationship). The system must have a chance to modulate the extension memory (Kuhl, 2000, 2001). If stress is too high, a patient may have no access to it (see the section on affective modulation of subsystems and insight). Promote a dialectical process of heating up and cooling down a system. Adapt your interventions to individual emotion regulation–coping abilities and characteristics (e.g., heat up the system more often with low-anxious patients, calm it down more often with high-anxious patients).

4. Try to think in an antagonistic way by promoting information processing styles a person does not use by habit or in a specific situation. Individuals differ in their habits or preferences to use specific subsystems to process information.

5. Stimulate the dialectical process as often as possible. A continuing change in subsystems used for information processing is expected to increase the frequency of insights. In addition, it is probable that the promotion of a dialectical process improves self–emotion regulation abilities: It strengthens the belief and ability to calm down again if negative experiences are considered. Therefore, the promotion of a dialectical process increases the chances that individuals will find insight on their own.

6. Use homework assignments to keep elements activated that may be important ingredients to a new insight. Have clients write notes, for example, related to their motives or fantasies about the future, or have clients talk to people, dig out memorabilia, watch movies, and so forth; however, do not forget assignments dedicated to freeing their spirit, such as relaxing or meditating, jogging, and walking in a park.

CONCLUDING COMMENTS

This chapter concentrates on concepts from cognitive psychology with the potential to contribute to an understanding of insight on a micro level. There are more concepts addressing relevant aspects, such as the construction integration model by Kintsch (1988), which addresses the individual's development of meaning in a dialogue. The relevance of such aspects is obvious, as most psychotherapeutic insight occurs in and through dialogue.

To dedicate sufficient space to making the most central concepts understandable, we concentrate on only a part of the abundant cognitive science literature that might be useful in advancing an understanding insight. We maintain that familiarity with basic psychological concepts enhances the chances of finding novel accesses to insight on the general as well as on the individual level, and we do not see this in contradiction to the observation that for some conclusions cross-validating coincidences are found between a cognitive science and a clinical approach.

REFERENCES

Ansburg, P. I., & Dominowski, R. L. (2000). Promoting insightful problem solving. *Journal of Creative Behavior, 34*(1), 30–60.

Bartlett, F. C. (1932). *Remembering: A study in experimental and social psychology.* Cambridge, England: Cambridge University Press.

Berger, T. (2005). *Die Dynamik psychischer Störungen. Strukturen und Prozesse aus der Perspektive konnektionistischer Netzwerke* [Dynamics of mental disorders: Structures and processes from a perspective of connectionist models]. Unpublished dissertation. Universität Freiburg, Freiburg, Germany.

Bowlby, J. (1969). *Attachment and loss: Vol. 1. Attachment.* New York: Basic Books.

Cannon, W. B. (1932). *The wisdom of the body.* New York: Norton.

Carver, C. S., & Scheier, M. F. (1998). *On the self-regulation of behavior.* New York: Cambridge University Press.

Carver, C. S., & Scheier, M. F. (2002). Control processes and self-organization as complementary principles underlying behavior. *Personality and Social Psychology Review, 6,* 304–315.

Caspar, F. (1995). *Plan analysis: Toward optimizing psychotherapy.* Seattle: Hogrefe & Huber.

Caspar, F. (1997). What goes on in a psychotherapist's mind? *Psychotherapy Research, 7,* 105–125.

Caspar, F. (2003). Psychotherapy research and neurobiology: Challenge, chance, or enrichment? (SPR Presidential Address, Santa Barbara, CA). *Psychotherapy Research, 13,* 1–23.

Caspar, F., Koch, K., & Schneider, F. (2005). Psychotherapie und ihre neurobiologischen Voraussetzungen [Psychotherapy and its neurobiological underpinnings]. In W. Senf & M. Broda (Eds.), *Praxis der Psychotherapie* (pp. 34–53). Stuttgart, Germany: Thieme.

Caspar, F., Rothenfluh, T., & Segal, Z. V. (1992). The appeal of connectionism for clinical psychology. *Clinical Psychology Review, 12,* 719–762.

Cohen, J. D., Braver, T. S., & Brown, J. W. (2002). Computational perspectives on dopamine function in prefrontal cortex. *Current Opinion in Neurobiology, 12,* 223–229.

Cohen, J. D., Dunbar, K., & McClelland, J. L. (1990). On the control of automatic processes: A parallel distributed processing account of the Stroop effect. *Psychological Review, 97,* 332–361.

Cohen, J. D., & Servan-Schreiber, D. (1992). Context, cortex, and dopamine: A connectionist approach to behavior and biology in schizophrenia. *Psychological Review, 99,* 45–77.

Deci, E. L., & Ryan, R. M. (1991). A motivational approach to self: Integration in personality. In E. Dienstbier (Ed.), *Nebraska symposium on motivation* (pp. 237–288). Lincoln: University of Nebraska Press.

Dominowski, R. L., & Dallob, P. (1995). Insight and problem solving. In R. J. Sternberg & J. Davidson (Eds.), *The nature of insight.* Cambridge, MA: MIT Press.

Duncker, K. (1945). On problem-solving. *Psychological Monographs, 58*(9), 113.

Epstein, S. (1985). The implications of cognitive–experiential self-theory for research in social psychology and personality. *Journal for the Theory of Social Behavior, 15,* 283–310.

Epstein, S. (1994). Integration of the cognitive and the psychodynamic unconscious. *American Psychologist, 49,* 709–724.

Gendlin, E. T. (1996). *Focusing-oriented psychotherapy: A manual of the experiential method.* New York: Guilford Press.

Grawe, K. (1998). *Psychologische Therapie* [Psychological Therapy]. Göttingen, Germany: Hogrefe & Huber.

Grawe K. (2004). *Neuropsychotherapie* [Neuropsychotherapy]. Göttingen, Germany: Hogrefe & Huber.

Gredler, M. E. (2001). *Learning and instruction: Theory into practice* (4th ed.). Upper Saddle River, NJ: Merrill.

Greenberg, L. S., Rice, L. N., & Elliott, R. (1993). *Facilitating emotional change: The moment-by-moment process.* New York: Guilford Press.

Greenberg, L. S., & Safran, J. D. (1987). *Emotion in psychotherapy: Affect, cognition and the process of change.* New York: Guilford Press.

Holyoak, K. J., & Spellman, B. A. (1993). Thinking. *Annual Review of Psychology, 44,* 265–315.

Kintsch, W. (1988). The role of knowledge in discourse comprehension: A construction–integration model. *Psychological Review, 95,* 163–182.

Knoblich, G., Ohlsson, S., Haider, G., & Rhenius, D. (1999). Constraint relaxation and chunk decomposition in insight problem solving. *Journal of Experimental Psychology: Learning, Memory & Cognition, 25*, 1534–1555.

Köhler, W. (1927). *The mentality of apes.* London: Routledge & Kegan Paul.

Kugler, P. N., & Turvey, M. T. (1987). *Information, natural law, and the self-assembly of rhythmic movement.* Hillsdale, NJ: Erlbaum.

Kuhl, J. (2000). A functional-design approach to motivation and self-regulation: The dynamics of personality systems interactions. In M. Boekaerts, P. R. Pintrich, & M. Zeidner (Eds.), *Handbook of self-regulation* (pp. 111–169). San Diego, CA: Academic Press.

Kuhl, J. (2001). *Motivation und Persönlichkeit: Interaktionen psychischer Systeme* [Motivation and personality: Interactions of mental systems]. Göttingen, Germany: Hogrefe & Huber.

Linehan, M. M. (1993). *Cognitive–behavioral treatment of borderline personality disorder.* New York: Guilford Press.

Linville, P. (1987). Self-complexity as a cognitive buffer against stress-related illness and depression. *Journal of Personality and Social Psychology, 52*, 663–676.

Mayer, R. E. (1995). The search for insight: Grappling with Gestalt psychology's unanswered questions. In R. J. Sternberg & J. Davidson (Eds.), *The nature of insight.* Cambridge, MA: MIT Press.

McClelland, D. C. (1985). *Human motivation.* Glenview, IL: Scott Foresman.

McClelland, J. L., McNaughton, B. L., & O'Reilly, R. C. (1995). Why there are complementary learning systems in the hippocampus and neocortex: Insights from the successes and failures of connectionist models of learning and memory. *Psychological Review, 102*, 419–457.

Metcalfe, J. (1986). Feeling of knowing in memory and problem solving. *Journal of Experimental Psychology: Learning, Memory, and Cognition, 12*, 288–294.

Metcalfe, J., & Wiebe, D. (1987). Intuition in insight and noninsight problem solving. *Memory & Cognition, 15*, 238–246.

Miller, E. K., & Cohen, J. D. (2001). An integrative theory of prefrontal cortex function. *Annual Review of Neuroscience, 24*, 167–202.

Miller, G. A., Galanter, E., & Pribram, K. H. (1960). *Plans and the structure of behavior.* New York: Holt.

Norman, D. A. (1981). Categorization of action slips. *Psychological Review, 88*, 1–15.

Norman, D. A. (1986). Reflections on cognition and parallel distributed processing. In J. L. McClelland, D. E. Rumelhart, & P. R. Group (Eds.), *Parallel distributed processing. Explorations in the microstructure of cognition* (pp. 531–546). Cambridge, MA: MIT Press.

Ohlsson, S. (1992). Information processing explanations of insight and related phenomena. In M. Keane & K. Gilhooly (Eds.), *Advances in the psychology of thinking* (pp. 1–44). London: Harvester-Wheatsheaf.

Powers, W. T. (1973). *Behavior and the control of perception.* New York: Aldine Publishing.

Read, S. J., Vanman, E. J., & Miller, L. C. (1997). Connectionism and Gestalt principles: (Re)introducing cognitive dynamics to social psychology. *Personality and Social Psychology Review, 1,* 26–53.

Reber, P. J., & Squire, L. R. (1994). Parallel brain systems for learning with and without awareness. *Learning and Memory, 1,* 217–229.

Rogers, C. R. (1961). *On becoming a person: A therapist's view of psychotherapy.* Boston: Houghton Mifflin.

Rumelhart, D. E., McClelland, J. L., & The PDP Research Group (1986). *Parallel distributed processing: Explorations in the microstructure of cognition: Vol. 1. Foundations.* Cambridge, MA: MIT Press.

Ryan, R. M. (1995). Psychological needs and the facilitation of integrative processes. *Journal of Personality, 63,* 397–427.

Ryan, R. M., Kuhl, J., & Deci, E. L. (1997). Nature and autonomy: An organizational view of social and neurobiological aspects of self-regulation in behavior and development. *Development and Psychopathology, 9,* 701–728.

Sapolsky, R. M. (1992). *Stress, the aging brain, and the mechanism of neuron death.* Cambridge, MA: MIT Press.

Schooler, J. W., Fallshore, M., & Fiore, S. M. (1995). Epilogue: Putting insight into perspective. In R. J. Sternberg & J. Davidson (Eds.), *The nature of insight* (pp. 559–587). Cambridge: MIT Press.

Showers, C. J., & Kling, K. C. (1996). Organization of self-knowledge: Implications for recovery from sad mood. *Journal of Personality and Social Psychology, 70,* 578–590.

Simon, D. P., & Simon, H. A. (1978). Individual differences in solving physics problems. In R. S. Siegler (Ed.), *Children's thinking: What develops* (pp. 325–348). Hillsdale, NJ: Erlbaum.

Smith, E. R., & DeCoster, J. (2000). Dual-process models in social and cognitive psychology: Conceptual integration and links to underlying memory systems. *Personality and Social Psychology Review, 4,* 108–131.

Smith, J. D., & Shapiro, J. H. (1989). The occurrence of holistic categorization. *Journal of Memory and Language, 28,* 386–399.

Smolensky, P. (1988). On the proper treatment of connectionism. *The Behavioral and Brain Sciences, 11,* 1–74.

Stein, D. J., & Ludik, J. (1998). *Neural networks and psychopathology.* Cambridge, England: Cambridge University Press.

Stinson, C. H., & Palmer, S. E. (1991). Parallel distributed processing models of person schemas and psychopathologies. In M. J. Horowitz (Ed.), *Person schemas and maladaptive interpersonal patterns* (pp. 334–378). Chicago: University of Chicago Press.

Sutherland, R.W., & Rudy, J. W. (1989). Configurational association theory: The role of hippocampal formation in learning, memory and amnesia. *Psychobiology, 17,* 129–144.

Teasdale, J. D., & Barnard, P. J. (1993). *Affect, cognition, and change: Remodeling depressive thought.* Hove, England: Erlbaum.

Watzlawick, P., Weakland, J. H., & Fisch, R. (1974). *Lösungen* [Solutions]. Bern, Switzerland: Huber.

Wegner, D. M. (2002). *The illusion of conscious will.* Cambridge, MA: MIT Press.

Wiener, N. (1965). *Cybernetics, or control and communication in the animal and the machine* (2nd ed.). Cambridge, MA: MIT Press. (Original work published 1948)

19

AN INTEGRATED DEVELOPMENTAL PERSPECTIVE ON INSIGHT

ELIZABETH A. BOWMAN AND JEREMY D. SAFRAN

This chapter presents a view of insight based on an influential model from developmental psychology: attachment theory. According to John Bowlby (1973), attachment theory is

> a way of conceptualizing the propensity of human beings to make strong affectional bonds to particular others and of explaining the many forms of emotional and personal disturbance, including anxiety, anger, depression, and emotional detachment, to which unwilling separation and loss give rise. (p. 127)

Attachment theory provides a framework for integrating recent theoretical conceptualizations from emotion, mentalization, and the therapeutic relationship. An integration of these perspectives leads to an appreciation of insight as a developmental process, an organizing of experience that unfolds over time in the context of psychotherapy relationships. It comes about through an active integration of emotions and mental representations of experience and it encourages reflective psychological processes. Insight is reflected in the ability to integrate dissociated emotional and conceptual knowledge (from an attachment perspective, the inclination to dissociate from affective and cognitive experience begins with early disturbances in primary

401

relational experiences). Integration of dissociated psychological information is symbolized and articulated through coherent and collaborative narratives. Collaboration and coherence in language are based on communication maxims proposed by the philosopher of language, H. P. Grice (1975; i.e., quality, quantity, relation, and manner). Grice's maxims were originally proposed as universal principles that provide a framework for optimal collaborative communication; coherent narratives are relevant, clear and orderly, succinct yet complete, and credible or easy to believe. According to attachment theorists (Hesse, 1999; Holmes, 1993; Main, 1991), narrative styles reveal the representational organization of psychological information about the self and the self in important relationships. Jeremy Holmes (2001) suggested that people who tell coherent stories about themselves and their relationships are able to synthesize experience, take ownership of the past, and integrate these into the context of their lives. The perspective we offer extends this explanation to highlight the need for integrating emotional knowledge within a reflective, conceptual framework of mental representations to achieve coherence in language. Within this new perspective, achieving insight is a dynamic process that synthesizes emotional awareness and mental reflection and is expressed through language (i.e., coherent stories about self and others).

The aim of this chapter is to present an integrated theoretical and clinical perspective combining developmental and other contemporary theories in psychotherapy. A previous chapter on cognitive approaches to insight (see chap. 18, this volume), emphasized reorganizing representations and promoting information processing that is consistent with our view; however, we present these themes in the context of a developmental literature emphasizing in-session process-oriented approaches. The social psychological perspective offered by Haverkamp and Tashiro (see chap. 17, this volume) discusses the importance of exploring and identifying multiple self-schemas to access more adaptive views of the self. Our view supports this notion by encouraging psychological reflective processes about the self; however, we emphasize the importance of using these same reflective processes for understanding others in close relationships (including relationships between clients and therapists). Our chapter brings together perspectives from attachment theory, emotion, mentalization, and the therapeutic relationship to provide an integrated approach to helping clients develop an increased capacity for insight.

ATTACHMENT THEORY AND PSYCHOTHERAPY

The starting point for attachment theory is John Bowlby's extensive clinical and theoretical writings on childhood psychopathology. Bowlby (1973) proposed the concept of the secure base that helps infants develop mental representations or *internal working models* based on the availability of important others early in life. Infants' experiences with caregivers create unique models for organizing the world. These models are based on the reciprocal relationship that evolves between a child and the environment and are internalized cognitive and emotional representations that guide expectations and ensuing psychological development. Security emerges when the infant's self-states (hunger, happiness, distress, etc.) are consistently acknowledged and mirrored back to the child. An environment that is consistent with the infant's experience forms the basis for a sense of self that is both certain and secure. Ultimately, securely attached infants will feel safe to explore the environment, effective in the world, and worthy of love. Bowlby's secure-base concept becomes applicable to adults with the realization that "the secure base can be seen not just as an external figure, but also as a representation of security within the adult psyche" (Holmes, 2001, p. 7).

Recognizing the role of mental representations in the context of adult security extends the applicability of attachment theory throughout the life span. Theorists in adult attachment understand the psychological health of adults in terms of secure and insecure states of mind with respect to how an adult represents his or her world, his or her relationships, and his or her sense of self (Hesse, 1999; & Holmes, 2001; Main, 1991). A person's state of mind (or mental state) at any given time combines the content of a representation and the affective experience this representation evokes. A secure state of mind is expressed through the coherence of a person's narrative in exploring important relationships with others from the past and in the present. We propose that insight is expressed in one's ability to openly reflect on these representations and to modulate emotion while remaining coherent in the context of communicating about one's state of mind (in the here and now as well as in a general sense). According to Holmes (2001), narrative coherence reflects a secure individual's ability to articulately express internal representations of meaningful relationships or attachments through language. Insight, from the perspective we propose, is the ability to assimilate dissociated affective experience and conceptual knowledge with respect to important mental representations and the ability to communicate a collaborative and coherent narrative. This understanding emphasizes the ability to help clients access dissociated aspects of experience and combine emotional and intellectual knowledge in their ability to explore and describe subjective experience.

In psychotherapy, therapists help clients actively organize thoughts and feelings related to mental states in a manner that is affectively authentic and coherent for the purpose of achieving insight. Therapists work at an affective level with clients to explore emotional experience, which leads to enhanced conceptual knowledge. The goal of this process is to enlarge the range of affective experience and emotional expression while allowing for increased complexity in ascribing meaning to motivation, intention, thoughts, and behavior of the self and others. A coherent narrative is a symbolic consequence of this process that brings both emotional and conceptual knowledge together. The application of this model in psychotherapy is a process of helping clients synthesize experience and diminish the need to defensively exclude or dissociate emotional and experiential information related to the representational world. Together, *representational* and *emotional dissociation* function defensively to protect a person from full access to the range of affective and conceptual information about oneself and oneself in relation to others. Obstructing psychological access to these aspects of experience diminishes the potentially painful affective consequences that these thoughts, memories, and feelings arouse. These defensive operations constrict and splinter mental states and diminish one's capacity for authentic relatedness; they reflect insecure states of mind characterized by incoherent narratives (i.e., overinclusive, vague, devaluing). The cost of dissociating this information is a disconnection from oneself and from others, leading to psychological distress and ineffective approaches to negotiating important relationships. From this perspective, the goal of psychotherapy is to facilitate the integration of dissociated emotional and conceptual knowledge and create narratives that are collaborative and coherent.

EMOTION AND MENTALIZATION

How do therapists help clients organize experience to achieve insight and reduce the need for emotional and representational dissociation created by attachment disturbances at important phases of development? We propose that insight comes about through two primary processes. The first process involves helping clients gain access to *emotion* or *action–disposition information* (Safran & Segal, 1990), whereas the second facilitates the client's capacity for *mentalization* or *reflective function* (Fonagy, Target, Steele, & Steele, 1998).

Emotion or Action–Disposition Information

Action–disposition information is emotional experience related to the self that leads to adaptive functioning in the world: "Emotion motivates adaptive behavior, providing people with information about their preparedness to act in certain ways" (Safran & Segal, 1990, p. 12). Thus, therapists encourage clients to access action–disposition information previously not present in awareness, which leads to enhanced recognition of inner emotional experience. A person who fails to integrate action–disposition information regarding a need for intimacy may be overly autonomous and independent and fail to engage in emotional closeness with others. As a consequence, meaningful relatedness is problematic. By acknowledging and fully accepting a part of the self that was previously out of awareness, a person develops the ability to contact inner emotions that can lead to adaptive behavior. Estrangement from affective experience or emotions not fully realized or made explicitly conscious is characteristic of insecure states of mind and represents a form of dissociation from the self and a restricted capacity for insight. Access to action–disposition information is the first step in integrating mental states and mental representations and emphasizes recognizing inner emotional experience.

Safran and Segal (1990) suggested that "the process of acknowledging emotion or action–disposition information is mediated by the interpersonal context in which it takes place" (p. 188). The therapeutic relationship can serve as an important arena in which clients can engage in this type of exploration. Clients who find their emotions and mental states accurately and supportively acknowledged by their therapists can develop increased comfort in acknowledging and subsequently addressing their own subjective experience in the context of close interpersonal relationships (e.g., the therapeutic relationship). Consider the following interaction between a patient, Jane, and her therapist. Jane held a central belief that she needed to be strong and independent; she had difficulty addressing feelings of despair or vulnerability. In the following example,[1] the therapist attempts to address Jane's difficulty experiencing painful emotions by making this the focus of the current interaction, in the here and now.

> Client: . . . things like that. Or my aunt saying like, 'Now, what have you got to be crying about?' You know, things like that. It kind of starts me thinking, 'Well, maybe I'm just feeling sorry for myself.' You know, 'You haven't got time to feel sorry for yourself.'
>
> Therapist: So you start to feel that pain.
>
> Client: Uh-huh.
>
> Therapist: And then it's like another voice chimes in saying, 'You're really feeling sorry for yourself.'
>
> Client: Uh-huh.
>
> Therapist: 'Be a fighter.'
>
> Client: Uh-huh.
>
> Therapist: 'Pull yourself together.'
>
> Client: I don't know if that's healthy or unhealthy or what but that's what I do anyway.
>
> Therapist: Uh-huh. And what about right now? Where are you?

[1]This clinical vignette is from *Interpersonal Process in Cognitive Therapy* (2nd ed., pp. 191–193), by J. D. Safran and Z. V. Segal, 1996, Northvale, NJ: Jason Aronson. Copyright 1996 by Jason Aronson. Adapted with permission.

Client: I guess I'm in the middle.

Therapist: In the middle?

Client: Yeah.

Therapist: Describe that to me. Being in the middle right now.

Client: I feel—like a sadness. And yet I don't want to show it. You know, it's just like a— just enough to let me feel something but not enough to keep me down.

Therapist: Uh-huh. Okay, so you say that you feel the sadness, and you don't want to show it?

Client: Uh-huh.

Therapist: Okay, what's your objection to showing it?

Client: Well, like my sister said, 'It doesn't look nice.' Appearances, you know.

Therapist: Wouldn't look good?

Client: Doesn't look good. Makes other people feel uncomfortable. Doesn't make me feel good. Just like a real negative situation. One to be avoided.

Therapist: If you showed your true feelings to me right now, it wouldn't look good to me?

Client: No. Then I wouldn't feel comfortable either. So, the reason is that I'm just not comfortable with it.

Therapist: Okay. Are you willing to explore this a little further?

Client: [*tentatively*] Yeah, all right.

Therapist: You sound hesitant.

Client: Yeah, but I'll try.

Therapist: Before you leap into something—what's your hesitancy?

Client: How I'm going to feel. How it's going to affect me. I guess I'm protecting me.

Therapist: Okay. That sounds sensible—to protect yourself. Like your concern is that if you explore it further, what might happen? You say, 'How I'll feel. . .'

Client: It might bring up feelings that I don't want to face. I don't want to feel, I don't want to face them. I don't know. And I don't know if I'm—you know—sometimes I just wonder, am I ready for it? Or, I have to be in the frame of mind for it.

Therapist: So this is important, I think, to pause here and not rush into something. To really respect where you are. You're saying, 'I'm not sure if I'm ready to look into this further.'

Client: Uh-huh.

Therapist: 'I might get into some feelings I'm not ready to deal with right now. And I feel like protecting myself.'

This vignette demonstrates several aspects of the processes involved in helping clients gain access to affective experience and develop the capacity for insight in terms of acknowledging inner emotional experience. First, the therapist helps the client acknowledge feelings of sadness. This is achieved, in part, by the client finding her subjective experience accurately reflected back to her from the therapist: "So you start to feel that pain." Recall Bowlby's (1973, 1988) claim that infants develop an authentic sense of self when inner experience is acknowledged and accurately reflected back from the environment; from the perspective we propose, recognition and confirmation of emotional states is essential for helping clients achieve insight and develop secure states of mind. Articulating emotional experience facilitates increased comfort for the client in recognizing and acknowledging painful emotions; this provides an essential foundation for facilitating insight and broader self-acceptance. Next, the therapist helps the client articulate her style of coping with feelings of pain: "be a fighter," and "pull yourself together." The unfolding exploration facilitates a more explicit conceptual awareness for the client about how she feels and the way she copes with uncomfortable feelings (i.e., the need to be strong and handle things on her own, not seek support from others). The therapist then tries to help the client address her feelings in the context of the immediate situation—in the here and now. She responds, "I don't want to show it." The therapist is working with Jane to articulate the way in which she dissociates from her emotional experience; she feels sadness and vulnerability, but simultaneously, she wants to protect herself and appear strong to others. The vignette concludes with the therapist recognizing and supporting the client's hesitancy about continued exploration. The therapist acknowledges her hesitancy and says, "I think it is important to respect where you are." This makes the interpersonal context in which this difficult exploration takes place one that recognizes and validates her experience in a general sense and in the here and now. Consistent with other developmental perspectives, the interaction described helps the client feel that "When I look, I am seen, so I exist" (Winnicott, 1971, p. 134). Supporting the client's hesitancy allows her to feel mastery over addressing her painful feelings; at the same time, she feels supported in the immediate interpersonal context. This type of affective attunement and recognition of the client's emotional experience (past and present) forms a building block for helping her access action–disposition information and place her emotional experience in a conceptual framework. In accessing action–disposition information, the emphasis remains one of discovery and emotional attunement on the therapist's part, which helps provide the acceptance and safety clients need to explore affective experiences of discomfort or distress. The therapist's empathy and attunement facilitates the client's ability to be open to internal experience and integrate this into her broader conceptual understanding of herself. Broader access to emotional information for the client enlarges subjective experience and, simultaneously, diminishes her automatic protective (in this case, avoidant) response when addressing painful emotions. Thus, emotions become explicit, and this recognition aids in the process of integrating emotions and mental states of the self and other. Thus, enhancing one's capacity for insight is a developmental process of self-discovery.

Mentalization or Reflective Function

The second process we propose for helping clients achieve insight consists of facilitating a client's capacity for mentalization or reflective function, as described by Fonagy, Target, Steele, and Steele (1998). These theorists propose that reflective function (RF) is an active form of mental processing that assumes flexibility in exploring important experiences of the self and of the self with others; "RF refers to the psychological processes underlying the capacity to mentalize" (p. 5). In their longitudinal work with families, Fonagy and Target (1998) recognized a common factor among their diverse population of children with emotional disorders. They observed that these children "lack the capacity to make use of an awareness of their own and other people's thoughts and feelings" (p. 92). They proposed that reflective functioning or mentalization is a developmental achievement and is contingent on an ability to ascribe intentionality and ultimately to make sense of the world. In effect, RF is the capacity to understand that beliefs, intentions, and desires are mental representations (of the self and others) that reflect current states of mind. As a state of mind, beliefs, intentions, and so forth are subject to change, reevaluation, or reinterpretation. The capacity for mentalization entails the ability to perform mental operations on representations of experience. RF highlights the notion (Fonagy et al., 1998) that insight is characterized by an openness to exploring mental representations, as well as by a fluid or flexible attribution process in organizing experience. From our perspective, this form of insight is expressed in one's openness and flexibility in reflecting on conceptual knowledge regarding mental representations of important interpersonal experiences. In contrast, representational dissociation and a lack of insight are characterized by rigid interpretations of experience and a diminished capacity to explore mental states. To illustrate the processes involved in mentalization, consider the following narrative[2] of a client describing the absence of her mother during childhood.

---

[2]This clinical vignette is from *Negotiating the Therapeutic Alliance: A Relational Treatment Guide* (pp. 130–139), by J. D. Safran and J. C. Muran, 2000, New York: Guilford Press. Copyright 2000 by Guilford Press. Adapted with permission.

It was really hard when I was growing up because my mother worked and was never around. I had to grow up quickly to take care of my brothers and sisters. I felt like I was responsible for dealing with problems that came up day to day. My mother was never there and it made me feel really alone and neglected. I remember when my brother Joe came down with the flu. I just wanted to cry because I saw how sick he was and I didn't know what to do. It was a really hard time. As I think about what that was like, I also realize that my mom needed to work to feed us and pay the bills after my father left. She couldn't work to pay the bills and be home at the same time. I think those were hard times for her too. When she got home from work in the evening she often ruffled my hair and said, "I don't know where I'd be without you."

In this example, the client's mental representation of her childhood relationship with her mother involved painful memories about feeling abandoned and on her own to take care of her siblings in everyday life; she describes feeling "alone and neglected." Although the memories described are difficult, her account demonstrates several aspects of mentalization and her capacity for insight. First, she is able to explore difficult memories and acknowledge the painful impact of these experiences on the self. Despite her negative feelings, she is able to attribute the absence of her mother during childhood to difficult life circumstances rather than to herself as undeserving of love and support. Finally, she is able to consider or imagine her mother's experience during this difficult time and reflect on her mother's view of her in the life of the family. According to Holmes (2001), "RF is related to autobiographical competence: To tell a story about oneself in relation to others one has to be able to reflect on oneself—to see oneself, partially at least, from the outside" (p. 69). In the context of recalling this period in her life, the client engages in an active and flexible attribution process in the context of exploring her difficult feelings of neglect. Consistent with narratives that reflect secure states of mind (Hesse, 1999), her description is relevant, easy to follow, consistent, and detailed enough to convey a discernable storyline. Her narrative demonstrates objectivity regarding the subject matter but is not affectively void or minimizing of the emotional implications of her experience. She also illustrates openness to her interpretations of her own experience (i.e., "As I'm thinking about this now"). Such openness or flexibility facilitates the integration of experience in the client's representational world and is the basis for achieving insight.

PSYCHOTHERAPEUTIC PROCESSES

Taken together, accessing action–disposition information and enhancing mentalization are two primary processes through which therapists work with clients to achieve insight. Therapists begin by helping clients contact and articulate affective experience to facilitate making emotions available for conceptual consideration. Recognizing inner emotional states broadens awareness of needs and desires in the self. In addition, therapists facilitate reflective processes for integrating emotion and conceptual knowledge and encourage clients to explore thoughts, feelings, desires, and beliefs in the self and others. Specifically, therapists can use therapeutic metacommunication to facilitate reflective processes and foster emotional access in an immediate interpersonal context (this is discussed further later in this chap.). In essence, therapists work with clients at affective and conceptual levels to engage in thinking about and sharing mental states. The narratives that evolve are co-constructed and symbolize these integrative processes. Holmes (2001) suggested that "the quest is always for a more elaborated, all embracing, spontaneous, individualized flexible story that encompasses a greater range of experience" (p. 84). Exploring mental states through these processes broadens self-awareness and helps clients find words for important subjective and relational experiences; the goal is to reduce defensive representational dissociation and improve the capacity for coherence. Gaining access to action–disposition information and enhancing mentalization highlight an important intersubjective program for the focus of therapy. Achieving insight is not merely conceptual or cognitive, but rather a process of integrating affective and conceptual representations of one's self and one's important experiences. Symbolized in coherent narratives, these processes enhance contact with the self and others. Ultimately, insight comes about through a dynamic, developmental process in which clients integrate emotion and experience in the way they represent themselves and others through language.

ATTACHMENT THEORY AND INSECURE STATES OF MIND: REPRESENTATIONAL DISSOCIATION

Representational dissociation, or the defensive need to exclude thoughts and feelings related to the self and others from awareness, is indicative of an atrophied capacity for insight or, according to attachment theorists, insecure states of mind. The exclusion of conceptual and emotional information defends one from difficult or contradictory aspects of experience; this disconnection is expressed through incoherent narratives (Hesse, 1999; Main, 1991). Insecure states of mind cluster in categories that exhibit characteristic forms of narrative incoherence; these states of mind function to fracture an individual's representational world. Attachment theorists (Bowlby, 1973; Holmes, 1993; Main, 1991) propose three general insecure styles: *dismissing* (defensive exclusion), *preoccupied* (overinclusive), and *unresolved* (disorganized). Each style demonstrates a diminished capacity for insight through problems accessing inner emotional experience and engaging in mentalization and is expressed in characteristic forms of narrative incoherence.

The first insecure style is associated with narratives that demonstrate a defensive exclusion (or a dismissing) of emotional and cognitive information that serves to protect the self from mental states associated with difficult or painful experiences. The dissociative process for these clients is a form of detachment from subjective experience and memories of the self and others. The dismissing form of narrative incoherence, as described in the literature on adult attachment (Hesse, 1999), is characterized by short, minimizing, or even curt descriptions of relationships, experiences, and emotions. These narratives are often inconsistent in their account; they idealize or devalue important attachment experiences (without a sufficient basis) and the effects of these experiences on the self. A dismissing client may describe an alcoholic parent in stereotyped ways, for example,[3] "You know the deal with alcoholics . . . they are all the same, their first priority is having a drink. I just learned to ignore it. He wasn't a bad father; he was just drunk all the time." In this narrative, it is striking that the client offers no explanation of the emotional impact of this experience on the self (reduced access to affective experience). There is a static, finalized quality to the description, as though it is not open for further interpretation or exploration (i.e., diminished capacity for mentalization). Finally, the description is inconsistent; he was drunk all the time, yet not a bad father. When clients defensively exclude meaningful information, it facilitates a sealing over of painful thoughts and feelings for the purpose of keeping difficult emotional experiences out of conscious awareness. For these clients, the lack of insight expresses itself in the diminished access to affective information and a limited attempt to reflect on or mentalize about subjective experience.

The second insecure style is associated with clients who provide overinclusive narratives and engage in a different manner of representational dissociation. These clients are preoccupied with negative affective experiences at the expense of other representational information. Immersion in a restricted range of emotional experience colors and distorts the narratives these clients provide; consequently, these clients demonstrate a characteristic limitation in their ability to mentalize or engage in flexible thinking with respect to mental states in the self and others. The person is so consumed or fixated with certain emotions that information related to broader thoughts, intentions, and desires in the self and others cannot be integrated and perspective taking and reflective processes are limited. The narratives of these clients are consistent, but their manner of communicating is often fractured and affectively charged (Hesse, 1999). Slade (1999) described preoccupied narratives as "so driven by feeling that they jump from one issue to the next without any sense of focus or inner purpose" (p. 586). The following

---

[3]The narrative presented is hypothetical; however, it demonstrates characteristic styles of narrative incoherence for dismissing clients.

narrative[4] demonstrates expected features of preoccupied or overinclusive narratives:

> You know my dad is a bastard and always has been. He was a miserable failure and I end up paying the price. He made me and my brother wait on the corner everyday while he was drinking away at John's. My life sucks because of him. He's always yelling at us. Sheila always said you can't trust alcoholics. My brother was sent away to military school and he made something of his life. He is married in Ohio with a couple of kids—his wife is really nice to me—she sends me a birthday present every year. I can't stand thinking about those times.

Here the client is angry and blames her father for the dissatisfaction in life that she currently feels. She appears emotionally entangled and, as a consequence, is unable to be objective or impartial. Her lack of insight is expressed in the restricted emotional range and the inhibited reflective processes. One can observe a mobilization of self-protective defenses in this narrative that reflect a sense of self that is vulnerable and damaged; as a result, her capacity to mentalize is limited. Specifically, the angry feelings are so pronounced that she cannot consider a broader or more nuanced range of emotions (e.g., sadness, vulnerability) or imagine other perspectives regarding her experience. This narrative is confused and circumstantial, moving from one topic to the next, introducing characters who are not known or essential to the story; at one point, it seems as though she confuses past and present (e.g., "he's always yelling at us"). The language incoherence for these clients indicates a preoccupation with intense emotion that inhibits the ability to communicate collaboratively. The restricted emotional access and limited reflective processes demonstrate her lack of insight regarding herself and her experience.

Clients with unresolved or disorganized states of mind are often those who have histories of trauma or loss. Insight, with respect to an integration of emotional awareness and conceptual knowledge, is the most impaired in clients who present unresolved narratives. According to Eric Hesse (1999), these clients appear to engage in more global dissociative processes in which narratives specific to trauma and loss seem implausible or irrational. An unresolved client may say, "My father was an alcoholic because I didn't work hard enough in school." Here the client demonstrates illogical thinking in the context of a potentially traumatic relationship. The attribution process is limited and faulty in describing the representation of this relationship and evidences a lack of reflection on the subjective experience of the self or the other. Holmes (2001) observed that in unresolved clients, "The incoherent narrative style associated with abuse presumably reflects traumatic memories threatening to break through into consciousness kept at bay by only partially

---

[4]The narrative presented is hypothetical; however, it demonstrates characteristic styles of narrative incoherence for preoccupied clients.

successful attempts at verbal papering over cracks" (p. 100). In unresolved clients, reflective processes are atrophied and severely impaired, whereas dissociation from affective experience is pronounced.

The form of one's narrative will reflect a current mental state with respect to the affective and conceptual interpretation of one's representational world. The styles described illustrate organized strategies for limiting access to emotional and representational information that restrict the capacity for insight. To help clients achieve insight in psychotherapy, therapists help clients organize and integrate experience to diminish the need to engage in emotional and representational dissociation. Insight is cultivated by helping clients engage in reflective processes to integrate emotional and conceptual knowledge and enhance coherence and collaboration in language.

THE THERAPEUTIC RELATIONSHIP AND THERAPEUTIC METACOMMUNICATION

Insight, from the perspective of gaining access to action–disposition information as well as enhancing mentalization, can be facilitated by metacommunication, a therapeutic intervention described by Safran and Muran (2000). Therapeutic metacommunication attempts to enhance the capacity for insight by encouraging an awareness of the nature and quality of communication between clients and therapists as it evolves in the here and now of the therapeutic relationship. Safran and Muran described metacommunication as a form of *mindfulness in action* in which therapist and client actively explore the here and now interaction to create a collaborative understanding of the current experience. This technique encourages exploration of emotions and mental states of both clients and therapists for the purpose of enhancing the capacity for mutual recognition, narrative coherence, and insight. Metacommunication enhances an intersubjective exploration by articulating the experience of clients and therapists in the current interpersonal context; it engages clients in this process of mentalizing and articulating affective experience of the self and the other in the here and now. Consider the following clinical vignette[5] with Sue, a 49-year-old woman who sought therapy because of social isolation and occupational problems. Her communication style demonstrates characteristics of an overinclusive or preoccupied style.

Client: I don't know . . . I just don't see the relevance of what we're doing.

Therapist: Do you have a sense of what would be relevant?

[5]This clinical vignette is from *Negotiating the Therapeutic Alliance: A Relational Treatment Guide* (pp. 137–139), by J. D. Safran and J. C. Muran, 2000, New York: Guilford Press. Copyright 2000 by Guilford Press. Adapted with permission.

Client:	Well, my occupational therapist, Sarah . . . is supposed to be working on my social skills, and you're supposed to be working on the thinking part . . . kind of a philosophy lesson. That's what I came here for.
Therapist:	Can you say more about what that 'philosophy lesson' would look like?
Client:	I don't know. You're the professional.
Therapist:	So you're kind of saying . . .
Client:	The ball's in your court, that's right, buster. I've led you by the nose as much as I can . . . I mean, cripes, you've got to do something.
Therapist:	Uh-huh.
Client:	If I can sit here and do it by myself, what do I need you for?
Therapist:	My sense is that when I try to run with the ball, I go off course.
Client:	Well, you start going really all over the place. I mean, you don't go deep enough. When you pick up something . . . you don't go deep enough . . . you don't stick to it so that it gets somewhere. I mean, I know the surface stuff, and I mean, you've got to go beyond that.
Therapist:	You weren't happy with the way things went last week?
Client:	Well, what did I get out of it?
Therapist:	Umm. . .
Client:	I mean, what was there that wasn't there before?
Therapist:	You're phrasing that as a question, but I think you're also saying that you didn't get anything out of it.

The session begins with the client expressing her anger about feeling as though the work she has been doing with her therapist has not been relevant. She places the blame for this lack of relevance squarely on the therapist. Consistent with an overinclusive style, her anger drives her narrative and she does not entertain alternative points of view. The therapist attempts to acknowledge the client's concern by asking the client to articulate her sense of what might be relevant. The client, still driven by frustration, places the responsibility on the therapist, insisting, "the ball's in your court." In response, the therapist attempts to metacommunicate by introducing his subjective experience to facilitate exploration of the current interaction. He suggests, "When I try and run with the ball, I go off course." In this statement the therapist validates the client's frustration and, simultaneously, offers his own experience to initiate the possibility of considering alternative points of view. After continued exploration of the client's experience, the therapist makes additional attempts to metacommunicate about the interaction taking place:

Therapist: See . . . my feeling is that it's tempting to try and convince you, but I have a sense that I wouldn't have much of a shot at it . . . that it would become a struggle about who's right . . . you or me?

Client: Well . . . unless I missed something. Although I realize when you mention the 'right' part . . . I mean . . . that's come up a couple of times before. I know I have a thing about always having to be right. But we're getting off track again. I don't think this is getting us anywhere.

Therapist: I'm willing to follow your lead right now. What direction would you like to go in?

Client: Well, there is something about me only being able to see things in black and white terms. Like I've said before, I know that's a problem for me. And I need you to help me see shades of gray.

Therapist: Any sense of what would be a useful way of going about that?

Client: Well . . . you once asked me what would happen if I were wrong, or whatever. You pursued that a little bit . . . but then you just dropped it.

Therapist: Okay, so what would happen if you were wrong?

Client: [*pause*] Well . . . I'd have trouble living with myself. I don't normally think of appearances being that big a deal to me, but obviously somewhere along the line I got this idea that I have to be right, and things have to be my way, or things have to be the way I think is right, which is the same, I suppose, as 'my way.' I mean, people say that I just need things to be my way. But I don't think that's necessarily true. I think it's more tied up with the 'right and wrong' deal. Of course, I know I have trouble accepting some things I don't like, and I know what a terrific rationalizer I am . . . so I can't always be sure . . . 'cause I do such a good job of rationalizing that I'm not always sure what's behind the rationalizing. I believe my rationalizing. That's my defense mechanism.

Therapist: Uh-huh. I have an impression that I think is related to the theme of 'right or wrong.' Are you open to some feedback?

Client: Okay.

Therapist: Okay. I get kind of a sense when you talk, right now, that it's kind of like you've got it all figured out.

Client: Well . . . so I just want you to give me a new way of looking at things, so I can throw the old way out. But the new way has to be as good as the old way.

Therapist:	My feeling is that . . .
Client:	You don't think that's possible.
Therapist:	Well, it feels like there's no room for me to, um, really, enter into a real dialogue with you because I have a sense from you that you've got it all figured out. That you've got yourself all figured out.
Client:	Well, I haven't got it all figured out, because I don't know where the original way of looking at things came from.
Therapist:	Uh-huh. But what about my experience of feeling that there's no room for a dialogue?
Client:	I see, I see, yeah, I would say that would be a reasonable observation.
Therapist:	Uh-huh.
Client:	And, of course, I don't like that because then that's the same garbage that I'm getting from everybody. 'Well, you don't want to change, you've already decided this,' and all the rest of it. You've said it slightly different, so it's not so . . . you know . . . it's not negative the way the rest of them say it . . . so I automatically attack them and defend myself. I mean . . . you've said it so that I don't automatically attack.
Therapist:	But it still feels not so nice, huh?
Client:	Well, it's not nice . . . but as I said . . . it certainly sounds like a reasonable observation.

In this segment, the therapist recognizes the client's frustration and, consequently, encourages collaboration from her with each intervention. This process facilitates insight by broadening Sue's awareness of her current subjective experience and helping her entertain new perspectives. The therapist works with the client at emotional and conceptual levels to acknowledge and articulate her current experience; he states that he is willing to follow her lead, asks her what might be helpful, and inquires about her openness to feedback. In the context of this difficult interaction, the therapist is careful to support the client's subjective experience and her sense of autonomy at each progressive phase in the interaction. In addition to his supportive stance, he begins to introduce his own experience of what is taking place here and now. His focus is on unpacking the current interaction and introducing his experience as a theme for consideration. He explains his feeling that the client "has it all figured out" and that there is no room to "enter into a real dialogue." Metacommunication facilitates mentalization or exploring different points of view; it encourages an articulation of the manner in which both Sue and her therapist experience and interpret the current relational interaction. Furthermore, it introduces Sue to the therapist's experience and to alternative ways of understanding how she negotiates relationships. These are formative processes for helping Sue develop insight by facilitating flexibility in the way she interprets herself in relation to others in an immediate interpersonal context. As this is a new experience, it provokes anxiety for Sue, and she wants proof that the new ways of considering things are "as good as the old."

Insight and narrative coherence are built on collaborative communication; consequently, the therapist emphasizes the notion that it feels like there is no room for a dialogue (i.e., his subjectivity and perspective). The client then begins to integrate the therapist's experience and she acknowledges that she has had similar feedback from others. She explains that typically this response from others produces "an automatic attack" on her part, but hearing it from the therapist seems reasonable. The therapist clarifies for the client not only her anxiety-provoking feeling but also her response to that feeling, thus helping her integrate her emotional experience with her understanding and response to that feeling. Metacommunication facilitates access to Sue's underlying affective experience and her ability to mentalize; the client and therapist work together to coconstruct a narrative that captures the current interpersonal context. Insight evolves though this intersubjective process by articulating and enhancing recognition of emotional and conceptual aspects of subjective experience (self and other) in the here and now. In the next segment, the therapist maintains a focus on the here and now by continuously checking in with the client regarding her concern about being "off topic" from the beginning of the session.

Therapist:	Okay. You'll tell me when we get off topic?
Client:	Well, it's always hard to tell where things are gonna go. But at least you've stopped asking me how I feel about stuff when I complained about that . . . after a few times. Now, you finally believe me that I don't really feel things. [*pause*] Or else you're not letting on . . . you're accepting it and letting it go . . . that's probably closer to the truth.
Therapist:	[*laughs*]
Client:	I analyze everything. The other day I was talking to somebody and they said, 'My goodness, you're thinking ahead all the time.' 'Cause I had correctly anticipated everything that happened in our relationship.
Therapist:	It's true; my sense is that you do think ahead all the time. It's an important ability . . . but I imagine that it can also get kind of tiring sometimes.
Client:	Yeah . . . my mind's never at rest. I'm always on guard.

Therapist:	Do you have a sense of being on guard right now?
Client:	Yeah . . . somewhat . . .
Therapist:	What does it feel like to be on guard right now?
Client:	Well . . . it's like a wall is up.
Therapist:	How high is that wall right now?
Client:	Well, it's only part way up right now. It's not that high or thick.
Therapist:	I'm going to suggest an experiment, if you're willing to try it.
Client:	Okay . . .
Therapist:	Can you think of the wall as part of you, and give that part a voice?
Client:	How do you mean?
Therapist:	Actually speak as the wall. For example, 'I'm Sue's wall, and this is what I do . . . etc.'
Client:	Okay . . . I'm Sue's wall . . . I'm tough on the outside and don't let people in. I've got spikes and electric fences . . . and if anybody comes too close . . . *zap!*
Therapist:	Now . . . can you actually speak to me as the wall?
Client:	Okay . . . I won't let you touch me . . . because if you actually did touch me you might find a weak spot.
Therapist:	It sounds as though your wall is serving an important function.
Client:	Yeah . . . it's allowing me to live. It's allowing me not to turn into a jellyfish. [*long pause*]
Therapist:	What are you experiencing?
Client:	I don't know. I feel kind of strange . . . kind of nervous. I never thought of it like that before.

In the beginning of this segment the client demonstrates how she interacts with the therapist and the world in that her defenses are continuously mobilized. Her self-protective style is at the forefront of her interactions with others; she feels a chronic need to be on guard, defended, and always strong. Although the client protests, "I don't really feel things," the angry and confusing nature of her narrative suggests magnified access to painful emotions at the expense of accessing her vulnerability or need for nurturance. The client's communications are angry and she places blame on the therapist. That she is overwhelmed with frustration diminishes her capacity to explore alternative perspectives, mental states, or reflect on the manner in which she represents her experience. The client describes "correctly anticipating everything that happened" in the course of a previous relationship; for Sue, the tentative and complex nature of subjective experience is anxiety provoking and creates a sense of uncertainty and insecurity in the context of relating to others. The dissociative processes for her are demonstrated in the opening of the segment; Sue has limited access to feelings other than anger and solid resistance to reflecting on and exploring her current mental state or the mental states of others.

In metacommunicating and focusing on the current interaction, the therapist works to develop Sue's capacity for insight by enhancing access to affective information through emphasizing a here and now exploration of the current subjective experience for him and his client. With this support and focus Sue begins to make contact with vulnerable, sensitive feelings toward the end of the segment; she articulates a vague, uncomfortable sensation. This broader self-awareness comes about in a progressive sequence. The therapist recognizes her self-state (i.e., the need to be on guard) and explores her defenses (i.e., wall is up); he asks her to "actually speak as the wall" she describes. Through this exercise the client gains access to inner emotional experience by acknowledging that she needs this wall because the therapist "might find a weak spot." With this recognition, her tone of voice softens and she is able to step back from the unremitting mobilization of her defenses. She is able to consider in a more objective and reflective manner, a new point of view. She admits, "I never thought of it like that before." Insight for this client comes about through making contact with her vulnerable emotions, reflecting on her understanding of things, and considering new or more elaborated perspectives. In this example, the therapist alternates between emphasizing emotional recognition and mentalization in an intersubjective process to help Sue contact inner emotional experience and to integrate this into a more flexible conceptual representation of her experience. Metacommunication facilitates insight by enlarging the range of subjective experience in the current interpersonal context and by providing a safe place to reflect on and negotiate relatedness to others.

Therapeutic metacommunication encourages clients to access action–disposition information (Safran & Segal, 1990) and engage in mentalization in the context of the psychotherapy experience. By recognizing and articulating mental states and acknowledging and fully accepting a part of the self in the context of the current interaction, clients begin to integrate experience in a developmental process for the purpose of achieving insight. Taken together, these processes enhance the insight by integrating emotional and conceptual knowledge and encouraging comfort in exploring broader, more nuanced aspects of experience in an immediate interpersonal context. These psychotherapeutic processes provide a foundation for intersubjective relatedness in sharing and exploring mental states and diminishing the need to dissociate from important representations of experience. Ultimately, these processes facilitate an integration of emotional and cognitive representations of experience, and this integration provides the foundation of insight.

CONCLUDING COMMENTS

This chapter presents a developmental point of view in conceptualizing and achieving insight. Using attachment theory as a foundation for incorporating contemporary theories in emotion, mentalization, and the therapeutic relationship, we hope to provide a nuanced clinical and theoretical contribution to this important volume. We emphasize the way in which therapists work at both affective and conceptual levels to help clients organize and integrate mental states and mental representations. The goal is a coherent narrative coconstructed by clients and therapists that symbolizes the integration of emotional and conceptual knowledge in the context of representational worlds that can be shared by the self and the self in relation to others. This emphasis on expanding awareness facilitates increased contact with the self and greater facility in negotiating important interpersonal experiences.

REFERENCES

Bowlby, J. (1973). *Attachment and loss: Vol. 2. Separation: Anger and anxiety.* New York: Basic Books.

Bowlby, J. (1988). *A secure base.* New York: Basic Books.

Fonagy, P., & Target, M. (1998). Mentalization and the changing aims of child psychoanalysis. *Psychoanalytic Dialogues, 8*(1), 87–114.

Fonagy, P., Target, M., Steele, H., & Steele, M. (1998). *Reflective-functioning manual, version 5.* Unpublished manuscript, University College, London.

Grice, H. P. (1975). Logic and conversation. In P. Cole & L. J. Moran (Eds.), *Syntax and semantics III: Speech acts* (pp. 41–58). New York: Academic Press.

Hesse, E. (1999). The adult attachment interview. In J. Cassidy & P. R. Shaver (Eds.), *Handbook of attachment: Theory, research, and clinical applications* (pp. 395–433). New York: Guilford Press.

Holmes, J. (1993). *John Bowlby and attachment theory.* London: Routledge.

Holmes, J. (2001). *The search for the secure base.* East Sussex, England: Brunner-Routledge.

Main, M. (1991). Metacognitive knowledge, metacognitive monitoring, and singular (coherent) vs. multiple (incoherent) models of attachment: Findings and directions for future research. In P. Harris, J. Stevenson-Hinde, & C. Parkes (Eds.), *Attachment across the life cycle* (pp. 127–159). New York: Routledge & Kegan Paul.

Safran, J. D., & Muran, C. (2000). *Negotiating the therapeutic alliance: A relational treatment guide.* New York: Guilford Press.

Safran, J. D., & Segal, Z. V. (1990). *Interpersonal process in cognitive therapy* (2nd ed.). New York: Basic Books.

Safran, J. D., & Segal, Z. V. (1996). *Interpersonal process in cognitive therapy* (2nd ed.). Northvale, NJ: Basic Books.

Slade, A. (1999). Attachment theory and research. In J. Cassidy & P. R. Shaver (Eds.), *Handbook of attachment: Theory, research, and clinical applications* (pp. 575–594). New York: Guilford Press.

Winnicott, D. W. (1971). *Playing and reality*. Middlesex, England: Penguin.

20

A PHILOSOPHICAL
ANALYSIS OF INSIGHT

R. FOX VERNON

What can philosophy offer a scientific inquiry into psychotherapeutic insight? The answer may well depend on how much time and patience one has, because philosophy, unlike science, often lacks the virtues of brevity and concreteness. It can be given to contemplation and abstraction, and it can drift from practical matters at hand. Yet such contemplation and drift is often the very point of philosophy, because at its best philosophical inquiry does not drift aimlessly, but downwardly, to the bottom or essence of things. What a philosophical analysis offers an inquiry into insight, then, is a look into the very depths of insight. In these depths, many enigmatic questions come to the fore. What is insight? Does it exist? Is it even possible? Can we have insights that are accurate and complete? Or is insight—by its very nature—inaccurate and incomplete, so that we are relegated to viewing mere representations, constructions, or distortions? These questions are troublesome, but they are nestled in the very fabric of our thinking, and they threaten every inquiry.

In the analysis of insight in this chapter, I invite my reader to join me in a brief, three-phase excursion into these questions, with each phase addressing one of three vexing philosophical issues: *epistemology, phenomenol-*

ogy, and *ontology*. In the first phase of this excursion, epistemology, I begin with the question, Is knowing possible? This question is the centerpiece of this study for two reasons. First, we want to know about insight, so it is reasonable to ask if knowing is possible in the first place. Of course, this would hold for any object of study. Can we know about rocks, or mathematics, or human behavior of any kind? But there is a second consideration that makes this epistemological discussion even more central. Insight is itself a form of knowing, so by exploring whether knowing is possible, we inevitably peer into the primary properties of insight. Thus, we are attempting to gain insight about insight. Is it flawed or distorted at its core? Or can insight at times remain free of flaws and distortions? Attempting to address these epistemological puzzles propels us into the second phase of this philosophical journey: phenomenology. Here, I argue that phenomenology—which is the study of the phenomena that pass before conscious awareness—provides a foundational epistemology; that is, basic phenomenological observations provide proof of knowing (or having insights), and this grounds all other ways of knowing (or having insights). Finally, in the third and final phase of this analysis, I rely on phenomenology (i.e., the examination of consciousness) to flesh out an ontology of insight. *Ontology* is a troublesome philosophical term that can mean many things. In this analysis I take the term to indicate the study of the basic properties of things, so in fleshing out an ontology of insight, I mean that I describe some of the fundamental properties of insight. These properties (such as sense-perceptibility or measurability) are so fundamental that we usually do not question them, for we have already assumed that they apply.

THE EPISTEMOLOGICAL QUAGMIRE

To put our present analysis in context, consider a question that might occur to any scientist embarking on an investigation of insight: Can we ever know whether someone has had one? At the center of this question is the issue of whether knowing itself is possible. This question is so foundational, and it so nearly ends things before they begin, that we need to contemplate its ramifications.

Methodism: The Bottomless Path

Modern psychology, when challenged as to whether it knows anything, seems to answer this challenge in the affirmative. Of course, the next question is, how does psychology know that it knows? And to that, modern psychology responds, with minor exceptions, by pursuing the epistemological route of *methodism*. Methodism is the assertion that methods—that is, certain specifiable criteria—are the foundational touchstones for attaining knowledge. The method that science has chosen is called, of course, the scientific method. Here, I also call this method *traditional empiricism*.

The assertion that traditional empiricism is epistemologically foundational usually suffices for researchers who are ready to go about the business of investigating (i.e., trying to know something), but for philosophers it simply will not do. If we aspire to be rigorous, we must ask whether the criteria of traditional empiricism are sound. That is, if we want to enter the depths of epistemology, we must ask, can traditional empiricism know that it knows? If it cannot, why should we respect any of its claims about insight? If traditional empiricism merely thinks it knows, this shouldn't carry any weight. After all, any of us can think we know. Why then turn to science if the best it can do is think it knows? The prize is in really knowing, and really knowing has been the claim of science since it came into ascendancy during the Enlightenment as a means of sweeping aside personal opinion and superstition.

That traditional science can only think it knows is at first not troublesome. After all, all that is needed is a method, or a criterion, to verify traditional science. But here is the rub: Methods cannot verify methods. Why? Because the project of assuring knowledge by means of a method requires that the method itself be validated (Why else should we trust it?), and the only way to do this (given the insistence on using method) is to use yet another method. But this method must also be validated with another method, and that method with yet another, and so on, such that we never reach an end. It is a bottomless path. Thus, all epistemologies based on method are ultimately arbitrary, because we must choose an arbitrary point at which we stop testing our method and simply accept that method as foundational. Of course, this is not a robust epistemology. It doesn't move us beyond opinion.

This is the epistemological quagmire that both traditional science and modern psychological inquiry find themselves in, and this is not recent news. Indeed, it is such old news that many of us (in philosophy, psychology, and larger intellectual circles) have grown weary of it—so weary that we have come to accept that when it comes to the heart of the matter, no truth can be verified absolutely. For the most part, we let matters rest there. Science is not perfect, we admit, but it is the best we have; it is a pragmatic compromise. So we no longer treat traditional empiricism with the reverence we once accorded it (e.g., during the Enlightenment), but nevertheless we push forward and conduct our research according to the assumptions and precepts of traditional empiricism.

Speaking as a philosopher, I can only ask, is this really okay? If we genuinely want to understand insight (or anything else for that matter), can we accept using science as a means of inquiry when science itself is unverified? Would we tolerate this of a finding in one of our studies? And if not, why tolerate it in the very method used in the bulk of our work?

I offer an even more unnerving observation about traditional empiricism: at its foundation, it refutes itself. That is to say that traditional empiricism, when subjected to its own criteria, fails to meet them. To examine this issue, I take a look at what those criteria are. For the most part, the underlying precepts of today's science are identical to the doctrine of empiricism that Hume (1748/1983) worked out in the 18th century. Hume put forward two criteria of indubitable knowledge: It must be either mathematical or sense-perceptible. A proposition that is neither, according to Hume, is merely thinking that we know, and in his words, we must "commit it then to the flames: for it can contain nothing but sophistry and illusion" (Hume, 1748/1999, p. 696).

Since Hume's day, traditional empiricism has not veered from either of the two criteria that Hume so eloquently distilled: sense perception and mathematical reasoning. This is a crucial point to appreciate, because these two criteria shape the underlying stance of traditional empirical inquiry toward the phenomenon of insight. On the basis of its epistemology, traditional empiricism insists that insight, if it is to be valid, must derive from and be verified by either mathematical reasoning or sense perception. What is problematic with these two tenets? Aside from the point already discussed—that method cannot justify itself without relying on further methods, and so on, ad infinitum—there is this: If traditional empiricism is to be taken seriously and its criteria applied to everything, then it ought to be applied to itself. That is, if the two criteria for verifying knowledge (or insight) are sense perception and mathematical analysis (or some combination of the two), then one ought to ask whether these criteria are themselves sense perceptible or mathematical; these are, after all, the most foundational of all knowledge claims.

It turns out they are not. One cannot sense perceive (i.e., hear, taste, smell, see, or touch) that sense-perception or mathematics are reliable methods of knowing, nor can one test this proposition through any mathematical reasoning (e.g., through calculation). To put this graphically, one cannot see with one's eyes that one is seeing with one's eyes (much less can one see with one's eyes that seeing with one's eyes is reliable). And one cannot mathematically verify that math is a reliable means of knowing. There is no such equation.

So back to the question: Can we ever know whether someone has attained an insight? It would seem not, at least not by means of any method. So at the outset of this analysis the use of methods as foundational epistemologies must be adandoned. This means the abandonment of traditional empiricism, the one method everyone thinks should be used. However, if we cannot use traditional empiricism, how can we ever set about knowing if someone has had an insight?

Skepticism: The Path of Doubt

Given the difficulties of authenticating any method of knowing, *skepticism*—which in many ways is a fair term for the basic tenets of most strands of postmodernism—may seem an attractive alternative. It is attractive, in part, because of an interesting similarity it holds with the scientific method, for a crucial feature of the scientific method is its skeptical attitude. Empiricism is quite satisfied to doubt everything, except perhaps its own criteria. In general, I think it is fair to say that the intellectual culture of the West is enamored with skepticism. We have been practicing it for quite a few centuries, and we are experts at it. This may lend particular appeal to the question, "Can we know?" And to this, one commonly answers—aloud or to oneself—"perhaps not." This is often quickly amplified to "probably not" or "certainly not." Most scholars, researchers, and philosophers alike usually arrive at the following skeptical conclusion:

> I may believe certain things about the world; and my experiments, surveys, or observations may even validate these beliefs—but I cannot really know if I am right or wrong. Others may agree with my theories and findings, perhaps everyone will agree with me; nonetheless, epistemologically speaking, I simply cannot know that I know.

This is skepticism. And it harbors this ultimate conclusion about insight: If insight indeed exists, the possibility of uncovering truth is simply not one of its fundamental properties. So, to the original question, "Can we ever know that someone has had an insight?", the skeptical answer would be either a staunch, "No, we cannot know," or a more guarded, "We do not know if we know."

Though I think it is true that Western culture is drawn to skepticism, it is also true that it is deeply troubled by it. We still want to know, and we believe, deep down, that knowing is possible and good. After all, what is an annual meeting of researchers, or a book on insight, if they are not at least places to share and celebrate knowledge, or bemoan the lack of it? What occurs, however, is a tremendous waffling. On the one hand, we want to know, and we want to believe in insights, and so we hold up science (or the traditional empirical method) as the great hope for knowing. On the other hand, we distrust the act of knowing, and we instinctively retract from claims of absolute certainty because of their apparent rigidity or dogmatism. Therefore, we take the position of uncertainty. Our insights, we claim, are fallible. But we tend to move even beyond this, to the claim not merely that knowing is fallible on occasion but that it fails in every occurrence.

What is wrong with the skeptical stance that knowing (or insight, for that matter) is inherently unachievable? The difficulty is that this stance refutes itself, for although it claims that knowing is inherently unachievable, it also claims to know something (that knowing is inherently unachievable). Skepticism cannot, metaphorically speaking, eat its cake and have it too. It cannot deny the possibility of knowledge, yet be itself a knowledge claim. In the end, the true skeptic is condemned not to believe skepticism (because not believing is the skeptical stance), or—if the skeptic insists on believing skepticism—she or he must believe it as an unknowable and thus ultimately unjustifiable and untestable opinion. Being the self-refuting epistemology that it is, skepticism allows us to believe anything, yet disbelieve anything too. It is not a robust epistemology.

PARTICULARISM: THE PATH OF PHENOMENOLOGY

If neither methodism nor skepticism can provide an adequate episte-mology—because methods cannot assure us that we do know and skepticism cannot assure us that we do not—where should one turn? I believe that one solution is the path that Chisholm (1973) labeled *particularism*. I'm not sure why Chisholm chose that term, but it may have been because he believed that a viable alternative to methodism and skepticism is to first find particu-lar cases of things that indubitably are known and then build epistemological criteria according to these cases. Phenomenology is just such an approach. From the phenomenological point of view—and here I build on Husserl's (1962, 1969) early view of phenomenology—epistemological doubt, as pre-sented in the question, "Can I know?" is the wrong place to start one's episte-mology. That is not to say that it isn't a fine place from which to begin questioning an epistemology. That it is. But questioning an epistemology, on one hand, and building one, on the other, are two different enterprises. Doubt simply cannot get an epistemology going. It is useful; however, it cannot construct, it only destroys.

From what, then, might an epistemology be built? Ironically, what might beget an epistemology is a reexamination of the question "Can one know?", but this time from a different perspective. Instead of focusing on the answer to this question, we focus on the asking of the question, for it is the asking—and the phenomenological witnessing of that asking—that answers the ques-tion. What do I mean by this? I mean essentially what Descartes (1641/1951) meant when he began his epistemology by doubting everything. He essen-tially asked, "Can we know anything?" He soon realized, however, that while asking this question, he could not doubt that he was indeed asking this ques-tion. Descartes thereby answered the question, "Can we know anything?" with the realization that we can know that we are questioning ourselves. That is, we can know that we are asking ourselves "Can I know anything?" This is a foundational and infallible insight.

Let us look more closely at this example of an infallible insight. In this example, the process of doubting (i.e., merely asking the question, "Can we know?") does not produce knowing. But when we do doubt, we also *see* (if we put our attention to it) that we are doubting. (I use the verb *to see* here to denote the mental act of grasping or recognizing, not the act of visually per-ceiving.) It is this seeing that produces knowing, the knowing of doubting. Indeed, this seeing is itself the very process—the very lived-through moment—of knowing or realizing something. It is this direct seeing that is at the core of insight. Not all seeing is of this kind. Sometimes what we think we see or know turns out not to be the case, so some types of seeing involve errors, omissions, misjudgments, and so on. The point is that even though some types of seeing are incomplete and flawed, there is a very important type that is not. When we see that we doubt, for example, we can see this directly and indubitably. Again, this is a foundational insight, or what I will call a *primordial* insight.

We now have a particular case of indubitable knowing (again, this is why phenomenology is a type of particularism), and we can examine this example of knowing to better understand its character. One of its crucial properties is the certainty that is inherent within it. That certainty does not arise from dogmatic theorizing, or from demanding or wishing that it be so, or from having already believed it to be so. Nor does it arise purely from logic (though it is no doubt logical). Perhaps most important, this certainty is not established by traditional empiricism or any other method. Rather, this certainty is a phenomenological *indubitability*—that is, it is a *lived-through, directly experienced* moment of consciousness. We live through this certainty not only when we see ourselves doubting, but perhaps more important, when we see that we see ourselves doubting. Descartes's (1641/1951) observation about witnessing his own doubt, then, is actually a witnessing of two truths: First, I see that I doubt, and second, I see that I see this! To test this, simply perform the phenomenological experiment of observing yourself doubting. My contention is that though you may think you see mere logic, theory, method, bias, or constructions, all of these are either dubitable or peripheral claims. The seeing of your doubting, however, will be unquestionable and central. It hits you right in the face, so to speak, in a way that none of the other claims do.

I used the word *test* previously, and it may lead you to think of phenomenology as a type of method with its own criterion and thus as problematic as all methods. Given the right context, it can be helpful to speak of phenomenology as a method. However, it is crucial to realize that the test that phenomenology depends on is not a test in the same way empiricism is. In traditional empiricism, one has an experience, and then filters (i.e., tests) that experience through the two foundational criteria of empiricism (sense-perception and mathematical reasoning). In phenomenology, one observes one's experience to see if something is present. What is indubitable (e.g., that I see my doubt) presents itself as such. It is experientially self-evident and remains unfiltered by any criteria.

The obvious character of these types of indubitable observations, then, resides within the witnessing itself. It is *experience-near*, to use the experiential continuum laid out by Pascual-Leone and Greenberg (see chap. 2, this volume). This obvious character, then, is not a theory but a lived experience. Husserl (1962, 1969) used several terms to convey these types of epistemological experiences. He spoke of *pure intuition*, the *primordial dator act*, the *self-evident*, the *given*, and the *purely self-given*. Husserl ultimately settled on the term *Evidenz* to denote these types of knowing. Evidenz are types of insight in which we know, and we know that we know. We do not check criteria to ascertain these types of insights; we simply see them. They are direct, lived observations of truth. They are foundational. This is a very different description of knowing and of insight than that of either methodism or skepticism. Methodism claims that insight is fundamentally a matter of a methodology that is tacked on to seeing. Seeing cannot be trusted, so to speak, but methods for testing seeing can. Furthermore, methodism claims that only sense-perception and mathematical reasoning are valid forms of seeing. Skepticism, however, simply asserts that no such seeing ever occurs.

An epistemological theory that is commonly opposed to Husserl's (1962, 1969) phenomenological account of Evidenz is a brand of skepticism usually known as *constructionism*. To oversimplify somewhat, constructionism is the view that we cannot know reality; we can only know our constructions of reality. A constructionist would likely assert that the seeing of doubt, as presented in the previous example, is merely the process of witnessing one's own constructions. But is this theory accurate? Does it describe our true experience? I don't think so. What has happened, I think, is that the constructionist has seen her- or himself doubting and has afterward attached the theory that this doubting was a mere construction. This supposed construction is really a theory imposed after the fact, not something witnessed in the moment. That is, the constructionist did not see a construction and then label it such, but rather saw actual doubt and labeled it a construction. I would not argue that constructions never occur within our experience, but I would argue that we should not presume constructions to exist where we have not witnessed them. To do so—to presume that all experience is constructed—is to prejudge experience rather than observe it. Furthermore, where constructions are actually seen, must not it be supposed that we indeed see these constructions (once we have constructed them)? If so, then mustn't we suppose a direct observation of sorts, a seeing that is indubitable, the seeing of constructions? If we do not allow for this, then insight must be a construction of constructions, and this neither makes sense nor does it match our lived-through experience.

In our actual observations of our experience, the facts that we can see ourselves doubting and we can see that we see this are indubitable evidence. These truths, these *knowings* or *insights*, come from a lived-through seeing and are available to anyone who is willing to examine or live through them. Thus, phenomenological speaking, seeing is believing. However, though seeing is believing, believing is not necessarily seeing. This is a crucial phenomenological point, and it speaks to what insight truly is. If I know something, then certainly I believe it. But I may believe something (e.g., that 1 + 1 = 2), and not know it. That is, I may think it is true, but not see that it is. To see that 1 + 1 = 2, to have that insight, I must actually think about 1 + 1, and then live through the experience, the *Aha!* moment, in which I recognize the truth that 1 + 1 = 2. Knowing or having an insight, is a lived-through moment of seeing something to exist or to be true. It is a moment of recognition. Thus, when we doubt, we can—if we wish to turn our attention to it—see (and thus know) that we are doubting. The skeptic might challenge this by simply demanding, "How do you know you are doubting?" The empiricist may ask, "What scientific criterion validates your observations of doubt?" But phenomenologically speaking—and for the sake of honesty and humility—the only recourse is to say, "I see it! I directly experience it!" And we might add, "You can too." If the skeptic and empiricist persist and claim they cannot see it (and thus cannot know it), we must wonder if they are blind. Perhaps they are. Blindness regarding matters that are plainly before us, is a common human condition. Surely where others are blind, we cannot force them to see. However, the opposite is also true. Where we see (as in the case of our own doubting), we must not force ourselves to be blind. It is precisely this pretense to be blind that both traditional empiricism and skepticism have adopted. With skepticism, this blindness is claimed regarding all things (for one can know nothing); with empiricism, it is claimed about whatever phenomena do not meet the criteria of being either sense-perceptible or mathematical. Phenomenology avoids both conceits.

Phenomenology as Foundational Epistemology

From this starting point—the point of personal experience, or subjective awareness—epistemology can be built; that is, we can answer the question, "Can I know?" and we can provide specific examples of knowledge. Where methods and skepticism have failed to provide grounding, phenomenology succeeds. Thus, the epistemology for a study of insight is itself founded on insight—that is, on personal, lived-through experience—not on science and not on skepticism (i.e., antiknowing postmodernisms). I label this starting point *phenomenological realism.*

I realize that phenomenological realism is a difficult epistemology to believe given the current philosophical and cultural climate. Very few are arguing for realisms of any kind, much less a phenomenological one. Even if phenomenological realism ultimately fails, however, I believe it deserves a good hearing, not least of all for this reason: Most of us, in our day-to-day lives—when we step away from our scientific journals or our postmodern deconstructions—seem to believe and abide by an underlying phenomenological realism. That is, we base our beliefs and our very lives on lived-through insights—on our own observations and our own reasoning.

Our clients do the same. Where we override our clients' insights with interpretations or ideas that run counter to their lived experience, we are unlikely to be doing our clients any favors, even if we are certain of our views. Of course, we may be right, but even if so, the key is to communicate to our clients in a way that helps them to see (from within their own experience) that we are right. If they do not see it, why should they believe it? We would not ourselves, and we would expect others to reveal their views in such a way that allowed us to evaluate and analyze those views for ourselves (and evaluating and analyzing, at their deepest levels, are processes of lived-through, personal experiencing).

However, I have veered from epistemology and into ethics. I will only add this brief observation: The path of phenomenological realism, if nothing else can be said for it, does at least honor the reasoning and experiencing of individuals. It does not encourage people to accept truths blindly, and in fact encourages them to challenge all truths—whether these come from religion, science, or elsewhere. Phenomenology values—as an inherent ethical stance—the power and dignity of human consciousness, however frail and fallible it may at times be.

Can It Ever Be Known Whether Someone Has Had an Insight?

Let's return to the original question: Can we ever know whether someone has had an insight? From the standpoint of phenomenological realism, the answer is a resounding yes—we can know when we ourselves have had an insight. Not only that, we can know that we know this. These are foundational claims about insight. It exists; and we can know, at times, that it does exist. Insight, then, is not inherently an illusion or construction or an arbitrary *meaning shift*.

We now have epistemological footing for our study of insight, a foundation or bottom, so to speak. Indeed, insight is a prescientific knowing that can substantiate science itself. That foundation rests on our subjective experiences of insight. However, we must be careful. This phenomenological foundation does not include all subjective experiences, all lived-through knowings; rather, only those that have the quality of Evidenz are included. Such experiences are self-evident or self-given; we see them, and we see that we see them.

I should perhaps pause at this point, for skeptical and empirical readers may immediately object: "Why should we trust another's subjective experience?" This is not what phenomenological realism requests. Rather, it asks that we test all knowledge on the basis of our *own* subjective and lived-through experience. Not only that, it requests that we take as knowledge only those experiences that appear as self-evident. Much experience does not appear as self-evident. For example, we hear a bird in the distance. What is self-evident in this experience is the very sound of the bird call. What is not self-evident is that it is a bird making that call. Here lies a maxim of phenomenological realism: We should take as knowledge only what we directly experience (the sound of the bird call) and remain neutral (in phenomenology, the term *bracketing* is sometimes taken to denote this) about whether it is an actual bird making that call (rather than, say, a recording of a bird).

Phenomenological realism, then, remains faithful to actual experience and does not move beyond what is contained within that experience. True, there are many phenomena that we want to know about but cannot directly see within our experience. We do not see the experiential processes of another, for example. Thus, we do not directly experience another's thoughts or insights. (This, of course, is self-evident in our experience of others!) We also do not directly see atoms. We must use tools and instruments to know about atoms. Therefore, when we make assertions about others' thoughts or about atoms, we must be careful to acknowledge that we are theorizing. When we theorize we hypothesize about things we do not directly experience, but when we *phenomenologize*, we describe things we do directly experience. We must be careful not to confuse the two.

To elaborate on this second point, modern empiricism often commends itself for avoiding the apparent dogmatism of absolute certainty. It zealously limits itself to theories, models, or—in the case of psychology—constructs. This, of course, is wise practice in certain domains of knowledge (e.g., when it comes to atoms or others' thoughts), but not everything is a theory (i.e., something we think is true but cannot directly observe and verify). Science can overlook these very things. Phenomenology, however, does not overlook them. It acknowledges them for what they are, and it acknowledges their abundance within everyday awareness of the world. We do not theorize that we doubt, for example. We see it directly. We do not theorize that $1 = 1$, or that $1 + 1 = 2$, or that a thing is what it is and not what it is not. We see these truths. No science can establish them (or ever has); no instruments verify them (or if they do, only because personal experience has verified those instruments); and no proofs can be found for them. We know them nonetheless, and we see that we do. Phenomenology, unlike science, allows these truths because they are subjectively experienced as self-evident. If we can trust our faculties to recognize that $1 = 1$, we should trust those same faculties to recognize other self-evident truths. That is really all that phenomenological realism asserts. It does not eliminate traditional empiricism as a methodology. Indeed, it gives traditional empiricism a foundation (something it could not do for itself). In doing so, it recognizes the limits of science. It allows traditional empiricism to speak about those things it can speak about (*publicly observable* sense-perceptions and measurements), and moves beyond science in those realms (such as that of subjective experience or mental activity) where science is simply blind and must prod about with its clumsy instruments. Insight is precisely such territory. It is a subjectively experienced phenomenon.

Having addressed the epistemological conundrum by turning to phenomenological realism, let us now delve into the issue of ontology, which has to do with describing the basic properties of insight. Ontology points to this foundational question: What is the nature of this stuff, insight, which we claim exists? Reason suggests that it would be wise to begin an inquiry of insight with an adequate description of what insight is (i.e., with its ontology). But have I followed this approach in this analysis? After all, didn't we begin with an epistemological analysis, rather than an ontological one? Haven't I, too, put method before description?

I don't think so. Indeed, a main concern in this chapter has been to get ontology right before moving on to an epistemology. Though we began by diving into epistemological concerns, success was not found there. Indeed, I attempted to demonstrate that the only way out of the initial epistemological quagmire (i.e., the concern, "Can we know if we know?") was to move beyond epistemology, for when we examined methods as a foundation for knowing, we found them to be wanting; and when we examined skepticism, we found it to be equally problematic. We then turned to particularism. Though I failed to point this out, particularism—in its essence—is an ontology, because particularism is based on particular examples and from these examples we then can build accurate descriptions of insight's basic properties.

The primary example obtained in the brand of particularism I put forward was that of *Evidenz*. Evidenz is a lived-through moment of seeing something to exist or to be true. Evidenz is the type of knowing that occurs when we see that we doubt or when we see that we see our doubt. Try seeing your own doubt now, and you will witness for yourself the properties of Evidenz. Indeed, any example of witnessing one's own mental events will hold the properties of Evidenz. The experience of Evidenz, I have argued, is a case of primordial insight. All types of Evidenz, or primordial insight, reveal at least the following ontological properties: *certainty* and *lived-through-ness*. The property of certainty is what might also be characterized as *truth*, and the property of lived-throughness is roughly captured in such synonyms as *personal awareness*, *human consciousness*, or *subjectivity*. This is not to say that all experiences of personal awareness or human consciousness are true. Many are not. But Evidenz is a particular case in which truth is present in a subjective, lived-through moment.

This example of primordial insight is, remember, "at the bottom of things." That is, it is a foundational example of insight, or what insight is at its core. I argue, then, that at its very core insight is a case of subjectively experiencing truth. Primordial insight, of course, is in many ways much less complex than the types of insight encountered from clients in psychotherapy. Such psychotherapeutic insights are often built on primordial insights (e.g., clients' witnessing of their own thoughts and feelings), but they may also be built on inaccurate, incomplete, or adulterated insights—that is, thoughts or perceptions that are not completely or indubitably true. There is much to be explored about such hybrid insights, not least of which is the issue of whether they can be differentiated from pure insights (i.e., primordial insights). I do not have space here to enter into this dialogue, but I should make this final, crucial point about the ontology of insight: Insight is not, at its core, necessarily and inherently incomplete, or inaccurate. Rather, a core property of insight, as witnessed in the example of Evidenz, is the possibility of unmistakably attaining truth.

Sense-Perceptibility and Measurability

Two additional properties are often presumed to be core properties of primordial insight: sense-perceptibility and measurability. Both have been presumed because the reigning epistemology, traditional empiricism, assumes them to be the case for all existing entities. Are these two properties attributable to insight?

Let us first examine the ontological concern of whether insights are sense-perceptible. When we observe our own insights, are we able to touch, smell, hear, feel, or taste them? The answers to this question is obviously negative. However, many insist that insights—at their foundational, ontological level—are in fact physical events that are sense-perceptible. It is often argued, for example, that they are electrochemical events of some sort that occur in the brain. Here, we need to be careful to separate theory from observation. This is a theory, and it has not been verified by science or experience. No one has ever witnessed an electrochemical occurrence and thus been able to comprehend (see, know, or realize) an insight. We do not look at brain scans to figure out what we are thinking or what we know. The best science has done so far is to argue that there are many physical (and quantitative, for that matter) correlates to insight. I insist that though it is fine to study the physical correlates of an object to get a better understanding of it (e.g., to study the footprints of an animal to track its whereabouts when we cannot witness it in the flesh), the goal in this analysis has been to get "to the bottom" of things, and that does not mean to study the correlates of a thing, but to study the thing itself! Can we not observe the "animal" when it is in the flesh; or in the case of insight, when it is occurring within our experience? Must we limit our explorations solely to physical correlates? Worse, must we then claim that correlates are more reliable and shed more light on the topic than actually viewing the thing itself? That, in my mind, is a strange way to proceed. Yet, it has been and still is the common practice of psychological science.

Now let us examine the ontological concern of whether insight is quantifiable or measurable. For that matter, can we measure any of our mental events? For example, is it possible to measure the meaningfulness of a recent insight we have had? Let us turn our attention to the number five and then to the meaningfulness of our recent insight. I think it is immediately and self-evidently present to us that the relation between the two is tenuous at best. Even were we to turn our attention to the number five in relation to a pencil that we hoped to measure, I would say that the relationship is somewhat tenuous. Were we to clarify, however, that the number five stood in relation to the unit of inches and that the unit of inches stood in relation to the length of pencil, then we would have a description that is not tenuous, but very precise: a 5-inch-long pencil.

However, to claim that an insight has a meaningfulness of five calls for a clarification of the units being used, and no one to date has identified units of any mental event. Perhaps the best that has been done is to say, "I am now having an insight," and later, "I have had another"; in this manner, one could count two insights. In this limited way, insights are quantifiable, but what is troubling in even this limited case is that insights have a habit of melding into one another (indeed, conscious experience has this foundational, onto-logical quality so that describing consciousness as a *stream* or *flow* makes sense, though this remains a metaphorical description).

To illustrate, imagine we are using a Likert scale of 1 to 7, with 1 being *no meaningfulness* and 7 being *extreme meaningfulness*. In this case, to describe or define the meaningfulness of an insight as a 5 actually holds some mean-ing. The number 5 does seem to capture—though still somewhat tenuously—an aspect of our insight's meaningfulness. And we could, of course, take mul-titudes of similar measurements to try to understand insight and correlate it with other phenomena. However, I hesitate to call this measurement. Con-sider once again the number five and its relation to the meaningfulness of our insight. I think it is immediately apparent that five, even as a measure of the intensity of the meaningfulness of our insight, is the loosest of correla-tions, and further, it is not a correlation that we witness. To repeat (or, to speak phenomenologically, to show that again), when I judge the meaning-fulness of the insight, I am not observing a direct relation between the num-ber five and meaningfulness. Rather, I am assigning a correlation. This is very different indeed, and to call it measurement is a misnomer, one that has ultimately derailed psychology, notwithstanding all the momentary pragmatic benefits of such subjective assignments.

This illustrates what I mean when I say that insights (and other mental events, such as meaningfulness, for example) are not quantifiable. I am not saying numbers cannot be assigned to such events. They can be, and there is some utility in this. But I am saying that the faculty of insight (or subjective knowing) can also be used to see that numbers and mental phenomena (such as insight) have only the loosest of relations. With physical phenomena, numbers can usually relate to them, through the intermediary of some type of unit, in a way that is meaningful and sensible. We see the relation between five, and inches, and length. With insight, however, we see no such relation, largely, I think, because insight and other mental events cannot be chopped into units. We see that this is so when we view insight or any other mental event. This irreducibly holistic quality of insight occurs as self-evident within our lived-through experience of insight. The only instance in which numbers provide so-called rigorous descriptors or indicators of insight (or other mental phenomena) is when science theorizes that such numbers tap or represent insights; but again, this is theory, and though theory can be rigorous, it cannot match the rigor of direct experience.

But this does not mean that Likert scales and other forms of mental measurement ought to be, to paraphrase the words of Hume, committed to the flames. These psychometric tools can be helpful when their limitations are properly understood. However, true rigor demands that we not allow psychometric epistemologies to determine our ontologies such that we begin to actually believe that personal experiences (insights, thoughts, feelings, beliefs, values, and so on) are nothing more than variables or constructs. To do this is to believe more in what we do not experience (e.g., quantities or variables roaming about in our minds) than what we do (i.e., actual insights, thoughts, and feelings) that roam about in our mental wilderness.

To get to the bottom of insight and build an inquiry on a rock steady foundation, we cannot ignore our direct observations of insight in favor of theories about it. We must "track" the animal we truly want to study and not merely limit ourselves to tracking its tracks. What would constitute tracking insight; how would we make direct observations of it? That is a question that phenomenological philosophy has struggled to explicate over the past century, and it is not without difficulties and controversies. Nonetheless, I think such direct observation can be described in a simple way: It is really nothing more than attending to our internal, lived-through experience of insight as it occurs within us. That is, we turn our subjective awareness upon our subjective awareness; we introspect "in the moment." And we do so with the aim of uncovering those aspects of our experience that are self-evident or self-given (as our doubt is self-evident to us when we turn our attention to it).

This may seem easy, but it is stunningly difficult. We often (in fact we usually) fail to attend rigorously to our own experience and differentiate its multifarious aspects. Rather, we go through much of our lives on autopilot, failing to notice the complexity and richness of our experience. To turn our attention to subjective experience requires great skill and discipline; to convey that experience in writing requires perhaps even greater skill and discipline. We often shy from the task and rely on our theories of experiences or on scientific descriptions that are already well accepted. We might describe an experience of insight, for example, as a change of schema regarding a certain issue. But no one, so far as I know, has ever witnessed a schema. What we have witnessed are our own beliefs. Beliefs can be directly experienced. Schemas, however, are theories about beliefs and other mental events. Theories are fine in their proper place. After all, we do want to build theories, and we want to rely on these theories in directing self-observations. But all theory must first be built upon and tested against actual lived-through experience. When our direct experience contradicts theory, we should at least respect both sides of this contradiction. We should not merely agree with what scientific theory proposes and simply impose that on our experience. Indeed, we should do the opposite and impose lived-through experiences upon our scientific theories. Those theories that crumble under the weight should be abandoned.

REFERENCES

Chisholm, R. M. (1973). *The problem of the criterion.* Milwaukee, WI: Marquette University Press.

Descartes, R. (1951). *Meditations.* New York: Liberal Arts Press. (Original work published 1641)

Hume, D. (1983). *An inquiry concerning human understanding.* Indianapolis, IN: Bobbs-Merrill. (Original work published 1748)

Hume, D. (1999). An enquiry concerning human understanding. In S. M. Cahn (Ed.), *Classics of Western Philosophy* (pp. 628–696). Indianapolis, IN: Hackett. (Original work published 1748)

Husserl, E. (1962). *Ideas: General introduction to pure phenomenology* (W. R. Boyce Gibson, Trans.). New York: Macmillan.

Husserl, E. (1969). *Cartesian meditations: An introduction to phenomenology* (D. Cairns, Trans.). The Hague: Martinus Nijhoff.

V

CONCLUSIONS

21

INSIGHT IN PSYCHOTHERAPY: DEFINITIONS, PROCESSES, CONSEQUENCES, AND RESEARCH DIRECTIONS

CLARA E. HILL, LOUIS G. CASTONGUAY, LYNNE ANGUS, DIANE B. ARNKOFF, JACQUES P. BARBER, ARTHUR C. BOHART, THOMAS D. BORKOVEC, ELIZABETH A. BOWMAN, FRANZ CASPAR, MARY BETH CONNOLLY GIBBONS, PAUL CRITS-CHRISTOPH, JOSLYN M. CRUZ, ROBERT ELLIOTT, MYRNA L. FRIEDLANDER, CHARLES J. GELSO, CAROL R. GLASS, MARVIN R. GOLDFRIED, LESLIE S. GREENBERG, MARTIN GROSSE HOLTFORTH, BETH E. HAVERKAMP, ADELE M. HAYES, JEFFREY A. HAYES, LAURIE HEATHERINGTON, SARAH KNOX, NICHOLAS LADANY, STANLEY B. MESSER, ANTONIO PASCUAL-LEONE, JEREMY D. SAFRAN, MICHELE A. SCHOTTENBAUER, WILLIAM B. STILES, R. FOX VERNON, AND BRUCE E. WAMPOLD

The chapters in this book provide a wealth of theoretical, empirical, and clinical information related to insight in psychotherapy. The task now is to integrate all this information in a coherent form to determine what is known and unknown about insight in therapy. One way to do this would be to summarize the chapters as they stand. Such a summary, however, would inevitably fail to do justice to the chapters, as the authors used different terminologies and approached the topic of insight from markedly different perspectives. In addition, the chapters speak for themselves and there really is no need to summarize them.

Instead, the editors opted to ask the authors to come together and debate the issues to combine their expertise and come to some consensus about responses to four core questions: What is insight? What leads to insight? What are the consequences of insight? What other issues need to be considered in thinking about insight?

This chapter is a distillation of these discussions and deliberations. In the interest of summarizing in a clear and succinct manner, we present our conclusions in bullet form without citing specific references (see the individual chaps. for specific references).

Before presenting the results of our discussions, though, we stress that these ideas are not offered as definitive statements because there is not enough empirical evidence to do so. Rather, these ideas are offered as heuristics about the phenomenon of insight that, in our collective opinion, deserve particular attention. We offer these ideas in the hope of spurring further theoretical and empirical investigation. Researchers, theorists, and practitioners might want to consider these factors and topics when they study, describe, or seek to foster insight.

It is also important to state that we are not trying to imply that insight is the only or best mechanism of change or the most desired outcome in therapy, and we are not trying to proselytize that every client should gain insight. Indeed, there was a fair amount of controversy among the authors about the importance of insight. Rather, we are interested in exploring the construct of insight, examining if and when insight is beneficial to clients, thinking about how insight might develop, and considering the consequences of insight as one potentially interesting and important mechanism of change in psychotherapy.

DEFINITION OF INSIGHT

Insight is an exciting but challenging construct, in part because it has many different meanings. Thus, our first task was to determine whether we could arrive at some agreement about what we mean by insight.

After much discussion, most of us agreed that insight usually is conscious (as opposed to unconscious or implicit) and involves both a sense of *newness* (i.e., the client understands something in a new way) and making *connections* (e.g., figuring out the relationship between past and present events, the therapist and significant others, cognition and affect, or disparate statements). Hence, most of us agreed that we could define insight as a conscious meaning shift involving new connections (i.e., "this relates to that" or some sense of causality).

Additional Possible Dimensions of Insight

A number of other elements of insight were suggested but were not added to the primary definition because we could not attain consensus about them, probably because of differences in theoretical orientation. Future researchers, however, may want to add these elements to their own definition of insight. The following dimensions were suggested:

1. Complexity (e.g., richness, number of neural connections, extent of elaboration of a schema, scope of understanding, degree of integration of various elements, level of abstraction or depth)
2. Intensity of feelings, emotions, or arousal related to the new meaning
3. Salience or centrality to client's conception of self
4. Suddenness (i.e., whether the insight is gained gradually or suddenly)
5. Conviction or belief in the new meaning
6. Manner in which insight is communicated (e.g., visual metaphors such as "I see" versus sensory metaphors such as "I feel," or verbally versus nonverbally)
7. Nearness to conscious awareness (conscious vs. unconscious, implicit vs. explicit) of the material prior to the insight event
8. Object of insight (e.g., emotion, cognition, external contingencies; past, present, future; about oneself, about others, about situation)
9. Quality of insight
   - Accuracy (how well the insight corresponds to the available information about the client or fits the client's sense of his or her experience)
   - Coherence (how internally consistent or elegant the insight is);
   - Consensus (how much the client, therapist, and significant others would agree on the truth of the insight)
   - Usefulness (the extent to which the client has a sense that the insight does or will lead to resolution of a problem he or she has been experiencing, or the extent to which it objectively leads to a resolution of the problem or generates further therapeutic work)

Because the effectiveness of insight depends on the needs of the client at a particular time within therapy, we were not willing to say that being at particular levels on any of these dimensions would necessarily make for better or more therapeutic insights. Hence, a simple insight might be best early in therapy for a given client, whereas a more complex insight might be better later in therapy when the client has assimilated more of the material that has emerged during treatment. However, we did think it possible (this is a good empirical question) that better or more therapeutic insights would involve the higher levels of at least several of these dimensions (e.g., higher or deeper level of complexity, emotional arousal or deepening, saliency, suddenness, believability, visual or sensory clarity, implicitness of material prior to insight, accuracy, coherence, consensus, usefulness).

We also caution that these dimensions are somewhat arbitrary. There is likely to be some overlap among them (e.g., complexity is probably related to centrality), whereas others may need to be divided (e.g., the different criteria of quality may not aggregate neatly within one construct). Furthermore, given that adequate measures do not exist to assess many of these dimensions, empirical research is needed to clarify these dimensions.

Other Ways of Conceptualizing Insight

We agreed to define insight as a conscious meaning shift involving new connections, which implies that insight is a process or state. We recognized, however, that other researchers might think of insight in other ways. Rather than a process or state, for example, they might think of insight in terms of an ability (i.e., capacity to engage in the insight process; insightfulness). Likewise, insight could be considered as a goal or outcome (a desirable achievement in itself) rather than as a process (i.e., means or task that helps one achieve another end, such as a way to achieve symptom change). People tend to differ on this issue primarily along theoretical lines (e.g., many psychoanalytic therapists consider insight a desirable outcome of therapy, whereas a large number of behavioral therapists consider the attainment of new understanding to be important only if it leads to other outcomes, such as behavioral change).

Related Constructs

In our discussion, we agreed that the terms *understanding* and *new meaning* are synonyms of insight and could be used interchangeably with insight. However, insight should be differentiated from other closely related constructs. Awareness, for example, may be seen as different from insight in that the former does not involve a sense of a new connection or causality (e.g., being aware of the sensation of feeling angry is not the same as understanding where the anger comes from). Not all participants agreed with this distinction, however, and it may be that awareness of newly emerging experiences is at one end of a continuum, whereas more causal types of insight are at the other end. In this way, the awareness–insight distinction may be one of degree as well as, or rather than, kind.

Another related construct is self-knowledge, which differs from insight both in terms of newness (i.e., self-knowledge is not necessarily new) and level of conscious awareness (i.e., self-knowledge can be implicit or unconscious). Finally, we also note that *hindsight* can be similar to insight as the making of new connections often involves looking back and constructing meaning (in fact, psychoanalytic therapists clearly value making connections between past and present events).

Caveats

The basic construct of insight is hard to pin down because the meaning of the term is socially constructed. The definition we proposed and the dimensions we delineated earlier should make it easier to measure insight, but it is still a complicated construct that is hard to capture completely.

In a related way, although insight appears to be valued across theoretical orientations, it is often described using different terms (e.g., psychoanalysts talk about insight whereas cognitive–behaviorists talk about understanding underlying assumptions). One should be cognizant of different terminologies when attempting to understand or investigate insight.

THE PROCESS OF GAINING INSIGHT

We suggest that clients are more likely to gain insight if several predisposing factors are present. The process of gaining insight often involves several stages (although these stages are certainly not invariant). We provide more details about these predisposing factors and process stages here. These conclusions come from our clinical experiences as well as from the empirical research (see individual chaps. for more detail).

Predisposing Factors

We identified two types of variables that likely enable clients to attain insight if the right conditions are present: client factors and therapist factors. These are participant characteristics that exist solely within the person of the client or therapist and are brought to the therapy situation. Although the presence of these variables might well be associated with the client subsequently attaining insight, these variables probably do not cause the attainment of insight. Furthermore, none of these variables should be viewed as absolutely essential for insight generation for every client. Instead, each one may increase the probability that insight will occur under certain circumstances.

    I.   Client factors
        A. Personality–dispositional factors
            1. Psychological mindedness (openness to experience, insightfulness, reflexivity, self-awareness)
            2. Cognitive ability (intelligence)
            3. Creativity–curiosity
            4. Readiness–motivation

5. Goal orientation
6. Lack of profound psychopathology or defensive functioning, absence of certain personality disorders such as para-
noid personality disorder
7. Level of functioning
8. Belief that insight is desirable
B. Environmental factors
1. Social support
2. Reliable feedback from others about one's behavior or impact on others
II. Therapist factors
A. Credibility
B. Skill–competence
C. Empathic capacity
D. Lack of hindering self-awareness or countertransference
E. Self-knowledge about own dynamics
F. Belief that insight is desirable or necessary for change

Stages of Insight Attainment

We postulated that insight attainment occurs through several stages within the process of therapy. Typically, clients and therapists have more immediate control over these variables than they do over the predisposing factors identified previously. Because these variables seem to occur in a se-quential manner, we divide them into five stages: setting the stage for in-sight, preparation for insight, marker of client readiness for insight, promo-tion of insight, and consolidation of insight.

Stage 1: Setting the Stage for Insight

There are probably some crucial elements that must be available in the therapy process before it is even possible to start the movement toward in-sight. The following would seem to be the most salient:

- state, mood, and stress-level of client (clients may be more re-ceptive to insight at some times more than others);
- belief of the therapist in the value of insight for this client at this time; and
- productive therapeutic alliance.

Stage 2: Preparation for Insight

Therapists might use one or more types of intervention to set the stage so clients are primed to gain insight. These interventions may be enough to generate insight in some clients. Most often, however, these interventions set the stage for later interventions that directly promote insight. Interven-tions might include such things as the following:

1. Reduce client inhibitors to insight by decreasing client avoidance, defenses, rumination, worry.
2. Motivate clients to seek insight by educating them about the benefits of gaining new understanding and by reinforcing attempts to gains insight.
3. Encourage client exploration to elicit material from which insight can develop.
   - Elicit memories, painful or puzzling stories, narratives or dreams from clients.
   - Help clients activate relevant schema (e.g., identify or monitor conscious thoughts; derive underlying assumptions about self from various conscious [automatic] thoughts; trigger core views of self by working in an emotionally immediate way with clients).
   - Increase client arousal to an optimal level (e.g., "strike while iron is hot" for many but "strike while iron is cold" for clients with borderline diagnoses).
   - Increase state of dissonance, disconnect, or self-incoherence to make client more aroused and ready for insight.

Stage 3: Markers of Client's Readiness for Insight

Clients often demonstrate a readiness for moving forward with the insight process. They may indicate puzzlement (e.g., "I just don't understand") or a desire for understanding (e.g., "I wish I understood why I do that"). Times when clients bring up recurrent dreams ("What could that dream mean? Why do I keep having that dream?) or problematic reactions ("I don't know why I reacted that way; it is so unlike me") are particularly good examples of when clients are confused and want to understand something about themselves. This client state of puzzlement seems to motivate active self-exploration, which can lead to new emotional awareness and insight.

Stage 4: Promotion of Insight

Most insights seem to be *coconstructed* (i.e., developed collaboratively between therapists and clients), although some emerge solely from the client and others are suggested by the therapist. Irrespective of the person who initiates the insight, the client ultimately must claim the insight as his or her own and integrate it into his or her schema. The therapist typically uses one of several different types of intervention to directly or indirectly help clients construct insight:

I. Interventions that may facilitate clients gaining their own insight
   A. Probes for insight (questions asking about causes or connections)
   B. Empathic reflections
   C. Pointing out or challenging discrepancies

    D. Pointing out or challenging conscious (or explicit) thoughts or behaviors
    E. Challenging underlying (frequently implicit) assumptions
  II. Interventions that may offer insight to clients
    A. Interpretations
    B. Reframing
  III. Interventions intended to help clients change specific behaviors, which in turn might facilitate insight
    A. Behavioral assignments
    B. Paradoxical directives

Stage 5: Consolidation of Insight

For insights to create lasting shifts in meaning, therapists often have to work with clients to help them consolidate the insights (what psychoanalysts refer to as *working through*). Therapists attempt to achieve such consolidation through various means:

- reinforcing the client for gaining insight;
- helping the client symbolize or articulate the insight in a clear or memorable form; and
- repeating the insight numerous times, in different ways, and applying it to multiple areas so the client generalizes the learning, incorporates the insight into existing schemas, and creates new, more adaptive schemas (new schemas have to be reinforced and strengthened through continued discussion and practice or they fade away and old schemas resurface).

Caveats

The process outlined here is hypothetical and will not apply to every client, given that the process of insight attainment probably varies widely across clients. Rather than being direct and clearly traceable, the process of insight attainment is undoubtedly complex and elusive. For example, a tentative insight may lead to action, which may lead to additional insight, which may lead to a corrective emotional experience, which may in turn lead to additional insight. As another example, a client may initially reject a therapist interpretation but then go home and think about it and later tell the therapist about discovering on his or her own exactly what the therapist earlier suggested.

CONSEQUENCES OF INSIGHT

As the contributors deliberated on the possible consequences of insight, they developed a long list of possible positive and negative effects. Obviously, not all of these consequences arise for every client. Rather, the outcome probably depends on the intensity, complexity, accuracy, content, and timing of the insight.

Furthermore, immediate and long-term outcomes may differ. For example, the immediate insight might be that the client reacts badly to her boss because the boss makes her feel as though she were an imposter, but she might later come to realize that the boss makes her angry because he criticizes her as her mother did. Sometimes the immediate outcome might seem dramatic and life-changing, but the client may later realize that in fact it is not true (or vice versa). Furthermore, sometimes the insight is an important product in and of itself, and sometimes insight is a mediator of other, more important changes (e.g., insight leads to behavioral change).

Possible Positive Consequences of Insight

Insight can have several possible positive consequences:

1. Insight can lead to symptom changes (e.g., reductions in depression or anxiety) or can serve as a preparation for behavior change (moving toward greater assimilation of the problem).
2. Insight can enable a client to make difficult decisions (e.g., if a client recognizes why she allows herself to stay in an untenable relationship, she may need to make a decision about whether to get out of the relationship).
3. Insight can increase client involvement in therapy.
4. Insight can evoke new memories or fantasies for a client in therapy.
5. Insight can engender more differentiated and meaningful emotional experiences.
6. Insight can facilitate a client's ability to articulate emotional experiences.
7. Insight can enhance therapeutic alliance.
8. Insight can foster the client's positive feelings about self (i.e., self-acceptance, authenticity, self-coherence).
9. Insight can increase the client's sense of hope, mastery, choice, freedom, self-efficacy, or agency.
10. Insight can increase client's ability to gain insight on his or her own outside of therapy.

Possible Negative Consequences of Insight

Insight can also potentially have several negative consequences:

1. A client may feel pain or regret over missed opportunities or lost time.
2. A client may feel forced to make decisions prematurely.

3. A client may feel stuck or paralyzed about making changes.
4. A client may become overinvolved in gaining understanding rather than (or instead of) making needed life changes.
5. A client may feel more negatively about self (e.g., becomes critical of self for past choices).
6. A client may proselytize (e.g., excessively or inappropriately try to convert others who share similar problems to his or her new way of thinking).

Caveats

Again, some words of caution are in order. First, the list of positive consequences may be too grandiose, implying that insight is a "cure-all" and has more far-reaching influence than is the case. In fact, insight may not be viewed as worthwhile or therapeutic by clients from cultures that value rituals, advice, interpersonal harmony, or detached mindfulness. Second, some of these consequences may overlap (e.g., increased client involvement and the therapeutic alliance), whereas others may need to be differentiated more (e.g., the sense of hope, mastery, choice, freedom, self-efficacy, and agency may not all cluster together). Third, the sequence with which these consequences of insight take place is likely to vary: Insight may lead to an emotional shift or to action or both, and either of these may lead to insight (e.g., once a person has made a major behavioral change or had a novel emotional experience, he or she may be in a better position to reflect on what caused his or her behavior or feeling). Furthermore, the sequence may be cyclical (e.g., insight leads to emotion or action, which leads to more insight, which then leads to more emotion or action, etc). Similarly, insight may be a desirable outcome in and of itself for some clients, whereas it may only be important as a means to an end (e.g., if it leads to symptom change) for others. Taking all of these caveats into consideration, we remind readers that these lists of positive and negative consequences are speculative at this time and in need of empirical validation. We urge readers to remember that these consequences are offered for their heuristic value rather than as fact.

RESEARCH QUESTIONS

Although this book's contributors were able to derive and agree on a long list of conclusions with regard to insight, a substantial number of questions were also raised and left unanswered. This outcome, in our opinion, clearly reflects that the field is ripe for investigations of insight. We divide our research questions into several categories: (a) definitional issues; (b) methodological issues; (c) investigations of the nature, process leading to, and consequences of insight; and (d) other research questions.

Definitional Issues

Because insight is such a slippery, elusive term, considerable attention is needed to define it carefully. More specifically, insight needs to be distinguished theoretically from related phenomena (e.g., awareness, explanation, revelation, self-knowledge, creativity). Further work is also needed in distinguishing insight as an experience, process, state, or ability. Finally, the prototypical insight (*Aha!*, "gold nugget") needs to be distinguished from less complete or smaller insights ("gold dust").

Measurement Issues

After insight is conceptualized and defined clearly, better methods are needed for assessing it. Having adequate measures will help in distinguishing insight from related phenomena. We stress the need for measures using different kinds of methods (self-report, observer ratings, interview methods) to reduce measurement bias and allow for testing consistency across methods.

Methodological Issues

All research methods have limitations. As such, it would be ideal to study insight using many different methods. For example, because the insight process appears to be idiographic and heavily context-bound, case studies are likely to be a suitable method of investigation. Qualitative methods may also be particularly useful for capturing the conscious inner processes of participants. In addition, quantitative studies will likely be useful for measure development and for assessing the overt presence of insight in therapy sessions. Furthermore, we encourage clinical trials researchers to include assessments of insight when investigating the effects of major theoretical approaches.

Moreover, it is important to recognize that therapists, clients, significant others, and trained judges will by definition have different perspectives on the phenomenon of insight. For example, therapists who believe fervently in insight might be motivated to overrate its frequency and significance. However, some clients might not understand what is meant by insight, or may not value insight unless educated about it. Likewise, judges might have their own biases (positive or negative) about insight, which would likely influence their evaluations. In addition, it is important to be aware that clients may have insights that they cannot or do not choose to articulate to therapists. Accordingly, the observable record of therapy (i.e., transcripts, audiotapes, videotapes) may not always be the best place to search for insights.

When and where to assess insight is another major methodological concern. Rather than being the consequence of specific and discrete events that immediately precede it, insight may result from many processes occurring over a long period of time. Therefore, the immediately preceding events most likely represent the final impetus for insight (the tipping point) rather than the whole process. Alternatively, the insight could have occurred (either inside or outside of the session) much earlier than when the client reports it. In such a case, the interventions immediately preceding the report of insight may have had little to do with the insight attainment. Hence, researchers need to examine the entire process (including both overt and covert factors) leading up to insight.

Investigations of the Nature of Insight

In terms of the nature of insight, several questions need to be addressed:

1. What is the role of schemas and schema changes in insight generation and maintenance (and how can we assess schemas and schema change from insight gains)?
2. Does insight need to be true or historically accurate? By providing an explanation for his or her problems, false insights could make the client feel good, but they may also lead to ineffective or self-defeating actions.
3. Does insight need to be related to current events that maintain problematic behaviors?
4. Does it make a difference if insight is sudden versus gradual?
5. Are insights better if they are client-generated, therapist-suggested, or coconstructed?
6. Do more complex, emotionally intense, or central insights lead to stronger and longer lasting changes?
7. Are insights involving previously unconscious (implicit) information more beneficial than insights involving previously conscious (explicit) information?
8. Is the degree of a client's conviction or belief in new meanings correlated with outcome?
9. Does insight that occurs within therapy differ from insight that occurs outside of therapy?
10. How similar is insight to other related phenomena, such as problem solving in cognitive science or religious conversion?

Investigations of the Process of Insight Attainment

Researchers could also investigate the processes involved in gaining insight. Several possible ideas include the following:

1. The stages previously described (i.e., setting the stage for insight, preparation for insight, markers of readiness for insight, promotion of insight, consolidation of insight) need to be in-

vestigated to determine if these stages exist or whether the process occurs in another manner.

2. The list of possible markers expressed by clients that indicate that they are ready for or eager to attain insight needs to be validated.

3. It needs to be determined whether different types of insight (e.g., in terms of object or target, the complexity or depth) are facilitated by different types of therapy. For example, it may be that psychoanalytic therapy stimulates insights relating past events to current experiences, whereas cognitive–behavioral therapy stimulates insights about underlying assumptions and their relationship with current events, and experiential therapy stimulates insights about the process of one's ongoing subjective experience.

4. Research is needed on the role of positive and negative emotion in insight generation and maintenance. For example, is emotional insight (as opposed to intellectual insight) necessary for long-standing change? If so, what are the optimal levels of emotional and intellectual arousal?

5. What is the therapist's role in initiating insight? Do therapists need to have insight to enable clients to attain insight? If therapists highly value self-examination, do they risk imposing their own values about insight on clients?

6. What is the role of supervision in helping therapists help their clients attain insight?

Investigations of the Consequences of Insight

In terms of the consequences of insight, it seems important to validate the list of positive and negative consequences presented earlier in this chapter, deleting ones for which no evidence is found and adding others that were overlooked. Also, researchers could study the possible interaction among potential consequences, particularly in determining whether insight plays a direct or mediating role in eventual treatment outcome (e.g., emotional well-being, symptom reduction, increased interpersonal functioning).

Other Research Questions

A number of other research questions, not clearly related to the afore-mentioned categories, also merit empirical attention:

1. Why is it that clients often do not come to therapy explicitly asking for insight, although many report posttherapy that they valued gaining insight?

2. What can be learned from other areas of psychology (social, cognitive, developmental, biological) and other disciplines (philosophy of science, sociology, anthropology, biology, history) about insight?
3. Does the insight process have an evolutionary value? Perhaps healthy people engage in insight processes (self-examination) on a regular basis as a way of solving problems. Perhaps it is when this process gets stuck that therapeutic intervention is needed.

CONCLUDING COMMENTS

We reached a number of agreements with regard to the nature, processes, and consequences of insight. In addition, there was a fair amount of consensus about future directions of research on insight. This level of agreement came as a pleasant surprise to the editors of the present book, who initially had fairly low expectations about the extent of consensus that could be achieved among so many individuals (of various theoretical affinities, no less) about a construct as complex as insight. We stress, of course, that research is needed to test the ideas that were generated by this process.

AUTHOR INDEX

Numbers in italics refer to listings in the reference sections.

Dare, C., 10, *29*
Dattilio, F., 90, 96, 98
Dattilio, F. M., 325, *330*
Davidson, J. E., 268, *277*
Davies, J. M., 12, *27*
Davis, C. G., 234, *252*
Davis, D. D., 239, *251*
Davis, M. K., 17, *28*
Davison, G. C., 60, *78*
Dayton, T., 228, *229*
Deane, F. P., 320, *331, 332*
Debbane, E. G., 155, *165*
de Carufel, F. L., 155, *165*
Deci, E. L., 390, *396, 398*
DeCoster, J., 378, *398*
Dematatis, A., 208, *229*
DeRubeis, R. J., 74, 80, 129, *137*
Descartes, R., 428, 429, *438*
Detert, N. E., 114, *116, 117*
Detweiler, J. B., 234, *253*
DeWitt, K. N., 318, *335*
Diamond, G., 91, 94, 96, 98
DiClemente, C. C., 264, *277*
Diemer, R. A., 147, 150, 152, *163*, 259, 261, *275*, 290, *292*
Dijksterhuis, A., 369, *371*
Dimaggio, G., 187, *203*
Dobson, K. S., 234, *252*
Dominowski, R. L., 270, *275*, 378, 385, 395, *396*
Downey, G., 364, *371*
Downing, J. N., 125, *136*
Dryden, W., 325, *330*
Duan, C., 280, *291*
Dunbar, K., 388, *396*
Duncker, K., 385, *396*
Durso, F. T., 228, 228, *229*
Dweck, C. S., 263, *275*
Dykman, B., 359, *371*
Dymond, R. F., 152, 153, *163*

Eagle, M. N., 18, *27*
Edelman, G., 61, *77*
Edelstein, S., 309, *311*
Edmonds, J., 321, 322, 323, *334*
Effrein, E. A., 360, *371*
Eissler, K., 9, 14, *27*
Ekman, P., 124, *135*
Elkin, I., 69, *78*, 127, *136, 137, 138*
Elliott, R., 41, 42, 43, 49, *52, 53*, 70, 73, *78, 79*, 80, 95, *98*, 107, *116, 117*, 154, 155, *163*, 168, 169, 170, 172, 173,

174, 176, 180, 182, 183, 184, *184, 185, 203*, 226, 229, *253*, 270, 271, *275*, 324, *331, 337, 351*, 390, *396*
Ellis, A., 36n, *52*, 59, *78*
Ellis, M. V., 339, *351*
Ellison, J., 51, *52*
Ellsworth, P. C., 357, *373*
Emery, G., 266, *274*, 320, *329*
Endres, L. M., 104, *116*
Engelstad, V., 148, *164*, 309, *310*
Ensink, K., 316, *330*
Epstein, M., 320, *330*
Epstein, N., 325, *330*
Epstein, N. B., 90, *98*
Epstein, S., 63, *78*, 378, *396*
Epston, D., 326, *335*
Escudero, V., 87, 96, *98*

Falender, V. J., 361, *371*
Fallshore, M., 270, *277*, 376, *398*
Farber, B. A., 319, 320, *331, 333, 335*
Fazio, R. H., 360, *371*
Feinsinger, J. E., 14, 19, *29*
Feldman, G. C., 233, 235, 239, *251, 252*
Feldman, S. I., 364, *371*
Festinger, L., 217, *229*
Fiedler, F. E., 289, *291*
Field, S. D., 106, *116, 117*
Fincham, F. D., 91, *98*
Fingarette, H., 272, *275*
Fiore, S. M., 270, *277*, 376, *398*
First, M., 190, *205*
Firth-Cozens, J. A., 70, *78, 79*, 107, *116, 117*, 155, *163, 165, 185, 203*, 229, *253*, *275*
Fisch, R., 85, *99*, 389, *399*
Fishman, S. T., 323, *333*
Foa, E. B., 231, 239, 249, *251*
Follette, V. M., 234, *252*
Fonagy, P., 315, 316, *329, 330*, 404, 408, *420*
Foreman, S. A., 155, *163*
Forgas, J. P., 362, *371*
Forrest, M. S., 324, *334*
Forster, J., 369, *371*
Frank, J. B., 3, 5, 119, 123, 124, 125, 127, 130, 131, 134, *136*
Frank, J. D., 3, 5, 119, 123, 124, 125, 127, 130, 131, 134, *136*
Frank, K. A., 9, *27*, 306, 309, 317, *330*
Frawley, M. G., 12, *27*
Frazier, P. A., 356, *372*
Fredrickson, B. L., 362, *372*

Kermer, D. A., 227, 230
Kernberg, O. F., 145, 162, 318, 332
Kernberg, P. F., 316, 330
Kerr, I. B., 325, 328, 333
Kerr, M., 82, 98
Kiecolt-Glaser, J. K., 234, 252
Kiesler, D. J., 34, 49, 50, 54, 55, 234, 252, 260, 276
Kihlstrom, J. F., 361, 371
Kim, D. M., 134, 137
Kintsch, W., 395, 396
Kipfer, B. A., 171, 185
Kirsch, I., 128, 129, 130, 137
Kivlighan, D. M., Jr., 36n, 52, 76, 79, 147, 148, 151, 152, 160, 163, 164, 294, 296, 305, 308, 309, 310
Klein, M. H., 34, 49, 54, 234, 235, 250, 252, 260, 267, 275, 276, 318, 332
Kling, K. C., 392, 398
Klosko, J. S., 239, 253
Kluckhohn, C., 288, 291
Knoblich, G., 385, 397
Knobloch, L. M., 104, 116
Knox, S., 319, 320, 327, 332
Koch, K., 383, 396
Kohlenberg, R. J., 306, 310
Köhler, W., 375, 397
Kohut, H., 16, 28
Korman, L. M., 50, 55, 241, 253
Korman, Y., 187, 191, 204
Kozak, M. J., 231, 249, 251
Krantrowitz, J. L., 315, 317, 332
Kris, E., 9, 14, 28
Krull, D. S., 364, 373
Krupnick, J. L., 131, 133, 137, 138
Kugler, P. N., 387, 397
Kuhl, J., 390, 391, 392, 394, 397, 398
Kuhlman, T. L., 72, 79, 321, 332
Kuhn, T. S., 264, 276
Kurtz, J., 163

Ladany, N., 338, 339, 340, 349, 350, 351, 352
Lakoff, G., 168, 169, 170, 172, 178, 179, 180, 182, 185
Lambert, M. J., 17, 28, 209, 229, 302, 311
Langley, N., 257, 276
Lanotte, M., 136
Laitila, A., 193, 204
Latour, B., 127, 137
Latts, M. G., 290, 291
Laurenceau, J. P., 233, 239, 251, 252
Lazar, A., 314, 329

Lazarus, A. A., 70, 79
Lecours, S., 315, 332, 333
Lee, T. W., 323, 331
Leggett, E. L., 263, 275
Leijssen, M., 39, 54
Leiman, M., 103, 104, 107, 116, 117
Lerner, J. S., 366, 373, 374
Leslie, L. A., 325, 332
Leventhal, H., 65, 79
Levitt, H., 188, 191, 203, 204, 234, 251, 269, 276
Levy, K. N., 260, 274, 316, 332
Levy, L. H., 217, 229
Lewin, A. E., 171, 185
Lewin, E., 171, 185
Lewin, J., 189, 203
Lewin, J. K., 204
Leykin, Y., 129, 137
Liberman, N., 369, 371
Lieberman, M. A., 271, 276
Lieberman, M. D., 356, 358, 368, 372
Lietaer, G., 49, 53
Lightsey, R., 229, 276
Linehan, M. M., 392, 397
Linley, P. A., 232, 241, 252
Linville, P., 392, 397
Llewelyn, S. P., 70, 74, 78, 79, 114, 116, 117, 163, 185, 203, 229, 253, 275
Lobell, L. K., 150, 163, 259, 275
Lopiano, L., 136
Lubetkin, B. S., 323, 333
Luborsky, E., 42, 54, 307, 311
Luborsky, L., 19, 28, 42, 54, 128, 136, 144, 145, 146, 148, 150, 155, 157, 159, 160, 162, 163, 164, 307, 309, 310, 311
Ludik, J., 379, 398
Lumley, M. A., 317, 334
Lundy, M., 319, 333
Lustman, P. J., 127, 138
Luxton, D. D., 234, 253
Lyddon, W. J., 127, 137
Lynch, G., 190, 204
Lyubomirsky, S., 233, 252

Machado, P. P. P., 187, 203, 204, 268, 275
Mack, L. M., 116
Mackay, H. C., 102, 117
Madanes, C., 87, 98
Maddever, H., 239, 252
Maggi, G., 136
Mahler, M. S., 318, 332

Mahoney, M. J., 60, 64, 68, *79*, 233, *252*, 325, *332*
Mahrer, A. R., 321, 323, *332*
Maidhof, C., 130, *139*
Main, M., 402, 403, 410, *420*
Malan, D. H., 32, 42, *54*, 156, *164*
Malcolm, W., 39, *54*
Malik, S., 259, *274*
Mann, C. H., 150, 159, *164*
Mann, J. H., 147, 150, 159, *164*
Maramba, G. G., 127, *137*
Margisa, R., *203*
Margison, F. R., *78, 116, 117, 163*, 185, 229, *253, 275*
Mark, D., 42, *54*, 307, *311*
Markus, H., 62, *79*, 357, 361, *372*
Marmar, C. R., 155, *163*
Marmor, J., *120, 124*, 135, *138*, 280, *291*
Marris, P., 264, *276*
Martin, D. J., 17, *28*
Martin, J., 260, 268, *276*
Marx, B. P., 232, *253*
Maslow, A. H., 282, *291*
Mathieu, P. L., 49, *54*
Mathieu-Coughlan, P., 34, 49, *54*, 234, *252*, 260, *276*
May, R., 34, 35, 41, *54, 55*, 287, *292*
Mayer, R. E., 375, *397*
McCallum, M., 19, *28*, 128, *138*, 156, 157, *164, 165*, 259, *276*, 317, *332*
McClanahan, M. K., *291*
McClelland, D. C., 390, *397*
McClelland, J. L., 378, 388, 392, 396, *397*, *398*
McClure, B. A., 289, *292*
McCracken, J. E., 290, *291*
McCready, T., 208, *229*
McDowell, N. K., 366, *373, 374*
McFarlane, A. C., 11, *29*
McGlaughlin, E. Q., *334*
McGuire, L., 234, *252*
McLeod, J., 189, 190, *204*
McMain, S., 339, *352*
McNaughton, B. L., 392, *397*
McNeill, B. W., 358, *373*
McWilliams, N., 314, *332*
Mechon Mamre, 170, *185*
Meehl, P., 160, *163*
Meichenbaum, D., 60, *79*, 129, 132, *138*
Menna, R., 261, *276*
Meshot, C. M., 104, *117*
Messer, S. B., 20, *28, 29*, 64, *79*

Metcalfe, J., 376, 389, *397*
Meyer, B., 133, *138*
Meyer, S., *334*
Miles, M. B., 271, *276*
Miller, A., 285, *292*
Miller, E. K., 387, *397*
Miller, G. A., 386, *397*
Miller, I. W., 239, 244, *252*
Miller, L. C., 379, *398*
Miller, L. S., 321, *332*
Miller, N. E., 295, 309, 314, *330*
Miller, W. R., 262, 264, 271, *276*
Mills, J., 364, *372*
Minami, T., 134, *136*
Mintz, J., 148, *164*, 309, *311*
Minuchin, S., 88, *98*
Mitchell, S. A., 16, *28*, 42, *53*, 314, 318, *331*
Moerman, D. E., 130, *138*
Mohr, J. J., 304, *310*
Mora, G. 3, *5*
Morgan, R., 148, *164*
Morgan, R. W., 19, *28*
Morris, W., 168, 170, 176, 178, *185*, 355, *372*
Morrison, L. A., 104, *117, 118*
Moyer, J., *137*
Mt. Zion Psychotherapy Research Group, 17, 18, *29*
Multon, K. D., 76, *79*, 151, *164*, 294, *310*
Muran, C., 408n, 413, 413n, *420*
Muran, J. C., 74, *79*
Murphy, G. E., 127, *138*
Murray, H. A., 288, *291*
Murray, P., 339, *352*

Najavits, L. M., 288, *292*
Nakayama, K., 46, *54*
Nelson, M. L., 338, *352*
Neubauer, P. B., 15, *29*
Newsom, G. E., 20, *27*
Nichols, M. P., 326, *332*
Niemeyer, R. A., 93, *98*
Nisbett, R., 357, 358, *372*
Nolen-Hoeksema, S., 233, 234, *252*
Norcross, J. C., 17, *29*, 218, 230, 264, *277*
Nordin, S., 321, *332*
Norman, D. A., 383, 387, *397*
Norman, W. H., 239, *252*
Normandin, L., 316, *330*
Norville, R., 157, *164*
Novotny, C. M., 133, *139*
Nurius, P., 357, *372*

Silberschatz, G., 50, *55*, 104, *116*, 157, 161, *165*
Sim, W., *229*
Simkin, J. S., 36, *56*
Simmens, S., *137*
Simon, D. P., 378, *398*
Simon, H. A., 378, *398*
Simons, A. D., 127, *138*
Singer, E., *36n*, *55*
Siqueland, L., 91, *98*
Slade, A., 411, *421*
Slatick, E., 173, *185*
Sloan, D. M., 232, *253*
Sloan, W. W., Jr., 104, *117*
Slovic, P., 358, *372*
Sluzki, C., 91, *99*
Smith, E. E., 154, 159, *165*
Smith, E. R., 361, 369, *373*, 378, *398*
Smith, J. A., *80*
Smith, J. D., 378, *398*
Smith, T. P., 323, *330*
Smolensky, P., 378, *398*
Smyth, J. M., 232, *253*
Snyder, D. K., 94, 96, 97, *98*, *99*
Snyder, M., 359, 364, *373*
Solomon, J., 19, *28*, 148, *164*
Sorbye, O., 148, *164*, 309, *310*
Sotsky, S. M., 78, 133, *137*, *138*
Souto, J., 232, *253*
Spangler, D. L., 320, *330*
Speanburg, S., 315, *334*
Speisman, J. C., 18, *29*
Spellman, B. A., 378, *396*
Spiegel, S. B., 155, *163*
Spiegler, M. D., 320, 322, *334*
Spillman, A., 18, 20, *28*, *29*
Spitzer, R., 190, *205*
Squire, L., 318, *334*
Squire, L. R., 378, *398*
St. Clair, M., 314, *334*
Stahl, J., *229*
Stanton, A. L., 233, *253*
Startup, M., 321, 322, 323, *334*
Staudinger, U. M., 260, *277*
Steele, H., 316, *330*, 404, 408, *420*
Steele, M., 316, *330*, 404, 408, *420*
Steer, R. A., 114, *115*, 190, *203*, 239, *251*
Stein, D. J., 379, *398*
Stelmaczonek, K., 260, *276*
Stern, D., 200, *205*
Sternberg, R. J., 268, *277*
Stevens, J. O., 36, 39, 45, 47, *55*

Steward, W. T., 234, *253*
Stewart, A., 93, *98*
Stiles, W., *203*
Stiles, W. B., 75, *78*, 80, 101, 102, 103, 104, 106, 107, 114, 115, *116*, *117*, *118*, 155, *163*, *165*, *185*, 188, *203*, 229, 232, 234, 235, 250, *253*, 264, *275*, *277*
Stinson, C. H., 379, *398*
Stoltenberg, C. D., 358, *373*
Strachey, J., 13, *29*, 295, *311*
Strauss, J. L., 233, 241, 248, 249, *252*
Strosahl, K., 234, *252*
Strupp, H. H., 20, *29*, 42, *52*, 132, *136*, 155, *165*, 307, *311*
Stukas, A. A., Jr., 364, *373*
Sue, D., 127, *139*
Sue, D. W., 127, *138*, *139*
Suh, C. S., 20, *29*
Sullivan, H. S., 294, 299, 300, *311*
Surko, M., 104, *116*
Sutherland, R. W., 392, *398*
Swann, W. B., Jr., 359, 363, 365, 366, *372*, *373*
Symons, C. S., 360, *373*

Tallman, K., 218, *229*, 257, 263, 274, 277, 285, 290
Talmon, M., 270, *277*
Tang, T. Z., 74, *80*
Target, M., 315, 316, *330*, 404, 408, *420*
Tarragona, M., 319, 320, *333*, *334*
Taylor, A. E., 366, *373*
Taylor, G. J., 259, *277*
Taylor, H. L., 259, *277*
Taylor, S. E., 366, *373*, *374*
Teasdale, J. D., 64, 65, *80*, 232, 233, 234, 249, *253*, 324, *334*, 388, *399*
Tedeschi, R. G., 241, *253*, 270, *277*
Thomas, J., 130, *137*
Thompson, B. J., 319, *331*
Thompson-Brenner, H., 133, *139*
Thwaites, R., 134, *139*
Tice, D. M., 367, *374*
Tichenor, V., 155, *163*
Tierney, S. C., 134, *136*
Tillich, P., 282, *292*
Tishby, O., 20, *28*, *29*
Todd, T., *164*
Tolor, A., 158, 159, *165*
Tompkins, M. A., 321, 322, 323, *334*
Torrey, E. F., 120, 124, 125, 134, *139*

464   AUTHOR INDEX

Toukmanian, S. G., 41, *52, 55*
Trijsburg, R. W., *333*
Trope, Y., 367, *373*
Truax, C. B., 49, *55*
Truax, P., 134, *135*
True, N., 232, *253*
Tsai, M., 306, *310*
Turner, C. W., 89, *99*
Turvey, M. T., 387, *397*
Tversky, A., 358, *372*
Twining, L., *79*

Urman, M., 173, *185*

van Balen, R., 31, 35, 36, 39, 46, 47, *53*
Van de Castle, R. L., 207, *230*
van der Kolk, B. A., 11, *29*
van Dijk, T. A., 168, *185*
Vanman, E. J., 379, *398*
Van Wagoner, S., 290, *292*
Vargas, M. J., 147, 149, 160, *165*
Varvin, S., 104, *118*
Versland, S., 148, *164*
Vighetti, S., *136*
Vivino, B. L., 150, *163*, 259, *275*
Voth, H., 145, *162*
Vygotsky, L. S., 264, *277*

Wachtel, P., 60, *80*
Wachtel, P. L., 295, 296, 297, 306, *311*, 324, *334, 335*
Wahlstrom, J., 193, *204*
Walach, H., 130, *139*
Wallas, G., 262, *277*
Wallerstein, R. S., 318, *335*
Wampold, B. E., 128, 130, 134, *136, 137, 139*
Warwar, S. H., 39, 50, *54, 56*
Watkins, E., 169, *185*, 233, *253*
Watkins, J. T., *78, 137*
Watson, J. C., 40, 41, 42, 43, 49, *54, 56*, 108, 110, *116*, 189, 190, 191, 193, *204*, 267, 268, 270, *277*
Watzlawick, P., 85, 87, *99*, 389, *399*
Weakland, J. H., 85, *99*, 389, *399*
Wegener, D. T., 358, *372*
Wegner, D. M., 389, *399*
Weisaeth, L., 11, *29*

Weisarth, L., *164*
Weishaar, M. E., 239, *253*
Weiss, J., 17, 18, *29*, 157, *164*, 309, *311*
Weiss, R. D., 288, *292*
Wenzlaff, R. M., 234, *251, 253*
Westen, D., 133, *139*
Westerman, M. A., 59, 77, *80*
Wetzel, R. D., 127, *138*
Whelton, W. J., 232, 242, *253*
White, M., 268, *277*, 326, *335*
Whorf, B. L., 167, *185*
Wickramasekera, I., 261, *277*
Wiebe, D., 376, 389, *397*
Wiener, N., 386, *399*
Wiesel, T. N., 62, *79*
Wilcoxin, L. A., 130, *137*
Wild, K. W., 157, *162*
Wilhelm, F. H., 129, *138*
Williams, E. N., 209, *229*, 319, *331, 338, 352*
Williams, J., 190, *205*
Williams, J. M. G., 234, *253*, 324, *334*
Wills, R. M., 94, *99*
Wilson, K. W., 234, *252*
Wilson, T. D., 227, *230*
Wine, B., 36n, *52*, 148, *163*, 296, *310*
Winnicott, D. W., 407, *421*
Winston, A., *79*
Winter, D. A., 261, *277*
Wise, J. C., 323, *331*
Wiser, S., 17, *27*, 50, *52*, 241, *251*
Wonnell, T. L., 308, *311*
Woodhouse, S., 319, *332*
Woods, S. W., *137*
Woolf, E. A., 257, *276*
Worthington, R. L., 127, *135*
Wright, J., 106, *117*
Wzontek, N., 320, *335*

Yalom, I. D., 34, 35, 41, *54, 56*, 124, *139*, 271, *276*
Yamaguchi, J. L., 127, *136*
Yontef, G. M., 36, *56*
Young, J. E., 239, *253*

Zack, J. S., 208, *229*, 304, *310*
Zheutlin, B., *334*
Zuroff, D. C., 17, *27*

SUBJECT INDEX

insecure styles, 410–413
model of psychopathology, 403
narrative construction in, 402, 403
schema formation and, 65–66
strategies to promote insight, 401–402, 404–409
therapeutic goals, 403–404, 420
therapeutic process, 409–410
therapeutic relationship, 405, 407–408
Attentional processes, 388
Avoidance
assessment, 235, 236, 237, 246
depression intervention, 238, 240, 241–242
as inhibiting insight, 233, 234

Behavioral psychology
action instigating insight, 299–300
concept of insight in, 58–59
promoting insight in conjoint therapy, 87–88
relational psychology and, 15
uses of insight and action, 307–308
See also Cognitive–behavioral theory/therapy
Belief modification, 60
Between-session change, 5
cognitive–behavioral therapy, 320–323, 328–329
family systems therapy, 325–326
future research, 326–328
humanistic–experiential therapies, 323–324
integrative approaches, 324–325
loss of insight, 328
psychodynamic theories, 314–320, 328
research needs, 313
See also Extratherapeutic insight
Bibliotherapy, 323
Bodily sentience, 65
Bohr, Neils, 262
Borderline personality disorder, 316
Bowen family systems therapy, 326
Brief dynamic therapy, 128
working through in, 302–303
Broad spectrum behavioral therapy, 70

CBT. *See* Cognitive–behavioral theory/therapy
Change
action–disposition information in, 404–405

action–insight feedback interaction for, 300–303
adaptive explanation as mechanism of, 123–133, 134–135
affective arousal in process of, 232–233
assessment of, 235. *See also* Change and Growth Experiences Scale
attachment theory, 403–404
behavioral theory, 58–59
in behavior and insight, 308
benefits of therapist insight, 285–286
between-session. *See* Between-session change
client education as common factor, 144
client readiness for, 264–265
client role as self-healer, 257–258
cognitive–behavioral theory, 59, 60, 76
condition of safety for, 17–18
consequences of insight, 448–450
as corrective experience, 14, 17, 67–68
emotional processing in, 234, 296
existential therapy, 35
experiential therapy, 31, 33, 34, 38, 48–49, 51
first order changes, 389
gains in insight during therapy and, 149–152, 160–161, 443–444
general insight vs. specific insight, 161
historical conceptualizations, 3–4
individual differences in capacity for, 14–15, 17
insight as common factor, 119–120, 121–123, 133–134, 135, 231–232
insight research in conjoint therapy, 94–97
insight through self-examination, 281–284
integrative insight and, 298–299
lack of therapist insight, 284–285, 290
memory processes in, 318
narrative coherence, case analysis of, 188–202
patient insightfulness as outcome predictor, 145–149, 160
posttraumatic, 232–233
process of productive thinking, 265–266
psychoanalytic conceptualization, 9, 12, 13, 15, 26, 155, 314, 315
relational theory, 15–16
research needs, 162
in response expectancies, 129–131

in schema-focused model of insight, 61, 62–68

second order changes, 389

stages of insight attainment, 446–448

symptom exacerbation before, 248

therapeutic focus and, 306–308

therapeutic relationship as mechanism of, 15–16, 17, 131

transference reactions in, 13

uses of insight for, 271–272, 293–294

without insight, 77

See also Assimilation model of change

Change and Growth Experiences Scale

case example, 243–249

change coding, 240–243

coding categories, 234–235, 236–238, 249–250

function, 233, 235, 242, 250

future directions, 250

insight–processing in, 234, 236, 240–241

interpretation of findings, 242

opportunities for improvement, 242–243

rater preparation, 235, 240

unit of analysis, 235

validity, 250

Charcot, J.-M., 11

Children

reflective functioning intervention, 316–317

therapeutic factors, 153

Circular causality, 89–90

Clarification of meaning, 67–68

Client-centered therapy

case analysis of insight and narrative process in, 188–202

concept of insight in, 32–33

outcome research, 70

self-awareness as outcome factor, 149–150

Client factors

active interpretation, 270

application of insight, 271

capacity for experiential learning, 259–260, 266–267

capacity for insight, 262

cognitive psychology models, 393

creativity, 261–262

exploration of experience, 272–273

goal orientation, 262–263

in insight gains in dream interpretation, 218–220

insight through self-examination, 281–284

interpersonal functioning, 260–261

involvement in therapy, 264

levels of cognitive development, 262

openness, 261

patient insightfulness, 145–149

patient insightfulness as outcome predictor, 145–149, 160

predisposing for insight, 445–446

probability of attaining insight, 263, 272, 273

productive thinking, 265–271

for psychoanalytic therapy, 259

psychological mindedness, 259, 273, 317

psychological states, 263–265

readiness for insight, 447

readiness to change, 264–265

receptivity, 268

self-healing, 257–258

social perspective taking, 261

stress levels, 263–264

Cognitive–analytic therapy, 325, 328

Cognitive–behavioral theory/therapy, 4, 123–124

conceptual basis, 59

conceptualizations of insight in, 57–61, 75

conjoint, 90–91

distinguishing features of insight in, 72–73, 75–76

effects of insight in, 73–75, 76, 120

evidence of insight in, 68–72, 75–76

family therapy, 325

homework assignments, 320–321, 328

learning theory, 67

meta-awareness and, 42

model of change, 59–60

research needs, 76–77

schema-focused model of insight in, 58, 61–68

between session change, 320–323, 328–329

therapy rational, 128–129

Cognitive contingencies, 60

Cognitive–experiential self-theory, 378

Cognitive functioning

abstraction, 36–45, 369, 370

attitude change, 358

automatic processes, 368–369

capacity for insight, 262

cognitive–behavioral theory, 59
conceptual linking, 35, 36, 38, 42–44, 51
confirmatory bias, 359
constraint relaxation, 385, 388
dissonance reduction strategies, 364, 365
distancing, 268
experiential focusing, 260
factors inhibiting insight, 233–234
implicational level, 232
incubation, 369
indications of insight, 21–22, 24–25
inference formation, 357–359
integration of perception and conceptual thinking, 65
learning through experiencing, 259–260, 266–267
meta-awareness, 38
mindful experiencing/being, 232
need for causal explanation, 124
processing of experience, 37
process of productive thinking, 265–266
productive reflection, 267–271, 272
promoting insight in conjoint therapy, 88–93
propositional level, 232
psychoanalytic model of insight, 13–14
psychological mindedness, 259, 317
in rational–emotional behavioral therapy, 59
reflective functioning, 315–317, 327, 408–409
self-verification, 363–365, 366–368
social psychology model, 356–368
top-down and bottom-up information processing strategies, 37–38, 41–42, 51
traditional cognitive psychological models, 376–377
See also Information processing, Perception
Cognitive psychology, 5, 395, 402
case conceptualization, 393
client role, 393
concept of insight in, 375–376, 377–385
connectionist models of information processing, 378–385
logical analysis of beliefs, 269
mindfulness-based, 324
models of motivational regulation, 386–392

strategies to promote insight, 393–395
Communication
assimilation model of change, 103–104
See also Discourse analysis; Language
Conditioning, 59, 67
Confirmatory bias, 359
Conjoint treatment
behavioral interventions, 87–88
circular causality, 89–90
concept of insight in, 81, 97
insight into causality, 85–86
insight research in, 94–97
manifestations of insight in, 82–86
promoting acceptance in, 94
promoting insight in conjoint therapy, 88–93
recognition of similar and reciprocal behaviors, 82–85
strategies for promoting insight in, 86–94
Consensual Qualitative Research, 319
Constructionism, 430
Construction/reconstruction of trauma experience, 12
Constructivist family therapy, 91–92, 93, 96
Core conflictual relationships, 148, 307
Corrective experiences, 14, 17, 67–68
Cortisol, 392
Countertransference, 221–222, 289–290
supervision, 345–347
Couples therapy. *See* Conjoint treatment
Courage, 283
Creativity, client capacity for, 261–262
Critical events-based model of supervision, 338–341
Cultural context
concept of insight, 168
resources for discussing insight, 167
role of discourse analysis, 168
Cyclical psychodynamics, 324

Defense(s)
attachment theory, 404
between-session change and, 314–315
in change process, 314, 315
inaccurate insight as, 23
insight and defensiveness, 154
intellectual insight as, 298
obstacles to insight, 282
psychoanalytic theory, 12, 13
representational dissociation, 410–413

Definition of insight, 4, 21, 119, 143, 144, 148, 159, 208–209, 258, 279–280, 294–295
  in assimilation model of change, 101, 115
  awareness and, 168–169
  cognitive–behavioral approach, 57–58
  in cognitive psychology, 375–376, 377–385
  common features, 144, 231–232, 442
  in conjoint treatment, 81
  dimensions of, 443
  for discourse analysis, 168
  as event, 168, 171, 180, 182
  in Gestalt psychology, 375
  interpersonal factors, 152–153, 159
  meaning construction in, 231, 232
  measurement of insight and, 445
  newness as quality of, 168, 181–182
  process conceptualization, 444
  psychoanalytic theory, 12, 14, 15, 18–19
  related constructs, 444–445
  research needs, 451
  schema-focused perspective, 68
  shortcomings of insight research, 159–160
  in social psychology, 355
  subjectivity in, 280, 432–433
  suddenness, 168, 226, 376
  in supervision setting, 337–338
Depression
  avoidance in, 238, 240, 241–242
  case example of integrative therapy, 243–249
  effects of insight in CBT, 74
  insight as common outcome factor, 120, 121–123
  insight inhibitors in, 238
  insight–processing in treatment for, 240–241, 247–249
  integrative therapy, 238–239, 243–249
  ruminative thinking in, 233, 241
Depth of insight, 22, 50
  in schema-focused model, 63–64, 66
Descarte, R., 428, 429
Desensitization procedures, 130, 321–322
  insight in, 58–59
Developmental psychology, 5
  assimilation model of psychopathology, 102–103
  readiness for change, 264–265

schema theory, 62, 65–66
  See also Attachment theory
Dialectical thinking, 269, 272, 388–389, 394
Discourse analysis
  client description of therapy events, 173–181, 182–183
  definition of insight for, 168–169, 181–182
  findings, 183–184
  purpose, 168, 183
  rationale, 167–168
  techniques, 168
Dissociation
  insecure attachment styles and, 410–413
  psychoanalytic theory, 12
Distancing, 268
Dopamine, 384
Downregulation, 391
Dream interpretation, 286
  action stage, 215–216
  client factors, 218–220, 227–228
  exploration stage, 213–214, 228
  Hill Dream model, case study of, 207–228
  insight outcomes in, 208
  insight stage, 214–215
  opportunities for research, 228
  psychotherapeutic approaches, 207
  therapeutic relationship in, 218
  therapist factors, 220–225, 227
  therapist skills, 222–225

Education and training of psychotherapists
  psychoanalysis in, 14
  sources of insight, 286–289
  See also Supervision
Ego psychology, 16
  conceptual and historical development, 12–15
Emotional attractors, 391
Emotional functioning
  in assimilation model of change, 104–107
  attachment theory of change, 403–404
  attachment theory of insight, 402, 404–408
  attentional processes and, 362
  bodily felt meanings, 267
  CBT conceptualization, 64
  in connectionist model of insight, 383
  corrective emotional experience, 14, 17

self-examination, 284
Goal oriented-behavior, 262–263
Group Counseling Helpful Impact Scale, 153–154

Hamilton Rating Scale for Depression (Modified), 239
Hartmann, Heinz, 13
Hebbian cell assembly, 61–62
Heraclitus, 3
Heuristics, 358–359
Hindsight, 444–445
Hippocampus, 391–392
Homework assignments, 320–321, 324, 328, 394
Hope
    assessment, 236, 237
    insight-processing in depression treatment and, 241
Humanistic–experiential therapies, 4, 121
    awareness and meta-awareness in, 31, 32, 33, 34, 35, 36–38, 38, 39, 41
    change in, 48–49, 51
    complexity of interpretation in, 265
    conceptualization of insight, 31–32, 36–38, 51
    conceptual variations, 32. See also specific variation
    emerging emotions in, 46–47
    experience-near vs. experience-distant insight in, 38–45
    focusing in, 33–34, 39, 45
    future directions, 50–51
    linking and connecting in, 36, 42–44, 51
    measurement of change in, 34
    mechanisms of experience-near insight, 45–48
    research findings, 49–50
    between session change, 323–324
    symbolization in, 33, 34, 39, 45
    therapist stance in, 47–48
Hysteria, 11–12

Idealization, psychoanalytic theory, 12
Implicit learning, 378
Implicit meaning, 63–64, 65–66, 68
Implicit motives, 390
Important Events Questionnaire, 151
Incubation, 369
Indications of insight, 21–22, 24–25
Indicators of insight
    critical event markers, 340, 343

critical events in, 339
client description of therapy events, 173–180, 182–183
Individual differences
    capacity for change, 17
    explanations of causality, 127
    insightfulness, 145–149, 160
    recognition of illness, 14–15, 17
    See also Client factors
Information processing
    automatic processes, 368–369
    cognitive–behavioral theory, 59
    connectionist models, 378–385
    internal focus in, 269
    schema model, 62
    social psychology conceptualization of insight, 355, 356
    strategies to promote insight, 394
    top-down and bottom-up strategies, 35, 37–38, 51
    traditional cognitive psychological models, 376–377
    See also Cognitive functioning
Inhibitors of insight
    alexithymia, 259
    avoidance, 233, 234
    client psychological states, 265
    defense mechanisms, 282
    first order changes, 389
    insecure attachment, 410–413
    interpersonal skills, 261
    mental blocks, 385
    motivation for cognitive consistency, 364–365
    representative heuristics, 358–359
    ruminative thinking, 233
    self-enhancement motivation, 365–366
    social psychology research, 370
    stress, 263–264
    supervisee experience, 349–350
    threat perception, 261
Insight Rating Scale, 151
Integrative insight, 296, 297–299
    action–insight feedback interaction, 300–303
Integrative theory, 4
    between-session change, 324–325
    developmental, 402
    experiential model, 36–37, 52
Integrative therapy
    depression treatment, 238–239, 243–249

uses of action and insight, 306–308
Intellectual insight
    change and, 298–299
    defensive function, 298
    definition, 148, 295
    emotional insight vs., 59, 295–296
    explicit–implicit meaning and, 65
    integrative insight vs., 296
    as outcome predictor, 148
    psychoanalytic model, 13–14
    in rational–emotional behavioral
       therapy, 59, 60
Intentionality
    differentiating effects and intents, 88
    in existential insight, 35
Intention memory, 390
Interacting Cognitive Systems, 65
Interactional behavioral therapy, 70
Interpersonal Process Recall, 95
Interpersonal psychotherapy, 15
Interpersonal relations
    assessment of self-understanding in, 151,
       152–154, 161
    attachment theory, 402–403
    capacity for insight and, 260
    in definition of insight, 152–153, 159
    in facilitating insight, 392
    meta-awareness in, 41
    narrative coherence and, 402
    psychodynamic interpretation, 156
    recognition of motivations of others, 22
    reflective functioning and, 316
    schema theory, 62
    social perspective taking, 261
    supervisor–supervisee, 339–340
interpersonal relations
    See also Family functioning
Interpretation
    accuracy of, 157, 158, 161
    conceptual linking in experiential
       therapy, 43
    depth of, 265
    dream work, case study of, 207–228
    frequency, 155–156, 161
    measurement of, 155
    measures of patient response to, 19
    outcome research, 155–156, 157–158,
       161
    psychoanalytic conceptualization, 10,
       155
    research needs, 161
    supportiveness and, 157–158

timing of, 156–157
transference, 156, 157, 158
Intersession Experience Questionnaire, 319
Intersubjective psychotherapy, 15
Intuition, 119, 378

Journaling, 269–270, 322–323, 324, 325
Joy, 66–67

Kris, Ernst, 13

Language
    finding the right word, 270
    implicit meaning and, 64
    resources for discussion of insight, 167
    significance of, 167
    verbalization of schema change, 68
    See also Discourse analysis
Learning
    CBT concepts, 67
    insight as, in schema-focused model,
       67–68
    through experiencing, 259–260, 266–
       267
Linking insights, 35, 36, 38, 42–44, 168
Loewenstein, Rudolph, 13
Logical analysis of beliefs, 269

Magic, 169–170
Marital therapy. *See* Conjoint treatment
Mastery and self-efficacy beliefs, 76
    outcome expectations and, 132–133
    predisposition to insight and, 262–263
Mastery/coping, 67
Meaning construction
    assimilation model of change, 103–104,
       110–113
    case analysis of insight and narrative
       process change, 188, 197–200, 201
    change process, 188–189
    connectionist models, 379
    in definition of insight, 231, 232
    evolutionary theory, 124
    experiential perspective, 41, 42
    learning theory, 67
    reframing strategy, 88–89
    social constructionist approach, 93
    through search of internal experience,
       266
Measurement of insight, 435–437
    in conjoint therapy, 95
    definition of insight and, 445

in discourse analysis, 168
in dream interpretation model, 210
in experiential therapies, 34
gains over course of therapy, 149–152
methodological analysis, 158–159
patient insightfulness, 145–149
psychodynamic approaches, 19–25, 26
in relation to therapeutic process variables, 152–155
research needs, 451
shortcomings of insight research, 159–160
stages of processing, 234
See also Assessment; Assimilation of Problematic Experiences Scale; Change and Growth Experiences Scale; Experiencing Scale; Insight Rating Scale; Patient Cognitive Change Scale; Patient Collaboration Scale; Patient Insight Scale; Q-Sort, self-awareness; Rutgers Psychotherapy Process Scale; Self-Understanding of Interpersonal Patterns Scale; Structural Change Scale

Memory
change process, 318
declarative, 318
explicit–implicit, 63–64, 66
extension memory, 390, 391
intention memory, 390
network theories, 361–362
reconstructive, 359
Mentalization, 315–317, 404, 408–409, 419
Meta-awareness, 32, 35, 36, 38, 41–42, 44, 48, 51
Metacommunication, therapeutic, 413–419
Metaphor/metaphorical thinking
lexical–metaphor analysis, 168
metaphors for insight, 169–172, 178–180, 182, 258, 270, 279–280
ontological metaphor, 172
penetration metaphors for insight, 170, 172
possession metaphors for insight, 170, 172
Modulation assumptions, 391
Motivation
for cognitive consistency, 363–365
emotional state and, 362–363
feedback loop, 386–388
recognition of, as indicator of insight, 22
reframing, 89
regulation, 385–392

for self-enhancement, 365–366
social psychology, 363

Narcissism,psychoanalytic theory, 12
Narrative construction
attachment theory, 402, 403–404
change process, 188–189
coherence, 187–188, 402, 403
distancing for, 268
emotional differentiation and, 188, 189, 196–197, 200–201
external processes, 188, 191
family therapy, 93
insecure attachment styles, 410–413
insight in, 188, 269–270
internal processes, 188–189, 191
narrative process change and insight, case analysis of, 188–202
process assessment, 189, 191–193
reflexive processes, 188, 189, 191, 194, 197–200
therapeutic goals, 410
three-stage model, 200–201
trauma effects, 188
Narrative Process Coding System, 189, 191
Narrative therapy, 326
Negative effects of insight, 449–450
Neural network models, 378–385
Neurophysiology
connectionist models, 378–385
extension memory, 391–392
neuromodulators, 384–385, 388
neurotransmitters, 384
schemas, 61–62
Novelty, in definition of insight, 376, 385, 442

Object relations theory, 15, 156, 157
between session change and, 318–320, 328
Ontology of insight, 434–438
Optimism, 76
Outcome research
between-session change, 326–327
cognitive psychology, 393
equal outcomes, 127–128
expectancy effects, 132–133, 134–135
experiential therapy, 49, 50
gains in insight during therapy, 149–152, 160–161
Hill dream interpretation model, 208
insight as common factor, 121, 133–134, 135

definitional issues, 451

dream work, 228

evidence of insight in CBT, 68–72, 75–76

experiential therapies, 49–51

on insight as common factor, 133–134

insight literature, 144–145, 160

insight measurement, 158–159

methodological issues, 451–452

needs, 25–26, 161–162, 450–454

psychodynamic, 17–18

psychological method, 424–425

shortcomings of insight research, 159–160

social psychology, 356

studying insight in conjoint therapy, 94–97

supervisee insight, 350

traditional empiricism, 425–426

See also Outcome research

Rogers, C., 11, 32–33, 282, 289, 323

Ruminative thinking, 270

assessment, 235, 236–237, 247, 250

depression intervention, 238, 240, 241

as inhibiting insight, 233, 234

Rutgers Psychotherapy Process Scale, 20–25

Safety, condition of, 17–18

Saint-Exupéry, A., 3

San Francisco Psychotherapy Research Group, 17–18

Schema-focused model of insight, 58, 75–76

change in, 61, 62–63

concept of schema in, 61–62

dimensions of insight in, 68, 72

distinguishing features, 61

emotional processes in, 64–65

as learning, 67–68

levels of representation in, 63–64, 68

limitations, 378

research findings, 68–72

Schemas

CBT conceptualization, 60, 61

change and, 60

family, 96

neurophysiology, 61–62

reconstruction, 361

research needs, 452

self-schemas, 62

social psychology model of cognition, 357–358

traditional cognitive psychological models, 377, 378

See also Schema-focused model of insight

Schizophrenia, 384

Scientific method, 424–426

Self-awareness

assessment of interpersonal relations and, 152–154, 159, 161

cognitive–behavioral therapy, 59, 60

concept of schema in, 58, 357–358

exercises, 283–284

existential therapy, 34, 35

experience-near and experience-distant insight, 32

experiential conceptualization, 51

in Gestalt therapy, 35–36

insight through self-examination, 281–284

manifestations of insight in conjoint treatment, 82–86

as meta-awareness, 41, 51

of motivation, 22, 24–25

as outcome factor, 149–150, 160

recognition of illness, 14–15, 17, 21

schema change, 64

supervisee, 341

Self-concept

assessment, 236, 237

depression intervention, 238

insight-processing in depression treatment and, 241, 246

public behavior vs. private behavior and, 367

self-enhancement motivation, 365–368

self-verification theory, 363–365, 366–368

social psychology model, 360–361

See also Self-awareness

Self-monitoring in CBT, 322–323

Self-organizing behavior, 387–388

Self psychology, 15

Self-reflexivity, 315

Self-schemas, 62, 63. *See also* Schemas

Self-Understanding of Interpersonal Patterns Scale, 151

Self-verification theory, 363–365, 366–368

Sequential analysis, 96

Shakespeare, William, 3

Similar behavior, insight into, 82–84

Skepticism, 426–428, 431

Social constructionism, 93, 96, 356–357

Social perspective taking, 261

Social psychology, 5

ABOUT THE EDITORS

Louis G. Castonguay completed his PhD at SUNY Stony Brook and his postdoctorate at Stanford University. He is currently an associate professor in the Department of Psychology at The Pennsylvania State University. His research focuses primarily on the process of change in different forms of psychotherapy and the efficacy of integrative therapies. He is also involved in the establishment of practice research networks aimed at facilitating collaboration between practitioners and researchers. He is former president of the North American Society for Psychotherapy Research and recipient of the Early Career Contribution Award from the Society of Psychotherapy Research, the David Shakow Early Career Award from Division 12 (Society of Clinical Psychology) of the American Psychological Association (APA), the Jack D. Krasner Memorial Award, and the Distinguished Psychologist Award from APA Division 29 (Psychotherapy), as well as other research awards.

Clara E. Hill earned her PhD at Southern Illinois University in 1974. She started as an assistant professor in the Counseling Psychology Program in the Department of Psychology at the University of Maryland, where she is currently a professor and codirector of the Counseling Psychology Program. She has been the president of the Society for Psychotherapy Research; editor of the *Journal of Counseling Psychology* and *Psychotherapy Research*; and winner of the Leona Tyler Award from Division 17 (Society of Counseling Psychology) of the American Psychological Association (APA), the Distinguished Psychologist Award from APA Division 29 (Psychotherapy), and the Outstanding Lifetime Achievement Award from the Section on Counseling and Psychotherapy Process and Outcome Research of APA Division 17. Her major research interests are dream work, psychotherapy process and outcome, training novice therapists in helping skills, and qualitative research. She has published 7 books and over 170 journal articles and book chapters.